Collected Papers on the *Tathāgatagarbha* Doctrine

Collected Papers on the *Tathāgatagarbha* Doctrine

JIKIDO TAKASAKI

MOTILAL BANARSIDASS PUBLISHERS
PRIVATE LIMITED • DELHI (INDIA)

First Edition: Delhi, 2014

ISBN: 978-81-208-3944-1

MOTILAL BANARSIDASS
41 U.A. Bungalow Road, Jawahar Nagar, Delhi 110 007
8 Mahalaxmi Chamber, 22 Bhulabhai Desai Road, Mumbai 400 026
203 Royapettah High Road, Mylapore, Chennai 600 004
236, 9th Main III Block, Jayanagar, Bengaluru 560 011
Sanas Plaza, 1302 Baji Rao Road, Pune 411 002
8 Camac Street, Kolkata 700 017
Ashok Rajpath, Patna 800 004
Chowk, Varanasi 221 001

MLBD Cataloging-in-Publication Data

Collected Papers on the Tathāgatagarbha Doctrine
by Jikido Takasaki
Includes bibliography and index
ISBN : 978-81-208-3944-1
I. Buddhism II. The Buddha
III. The Buddha Nature
IV. The Tathāgatagarbha Doctrine

Printed in India

by RP Jain at New Age Books Printing Unit
A-44, Naraina Industrial Area, Phase I, New Delhi–110028
and published by JP Jain for Motilal Banarsidass Publishers (P) Ltd,
41 UA Bungalow Road, Jawahar Nagar, Delhi-110007

Contents

IV. *TATHĀGATAGARBHA* DOCTRINE IN GENERAL

V. JAPANESE AND EAST ASIAN BUDDHISM

Preface

This volume brings together a selection of my previously published papers written in English (and one in German). Their subject matter relates by and large to the *tathāgatagarbha* theory or the idea of Buddha-nature, which have been my main subjects of research over the years. Now at the age of eighty-six, a little beyond the age reached by the Buddha Śākyamuni, I felt that it would be appropriate to publish a volume of this kind for the benefit of future researchers. A similar selection of papers written in Japanese has already been published in nine volumes.

My main works on the *tathāgatagarbha* theory are the following two books:

A Study on the Ratnagotravibhāga (Uttaratantra), Being a Treatise on the Tathāgatagarbha Theory of Mahāyāna Buddhism, S.O.R. XXXIII, Rome: Is.M.E.O., 1966.

Nyoraizō shisō no keisei (The Formation of the *Tathāgatagarbha* Theory) (in Japanese), Tokyo: Shunjūsha, 1974.

The former is basically my Ph.D. dissertation submitted to the University of Poona, the late Prof. Giuseppe Tucci having been one of the examiners. It consists mainly of an English translation of the *Ratnagotravibhāga* (*Uttaratantra*) from the original Sanskrit as edited by E. H. Johnston in 1950 on the basis of newly discovered manuscripts. In the introduction to my study, I give a rough sketch of the history of the *tathāgatagarbha* theory. I found the first use of the term *tathāgatagarbha* in the *Tathāgatagarbha-sūtra*, which declares "*sarvasattvās tathāgatagarbhāḥ*" (all living beings are possessed of the germ of the Buddha [in their womb]) and presents nine analogies.

The second above work was the result of further investigations into the formation and development of the *tathāgatagarbha* theory. It was originally submitted to the University of Tokyo as my D.Litt. dissertation. In this volume, basing myself mainly on the structure of the *Ratnagotravibhāga*, I traced the formation of the system of the *tathāgatagarbha* theory on the basis of Mahāyāna scriptures quoted in the *Ratnagotravibhāga*.

In part 1, I singled out those scriptures that use the term *tathāgatagarbha* as their principal term and identified three scriptures —*Tathāgatagarbha-sūtra*, *Anūnatvāpūrṇatvanirdeśa*, and *Śrīmālādevīnirdeśa*—as the basis for the formation of the *tathāgatagarbha* theory. Next, I placed the Mahāyāna *Mahāparinirvāṇasūtra*, which uses the term *buddhadhātu* for the first time as a synonym of *tathāgatagarbha*, and associated scriptures in a second group, while in the third group we have the *Laṅkāvatārasūtra* and so on, in which the concept of *tathāgatagarbha* is identified with *ālayavijñāna*, the basic concept of the Vijñānavāda.

In part 2, I dealt with the prehistory of the *tathāgatagarbha* theory in Mahāyāna scriptures that use terms synonymous with *tathāgatagarbha*, such as *gotra* and *dhātu*, *tathāgatagotra*, *tathāgatotpattisaṃbhava*, *āryavaṃśa*, *buddhaputra*, *dharmadhātu* and *dharmakāya*, *cittaprakṛti*, and so on. The main points made in this work are discussed in the papers that have now been brought together in the present volume.

This volume has for convenience' sake been divided into seven parts according to subject matter. Part 1 presents a textual study, namely, a critical edition of chapter 6 of the *Laṅkāvatāra*. Part 2 deals with subjects concerning scriptures such as the *Laṅkāvatāra*, part 3 with technical terms and basic concepts of the *tathāgatagarbha* theory, part 4 with *tathāgatagarbha* doctrine in general, and part 5 with Japanese Buddhism and Buddhism in East Asia (on the basis of scriptures translated into Chinese). Part 6 presents a historical survey of Japanese scholarship on Buddhism, and part 7 consists of several book reviews.

Editorial Note

The articles in this volume have been reprinted by and large in the form in which they originally appeared. However, in addition to minor corrections and slight modifications in wording and punctuation, some changes have also been made to minimize the lack of stylistic uniformity, including the conversion of endnotes to footnotes, the use of a single citation format as far as was reasonably practicable, and consistency in the romanization of Chinese in accordance with the Wade-Giles system. But some inconsistencies remain in, for example, spelling, the romanization of Sanskrit and Tibetan, and the inclusion of Chinese characters, and for these the reader's indulgence is requested.

Abbreviations

Ch.	Chinese
HOS	Harvard Oriental Series
IIJ	*Indo-Iranian Journal*
JA	*Journal asiatique*
JAOS	*Journal of the American Oriental Society*
JIBS	*Journal of Indian and Buddhist Studies* (*Indogaku Bukkyōgaku Kenkyū*)
Jp.	Japanese
LAS	*Laṅkāvatāra-sūtra*
Ms(s).	Manuscript(s)
RGV	*Ratnagotravibhāga*
Skt.	Sanskrit
T.	Taishō edition (*Taishō shinshū daizōkyō*)
Tib.	Tibetan
ZDMG	*Zeitschrift der Deutschen Morgenländischen Gesellschaft*

PART I
TEXTUAL RESEARCH

A Revised Edition of the *Laṅkāvatāra-sūtra* "Kṣaṇika-parivarta"

Introduction

The *Laṅkāvatāra-sūtra* has had an enormous influence over a long period of time in China ever since its first translation into Chinese in A.D. 443 by Guṇabhadra (*Leng-ch'ieh a-pa-t'o-lo pao-ching*, 4 fascs., Sung version), especially among Zen Buddhists, as is shown by the legend of Bodhidharma, the founder of Chinese Zen Buddhism. According to legend, he brought the *Laṅkāvatāra* to China as proof of the Zen doctrine of "no reliance on written characters." This tendency was transmitted as far as Tibet via Tun-huang, and in the ninth century Chos grub translated this Sung version into Tibetan (Peking Ed., no. 776). (On this, see "Some Problems in the Tibetan Translations from Chinese Materials," pp. 525–536 below.)

Apart from this version, there has also been preserved in Tibet a version that was translated directly from Sanskrit (Peking Ed., no. 775), the contents of which are almost identical with the present Sanskrit edition. As for Chinese translations, there are two furthers versions, namely, the Wei version in 10 fascicles translated by Bodhiruci (*Ju leng-ch'ieh ching*) and the T'ang version in 7 fascicles translated by Śikṣānanda (*Ta-ch'eng ju leng-ch'ieh ching*). In contrast to the Sung version, which is shorter, they cover the same ground as the Sanskrit edition but were not utilized in China to the same extent as the Sung version.

The *Laṅkāvatāra* has been traditionally revered in Nepal as one of the Nine Treasures of Mahāyāna Buddhism, and this remains the case even today. Sanskrit manuscripts are preserved in

Nepal as well as in universities and institutes around the world.

The first critical edition of the Sanskrit text was published by S. S. Das and S. C. Vidyabhusana (Darjeeling, 1900), and it contains only the first part of the text, as far as p. 144, *l*. 5 in the Nanjio Edition. Next, Bunyiu Nanjio of Japan edited the entire text on the basis of a manuscript kept at the Royal Asiatic Society in London, two manuscripts kept in Cambridge University Library, which had been brought from Nepal by J. Takakusu (Tokyo University Catalogue, no. 333 (I)), and another manuscript that had been brought from Nepal by Rev. Ekai Kawaguchi (Otani University, Kyoto, 1923). This so-called Nanjio Edition is that which is most commonly used today. There is another, newer edition that was published on the occasion of the 2,500th anniversary of the Buddha's *mahāparinirvāṇa* and is included in the Buddhist Sanskrit Series (B.S.S., no. 3, ed. by P. L. Vaidya, Mithila Institute, Darbhanga, 1963). This text is, however, merely a reissue of the Nanjio Edition with a few corrections.

The Nanjio Edition, though usually regarded as being of a normal standard for such an edition, contains various mistakes in comparison with the Tibetan version translated directly from the Sanskrit. These would seem to be due rather to the doctrinal difficulties of the *Laṅkāvatāra*, and even modern Nepalese manuscripts have the same errors. Therefore, it could be said to have been only natural that Nanjio made certain mistakes.

Now, however, we have access to many other manuscripts that have been found since then. Namely, in Tokyo University Library there are, in addition to the two manuscripts mentioned above, five further manuscripts, i.e., one acquired by Dr. Takakusu (no. 332) and four acquired by Rev. Kawaguchi (nos. 327–330). Further, in Germany in recent years scholars of Sanskrit philology have initiated the Nepal-German Sanskrit Manuscript Preservation Project with the support of the Nepalese Government. In this collection, we find several manuscripts of the *Laṅkāvatāra*. This project was originally meant for German scholars, but thanks to Dr. Akira Yuyama, the former Chief Librarian of the Reiyukai Library who is acquainted with many German scholars, we were able to make use of the necessary microfilms from the collection which Dr. Yuyama obtained for the Reiyukai Library through Prof. Michael Hahn, head of the said project. We have heard that there are other manuscripts too in the United States and elsewhere, but we were unable to utilize them on this occasion.

The purpose of our present project is to re-edit the Nanjio Edition on the basis of the following manuscripts: seven manuscripts kept at Tokyo University Library (T1–7), seven manuscripts in the possession of the Nepal-German Sanskrit Manuscript Preservation Project (N11–17), and also two manuscripts kept at Cambridge University Library (C1–2) and one manuscript kept at the Royal Asiatic Society (R10).

For our present project, J. Takasaki, head of the project, received a grant-in-aid from the Ministry of Education for three years. For the final report on our research, we decided to publish a new edition of Chapter 6, the "Kṣaṇika-parivarta" (corresponding to Nanjio Ed., pp. 220–239).

In editing the text, the editor has tried to record as many different readings as possible in the notes and has limited revisions to those based on manuscript readings. Generally speaking, most Nepalese manuscripts date from the modern period since the nineteenth century, and the situation is no different for the *Laṅkāvatāra*. That is to say, apart from three manuscripts that clearly date from the eighteenth century, all the rest seem to belong mostly to the nineteenth century. There is a palm leaf (*pattra*) manuscript among the Tokyo collection (no. 333 (I) = T1), but the date is not recorded, and judging from the script, it cannot be expected to be of an early date.

Thus the manuscripts of the *Laṅkāvatāra* are all Nepalese, and there seems no difference of recension. But as far as the portion edited this time is concerned, we may divide the manuscripts in the following manner:

A. T1 ("T") — T6 — N11
B. C8 ("C") — R10 ("A") — N12
C. T2 ("K") — T4 — N13
D. T3 — T5 — C9 — N14 — N16 — N17

(Quotation marks indicate the manuscripts used in the Nanjio Ed.)

Nepalese Sanskrit manuscripts written in the Newari script are generally said to have the following characteristics:

(1) doubling of consonants after *r* (e.g., *dharmma*, *varttate*, etc.).
(2) *satva* for *sattva* and *tatva* for *tattva*.
(3) use of *anusvāra* at the end of a sentence.
(4) irregular use of punctuation (*daṇḍa*), which is usually omitted.

Among these characteristics, (2) is present in all our manuscripts, as is (3). As for (1), however, there are differences between the groups of manuscripts. Among the above four groups, D has the doubling of consonants in most cases, sometimes even between two words, such as *punarmmahāmate* for *punar mahāmate*. Group B and T1 in group A, on the other hand, do not double consonants after *r* except in *varttate* and other words containing the consonants *rtt*. This doubling is observed in all groups. Group C and N11 in group A occupy an intermediate position in the use of double consonants, using it in *dharmma*, *āryya*, and *sarvva*. (T4 belongs to the same group in most cases.)

As for punctuation, group B is the most faithful to the rules, followed by N16 and T1. But Nepalese manuscripts usually mark the end of a sentence with *anusvāra* before a sentence starting with a vowel. Also noticeable is the use of *visarga* before a voiced consonant as a sign of the end of a sentence. If the use of *sandhi* is observed where punctuation is neccesary, we should consider it the result of a misunderstanding on the part of the copyist of the manuscript.

As well as the characteristics mentioned above, we often observe cases where a nasal is unnecessarily identified with the next consonant and, in contrast, cases where *anusvāra* is used almost throughout. To the former belong groups C and D except for T4, while to the latter belongs group B, which uses, e.g., *aṃti* for *anti.* As for *gaṅgā*, all manuscripts have *gaṃgā.*

To determine the recension or group of a particular manuscript, a useful method is to single out a unique variant reading among the manuscripts. For example, "sand" in the phrase "sands of the Gaṅgā" is given as either *vālikā* or *vālukā.* In the initial sections, the three manuscripts T1, T6, and N12 always use *vālukā* while all the other manuscripts have *vālikā*, but in the middle section all manuscripts use *vālukā*. In the latter part of the text, the groups are again divided into two, and this time manuscripts C8 and R10 of group B join those using *vālukā*. From this fact we may suppose that *vālukā* shows the old reading, which later changed in some groups. If this is so, then we could suppose that groups A and B retain a comparatively old reading.

As a similar case, we may mention the following example in Chapter 7. In manuscripts T3 and T5, the name of the questioner Mahāmati is replaced by Subhūti. This may indicate an intimate relationship between these two manuscripts. Also in the same chapter, we observe the substitution of *parivrājika* for *pravrājika* only in T1 and T6. T1 confuses *ś* and *s*, using mostly *s* for *ś*. This usage is also observed to some extent in T6.

What is also frequently observed is different readings in the manuscripts and in the Tibetan translation from the Sanskrit, and in most cases the latter gives a better reading when considered from the content. Especially when the latter's reading is identical with the first Chinese translation, the Sung version, we can recognize this as the original reading. In such cases, we will be required to correct the reading even against the manuscript reading. For example, *kṣayavarjitam* in v. 10 of chap. 6 (Nanjio Ed., p. 239, *l*. 9) is found in most manuscripts, but the Tibetan translation and all three Chinese translations have the equivalent of *kriyāvarjitam*. Only N11 has the reading *kriya-*, and since the same verse in the "Sagāthakam" supports this reading, we should accept this reading *kriyavarjitam* (*kriya* short for regular *kriyā* is here required by the metre). Among the Chinese translations, the Sung version sometimes gives a literal translation, which helps one surmise the original form, and in view of its early date, we consulted it frequently. The Wei version has many misreadings due to its distinctive understanding of the text, while the T'ang version sometimes uses the Sung version in important parts and is not as good as it claims to be.

In publishing this edition, I am grateful to Mr. Edgar Cooke, Mr. Yukihiro Okada, and Mr. Michihiko Yajima (all of the Department of Indian Philosophy, University of Tokyo), who assisted me in reading and romanizing the manuscripts. Many thanks are also due to Mrs. Maeko Okada of the same department, who produced a basic typescript for the printer.

1 February 1981
Jikido Takasaki, Editor

Preliminary Notes

1. The following is a tentative revised edition of the *Laṅkāvatāra-sūtra* (Chap. VI: Kṣaṇikaparivartaḥ) originally edited by B. Nanjio (Kyoto, 1923) (abbr. Nj.).

2. The manuscripts used in this edition together with their abbreviations are as follows.

T Sanskrit Mss. kept in the Tokyo University Library.

T1 Matsunami Catalogue, no. 333 (I) (originally collected by J. Takakusu).
"T" in Nj.
Palm-leaf, 67 leaves, 6 lines, 23 in. × 2¼ in., Siddhānta (Kuṭila characters?), no date.

T2 Ibid., no. 331 (originally collected by E. Kawaguchi).
"K" in Nj.
Paper, 145 leaves, 6 lines, 14⅕ in. × 3⅕ in., Newari script, dated Saṃvat 857 (= A.D. 1737).

T3 Ibid., no. 328 (originally brought back by Kawaguchi).
Paper, 217 leaves, 5 lines, 14¼ in. × 3¼ in., Newari script, no date.

T4 Ibid., no. 329 (originally brought back by Kawaguchi).
Paper, 141 leaves, 7 lines, 14¾ in. × 4½ in., Newari script, no date.

T5 Ibid., no. 330 (originally in Kawaguchi Collection).
Paper, 115 leaves, 6–7 lines, 14½ in. × 3½ in., Newari script, modern.

T6 Ibid., no. 332 (originally collected by J. Takakusu).
Paper, 172 leaves, 6 lines, 14 in. × 3¼ in., Newari script, no date.

T7 Ibid., no. 327 (originally collected by Kawaguchi).
Fragments, up to the middle of Chap. II (Nj. 105.2).
Paper, 67 leaves, 5 lines, 13¼ in. × 3¼ in., Newari script,

modern.

C Skt. Mss. kept in Cambridge University Library.

C8 Bendall Catalogue, Add. no. 915.
"C" in Nj.
Paper, 160 leaves, 8 lines, 14 in. × 4½ in., Newari script, dated Saṃvat 916 (= A.D. 1796).

C9 Ibid., Add. no. 1607.
Paper, 222 leaves, 6 lines, 12½ in. × 3 in., Newari script, dated Saṃvat 902 (= A.D. 1782).

R10 Ms. in possession of the Royal Asiatic Society, London, Hodgson Skt. Ms. no. 5.
"A" in Nj.
Paper, 157 leaves, 6 lines (7 or 8 lines in parts), size not recorded, Newari script, no date.

N Mss. photographed under the Nepal-German Manuscript Preservation Project, Kathmandu.

N11 [Reel No. E 406/2 (photographed 22.11.1977)] (I).
Paper, 140 leaves, 9 lines, 44 cm. × 12 cm., Newari script, no date.

N12 [Reel No. E 3/3 (8E 1), E 4/1 (8E 2) (18.3.1976)] (II) (III).
Paper, 201 leaves, 6 lines, 29.8 cm. × 8.4 cm., Newari script, no date.

N13 [Reel D 73/8 (2.7.1976)] (1273D) (IV).
Paper, 59 leaves, 12 lines, 45.2 cm. × 18.9 cm., Newari script, no date.

N14 [Reel D 52/5 (19.4.1976)] (1027D) (V).
Paper, 127 leaves, 7 lines, 43.6 cm. × 11.4 cm., Newari script, no date.

N15 [Reel D 58/4 (18.5.1976)] (1046D) (VI).
Paper, 231 leaves (folios 65–197 missing), 5 lines, 38 cm. × 8.4 cm., Newari script, no date.

N16 [Reel D 16/2 (9.1.1976)] (289D) (VII).

Paper, 158 leaves, 7 lines, 38 cm. × 11 cm., Newari script, modern (probably copy of old Ms.).

N17 [Reel No. C 13/7 (2.12.1975), Kaiser Library No. 119] (VIII).
Paper, 150 leaves, 6 lines (up to folio 68), 7 lines (folio 69 onwards), 35.5 cm. × 9.5 cm., Newari script.

3. Abbreviations (for Mss. see above)

Nj. Nanjio Ed. of *Laṅkāvatārasūtra*.

Vd. *The Saddharma-Laṅkāvatārasūtra*, ed. by P. L. Vaidya, Buddhist Sanskrit Texts, No. 3, Darbhanga, 1963.

v. verse (numbers follow Nj.).

Sag. "Sagāthakam" (Chap. X) of the *Laṅkāvatāra*.

Tib. Tibetan translation from Sanskrit source.
Peking Ed. No. 775 (Reprint Vol. 29, pp. 26.3–86.4).

Ch. Chinese translations.
(S) 1. Sung version, in 4 fascs., Taisho No. 670.
(W) 2. Wei version, in 10 fascs., Taisho No. 671.
(T) 3. T'ang version, in 7 fascs., Taisho No. 672.

4. Editorial marks

_____ Emendation based upon sources other than Mss.

~~~~ Revision of the Nj. Edition.

- - - - Emendation based upon sources other than Mss. & revision of Nj. Edition.

[ ] Insertion in revision.

( ) Portion to be omitted after revision.

\+ Added (punctuation, etc.).

5. Section divisions and their numbers follow the *Butsugo shinron* 佛語心論 by Kokan Shiren. See "An Analysis of the *Laṅkāvatāra*" [pp. 101–117 below]; J. Takasaki, *Ryōgakyō*, Butten kōza 17 (Tokyo: Daizō Shuppan, 1980).
~~~~

Chapter VI Kṣaṇikaparivarta*

§ tathāgatagarbha (80)

[Nj. 220.1]

atha khalu mahāmatir[1] bodhisattvo[2] mahāsattvaḥ[3] punar api bhagavantam adhyeṣate[4] sma /[5] deśayatu me bhagavān[6] deśayatu me sugataḥ[7] skandha[8]dhātvāyatanānāṃ[9] pravṛttinivṛttim[10] /[11] asaty ātmani kasya pravṛttir[12] vā[13] nivṛttir vā[14] bālāś ca[15] pravṛttinivṛttyāśritā[16] duḥkhakṣayānavabodhān[17] nirvāṇaṃ[18][19] na[20] prajānanti[21] /[22]

* Entire chapter missing in T7 and N15; T1 lacks as far as 'tathāgatagarbha' in Nj. 222.10.

1. °ti] N14,17.
2. °satvo] in all Mss.
3. °satvaḥ] in all Mss. (Hereafter an asterisk [*] is used in similar circumstances.)
4. adhyeṣante] T4,5, N14,16.
5. om. /] T2,3,4,5, C9, N13,14,17; //] T6, C8, R10, N14,16.
6. bhagavan] T6, C8, R10.
7. gata] T2,6, C8,9, R10, N11,12,13,16; gatas] N14,17; gaka] T4.
8. skaṃdha] C8, N12.
9. °āyatanā] T5; °nāṃ //] N14.
10. pravṛttim] C9 (om. nivṛtti).
11. om. /] in all Mss.
12. prabhitvā] T5.
13. °vvā] N11 (for vā twice).
14. om. nivṛttir vā] T5, C9; om. vā] T6; °tti] R10, N14.
15. om. bālaś ca] C8, R10, N16 (vā śca?).
16. tyā°] T2,4, N11,13,14,16,17.
17. om. °kṣa°] T6.
18. nirvvā°] T3,5, C9, N11,14,16,17.
19. °ṇan] T2,3,4,5, C9, N12,13,16,17.
20. om. na] N14.
21. jānanti (om. pra)] R10; °aṃti] C8, R10, N11.
22. om. /] T2,3,5, N13,14,17; //] T4,6, C8,9, R10, N11,16.

[Nj. 220.6]

bhagavān āha [1]/ tena hi mahāmate śṛṇu sādhu ca suṣṭhu ca manasikuru [2]/ bhāṣiṣye[3] 'haṃ[4] te [5]/ sādhu bhagavann[6] iti[7] mahāmatir[8] bodhisattvo mahāsattvo[9] bhagavataḥ pratyaśrauṣīt[10] [11]// bhagavāṃs[12] tasyaitad[13] avocat[14] [15]/ tathāgatagarbho mahāmate kuśalākuśalahetukaḥ[16] sarvajanmagatikartā[17] [18]/[19] pravartate[20] naṭavad[21] gatisaṃkaṭa[22] ātmātmīyavarjitaḥ[23] [24]/

1. //] T2,4,6, C8,9, R10, N11,12,13,16.
2. om. /] in all Mss.
3. bhāṣi] T5.
4. han] T2,3,4,5, C8,9, R10, N11,12,13,14,16.
5. om. /] in all Mss.
6. bhagavānn] T3,4, C9, N11,13,14,16,17.
7. + //] N11.
8. mahāmati] T5, R10, N13.
9. °satvaḥ /] C8, R10; om. mahāsatvo] N12.
10. prati aś°] T2; pratiaśroṣīd] T3; pratiśroṣīd] T4,5, R10, N11,13,14,16,17; pratiśroṣī] C9; pratyaśrauṣīd, and om. //] T6, N12.
11. om. //] in all Mss.
12. °vāns] T2,3,4,5, N14,17; °vāms] C9.
13. tad (om. tasyai)] N11.
14. avoca] T2.
15. om. /] T2,3,4,5, C9, R10, N13,14,17; //] T6, C8, N11,12,16.
16. kuśalahetukaḥ (om. akuśala-)] T4, R10, N11.
17. sarvva°] T2,3,5, C9, N11,14,16,17.
18. karttā] T2,3,4,5, C8,9, R10, N11,12,13,14,16,17.
19. om. /] T2,3,5,6, C8,9, R10, N11,12,13,14,16,17. Vd. om. /.
20. °vartta] T2,3,4,5,6, C8,9, R10, N11,12,14,16; °varttate] N13.
21. natāvan] T6; naṭavaṃ] T4; naṭaṃ] N16; naṭaṅ] N17.
22. saṃkaṭe] T3,4, C8,9, R10, N11,12,13,14; saṃkato] T6, N16.
23. °rjji°] T2,3,5, C9, N14,16,17; °rjītaḥ] T4.
24. Nj. °varjitastad° (om. /), but //] C9; /] N11,16. Vd. has *daṇḍa*.

[Nj. 220.11]

tadanavabodhāt[1] trisaṅgati[2]pratyayakriyāyogaḥ[3] pravartate[4] /[5] na[6] ca tīrthyā avabudhyante[7] kāraṇābhiniveśābhini[8]viṣṭāḥ[9] /[10] anādikā-[11]lavividhaprapañca[12]dauṣṭhulyavāsanāvāsita ālayavijñāna[13]saṃśabdito [14]'vidyāvāsanā[15]bhūmijaiḥ saptabhir[16] [17]vijñā[18...]naiḥ saha[...18] mahodadhitaraṅga[19]van[20] nityam [21]avyucchinnaśarīraḥ[22] pravar[23]tate /[24]

1. °dhā] R10.
2. tṛsaṃgati] T2,3,4,5, C9, N13,16,17; tṛsaṅgati] T6; trisaṃgati] C8, N12; trisagati] R10; tisaṅgati] N11; tṛsagati] N14.
3. °yoga] C9.
4. °vartta°] in all Mss. except R10, N17.
5. + //] C8, R10; om. /] T2,3,4,5,6, C9, N11,12,13,14,16.
6. tena] N13.
7. + //] N12.
8. °nibhiśobhini°] T2,3,4,5, C9, R10, N13,14,16,17.
9. °ṣṭaḥ] T6.
10. om. /] T2,3,4,5, C8,9, R10, N12,13,14,16,17.
11. °kāra°] N16.
12. paṃca] in all Mss. except N11.
13. vijñānaṃ] T6.
14. °taḥ avi°] in all Mss. A *daṇḍa* may be inserted here (°taḥ / avidyā°).
15. Nj. vāsana°, but vāsanā in all Mss. (Tib. *gnas kyi sa* suggests 'vāsabhūmi' as in the *Śrīmālā*.)
16. °bhi] T6, N17.
17. (bhir)vvi°] N11.
18. °nairmma° (om. saha)] T2,3,5, C9, N11,13,14,17; nairma°] C8, R10, N12,16; °nai ma°] T6 (but Tib. ... *daṅ lhan cig tu* = -naiḥ saha), Ch(S) 俱.
19. taraṃga] T4,6, C8, R10, N12,16.
20. °va] T2, N13, 17; °vaṃ] N14.
21. avi°] T6.
22. sarīraḥ] T2,3,4,5, C9, N13,14,17.
23. °rtta°] in all Mss.
24. //] T6, C8, R10, N12; /] N11 (om. / in Nj.). Tib. takes 'pravartate' as governing up to '-pariśuddhiḥ'.

[Nj. 220.16]

anityatādoṣarahita[1] ātma[2]vādavi[p. 221]nivṛtt[3]o 'tya[3]ntaprakṛtipariśuddhiḥ[4] /[5] tadanyāni vijñānāny utpannāpavargāni[6] manomanovi[7]jñānaprabhṛtīni[8] kṣaṇikāni saptāpy[9] abhūtaparikalpahetujanita[10]saṃsthānākṛtiviśeṣasamavā[11]yāvalambīni[12] nāmanimittābhiniviṣṭāni[13] svacittadṛśyarūpalakṣaṇā[na][14]vabodhakāni sukhaduḥkhā[15]pratisaṃveda[16]kāny[17]

1. °taḥ pravattate] T2,3,4,5; pravarttate] N11,12,13,14,16,17; pravartante] T6; + // after °varttate] N12.
2. ātmā°] T6.
3. °vṛttaḥ atya°] T2,4,5,6 C9, N12,16,17; + // after ttaḥ] C8, R10; /] N11.
4. °is] T2,3,4, C8,9, R10, N11,12,13,14,16,17; °as] T5; °es] T6. (It is possible to have '°śuddhaḥ' as an adjective qualifying 'tathāgatagarbhaḥ'; Vd. °śuddhaḥ.)
5. om. /] in all Mss.
6. °apargāṇi] T6; °apavagāni] R10; °rggā] T5, C9, N16,17.
7. mana°] T6, N11.
8. °tīnī] T6; tini] N11,14.
9. pi] in all Mss.
10. °janitaṃ] T2,3,4,5, C8,9, R10, N12,13,14,16,17.
11. °saṃā] N11; °samavā ā] N17.
12. °laṃbī°] T6, N12; + /] C8. Tib. *dbyibs kyi bya ba daṅ bye brag la dmigs pa* = *saṃsthānakriyāviśeṣāvalambīni.
13. nāmatināmanimittāniviṣṭāni] N17. Tib. nāmanimittābhiniveṣābhiniviṣṭāni.
14. Tib. *khoṅ du ma chud pa* = °anavabodhakāni, which is acceptable here.
15. °khāṅaprati°] T4.
16. samveda] N11.
17. °kāṃny°] C9, N14,16.

[Nj. 221.5]

amokṣakāraṇāni nāmanimittaparyutthāna[1]rāga[2]janitajanakataddhetvālamba[3]nāni / [4] teṣāṃ copāttānām indriyākhyānāṃ[5] parikṣayanirodhe samananta[6]rānutpatter[7] anyeṣāṃ svamativikalpasukhaduḥkhāpratisaṃ[8]vedi[9]nāṃ saṃjñāvedita[10]nirodhasamāpattisamāpannānāṃ catur[11]dhyānasatyavimokṣakuśalānāṃ yogināṃ[12] vimokṣabuddhir bhavaty[13] apravṛtteḥ[14] //

1. paryyutthāna°] T2,3, C9; paryyusthāna°] T4,5,6, N11,13,16 (sthā?).
2. om. ga] N12.
3. laṃba] C8, R10, N12 (Nj. ālambāni, 'na' missing).
4. om. /] T2,3,4,5,6, C9, N11,12,13,14,16, 17; //] C8, R10 (teṣā for teṣāṃ).
5. nām pa°] T3,4,5, C9, N13,14,16,17.
6. samanaṃta°] C8; samanata] R10.
7. °ttir eṣāṃ] T6.
8. samve°] N11.
9. dinā] R10.
10. °vādita°] N11; °vadita°] N16.
11. catu-] N16.
12. om. yoginām] N14.
13. °ti] in all Mss; + //] C8, R10, N12,16; + /] T6, N11.
14. apravṛtte] in all Mss. (T2, vṛrtte?) and om. // (probably taken as first word of next sentence: apavṛtte aparāvṛtte ca). The position of this word is unusual. Tib. *gshan dag kyaṅ mi ḥjug paḥi phyir* = anyeṣāṃ cāpravṛtteḥ. But Ch(S) supports Mss. reading (不離不轉).

[Nj. 221.12]

aparāvṛtte[1] ca[2] tathāgatagarbha(śabda)[3]saṃśabdita[4][5] ālayavijñāne[6] nāsti saptānāṃ[7] pravṛtti[8]vijñā[9]nāṃ[10] nirodhaḥ[11] / [11] tat kasya hetoḥ [/][12] taddhetvā[13]lamba[14]napravṛttatvād[15] vijñānānām aviṣayatvāc[16] ca sarva-[17]śrāvakapratyekabuddhatīrthyayogayoginām[18] [/] svapu[19]dgalanairātmyāva[20]bodhāt svasāmānya[21]lakṣaṇaparigrahāt skandha[22]dhātvāyatanānāṃ[23] pravarta[24]te

1. aprāvṛtte] T2; apavṛtte] R10; aprarā°] N17. Tib. *rab tu ma gyur na* = apravṛtte (?) (and 'ca' seems to have been omitted).
2. -vat //] R10; + //] C8.
3. śabdaṃ] T3,4,5, C9, N13,16,17; om. śabda] N14, which is supported by Tib. and is preferable here.
4. saśa°] T4, R10.
5. te] in all Mss. except T2.
6. + /] T5.
7. satvānām] T3,4,5,6, C8, N13,14,16,17.
8. saṃvṛtti] T6.
9. °jñānān] N12.
10. nān ni] T2,3,4,5, C9, N13,14,16,17.
11. °as, and om. /] T3,4,5, C8,9, R10, N12,13,14,16,17; aḥ //] T6, N11.
12. °toḥ //] T6, C8, R10, N11 (which is preferable).
13. tatvāla°] T3,4,5, C9, N14; tabhitvāla] T6.
14. °laṃba°] C8, R10, N12.
15. °tvā] T2, N13,17; tvāt] T6, N11 (+ /).
16. °ṣayayatvāc] N13.
17. °rvva°] T3,5, C9, N11,14,16,17.
18. °nāṃ, and om. /] in all Mss. So too Nj. From the context, however, a short punctuation mark is expected here. Tib. seems to have it.
19. °puṃga°] T2,3,4,6, C8,9, R10, N12,13,14,16,17; vapuṃga°] T5.
20. °tmyava°] T5. Is this °tmyānava°? Ch(S) 不覺無我, but Tib. as the text.
21. nye] R10.
22. skaṃdha°] C8, R10, N12.
23. °nām pra] T2,3,4,5, C9, N13,14; nānmam] N17.
24. °rtta°] in all Mss. except N13; + //] N12.

[Nj. 221.17]

tathāga[1]tagarbhaḥ pañca[2]dharma[3]svabhāvadharma[3]nairātmyadarśa-
nān[4] nivarta[5]te bhūmikramānusaṃdhi[6]parāvṛttyā[7] [/][8] nānya[9]tīrthya-
marga[10]dṛṣṭibhir[11] vicārayitum[12] śakyate /[13] tato[14] 'calāyāṃ (bhūmau)[15]
bodhisattvabhūmau[16] pratiṣṭhito [p. 222] daśasamādhisukha[17]mukha-
mārgān[18] pratilabhate /[19] samādhibuddhaiḥ saṃdhā[20]rya[21]māṇo[22] 'cin-
tyabuddhadharma[23]svapraṇidhānavyavaloka[24]natayā

1. om. gata] N12.
2. paṃca] in all Mss. except T6.
3. °rmma] T2,3,5, C9, N11,13,14,16,17.
4. °nāt /] T6.
5. rtta°] in all Mss. (+ //, N12).
6. sandhi°] T5,6.
7. vṛttyāḥ] T2, N12,13; vṛtyāḥ] T3,4,5, C9, N14,16,17; vṛttir] T6; vṛtyā] R10; vṛttaḥ /] N11. Nj. has no *daṇḍa*, but most Mss. seem to end sentence here (*visarga* is a kind of sign for a period!).
8. mānya°] N11. 'mā' as a negative particle.
9. °tīrtha°] T6, N11.
10. rgga] T5, C9, N11,16,17.
11. °ṣṭir] T3, C8,9, N12,16; °ṣṭi] T5, R10, N14; °ṣṭibhi] T6, N11.
12. vināraśayitum] T4, N16; vicāraśeyitum] T5; vicālayi°] N11; °tu] T2, N13,17.
13. om. /] in all Mss. except N12 (//).
14. tathāca°] T6 (*avagraha* is not used in any Mss.).
15. om. bhūmau] T6, N11 (supported by Tib.).
16. °mo] R10.
17. om. sukha] N12 (supported by Tib.), but Ch(S) has sukha (樂門).
18. °rggām] T3, C9, N11,14,16; gām] T5; gā] T6.
19. om. /] in all Mss. except N16 (//).
20. sandhā] T2,3,4, C9, N11,12,14,16,17; sadhā] T5; satvā] T6.
21. °ryya°] T2,3,4,5, C9, N11,13,16,17.
22. °naḥ aci°] in all Mss. (+ /, N11); °ciṃtya] N16.
23. °rmma (as in n. 3 above).
24. om. loka] N12.

[Nj. 222.2]

samādhisukha[1]bhūtakoṭyā vinivārya[2] pratyātmārya[3]gati[4]gamyaiḥ
sarva[5]śrāvakapratyekabuddhatīrtha[6]karāsā[7]dhāraṇair[8] yogamārga[9]i[10]r
deśārya[11]gotramārgaṃ[12] pratilabhate,[13] [14]kāyaṃ ca[15] jñānamanomayaṃ[16]
samādhy[abhi][17]saṃskārarahitam /[18] tasmāt tarhi mahāmate tathā-[19]
gatagarbha[20] ālayavijñāna[21]saṃśabdito[22] viśodhayitavyo[23] viśeṣārthi-[24]
bhir[25] bodhisattvair[26] mahāsattvaiḥ[27] //[28]

1. mukha] N12.
2. °ryya] T2,3,5, C9, N11,13,14,17; °vāya] N16.
3. āryya] T2,3,5, C9, N11,13,14,16,17.
4. gata] T2, N13; gatagata] N17.
5. °rvva°] T2,3,5, C9, N11,14,16,17.
6. Nj. tīrthya, which is supported by all Mss. except T2, N13 (°rthīka°), N11 and N17 (°rthaka°). The term for 'heretics' is usually 'tīrthya' or 'tīrthakara'. Vd. tīrthakara.
7. saṃdhā°] C8.
8. °ṇai] C9, N14; sādharaṇar yyoga] N16; yyoga] T5, N11.
9. °rgga°] T3, C9, N11,14,17.
10. aiḥ] T2,5, C8, N11,13; °rgaḥ] R10.
11. °ryya] T2,3,5, C9, N11,13,14,16,17.
12. °rgan na] T2,5,6, C8, R10, N12,13; °rggan na] C9, N14,16,17; °rrgan] T3,4; °rggān] N11.
13. patilabhate] N14; + //] T6, C8, R10, N12,16; + /] N11.
14. + kāryya (before kāya)] T5, C9, N11,14,16; + kāryyaṃ] T2,3, N13,17; + kāryaṃ] T4, C8, N12; + kārya] R10.
15. kāyañ ca] T2,3,4,5, C9, N11,13,14,17.
16. maya] T6.
17. abhi] missing in all Mss., but Tib. *mṅon par ḥdu byed.*
18. taṃ, and om. /] T2,3,4,5, C8,9, N11,13,17; taṃ /] N12,14; taṃ //] N16;

om. /] R10.

19. om. °thā] T6.

20. °bhaḥ] in all Mss. (°gabhaḥ, R10; + //, N11).

21. jñānaḥ] T6, N11.

22. saṃśabditaḥ] T2,3,4,5, C8,9, N12,13,14,16,17; saśabditaḥ] R10; °ta] N11.

23. °vyā] T6.

24. °rtha°] T6.

25. °bhiḥ] T2,4,5, C9, R10, N13,14,16,17.

26. °rmma°] T5, N11,14,16,17.

27. °tvair] T2,3,4,5, C8,9, R10, N11,12,16,17; °tvai] T6, N13,14.

28. om. //] in all Mss.

[Nj. 222.9]

yadi[1] hi mahāmate ālayavijñānasaṃśabditas[2] tathāgatagarbho 'tra[3] na syād [4...]ity asati[...4] mahāmate tathāgatagarbha[5] ālayavijñānasaṃ-śabdite[6] na[7] pravṛttir[8] na[9] nivṛttiḥ[10] syāt[11] / bhavati ca mahāmate pravṛttir[12] nivṛttiś[13] ca bālāryāṇāṃ[14][15] / svapratyātmārya[16]gatidṛṣṭa[17]-dharma[18]sukhavihāreṇa ca viharanti[19] yogino[20...] '[...20]nikṣipta-

1. yyadi (after -tvair)] N11.
2. taḥ] C8; (+ //)] T6, N11.
3. om. *avagraha* in all Mss.
4. asat iti] T3,4, N14,16; asati iti] C9, N14; iti (om. asati)] T2,5, N13,17; iti asati] C8, R10; om. ity] T6, N12; aśati (om. ity)] N11.
5. tathāgarbha (om. gata)] T5, R10; °bhaḥ] T5.
6. °sabdi] T1 (T1 starts after ālaya); °tai] N11.
7. om. na] T6.
8. °tti] T3,6, N13.
9. om. na] T6.
10. °tti] T5.
11. syād (om. /)] in all Mss.
12. °tti] T1, N13.
13. °ttim] R10.
14. °ryyā] T2,3, C9, N11,13,14,16,17.
15. °ṇāṃ, and om. /] T2,3,4,5,6, C8,9, R10, N12,13,14,16,17; om. /] T1, N11.
16. °ryya] T2,3,5, C9, N11,13,14,16,17.
17. dṛṣṭi] T1.
18. °rmma°] T2,3, C9, N11,14,16,17.
19. °raṃti] R10.
20. °naḥ ani°] in all Mss. except T1.

[Nj. 222.14]

dhurāḥ [1]/ duṣprativedhaś[2] ca mahāmate ayaṃ[3] tathāgatagarbhāla-ya[4]vijñānagocaraḥ sarva[5]śrāvakapratyeka[6]buddhatīrthyavitarka[7]dar-śa[8]nānām[9] [/] prakṛtipariśuddho 'pi[10] sann aśuddha ivāgantūpakleśo-pakliṣṭa[11]tayā teṣām ābhāti,[12] na tu tathāgatānām[13] / tathāgatānāṃ[14] punar mahā[15]mate karatalā[16]mala[17]kavat pratyakṣagocaro bhavati [18]//

1. om. / after °rāḥ] in all Mss.
2. duṣpratiśedhās] T5, N12,13,14,16,17; duḥpratiśedhaś] T6; °pratidhāś] C9; dupratiṣedhyaś] N11. Nj. °dhurā duṣprativedhāś ca and / after ca.
3. ayan] T1,2,5, C8, R10, N12,16,17; ṣuyan] N13.
4. °gatagalaya (om. rbha)] N12; °bhāya (om. la)] N14.
5. °rvva°] T2,3,5, C9, N11,14,16,17.
6. om. pratyeka] N13.
7. °rkka°] T1, C9, N11; °vigatakṣa°] T6.
8. °daśa] R10.
9. °nāṃ] T1,6, C8, R10, N11,12,17; °nām] T2,3,4,5, C9, N13,14,16. om. / after °nām in all Mss. Nj. °nāṃ and om. /, but Tib. sentence ends here (... *dpyod paḥi lta ba can rnams kyis dkoṅ du chud par dkaḥo* // for duṣprativedhaś ca ... vitarkadarśanānām /).
10. om. *avagraha* in all Mss.
11. °gantupakleśopaklista] T1; gantupakleśopaparikliṣṭa] N11; ivākleśoparikliṣṭa°] T2, C8, R10, N12,13; ivākleśaparikliṣṭa] N17; ivāśeyakleśoparikliṣṭa] T3,4,5, C9, N16; ivāśeyakleśāparikliṣṭa] N14; ivāśeyakleṣṭa°] T6. Nj. °gantukleśo° (om. upa).
12. + /] T1,2,3,4,5, C9, N14,17; + //] C8, R10, N13,16.
13. °nāṃ] T1,6, C8,9, R10, N11,12; °nān] T2,3,4,5, N13,14,16,17. om. /] in all Mss. except N12 (+ //).
14. °nām] T2,3,4,5, C9, N14,16,17; °nā] R10; om. tathāgatānāṃ] T1,6.
15. °mma] T5, C9, N11,14,16,17.
16. karatarā°] T2,3,4,5, C8,9, R10, N12,14,16,17.
17. °mara] T6.
18. om. //] T2,3,4,5, C9, N13,14,17; /] T1,6, N11.

[Nj. 222.19]

etad eva [1...]mahāmate mayā[...1] śrīmālāṃ[2] devīm adhikṛtya deśa[p. 223]-
nāpāṭhe 'nyāṃś[3] ca sū[4]kṣmanipuṇa[5]viśuddha[6]buddhī[7]n bodhisattvā[8]n
adhiṣṭhāya tathāgatagarbha[9] ālayavijñānasaṃśabdi[10]taḥ saptabhi[11]r
[12]vijñānaiḥ saha pravṛ[13]ttyabhiniviṣṭānāṃ[14] śrāva[15]kāṇāṃ[16] dharmanair-
ātmyapradarśa[17]nā[18]rthaṃ śrīmālāṃ[19] devīm adhiṣṭhāya tathāgata-
viṣayo deśi[20]to,[21] na śrāvakapratyeka[22]buddhā[23]nyatīrthakaratarka[24]viṣa-
<u>[25...]yaḥ / anyatra[...25]</u>

1. mayā mahāmate] T2,3,4,6, C8, N11,12,13,14,16,17; om. mayā] T1,5.
2. °lā] R10; °śrīmāṃ] N13; °mālī] N17.
3. anyāṃ] in all Mss. except N11,12 (N11, anyā).
4. sū°] T3,4,5, C9, R10, N12,13,14,16,17.
5. °puna°] T2,3,4,5,6, C9, N12,13,14,16,17.
6. śuddhā°] R10.
7. °buddhi-] T2,3,4,5, C8,9, R10, N12,13,14,16,17.
8. °tvā] in all Mss. except N11.
9. °bhaḥ] T1,2,3,4,5, C9, N11,13,14,16,17.
10. °naṃ] T1.
11. °bhi] N13,14.
12. (r)vvi] N11.
13. pravṛtya°] T6, C8, R10.
14. °nā] R10.
15. °nāṃ] T6.
16. °rmma] T2,3,5, C9, N11,12,14,16,17.
17. pradeśanā°] N13.
18. °tha] T1, R10, N11.
19. °lān] N11; °lā] N12.
20. °padeśi° (upadeśi)] T3,4, C9, N13,14; °vadeśi°] N12.
21. °taḥ] in all Mss.; + //] C8, R10, N12; /] N11.
22. om. pratyeka] T6.
23. °ddha°] R10.
24. °rkka] N11.
25. Nj. viṣayo 'nyatra, but °yaḥ anya° in all Mss.; + // (after yaḥ)] N16. Tib. ends sentence before 'anyatra'.

[Nj. 223.6]

mahāmate tathāgataviṣaya[1] eva tathāgatagarbha ālayavijñānaviṣa-
[2...]yas tvat[...2]sadṛśānāṃ[3] [4...]ca [5]sūkṣmanipuṇa[6]matibuddhi[7]pradeśakānāṃ
bodhisattvānāṃ[8] mahāsattvānām[9] arthapratisaraṇānāṃ[10], no tu ya-
thārutadeśanā[11]pāṭhābhiniviṣṭānāṃ sarvā[12]nyatīrthya[13]śrāvakapratye-
kabuddhānām[14] /[15] [...4] tasmāt tarhi mahāmate tvayānyaiś ca

1. °yaḥ] T1.
2. yaḥ tvat°] T5, N12; yatvat] N16; yatvāt] T2,3,4, C9, N11,13,14,17.
3. °nāñ] N11.
4. T5 om. from 'ca' to '°buddhānām'.
5. śū°] T3, C9, N14,16,17.
6. °puna°] T6, C9, N11,14.
7. buddha] T2, N17.
8. °nām] T2,3, C8, N13,14,16,17.
9. °nāṃ] T1; om. mahāsattvānām] T6.
10. °nān] T3, C9, N17; °nan] N16; °saraṇān] C8; śaraṇān] N13; śaraṇānām] N11; saṇānāṃ] T6. Vd. pratiśaraṇa°.
11. °pāṭha°] R10.
12. °rvvā°] T2,3, C9, N11,14,16,17; °rvanya°] T1.
13. °rtha°] T3, C9, N13,14,16.
14. °nāṃ] T2,3,6, C8,9, N11,13,14,17; °nān] N12; °nā + //] N16.
15. om. /] T1,2,3,4, C8,9, R10, N11,12,13,14,17.

[Nj. 223.10]

bodhisattvair[1] mahāsattvaiḥ sarvatathāgatavişaye[2] 'smiṃs[3] tathāgatagarbhālayavijñānaparijñāne[4] yogaḥ[5] karaṇīyaḥ[6] / na śrutamā[7]trasaṃ[8]tuṣṭair[9] bhavitavyam[10] //[11] tatredam[12] ucyate //[13]

garbhas[14] tathāgatānāṃ hi vijñānais[15] saptabhi[16]r yu[17]taḥ[18] /[19]
pravartate[20] dvayagrāhāt[21] parijñānān nivartate //[22] 1 //

1. rmma°] T4,5, N11,14,16,17.
2. °rvva°] T2,3,5, C9, N11,14,16,17.
3. No *avagraha* in any Mss. (except N12?).
4. °na] T6, N13; jñāne (om. parijñāne)] N12.
5. gas] T3,4,5, N13,14,16,17.
6. Nj. °yo, but °yaḥ in all Mss. and + //] C8, N12; + /] T1, N11. So too Vd.
7. mātraṃ] N11.
8. santu°] T2,3,4,5, C9, N13,14,16,17; satu] R10, N11.
9. °ṣṭai] T5; °ṣṭaiḥ] C8; °stair] T4.
10. vyaṃ] in all Mss.
11. /] T2,3,4,5, C9, N14,17.
12. °dan] T3.
13. /] T1,2,3,5, C9, N14, 17.
14. °bha] N11; °rbbha°] N14.
15. °naiḥ] T6, N11,12; °nai] N16.
16. °bhi] N12.
17. yyu°] T5, C9, N11,14,16,17.
18. °ta] T2,3,4,5, C9, N13,14,16,17.
19. om. /] T3,4, C9, N13,14,17; //] C8, R10, N12,16.
20. °rtta] in all Mss. except T2.
21. Nj. dvayo, but dvaya- in T1, C8,9, N12,14,16 (supported by Tib.); dva-] T2, N13,17. 'dvayo in Vd. is inappropriate.
22. //] T1,6, C8, R10, N11,12,16; om. /] T2.

[Nj. 223.16]

bimbavad[1] dṛśyate[2] cittam[3] anādim atibhāvitam[4] /[5]

arthākāro[6] na[7] cārtho[8] 'sti[9] yathābhūtaṃ vipaśyataḥ[10] //[11] 2 //[a]

aṅgulyagraṃ[12][13][14] yathā bālo[15] na[16...] gṛhṇāti[...16] niśākaram[17] /[18]

[p. 224]

tathā hy akṣarasaṃsaktās[19][20] tattvaṃ[21] nāyenti[22][23...] [...23] māmakam[24] //[25] 3 //[b]

naṭavan[26...] nṛtyate[27] cittaṃ[...26] mano[28] vidūṣasādṛśam[29][30][31] /[32]

vijñānaṃ pañcabhiḥ[33] sārdhaṃ[34] dṛśyaṃ[35] kalpeti[36] raṅgavat[37] // 4 //[c]

1. Nj. vi°, but *ba* and *va* are not distinguished in any Mss. throughout the text; viṃ°] T6.
2. vat°] T2, N13,17.
3. °ttaṃ] T6.
4. °taṃ] T1,6, C8, R10, N11,12.
5. om. /] T2,3,4,5, C9, N13,14,16,17; //] C8, R10,N12.
6. atha] T2; athā] N13.
7. °karo] T1; °kāran] T2,3,4,5, N14,16,17; °kāraṃ] T6, C8,9, N11,12,13.
8. nna] C9, N13.
9. No *avagraha* in any Mss. except T3.
10. vipasyataḥ] T1; vipataḥ] T2,5, N13.
11. /] T1, R10.
12. aṃgu°] T2,3,4,5,6, C8,9, R10, N12,13,14,16,17; agu°] T1.
13. °lyā] T2,3, C8,9, R10, N13,14,16,17.
14. °grā] T1.
15. bālāḥ] T6.
16. gṛhṇāti na] T1.
17. nisā°] T1, N11; viśā°] R10.
18. ran (before t) and om. /] T2,3,4,5, C9, N13,14,16,17; raṃ + //] C8, R10, N12.
19. sasa°] R10; saṃśa] T6.
20. °ktas] T1; °ktaḥ] T6 (Tib. indicates plural).
21. °tva] in all Mss. except T6.

22. tatvan] N11.

23. Nj. reads na vetti, but nā° in all Mss., which is to be accepted; nāveti] C8,9, R10, N11; nāvaiti] T2,3,4,5, N12,13,14,16,17; nāceti (nāveti?)] T1; nāvetti] T6. Cf. Sag. 715: nāveti (BHS form for 'avayanti'), which may show the original reading (alternative reading: akṣarasaṃsaktas tattvaṃ nāveti māmakam //).

24. mama°] T1.

25. °kan (before °naṭa) and om. //] T2,3,4,5, N13,14,16,17; °kaṃ //] T6, C8,9, R10, N11,12.

26. naṭavate (om. nṛtyate)] T5; naṭāvad dṛśyate] T1.

27. °vat] T6.

28. °ttam] T2,3,4,5, C9, N13,14,16,17 (before ma°); citta] R10.

29. viṣaya°] N12.

30. śā°] T2,4,5, C9, N13,14,17.

31. śaṃ] T1,3,5,6, C8, N14; śiṃ] N13,17.

32. om. /] T2,3,4,5,6, C9, R10, N13,14,16,17; //] C8, N11,12.

33. paṃca] T2,3,4,6, C8,9, R10, N11,13,14,16,17.

34. rdhan] T3,4,5, C9, N11,14,16; rdha] R10.

35. śyaṅ] T3,5, C9, N14,17; śya] R10.

36. °lpenti] T1,4,6; °lepenni] C8,9, R10, N11,12,14,16,17; °lpanti] N13.

37. raṃ°] T4,6, R10, N11; ra°] T1.

a. Cf. Sag. 708:

bimbavad dṛśyate cittamanādim abhiḅhāvitam /
arthākāraṃ na cārtho 'sti yathābhūtaṃ vibhāvayet //

b. Cf. Sag. 715:

aṅgulyagraṃ yathā bālaiś (sic.) candraṃ gṛhṇanti durmatiḥ /
tathā hy akṣarasaṃsaktās tattvaṃ nāveṃti māmakam //

c. Cf. Sag. 433:

naṭavat tiṣṭhate cittaṃ mano vidūṣasādṛśam /
vijñānapañcakaiḥ (sic.) sārdhaṃ dṛśyaṃ kalpati (sic) raṅgavat //

§ Pañcadharma (81)

[Nj. 224.4]

atha khalu mahāmatir[1] bodhisattvo mahāsattvaḥ punar api bhagavantam adhyeṣate[2] sma[3] /[4] deśayatu me [5...]bhagavān deśayatu me[...5] sugataḥ[6] pañca[7]dharma[8]svabhāvavijñānanairātmyadvayaprabheda-[9...]gatilakṣaṇam[10] (/) yena nairātmyadvayaprabhedagati[...9]lakṣaṇenāham[11] cānye ca bodhisattvā mahāsattvāḥ sarva[12]bhūmikramā[13]nusaṃdhi[14]ṣv[15] etān[16] dharmān[17] vibhāvaya[18]ema[19] (/)

1. mati] N13,14.
2. °ṣante] T2,3,4,5, C9, N13,14,16,17.
3. om. sma] N16.
4. om. /] T2,3,4,5, C9, N13,14,16,17; //] T6, C8, R10, N11,12.
5. om. bhagavān deśayatu me] T2,3,4,5, C8,9, R10, N12,13,14,16,17; om. me] T6.
6. °ta] in all Mss.
7. paṃca°] in all Mss. except T1.
8. °rmma°] T3,5, C9, N11,13,14,16,17.
9. om. from lakṣaṇaṃ to gati] T6.
10. Nj. adds /, + //] C8, R10. Better replaced with semi-*daṇḍa* or comma. Vd. has comma.
11. N11 repeats nairātmyadvayaprabhedagatilakṣāṇena.
12. °rvva°] T2,3,5, C9, N11,14,16,17.
13. °krāmā°] R10.
14. °sandhi°] N11.
15. °ṣu] in all Mss. except T1.
16. etā] T1.
17. °rmmān] T2,3, C9, N14,16,17; °rmmatā] N11.
18. °vaya°] N14.
19. Nj. + /, and N11,12 //, but all other Mss. om. Vd. has comma.

[Nj. 224.9]

yathā[1] tair[2] dharmaiḥ[3] sarva[4]buddha[5]dharmā[6]nu[7]praveśo bhavet[8](,)[9] sarva[4]buddhadharmā[10]nupraveśāc[11] ca yāvat tathāgatasvapratyātma-[12]bhūmipraveśaḥ[13] syād iti[14] /[15] bhagavān āha /[15'] tena hi[16] mahāmate śṛṇu sādhu ca suṣṭhu ca manasikuru /[17] bhāṣiṣye ’[18]haṃ[19] te /[20] sādhu bhagavann[21] iti[22] mahāmatir bodhisattvo mahāsattvo[23] bhagavataḥ pratyaśrauṣīt[24] //[25]

1. thā (om. ya°)] N14.
2. taiḥ] T6; tai] N13.
3. °rmma°] T2,3,5, C9, N11,14,16; °rmmaḥ] N17.
4. °rvva°] T2,3,5, C9, N11,14,16,17.
5. om. buddha] T6.
6. °rmmā°] T2,3, C9, N11,14,16,17.
7. °ṇu°] T6.
8. vet (om. bha)] N14.
9. + /] in all Mss. (//, C8, R10, N12,13,16). Semi-*daṇḍa* is preferable.
10. °rmmā] T3, C9, N11,14,16,17.
11. °sāc] T1.
12. °tmā°] N12.
13. °śaś ca] T1,6, N11.
14. syādiḥ] C9.
15. //] in all Mss. except T1.
15'. //] in all Mss. except T1, which has / ; + // before bhagavān] N11,12
16. om. hi] N11.
17. om. /] in all Mss.
18. om. *avagraha* in all Mss.
19. han] in all Mss. except T1, which has ham.
20. om. /] in all Mss.
21. °vānn] T4,5, C9, N11,13,14,16,17.
22. + //] T6, N11; /] T1.
23. om. mahāsattvo] C8, R10.
24. °śro°] T3,4,5, C8,9, R10, N13,14,16,17.
25. om. //] T1; °īd and om. //] T2,3,4,5,6, C9, N11,12,13,14,16,17.

[Nj. 224.14]

bhagavāṃs[1] tasyaitad avocat[2] /[3] pañcadharma[4]svabhāvavijñānanai-
rātmyadvayaprabheda[5]gatilakṣaṇaṃ[6] te mahāmate deśayiṣyāmi[7] /[8]
yad uta nāma nimittaṃ vikalpaḥ[9] samyagjñānaṃ[10] tathatā[11] ca[12]
tathāgatapratyātmārya[13]gatipraveśaḥ[14] śā[15]śvatocchedasadasad[16]dṛṣṭi-
vivarjito[17][18] dṛṣṭadha[p. 225]rma[19]sukhasamāpattisukhavihāra āmukhī-
bhavati yogayoginām[20] /[21]

1. °vān] T3,5,6, C9, N11,13,14,16,17; °vaṇ (?)] T4.
2. //] T2,4,6, C8, R10, N12,13,16,17.
3. °paṃ°] T1,2,3,4,5,6, C9, N12,13,14,16,17.
4. °rṃma°] T2,3,5, C9, N11,14.
5. dvayacittadṛśyavāhlabhāvāprabheda] R10.
6. °nan] C8.
7. deśayāmi] R10.
8. //] C8, R10, N12; om. /] T1,2,3,4,5, C9, N11,13,14,16,17.
9. °lpa°] T5, N16.
10. °nan] T2,3,4, C9, N12,13,14,17; samyaganan] T5; samyagnaṃ] N16.
11. tathān] T5.
12. om. ca] T5; ca nu] T2, N13,17; nu (om. ca)] N16.
13. °rẏya°] T3,5, C9, N11,14,16.
14. + / after °śaḥ] N11.
15. sā°] T1.
16. °satdṛ] T2; om. asad] T6; °saḍasatadṛ°] N13.
17. °rjji] T2,3,5, C9, N16.
18. taḥ] Nj., all Mss. except T6, which has °to; + /] N11; + //] N12. Vd. °to.
19. °rmma°] N11,14,16,17.
20. °yogī] T3, C9, N14.
21. °nāṃ, and om. /] in all Mss.

[Nj. 225.2]

tatra mahāmate pañca[1]dharma[2]svabhāvavijñānanairātmyadvayasva[3]-cittadṛśyabāhyabhāvā[4]bhāvānavabo[5]dhād vikalpaḥ pravarta[6]te bālā-nāṃ, na tv āryā[7]ṇāṃ[8] //

mahāmatir āha /[9] katham[10] punar bhaga[11...]van bālā[...11]nāṃ vikalpaḥ pravarta[12]te,[13] na tv āryā[14]ṇāṃ /[15] bhagavān āha /[16] nāmasaṃjñā[17]saṃ-ke[18]tābhinive[19]śena mahāmate bālāś[20] cittam anusaranti[21] /[22]

1. °paṃca°] T2,3,4,5,6, C8,9, R10, N12,13,14,16,17.
2. °rmma] T2,3,5, C9, N11,14,16,17.
3. om. sva] C8, R10.
4. om. bhāvā (abhāva)] in all Mss. except T1.
5. bhāvanābo°] T6.
6. °rtta°] T1, C8, R10, N11,12; varttate] T2,3,4,5,6, C9, N13,14,16,17.
7. °ryyā°] T2,3,5, C9, N11,13,14,16,17.
8. °ṇāṃ and om. //] T2,3,4,5, C9, N13,14,17; + /] T1,6, C8, R10, N11.
9. om. /] T4,5; //] T6, C8,9, R10, N12,13,14,16,17.
10. °tham°] T2,3,4,5, C9, N14,16,17.
11. °vaṃ balā°] T6.
12. °rtta°] T1,3,4,5,6, C9, N11,12,13,16,17.
13. + //] C8, R10, N12.
14. °ryyā°] T2,3, C9, N11,13,16,17.
15. °ṇāṃ //] T2,6, C8, R10, N11,12,16; °nām //] N13,17; om. /] T3,4,5, C9, N14.
16. //] T2,4,6, C8,9, R10, N11 (+ // before bhagavan too),12,13,16.
17. °sajñā] C9.
18. saketā] R10; om. saṃketā] T4.
19. °se°] T1.
20. °lāḥ] T2,3,4, C8,9, R10, N13,14,16,17; °lā] T5, N11.
21. anusmara°] T6, N11.
22. //] T6, C8, R10 (°raṃti), N12; om. /] T1,2,3,4,5, C9, N13,14,16,17.

[Nj. 225.7]

anusaranto[1] vividhalakṣaṇopacāreṇātmātmīyadṛṣṭipatitāśayā[2][3][4] var-ṇapuṣkalatām[5][6] abhiniviśante[7] /[8] [9...]abhiniviśantaś cā[...9]jñānāvṛtāḥ[10] saṃ-rajyante[11] [/][12] saṃraktā[13][ś ca][14] rāgadveṣamohajaṃ[15] karmābhisaṃs-[16]kurvanti[17][18] /[19] abhisaṃskṛtya punaḥ punaḥ[20] kośakārakīṭakā[21] iva svavikalpapariveṣṭitamatayo[22] gatisamudrakāntāraprapatitā [23...]ghaṭī-yantravan[...23] nāti[24]pravartante[25] /[26]

1. anusmara°] T6, N11.
2. °dhaṃ] N12.
3. °ātmatmīya°] N17.
4. °sayā] N11.
5. °rṇṇa] T3,4,5,6, C8,9, R10, N11,13,14,16,17.
6. °latayām] N11.
7. abhiniśante] T5,6.
8. om. /] T1,2,3,4,5,6, C9, N11,13,14,16,17; //] C8, R10, N12.
9. °visyā°] T1; °viśaś cā°] N11; °visantoś cā°] N14.
10. °vṛttāḥ] T1.
11. sara°] N13.
12. From the context it is better to add a *daṇḍa* here (supported by Tib.). So too Vd.
13. sara°] T2,3,4, C8,9, R10, N13,14,16,17.
14. From the context it is better to insert 'ca'.
15. mohaja-] T4.
16. °rmmā] T2,3, C9, N11,14,16,17.
17. saṃku°] T6.
18. °rvva°] T2,3,5, C9, N11,14,16,17.
19. om. /] T1,2,3,4,5,6, C9, N12,13,14,16,17; //] C8, R10 (/, N11).
20. puna] T6.
21. °ṭakāra] T6; °ṭakī] N13.
22. °tatayo (om. ma)] T5.
23. ghaṭīyantraghatīvan] T2,3; ghaṭīyantraghaṭīvan] C8,9, R10, N12,13,14, 16,17; prapaṭiyantraghaṭīvann] T5; ghaṃtī°] N11.
24. nābhi] T3,5, C8,9, R10, N12,13,14,16,17.
25. °rtta°] T3,4,5, C8, N13,14,16,17; varttate (om. pra)] T6, N11.
26. om. /] T3,4,5,6, C9, N11,14,17; //] C8, R10.

[Nj. 225.13]

na ca prajānanti[1] mohān[2] māyāmarīcyudaka[3]candra[4]svabhāvakalpa-
nātmātmīyarahitān[5] sarva[6]dharmān[7] abhūtavi[8]kalpodi[9]tāṃlla[9]kṣya[10]-
lakṣaṇāpagatān[11] bhaṅgo[12]tpādasthitigati[13]vinivṛttān[14] svacittadṛśya-
vikalpaprabhavān[15] ne[16]śvarakālā[17]ṇu[18]pradhānaprabhāvān [/][19] nāma-
nimi[20]ttānu[21]plavena mahāmate bālā nimittam [22]anusaranti[23] //[24]

1. °naṃti] C8; + //] N12.

2. °hāt] T5,6, C9, N11,14,16,17.

3. °marīcidaka°] T1,5,6, C9, N11,13,14,16,17 (this reading is also possible); °marīciudaka] T2,3.

4. °draṃ /] T1,6.

5. °taṃ] in all Mss.; + /] T3, N14.

6. °rvva°] T2,3,5, C9, N11,14,16,17.

7. °rmmā°] T3, C9, N11,14,16,17.

8. om. vi] T1,4, R10.

9. °tāṃ la°] in all Mss. except R10, which has °tā la°. '°tāṃ la' is also possible.

10. °lakṣa°] C9.

11. °tāṃ] T1,6, C8, R10, N11,13,16; °tām] T2,4,5, C9, N14,17.

12. bhaṃgo] T1,4,5,6, C8, R10, N11,12.

13. om. gati] N11.

14. °ttām] T1,2; °ttāṃ] T3,4,5, C8, N12,14,17; °ttāt] T6; °ttaṃ] C9, N16; °ttā] R10, N13.

15. °bhān] T5.

16. Nj. ī(śvara), but ne° (na+ī°)] T5,6, C8,9, R10, N11,12,13,14,17; (°vān)e°] N16. From the context a negative is required (supported by Tib.).

17. °kārā°] T2,3,4,5, C8,9, R10, N12,13,14,16,17.

18. (kāl)ānu°] T1,6.

19. From the context it is better to add a *daṇḍa* here (supported by Tib.). So too Vd.

20. om. nu (°ttāpla°)] T1.

21. °pra°] T2, N13.

22. om. anu] T6.

23. anusmaranti] N11.

24. om. //] T2,3,4,5,6, C9, N11,13,14,17; /] T1.

[Nj. 225.18]

tatra[1] nimittaṃ[2] punar mahāmate[3] yac cakṣurvijñānasyābhāsam[4] āga[p. 226]cchati[5] rūpa[6]saṃjñakam[7], evaṃ śrotraghrāṇajihvākāya[8]-manovijñānānāṃ [9]śabda[10]gandharasa[11]spraṣṭa[12]vya[13]dharmasaṃjñakam[14], etan̲[15] nimittam iti vadāmi[16] /[17] tatra vikalpaḥ punar[18] mahāmate[19] yena nāma samudīrayati[20] / nimittavyañjakam[21] idam, evam idaṃ[22] nānyatheti[23] hastyaśvarathapadātistrīpuruṣādisaṃjñaka[24...]<u>m etad</u>[...24] vikalpaḥ (<u>pravartate</u>)[25] /[26]

1. tatrā] T2, N13. 2. °ttam] T3,4,5, Ç9, N13,14,17; °ttan] N11.
3. (r)mma] C9, N11,16,17. 4. °kṣuvi°] T4,6, N11,14.
5. cchanti] T5; + //] C8, R10. 6. rūpaṃ] R10.
7. °kaṃ] T5; + /] T1. Vd. has *daṇḍa*.
8. jihvāya°] R10; jihvākāyāya°] N14.
9. om. śabda] T6; ge śabda°] N13. 10. gaṃdha] C8, R10.
11. °pra (om. s)] T2,3,4,5, C9, N12,13,14,16,17.
12. + // after °vya] N16.
13. °rmma°] T3,5, C9, N11,13,14,16,17. 14. °kaṃ] N11.
15. °tan] in all Mss. except T3. Nj. etaṃ, but Vd. etan (etan < etad).
16. itivadāmītivadāmi] T6.
17. om. /] T2,3,4,5,6, C8,9, R10, N11,13,14,17; //] N12,16.
18. puna] R10. 19. (r)mma°] T5, C9, N11,14,17.
20. om. /] T1,2,3,4,5,6, C9, N11,13,14,16,17; //] C8, R10, N12.
21. °vyaṃja°] T1,2,3,4,5,6, C9, N12,14,16,17.
22. °dan] T2,3,4,5, C8,9, R10, N13,14,16,17.
23. + // after °ti] T6; /] N11.
24. °kaṃ tad] T1, which is adopted by Nj.; °ka etad] in all Mss. The reading 'etad' is preferable, but 'tad' is also possible.
25. pravarttate only in T1; om. in other Mss. Tib. supports the latter.
26. om. /] in all Mss.

[Nj. 226.5]

samyag[1]jñānaṃ[2] punar[3] [4]mahāmate yena nāmanimittayor [5]anupalabdhir, anyonyāgantu[6]katvād[7] apravṛttir[8] [9]vijñānasyānucchedāśā[10]śvatataḥ[11] sarva[12]tīrthakara[13]śrāvakapratyekabuddhabhūmyapātana[14]tvāt[15] samya[16]gjñānam ity ucyate /[17] punar aparaṃ[18] mahāmate yena samyag[19]jñānena bodhisattvo mahāsattvo[20] na nāma

1. samyak°] C8, R10; saṃyag°] N14.
2. °nam] T2,3,4, C9, N13,14,16.
3. puna] T6.
4. (°r)mma°] T3,5, C9, N11,16,17.
5. aṇu] T6.
6. anyogaṃtu] T6; anyonyāgaṃtu] N12,16. Vd. has *daṇḍa* before 'anyonya°'.
7. °tvāt / (or //)] in all Mss. (//, C8, R10, N12,13,16). The reading here follows Tib.
8. °ttiḥ] T1,2,3,4,5, C9, N12,13,14,16,17; °tti] T6.
9. (r)vvi°] N11.
10. °sā°] T1.
11. °svatataḥ] N11; °śvataḥ tataḥ] T2,3,4,5, N12 (// after °śvataḥ),13,16, 17; °śvataḥ tata] C9; °svatas tataḥ] C8, R10.
12. °rvva°] T2,3,5, C9, N11,14,16,17.
13. °karā°] N11.
14. °pāta°] T1; °pātata°] N12.
15. °tvān] T5, C9, N11,14,16.
16. °yak] C8, R10.
17. //] in all Mss. (doubled in N11).
18. apaṃ] N11; °ram] T3,4,5, N13,14,17.
19. °yak°] C8, R10, N12.
20. °tvaḥ] T1,2,3,4,5, C8,9, R10, N13,14,16,17.

[Nj. 226.9]

bhāvīkaroti[1] na ca [2]nimittam abhāvīkaroti[2] /[3] samāropāpavādānta[4]-dvayakudṛṣṭivivarjitaṃ[5][6] nāmanimittārthayor apravṛttivijñānam[7] evam[8] etāṃ[9] tathatāṃ[10] vadāmi[11] /[12] tathatāvyavasthitaś ca mahāmate bodhisattvo mahāsattvo[13] nirābhāsagocarapratilābhitvāt[14] pramuditāṃ[15] bodhisattvabhūmiṃ[16] pratilabhate[17] //[18]

1. °vībhavati //] N12; °vikaroti] N14.
2. °tta bhāvī°] T3,4,5,6, C9, R10, N12,13,16,17; °ttaṃ bhāvī°] C8; °tta bhāvi°] N14.
3. //] C8, R10; om. /] in other Mss.
4. °ntar°] T3,4, C8, R10, N12,14; daṃtar°] N16.
5. °rjji°] T2,3,5, C9, N14,16,17.
6. °tan] T2,3,4,5, C8,9, R10, N12,13,14,16,17.
7. °vṛṣṭa°] T2,3,4,5, C9, N13,14,16,17.
8. om. evam] T6. Vd. inserts *daṇḍa* before 'evaṃ'.
9. etān] T2,3,4,5, C8,9, R10, N12,14,16,17; etām] N11; etātān] N13.
10. om. tathatāṃ] T1,6, N11.
11. vami] N13.
12. //] N12; om. /] in other Mss.
13. mahāmate] T2,3,4,5, N14,16,17; + mahāmate after mahāsatvo] N12; om. bodhisattvo mahāsattvo] C9.
14. °tvān] T5, C9, N14,16,17.
15. °tām] T2,3,4,5, N12,14,17; °tān] C9; °tā] N11.
16. °mim] T2,3,4,5, C9, N11,14,16,17; °mi] R10.
17. om. prati] T6.
18. /] T6, N11; om. //] T1,2,3,4,5, C9, N13,14,17.

[Nj. 226.15]

sa pratilabhya pramuditāṃ[1] bodhisattvabhūmiṃ[2] vyāvṛttaḥ[3] sarva-[4]
tīrthyāpāyagati[5...]bhyo bhavati[...5] loko[6]ttaradharma[7]gatisamavasṛtaḥ /[8]
lakṣaṇaparicayān[9] māyādipūrvi[10]kāṃ sarva[11]dharma[12]gatiṃ[13] vibhāvay-[14]
an svapratyātmārya[15]dharma[16]gati[17]lakṣaṇaṃ[18] tarka[19]dṛṣṭivinivṛtti[20]kau[21]tu-
ko [*]'nu[p. 227]pūrve[22]ṇa yāvad dharma[23]meghā bhūmir iti /[24] dharma-[25]
meghānantaraṃ[26] yāvat

1. °tām] T2,3,4,5, C9, N13,14,16,17.
2. °mim] T3,4,5, C9; °mi] N11.
3. + // after vyāvṛttaḥ] C8, R10.
4. °rvva] T2,3,5, C9, N11,14,16,17.
5. om. °bhyo bhavati] T2,3,5, C9, N12,13,14,17; °bhavanti] N16.
6. om. loko°] N16.
7. °rmma°] T2,3,5, C9, N11,14,16,17.
8. //] C8, R10; om. /] in other Mss.
9. °yāt] C9, N11,13,14,16,17.
10. °rvva°] T2,3, N11; °rvvi°] T5, C9, N14,16,17; °rvi°] in other Mss. Nj. °rva°.
11. °rvva°] T2,3,5, C9, N11,14,16,17.
12. °rmma°] T2,3,5, C9, N11,13,14,16,17.
13. °ti] N11.
14. bhāva° (om. vi)] T5; vibhava°] R10.
15. °ryya] T2,3,5, C9, N11,14,16,17.
16. °rmma°] T3,5, C9, N11,14,17.
17. °gativibhāvayan la°] R10; °gatidhamila°] N13; °dhatila°] N17.
18. °nan] T2,3,4,5, C9, N13,14,16,17.
19. °rkka°] T2,3,5, C9, N11,14,16,17.
20. °tti°] T3, C8,9, R10, N14.
21. °cau° (?)] T1; °kā°] N13.
* No *avagraha* in any Mss. (No further instances of this will be noted.)
22. °rvve°] T2,3,5, N14,16,17.
23. °rmma°] T2,3, C9, N11,14,16,17.
24. //] T6, C8, R10; om. /] in other Mss.
25. °rmma] T2,3,5, C9, N11,16,17; rmaṃ] R10.
26. °ghāntaraṃ] N16.

[Nj. 227.1]

samādhibalavaśitā[1]bhijñākusumitāṃ[2] tathāgatabhūmiṃ[3] pratilabhate[4] / sa pratilabhya[5] sattvaparipācanatayā vicitrair[6] nir[7]mā[8]ṇakiraṇair[9] virājate[10] jalacandravat[11] / aṣṭāpadasunibaddha[12]dharmā[13] nānādhimuktikatayā sattvebhyo dharmaṃ[14] deśayati[15] / kāyaṃ[16] manovijñaptirahitam etan[17] mahāmate tathatā[18]praveśāt[19] pratilabhante[20] bodhisattvā mahāsattvāḥ[21] //

1. °vasitā°] T1; vaśavaśitā] N11; balavasitān and om. abhijñākusumitān] C9.
2. °tān] T2,3,4,5, N11,13,14,16,17; °tā] T1, R10.
3. °mim] T2,3,4,5, C9, N13,14,17; °mi] N11.
4. //] C8, R10, N12; om. /] T2,3,5, C9, N11,13,14,16,17.
5. °labhyaḥ] N11.
6. °trai] N11.
7. (r)nni°] T5.
8. °rmma°] T2,3, C9, N11,14,17.
9. nirvāṇair for nirmāṇakiraṇair] T6.
10. (r)vvirājyate] N11.
11. //] T6, C8,9, R10, N12,13,16,17.
12. °samuniboddhi°] N11; °sunibad° (om. dha)] N13. Cf. Nj. 122: daśaniṣṭhāpadasunibaddhadharmāṇaḥ.
13. °rmmā] T2,3, C9, N11,13,16,17.
14. °rmmaṃ] T2, N11; °rmman] T3,5, N14,16,17; °rmma] C9; °rman] T4, C8, R10, N12,13.
15. //] C8, R10, N12,16; om. /] T2,3,4,5, C9, N13,14,17.
16. °yam] T3,4,5, C8,9, R10, N13,14,16,17.
17. etat] T3,4,5,6, N13,14,16,17. Vd. inserts *daṇḍa* before 'etan'.
18. tathāgatā°] T6.
19. °śān] T2,3,5, C9, N11,13,14.
20. °bhate] T1; + // after te] T6, C8, R10, N11,12.
21. om. //] T2,3,4,5,6, C9, R10, N12,13,14,16,17.

[Nj. 227.8]

punar api mahāmatir āha /[1] kiṃ punar[2] bhagavan[3] pañcasu[4] dharmeṣv[5] antargatās[6] trayaḥ[7] svabhāvā[8] uta svalakṣaṇasiddhāḥ[9] /[10] bhagavān āha /[11] atraiva mahāmate trayaḥ svabhāvā[12] antargatā[13] aṣṭau ca vijñānāni[14] dve ca nairātmye[15] /[16] tatra nāma[17] ca nimittaṃ[18] ca parikalpitaḥ[19] svabhāvo veditavyaḥ[20] /[21]

1. //] in all Mss. except T1, which om. *daṇḍa*.
2. punar punar] N14.
3. °vaṃ] N11.
4. °paṃcasu] T4,5,6, C8,9, R10, N12,16; °paṃca] T2,3, N13,17.
5. °rmme°] T2,3,5, C9, N11,14,16,17.
6. °rgga°] T3,5, C9, N14,16,17; ga° (om. r)] R10.
7. + / after °yaḥ] T6; //] N11.
8. om. °vā°] N12.
9. °siddhāntaḥ] T6, N11.
10. //] T4,6, C8, R10, N11 (doubled),12,13; om. /] T3, C9, N14.
11. //] T2,4,5,6, R10, N11,12,13,14,16,17.
12. °vāḥ] T6, C8, R10.
13. °tāḥ] T1,2,3,4,5,6, C8,9, N14,17; rantagarāḥ] N11; antargantatāḥ] N13; antarggatāḥ] N16.
14. + / after °ni] R10.
15. °tmyaṃ] T2,3,4,5, C8,9, R10, N11,12,13,14,16,17.
16. Only N12 has *daṇḍa*.
17. nāmaṃ ca] T6; ca nāma] N12; om. ca] T1.
18. °ttañ] T2,3,5, C9, N13,14,16,17.
19. kalpiḥ] R10.
20. °vya] T3,4,5, C9, N14,16.
21. //] C8, R10, N11 (doubled),12,13,16; om. /] T1,6.

[Nj. 227.12]

yaḥ[1] punar[2] [3]mahāmate tadāśrayapravṛtto[4] vikalpaś[5] cittacaittasaṃ[6]-[7]śabdito[8] yugapatkālodita[9] āditya iva raśmi[10]sahito[11] vicitralakṣaṇa-svabhāvo[12] vikalpā[13]dhārakaḥ[14] sa mahāmate svabhāvaḥ[15] paratantra ity ucyate /[16] samyagjñānaṃ[17] tathatā ca mahāmate avinā<u>ṣi</u>[18]tvāt svabhāvaḥ pariniṣpanno[19] veditavyaḥ //[20]

1. yāṃ] C8.
2. puna] T6.
3. (°r)mma°] T3,5, C9, N11,13,16,17.
4. om. pra] T1; °vṛtta] T6.
5. °lpaḥ] T1; °lpa-] N11.
6. caita] N11; om. caitta] T6.
7. °sa°] T1.
8. °taḥ] in all Mss.; + /] T1; //] C8, R10.
9. yugavat°] T4; yugat°] N16.
10. rasmi°] T2,3,4,5, C9, N11,13,14,16,17.
11. sahitaḥ] in all Mss. except R10, which reads 'sahataḥ'; + //] C8, R10.
12. °vaḥ] T1,2,3,4,5, C9, N12,13,14,16,17.
13. vikalpāva] T1.
14. + // after °kaḥ] C8, R10.
15. + / after °vaḥ] T2,3, C9, N14,17; //] N13.
16. //] N16; om. /] T2,3,4,5, C8,9, R10, N12,13,14,17.
17. °nan] N11,12.
18. °śa°] Nj.; but °śi°] C8, R10, N11,12,13; °śi°] T1,2,3,4,5,6, C9, N13,14, 16,17. 'avināśitvāt' is acceptable here.
19. °nni] T6.
20. /] C9.

[Nj. 227.18]

punar aparaṃ[1] mahāmate svacittadṛśyam abhiniviśya[2]mānaṃ[3] vikalpo 'ṣṭadhā[4] bhidyate[5] /[6] nimittasyābhūtalakṣaṇaparikalpita-[p. 228]tvād ātmātmīya[7]grāha[8]dvayavyupaśamān[9] nairātmya[10]dvayam[11] ājāyate[12] /[13] eṣu mahāmate pañ[14]casu dharmeṣu[15] sarvabuddha[16]dharmā[17] antargatā[18] bhūmivibhāgānusaṃ[19]dhiś ca śrāvakapratyekabuddhabodhisattvānāṃ[20] tathāgatānāṃ[21] ca[22] pratyātmārya[23]jñānapraveśaḥ //[24]

1. °ram] R10, N12.
2. °niveśaya] T2, N13,17; °nivisya] T1.
3. nam] T2,3,4,5, C8,9, R10, N11,13,14,16,17 (on the assumption that it was preceding *ba*?).
4. ṣṭayo] C9.
5. vidyate] N16.
6. om. /] T1,2,3,4,5,6, N12,13,14,16,17.
7. ātmītmīya°] T2,3, N14,17; rvātmātmīya] N12 (om. °dā).
8. grāhaya°] N13.
9. vyupasamān] T1,6, N11,16; °mā] T5.
10. narātmya] N17.
11. °yām] R10.
12. ājayate] R10.
13. //] C8, R10, N16; // //] N11; om. /] T2,3,4,5, C9, N13,14,17.
14. paṃ°] T3,4,5,6, C9, R10, N12,13,14,16,17.
15. °rmme°] T2,3,5, N11,14,16,17.
16. om. buddha] T2, N13,17.
17. °rmmā] T2,3, C9, N11,14; °rmo (?)] T1; °rma°] T6; °rmām] R10.
18. antaragatā] T5, C9, N14,16,17.
19. °san°] T2,6, C8, N11,13,17.
20. °nān] T2,3,4,5, C9, N11,13,14,16,17.
21. °nāñ (ca)] T2,3,4,5, C9, N11,13,16,17.
22. om. ca] T6.
23. °ryya°] T2,3,5, C9, N11,14,16,17.
24. /] T3,4,5,6, R10; om. //] C8,9, N11,13,14.

[Nj. 228.5]

punar aparaṃ[1] mahāmate[2] pañcadharmā[3] nimittaṃ[4] nāma vikalpas[5] tathatā samyag[6]jñānaṃ[7] ca /[8] tatra mahāmate nimittaṃ yat saṃsthānākṛtiviśeṣākārarūpādilakṣaṇaṃ dṛśyate[9] tan nimittam[10] /[11] yat tasmin nimitte ghaṭādi[12]saṃjñākṛtakam evam idaṃ[13] nānyatheti[14] tan nāma /[15] yena tan[16] nāma samudīrayati[17] nimittābhivyañjakaṃ[18] sa-ma[19]varmeti[20]

1. °ram] T2,3,4, N13,14,16,17; °ra] T5.
2. paṃ°] in all Mss. except T1.
3. °rmo] Nj., but °rmā] T2, N12,13; °rmmā] T3, which is preferable (supported by Tib.); °rmma] C9, N11,14,16,17; °rma] T6, C8, R10. Vd. °rmāḥ.
4. °ttan] T2,3,4,5, C8,9, R10, N13,14,16,17.
5. °lpa-] in all Mss.
6. °yak°] C8, R10.
7. °nañ] T2,3,4,5,6, C8,9, R10, N11,14,16,17.
8. om. /] in all Mss.
9. + / after °te] T1; //] T6.
10. °ttaṃ] in all Mss.
11. /] only in N11.
12. ghaṭāṭi°] T5, N13.
13. idan] T2,3,4,5, C9, N13,14,17.
14. // after °ti] N11.
15. om. /] T1,3,4,6, C8,9, R10, N11,12,13,14,16,17.
16. taṃ] T6.
17. samudira°] N11; mudīra° (om. sa) and // after °ti] N12.
18. °vyaṃja°] T3,4,5,6, C9, N12,13,14,16,17.
19. Reading uncertain. same] T1; śanma°] T2,3,4,5, C8,9, R10, N12,13,14, 16,17; śamma] N11. Tib. (Peking Ed.) *bde ba she* (?). For śama?
20. dharmeti] Nj. and T4,6, C8, R10, N12,13; dharmmā°] T2,3,5, C9, N14, 16,17. But varmeti] T1, and varmmati] N11. Tib. *go cha* supports 'varman'.

[Nj. 228.10]

vā[1] sa mahāmate citta[2]caitta[3]saṃśabdito[4] vikalpaḥ /[5] yan nāmani-
mittayor[6] atyantā[7]nupalabdhitā[8] buddhi[9]pralayād[10] anyonyā[11]nanubhū-[12]
tāparikalpitatvād[13] eṣāṃ[14] dharmāṇāṃ[15] tathateti[16] (/)[17] tattvaṃ bhūtaṃ[18]
niścayo niṣṭhā[19] prakṛtiḥ svabhāvo[20...20] 'nupalabdhiḥ[21] /[22] tat tathatālak-[23]
ṣaṇaṃ[24] (/) mayānyaiś ca tathāgatair[25...25] anugamya yathāvad deśitaṃ[26]
prajñaptaṃ vivṛtam[27] uttānīkṛtam[28] [/][29]

1. vā ma sa] R10.
2. cittaṃ] T1.
3. caittaṃ] R10.
4. °sabdhi] T1.
5. //] C8, R10, N12; om. /] T1,2,3,4,5, C9, N13,14,16,17.
6. °ttar] N14.
7. atyaṃtā°] C8; atyanta°] N16.
8. °tā upa°] N12.
9. °dhinā] T2, N13,17; om. tā] T1.
10. buddha°] T2, N13,17.
11. °layad] T4.
12. anyonyā (om. na)] T3,6, C8,9, R10, N11,13,14,16,17.
13. °ta (om. negative a-)] T1,3,6, C9, N12.
14. eṣān] T2,3,4,5, C9, N11,12,14,16.
15. °rmmā] T2,3, C9, N11,14,16,17.
16. dharmateti] T4, N13; dharmmateti] T2,3, C9, N11,14,16,17; dharmata-thateti] C8; dharmatatheti] N12; dharmmatathateti] T5. Cf. Tib. 'tathatā'.
17. om. /] in all Mss. (which is preferable).
18. °tan] T2,3,4,5; bhūtatvaṃ bhūtaṃ] N13.
19. + pratiṣṭhā after niṣṭhā] T1.
20. °vanu°] T6; °vānu] C9, R10, N11,12,13,14,16,17.
21. °is] T6; but all other Mss. have °iḥ, and C8, R10, + //; /] N11. Short

punctuation mark is required here (subordinate *yad* clause ends here).

22. tan] T2,3,4,5, C9, N13,14,16,17.
23. °tathāla] Nj. and T6, C9; tathatāla°] in all Mss. 'tathālakṣaṇa' is unlikely.
24. Nj. + / here, but not supported by Mss. (°ṇammayā° in all Mss. except T6, N11); °(la)yaṃ (for lakṣaṇaṃ)] T6.
25. °gatena nu°] T2, N17; °gataranu°] N13.
26. °tam] T2,3,4,5, C9, N14,16,17; + /] T6, N11.
27. vivattam] N11.
28. uttākṛtaṃ] T3, C9; uttākṛṃ] N14; °kṛta] N11.
29. *Daṇḍa* is required here (accordingly °tam instead of °taṃ). N11 has /.

[Nj. 228.15]

[1...]yo 'trānugamaḥ[...1] [2]samyagavabo[3]dho 'nucchedā[4]śā[5]śva[6]tato vikalpas-
yāpravṛttiḥ svapratyātmā[7]ryajñānānu[8]kūlaṃ tīrthakarapak[9]ṣapara-
pak[10]ṣaśrāvakapratyekabuddhāgatilakṣaṇaṃ [11]tat [12]samya[13]gjñā[p. 229]-
nam[14] [15]/ ete ca[16] mahāmate pañca[17]dharmā[18]ḥ [19]/ eteṣ[20]v eva trayaḥ sva-
bhāvā[21] aṣṭau ca vijñānāni dve ca nairātmye[22] sar[23]va[24]buddhadharmā[25]ś
cāntar[26]gatā[27]ḥ [28]/

1. Nj. yatrānugamya. °yamyaḥ] T2,3,5, C8,9, R10, N12,13,14,16,17, but yātrānugamaḥ] T1; yotrānugamaḥ] T6, N11. This last reading is acceptable here.
2. om. samya°] T4.
3. Nj. °bodhānu°, but °bodhaḥ anu° in all Mss. (cf. Tib. *gaṅ gis khoṅs su chud ciṅ yaṅ dag par rdsogs pa daṅ* = yenāvagamya samyagavabodhaḥ).
4. °sā°] T1.
5. °sva°] T2,3,4,5, C9, N11,13,14,17.
6. °śvato] T6.
7. °ryya°] T2,3,5, C9, N11,13,14,16,17.
8. anukukūlaṃ] T2, N17; + /] N11.
9. °kṣā°] T2,4,6, C8,9, R10, N11,12,13,14,16,17 (-pakṣa + aparapakṣa; does aparapakṣa mean 'Buddhist'?). Tib. om. °pakṣa° (tīrthakaraparapakṣa-).
10. °kṣaṃ] T2.
11. tan] T3,4, C9, N11,14,16.
12. saṃ°] C9, N17.
13. °yak°] C8, R10.
14. °naṃ] T1.
15. om. /] T1,2,3,4,5,6, C8, R10, N12,13,16,17.
16. na] N11.
17. paṃ°] 2,3,4,5,6, C9, N13,14,16,17.
18. °rmmāḥ] T2,3, C9, N14,16; °rmmaḥ] T5; °rmaḥ] N13; °rmā] T6;°rmmā] N11.
19. //] N13; om. /] T1,3,5,6, C8,9, R10, N11,14,16.
20. esv] T1; eṣv.] T6, N11.
21. °vāḥ] in all Mss.
22. °tmya] C9.
23. °rvva] T2,3,5, C9, N11,14,17.
24. om. buddha] T6.
25. °rmmā] T2, C9, R10, N11,16,17.
26. °rgga] N16,17.
27. °tā] N13.
28. //] C8, R10, N12; om. /] in other Mss.

[Nj. 229.3]

atra te mahāmate[1] svamatikauśalaṃ[2] karaṇīyam anyaiś ca kārayitavyaṃ,[3] na parapraṇeyena[4] bhavitavyam[5] //[6] tatredam ucyate //[7]

[8]pañcadharmāḥ[9] svabhāvaś[10] ca vijñānāny[11] aṣṭa[12] eva ca /[13]
dve nairātmye[14] bhavet kṛtsno[15] mahāyānaparigrahaḥ //[16] 5 //[a]

1. tremate] N13.
2. °aṅ] T3,5, C9, N14,16,17; °śalyaṃ] N12.
3. + /] T1,2,3,4,5, C9, N14,17; //] C8, R10, N11,12,13,16. Vd. has *daṇḍa*.
4. °yeṇa] N12.
5. °vyaṃ] T3,4,5, C8,9, R10, N11,14,16,17; °vyaḥ] T1; °vya] N13.
6. /] T1; // //] N11; om. //] in other Mss.
7. /] T2,3,5, C8,9, N14,17.
8. paṃ°] T2,3,4,5, C9, N12,13,14,16,17.
9. °rmmāḥ] T2, C9, N14,16; °rmmā] N11.
10. °vāś] N11. Is this preferable? Cf. Sag. 638.
11. vijñānānāny] N16.
12. om. aṣṭa] N16.
13. //] C8, R10, N12; om. /] T2,3,4,5, C9, N13,14,16,17.
14. °yaṃ] T2,3,4,5, C9, N12,13,14,16,17.
15. kṛṣṭo] N16.
16. //] T6, C8, R10, N11,12; /] T1; other Mss. have no *daṇḍa*.

a. Cf. Sag. 638:

pañcadharmāḥ svabhāvāś ca vijñānāny aṣṭa eva ca /
dve nairātmye bhavet kṛtsno mahāyānaparigrahaḥ //

[Nj. 229.8]

nāmanimitta[1]saṃkalpāḥ[2] svabhāvadvaya[3]lakṣaṇam[4] /[5]

samyag[6]jñānaṃ[7] tathātvaṃ[8] ca pariniṣpannalakṣaṇam[9] // 6 //[b]

1. °ttaṃ] T1,2,3,4,5, C8,9, N12,13,14,16,17.
2. Short *a* in all Mss. (°lpa, T5). Most Mss. probably read: nāma nimittaṃ saṃkalpaḥ. But a short syllable is required for the fifth syllable. An alternative reading is as in v. I.134: nimittaṃ nāma saṃkalpaḥ. In this case, however, 'ca' is required after 'saṃkalpa'. Thus the Nj. reading is acceptable after all.
3. dvayā] T5, N16.
4. °ṇaṃ] T2,3,4,5,6, C8,9, R10, N12,13,14,16,17; °ṇa] N11.
5. //] C8, R10, N12; om. /] T2,3,4,5, C9, N11,13,14,16,17.
6. °yak] C8.
7. °nan] T2,3,4,5, C9, N14,16,17.
8. tathatvaṃ] T4,5,6, C9, N12,14,16,17; tathatvañ (ca)] N11. 'tathatva' is more usual in BHS.
9. ṇaṃ] T2,3,4,5,6, C8,9, R10, N12,13,14,16,17; ṇa] N11.

b. Cf. v. II.134:
nimittaṃ nāma saṃkalpaḥ svabhāvadvayalakṣaṇam /
(sic.)
samyagjñānaṃ hi tathatā pariniṣpaṇṇalakṣaṇam //

Sag. 156bc:
nāmanimittasaṃkalpaḥ svabhāvadvayalakṣaṇam /
samyagjñānaṃ hi tathatā pariniṣpannalakṣaṇam //

§ Gaṅgānadīvālukāsamās tathāgatāḥ (82)

[Nj. 229.10]

atha khalu mahāmatir [1] bodhisattvo mahāsattvaḥ [2...] punar api bhaga-vantam [...2] etad avocat [3] / yat punar [4] etad [5] uktaṃ [6] bhagavatā deśanā- [7] pāṭhe yathā [8] gaṅgā[9]nadī[10]vālukāsamās tathāgatā [11] atītā [12...] [...12] anāgatā [13] var-[14]tamānāś ca [15] / tat kim [16] idaṃ [17] bhavan yathārutārthagrahaṇaṃ [18] kar-[19]tavyam [20] / [21] āhosvid anyaḥ kaścid arthāntaraviśeṣo [22] 'stīti tad ucya-tāṃ bhagavan [23] /

1. °ti] T2, N13,17.
2. bhagantaṃ punar] C8, R10 (om. api).
3. //] T4,6, C8,9, R10, N12,13,16; om. /] T5.
4. puna] T1.
5. eta] T4,5, N14.
6. °taṃ] T2,3,4,5, C8,9, R10, N16,17.
7. bhagavan sa] T1.
8. gaṃ°] in all Mss. except T5.
9. gagādī°] T5.
10. Nj. bālukā. vālukā°] T1,6, N12; vālikā°] T2,3,4,5, C8,9, R10, N11,13,14, 16,17. Both forms are possible. Vd. vālukā°.
11. °tāḥ] in all Mss. except N12; + /] T1.
12. °tānā°] T2,6, N11,13,17.
13. °ta] R10.
14. °rtta°] in all Mss. except R10; varṇṇa (?)] R10.
15. om. /] in all Mss.
16. °dam] T2,3,4, C9, N14,17.
17. + /] T6.
18. °ṇaṅ] T3, C9, N14,17.
19. °rtta°] in all Mss.
20. °vyaṃ // ā°] T2,3,4, C8,9, R10, N12,13,14,16,17; °vyaṃ ā°] T5; °vyaṃ a] T6; (vyam ā] T1, N11). Better to have punctuation. Vd. has comma.
21. °hāsvid] T5.
22. °seṣo] T1.
23. //] T2,3,4,5,6, C8,9, R10, N11 (doubled), 12,13,14,16,17.

[Nj. 229.15]

bhagavān āha /[1] na mahāmate yathārutārthagrahaṇaṃ[2] kartavyam[3] /[4] na ca mahāmate gaṅgā[5]nadīvālukā[6]pramāṇatayā tryadhvaka[7]buddha[8]pramāṇatā bhavati /[9] tat kasya hetor[10] yad uta[11] lokātiśayāti[12]krāntatvān[13] mahāmate[14] dṛṣṭānto[15] [16]'dṛṣṭāntaḥ sadṛ[17]śāsa[18]dṛśatvāt /[19]

1. //] T2,3,4,5,6, C8,9, R10, N11,12,13,14,16,17.
2. °rtta°] in all Mss.
3. °vyaṃ] in all Mss.
4. //] T3,4,5, C8,9, R10, N11,12,13,14,16.
5. gaṃ] in all Mss.
6. Nj. bālukā. valukā] T1,6, N12; vālikā] in other Mss.
7. tryadhvaika°] T1,2,6, C8, R10, N17; tryadhaika] T3,4, C9, N11,12,13,14; tryaka] T5, N16.
8. om. buddha] T2,3,4,5, C8,9, R10, N12,13,14,16,17.
9. //] T6, N11,13,16; om. /] T3,4,5, C8,9, R10, N12,14.
10. °taḥ] T1,6 (+ //), N11 (+ /); °to] T5, N14. Vd. has '?'.
11. utā] C9.
12. °sayā°] T6, N11; lotiśayā°] N12.
13. °tāt /] T2,3,4,5,6, N14,17; °tāt //] C8, R10, N11,12,13,16; krāntan] C9.
14. om. mohāmate] C9.
15. °ntaḥ] C9.
16. *Avagraha* only in N11.
17. śadṛ°] R10; om. sa°] T3, N14; om. °ṣṭāntaḥ sadṛ°] C9.
18. śāśa] N17.
19. //] T4, C8, R10, N12,13,17.

[Nj. 230.1]

na ca mahāmate tathāgatā arhantaḥ samyaksaṃ[1]buddhāḥ[2] sadṛśāsadṛśaṃ lokātiśaya[3]ātikrāntaṃ[4] dṛṣṭāntaṃ[5] prāvi[6]ṣkurvanti[7] /[8] anyatra upamāmātram[9] etan[10] mahāmate [11]mayopanyastaṃ[11] taiś[12] ca tathāgatair yathā[13] gaṅgā[14]nadīvālukā[15]samās tathāgatā arhantaḥ samyaksaṃ[16]buddha iti nityānityābhiniveśābhiniviṣṭānāṃ[17]

1. saṃ°] T6, N14.
2. °ddhaḥ] T1; °ddhā] N13.
3. lokāti (om. atiśaya), N13.
4. °tan] T2,3,4,5, C9, N17; °krān (om. taṃ)] N14.
5. °tan] T2, N13,17; °tam] T3,4,5, C9, N11,14.
6. prāviku°] T6.
7. °rvva°] T2,3,5, C9, N11,14,16,17.
8. //] T6, C8, R10, N12,16; om. /] T2,3,4,5, C9, N13,14,17.
9. umā° (om. pa)] R10. All Mss. separate anyatra and upamā°.
10. etat] T3,4,6, C9, N11,13,14,16,17.
11. mayā upa°] T1,2,3,4,5,6 (°sta), C9, N11,12,13,14,16,17; upanyastam mayā] C8, R10 (which is preferable).
12. tais] T6 (om. ca); taiḥ] C8.
13. (r)yya°] N11. Vd. inserts *daṇḍa* before 'yathā'.
14. gaṃ°] T2,3,4,6, C8,9, R10, N11,12,13,14,16,17.
15. Nj. bāluka°. vālukā] T1,6, N12; vālikā] T2,4,5, C8, R10, N11,13,16,17; vālikāḥ] T3, C9, N14.
16. saṃ°] T6.
17. °nām] T3,4,5, N11,13,14,17; °niveśanti nirviṣṭānāṃ] T6.

[Nj. 230.5]

bālapṛthagjanānāṃ[1] tīrthakar[2]āśay[3]akudṛṣṭiyuktānāṃ[4] saṃ[5]sārabha-
vacakrānusā[6]riṇām udve[7]janārthaṃ[8] katham eta[9] udvignā bhavaga-
[10]ticakra[11]saṃkaṭād [12]...viśeṣārthino viśeṣam...[12] ārabherann iti[13], sulabha-
buddhatva[14]pradarśanārthaṃ ca[15] nodum[16]barapuṣpatulyas[17] tathāgatā-
nām utpāda iti kṛtvā vīrya[18]m nā[19]rapsyante[20] /[21]

1. °nān] T2,3,4,5, C9, N13,14,16,17.
2. °karāṃ] T4.
3. °saṃśaya°] T2,4,5, N13,17.
4. °yuṣṭānāṃ] T4,5,6, N17; puṣṭānāṃ] C9, N12,13,14,16.
5. san°] N12.
6. °śā] T6, N11.
7. udvaija°] N13,16.
8. °rtham vā] T2,3,4,5, C8,9, R10, N13,14,16,17.
9. ete] T2,3,4,5,6, C9, R10, N11,13,16,17.
10. bhavati°] T6; bhagavati] C8, R10, N16.
11. °kraṃ°] T1.
12. viveṣārthino (?) viseṣam] T1.
13. °rantiti] C9, N14; + /] T1; + //] T6.
14. sulabhabuddhabuddhatva°] T6.
15. Nj. na. But all Mss. have ca (°añ ca in all Mss. except T1, N12).
16. °duṃ] N12.
17. °yaḥ /] N11.
18. °ryya°] T2,3,5, C9, N16,17.
19. Nj. vīryam ā°. But all Mss. have nā°. °yaṃ] T1,6; °yan] in other Mss. Tib. has neither negative (here and before 'udumbara').
20. °ate] T4; °aṃte] T5, N16; lapsyante] T6.
21. //] N11,12; om. /] T2,3,4,5,6, C8, R10, N13,14,16,17.

[Nj. 230.10]

deśanāpāṭhe tu mayā vaineyajanatāpekṣa[1]yo[2]dumbarapuṣpasudur-
la[3]bhaprādurbhā[4...]vās tathā[...4]gatā iti deśitam[5] [6]/ [7...]na ca[...7] mahāmate
udumbarapuṣpaṃ[8] kenacid[9] dṛṣṭapūrvaṃ[10] na[11] drakṣyate[12] /[13] tathā-
gatāḥ punar [14]mahāmate loke dṛṣṭā[15] dṛśyante[16] caitarhi /[17] na sva[18]-
naya[19]pratyava[20]sthānakathām adhikṛtyo[21]dumbarapuṣpasudurlabha-
prādurbhāvās tathāgatā iti /[22]

1. °nāyā°] N12.
2. °yā udu°] in all Mss. So too Vd.
3. °rlla°] T2, N11,14,17.
4. °vās tacās tathā°] T6.
5. °taṃ] T1,6, N12; °tan] T2,3,4,5, C8,9, R10, N11,13,14,16,17.
6. om. /] in all Mss.
7. tatra] T6.
8. °ṣpaṅ] T3,5, C9, N14,17; °ṣpa] N11.
9. °ci] T6, N14.
10. °rvvan] T2,3,5, C9, N11,14,16,17; °rvan] T4, N12,13; om. pūrvaṃ] T6.
11. na ca] T6.
12. °anti] T1,2,3,4,5, C8,9, R10, N11,13,14,16,17; °aṃti] N12; °ati] T6.
13. //] C8, R10; om. /] in other Mss.
14. °(r)mma] T3,5, C9, N11,14,16,17.
15. om. dṛṣṭā] R10; repeat loke dṛṣṭā] T2, N13.
16. + /] T1; + //] T6.
17. om. /] in all Mss.
18. 'sva°] T6.
19. om. naya] N12.
20. °tyāva°] N11.
21. °tya udu°] in all Mss. So too Vd.
22. om. /] in all Mss. except N11.

[Nj. 230.15]

svanayapratyava[1]sthānakathāyā[2]ṃ mahāmate nir[3]diśyamānāyā[4]ṃ lo[5]kātiśa[6]yātikrāntā dṛṣṭāntāyuktāḥ[7] kriyan[8]te '[9]śraddheyatvā[10]t /[11] aśraddheya[12]ṃ syād bālapṛthagjanānā[13]ṃ ca[14] /[15] [p. 231] svapratyātmār[16]yajñānagocare ca[17] dṛṣṭāntā[18] na pravar[19]tan[20]te /[21] cittamano[22]manovijñānadṛṣṭa[23]lakṣaṇātikrānta[24]tvāt tattvasya /[25] tattva[26]ṃ ca tathāgatā atas teṣu dṛṣṭāntā[27] nopanyasyante[28] //[29]

1. °pratyayasthāna°] N16.
2. °yām] T2,3,5, C9, N13,14,16,17.
3. °rddhi] C9, N11,16,17.
4. °yā] N14.
5. lokātiti°] T4.
6. °sa°] T1.
7. dṛṣṭāyuktāḥ] T5; dṛṣṭāntāḥ] C8, R10; dṛṣṭānāyuktāḥ] C9. Vd. dṛṣṭāntā yuktāḥ.
8. °yaṃte] C8, R10; + //] N12.
9. aśra°] T1,2,3,4,5,6, C8,9, N11,12,13,14,16,17.
10. °tvād] T2,3,4, C9, N11,12,13,16,17.
11. om. /] in all Mss.
12. śraddheya] T6.
13. °nāṃñ] T2,3, C9; °nāñ] T4,5, N14,17; °janāṃ] T1.
14. om. ca] T1,6, C8, R10, N11.
15. om. /] in all Mss.
16. °ryya] T2,3,5, C9, N11,13,16,17; °tmāya°] T6.
17. om. ca] C9.
18. °nto] C9, N14.
19. °rtta°] in all Mss.
20. °aṃte] C9; °ate] N17.
21. //] C8, R10, N12; om. /] in other Mss.
22. mana°] T6, N11; om. mano] T5, R10.
23. °dṛṣṭi°] N11. Tib. om. dṛṣṭalakṣaṇa.
24. °krāṃta] N12.
25. om. /] in all Mss.
26. °tvañ] T1,2,3,4,5,6, C9, N13,14,17.
27. dṛṣṭantvā] T6.
28. °syaṃte] C8, R10; nopanamyante] N11.
29. om. //] T1,2,3,4,5,6, C9, N11,13,14,17.

[Nj. 231.4]

kiṃ[1] tu[2] upamāmātram[3] etan[4] mahāmate kṛtaṃ,[5] yad[6] uta[6] gaṅgā-[7] (sic.) nadī[8]vālukā[9]samās[10] tathāgatāḥ,[11] samā na viṣamā[12] akalpāvikalpana[13]taḥ[14] /[15] tad yathā mahāmate, gaṅgā[16]yāṃ[17] nadyāṃ[18] vālukā[19] mīnakaccha-paśiśu[20]māranakramahiṣasiṃhahastyādibhiḥ saṃkṣobhyamāṇā[21] na kalpayanti[22] na vikalpayanti[23] saṃkṣobhyāmahe na veti nirvi[24]kalpāḥ[25] svacchā malavyapetāḥ [/][26]

1. kim°] T2,3,4,5,6, C9, N11,13,16,17.
2. °tu upa°] in all Mss. and Nj.
3. upamātram] N11.
4. etat] T3,4,5, C9, N11,13,14,16,17.
5. kṛta] N11,12; + /] T6.
6. ya (om. uta)] N12.
7. gaṃ°] in all Mss.
8. Nj. bā°. Hereafter the same usage in Nj. has been silently corrected.
9. vālikā°] T2,3,4,5, C8,9, R10, N11,13,14,16,17.
10. Nj. °statathā° (°ta° redundant).
11. tagatāḥ] N16.
12. viṣā] T6; viṣamo] C8.
13. akalpavikalpa°] T2,3,4,5,6, C8, R10, N13,14,16; akalpa° (om. avikalpa)] C9, N17; avikalpa° (om. akalpa)] N12.
14. °tas] T2,3,4,5, C8,9, R10, N13,14,16,17; °lpas (om. °nata°)] N12.
15. om. /] T2,3,4,5, C8,9, R10, N12,13,14,16,17; // //] N11. New paragraph is preferable here (instead of before 'kiṃ tu', where Tib. continues the sentence with *mod kyi*).
16. gaṃ°] in all Mss.
17. °yān] T2,3,4,5, C9, N14,16,17.
18. °dyām] T3,4,5, C9, N14,16,17 (on the assumption that it was preceding *ba*?).

19. vālikā] T2,3,4,5,6, C8,9, R10, N11,13,14,16,17.
20. °sisu] T1; °siśu°] T6; °śisu°] N12.
21. °ṇo] C8; °nā] T3,4,5, C9, N12,14,16,17; °no] T2, R10, N13
22. + //] N16.
23. °yaṃti] C8; + //] N16.
24. °rvvi°] T3,5, C9, N14,16,17.
25. °kalāḥ] N12.
26. Nj. has no *daṇḍa*; + /] T6, N11,16. Ending of word with *visarga* before e° in all Mss. may mean that the sentence ends here. Vd. has *daṇḍa*.

[Nj. 231.9]

evam eva mahāmate tathāgatā[1...]nām [...1]arhatāṃ sa[2]myaksaṃbuddhā[3]nāṃ svapratyātmār[4]yajñānaga[5]ṅgā[6]ma[7]hānadībalābhijñāva[8]śitāvālu[9]kāḥ sa[10]rvatīrthakarabālamī[11]napara[12]pra[13]vādibhiḥ saṃkṣobhyamāṇā[14] na kalpayanti[15] na[16] vikalpayanti[17] [18]/

1. °nā arha°] T4; °nārha] N16.
2. saṃ°] N14.
3. samyagbuddhā°] T5.
4. °ryya°] T2,3,5, C9, N11,13,14,17.
5. gaṃ°] in all Mss.
6. om. mahā] T4.
7. om. gaṅgāmahāna°] R10.
8. vasi°] T1.
9. °kā (om. ḥ)] T3,4,5, C9, N14,16. Hereafter the form 'vālukā' is used in all Mss. with the exception of two cases below (Nj. 233.6, 234.5 [v. 8]).
10. °rvva°] T2,3,5, C9, N11,14,16,17.
11. mīra°] N12.
12. paraḥ] N11; om. para°] T5.
13. pavādi] T5.
14. °nā] T3, N11; + //] N16.
15. kalpanti] T6.
16. nā°] T6.
17. °yaṃti] C8, R10; om. na vikalpayanti] T1.
18. //] C8, R10, N12,16; om. /] T1,2,3,4,5,6, C9, N11,13,14,17.

[Nj. 231.13]

tathāgat[1]a pūrv[2]a praṇihitatvāt[3] sarv[2]a sukhasamāpattiparipūry[4]ā sattvānāṃ[5] na kalpayanti[6] na vikalpayanti[7] /[8] atas te[9] gaṅ[10]gānadīvālukāsamās[11] tathāgatā nirvi[12]śiṣṭā[13] anunayapratighā[14]pa[15]gatatvāt //[16]

1. °gatā°] T5, R10.
2. °rvva°] T2,3,5, C9, N11,14,16,17.
3. + /] T1,4, N11; + //] T6, C8, N12.
4. °ryyā°] T2,3, C9, N11,14,16,17.
5. °nān] N11.
6. °yaṃti] C8, R10; vikalpayanti] T6; + /] N12.
7. °yaṃti] C8, R10.
8. //] C8, R10; N12,16; om. /] T2,3,4,5,6, N13,14,17.
9. teṣāṃ] N11,13.
10. gaṃ°] in all Mss.
11. vālikā] R10 only.
12. nivi°] R10; nirvvi°] N14.
13. °ṣṭāḥ] T6; + /] T1, R10.
14. °ghāta°] C9, N14,16; °ghāva°] N12; °ghāca°] N17.
15. om. paga] R10 (°pratighātatvāt).
16. /] T1,3,4,5,6, C9, N14; // //] N11.

[Nj. 231.17]

tad yathā mahāmate gaṅgāyāṃ[1][2] nadyāṃ[3] vālukā pṛthivīlakṣaṇa-svabhāvātvāt[4] pṛthivī [5]kalpoddāhe dahyamānāpi[5] na pṛthivīsvabhāvaṃ[6] vijahāti /[7] na ca mahāmate pṛthivī dahyate[8] tejo[p. 232]dhātu-pratibaddhatvād anyatra bālapṛthagjanā vitathapatitayā[9] saṃtatyā[10] dahyamānāṃ[11] kalpayanti[12] na ca dahyate tad[13]agnihetubhūtatvāt /[14] evam eva mahāmate tathāgatānāṃ[15] dharma[16]kāyo gaṅ[17]gānadīvālu-kāsamo[18] 'vināśī[19] /[20]

1. gaṃ°] in all Mss.
2. °yān] T2,3,4,5, N11,13,14,16,17.
3. °dyān] T2; °dyām] T4,5, C9, N13,14,17.
4. °tvān] N14; om. pṛthivīlakṣaṇasvabhāvatvāt] T6.
5. kalpoddāhye vahyanānādhi] N11.
6. °vam] T2,3,4,5, C9, N13,14,16,17.
7. //] C8, R10, N12; om. /] T2,3,4,5, C9, N13,14,16,17.
8. + /] T6, N11.
9. Nj. vitathatāpatitayā, on the basis of T2, C8, R10, etc. But vitathapa° (om. tā), T1, N11. Tib. *log par lhuṅ ba* suggests this reading (vitathapatita). Cf. Nj. 162.11–12: vitathapatitayā buddhyā, where Tib. has the same translation.
10. san°] T2,3,4,5, C8, R10, N12,13,14,16,17.
11. °nāṅ] T3,5, C9, N14.
12. °yaṃti] T3, C8,9, R10; + //] C8, R10, N12.
13. ted°] N13.
14. //] T4, C8, R10, N12,16; om. /] T1.
15. °nān] T2,3,4, C9, N14,17.
16. °rmma°] T2,3,5, C9, N11,14,16.
17. gaṃ°] in all Mss.
18. °maḥ] T2,3,4,5, C8 (+ //), C9, N12 (+ /), N13,14,16,17; °mā] T6, N11; °ma //] R10.
19. avināśī] C8, R10, N12; avināsī] T1,2,3,4,5,6, C9, N11,13,14,16,17.
20. //] N13,16; om. /] T2,3,4,5, C8,9, R10, N11,14.

[Nj. 232.4]

tad yathā mahāmate nadyāṃ[1] gaṅgā[2]yāṃ[3] vālukā apramāṇāḥ[4] [/][5] evam eva mahāmate tathāgatānāṃ raś[6]myāloko[7...] ’pra[...7]māṇaḥ[8], sattvaparipākasaṃcodanam upādāya[9] sarva[10]buddha[11]parṣan[12]maṇḍaleṣu prasarpyate[13] tathāgataiḥ[14] /[15] tad[16] yathā mahāmate gaṅ[17]gā[18]yāṃ[19] nadyāṃ[20] vālukā[21] na vālukā[22]svabhāvāntaram ārabhante[23], vālukāvasthā eva vālukāḥ[24] [/][25]

1. °dyā] T1,2,3,4,5, C9, N12,14,16,17; om. mahāmate nadyāṃ] R10.
2. gaṃgā°] in all Mss.
3. °yā] T5, C8,9, R10, N11,12,13,14,16,17.
4. °ṇa] T1; °ṇā] in other Mss.; + apramā before apramāṇā] N12.
5. /] only in T1. Nj. has no *daṇḍa*, but it is expected. Vd. has comma.
6. rasmy°] T2,3,4,5, C9, N13,16,17; ramy°] N11,14.
7. °ke / pra] T3, C9, N14.
8. + //] C8, R10.
9. upāya] T2, N13,17.
10. °rvva°] T2,3,5, C9, N11,14,16,17.
11. buddhadharm(m)a°] in all Mss. But Tib. and all Ch. versions omit °dharma°.
12. parṣa°] T2; patṣa°] T3,4,5, C9, N11,14,16,17; parṣat°] T6; paṣan] R10; paṃṣan] N12.
13. pravarttante] T1; pravarttate] in other Mss. (+ //] C8, R10). But Tib. *gton no* suggests pra-sṛ- here. (If ‘pravartate’ is accepted, ‘tathāgataiḥ’ will be redundant.)
14. °tais] T2,3,4,5, C8,9, R10, N12,13,14,16,17.
15. // //] N11; om. /] in other Mss.
16. tan tad] T3; tat tad] C9.
17. + //] C8, R10.
18. gaṃ°] in all Mss.

19. °yān] T2,3,4,5, C8,9, R10, N13,14,16,17; °yā] T1.
20. °dyām] T2,3,4,5, C9, N13,14,17; nadyāṃ gaṃgāyāṃ] T6.
21. om. na] T6.
22. vālu°] N16.
23. °bhaṃte] T2,3,4,5, C9, N12,13,14,17; + /] T6; + //] N11,16.
24. om. eva vālukāḥ] R10.
25. om. /] in all Mss. and in Nj. *Daṇḍa* added to conform to previous instances. Vd. has comma in similar circumstances below.

[Nj. 232.9]

evam eva mahāmate tathāgatānām arhatāṃ[1] samyaksaṃbuddhān-
āṃ saṃsāre na[2] pravṛttir[3] na[4] nivṛttir[5][6] bhavapravṛttyucchinnahetu-[7]
tvāt[8] /[9] tad yathā mahāmate gaṅgāyāṃ[10][11] nadyāṃ[12] vālukā[13] apakṛṣṭā[14]
api na prajñāpayante,[15] prakṣiptā api na prajñāyante [/][16] evam eva
mahāmate tathāgatānāṃ[17] jñānaṃ[18] sattvaparipākayogena[19...] na[...19] kṣī-
yate[20] na vardhate[21] 'śarīratvād[22][23] dharmasya[24][25] /[26]

1. arhatā] N11.
2. ṇa (saṃsāreṇa)] T6.
3. °tti] N12,14.
4. (r)nna] C9, N11,13,14,17; om. na] T4,5, N12.
5. °vṛti°] N11.
6. °ḥ] in all Mss. except N12, which om. nirvṛtti; + //] C8, R10; + bhavati] T6.
7. °vṛtyu°] T6, N11,12,13.
8. °hetvāt] N12.
9. //] T4, C8, R10, N12,13,16; om. /] T3,5, C9, N14.
10. gaṃ°] in all Mss.
11. °yān] T2,3,4,5, N11,13,16,17; °yā] T1, C9, N14.
12. °dyām] T2,3,4,5, C9, N11,13,14,16,17; dyā] T1.
13. °luvā] N16; + vā] T5.
14. aparikṛṣṭā] T2, N13,17.
15. Nj. prajñāpayante on the basis of T2. N13 and N17 have same reading. But prajñāyante in other Mss. Tib. *mṅon med pa* for 'na prajñāyante' here and below. Vd. prajñāyante.
16. Nj. om. /. But + /] T1, N11; + //] T4,6, C8, R10.
17. °nā] N14.
18. °na] N14; om. jñānaṃ] T6.
19. om. na] T1,2,3,4, N12; yoga na] T5,6, C9, N11,13,14,16,17.
20. °yante] N17.
21. °yante] N17; + //] C8, R10.
22. aśa°] T2,3,4,5,6, C8,9, R10, N12,13,14,16,17; asa°] T1, N11.
23. °tvāt] T1,2,3,4, C9, R10, N12,13,14,16; °tvā] T5; aś ariratvāt] N17; aśarīravatām, and om. up to śarīravatāṃ] T6; + /] T1; + //] C8, R10, N12.
24. °rmma°] T2,3,5, C9, N11,14,16,17.
25. °syā] T5, C8, R10, N12,14.
26. om. /] T1,2,3,4,5, N12,13,14,16,17.

[Nj. 232.14]

[1]śarīravatāṃ[2] hi mahāmate nāśo[3] bhavati[4] nā[5]śarīravatāṃ[6], dharmaś[7] cā[8]śarīraḥ /[9] tad yathā mahāmate gaṅ[10]gāyāṃ[11] nadyāṃ[12] vālukā niṣ-[13]pīḍyamānā ghṛ[14]tatailārthibhir[15] ghṛ[14]tatailādivirahitāḥ[16] [/][17] evam eva [p. 233] mahāmate tathāgatāḥ[18] sattvaduḥkhair[19] niṣpīḍ[20]yamānā[21] dharmadhā[22]tusva[23]rasa[24]praṇidhānasukhaṃ[25]

1. sa°] T1.
2. °rīratāṃ] T2; °rīravatā] C9; °rīrasamvā] N11; °rīratvāt dharmaśarīravatā] T3,4, N14; °rīratvā // dharmaśarīravatāṃ] R10; °rīratvāt // dharmmaśarīravatī] N16; °rīrasasvā hi tvāt dharmaśarīravatāṃ] N12; °rīrasamvā hi dharmaśarīratāṃ] N14,17 (°rmma°, N17).
3. nāso] T1.
4. bhavanti] N16.
5. naśa°] T1, N12.
6. °tān] T2,3,4,5, C9, N13,14,16,17; °ratāṃ (om. va)] R10.
7. °rmma] T2,3,5, C9, R10, N14,16,17.
8. °sa°] T1.
9. // //] N11; //] N12; °ras, and om. /] T2,3,4,5, C8,9, R10, N13,14,16,17.
10. gaṃ°] in all Mss.
11. °yān] T2,3,4,5, N13,14,17; °yāṃn] C9; gaṃgādyāṃ] N12; gaṃgān] N16.
12. °dyām] T2,3,4,5, C9, N11,13,14,16,17; °dyā] R10.
13. °ṣpi°] T1.
14. (twice) ghṛta] T4,5,6, C8,9, R10, N11,12,13,14,16,17.
15. °bhiḥ] T1,2,3,4, N11(+ /),14,16,17; °bhi] R10; °lāccithibhiḥ] T5; lārccitibhiḥ] C9; om. ghṛtatailārthibhir] T5.
16. °tā] in all Mss. except T1, which has °ta /.
17. Nj. om. /. /] T1 only.
18. °tānāṃ] T1.
19. °khai] T5.

20. °ṣpīdya°] T3,6, C9, N16.
21. °nāḥ] T1,6, C8, R10, N11(+ //),12; °no] C9; °nānā] N16.
22. °rmma] T2,3,5, C9, N11,13,14,17.
23. °tva] T1; °tvi] T2,3,4,5, N13,14,16,17; °tu] N11; °tvī] T6, C8,9, R10, N13. Nj. °tvī. See n. 24 below.
24. Nj. (°tv-ī)śvara, on the basis of T2, C8, R10. So too T3,4,5, C9, N12,13, 14, 16,17. But °svarasa°] T1, N11; °svara°] T6. N11 has 'dharmadhātu-svarasapraṇidhānasukham', which is confirmed by Tib. *chos kyi dbyiṅs kyi raṅ gi ṅaṅ gi smon lam gyi bde ba* and C(W) 自法界相…自法味相. 'dharmadhātvīśvarapraṇidhānasukha' is, however, better regarded as a variant reading of later times.
25. °khan] T2,3,4,5, C9, N13,14,16,17.

[Nj. 233.2]

na vijahati[1] (mahāmate)[2] mahākaruṇopetatvād,[3] yāvat sarva[4]sattvā na nirvāsyante[5] tathāgataiḥ /[6] tad yathā mahāmate gaṅ[7]gāyāṃ[8] nad-yāṃ[9] vālukāḥ[10] pravāhānukūlāḥ[11] pravahanti[12] nā[13]nudake[14] [/][15] evam eva mahāmate tathāgatānāṃ sarva[16](buddha)[17]dharma[18]deśanā nirvā[19]-ṇapravāhānukūlā saṃvartate,[20][21] tena[22] gaṅ[23]gānadīvā[24]lukāsamās[25] tathā-gatā ity ucyante[26] /[27]

1. °hāti] in all Mss. except N13 (vijihāti, R10); + //] C8, R10; + /] N12.
2. om. mahāmate] T1,6. This vocative is unnecessary. Tib. confirms this.
3. tvāt] in all Mss. and + //] T4, C8, R10, N12; + /] T6, N11.
4. °rvva°] T3,5, C9, N11,14,16,17.
5. °rvvā°] T2,3,5, C9, N11,14,17. T4 om. from 'nirvāsyante' to 'sarvabud-dhadharmadeśanā' in Nj. 233.6. Vd. nirvāpyante.
6. om. /] T1; °tais, and om. /] T2,3,5, C8,9, R10, N12,13,14,16,17; tathāga-te tathāgataḥ] N11.
7. gaṃ°] in all Mss.
8. °yān] T2,3,5, C8,9, R10, N13,16,17.
9. °dyām] T2,3,5, C9, N12,14,16,17; °dyā] R10.
10. °kā] T1,2,5,6, C8,9, N11,12,13,14.
11. °lā] in all Mss. (°nulā, T6).
12. °vahati] N12; + /] T1.
13. °tā°] C8, R10.
14. °daka /] N11. Nj. om. /.
15. om. evam] N17.
16. °rvva] T3,5, C9, N11,14,16,17.
17. om. buddha] T1,6, N11. Tib. confirms this omission. From the context 'buddha' is redundant and better left out.
18. °rmma°] T4, C9, N14,16,17.
19. °rvvā°] T3,5, C9, N11,14,16,17.
20. °rtta°] in all Mss.
21. °nte] C8, N11. Vd. has *daṇḍa* after 'saṃvartate'.
22. yena] in all Mss. except T1, N16 (saṃvarttate na, om. either 'te').
23. gaṃ°] in all Mss.
24. °vāli] T2,3,4,5, C9, N14,16,17.
25. °samas] R10.
26. ucyaṃte] C9; ucyate] N11.
27. //] N12,16; om. /] in other Mss.

[Nj. 233.7]

nāyaṃ[1] mahāmate gatyarthas[2] tathāgateṣu pravartate[3][4] /[5] vināśo[6] mahāmate[7] gatyartho bhavati /[8] na ca mahāmate saṃsārasya pūrvā[9] koṭiḥ prajñāyate[10] /[11] aprajñāyamānā[12] kathaṃ[13] gatyarthena nirdekṣyāmi /[14] gatyartho mahāmate[15] ucchedo, na ca bālapṛthagjanāḥ[16] saṃ[17]prajānanti[18] //[19]

1. yam] T3,4,5, N14,16; yaṇm] C9.
2. + /] T1; + //] N11,12 (°thaḥ in all Mss. and Nj., but Vd. tas).
3. °rtta] in all Mss.
4. °nte] T6.
5. //] C8, R10; om. /] in other Mss.
6. vināso] T6.
7. om. vināśo mahāmate] T1; om. mahāmate gatyartho bhavati / na] N11.
8. //] N16; om. /] T2,3,4,5, C8,9, R10, N12,13,14,17.
9. °rvvā°] T2,3,5, C9, N11,14,16,17; pūrvakoṭiḥ] T1.
10. °yante] T6.
11. //] C8, R10, N12,13,16; om. /] T3,4,5, C9.
12. °mānāṃ] T2, N11,12,13,16; °mānāṅ] T3,4, C9, N14; °māṇāṃ] T6; °māṅ] T5; jñāpayamānaṃ] N17.
13. kaṃ] R10; om. kathaṃ] T6.
14. //] C8, R10; om. /] in other Mss.
15. + /] T2,3,4, C9, N14,17; + //] C8, R10, N16.
16. °pṛg°] N12. Vd. has *daṇḍa* before 'na ca'.
17. sam°] T3,4,5, R10.
18. samprananti (om. jā)] R10.
19. /] T1, C8,9, R10; om. //] T2,3,5, N12,13,14; // //] N11.

[Nj. 233.12]

mahāmatir āha[1] /[2] tad yadi[3] bhagavan pūrvā[4] koṭir[5] na[6] prajñāyate[7] sattvānāṃ[8] saṃsaratāṃ[9], tat kathaṃ[10] mokṣaḥ prajñāyate[11] prāṇinām[12] /[13] bhagavān āha /[14] anādikālaprapañ[15]cadauṣṭhulyavikalpavāsanāhetuvinivṛttir[16] mahāmate svacittadṛśyabāhyārthaparijñānāt[17] [/] vikalpasyāśraya[18]parāvṛttir[19] mahāmate[20] mokṣo, na nāśaḥ /[21] ato nānāntakathā mahāmate kiṃcit kārī[22] bhavati /[23]

1. mahāmati //] N12 (om. āha).
2. //] in all Mss. except T1 (/), T5 (om. /).
3. yathā] T3,5, C9, N16.
4. °rvvā°] T2,3,5, C9, N11,14,16,17.
5. °ṭi] T5.
6. ca] T2, N17.
7. + /] T2,N17; + //] N13.
8. san°] N11,12.
9. °tān] T2,3,4,5, C9, N14,16,17; °tā] R10.
10. °tham] T3,5, C9, N11,13,14,16,17.
11. °yante] T1; + //] C8, R10.
12. °nāṃ] in all Mss.
13. //] in all Mss. except T1,3 (//, doubled N11).
14. //] in all Mss. except T1,6.
15. °paṃ°] T2,3,4,5,6, C9, N12,13,14,16,17.
16. °(r)mma] N11.
17. °nāt] T1,2,3,4,5,6, C9, N11,13,14,16,17; + /] T6, N11. Better to add *daṇḍa* here, although Nj. does not.
18. °sraya] T1; kalpaśraya] T6.
19. °tim] T3,4,5, C9, N13,14,16,17.
20. °(r)mma] N11.
21. //] C8,9, N11,12; om. /] T1,2,3,4,5,6, N13,14,16,17.
22. karī] T1,3,4,5,6, C8,9, R10, N11,14,16.
23. //] C8, R10, N11,12,16; om. /] T1,2,3,4,5, C9, N13,17. N14 om. from 'bhavati' to 'bahirdhā vā parī°' in Nj. 234.1.

[Nj. 233.17]

vikalpasyaiva mahāmate paryā[1][2...]yo 'nanta[...2]koṭir iti [3]/ na cātra vikal-
pā[p. 234]d anya[4]t ki[5]ṃ cit sattvāntara[6]m as[7]ty adhyātmaṃ vā bahir-
dhā[8] vā[9] parik[10]ṣyamā[11]ṇaṃ buddhyā [12]/ jñānajñeyavi[13]viktā hi mahā-
mate sarva[14]dharmā[15][16]ḥ [17]/ anyatra svacittavikalpā[18]parijñānād[19] vikal-
paḥ [20]pravartate tad [21]avabodhān[22] nivar[23]ta[24]te [25]// tatredam ucyate [26]//

1. °ryyā] T2,3,5, C9, N11,16,17.
2. yo ananta°] N11 (no *avagraha* in other Mss.); °yānanta°] N13.
3. om. /] in all Mss.
4. anya] T3.
5. °ñci°] T6, C8, R10, N13,16.
6. sandhāntaram] T3, C8, R10; saṃdhāntaram] N12; santaram] C9; (kiṃ cin) dhāntaram] N16.
7. sati] T1,2,3,5,6, C8,9, R10, N11,12,13,16,17; °ntara kiṃ ci] T4; + /] T1,6, N11.
8. bahidhā] T3,4,5, C9.
9. vā cā] T2, C8,9, N12,17.
10. °kṣa] R10; (karī)kṣya] N14.
11. °mānaṃ] C9.
12. om. /] in all Mss.
13. °jñesaya°] T3; °jñāsaya] C9.
14. °rvva°] T2,3,5, C9, N11,14,16,17.
15. °rmmā°] T3, C9, R10, N11,14,16,17.
16. °ā] T6, N11,12.
17. om. /] in all Mss.
18. °lpapa°] T6.
19. °nā] T1.
20. °rtta°] in all Mss.; + //] C8, R10, N12.
21. anava°] R10.
22. °dhā] T4.
23. °rtta] in all Mss.
24. °nte] T2, N13.
25. /] T1; // //] N11; om. //] T2,3,4,5, C9, N13,14,16,17.
26. /] T2,3,5, C9, N14,17.

[Nj. 234.5]

gaṅ[1]gā[2]yāṃ vā[3]lukāsamānye[4] paśyanti vināyakān /[5]

a[6]nā[7]śagatiniṣṭhān[8] vai[9] te[10] paśyanti[11] tathāgatān[12] //[13] 7 //

gaṅ[14]gāyā[15]ṃ vālukā[16] yadvat[17] sarva[18]doṣai[19]r [20]vivarji[21]tā[22]ḥ[23] /

[24]vā[25]hānukūlā nityāś[26] ca[27] tathā buddhasya[28] buddhatā // 8 //

1. gaṃ°] in all Mss.
2. °yā] T2,4, C8, R10, N12,17; °ya] T1.
3. vāluka] C8, R10, N12; vālikā°] N11; vālika°] T2,3,4,5,6, C9, N13,14,16, 17.
4. °samānaye] R10; °sanye] T5; (°ka)mānye] T3, N14; (°ka)māne] C9.
5. //] C8, R10, N11,12,16; om. /] T2,3,4,5, C9, N13,14,17.
6. avinā°] in all Mss., but one syllable extra. There is no difference in meaning without 'vi'.
7. °sa°] T1,6.
8. °ṣṭhā] R10, N13; °ṣṭhāt] C9; °viṣṭhān] N16.
9. vi] T1 (°ānivite).
10. om. te] T6.
11. °yaṃti] N11.
12. °tāṃ] T2,3, C9, N13,14,17; °tā] N11.
13. /] T1; om. /] T2,3,4,5, N13,14,17 (°tānga°, T4,5!).
14. gaṃ°] in all Mss. except 17. T16 om. gaṅgā.
15. °ya] T1; °yā] T2,3,4,5,6, C9, R10, N11,13,16,17.
16. vālilā] T2,3,4,5, C9, N11,13,14,16,17.
17. °van] N16.
18. °rvva] T2,3,5, C9, N11,14,16,17.
19. °ṣai] T5,6.
20. (r)vvi] N11.
21. °rjji] T2,5, C9, N14,16,17.
22. °tā] T1,2,3,4,5,6, C9, N11,13,16,17. This form is possible if 'vālukā' is regarded as singular. See n. 26 below.

23. //] C8, R10, N12,16; om. /] T2,3,4,5, C9, N13,14,17.

24. + pra° before vā (va)] in all Mss., but one syllable extra. There is no difference in meaning without 'pra°'.

25. °vahā°] T2,3,4, C8,9, R10, N13,14,16,17.

26. nityās (tā°)] T1; nityā] T2,4,6, C8, R10, N12,13,17; mityā] T3,5, C9, N14,16. Mss. with agreement in number (f. sg.) in both lines are T2,3,4, 5,6, C9, N13,14,16,17. Tib. has no plural mark.

27. om. ca] T1,6. From this the reading 'pravāhānukūlā nityā(s)' in *pāda* c is not impossible, although 'ca' is required from the context. Both 'vāhānukūlā nityā(ś) ca' and 'pravāhānukūlā nityā(ś)' have the same *vipulā* form (*ma vipulā*).

28. busya] T3, N14; om. buddhasya] T1; tathāgata (om. buddhasya)] N16.

§ Sarvadharmakṣaṇikatva (83)

[Nj. 234.9]

atha khalu mahāmatir[2] bodhisattvo mahāsattvaḥ punar api bhagavantam etad avocat /[3] deśayatu[4] me[5] bhagavān[6] deśayatu me[7] sugatas[8] tathāgato 'rhan[9] [10]samyaksaṃbuddhaḥ[11] sarva[12]dharmāṇāṃ[13] kṣaṇabhaṅgaṃ[14] [15]bhedalakṣaṇaṃ [16...]caiṣāṃ / tat kathaṃ[...16] bhagavan sarva[17]dharmāḥ[18] kṣaṇikāḥ /[19]

1. + // before atha] C8, R10, N11.
2. °ti] T4,5, C9, N11,13,14,16.
3. //] T4,6, C8, R10, N11,12,13,16.
4. °yaṃtu] T2, N17.
5. Nj. om. me. T1 has 'me' as usual after 'deśayatu'.
6. bhagavan] C8, R10, N12.
7. om. me] R10.
8. °ḥ] T1; om. s] T6, C8,9, R10, N12.
9. rha] N11.
10. saṃ°] N14.
11. °bubuḥ] T3.
12. °rvva°] T2,3,5, C9, N11,14,16,17.
13. °rmma°] T2,3, C9, N11,14,16,17.
14. °bhaṃga-] T1,2,3,4,5,6, C8,9, R10, N11,12; kṣaṇaṃ bhaṅga] N14.
15. (°ga)debhedabha° (?)] T5. Tib. om. 'bhedalakṣaṇaṃ caiṣām' and 'tat'.
16. sarvadharmām (bha°)] T2,3, C9, N14,16,17; sarvvadharmasta(gavan)] T5; sarvadharmam (bha°)] N13; sarvadharmāt kathaṃ (bha°)] T4, C8, R10; sarvadharmān kathaṃ (bha°)] N12; sarvvadharmāś ca (bna°)] N11; sarvadharmāś ca caiṣāṃ / tat kathaṃ (bha°)] T6.
17. °rvva] T2,3,5, C9, N11,14,16,17.
18. °rmmā°] T2,3, C9, N11,14,16,17.
19. //] T4,6, C8,9, R10, N11,12,13,14,16; om. /] T1.

[Nj. 234.13]

bhagavān āha[1] / tena hi mahāmate śṛṇu sādhu ca suṣṭhu ca[2] manasikuru[3] /[4] bhāṣiṣye[5] 'haṃ[6] te /[7] sādhu bhagavann[8] iti[9] mahāmatir[10] bodhisattvo mahāsattvo[11] bhagavataḥ pratyaśrauṣīt[12] //[13]

1. //] T2,3,4,6, C9, R10, N11 (+ // before bhagavān),12,13,14,16,17.
2. om. suṣṭhu ca] N11,12.
3. °ku] N17.
4. om. /] in all Mss.
5. bhiṣi°] R10
6. han] T1,2,3,4,5, C8,9, R10, N11,12,13,14,16,17.
7. //] C8, R10; om. /] T1,2,3,4,5,6, C9, N11,12,13,14,16,17.
8. °vānn] T2,4,5, C9, N11,13,14,16,17.
9. + /] T1, N11; + //] T6.
10. °ti] T4,6, C9, N13,14.
11. °tvaḥ] C9.
12. °ṣīd] T2,4,6; pratyaśroṣīd] T3,5, C9, N11,12,13,14,16,17; °śroṣīt] C8, R10.
13. oṁ. //] in all Mss.

[Nj. 234.16]

bhagavāṃs tasyaitad avocat /[1] sarva[2]dharmāḥ[3] sarva[4]dharmā[5] iti mahāmate[6] yad uta kuśalākuśalāḥ[7] saṃskṛtā[8]saṃskṛtā[9] laukikalo-[p. 235]kottarāḥ sāvadyānavadyāḥ[10] sā[11]sra[12]vā[13]nāsravā upāttānupāttāḥ[14] /[15] saṃkṣepeṇa[16] mahāmate pañco[17]pādānaska[18]ndhāś[19] cittamanomanovijñānavāsanāhetukāś[20] cittamanomanovijñāna[21]vāsanā[22]puṣṭair[23] bāla[24]pṛthagjanaiḥ kuśalākuśalena[25] parikalpyante[26] /[27]

1. //] T6, C8,9, R10, N12,13,16,17.
2. °rvva°] T2,3,5, C9, N11,14,16,17.
3. °rmmāḥ] T2,3, C9, N11,14,16,17; °rmā] T6.
4. °rvva°] T2,3,5, C9, N11,14,16,17.
5. °rmmā] T2,3,5, C9, N11,14,16,17.
6. om. mahāmate] in all Mss. except T1.
7. °lāṃ] T4; kuśalāḥ kuśalāḥ] T1; kuśalāḥ (om. akuśala)] N14.
8. °kṛte saṃ°] N13.
9. °tāḥ] T1,3,4,5,6, C8,9, R10, N11 (+ /),12,13,14,16.
10. sāvadyāḥ (om. anāvadya)] T2, N13,17; sarvadyānavadyāḥ] T6.
11. sāśra°] T1,5,6, C8, R10, N11,12,13; srāsra°] T4, C9.
12. °śra°] T1,2,3,4,6, C8,9, R10, N11,12,13,14,16,17.
13. °vāḥ] T2,3,4,6, C8,9, R10, N11,12,13,14,16,17.
14. °pāttā] T4,5, R10; upāttā (om. anupātta)] T3, C9, N14; upāntānupāntāḥ] T6; upārttānupāttāḥ] N11 (Nj. °pattaḥ).
15. om. /] in all Mss. except N11.
16. °pe (om. ṇa)] N14.
17. paṃco°] T2,3,4,5,6, C8,9, R10, N11,13,14,16,17.
18. °skaṃ°] R10.
19. °ndhāḥ] T1, N11.
20. °kāḥ] T1,2,3,4,5,6, C9, N11 (+ /),13,14,16,17.
21. vijñānaṃ (vā)] N13.
22. vāsanāḥ (pu°)] T6, N11.
23. °puṣṭai] T3, C9, N13,14,17; °puṣyair] T1; °kṣuṣṭair] C8; °juṣṭair] R10.
24. bālā°] R10; bāli°] N17; bali°] N13.
25. °laina] R10.
26. °kalpante] T6, C9.
27. //] C8, R10, N12; om. /] in other Mss.

[Nj. 235.4]

samādhisukhasamāpattayo mahāmate[1] dṛṣṭadharma[2]sukhavihāra-
bhāvenā[3]ryā[4]ṇāṃ[5] kuśalānāsravā[6] ity ucyante[7] /[8] kuśalākuśalāḥ pun-
ar[9] mahāmate yad utāṣṭau[10] vijñānāni [/][11] katamāny aṣṭau,[12] yad uta
tathāgatagarbha[13] ālayavijñānasaṃśa[14]bdito[15] mano[16] manovijñānaṃ[17]
ca pañca[18] ca vijñā[19]nakāyās[20] tīrthyā[21]nuvar[22]ṇitā[23]ḥ /[24]

1. mahāmahāmate] N16.
2. °rmma°] T2,3,5, C9, N11,14,16,17.
3. °bhāveṇā°] C8,9, R10, N14,16; °bhavanā°] N13.
4. °ryyā°] T2,3, C9, N11,14,16,17.
5. °ṇāṅ] T2,3,5, C9.
6. °śra°] T2,3,5, C8, R10, N11,12,13,14,16,17; nāṃśra°] T6.
7. ucyaṃte] T3,6, C9, N14.
8. //] N16; om. /] in other Mss.
9. (r)mma°] T3,5, C9, N14,16,17.
10. °ṭa aṣṭau] T1,3,4,5,6, C8,9, R10, N11,14,16.
11. Nj. om. /. /] T1; //] N12. Vd. has *daṇḍa*.
12. + ʾ] T6. Vd. has '?'.
13. °rbhaḥ] in all Mss. except T6; + /] N11.
14. °sa°] T1.
15. °taḥ] T1 (+ /),2,3,4,5, C8,9, R10, N11,12,13,14,16,17; °śabdir] T6.
16. manaḥ] in all Mss. except T6, N11.
17. nañ] T2,3,4,C9, N14,16,17.
18. paṃ°] T2,3,4,5,6, C8,9, R10, N12,14,16,17; paca] N13; om. manovijñā-naṃ ca pañca] N12.
19. monovijñā] N12.
20. °yāḥ] in all Mss. except T6; + /] N12.
21. °āvu°] C9.
22. °rṇṇi] T2,3,4,5,6, C8,9, R10, N13,14,16,17.
23. °tās] T2,3,4,5,6, C8,9, R10, N12,13,14,17; °tā] N16 (°tā // statra). T6 adds 'tatra mahāmate pañcavijñānakāyās' (redundant) before 'tīrthyā°'.
24. //] N11,16; om. /] in other Mss.

[Nj. 235.9]

tatra mahāmate[1] pañca[2] vijñānakāyā[3][4] manovijñānasahitāḥ[5] kuśalākuśalakṣaṇa[6]paramparā[7]bhedabhinnāḥ[8] saṃtati[9]prabandha[10]nābhinnaśarīrāḥ[11] pravartamānāḥ[12][13] pravartante[14] (/)[15] pravṛtya[16] ca vinaśyanti[17] [/][18] svacittadṛśyānavabodhāt[19] samanantaranirodhe[20][21] 'nyad[22] vijñānaṃ[23] pravartate,[24][25] saṃsthānākṛti[26]viśeṣa[27]grāhakaṃ[28]

1. om. mahā°] N13.
2. paṃca°] T2,3,4,6, C8,9, R10, N11,12,13,14,16,17.
3. nākā°] T3, C9, N14.
4. °yāḥ] T1,3,5,6, C9, N14; °yāṃ] T2,4, N13; °yaṃ] N16,17; yam(ma)] N11. Nj. pañcavijñānakāyā; Vd. pañca vijñānakāyā (here and below [Nj. 236.4]). The latter is preferable. Cf. pañca ca vijñānakāyās (Nj. 235.8–9); pañcabhir vijñānakāyaiḥ saha (Nj. 235.14]).
5. °tā] T2, C8, R10, N13,17.
6. kuśalakṣaṇa° (om. akuśala)] T2, N13,17; kuśalākuśalākuśalakṣaṇa (kuśalā, redundant)] N16.
7. paraṃparā] N11; paraṃpara] T1; parasparā] T4,6, C8,9, R10, N12,13, 14,16,17 (cf. Tib. *gcig nas gcig tu*).
8. °nnā] T1.
9. santati] in all Mss.
10. °baṃdha°] T6, C8, R10, N12.
11. °sarī°] T2,3,4,5, C9, N14,16,17.
12. °rtta°] in all Mss.
13. °nā] T1.
14. °rtta°] in all Mss.
15. //] C8, R10, N12; om. /] in other Mss. See n. 18 below.
16. pravṛttya] T6. N13 adds 'pravarttante' (redundant) before 'pravṛtya'.
17. °sya°] T1,2,3,4,5,6, C9, N11,13,14,16,17.
18. /] T6; //] N12; om. /] in other Mss. and Nj. A *daṇḍa* is better here

instead of before 'pravṛtya ca'.

19. °śya°] N13.
20. °dhān°] T5, C9, N13,14,16,17.
21. samantara] T6; samanantarara] N11; pamanantara] N17.
22. °ruddhe] T1; om. *avagraha* in all Mss. except T1.
23. °nam] T2,3,4,5, C9, N13,14,16,17; °na] T6.
24. °rtta°] in all Mss.
25. + //] C8, R10, N12. A short punctuation mark is required here. Vd. has *daṇḍa*.
26. saṃsthākṛ] T3,4,5, C9, R10, N13,14,16,17; sasthākṛ] T2.
27. °viseṣa°] T1.
28. °kam] T2,3,4,5, C9, N13,14,16,17.

[Nj. 235.14]

manovijñānaṃ[1] pañcabhir[2] vijñānakāyaiḥ[3] saha saṃprayuktaṃ[4] pravartate[5] /[6] kṣaṇa[7]kālā[8]navasthāyi[9] tat[10] kṣaṇikam iti vadāmi /[11] kṣaṇikaṃ[12] punar[13] mahāmate ālayavijñānaṃ[14] tathāgatagarbha[15]saṃ-[16]śabditaṃ[17] manaḥ[18]sahitaṃ[19] pravṛttivijñānavāsanābhiḥ[20] kṣaṇikam,[21] [22...]anāsravavā[p. 236]sanābhir akṣaṇikam[...22] /[23] na ca bālapṛthagjanā[24] avabudhyante[25]

1. °nam] T3,4,5, C9, N14,17.
2. paṃca] T2,3,4,5,6, C8,9, R10, N12,13,14,16,17.
3. vina° (om. jñā)] T4.
4. °tam] C9; saṃyuktam] T2,3,4,5, N13,14,16,17.
5. °rtta°] in all Mss.
6. //] C8, R10; /] T1; om. /] in other Mss.
7. kṣaṇi°(ka)] N12.
8. °kālya°(na)] T2, N13,17.
9. °yitaṃ] T2, N13,17. Vd. has *daṇḍa* here instead of after 'pravartate'.
10. ta] T6; tata] N11.
11. //] N16; om. /] in other Mss.
12. °kam] T2,3,4,5, C9, N13,14,17. Tib. om. kṣaṇikam, but Ch(S) has it. Ch(S) seems to read 'kṣaṇikam iti punar°', which is a better reading.
13. (r)mma°] T3,5, C9, N14,16,17.
14. °nan] T2,3,4,5, C9, N13,14,16,17.
15. Nj. °rbhaḥ, but not so here. °rbha(saṃ°)] T1,6, which is to be accepted. °rbhaṃ] N11; °rbhaḥ] in other Mss. Vd. rbhasaṃ°.
16. śaṃśab°] T3,4,5, C9, N14,17; saṃsab°] T1.
17. °tam] T1,3,4,5, C8,9, R10, N14,16,17.
18. mana°] T3, C9, N14.
19. °saṃhi°] T2,3,4, C8,9, N12,13,14,16,17.
20. °bhi] T5, N16.
21. °kan (before na)] T3,4,5, C8,9, R10, N12,13,14,16,17; kaṃ] N11.
22. °kaṃ] T1; om. anāsravavāsanābhir akṣaṇikam] in other Mss. Ch(S) and Tib. confirm T1 reading.
23. om. /] in all Mss.
24. kāla°] N13.
25. + //] C8, R10, N12.

[Nj. 236.2]

kṣaṇikavādābhiniviṣṭāḥ kṣaṇikākṣaṇikatām[1] imāṃ sarvadharmā-[2][3]
ṇāṃ[4], tad anavabodhād[5] ucchedadṛṣṭyāsaṃskṛtān[6] api dharmān[7]
nāśayiṣyanti[8] /[9] asaṃsāriṇo mahāmate pañca[10] vijñānakāyā ananu-
bhūtasukhaduḥkhā[11][12] anirvāṇahetavaḥ[13][14] /[15] tathāgatagarbhaḥ punar
mahāmate[16] anubhūtasukhaduḥkhahetusahitaḥ pravartate[17] nivartate[18]
ca[19] catasṛbhir[20] vāsanābhiḥ[21] saṃmūrcchitaḥ[22] /[23]

1. °kāḥ°] T2,3,4,5, C8,9, R10, N12,13,14; om. kṣaṇikā°] T6, N17.
2. °rvva°] T2,3,5, C9, N11,14,16,17.
3. °ṛmmā°] T2,3,5, C9, N11,14,16,17.
4. °ṇān] T2,3,4,5, C9, N11,13,14,16,17. Vd. has *daṇḍa*.
5. °dhāt] T4,5,6 (+ /), C9, R10, N11 (+ /),12,13,14 (om. °an°),16,17.
6. °ṣṭyā asaṃ°] in all Mss.
7. °rmmān] T2,3,5, C9, N11,14,16,17; °rman] N12.
8. nāsa°] T1,2,3,4,5, C9, N13,14,16,17.
9. //] C8, R10, N12,13,16; om. /] C9, N14.
10. paṃca] T2,4,5,6, C8,9, R10, N12,13,16,17; paṃcabhi°] T3, N14.
11. bhūtā°] T3,4,5,6, C8,9, N11,13,14,16; bhūtāḥ] N12.
12. °khā°] T3, C9, N14.
13. °rvvā°] T2,3,5, C9, N11,14,16,17.
14. °vas] T2,3,4, C8,9, R10, N12,13,16,17; °hetuvas] T5, N14.
15. om. /] in all Mss.
16. (r)mma°] T2,3,5, C9, N14,16,17.
17. °rtta°] in all Mss.
18. °rtta°] in all Mss.
19. na vivarttate] T1; + //] C8, R10; om. nivartate ca] T4; add nivartate (redundant) before ca] T3, N14.
20. (r)vvā°] T3,5, C9, N11,14,16,17.
21. °bhi] C8, R10.
22. sanmūr°] T2; sammūr°] T3,5, C9, R10, N13,14,16,17; samur°] T4.
23. om. /] in all Mss.

[Nj. 236.7]

na ca bālā avabudhyante[1] kṣaṇikadṛṣṭivikalpavāsita[2]matayaḥ //[3] punar aparaṃ[4] mahāmate samadharaṇa[5](m)kalpasthitāḥ[6] suvarṇa[7]vajrajina[8]dhātuprāptiviśeṣā[9] abhaṅginaḥ[10] /[11] yadi punar mahāmate[12] abhisamayaprāptiḥ[13] kṣaṇikā[14] syād, anāryatvam[15] āryāṇāṃ[16] syān,[17] na cānāryatvam[18] āryā[19]ṇāṃ[20] bhavati /[21]

1. + //] N11.
2. °vasita°] T4.
3. /] T1,2,3,4,5, N14,17; om. //] T6, C9, N11.
4. °ram] T3,4,5, C8, R10; om. aparaṃ] T6.
5. Nj. samadhāraṇaṃ, but °dharaṇa° in all Mss. (°aṅ, T2,3,5, C9, N14,17). Tib. om. 'samadharaṇaṃ kalpasthitāḥ', but at the next occurrence has *skal par gshal* (*kyaṅ*) ('measured as *kalpa*'; seems to have no word for 'samadharaṇaṃ'). 'dharaṇa' (holding, bearing, comprising) may signify a particular high number (cf. *Mahāvyutpatti*, no. 7726) or a unit of weight. Although the meaning is not clear, 'samadharaṇa' may be better connected with *kalpa* as an adjective rather than separated as an adverb.
6. °tā] N12; °saṃsthitāḥ] T6.
7. °rṇṇa°] T2,4,6, C8,9, R10, N11,13,14,16,17.
8. °vaja] N14; savarṇṇavajra] C9, N16; savajra] T5.
9. °viseṣā] T1.
10. abhaṃgi°] T1,2; bhaṃgino] T6; asaṃginaḥ] T3,4,5, C8,9, R10, N12,13, 14,16,17.
11. //] R10, N11; om. /] T1,3,4,5,6, C9, N13,14,16,17.
12. (r)mma°] T2,3,5, C9, N11,14,16,17.
13. °pti] N17.
14. °kā] T6, N11; °kaḥ] in other Mss. Nj. °kaḥ, but Vd. °kā.
15. °ryy°] T2,3,5, C9, N11,13,14,16,17.
16. °ryy°] T2,3,5, C9, N11,13,14,16,17.
17. Vd. syāt / na.
18. °ryyā°] T2,3,5, C9, N11,14,16,17.
19. °ryyā°] T2,3, C9, N14,16,17.
20. °ṇām] T2,3,4,5, N13,14,16,17; om. syān na cānāryatvam āryāṇāṃ] T1.
21. //] C8, R10, N11,16; om. /] in other Mss.

[Nj. 236.12]

suvarṇaṃ[1] vajraṃ[2] ca mahāmate samadharaṇa(m)[3]kalpasthitā api[4] tulyamānā na hīyante[5] na[6] vardhante[7] /[8] tat kathaṃ bālaiḥ[9] kṣaṇikārthe[10] vikalpyata[11] ādhyātmikabāhyānāṃ sarva[12]dharmāṇām[13] asaṃdhyābhāṣya[14]kuśalaiḥ[15] //

1. °rṇam] T5; °rṇṇam] T4, C8,9, R10, N11,13,14,16,17; °rṇṇaṃ] T2,3; °rṇṇa] T6.
2. °jrañ] T2,3,4,5, C9, N13,14,17.
3. Nj. dhāraṇaṃ; dharaṇa°] in all Mss. See p. 67, n. 5.
4. 'pi'] T6.
5. hāyante] in all Mss. (°yaṃte, T2,3,5, C9, N11,13,14).
6. om. na] C8, R10.
7. varddhante] T6; varddhanante] T1; baddhante] N15,17; baddhaṃte] T2; valaṃ vate (?)] N11; dhāryante] N12; om. vardhante] T3,4,5, C8,9, R10, N14,16.
8. //] N13; om. /] T2,6, N13,17.
9. °lai]] T5, N16.
10. °rtho] T1,6.
11. te] in all Mss. (°lpate, N11); + //] C8, R10, N12; + /] T1,6, N11.
12. °rvva°] T2,3,5, C9, N11,14,16,17.
13. °rmmā°] T2,3, N11,14; °rmāṃ] T5; °rmmān] N16; °rmmānām] N17; rmmānāṃm] C9.
14. °pya°] R10.
15. /] T1,4, C8, N16; om. //] T2,3,5, R10, N11,13,14,17.

§ Ṣaṭpāramitā (84)

[Nj. 236.16]

punar api[1] mahāmatir āha /[2] yat punar [3..]etad uktaṃ[..3] bhagavatā[4] ṣaṭpāramitāṃ[5] paripūrya[6] buddhatvam avāpyata iti /[7] tat katamās tāḥ ṣaṭpā[p. 237]ramitāḥ[8], kathaṃ[9] ca[10] paripūriṃ[11] gacchati[12] /[13] bhagavān āha /[14] traya[15] ete[16] mahāmate pāramitābhedāḥ [/][17] katame trayo[18], yad uta laukika[19]lokottara[20]lokottaratamāḥ[21] /[22]

1. om. punar api] in all Mss. except T1,6, N11.
2. //] T2,3,4,5,6, C8, N11,13,14,16,17; // //] C9.
3. evaṃ tad uktaṃ] T6.
4. °ta] T6.
5. °tā] T2,4,5,6, C8,9, R10, N11,12,13,14,16,17; + //] N12.
6. °ryya] T2,3,5, C8,9, R10, N11,13,14,16,17.
7. //] T6; // //] N11; om. /] T2,3,4,5, C8,9, R10, N12,13,14,16,17.
8. °tā] T6, N11.
9. °thañ] T5, R10; °tham] T3,4, C9, N14.
10. vā] T1,2,3,6, C9, N11,12,13,14,16,17; cā] C8, R10.
11. °riṅ] T2,3,5, C9, N14,16,17; om. °riṃ] R10.
12. °cchaṃti] T4,5, N11; °cchanti] T3, C8, R10, N12,14,16.
13. //] T5,6, C8, R10, N12,13,14,16,17; // //] N11.
14. //] T3,5,6, C8,9, R10, N11,12,13,14,16,17.
15. om. traya] R10.
16. ime] T1,2,3,4,5,6, C9, N11,12,14,16,17.
17. om. /] in all Mss. and Nj. From the context it is better to have a *daṇḍa*, as does Vd.
18. °yaḥ] T1,6 (+ /), N11 (+ //); °yor] T2,4,5, N13,16,17.
19. loki°] N11.
20. om. lokottara] T1,5.
21. °mās] T3,4, C8,9, R10, N12,14,16; °rakatās] T2, N13,17; °ramās (?)] N11; °ras (om. tama)] T5; tamāḥ] T1,6.
22. //] N11; om. /] T2,3,4,5,6, C8,9, R10, N12,13,14,16,17.

[Nj. 237.3]

tatra mahāmate[1] laukikyaḥ[2] pāramitā[3] ātmātmīya[4]grāhā[5]bhiniveśābhiniviṣṭā[6] anta[7]dvayagrāhiṇo[8] vicitrabhavopapattyā[9]yatanā[10]rthaṃ rūpādiviṣayābhilāṣiṇo[11] dānapāramitāṃ[12] paripūrayanti[13] /[14] evaṃ[15] śīla[16]kṣānti[17]vīrya[18]dhyānaprajñāpāramitāṃ[19] mahāmate paripūrayanti[20] bālāḥ[21] /

1. + //] N12.
2. lokikṛḥ] N14; lokikyaḥ] N16.
3. °tāḥ] in all Mss. except N11, which has °ramirātmā°.
4. °tmāya] T3, C9, N14; ātmāmīya°] R10; ātmīya (om. ātma)] T5.
5. °grahā°] N11.
6. °ṣṭāḥ /] T6, N11 and also Vd. But not so here. The compound 'ātmātmīyagrahābhiniveśābhiniviṣṭa' is in apposition to 'antadvayagrāhin' and 'rūpādiviṣayābhilāṣin' (cf. nityānityābhiniveśābhiniviṣṭānāṃ bālapṛthagjanānāṃ [Nj. 230.5]). Here 'laukiyaḥ pāramitā' is probably mentioned merely as the topic of the following and is not the actual subject of the sentence. Tib. treats it in this way.
7. antar°] C8, R10.
8. °ṇaḥ] in all Mss.
9. °patyā°] T3,5, C9, R10, N11,12,13,14,16,17.
10. °āyanā°] T6.
11. lābhiṇo] T6.
12. °tām] T2,3,5, C9, N11,13,14,17.
13. °yati] T2,3,4,5, C9, N12,13,14,16,17.
14. //] C8, R10, N12,13,16.
15. eva] N11,14.
16. śīlapāramitākṣā-] T2,3,4,5, C8,9, R10, N12,13,14,16,17.
17. om. kṣānti] T6; + pāramitā] N14.
18. °ryya°] T3,5, C9, N11,14,16,17.
19. °tā] T3,4,5, C8,9, R10, N12,14,16.
20. yaṃti] C8, R10; + /] T6; + //] C8, R10, N12,16.
21. lā, and om. /] in all Mss.

[Nj. 237.8]

abhijñāś cābhinirharanti brahmatvāya [1] / tatra [2] lokottarābhiḥ pāramitābhiḥ śrāvakapratyekabuddhā nirvā[3]ṇa[4]grāha[5]patitāśayā[6] dānādiṣu prayujyante[7], yathaiva bālā ātmasukhanirvā[8]ṇābhi[9]lāṣiṇaḥ[10] /[11] lokottaratamāḥ[12] punar ma[13]hāmate svacittadṛśyavikalpamātragrahaṇāt[14] svacittadvayāvabodhād apra[15]vṛtter[16]

1. om. /] T1,2,4,5,6, R10, N11,12,13,14,17.
2. tra (om. ta°)] T1.
3. °rvvā°] T3,5, C9, N11,14,16.
4. °ṇaṃ (grā°)] C8, R10.
5. om. grāha] T3, N14; om. grā°] T4, C9.
6. patināśeyā] T5, C9, R10, N14; patimāśayā] T4, N16.
7. + /] T1.
8. °rvvā] T3,5, C9, N11,14,16.
9. °ṇāṃ bhi°] R10.
10. °ṇo] C8, R10, N12.
11. om. /] T1,2,4,5, C8,9, R10, N11,12,13,14,16,17.
12. °mā] C9; °rakatamāḥ] T2, N13,17.
13. (r)mma°] T3,5, C9, N14,16,17.
14. + /] T6, N11.
15. apapra°] T6.
16. °tte] T6, C9, N11,14.

[Nj. 237.13]

vikalpasyopādāna[1]grahaṇābhāvāt[2] svacittarūpalakṣaṇā[3]nabhini[4]veśād dānapāramitā sarva[5]sattvahitasukhārtham[6] ājāyate[7] bodhisattvānāṃ[8] mahāsattvānāṃ[9] paramayoga[10]yoginām[11] / yat tatraivālam[12]bane vikalpasyāpravṛttiṃ[13] śīlayanti,[14] tac chīlaṃ[15] pāramitā[16] ca sā /[17] yā tasyaiva[18] vikalpasyāpravṛttikṣamaṇatā[19]

1. °sya upā°] in all Mss. except N12. So too Vd.
2. + /] T1,6, N11.
3. °pakṣa° (om. la)] T2, R10, N11.
4. °ṇābhi° (om. an-)] in all Mss., but Tib. *ma chags pa* = anabhiniveśa; Ch(S) and other two versions also support Tib.
5. °rvva°] T3,5, C9, N11,14,16,17.
6. °amm] N17.
7. + /] T1; + //] T6, C8, R10, N12.
8. °nām] C8,9, R10, N13,14,16,17.
9. °nām] T2,3,4, C9, N14,16,17; om. mahāsattvānāṃ] T1.
10. om. yoga] N13,16,17.
11. °nāṃ, and om. /] in all Mss.
12. °laṃ°] T1, C8,9, R10. R10 adds °vala° between °laṃ° and °bane.
13. °tti] T6, N13,17.
14. yaṃti //] C8, R10.
15. °la] in all Mss. except T1.
16. pāla°] T4.
17. om. /] in all Mss.
18. °sya°] T6.
19. °kṣagaṇatā] N17. N13 om. from '°kṣamaṇatā' to 'āśrayaparāvṛtti' in Nj. 238.6.

[Nj. 238.1]

grāhyagrāhakaparijñayā[1] sā kṣāntipāramitā[2] / yena vīryeṇa[3] pūrva[4]-
rātrāt[5] pararātraṃ[6] ghaṭate[7] yogānukūla[8]darśād[9] vikalpasya[10] vyāvṛt-
teḥ[11] sā vīrya[12]pāramitā[13] /[14] yad vikalpanivṛttes[15] tīrthya[16]nirvāṇa[17]grāhā-
patanaṃ[18] sā[19] dhyānapāra[20]mitā[21] /[22] tatra prajñāpāramitā yadā svacit-
tavikalpābhāvād ā buddhipravicayāt[23] prativicinvann[24] antadvaye[25]

1. °jñāyā] T3,6, C9, R10, N16,17.
2. //] T3,4,5, C8,9, R10, N11,12,14,16.
3. °ryye°] T2,3,5, C9, N11,14,16,17; vīryena] T4.
4. °rvva°] T3,5, C9, N11,14,16,17.
5. °trā] T6, N11. Vd. adopts this reading (pūrvarātrāpararātraṃ).
6. pari°] T2,3,4,5, C8,9, R10, N14,17.
7. ghaṭa (om. te)] T4; + //] N12.
8. °kūlā°] N11.
9. °darśāt] N12; °darśanād] T3,4, C9, N14,17; darśanā] T6. Vd. darśanād.
10. + /] C8.
11. °ttaḥ] T6; + /] N11; + //] C8, R10.
12. °ryya°] T2,3,5, C9, N11,14,16,17.
13. °tāḥ] T1,3,4,5,6, C9, N11,14,16,17.
14. //] C8, R10, N11,12; om. /] T1,6, C9.
15. °ttīs] T2,3,4,5, C9, N11,12,14,16,17; °ttas] T6.
16. tīrthyā] T5, C9.
17. °rvvā°] T2,3,5, C9, N11,14,16,17.
18. °na] R10.
19. om. sā] N12.
20. °pāri°] N11.
21. °tāḥ] T6.
22. //] C8, R10, N12,16; om. /] N17.
23. °yān] T1,3,4,5, C8,9, R10, N11,14,16,17.
24. °cinvaṃnn] C8; °canvann] T1; °cintyatvann] T2, N17; °citvan] T5; °citva(nta)] T6; °cinva] N11; °cicann] N12; °cintanvann] T3,4; pravicintanvann] N14.
25. antar°] C8, R10.

[Nj. 238.6]

na pataty,[1] āśrayaparāvṛttipūrva[2]ka[3]rmavināśataḥ[4] svapratyātmārya[5]-gatipratila[6]mbhāya prayujyate, sā prajñāpāramitā [7] / etā mahāmate pāramitā,[8] eṣa pāramitārthaḥ[9] //[10] tatredam ucyate //[11]

1. °ti] T1 (+ /),3,4,5,6, C8,9, R10, N11,14,17; patita] T2, N12 (+ //),16.
2. °rvva°] T2,3,5, C9, N11,14,16,17.
3. °kam a°] T1,3,4,5,6, C8, R10, N12,16; °karmma°] T2, N17; °karma°] C9, N13,14 (T3?). Tib. and Ch(S) seem to support the reading 'āśrayaparāvṛttipūrvakam avināśataḥ' (Tib. *gnas gyur pa sṅon du ḥgro ba mi ḥjigs pas*; Ch(S) 先身轉勝而不可壞). But this latter reading is grammatically doubtful. Further investigation is needed.
4. °ta] R10; + /] T2,3, C9, N14,16,17; + //] T4,8, R10, N12,13.
5. °ryya°] T2,3,5, C9, N11,13,14,16,17.
6. °laṃ°] T3,5,6, C9, N13,14,16.
7. //] T6, C8, R10, N12; om. /] T2,3,4,5, C9, N13,14,17.
8. + /] C8; + //] R10. Vd. has *daṇḍa*.
9. °as] T2,3,4,5, C8,9, R10, N12,13,14,16,17.
10. // //] N11; om. //] T2,3,4,5, C8,9, R10, N12,13,14,16,17.
11. ucyat] T5. The following verses actually belong to the section on *kṣaṇikatva*.

§ Verses on Kṣaṇikatva (84A)

[Nj. 238.9]

śūnyam anityaṃ kṣaṇikaṃ[1] bālāḥ kalpenti[2] saṃskṛtam[3] /[4]
nadīdīpa[5]bīja[6]dṛṣṭāntaiḥ[7] kṣaṇi[8]kārtho vikalpyate //[9] 9 //[a]
nirvyā[10]pāraṃ[11] [ca][12] kṣaṇikaṃ viviktaṃ[13] kriya[14]varji[15]tam[16] /[17]
anutpattiś[18] ca dharmāṇāṃ[19] kṣaṇikārthaṃ[20] vadāmy aham[21] //[22] 10 //[b]

1. °kam] T2,3,4,5, N12,13,14,16,17; kaṃm] C9; °ka] R10, N11.
2. kalpanti] R10; kalpyanti] N12.
3. °taṃ] in all Mss. except N11, which has °taḥ.
4. //] C8, R10, N12,13,16; om. /] T1, N14.
5. nadīpa] T6, C8, R10.
6. °vītaja] T3, C9, N14 (Nj. vīja).
7. This *pāda* has one extra syllable. Tib., Ch(S), etc., agree with this reading. Cf. Sag. 116c: nadīdīpādidṛṣṭāntaiḥ.
8. kṣāṇi°] N14.
9. /] N12; om. //] T1,2,3,4,5, C9, N13,14,16,17.
10. nivyā°] N13.
11. °ra] T2, N12,17; + ca] T6.
12. Nj. om. ca. Only T6 has ca. But metrically one more syllable is required in this *pāda*. Cf. Sag. 117a: nirvyāpāraṃ tu kṣaṇikam (*ma vipulā*).
13. °kta] T6, R10.
14. Nj. kṣaya°. So in all Mss. except N11, which has kriya°. Tib. *byed pa spaṅ pa* and Ch(S) 離所作 suggest 'kriyāvarjita'. Here kriya° *metri causa*. Cf. Sag. 117: kriyavarjitaṃ.
15. °rjji] T2,3,4,5, C9, N14,16,17.
16. °taṃ] T1,6, C8, R10, N12; °ta] N11.
17. //] C8, R10, N12,16; om. /] T2,3,4,5, C9, N13,14,17.
18. °ttis ca] T6.
19. °rmmā] T2,3, C9, N11,14,17.

20. °kārtham] N11,12; °kāthaṃ] N13.
21. °haṃ] in all Mss.
22. //] T6, C8, R10, N12,13,16; /] T1,2,3,5, C9, N14,17.

a: Cf. Sag. 116:
śūnyam anityaṃ kṣaṇikaṃ vālāḥ kalpanti saṃskṛtam /
nadīdīpādidṛṣṭāntaiḥ kṣaṇikārtho vikalpyate // 116 //
b. Cf. Sag. 117:
nirvyāpāraṃ tu kṣaṇikaṃ viviktaṃ kriyavarjitam /
anutpattiṃ ca dharmāṇāṃ kṣaṇikārthaṃ vadāmy aham // 117 //

[Nj. 238.13]

utpattya[1]nan[2]tara[3]ṃ bhaṅgaṃ[4] na vai deśemi[5] bāliśān[6] /[7]
nairantarye[8]ṇa[9] bhāvānā[10]ṃ vikalpāḥ[11] spanda[12]te gatau[13] //[14] 11 //
sāvidyā kāraṇa[15]ṃ teṣāṃ[16] cittānāṃ[17] saṃpravartikā[18] /[19]
antarā[20] kim[21] avasthāsau yāvad rūpaṃ[22] na jāyate[23] //[24] 12 //[c]

1. °tya] T1,2, R10, N13,17.
2. °naṃta°] N12.
3. °ram] T3,4,5, C9, N13,14,17; °ra] N16.
4. bhaṃgaṃ] T1,6; bhaṃga] N11,13; bhagaṃ] T2,3,4, N17; bhagava] T5, C9, N14; bhagavan] C8, R10, N12; bhagavaṃ] N16.
5. desemi] T1; desé //] N14.
6. °śāṃ] T3,4,5, C9, N11,13; °śām] N14,17; °śā] N16; °śāṃ] T1,2; mālisāṃ] T6.
7. //] C8, R10, N12; om. /] T2,3,4,5, C9, N13,14,17.
8. °ryye°] T2,3,5, C9, N11,14,16,17.
9. °na] T3, C9, N14.
10. °nā] T2,3,4,5, C9, N11,13,14,16,17.
11. °pa] T5.
12. °dane] T4,5.
13. gato] N11.
14. //] T6, C8, R10, N11,12,16; /] T1; om. //] in other Mss.
15. °ṇan] T3,4,5, C8, R10, N12,13,14,16,17.
16. °ṣāñ] T2,3,4,5, C9, N13,14,17.
17. citānām] N13,14.
18. saṃpravarttikā] T2,3,6, C8, N11; sampravarikā] N12; sapravarttikā] T1, 5; saṃpravṛttikā] T4, C9, N13,14,16,17; sapravṛttikā] R10. Cf. Sag. 823: saṃpravartitā. The reading 'saṃpravartakaṃ' (in apposition to 'kāraṇa') is possible, but not Nj. °vartikam.
19. //] C8, R10, N12,16; om. /] T4,5,C9, N13,14,17.
20. aṃta°] N11.

21. kim arākim] R10.
22. °pan] T3,4,5, C8,9, R10, N12,13,14,16,17.
23. °ti] T1. Tib. *mi śes pa* = na jānāti. But Ch(S) 未生, which supports the text reading.
24. //] T6, C8, R10, N11,12,16; /] T1; om. /] in other Mss.

c. Cf. Sag. 823:

tasyāvidyā kāraṇaṃ teṣāṃ cittānāṃ saṃpravartitā /
antarā kim avasthāsau yāvad rūpaṃ na jānati // 823 //

[Nj. 238.17]

samanantara[1]pradhvastaṃ[2] cittam anyat[3] pravartate[4] /[5]
[p. 239] rūpaṃ[6] na tiṣṭhate kāle[7] kim ālambya[8] pravartsyate[9] //[10] 13 //[d]
yasmād[11] yatra[12] pravarteta[13] cittaṃ vitathahetukam[14] /[15]
na prasiddhaṃ[16] kathaṃ[17] tasya kṣaṇa[18]bhaṅgo[19] 'vadhāryate[20] //[21] 14 //[e]

1. °naṃta°] C8, R10. 2. °prastaṃ] T3, N14; °prathastaṃ] N11; °prasta] T5.
3. amyat] N11. 4. °rtta°] in all Mss.
5. //] C8, R10, N12,16; om. /] T1,2,3,4,5, C9, N13,14,17.
6. °pan] T2,3,4,5, C9, R10, N12,13,14,16,17.
7. kāki] T3, C9, N11,14,16; ki (kim)] T2, N17.
8. °laṃ] T1,6, N12,16. 9. °vatsya] T4,5, C9, R10, N11.
10. //] T6, C8, R10, N11,12,16; /] T1; om. //] in other Mss.
11. yasmāt] N12. 12. yantra] T1. N12 has 'yatra' after 'cittam'.
13. °rtt°] in all Mss.; pravartteta] T1,6; pravarttata] T4, N11; pravarttate] in other Mss. Nj. adopts 'pravartate', but 'pravarteta' is metrically better (⏑ – – ⏑). Sag. 825 has same reading. 14. °kaṃ] in all Mss.
15. //] C8, R10, N12; om. /] T1,2,3,4,5, C9, N13,14,16,17.
16. °ddhaḥ] T1,5,6, N11; °ddha] T3,4, C9, R10, N14,16 (+ //).
17. °than] T2,3,5, C8,9, R10, N14,16,17. 18. °ṇaṃ] C9, N14.
19. °bhaṃgo] in all Mss. except N14, which has 'bhago'.
20. °dhāryya°] T2,5, N11,13,17; °tāryya°] T3, C9, N14; °dhāyete] R10; °dhāyya° (?)] N16.
21. //] T6, C8, R10, N11,12; /] T1; om. //] in other Mss.

d. Cf. Sag. 824:
samaṇantarapradhvastaṃ cittam anyat pravartate /
rūpaṃ na tiṣṭhate kiṃ cit kim ālambya pravartsyate // 824 //
e. Cf. Sag. 825:
yasmād yatra pravarteta cittaṃ vitathahetukam /
na prasiddhaṃ kathaṃ tasya kṣaṇabhaṅgo 'vadhāryate // 825 //

[Nj. 239.4]

yogināṃ[1] hi samāpattiḥ suvarṇaṃ[2] jinadhātavaḥ[3] /[4]
ābhāsvara[5]vimānāś ca abhedyā loka[6]kāraṇāt //[7] 15 //[f]
sthitayaḥ[8] prāptidharmāś[9] ca[10] buddhānāṃ jñānasaṃ[11]padaḥ /[12]
bhikṣutvaṃ[13] samayaprāptir[14] dṛṣṭā vai kṣaṇikāḥ[15] katham[16] //[17] 16 //[g]

1. °nā] T2, N13,17.
2. °rṇṇañ] T2,3,4, C8,9, R10, N11,13,14,16,17; °rṇṇaṃ] T6; °rṇañ] T5.
3. °tuvaḥ] T3,5, C9, N14; tāvaḥ] R10.
4. //] C8, N12; om. /] T2,3,4, C9, R10, N13,14,16,17.
5. °svarā] T2,3,4,5,6, C8,9, R10, N11,13,14,16,17.
6. loke] N12.
7. //] T6, C8, N11,12; /] T1; om. //] in other Mss.
8. °ya] T1.
9. prāptiḥ] T1.
10. °rmmā°] T2,3,5, C9, N11,14,16,17.
11. °sam°] T2,3, C9, N11,12,13,14,17; °dam° (?)] T4.
12. //] C8, N11; om. /] T2,3,5,6, C9, R10, N13,14,16,17.
13. bhikṣadaṃtvaṃ (?)] T4.
14. °tiḥ] T6; °ti] N11,13,14,16,17.
15. °kā] T6, N11. 'kṣaṇikā' is not impossible (in apposition to 'samaya-prāpti'). Cf. Sag. 827.
16. thaṃ] in all Mss.
17. //] T6, C8, R10, N11,12; /] T1; om. //] in other Mss.

f. Cf. Sag. 826:
yogināṃ hi samāpattiḥ suvarṇajinadhātavaḥ /
ābhāsvaravimānāni abhedyā lokakāraṇāt // 826 //

g. Cf. Sag. 827:
sthitayaḥ prāptidharmāś ca buddhānāṃ jñānasaṃpadaḥ /
bhikṣutvaṃ samayaprāptir dṛṣṭā vai kṣaṇikā katham // 827 //

[Nj. 239.8]

gandharva[1]puramāyādyā rūpā vai kṣaṇikā[2] na kim[3] /[4]

abhūtikāś ca bhūtāś ca[5] bhūtāḥ[6] kecit <u>karā gatāḥ</u>[7] // 17 //[h]

iti[8] kṣaṇika[9]parivarta[10]ḥ ṣaṣṭhaḥ[11] //

1. °rvva°] T2,3,5, C9, N11,14,16,17.
2. °ka] R10.
3. kiṃ] T1,3,4,5,6, C8,9, N13,14,16,17; ki] R10, N11,12; kim] T2.
4. //] C8, R10, N12; om. /] T2,3,5, N13,14,16,17.
5. om. bhūtāś ca] T1, R10.
6. °tā] T2,3,5,6, C9, N13,14,16,17.
7. For *pāda* cd, Tib. *ḥbyuṅ ba ma yiṅ gzugs rnams daṅ // ḥbyuṅ po de dag gaṅ du soṅ* /, which suggests 'rūpāṇi' or 'rūpāś ca' (rūpa, m., as in previous line) for 'bhūtāś ca', and '*bhūtāḥ kvacana te gatāḥ' for *pāda* d. Cf. Sag. 828: kiṃcit kva cāgatau. Ch(S) and (W) also suggest 'rūpa' (色) in *pāda* c, while Ch(W) and (T) seem to have a word relating to 'kara' in *pāda* d. Nj. karāgatāḥ, but it should be 'karā gatāḥ', in the sense "which elements are understood as makers?"
8. om. iti] T1,2,3,4,5, C9, N11,13,14,16,17; + // before the sentence] in all Mss.
9. kṣaṇa°] N13,17; āsyasaddharmalaṅkāvatārakṣaṇika] T1; āryasaddharmmalaṃkāvatārakṣaṇika°] N11; śrīlaṃkāvatāre kṣaṇika°] T6, N12.
10. °rtt°] in all Mss. (°rtto nāma, T6).
11. ṣaṣṭhamaḥ] T6; ṣaṣṭataṃaḥ] N13.

h. Cf. Sag. 828:

gandharvapuramāyādyā rūpā vai kṣaṇikā katham /
abhūtikā ca bhūtāni bhūtāḥ kiṃcit kva cāgatau // 828 //

PART II

THE *LAṄKĀVATĀRA* AND OTHER TEXTS

An Analysis of the *Laṅkāvatāra*: In Search of Its Original Form*

The transmitted text of the *Laṅkāvatārasūtra*[1] is peculiar in various respects in comparison with other Mahāyāna scriptures.

First of all, it has no typical conclusion beginning with the cliché '*idam avocad bhagavān...*', as is usually found at the end of such sūtras.[2] Nor is any *parīndanā* chapter or the like attached to the sūtra. Secondly, the sūtra consists of two parts: one in mixed prose and verse and forming the main body of the sūtra, and the other, a section exclusively in verse which was named "Sagāthakam" by Nanjio, the editor of the Sanskrit text. While both parts have a certain number of verses in common, 205 verses out of 432 in the main body of the sūtra and 664 verses out of 884 in the "Sagāthakam" section are left unmatched in the other part.[3]

---

* Originally published in *Indianisme et Bouddhisme: Mélanges offerts à Mgr Étienne Lamotte* (Louvain-la-Neuve: Institut Orientaliste, 1980), pp. 339–352. I would like to express my thanks to Mr. Edgar Cooke, a graduate student at the University of Tokyo, who took the trouble to read through my original manuscript and correct my English.

1. (Text) *The Laṅkāvatāra Sūtra*, ed. by B. Nanjio (Kyoto, 1923); *Saddharmalaṅkāvatārasūtra* (Buddhist Sanskrit Texts, No. 3), ed. by P. L. Vaidya, with an Introduction by S. Bagchi (Darbhanga, 1963).

(English translation) D. T. Suzuki, *The Laṅkāvatāra Sūtra: A Mahāyāna Text* (London, 1932). (Index) D. T. Suzuki, *An Index to the Lankavatara Sutra (Nanjio Edition) with the Chinese and Tibetan Equivalents* (Kyoto, 1933). (Study) D. T. Suzuki, *Studies in the Lankavatara Sutra* (London, 1930). (Japanese translation) Kōsai Yasui, *Bonbun wayaku Nyūryōgakyō* (Kyoto: Hōzōkan, 1976).

2. At the end of the Wei-dynasty Chinese translation, a few lines in verse are added as a concluding formula (T. vol. 16, p. 586b), but this is not found in any of the other versions.

3. See List of Verses below (p. 115). The difference in the number of verses

Furthermore, the order of the verses in the "Sagāthakam" has no connection with their arrangement in the main body. In the third place, the sūtra has no system to its contents, nor has it any unifying story to regulate the whole. It is, as is often said, merely a mosaic collection of small parts put at random within the frame of a sūtra.

The present Sanskrit text consists of ten chapters, of which the all-verse section is the tenth. According to the colophon, the sūtra is entitled "*āryasaddharmalaṅkāvatāro nāma mahāyānasūtraṃ sagāthakaṃ*," probably because the gāthā chapter is attached to the main body of mixed prose and verse. The term *sagāthaka*, being appositional to the term *mahāyānasūtra*, does therefore not stand for the verse section as has been assumed by Nanjio.[4] This all-verse section is otherwise called "*laṅkāvatārasūtrokta-gāthā-ratnamaya-mahāyānanaya*," as may be observed in its introductory verse. It would be better called *gāthāgrantha* or *gāthāmaya-laṅkāvatāra*. Or otherwise can we not regard the whole title in the colophon mentioned above as denoting this *gāthāgrantha* exclusively? If we can, '*sagāthako laṅkāvatāraḥ*' would imply a different text from the main body.

Besides the Sanskrit text, which is based upon manuscripts transmitted among Nepalese Buddhists, there are several versions preserved in the Chinese and Tibetan Tripiṭakas.[5] Of them, the Liu-Sung–dynasty Chinese translation (Sung version) retains a quite different form in comparison with the other versions. Namely,

---

common to both divisions (namely 227 for the main body of the sūtra against 220 for the "Sagāthakam") is due to the occasional doubled use of verses and a different way of counting verses in the main body.

4. D. T. Suzuki, *Studies in the Lankavatara Sutra* (hereafter *Studies*), p. 22.

5. (Chinese translations) 1. (Liu) Sung version, 4 fascs., T. no. 670; 2. Wei version, 10 fascs., T. no. 671; 3. T'ang version, 7 fascs., T. no. 672. (Tibetan translations) 1. Peking Edition, no. 775 (translated from Sanskrit); 2. Peking Edition, no. 776 (translated from the Chinese Sung version): both are included in the Peking Edition, vol. 29 (Tokyo, 1958).

in this version the first chapter, called "Rāvaṇādhyeṣaṇā" in the present Sanskrit text, and the ninth chapter, "Dhāraṇī," together with the "Sagāthakam" section are completely missing except for the beginning paragraph of the first (*evaṃ mayā śrutam*...). Instead, the whole text is here called the chapter of *Sarvabuddhapravacanahṛdaya*, the same term being used in the same way at the end of chapter VIII in the transmitted Sanskrit text. This fact seems to show that the original of the Sung version was a text ending with the section concerning meat-eating and entitled or characterised as the *Sarvabuddhapravacanahṛdaya*. As this version was translated in 443 A.D., or about 70 years earlier than the Wei version, which retains the same structure as the present Sanskrit text, it is usually supposed that it shows an older form of the sūtra and that the "Sagāthakam" and the rest are to be regarded as later additions. But if the "Sagāthakam" is a later addition, why then are about 200 verses doubles of those in the older part? And what was the purpose of the addition of such a mere collection of verses to the main body?

Prior to answering these questions, let us first analyze the structure of the Sung version in comparison with the main body (chaps. I-IX) of the present Sanskrit text and the "Sagāthakam" side by side. As has been said above, this sūtra has no system at all. The best way to analyze such a mosaic scripture is to divide the whole text into small parts or sections according to their subjects. In his *Butsugo shinron* (*Buddhapravacanahṛdayaśāstra*),[6] Kokan Shiren,[7] a fourteenth-century Japanese commentator on the Sung version, tried for the first time to divide the text in this way and made 86 sections together with titles showing the subject matter for the main body of the text, including the portion

6. (Edition) *Nihon Daizōkyō*, *Hōtōbu shōso*, vol. 3, pp. 175–353 (Tokyo, 1916).

7. D. T. Suzuki, *Studies*, pp. 43–44, 64. Shiren (1278–1346) was a Zen monk of the Kamakura period, and is also famous for his book on the history of Buddhism in Japan called *Genkō shakusho*.

corresponding to the "Māṃsabhakṣaṇa" chapter. In addition, the introductory part covering up to the *aṣṭottaraśatapada* (108 clauses) section is treated as the introduction with five divisions. A table of the sections with pagination referring to the Nanjio edition and other information is given below.[8]

Many of these sections consist of a prose part followed by a verse or verses which repeat the contents of the former (in other words, *geya*), but there are more than 20 sections without verse, most belonging to the part corresponding to chap. II of the Sanskrit text. Out of 53 sections which have a verse or verses, there are 11 sections mostly found in the part covered by the Sanskrit text's chaps. III to VIII that have verses which are lacking in the "Sagāthakam." In a few cases we may feel that some neighbouring sections would be better combined (e.g., sections 4–5, 8–9, 36–38, 67–69, 72–75), but for the most part Kokan's division is acceptable in content and structure.[9] As for the introductory part, only the six verses out of eight in the section of the praising of the Bhagavat are identical with the beginning six verses in the "Sagāthakam," while none of the rest concerning the 108 questions and answers are found in the "Sagāthakam." The fact that the Sung version has the same six verses as the "Sagāthakam" in the section of the praising of the Bhagavat but is missing two verses that are in the Sanskrit text seems to show that the latter two verses are a later insertion to the main body after the compilation of the "Sagāthakam."

Among the sections without verse, some discuss relatively advanced or newly-introduced subjects. For example, the first three sections deal with two kinds of *vijñāna*s, seven *svabhāva*s and seven *paramārtha*s, and the distinction between true and wrong

8. The titles given to each section have been omitted and instead remarks on the content are given, mostly in Sanskrit when available.

9. Hereafter in this article, the section numbers given by Kokan Shiren will be used for references to the main body of the *Laṅkāvatāra*.

conception, respectively, and are probably a somewhat later addition judging by their contents as well as the style of the beginning of the section. For instance, section 1 starts suddenly after the 108 clauses with Mahāmati's question: '*katividho...vijñānānām utpādasthitinirodho bhavati*', and its contents have no counterpart either in the "Sagāthakam" or in the 108 questions and answers. In contrast, section 4 seems to be directly connected with the introductory part. The reason is that this section shares expressions concerning the name of the preaching place and the subject matter similar with the beginning paragraph of the sūtra. Namely:

> (Introduction) *evaṃ mayā śrutam / ekasmin samaye bhagavāṃllaṅkāpure samudramalayaśikhare viharati sma ... sārdhaṃ, mahatā ca bodhisattvagaṇena ... pañcadharmasvabhāva-vijñāna-nairātmyadvayagatiṃgataiḥ /*
>
> (Section 4) ... / *deśayatu me bhagavāṃś cittamanomanovijñāna-pañcadharma-svabhāvalakṣaṇakusumadharmaparyāyaṃ sarvabuddhapravacanahṛdayam / laṅkāpurigirimalaye nivāsino bodhisattvān ārabhyodadhitaraṅgālayavijñānagocaraṃ dharmakāyaṃ tathāgatānunītaṃ prabhāṣasva //*

Also remarkable in section 4 is the use of the term *sarvabuddhapravacanahṛdaya*, which corresponds to the title given at the end of chap. VIII and is accepted by the Sung version as denoting the contents of the whole text. From these points, section 4 can more rightly stand at the top of the main part.

There is another section that also can stand at the head but for a different reason. Section 8, of which the title is given in the sūtra itself as *āryajñānavastupravicayo nāma dharmaparyāyaḥ*, is characterized as *aṣṭottarapadaśataprabhedāśraya*, as is stated at the beginning:

> *atha khalu mahāmatir bodhisattvo mahāsattvaḥ punar eva tasyā bodhisattvaparṣadaś cittāśayavicāram ājñāya āryajñānavastupravicayaṃ nāma dharmaparyāyaṃ sarvabud-*

dhādhiṣṭhānādhiṣṭhito bhagavantaṃ paripṛcchati sma /

This section thus clearly presupposes the sections concerning the 108 clauses. It would not be strange if this section came immediately after the 108 clauses. Section 8 has no verse, but verses at the end of section 9 include three which seem to be proper to this section. Of them the last one (v. 129) runs as follows:

tārkikāṇām aviṣayaṃ śrāvakānāṃ na caiva hi /
yaṃ deśayanti vai nāthāḥ pratyātmagatigocaram //

The term *pratyātmagatigocara* is a kind of key word denoting the fundamental standpoint of the sūtra and is used in various passages with similar expressions. We find the same term in the section on Mahāmati's request in the introduction, as follows:

mahāmatir ahaṃ bhagavan mahāyānagatiṃgataḥ /
aṣṭottarapraśnaśataṃ pṛcchāmi vadatāṃ varam //9//
tasya tadvacanaṃ śrutvā buddho lokavidāṃ varaḥ /
nirīkṣya pariṣadaṃ sarvāṃ alapī sugatātmajam //10//
pṛcchantu māṃ jinasutās tvaṃ ca pṛccha mahāmate /
ahaṃ te deśayiṣyāmi pratyātmagatigocaram //11//

This may be further proof of a direct connection between section 8(–9) and the introductory part.

There is another problem relating to the sections just referred to. There is a verse the same as v. 129 utilized at the end of section 5, which is to be combined with section 4 judging by their content (a discourse on the *udadhitaraṅga-ālayavijñāna*). It is also identified with v. 437 in the "Sagāthakam." However, its position in the "Sagāthakam" is in a series of five verses identified with those in section 9. This means that sections 8–9 follow a more natural flow than sections 4–5, where only one verse was picked up out of the five forming a set in the "Sagāthakam." It also seems to suggest that the "Sagāthakam" was a collection of source materials from which certain verses were picked up and furnished with prose explanations and from which the same verse was sometimes utilized in different sections.

Then which section, section 4 or section 8, can claim priority in using the verse equivalent to "Sagāthakam" v. 437? The two verses preceding v. 437 run as follows:

> *dṛśyaṃ na vidyate cittaṃ cittaṃ dṛśyāt pravartate* /
> *dehabhogapratiṣṭhānam ālayaṃ khyāyate nṛṇām* //435//
> (= II.125)
> *cittaṃ manaś ca vijñānaṃ svabhāvaṃ dharmapañcakam* /
> *nairātmyaṃ dvitayaṃ śuddhaṃ prabhāṣante vināyakāḥ* //436//
> (= II.126)

Of these, the first one can represent a portion of section 8 but is also applicable to section 4, while the second one has no counterpart in section 8 or 9 but is more suitable to section 4, which is called *cittamanomanovijñānapañcadharmasvabhāvalakṣaṇakusumadharmaparyāya*.

On further examination, however, these three verses express the core doctrines of the sūtra and their use is not restricted to only small portions in special passages.[10] The same can be said of the titles of sections 4 and 8. Their names are too vast to be applied to one section only.

Both sections are thus almost equal in their right to stand at the top of the main part accompanying the three verses referred to above. The only difference is that section 8 presupposes the passage of 108 clauses but section 4 does not. The problem now

10. The eight *vijñāna*s, three *svabhāva*s, five *dharma*s, and two kinds of *nairātmya* are often referred to as indicating the main subjects of the *Laṅkāvatāra*, but at the same time each of these subjects appears in a different section, and roughly speaking, they are covered in the segment of the text between sections 1 and 21. As to the term *dehabhogapratiṣṭhānam ālayam*, there is no special section for it, but similar terms are found in many passages, as in the case of the term *pratyātmagatigocara*. Cf. Jikido Takasaki, "Nyūryōgakyō no yuishikisetsu," *Bukkyōgaku* 1 (1976). (This article specially refers to the term *dehabhogapratiṣṭhābhaṃ vijñānam*.)

transfers to the position of the 108 clauses in the sūtra.

As has been said above, the verses concerning the 108 questions and answers are not found in the "Sagāthakam." There is only one verse that refers to a similar term in the "Sagāthakam," i.e., v. 317, which runs as follows:

> *aṣṭottaraṃ nayaśataṃ śrāvakāś ca trayas tathā /*
> *kṣetram ekaṃ hi buddhānāṃ buddhaś caikas tathā bhavet //*

This *aṣṭottaraṃ nayaśataṃ* does not mean the same set of 108 clauses.

Use of a similar term in the main part of the sūtra is also very limited. Besides the example in section 8, the following two cases are found:

1. *punar aparaṃ mahāmate kleśajñeyāvaraṇadvayaviśuddhyarthaṃ sārthavāhavad ānupūrvyā aṣṭottare nirābhāsapadaśate pratiṣṭhāpayanti yānabhūmyaṅgasuvibhāgalakṣaṇe ca //* (*tathāgatānāṃ dharmadeśanā*) (Section 29)

2. *saced viṣamagraho bhaviṣyati so 'syāṣṭottaraśatābhimantritena rodan krandan ekāṃ diśaṃ dṛṣṭvā yāsyati //* ("Dhāraṇī-parivarta")

In the first, the term *nirābhāsapada* may mean the 108 clauses in the introductory part, as the latter consists of pairs of contradictory concepts and aims to indicate the sphere of *nirābhāsa*. But section 29 has no verse and it is not impossible to regard this section as a later addition. The second is found in chap. IX, which is no doubt a later addition. Further, it has no connection with the 108 clauses.

Thus examining, we have come to know that the 108 clauses have almost nothing in common with the sections in the main part except for their great significance in denoting the ultimate point of doctrine,[11] nor have they any root in the "Sagāthakam." In this

11. The 108 clauses represent in a way the Madhyamic standpoint of the

sense, section 4, which does not presuppose the existence of the 108 clauses, can claim priority in the use of v. 437 as having been formed earlier than section 8, which does presuppose their existence.

It may still be too early to discuss the original form of the *Laṅkāvatāra* out of the limited materials referred to above. As a temporary hypothesis, however, it would be allowable to suppose that the "Sagāthakam" and the main body of the *Laṅkāvatāra* were different texts in the beginning—different texts from the same source materials. Development took place in both independently until finally they were combined into one volume.

In this supposition, the role of the verses will be greatly emphasized as helping to indicate the period of formation of a section. More specifically, those verses which are found in both the main body and the "Sagāthakam" can claim their antiquity as forming the original text of the *Laṅkāvatāra*. And those sections in the main body which relate to these verses in content (not necessarily having to be in the same section as was shown for sections 4 and 8) can also claim antiquity, while other sections which have no verses (e.g., section 1, or section 84 on *ṣaṭpāramitā*) or which have verses that do not correspond to the "Sagāthakam" (e.g., the sections on the 108 questions and answers) are to be regarded as of somewhat later development or insertion. In this way, we can assume the original form of the main body of the *Laṅkāvatāra* to have started with the general introduction followed by Mahāmati's praise of the Buddha and then by sections 4–5. As for the "Sagāthakam," on the contrary, we have no definite way of presuming how far the original text extended. There may be many later additions in it, but we cannot limit the original to those verses in common with the main body. There are many verses which express the core of the doctrine although not utilized in the main body (e.g., "Sagāthakam" v. 77: *vijñaptimātraṃ tribhavaṃ*..., etc.).

Laṅkāvatāra in contrast to the Yogācāra-like tendency in many sections.

From these points and from the fact that some verses in the "Sagāthakam" were used twice in different sections in the main body as mentioned above, we come to make the further supposition that the original form of the *Laṅkāvatāra* was in verses akin to the "Sagāthakam." These verses may be called the source material for the *Laṅkāvatāra*. They were probably transmitted within a group[12] of Mahāyāna yogins to which the author or authors of the *Laṅkāvatāra* belonged. Verses were only loosely bound together, and the author or authors picked up a certain verse or several verses in a series, providing a prose explanation of the doctrine therein and furnishing it with the form of a question-and-answer dialogue between the Bhagavat and the Bodhisattva Mahāmati. Even after the initial formation of the text in prose and verse, to which the title was given as *Laṅkāvatāra* for the first time,[13] the text continued to be enlarged, sometimes by adding verses newly picked up from the source material, sometimes by composing new verses when necessary, and sometimes by introducing materials from other sources. As an example of this last type, we can mention section 86, i.e., the chapter on meat-eating. A fairly long passage discussing the concept of Nirvāṇa in various heretical doctrines (section 70) also has no counterpart in the "Sagāthakam" and is therefore probably a later addition. The same contents as this passage are found in the Chinese Tripiṭaka as an independent work in the form of a commentary on the *Laṅkāvatāra* allegedly by Āryadeva.[14] Attribution of this work to Āryadeva is usually regarded as spurious, but based upon the present assumption, Āryadeva may be the real author of this work, it afterward having been introduced into the *Laṅkāvatāra*

12. It must have been a group which had a fairly intimate connection with the Yogācāra but did not belong to the orthodox or main group.

13. Neither the name of the questioner nor the name of the preaching place are found in the "Sagāthakam."

14. T. no. 1640, in vol. 32. Translated by Bodhiruci, the translator of the Wei version of the *Laṅkāvatāra*.

in the same way as section 86. (From a doctrinal point of view the *Laṅkāvatāra*, which expresses the Vijñānavāda standpoint, is no doubt a composition later than Nāgārjuna and Āryadeva.)

At the beginning of its compilation, the author may have had a plan to complete the sūtra with the usual cliché as the ending. But he did not do so and left the text open to further enlargement, probably because there were many verses left unused in the source material. At some stage, however, the original author or his successors had the intention to sum up the contents of the text. Thus was made section 85, i.e., chap. VII in the Sanskrit text, which expresses the hidden meanings of doctrines mostly referred to in previous passages and also makes clear the function of the Tathāgata.[15] Another way of summing up the core of the doctrines is observed in the chapter "Rāvaṇādhyeṣaṇā" added at the top of the text by another author of a slightly later period.[16]

As for the source material in verse, the first author of the *Laṅkāvatāra* or his early successors perhaps never regarded them as the finalized text and so kept them from the public. The original for the Sung version was perhaps in this way transmitted without the *gāthā* text. Later on, after the completion of the expansion of the text, the transmitters of the *Laṅkāvatāra* made the source material open to the public and called it the *Laṅkāvatāra-sūtraṃ Sagāthakam*.

The foregoing is the present author's supposition concerning the process of formation of the *Laṅkāvatāra* made on the basis of a hypothesis that the "Sagāthakam" and the main body were originally different texts. To validate this supposition, we are required to examine the content of each section in detail from a doctrinal standpoint. We cannot but postpone this until a later article.

15. See Jikido Takasaki, "*Nyūryōgakyō* no ito suru mono" [The aim of the *Laṅkāvatāra*: A study of the *Nairmāṇika-parivarta*], *IBK* 26-1 (1977).

16. See D. T. Suzuki, *Studies*, pp. 65–85. The passage is incorporated there especially to give a summary of the *Laṅkāvatāra*.

Table of Sections in the *Laṅkāvatāra* Given by Kokan Shiren

Section number	Page & line in Nanjio Edition	Verse number	Equivalent verses in "Sagāthakam"	Remarks
Introduction				
i.	1.6-2.2	...		general introduction
...	2.3-21.6	I.1-44	...	Rāvaṇādhyeṣaṇa
Chap. II				
ii.	22.1-23.7	II.1-8	S. 1-3, ..., 4-6	Buddhābhiṣṭuti
iii.	23.8-23.16	9-11	...	Mahāmati's request
iv.	23.17-29.8	12-59	...	108 questions
v.	29.9-34.10	60.98	...	108 answers
vi.	34.11-37.5			aṣṭottarapadaśataka
Main Part (Questions & Answers)				
1.	37.6-39.8	...		dvividho vijñānām utpatti-sthitinirodhaḥ
2.	39.9-40.10	...		saptavidho bhāvasvabhāvaḥ, saptavidho paramārthaḥ
3.	40.11-43.13	...		
4. 5.	43.14-46.18 47.1-49.5	99-106 107-124	S. 56-57, 385-390 S. 391-406, 437 (= II.129)	cittamanomanovijñānapañca-dharmasvabhāvalakṣaṇa-kusumadharmaparyāyaḥ
6.	49.6-49.12	...		
7.	49.13-50.12	...		āryajñānalakṣaṇatraya
8.	50.13-52.8	...		āryajñānavastupravicayaṃ nāma dharmaparyāya
9.	52.9-55.1	125-129	S. 435-439	
10.	55.2-56.13	...		svacittadṛśyadhārāviśuddhi
11.	56.14-58.1	...		(dharmatābuddhādi)
12.	58.2-59.9	...		dvividhaṃ śrāvakayānanaya-prabhedalakṣaṇaṃ
13.	59.10-61.14	...		nityācintyatā
14.	61.15-62.6	...		
15.	62.7-63.1	...		anutpannāḥ sarvadharmāḥ
16.	63.2-65.16	130-133	S. 115 (= II.177), 245, 104, 114 (= II.176)	pañcābhisamayagotrāṇi
17.	65.17-67.1	...		icchantikānām anicchantikatā mokṣaṃ
18.	67.2-68.7	134	S. 156 (= VI.6)	svabhāvalakṣaṇatraya
19.	68.8-70.8	...		nairātmyadvayalakṣaṇa-pravicaya
20.	70.9-72.11	135	...	samāropāpavādalakṣaṇa
21.	72.12-73.10	136	S. 92	

22.	73.11-77.1	137-138	…	śūnyatānutpādādvayaniḥsvabhāvalakṣaṇa
23.	77.2-77.12	…		
24.	77.13-79.12	139	S. 133	tathāgatagarbha-upadeśa
25.	79.13-82.7	…		yogābhisamaya
26.	82.8-85.9	140-144	S. 85, 90, …, 24, 89	hetupratyayalakṣaṇa
27.	85.10-88.13	145-148	S. 265, …, 54, 55	vāgvikalpalakṣaṇahṛdayaṃ nāma dharmaparyāya
28.	88.14-96.13	149-160	S. 11, 130, 7-8, 209, 12, …, 23, 443-444, 186-187	
29.	96.14-97.4	…		catuṣṭayavinirmuktā dharmadeśanā
30.	97.5-98.13	161-164	S. 149, 352-354	caturvidhaṃ dhyānaṃ
31.	98.15-99.16	…		nirvāṇādhivacana
32.	99.17-100.5	…		dviprakāraṃ svabhāvadvayalakṣaṇaṃ
33.	100.6-103.6	165	S. 452	adhiṣṭhānadvaya
34.	103.7-104.12	…		pratītyasamutpāda
35.	104.12-106.1	166-167	S. 453, 47	abhilāpa--asadbhāva
36.	106.2-107.2			(bhrānti)
37.	107.3-108.15			(bhrānti)
38.	108.16-109.14	168-169	S. 127-128	(bhrānti)
39.	109.15-110.16	170	S. 88	sarvadharmāṇāṃ mayopamatvaṃ
40.	110.17-112.9	171	S. 244	
41.	112.10-113.14	172	S. 456	nāmapadavyañjanakāya
42.	114.1-115.6			
43.	115.7-116.10	173-175	S. 119, 118, 167	sarvadharmalakṣaṇāḥ
44.	116.11-121.17	176-178	S. 114 (= II.133), 115 (= II.130), 9	(srotaāpannādicatuṣphalāni)
45.	122.1-123.9	…		dviprakārā buddhiḥ
46.	123.10-124.16	…		mahābhūta-bhautika
47.	124.17-126.5	…		skandhānāṃ skandhasvabhāvalakṣaṇa
48.	126.6-127.13	179-181	S. 25, 210, 26	caturvidhaṃ nirvāṇaṃ
49.	127.14-133.1	182-202	S. 286 (= III.39), 289, 296-302, 305-310, 373-378	parikalpitasvabhāvaprabhedanayalakṣaṇa
50.	133.2-135.16	203-210	S. 457-458, 445-450	pratyātmāryajñānagatilakṣaṇaṃ ekayānaṃ ca
Chap. III				

51.	136.1-137.17	III.1-2	S. 188-189	manomayakāyagatiprabheda-nayalakṣaṇa
52.	138.1-148.8	3-4	S. 462-463	pancānantaryāṇi
53.	140.9-140.17	5	S. 464	buddhānāṃ buddhatā
54.	141.2-141.15	6	…	caturvidhā samatā
55.	142.16-144.13	7-8	S. 470-471	avacanaṃ buddhavacanaṃ
56.	144.14-147.14	9-14	S. 176-177, 180, 194-196	nāstyastitvalakṣaṇaṃ sarva-dharmāṇāṃ
57.	147.15-149.11	15-19	S. 465-469	siddhāntanayalakṣaṇa
58.	149.12-154.6	20-33	S. 474-487	abhūtaparikalpalakṣaṇa
59.	154.7-156.10	34-37	S. …, 135-137	yathārutārthagrahaṇaṃ na kartavyaṃ
60.	156.11-158.15	38-43	S. 285-288, 292, 294 (S. 286 = II.182)	jñānavijñānalakṣaṇa
61.	158.16-160.7	44-45	S. 183-184	navavidhā pariṇāmadṛṣṭiḥ
62.	160.8-163.9	46-47	…	sandhyasandhilakṣaṇa
63.	163.10-166.5	…		sarvabhāvasvabhāvānava-dhāraṇatva
64.	166.6-169.3	48-57	S. 91, …, …, 79, 86, 94bc, 199-200, 207-208	pratijñā na kartavyā
65.	169.4-171.9	58-60	…	vijñaptimātravyavasthāna
66.	171.10-172.18	61		deśanāsiddhāntanayalakṣaṇa
67.	173.1-175.8			lokāyatika
68.	175.9-179.17			(lokāyata)
69.	179.17-182.6	62-68	S. 656b-662	tryāmiṣaṃ dharmasaṃgrahaś ca
70.	182.7-187.2	69-78	…	tīrthakarāṇāṃ nirāṇavikalpāḥ
71.	187.3-191.2	79-85	S. 63-64, …, 500-501, …, …	svabuddha-buddhatā
72.	191.3-193.13			tathāgatasyādhivacanaṃ
73.	193.13-197.8			(arthapratiśaraṇa)
74.	197.9-201.4	86-91	S. 581-587a	(anirodhānutpāda)
75.	201.5-204.10	92-117	S. 587b-613	
76.	204.11-210.3	118-122	…	anityatā
Chap. IV				
77.	211.1-213.15			abhisamaya (nirodhakra-mānusandhi)
78.	213.16-216.5	IV.1-7	S. 105-109, 205-206	(paramārthe na kramānu-sandhiḥ)
Chap. V				
79.	217.1-219.10	V.1-3	…	tathāgatanityānityaprasaṅga
Chap. VI				
80.	220.1-224.3	VI.1-4	S. …, 708, 715, 433	skandhadhātvāyatanānāṃ pravṛttinivṛttiḥ

81.	224.4-229.9	5-6	S. 638, 156bc (= II.134)	pañcadharma-svabhāvaprabhedagatilakṣaṇa
82.	229.10-234.8	7-8	…	gaṅgānadibālukāsamās tathāgatāḥ
83.	234.9-236.15	9-17	S. 116-117, …, 823-828	sarvadharmāṇāṃ kṣaṇa-bhaṅgabhedalakṣaṇaṃ
84.	236.16-239.10	…		ṣaṭpāramitā
Chap. VII				
85.	240.1-243.14	VII.1-5	…	nairmāṇika
Chap. VIII				
86.	244.1-259.7	VIII.1-24	…	māṃsabhakṣaṇe guṇadoṣaḥ
Chap. X				
…	206.1-263.3	…		dhāraṇī
"Sagāthakam"				
…	264.1-376.1	S. 1-884		

List of Verses in the "Sagāthakam" Equivalent to Those in Other Chapters

Verse numbers in "Sagāthakam"	Equivalent verse numbers in (section numbers in parentheses) Chap. II	Chap. III	Chap. IV	Chap. VI
S. 1-6	II.1-3, 6-8 (Introduction)			
7-8	151-152 (28)			
9	178 (44)			
11-12	149, 154 (28)			
23	156 (28)			
24	143, 144ab (26)			
25, 26	179, 181 (48)			
47	167 (35)			
54-55	147-148 (27)			
56-57	99-100 (4)			
63-64		III.79-80 (71)		
79		51 (64)		
85	140 (26)			
86		52 (64)		
88	170 (39)			
89, 90	144bc, 141 (26)			
91		48 (64)		

92	136 (21)			
94bc		53 (64)		
104	132 (16)			
105-109			IV.1-5 (77-78)	
114-115	133, 130 (16)			
114-115	176-177 (44)			
116-117				VI.9-10 (83)
118-119	174, 173 (43)			
127-128	168-169 (38)			
130	150 (28)			
133	139 (24)			
135-137		35-37 (59)		
149	161 (30)			
156bc	134 (18)			6 (81)
167	175 (43)			
176-177, 180		9-10, 11 (56)		
183-184		44-45 (61)		
186-187	159-160 (28)			
188-189		1-2 (51)		
194-196		12-14 (56)		
199-200		54-55 (64)		
205-206			6-7 (77-78)	
207-208		56-57 (64)		
209	153 (28)			
210	180 (48)			
244	171 (40)			
245	131 (16)			
265	145 (27)			
285-288		38-41 (60)		
(286), 289	182-183 (49)			
292, 294		42-43 (60)		
296-302	184-190 (49)			
305-310	191-196 (49)			

352-354	162-164 (30)			
373-378	197-202 (49)			
385-406	101-123 (4-5)			
433				4 (80)
435-439	125-128 (9)			
(437)	124 (4-5)			
443-444	157-158 (28)			
445-450	205-210 (50)			
452	165 (33)			
453	166 (35)			
456	172 (41)			
457-458	203-204 (50)			
462-463		3-4 (52)		
464		5 (53)		
465-469		15-19 (57)		
470-471		7-8 (55)		
474-487		20-33 (58)		
500-501		82-83 (71)		
581-613		86-117 (74-75)		
638				5 (81)
656b-662		62-68 (69)		
708				2 (80)
715				3 (80)
823-828				12-17 (83)

The Concept of *Manas* in the *Laṅkāvatāra**

I

The *Laṅkāvatārasūtra* (*LAS*) is noted by scholars for its eightfold *vijñāna* theory. Among the eight *vijñāna*s, however, the character of *manas* is not clear and sometimes it is held that there is no reference in the *LAS* to *kliṣṭa-manas*, which is generally regarded as its fundamental character.[1] To examine this claim we must first of all make a list of all occurrences of the term *manas* in the *LAS*.

II

For our present purpose, the term *manas* will be classified into two groups according to its use in the *LAS*, namely:

A. general use as observed in the case of *manas-karman* in contrast to *kāya-* and *vāk-karman*;

B. use unique to the Vijñānavāda, namely, as distinguished from *citta* (= *ālayavijñāna*) and *vijñāna* (= 6 *vijñāna*s).

In the following list, each section is again divided conventionally into several parts in accordance with its context.

For occurrences in prose, the page and line in the Nanjio Edition (Kyoto, 1923), and for those in verses, the verse number adopted by the same text together with the chapter number (for chap. X, the "Sagāthakam," with the abbreviation Sag.) are given. For reference, the section number adopted by the *Butsugo shinron*,[2] a Japanese commentary on the Sung version of the Chinese

---

* Originally published in *JIBS* 29-2 (1981), pp. 977–970.

1. Shunkyō Katsumata, *Bukkyō ni okeru shinshikisetsu no kenkyū* [A study of *citta-vijñāna* thought in Buddhism] (Tokyo, 1961), pp. 660, 662.

2. *Butsugo shinron* (Commentary on the *Buddhapravacanahṛdaya*), by Kokan Shiren (1287–1346), *Nihon Daizōkyō*, Hōtōbu 3 (Kyoto, 1916). See J. Takasaki, *Ryōgakyō* [The *Laṅkāvatārasūtra*], Butten kōza 17 (Tokyo:

translation of the *LAS*, is given in brackets. (For the introductory part of the *LAS* up to the end of the 108 *pada*s, Nanjio Edition, p. 37.5, [0] is used.)

A. The mind in general

1. one of the three kinds of actions: *manasā na…kriyate śubham*, Sag. 419.
2. *manomaya-kāya* (spiritual body):
   a. (definition): *manovad apratihataśīghragāmitvān ity ucyate*, [25] 81.7-8; *manojavasadṛśaṃ…kāyaṃ…*, [51] 137.5.
   b. (three kinds of spiritual bodies): [25] 18.6-16; [51] 136.8-10, 11-14; 137.1-8.
   c. (other occurrences): [47] 125.18–126.1; [51] III.2; [58] III.31 (*kāyo manomayaḥ*); [72] 192.1 (*manomaya-dharma-kāya*); 193.3; [81] 222.5 (*kāyaṃ jñāna-manomayaṃ* [*pratilabhante*]); Sag. 68; 189 (= III.2); 226; 420.
3. *mano-vispandita* (motion of the mind): [64] III.53 = Sag. 94bc (*manovispanditaṃ…atikramya*); [68] 178.1-3 (*yāvad …manovispanditaṃ…tāvad lokāyatam*); [70] 185.11-14 (*manasa āgatigati-vispandanān nāsti…nirvāṇaṃ*).
4. (other occurrences): *mana-varjitaṃ* (*nirvāṇam*), [57] III.18 = Sag. 468; *manohara*, [78] IV.4 = Sag. 108.

B. *Manas* as one of eight *vijñāna*s

(I) *citta*, *manas*, and *vijñāna*:

1. *cittaṃ manaś ca vijñānaṃ* (in verse only):
   a. (together with five *dharma*s, three *svabhāva*s, etc., showing topics of the text): [0] II.68; [9] II.126 = Sag. 436; Sag. 415.
   b. (other occurrences): [4] II.104 = Sag. 388; [60] III.40 = Sag. 287; Sag. 414.

Daizō Shuppan, 1980) (includes a comparative list of section numbers and pages in various versions of the *LAS*).

2. *citta-mano-manovijñāna-* (in compound):
   a. (together with five *dharmas*, three *svabhāvas*, etc., showing topics of the text): [4] 43.14; [19] 69.11; [21] 72.12-13; [25] 81.3-4.
   b. (together with *vāsanā*, etc.): [37] 108.10 (~ *-dauṣṭhulya-vāsanāsvabhāvadharma-*); [77] 213.4 (~ *-lakṣaṇapari-cayakauśalya-*); [78] 214.7 (~ *-bāhyabhāvasvabhāva-lakṣaṇâbhiniveśa*).
   c. (to surpass, remove or change *citta-*, etc.): *citta-mano-manovijñānaṃ...tartuṃ śakyaṃ*, [4] 45.14-16; ~ *-citta-parāvṛttyāśrayānāṃ yogināṃ*, [28] 93.2-5; ~ *...-parā-vṛttibhāvāt*, [37] 108.10 (see above); ~ *-rahita*, [3] 43.1; ~ *-atīta*, [66] 172.11; ~ *-vyāvṛtti*, [69] 108.16-17; [70] 185.5; [77] 212.6 (~ *-vikalpa-* ~); ~ *-vigamāt*, [78] 215.5 (~ *-vikalpasaṃjñā-* ~); ~ *-atikrānta*, [82] 231.1-3 (~ *-dṛṣṭalakṣaṇa-* ~).
3. (miscellaneous forms): *cittaṃ manaś ca ṣaḍ vānyavijñā-nāni*, Sag. 722; *cittaṃ manaś cāpi vijñānaṃ*, Sag. 226; *cittaṃ mano vijñānam eva ca*, Sag. 417; *cittaṃ manaś ca samāśritya vijñānaṃ saṃpravartate*, Sag. 269; *ālaya-mano-manovijñāna(-dṛṣṭivāsanā-parāvṛttiḥ)*, [31] 98. 17.
4. (explanations of terms *citta*, *manas* and *vijñāna*): [4] II.106 = Sag. 390 (*manasā vicīyate*); [80] VI.4 = Sag. 433 (*manas = vidūṣakasādṛśa*); Sag. 102-103 (*manas = manyanâtmaka*); Sag. 216 (*manas = kaluṣakāraka*); Sag. 217 (*manaḥ prārthayate gatiṃ*); Sag. 687 (*manas = parikalpa*, cf. *citta = saṃkalpa, vikalpa*); [5] II.116 = Sag. 400 (*manasā manayate*, no reference to *citta*).

Cf. In Sag. 459–460, *manas* is counted as one of the synonyms of *citta* and one of the special forms of *vikalpa*, namely:

cittaṃ vikalpo vijñaptir mano vijñānam eva ca /
ālayaṃ tribhavaś ceṣṭā ete cittasya paryāyaḥ //459//

āyur uṣmâtha vijñānam ālayo jīvitendriyam /
manaś ca manavijñānaṃ vikalpasya viśeṣaṇam //460//

(II) eight *vijñāna*s, seven *pravṛttivijñāna*s, and their interrelations:

1. eight *vijñāna*s: [1] 37.14 (*vijñānaṃ...aṣṭalakṣaṇoktaṃ*); [4] II.104 (*cittaṃ manaś ca vijñānam aṣṭau*); [48] 126.13 (*aṣṭau vijñānāni*); [52] 139.1 (*aṣṭānāṃ vijñānakāyānāṃ*); [81] 227.10 (*aṣṭau...vijñānāni*); [81] VI.6 = Sag. 638 (*vijñānāny aṣṭa eva ca*); Sag. 733 (*vijñānaṃ...aṣṭavad*); [83] 235.6-9 (*aṣṭau vijñānāni = tathāgatagarbha ālayavijñānasaṃśabdito mano manovijñānaṃ ca pañca ca vijñānakāyās tīrthyânuvarṇitāḥ*).

2. a. 7 *pravṛttivijñāna*s: [48] 126.17-18 (*saptānāṃ vijñānānāṃ pravṛttiḥ tad*[= *manovijñāna*, or *ālayavijñāna*]-*hetvālambanatvād bhavati*); [80] 220.15 (*avidyā-vāsanabhūmijaiḥ saptabhir vijñānaiḥ saha...pravartate* [*ālayavijñānasaṃśabdito, tathāgatagarbhaḥ, mahodadhitaraṅgavan nityam avyucchinnaśarīraḥ...*]); [80] 221.2 (*tadanyāni vijñānāni...mano-manovijñānaprabhṛtāni...sapta*); [80] 221.13 (*saptānāṃ pravṛttivijñānānāṃ nirodhaḥ*); [80] VI.1 (*vijñānais saptabhir yutaḥ* [*garbhas tathāgatānāṃ*]); [85] 242.2 (*sapta...mano-manovijñāna-cakṣurvijñānâdayaḥ kṣaṇikāḥ*).

   b. *manādi-*

   ...*-pravṛttivijñānāni*, [1] 38.18 (↔ *ālayavijñāna*).

   ...*bhiḥ*, Sag. 726 (*visaṃyuktaṃ sattvaṃ*) (↔ *cittena saha saṃyutaṃ*); Sag. 740 (*saha...anyatvaṃ*) (↔ *cittena saha ekatvaṃ*); Sag. 753 (*saha saṃyutaṃ* [*prakṛtiprabhāsvaraṃ cittaṃ*]).

   ...*ādyaḥ*, Sag. 754 (↔ *prakṛtiprabhāsvaraṃ cittaṃ*).

3. (*ālayavijñāna* and *manas*, *vijñāna*, etc.):
vāsanā...manovijñānasaṃbhūtā, ālayaṃ ca maṇaḥ sthitāḥ (sic), [85] VII.4; *cakṣuś ca rūpam āloka ākāśaś ca*

manas tathā / ebhir utpadyate nṛṇāṃ vijñānaṃ hy ālayodbhavam //, Sag. 262; *ālayaṃ hi samāśritya mano vai saṃpravartate / cittaṃ manaś ca saṃśritya vijñānaṃ saṃpravartate //*, Sag. 269; *mano hy ālayasaṃbhūtaṃ vijñānaṃ ca manobhavam //*, Sag. 870.

4. (*ālayavijñāna* and *manas*):
ālayavijñānam...manaḥsahitaṃ pravṛttivijñānavāsanābhiḥ kṣaṇikaṃ, [83] 235.16-17 (↔ *anāsravavāsanābhir akṣaṇikaṃ*); *ālaya-mana-saṃyutam*, Sag. 157 (*mātāpitṛsaṃyogād...vardhate*) (stem: *mana-*); *ālayaṃ hi manasyātmā ātmīyaṃ jñānam eva ca /*, Sag. 645 (stem: *mana-*).

5. (*ālayavijñāna* = *citta* and *manovijñāna*, etc.) (no mention of *manas*):
ālayaṃ ca kathaṃ kasmān manovijñānam eva ca / [0] II.20;
oghāntarajalasthānīyād ālayavijñānāt pravṛttivijñānataraṅga utpadyate / yathā...cakṣurvijñānam evaṃ...pañcavijñānakāyāḥ pravartante / saha tair eva...pañcabhir vijñānakāyair hetuviṣayaparicchedalakṣaṇâvadhārakaṃ nāma manovijñānaṃ taddhetujaśarīraṃ pravartate /, [4] 44.8-16;
ṣaṇṇāṃ vijñānakāyānāṃ nirodhād ucchedadṛṣṭim āśrayanti bālapṛthagjanāḥ, ālayânavabodhāc chāśvatadṛṣṭayo bhavanti, [85] 242.15-16, cf. VII.5; *manovijñānavyāvṛttaṃ cittaṃ kāluṣavarjitam*, Sag. 239;
manovijñānaṃ...viṣayaparicchedâbhiniveśena pravartamānaṃ vāsanābhir ālayavijñānaṃ prapuṣṇāti, [48] 126.18-127.1;
cf. [48] II.180 = Sag. 210 (*taddhetukaṃ tadālambya manogatisamāśrayaṃ / hetuṃ dadāti cittasya vijñānaṃ ca samāśritam //*, *tad* = *vikalpahetuvijñāna* in II.179 = *manovijñāna*? *manas* in *manogati* means simply mental organ?); (*manovijñānam*) *ālayavijñāna-hetvālambanam* (*abhinna-*

śarīralakṣaṇam), [48] 127.2-3, cf. below.

6. (*manas* and *manovijñāna*):

(*manovijñānaṃ*) *manaḥsahitam *ātmâtmīyagrāhâbhiniveśa-manyanākāreṇânupravartate*, [48] 127.1-2 (*ālayavijñānahetvālambanam*);

*Nanjio Edition separates *manaḥ* and *sahitam*, but Tib. *yid daṅ lhan cig tu*. See also example under B (II) 4 above.

jñānâtmakās tathāgatā...kena na kalpante manasâtmato jīvataḥ pudgalataḥ / kathaṃ na vikalpante manovijñānena, chap. I, p. 20.2-5, cf. Sag. 687 (under B (I) 4); *cakṣū rūpe manaś câpi āvilasya manas tathā*, Sag. 884 (meaning of *manas* here uncertain).

7. (*manovijñāna*):

a. (definition): = *vastuprativikalpavijñāna*, [1] 37.15 (according to the commentary of Jñānaśrībhadra, in contrast to *khyātivijñāna* being *cakṣurādi-pañcavijñānakāyāḥ*); = *hetuviṣayaparicchedalakṣaṇâvadhāraka*, [4] 44.14, cf. above under B (II) 5; = *viṣayaparicchedâbhiniveśena pravartamāna*, [48] 126. 19, cf. above under B (II) 5; = *viṣayârthahetuka*, [0] 20.5; = *vikalpahetuvijñāna*, [48] II.179 = Sag. 25; *vikalpo manavijñānam*, Sag. 687.

b. (other occurrences): *kāyaṃ manovijñapti-rahitaṃ* (*labhante bodhisattvāḥ*), [81] 227.5; *manovijñāna-saṃçannāḥ* (*śāsāḥ*), Sag. 862.

(III) other established doctrines of the Vijñānavāda:

1. threefold *pariṇāma*: cf. *Triṃśikā Vijñaptimātratāsiddhi*, v. 1.

vipāka-pariṇāmaś ca vijñānasya manasya ca / mano hy ālayasaṃbhūtaṃ vijñānaṃ ca manobhavam // Sag. 870;

2. threefold *grāhaka*: cf. *Mahāyānasūtrālaṃkāra*, p. 65 (*Bhāṣya* ad. XI.40).

dehaḥ pratiṣṭhā bhogaś ca grāhyavijñaptayas 'trayaḥ /

mana-udgraha-vijñapti-vikalpo grāhakās trayaḥ // Sag. 72.

III

In the following we shall comment on some notable points to be observed in the list.

1. The *LAS* uses the three terms for the mind, i.e., *citta*, *manas* and *vijñāna*, as showing different functions distinguished from each other as observed in the works of the Vijñānavāda. This is especially clear from the compound *citta-mano-manovijñāna-*. Here *manovijñāna* represents the six *vijñāna*s, or *manovijñāna* accompanied by the *pañcavijñānakāyāḥ*, and thus is made the whole mental system consisting of eight *vijñāna*s.
2. *manas* is one of the seven *pravṛttivijñāna*s (acting consciousnesses), which are the wave-like *pariṇāma* on the ocean-like *ālayavijñāna*, or *citta*, and are *avidyāvāsanabhūmija* and perishable. The *ālayavijñāna* is, on the contrary, not perishable as it is the *tathāgatagarbha*, which represents the *prakṛtiprabhāsvara-citta*. In other cases, however, when referred to by *citta-mano-manovijñāna*, *citta* is said to be surpassed or to have changed its basis (*parāvṛtti*) in *nirvāṇa*, or at the completion of practice. This latter doctrine is closer to the orthodox Vijñānavāda.
3. The functions of *manas* in the whole system are not clear. In some passages it is completely neglected in the explanation of the evolution of the *vijñāna*s (e.g., sections [1], [4–5]), and sometimes its function is minimized (e.g., section [48], where *manovijñāna* plays the most important role). Also its definitions vary passage by passage. This seems to show that *manas* as an independent mental function is not yet established in the *LAS*, especially in the main part.[3]

3. The "main part" here means chapters II to VIII, together with the first paragraph of chap. I in the Sanskrit text, of which the corresponding passages are found in the Sung version of the Chinese translation. They are

(*Manas* is once defined as *kaluṣakāraka*, 'maker of dirtiness', but this function is also ascribed to *manovijñāna*; see Sag. 237 under B (II) 5. Also *āvilasya manas* in Sag. 884 suggests *kliṣṭa-manas*, but the context is not clear.)

4. Among definitions of *manas*, the most important is *manyanâtmaka* in Sag. 102, which runs as follows:

   cittam ālayavijñānaṃ mano yan manyanâtmakam /
   gṛhṇāti viṣayān yena vijñānaṃ hi tad ucyate //

   This verse is quoted in Hsüan-tsang's translation of the *Vijñaptimātratāsiddhi*[4] as the scriptural proof (*āgama*) of the seventh *vijñāna*, *manas*, which is defined in Vasubandhu's *Triṃśikā-kārikā* as "*mano nāma vijñānaṃ mananâtmakam*" (v. 5). This *manyanā* and *manana*, both translated into Tibetan by *ṅar sems*, seem to have the same meaning of "conceit," or more precisely "self-conceit" (thinking something as self).

   The same translation is used in an example under B (II) 6 in the list. In this example *manovijñāna* is said to have originated (having *ālayavijñāna* as its cause and basis of cognition) together with *manas* in the form of conceit, which affects the concept of the ego and its belongings. The function of *manas* is not directly mentioned here, but we may be allowed to regard *manyanā* as the *ākāra* proper to *manas*.

   There are other cases where the term *manyanā* is translated into Tibetan by *(b)rlom(s) sems*, for example Sag. 10:

   asārakā ime dharmā manyanāyāḥ samutthitāḥ /
   sāpy atra manyanā śūnyā yayā śūnyeti manyate //

   The meaning of this verse may be rendered as follows:

   Being arisen from conceit, these dharmas are of no substantial core;

---

regarded as the old portions of the *LAS*. See Takasaki, op. cit. (Introduction).

4. *Ch'eng wei-shih lun*, fasc. 5, T. vol. 31, p. 24c.

The conceit by which man thinks them void is again void.

In this case *manyanā* is not directly connected with *manas* or with the ego concept. The basic meaning of *manyanā* known from this example is "thinking something which is unreal as being real," and hence it is better rendered as "illusory imagining."[5] Tibetan *rlom sems*, usually translated as "pride," is used in order to show this special sense attached to the verb *man-* and its derivatives (e.g., *manyati* = *rlom sems byed*, Sag. 461). Tibetan *ṅar sems* seems to indicate a special case when its function is limited to the ego concept. The term *manyanā* goes back to Pāli *maññanā*, but is not found in classical Sanskrit. A further restriction of this function to *manas* with a special sense of self-conceit was probably introduced by the Vijñānavādins, who were seeking a unique function of *manas* as distinguished from *citta* and *vijñānas*.

5. There are two notable verses which show visible influence of the established doctrines of the Vijñānavāda (B (III) 1 & 2). They are notable because of their similarity with the doctrines found in Vasubandhu's works. Namely, the first refers to the *vijñānapariṇāma* theory ascribed to Vasubandhu, but it is quite doubtful whether the compiler of this verse understood the same doctrine implied in the term *pariṇāma*! As for the second verse, the threefold concept of *grāhaka*, i.e., *mana-udgraha-vikalpa*, belongs to Vasubandhu's terminology, but the fundamental doctrine of the threefold manifestation (*ābhāsa*) of *vijñāna* in terms of *deha*, *bhoga* and *pratiṣṭhā* is proper to the main part of the *LAS* and was probably established by borrowing the idea from the *Mahāyānasūtrâlaṃkāra*, the *Madhyāntavibhāga* and other early works of the Vijñānavāda.[6] The relationship between

5. F. Edgerton, *Buddhist Hybrid Sanskrit Dictionary*, s.v. *manyanā*.

6. J. Takasaki, "Nyūryōgakyō no yuishikisetsu" [*Vijñaptimātra* doctrine of the *Laṅkāvatāra*], *Bukkyōgaku* 1 (1976), pp. 1–26 (on the concept *deha-bhoga-pratiṣṭhābhaṃ vijñānam*).

the *LAS* and the works of the Vijñānavāda is still obscure, and to delve deeply into this issue is beyond our present purpose. We shall only indicate here that these two verses belong to the "Sagāthakam" and are not found in the oldest Chinese version, and there remains the possibility of their composition after Vasubandhu.

(This research was partially supported by a grant-in-aid for scientific research from the Ministry of Education.)

Sources of the *Laṅkāvatāra* and Its Position in Mahāyāna Buddhism*

Determining the date of Mahāyāna sūtras is one earnest concern of modern scholars of Indology, and in most cases a difficult and troublesome task. It is usually held that the first appearance of Mahāyāna sūtras was between the first century B.C. and the first century A.D., and that most of the important sūtras such as the *Prajñāpāramitā*, the *Saddharmapuṇḍarīka*, the *Gaṇḍavyūha*, and the *Daśabhūmika*, as well as some other sūtras belonging to the *Avataṃsaka* groups, the *Kāśyapaparivarta* (*Ratnakūṭa*), the *Vimalakīrtinirdeśa*, the larger and smaller *Sukhāvatīvyūha*s, and others were already in vogue before Nāgārjuna (A.D. 150–250). There are some other sūtras which were probably unknown to Nāgārjuna and Āryadeva, the early teachers of the Mādhyamika, but clearly known to Asaṅga and Vasubandhu, the founders of the Vijñānavāda of the Yogācāra, such as the *Saṃdhinirmocana* and the *Mahāyānâbhidharmasūtra*. Such is also the case with regard to the group of sūtras which teach the *tathāgatagarbha* (or Buddha-nature) doctrine such as the *Tathāgatagarbhasūtra*, the *Śrīmālāsūtra*, the *Anūnatvâpūrṇatvanirdeśa*, and the *Mahāparinirvāṇasūtra*.

The *Laṅkāvatāra*,[1] to which we are now going to refer, is also one of the later compositions, since it expresses concurrently the *vijñaptimātra* theory and the Tathāgatagarbha theory, two theories

* I would like to express my thanks to Rev. Ruben Habito, Lecturer, Sophia University, Tokyo, who took the trouble to read through my original manuscript and to assist with my English. First published in L. A. Hercus et al., eds., *Indological and Buddhist Studies: Volume in Honour of Professor J.W. de Jong on His Sixtieth Birthday* (Canberra: Faculty of Asian Studies, 1982), pp. 545–568.

1. *The Laṅkāvatāra Sūtra*, ed. B. Nanjio (Kyoto, 1923) (abbr. *LAS*).

unknown to Nāgārjuna. Furthermore, because of its unique doctrine of the identification of *ālayavijñāna* with *tathāgatagarbha*, a doctrine that is not found even in the works of Asaṅga and Vasubandhu, the *Laṅkāvatāra* is sometimes regarded as of a date later than Vasubandhu.[2]

There is another criterion for deciding the date of composition of a sūtra besides the reference to the date of great teachers to whom it was or was not known. The date of the first translation of a sūtra into Chinese, if this were extant, gives the lower limit of composition of that sūtra. In cases where the first translation is non-extant, the degree of certainty is reduced, but this date is taken into consideration. As for the *Laṅkāvatāra*, three translations are preserved in the Chinese Tripiṭaka, of which the oldest is the so-called Sung version in four fascicles translated by Guṇabhadra in 443. According to the Chinese catalogues of the Tripiṭaka, there was a translation of this sūtra by Dharmakṣema, who engaged in the work of translation between 412 and 433.[3] If this is true, the lowest limit of the date of the *Laṅkāvatāra* would be a bit earlier. In any case, we suppose from these facts that the *Laṅkāvatāra* probably already existed by the end of the fourth century A.D., or at the latest by the early fifth century.

The late Dr. H. Ui was of the opinion that the *Laṅkāvatāra* belongs to the group of Mahāyāna sūtras in the third period, i.e., the period after Asaṅga and Vasubandhu, and that since it already existed at the end of the fourth century A.D., the date of Vasubandhu, to whom it was unknown, should be some time in the fourth century. Thus Ui assumed the dates of Asaṅga to be 300–380 and those of his younger brother Vasubandhu to be 320–400. (Another piece of evidence for deciding this date is that the

2. H. Ui, *Indo tetsugakushi* [A history of Indian philosophy] (Tokyo, 1932), p. 418. See below.
3. The *K'ai-yüan lu*, T. vol. 55, p. 520a. Cf. D. T. Suzuki, *Studies in the Lankavatara Sutra* (London, 1930), p. 4.

Bodhisattvabhūmi was translated by Dharmakṣema in approximately 420.)[4]

To this supposition an objection was raised by the late Dr. S. Yamaguchi, who, after examining the Tibetan translation of the *Vyākhyāyukti* attributed to Vasubandhu, found a series of verses identified with vv. 135–137 in the "Sagāthakam" of the *Laṅkāvatāra*.[5] If the *Vyākhyāyukti* is really a work of Vasubandhu, the *Laṅkāvatāra*, or at least a certain number of verses in it, might have been known to Vasubandhu. There are two possible assumptions that can be made concerning this problem: to suppose the date of composition of the *Laṅkāvatāra* to be in the early fourth century or earlier, or else to suppose that Vasubandhu lived in the fifth century. Yamaguchi seems to have supported the latter possibility, although he did not say this explicitly in his article. The date of Vasubandhu is still a point of issue among scholars, but presently it is generally assumed to be the fifth century (approximately 400–480). For further verification, however, we will have to examine the internal evidence of the *Laṅkāvatāra*.

As to internal criteria for deciding the date of composition of a sūtra, we may note, roughly speaking, the following three kinds of cases:

I. Proper names appearing in the sūtra: a) names of sūtras; b) names of principal *personae* in certain sūtras; c) other names peculiar to certain sūtras; d) names of historical persons.

II. Idiomatic phrases which seem to indicate that sentences following them are quotations of or references to some sūtra passages. In the case of the *Laṅkāvatāra* we often meet such phrases as '*uktaṃ deśanāpāṭhe...*,' '*sūtrāntapāṭhe*,' '*yat punar idam (etad) uktaṃ bhagavatā...*,' etc.

---

4. H. Ui, *Indo tetsugaku kenkyū* [Studies in Indian philosophy], vol. 1 (Tokyo, 1924), p. 406.

5. S. Yamaguchi, *Bunshū* [Collected minor works], vol. 2, p. 312 (originally appeared in *Tōhōgaku ronshū*, July 1962).

III. Technical terms or important key words unique to certain sūtras or systems of doctrine, e.g., Yogācāra-vijñānavāda, Mādhyamika, and the like.

Below, we shall examine the contents of the *Laṅkāvatāra* in the light of these criteria.

I. Proper Names

a) Names of sūtras:

1. Verse 16 of chapter VIII runs as follows:

Hastikakṣe mahāmeghe nirvānâṅgulimālike /
Laṅkāvatārasūtre ca mayā māṃsaṃ vivarjitam //

In this verse we can observe the names of five Mahāyāna sūtras, including the *Laṅkāvatāra*, which are said to teach the prohibition of meat-eating. The other four sūtras are:

1) the *Hastikakṣasūtra* (equivalent to T. nos. 813, 814),
2) the *Mahāmeghasūtra* (equivalent to T. no. 387),
3) the *Mahāparinirvāṇasūtra* (equivalent to T. nos. 374–376),
4) the *Aṅgulimālikasūtra* (equivalent to T. no. 120),

and, indeed, we find the prohibition of meat-eating in all of them.[6]

Chapter VIII of the *Laṅkāvatāra* is specially dedicated to the subject of meat-eating ("Māṃsabhakṣaṇa-parivarta"). This subject is not necessarily connected with the main body of the sūtra and is regarded as a supplementary chapter. No verses belonging to this chapter have corresponding verses in the "Sagāthakam," i.e., the section consisting of Gāthās of the *Laṅkāvatāra*. These facts, together with the mentioning of its own name in the verse, enable us to suppose that this chapter is a later addition. At the same time, however, as this subject of meat-eating is mentioned

6. 1) T. vol. 17, p. 781b = ibid., p. 87a; 2) vol. 12, p. 1099c; 3) vol. 12, pp. 868c–869b = ibid., p. 386a-c; 4) vol. 2, p. 541a.

among subjects in question at the beginning of chapter II, and moreover, the oldest extant Chinese version retains this portion, including this very verse, it is certain that this verse shows the clear historical background of the doctrine of the prohibition of meat-eating in Mahāyāna Buddhism before the *Laṅkāvatāra*.

Of the sūtras mentioned above, the *Mahāparinirvāṇa* is one of the important sūtras of the Tathāgatagarbha theory. The *Mahāmegha* and the *Aṅgulimālika* have an intimate connection with it, probably influenced by it in their doctrine concerning *tathāgatagarbha*.[7] From this we may suppose that the *Hastikakṣasūtra* (which has no connection with the Tathāgatagarbha theory) was included among these sūtras because it too prohibits the eating of meat, a prohibition which is in accordance with the doctrine of *tathāgatagarbha*, which recognises and teaches the possibility of every living being without exception becoming a Buddha.

b) Names of principal *personae*:

1. Śrīmālā Devī

The *Laṅkāvatāra* refers to Śrīmālā Devī, the heroine of the *Śrīmālādevīsiṃhanādasūtra*, twice in chapter VI, namely:

> *etad eva Mahāmate mayā Śrīmālāṃ devīm adhikṛtya deśanāpāṭhe 'nyāṃś ca sūkṣmanipuṇaviśuddhibuddhīn bodhisattvān adhiṣṭhāya tathāgatagarbha ālayavijñānasaṃśabditaḥ saptabhir vijñānaiḥ saha pravṛttyabhiniviṣṭānāṃ śrāvakāṇāṃ dharmanairātmyapradarśanârthaṃ Śrīmālāṃ devīm adhiṣṭhāya tathāgataviṣayo deśitaḥ* (*LAS*, pp. 222.19–223.5)

The *Śrīmālāsūtra* is also an important sūtra in the history of the Tathāgatagarbha theory, and is regarded as being contemporary with the *Mahāparinirvāṇa*. Besides this passage, it had other influences on the *Laṅkāvatāra* regarding a number of points to which I shall refer later.

7. J. Takasaki, *Nyoraizō shisō no keisei* [Formation of the Tathāgatagarbha theory] (Tokyo, 1974), pp. 219 and 295.

2. Vajragarbha

yathā Mahāmate Vajragarbhasya bodhisattvasya mahāsattvasyânyeṣāṃ ca tādṛglakṣaṇaguṇasamanvāgatānāṃ bodhisattvānāṃ mahāsattvānām evaṃ Mahāmate prathamāyāṃ bhūmau bodhisattvā mahāsattvāḥ samādhisamāpattyadhiṣṭhānaṃ pratilabhante / (*LAS*, pp. 100.16–101.3)

Vajragarbha is the representative Bodhisattva in the *Daśabhūmika* who preaches the doctrine of the ten stages of the Bodhisattva in place of the Buddha, though with his support (*adhiṣṭhāna*). Here in the section on the two kinds of *adhiṣṭhāna* of the Buddha (section no. 33, pp. 100.6–103.6),[8] this precise point is referred to, and we come to know that the *Laṅkāvatāra* owes its ten-stages theory, scattered across various pages, to the *Daśabhūmika*. This may be a natural consequence of its acceptance of the *cittamātra* theory of the latter as its fundamental standpoint.

3. Vajrapāṇi

In chapter VII, the section on the activity of the *nirmāṇakāya* of Tathāgatas (section no. 85), there is found the following question and answer:

(kiṃ kāraṇaṃ) Vajrapāṇiś ca satatasamitaṃ nityânubaddhaḥ / (*LAS*, p. 240.10)

nirmitanairmāṇikānāṃ Mahāmate tathāgatānāṃ Vajrapāṇiḥ pārśvânugato, na maulānāṃ tathāgatānām arhatāṃ samyakṣaṃbuddhānām / ... / dṛṣṭadharmasukhavihāriṇas tam (= maulaṃ tathāgatam) āgacchanty abhisamayadharmajñānakṣāntyā / ato Vajrapāṇis tān anubadhnāti / (*LAS*, p. 242.6-11)

Vajrapāṇi is not a figure peculiar to any particular sūtra, but here special reference is made to Vajrapāṇi, the Guhyapati, as the representative Bodhisattva of the *Tathāgatâcintyaguhyanirdeśa*,

---

8. On the section numbers adopted here, see J. Takasaki, "An Analysis of the *Laṅkāvatāra*" [pp. 101–117 above].

also called the *Guhyapatipariṣat* of the *Mahāratnakūṭasūtra* (T. nos. 310 (3), 312; Tib. Peking, no. 760 (3)). In this sūtra, Vajrapāṇi is said to be always standing at the right hand of the Buddha, and, because of his position, he was asked by another Bodhisattva to preach the secret doctrine of the Tathāgata (T. 11, p. 705c).

That this sūtra influenced the *Laṅkāvatāra* is guaranteed by the fact that the doctrine '*avacanaṃ buddhavacanaṃ*', which became famous as a unique standpoint of the *Laṅkāvatāra* through later propagation by Zen Buddhism, is in this sūtra said to have been (previously) taught by the Bhagavat (*yad idam uktaṃ bhagavatā*), and actually it is found in the section on the secret act of speech (*vākkarmaguhyaka*) of the Tathāgata in the *Tathāgatâcintyaguhyanirdeśa* (T. vol. 11, p. 719b = p. 55a). I shall refer to this below.

c) Other names peculiar to certain sūtras:

1. Buddha Amitābha

> *vaipākikāś ca ye buddhā jinā nairmāṇikāś ca ye /*
> *sattvāś ca bodhisattvāś ca kṣetrāṇi ca diśe diśe* //140//
> (sic)
> *nisyandadharmanirmāṇā jinā nairmāṇikāś ca ye /*
> *sarve te hy Amitābhasya Sukhāvatyā vinirgatāḥ* //141//
> (*LAS*, p. 283.4-7)

As is well-known, Buddha Amitābha and his cult go back to the *Sukhāvatīvyūha*, and this passage is an expression of the cult of Amitābha. But as this cult is fairly widely referred to in Mahāyāna sūtras,[9] it is not necessary to regard the *Laṅkāvatāra* as belonging specially to Pure Land Buddhism.

d) Names of historical persons:

1. Nāgāhvaya (= Nāgārjuna)

> *dakṣiṇāpatha-vedalyāṃ bhikṣuḥ śrīmān mahāyaśāḥ /*

9. Gregory Schopen, "Sukhāvatī as a Generalized Religious Goal in Sanskrit Mahāyāna Sūtra Literature," *IIJ* 19 (1977), pp. 177–210.

nāgāhvayaḥ sa nāmnā tu sadasatpakṣadārakaḥ //165//
prakāśya loke mad-yānaṃ mahāyānam anuttaram /
āsādya bhūmiṃ muditāṃ yāsyate 'sau sukhāvatīm //166//
(*LAS*, p. 286.12-15)

These verses in the "Sagāthakam" are famous as a prophecy (*vyākaraṇa*) about Nāgārjuna, and because of this prophecy, the sūtra gained renown among the Mahāyānists of later India.[10] We may regard this, too, as further evidence that the *Laṅkāvatāra* was composed after Nāgārjuna.

There are many other names belonging to categories c) and d) in the "Sagāthakam": for instance, Vyāsa, Kāṇada, Kapila (v. 784); Pāṇḍavāḥ, Kauravāḥ, Rāma (v. 785); Mauryāḥ, Nandāḥ, Guptāḥ (v. 786), etc. The name *guptāḥ* may be an indication that this sūtra is a product of the Gupta Age. But the other examples are not too important for our present concern. Moreover, these verses in the "Sagāthakam," including the one referring to Amitābha and the one referring to Nāgāhvaya, have no equivalents among the verses in the main body of the *Laṅkāvatāra*, and this leaves some doubt about their existence before the date of the first Chinese translation of this sūtra.

II. Passages with Conventional Initiating Phrases ('*yad uktaṃ bhagavatā*', etc.)

1. The saying *avacanaṃ buddhavacanam*

yad idam uktaṃ bhagavatā yāṃ ca rātriṃ tathāgato 'bhisambuddho, yāṃ ca rātriṃ parinirvāsyati, atrântara ekam apy akṣaraṃ tathāgatena nôdāhṛtaṃ na prakhyāhariṣyati, avacanaṃ buddhavacanam iti, tat kim idaṃ saṃdhāyôktaṃ tathāgatenârhatā samyaksambuddhenâvacanaṃ buddhavacanam iti / (*LAS*, pp. 142.16–143.3)

This 'saying of the Bhagavat' comes, as mentioned earlier,

10. E.g. *Madhyamakāvatāra*, ed. L. de La Vallée Poussin, p. 76.11-16.

from the *Tathāgatâcintyaguhyanirdeśa*, and the *Laṅkāvatāra* intends to resolve the hidden meaning (*saṃdhi*) of this saying. The answer given is that there are two aspects of *dharmatā*, the truth, namely, *pratyātmâdhigamadharmatā* and *paurāṇasthitidharmatā*. The saying *avacanaṃ buddhavacanam* refers especially to the latter aspect, which means *pratītyasamutpāda* as the nature of things regardless of the appearance of Tathāgatas or the non-appearance of them (*utpādād vā tathāgatānām anutpādād vā tathāgatānāṃ sthitaivaiṣā dharmāṇāṃ dharmatā*). This last phrase is again a cliché commonly found since the Āgamas and the Nikāyas of Early Buddhism, referring to the eternity of the truth.

1.2 The same saying is referred to in another passage:

> *ata etasmāt kāraṇān Mahāmate uktaṃ deśanāpāṭhe mayânyaiś ca buddhabodhisattvair yathaikam apy akṣaraṃ tathāgatā nôdāharanti na pratyāharantîti* / (*LAS*, p. 194.6-8)

This is with special reference to the teaching that one should rely upon the meaning but not upon letters (as one of the four reliances [*pratiśarana*]).

1.3 The very same saying is discussed in chapter VII, again in relation to its hidden meaning as one of the problems of the role of the Buddha.

> *yasyāṃ ca rātrau tathāgato 'nuttarāṃ samyaksambodhim abhisambuddho yasyāṃ ca rātrau parinirvṛta etasminnantare bhagavataikam apy akṣaraṃ nôdāhṛtaṃ na pravyāhṛtam* /
> (*LAS*, p. 240.4-6)

These frequent references show the serious concern of the sūtra in regard to this fundamental point.

2. *ābhimānikasya śūnyatādṛṣṭiḥ*

Another example of reference to a doctrine taught by the Bhagavat, together with a new interpretation of its hidden meaning, is the following:

idaṃ Mahāmate nāstyastitvasya lakṣaṇam / idaṃ ca Mahāmate saṃdhāyôktaṃ mayā varaṃ khalu sumerumātrā pudgaladṛṣṭir na tv eva nāstyastitvâbhimānikasya śūnyatādṛṣṭiḥ / nāstyastitvâbhimāniko hi Mahāmate vaināśiko bhavati / (*LAS*, p. 146.10-14)

This saying *varaṃ khalu … śūnyatādṛṣṭiḥ* is found in a similar form in the *Kāśyapaparivarta*, i.e., the old *Ratnakūṭasūtra.*[11]

3. Tathagātagarbha theory

The concept of *tathāgatagarbha* is also said to be from a previous sūtra, namely:

tathāgatagarbhaḥ punar bhagavatā sūtrāntapāṭhe 'nuvarṇitaḥ / sa ca kila tvayā prakṛtiprabhāsvara-viśuddhy-ādiviśuddha eva varṇyate, dvātriṃśallakṣaṇadharaḥ sarvasattvadehântargataḥ / mahārghamūlyaratna-malina-vastraparivеṣṭitam iva skandhadhātvāyatanavastraveṣṭito rāgadveṣamohâbhūtaparikalpamalamalino nityo dhruvaḥ śivaḥ śāśvataś ca bhagavatā varṇitaḥ / (*LAS*, pp. 77.14–78.1)

Actually, however, we have as yet not found any particular sūtra which has this long series of qualifications of *tathāgatagarbha* in this exact order and with these exact expressions. Among these qualifications or characteristics, the first one, *prakṛtiprabhāsvaratā*, is the most basic characteristic of *tathāgatagarbha* and is rather commonly found in many sūtras. This concept *prakṛtiprabhāsvaratā* is usually accompanied by another characteristic, *āgantukair upakleśair upakliṣṭaḥ*, and this latter concept is here referred to by the expression *rāgadveṣamohâbhūtaparikalpamalamalinaḥ*, together with the simile of *mahārghamūlyaratna* enveloped by a *malinavastra*. A similar example is found among the nine illustrations of *tathāgatagarbha* taught in the

11. A. von Staël-Holstein, *The Kāśyapaparivarta*, §64.

Tathāgatagarbhasūtra,[12] which declared for the first time that all living beings are embryos of the Tathāgata, i.e., are possessed of the *tathāgatagarbha.*[13] This most important concept is again referred to here by the expression *sarvasattvadehântargataḥ.* On the other hand, the four characteristics of *nitya-dhruva-śiva-śāśvata* are found in a set, and exactly in the same order, in both the *Anūnatvâpūrṇatvanirdeśa* and the *Śrīmālā.*[14]

From the above observations, we may suppose that this passage is a kind of summary of '*tathāgatagarbha-upadeśa*' (cf. *LAS*, p. 78.6) collected from various sūtras preceding the *Laṅkāvatāra.*

The following two examples are worth considering for their remarkable similarity with the doctrine of Vasubandhu in the *Triṃśikā.*

4. *parikalpita evâsau*

yat punar etad uktaṃ bhagavatā yena yena vikalpena ye ye bhāvā vikalpyante, na hi sa teṣāṃ svabhāvo bhavati / parikalpita evâsau, tad yadi bhagavan parikalpita evâsau na bhāvasvabhāvalakṣaṇâvadhāraṇam, nanu te bhagavan nêvaṃ bruvataḥ saṃkleśavyavadānâbhāvaḥ prasajyate parikalpitasvabhāvabhāvitatvāt sarvadharmāṇām / (*LAS*, p. 163.10-15)

5. *vijñaptimātrâvasthāna*

yat punar idam uktaṃ bhagavatā yadā tv ālambanam arthaṃ nôpalabhate jñānaṃ tadā vijñaptimātravyavasthānaṃ bhavati, vijñapter grāhyâbhāvād grāhakasyâpy agrahaṇaṃ bhavati / tadagrahaṇān na pravartate jñānaṃ vikalpasaṃśabditam / (*LAS*, p. 169.4-7)

Parallel passages to these in the verses of the *Vijñaptimātratā-*

12. The seventh illustration (*pūtivastra* on an image of the Buddha). Cf. *Ratnagotravibhāga*, ed. E. H. Johnston (abbr. *RGV*), vv. I.118–120.

13. See *RGV*, p. 26.7-10.

14. See quotations in the *RGV*, p. 54.12-15 (*Anūnatvâpūrṇatvanirdeśa*) and p. 12.10-14 (*Śrīmālā*).

triṃśikā are, respectively, as follows:

> *yena yena vikalpena yad yad vastu vikalpyate /*
> *parikalpita ẹvâsau svabhāvo na sa vidyate //20//*
>
> *yadā tv ālambanaṃ vijñānaṃ naivopalabhate tadā /*
> *sthitaṃ vijñānamātratve grāhyâbhāve tad agrahaṇāt //28//*

Based on the common supposition that śāstras come after sūtras, Vasubandhu's treatise can be regarded as based upon the *Laṅkāvatāra*. But the phrase *yat punar idam* (or *etad*) *uktaṃ bhagavatā*, which precedes these most important doctrines of *vijñaptimātratā*, leads us to suppose that these passages too, as in other cases mentioned above, are quotations of other texts. We may then assume, or at least the possibility cannot be denied, that Vasubandhu's *Triṃśikā* is the very source of these passages in the *Laṅkāvatāra*.

One reason for this assumption is that Sthiramati, commenting on v. 20 of the *Triṃśikā*, refers to a sūtra passage as the authority, a passage that runs as follows:

> *uktaṃ ca sūtre / na khalu punaḥ Subhūte dharmās tathā vidyante yathā bālapṛthagjanā abhiniviṣṭā iti /* (Lévi's ed., p. 39)

This quotation is probably from a certain *Prajñāpāramitāsūtra*. If Vasubandhu composed the verse on the basis of the *Laṅkāvatāra*, and if it was handed down among Yogācāra teachers, Sthiramati could have quoted the said passage of the *Laṅkāvatāra* as the authority. But he did not do so in spite of his knowledge of the *Laṅkāvatāra*, proved by his quoting it in his *Sūtrâlaṃkārabhāṣyaṭīkā*.[15] For this assumption, however, the date of Vasubandhu must again be called into question, and we must postpone a decision on this point until after we have examined the doctrinal sources of the *Laṅkāvatāra* concerning the *vijñaptimātratā* theory.

---

15. Sthiramati ad *Sūtrâlaṃkārabhāṣya* XI, v. 40, Peking Edition (reprint), vol. 108, p. 283.2.7 (quotation of *LAS*, v. III.33).

There are other examples of previously preached doctrines or analogies with the initial phrases *uktaṃ bhagavatā* and the like. These examples are not necessarily to be regarded as from some particular sūtra, but are rather commonly accepted doctrines or analogies.

6. One should not take the meaning as it is written by letters

yat punar uktaṃ bhagavatā yathārutârthagrahaṇaṃ na kartavyaṃ bodhisattvena mahāsattvenânyaiś cêti / (*LAS*, p. 154.8-9)

The teaching that one should rely upon the meaning (*artha*) but not upon letters (*vyañjana*) is one of the four reliances (*pratiśaraṇa*), the other three being *dharma* instead of *pudgala*, *jñāna* instead of *vijñāna*, and *nītârthadeśanā* instead of *neyârthadeśanā*. Among the sūtras mentioned above, the *Mahāparinirvāṇa* has a section specially dedicated to the four *pratiśaraṇa*s (T. no. 376, chap. 9, vol. 12, p. 880a). This teaching has, of course, an intimate relation to the doctrine of *avacanaṃ buddhavacanam* mentioned above.

7. Tathāgata is *anirodhânutpāda*

deśayatu me bhagavān deśayatu me sugato yad deśanāpāṭhe bhagavatânirodhânutpādagrahaṇaṃ kṛtam, uktaṃ ca tvayā yathā tathāgatasyaitad adhivacanam anirodhânutpāda iti / (*LAS*, p. 191.4-6)

Non-origination and non-destruction as characteristics of the Tathāgata are the main subject of the *Jnānâlokâlaṃkārasūtra*, the core of whose doctrines has come to be known to us through the *Ratnagotravibhāga.*[16] It is not unnatural to suppose that the *Laṅkāvatāra* adopted this saying from the *Jṇānâlokâlaṃkārasūtra*, which emphasises the eternity of the Tathāgata (Dharmakāya, as observed likewise in the *Mahāparinirvāṇa* and the *Śrīmālā*).

16. This sūtra is used as source material for the *RGV*, chapter I, on *buddhatva*, and chapter IV, on *buddhakarman*.

8. *anityā vata saṃskārāḥ*

anityatānityatêti bhagavan sarvatīrthakarair vikalpyate / tvayā ca sarvadeśanāpāṭhe deśyata anityā vata saṃskārā utpāda-vyayadharmiṇa iti / (*LAS*, p. 204.12-14)

This quotation is the first half of the famous verse on *anityatā*.[17]

9. Tathāgatas are innumerable like the sands of the Ganges

yat punar etad uktaṃ bhagavatā deśanāpāṭhe yathā gaṅgā-nadīvālukāsamās tathāgatā atītā anāgatā vartamānāś ca / tat kim idaṃ bhagavan yathārutârthagrahaṇaṃ kartavyam āhosvid anyaḥ kaś cid arthântaraviśeṣo 'stîti tad ucyatāṃ bhagavan / (*LAS*, p. 229.11-15)

The innumerability of Tathāgatas is often referred to in various sūtras, but we do not yet know the precise source of this analogy.

10. Appearance of a Tathāgata is as rare as the Udumbala flower

deśanāpāṭhe tu mayā vaineyajanatâpekṣayôdumbalapuṣpa-sudurlabhaprādurbhāvās tathāgatā iti deśitam / na ca Mahā-mate udumbalapuṣpaṃ kena cid dṛṣṭapūrvaṃ na drakṣyate / tathāgatāḥ punar Mahāmate loke dṛṣṭā dṛśyante caitarhi / na svanayapratyavasthānakathām adhikṛtyôdumbalapuṣpasu-durlabhaprādurbhāvās tathāgatā iti / (*LAS*, p. 230.10-13)

The difficulty of obtaining the Udumbala flower is taught in the *Mahāparinirvāṇa* as an analogy for the opportunity of meeting the Buddha,[18] while in the *Saddharmapuṇḍarīka* and in the *Mahādharmabherīsūtra* it is given as showing the difficulty of obtaining the opportunity to hear the Dharma taught in these sūtras.[19]

11. *ṣaṭpāramitā*

---

17. *aniccā vata saṅkhārā uppāda-vaya-dhammino / uppajjitvā nirujjhanti tesaṃ vūpasamo sukho //* (*Mahāparinibbānasuttanta*, DN, vol. 2, p. 157).

18. T. no. 374, vol. 12, p. 372b.

19. T. no. 262, vol. 9, p. l0ab; T. no. 270, vol. 9, p. 290c.

yat punar etad uktaṃ bhagavatā ṣaṭpāramitāṃ paripūrya buddhatvam avāpyata iti / (*LAS*, p. 236.16-17)

Generally speaking, this saying is based upon the *Prajñāpāramitā* and other sūtras, although no passage with exactly this wording has been traced as yet.

The following two examples (nos. 12, 13) have no such initial phrase as '*yad uktaṃ bhagavatā*' or the like, but are clearly borrowed from the Āgamas together with their cliché and analogy.

12. *itaretaraśūnyatā*

itaretaraśūnyatā punar Mahāmate katamā, yad uta yad yatra nāsti tad tena śūnyam ity ucyate / tad yathā Mahāmate Mṛgālamātuḥ prāsāde hastigavaiḍakâdyā na santi / aśūnyaṃ ca bhikṣubhir iti bhāṣitam mayā, sa ca taiḥ śūnyam ity ucyate / na ca punar Mahāmate prāsādaḥ prāsādabhāvato nāsti, bhikṣavaś ca bhikṣubhāvato na santi / na ca te 'nyatra hastigavaiḍakâdyā bhāvā nâvatiṣṭhante / idaṃ Mahāmate svasāmānyalakṣaṇaṃ sarvadharmāṇām itaretaraṃ tu na saṃvidyate

(*LAS*, p. 75.10-19)

This teaching, together with the analogy of Mṛgālamātuḥ *prāsāda*, is the subject of the *Cūlasuññattasutta* of the *Majjhima Nikāya*.[20] The *Mahāsuññattasutta* of the same Nikāya also teaches this doctrine of *śūnyatā* with the detailed process of annihilation of outer concepts from our mind in meditation by repeating the formula '*yad yatra nāsti tad tena śūnyam*' and so on. The same formula is often found in Yogācāra works such as the *Yogācārabhūmi*, the *Madhyântavibhāga*, the *Abhidharmasamuccaya*, and also the *Ratnagotravibhāga*.[21] The unique contribution of the *Laṅkāvatāra* to this teaching is that it defines this concept as *itaretaraśūnyatā*, i.e., relative emptiness, and that it regards this

20. MN, vol. 3, pp. 104–105, etc.

21. See Gadjin Nagao, "Kūshō ni okeru amareru mono (*avaśiṣṭam*)," in id., *Chūgan to yuishiki* (Tokyo, 1978), pp. 542–560.

as something to be rejected by Bodhisattvas.

13. *dharmāṇāṃ dharmatā*

tatra paurāṇasthitidharmatā katamā, yad uta paurāṇam idaṃ Mahāmate dharmatāvan me hiraṇyarajatamuktâkaravan Mahāmate dharmadhātusthititôtpādād vā tathāgatānām anutpādād vā tathāgatānāṃ sthitaivaiṣā dharmāṇāṃ dharmatā dharmasthititā dharmaniyāmatā paurāṇanagarapathavan Mahāmate / tad yathā Mahāmate kaś cid eva puruṣo 'ṭavyāṃ paryaṭan paurāṇaṃ nagaram anupaśyed avikalapathapraveśam, sa taṃ nagaram anupraviśet, tatra praviśya pratiniviśya nagaraṃ nagarakriyāsukham anubhavet / tat kiṃ manyase Mahāmate, api nu tena puruṣeṇa sa panthā utpādito yena yathā taṃ nagaram anupraviṣṭo nagaravaicitryaṃ ca // āha — no bhagavan / bhagavān āha /evam eva Mahāmate yan mayā taiś ca tathāgatair adhigataṃ sthitaivaiṣā dharmatā dharmasthititā dharmaniyāmatā tathatā bhūtatā satyatā /

(*LAS*, pp. 143.9–144.5)

As has been mentioned above, this teaching concerning the eternity of the truth refers to the doctrine of *pratītyasamutpāda*. The same is found along with the analogy of an old castle in the *Saṃyutta Nikāya* (*Nidāya Saṃyutta*, "Nagara"), which must be the original version of this passage. As for the formula *sthitaivaiṣā dharmāṇāṃ dharmatā utpādād vā tathāgatānām anutpādād vā (tathāgatānāṃ) dharmasthititā dharmaniyāmatā*, it is widely used in Mahāyāna sūtras, with minute variants, for instance, the *Śālistambha*, the *Saddharmapuṇḍarīka*, the *Jnānâlokâlaṃkāra*, the *Dhāraṇīśvararājaparipṛcchā*, the *Tathāgatâcintyaguhyanirdeśa* (T. vol. 10, p. 746c), the *Tathāgatagarbhasūtra* (concerning *tathāgatagarbha*, cf. *RGV*, p. 72), and the *Saṃdhinirmocana* (which defines it as *dharmatāyukti*, one of the four kinds of *yukti*, reasoning).[22]

---

22. See J. Takasaki, "*Dharmatā, Dharmadhātu, Dharmakāya* and *Buddhadhātu*" [pp. 228–245 below].

III. Technical Terms and Key Words

There are innumerable words and phrases that have been transmitted from the early period among Buddhist Āgamas. Many sentences in the *Laṅkāvatāra* include, or are composed of, such words and phrases. What we want to notice here are not all such words and phrases but only some particulars which are especially important for determining its date of composition. This naturally leads us to examine the doctrines around the Vijñānavāda.

Prior to discussing the doctrine of *vijñānavāda*, I shall refer first of all to the basic doctrine common to both the *vijñaptimātratā* theory of the Yogācāra and the *Laṅkāvatāra*, that is, the *cittamātra* theory found in the *Daśabhūmika*. Then, I shall refer to various terms which have come from the *Śrīmālā* as another important source of the *Laṅkāvatāra*.

a. *cittamātra*

There are many verses referring to the term *cittamātra* in the *Laṅkāvatāra*, while in the prose this term is replaced by other explanatory words such as *svacittadṛśyamātra*, *svacittavikalpavikalpita*, etc.[23] Of these the following two examples are the nearest expressions to the original in the *Daśabhūmika*.

1. *tatra kathaṃ Mahāmate bodhisattvo mahāsattvaḥ svacittadṛśyabhāvanākuśalo bhavati / yad uta sa evaṃ pratyavekṣate svacittamātram idaṃ traidhātukam ātmâtmīyarahitaṃ nirīham āyūhaniryūhavigatam anādikālaprapañcadauṣṭhulyavāsanâbhiniveśavāsitaṃ traidhātukavicitrarūpôpacārôpanibaddhaṃ dehabhogapratiṣṭhāgativikalpânugataṃ vikalpyate khyāyate ca / evaṃ hi Mahāmate bodhisattvo mahāsattvaḥ svacittadṛśyavibhāvanākuśalo bhavati /* (*LAS*, p. 80.5-13)

In this long explanation, the terms after *anādikālaprapañca-*

23. On the examples of the *cittamātra* theory in the *Laṅkāvatāra*, see J. Takasaki, "Yuishin to nyoraizō" [*Cittamātra* and *tathāgatagarbha*], *Bukkyōgaku* 9/10 (1980), pp. 53–78.

and so on are unique to the *Laṅkāvatāra* (and are used under the influence of the Vijñānavāda; see below), but others are taken from the *Daśabhūmika*.

2. *cittamātram idaṃ sarvaṃ dvidhā cittaṃ pravartate /*
   grāhyagrāhakabhāvena ātmâtmīyaṃ na vidyate //121//
   (*LAS*, p. 209.15-16)

This verse is located in the section on *anityatā* in chapter III. Together with the next verse, which also refers to *cittamātratā*, however, it has no direct relation to the doctrine of *anityatā* discussed there. Also, it has no corresponding verse in the "Sagāthakam." The term *grāhyagrāhaka* is again from the Yogācāra.

b. Doctrines taught in the *Śrīmālā*

Besides the passage where the name of Śrīmālā Devī is referred to, there are a certain number of sections where we observe the influence of the *Śrīmālā*, or at least the use of its terminology.

1. *cyutidvaya, caturvāsanābhūmi, avidyāvāsanābhūmi* and *manomayakāya*

   (tathāgato) na vitarkayati na vicārayati, caturvāsanābhūmiprahīṇatvāc cyutidvayavigamāt kleśajñeyâvaraṇadvayaprahāṇāc ca // (*LAS*, pp. 241.17–242.1)

The names of these four kinds of *vāsanābhūmi* are given in the verse attached to the same section (chapter VII) in the following way:

bhava-kāma-rūpa-dṛṣṭīnāṃ[24] *vāsanā vai caturvidhā /*
manovijñānasaṃbhūtā ālayaṃ ca manaḥ sthitāḥ //4//
(*LAS*, p. 243.10-11)

In the *Śrīmālā*, these four *vāsanābhūmi* (originally probably *vāsabhūmi*, dwelling place) are counted as showing subtle defilements underlying superficial active defilements, according to the

24. *bhāva* in the Nanjio edition is to be corrected in the light of the Mss., as well as from the context.

stages of living beings in the threefold sphere of transmigration.[25] They are said to be quite strong and difficult to annihilate, but stronger and more difficult to annihilate is the *avidyāvāsabhūmi*, which is an underlying preserve even in the mind of saints. This *avidyāvāsabhūmi* (this form is known through quotations in the *Ratnagotravibhāga*)[26] is again referred to here by the name of *avidyāvāsanabhūmi* (*LAS*, p. 220.14-15).

As for the *cyuti-dvaya*, two kinds of death or transformation, the *Laṅkāvatāra* notes only one of them by the term *acintyapariṇati-cyuti*, which is, according to the *Ratnagotravibhāga*,[27] *acintyā pāriṇāmikī cyutiḥ* in the original. This is said to be a form of death especially for saints, the other being for ordinary living beings, probably named **pariccheda-cyuti* in Sanskrit[28] although the term is recorded nowhere else.

In this connection the concept *manomayakāya* is to be mentioned. This concept is used in the *Śrīmālā* in a pair with *acintyā pāriṇāmikī cyutiḥ* as indicating the form of birth or life of the saints of three kinds, namely, *arhat*, *pratyekabuddha* and *vaśitāprāptā bodhisattvāḥ*.[29] In the *Laṅkāvatāra*, however, it especially means the Bodhisattva's state and is discussed in detail with three kinds of characteristics (section 51, chapter III, pp. 136–137).

2. *Tathāgatagarbha*, being the substratum of *saṃsāra* and *nirvāṇa*, is not understood by those whose mind has deviated from *śūnyatā*

sapta Màhāmate mano-manovijñāna-cakṣurvijñānâdayaḥ kṣaṇikā vāsanāhetutvāt kuśalânāsravapakṣaràhitā na saṃsāriṇaḥ /

25. Tib. 1) *lta ba gcig la gnas paḥi gnas kyi sa*, 2) *ḥdod paḥi ḥdod chags la gnas kyi sa*, 3) *gzugs kyi ḥdod chags la gnas kyi sa*, 4) *srid paḥi ḥdod chags la gnas kyi sa*, Peking Edition (reprint), vol. 24, p. 256.3.2-4.
26. *RGV*, p. 32.17.
27. *RGV*, p. 33.2-3.
28. Tib. *rgyun chad paḥi ḥchi pho*, Peking Edition, vol. 24, p. 256.1.7.
29. *Śrīmālā*, p. 256.4.3-6; *RGV*, pp. 33.15–34.4.

tathāgatagarbhaḥ punar Mahāmate saṃsarati nirvāṇasukhaduḥkhahetukaḥ / na ca bālapṛthagjanā avabudhyante śūnyatāvikṣiptamatayaḥ / (*LAS*, p. 242.2-6)

This passage in chapter VII gives a summary of the Tathāgatagarbha theory given in chapter VI, which is based fundamentally upon the *Śrīmālā*. (Cf. quotations and references in the *Ratnagotravibhāga*, e.g., *tathāgatagarbho — śūnyatāvikṣiptacittānām agocaraḥ.*)[30]

Of these 'seven *vijñāna*s', however, the *Śrīmālā* merely says that six *vijñāna*s and *vijñāna* itself (or that which knows)[31] are not the substratum which experiences *duḥkha* and *sukha* because they are momentary, while only *tathāgatagarbha* can be the substratum of *nirvāṇa* and *saṃsāra*. On the other hand, here the concept of *ālayavijñāna* is newly introduced as identical with the *tathāgatagarbha*, and the Tathāgatagarbha theory is thus construed by means of the Vijñānavāda. This is a really unique point of the *Laṅkāvatāra*.

c. Vijñānavāda

The *Laṅkāvatāra* is sometimes referred to as a work which elucidates the doctrines of the Vijñānavāda as expressed at the beginning of the sūtra: *pañcadharma-svabhāva-vijñāna-nairātmyadvaya* (*LAS*, p. 2.2). These are the *pañcadharma—nāman, nimitta, vikalpa, samyagjñāna*, and *tathatā*; the *trisvabhāva—parikalpita-*, *paratantra-*, and *pariniṣpanna-svabhāva*; the *aṣṭa-vijñānāni—ālayavijñāna* or *citta, manas, manovijñāna*, and *cakṣurādi-pañca-vijñānakāyāḥ*; and the *nairātmyadvaya—pudgalanairātmya* and *dharmanairātmya*. These categories are really the core of the Vijñānavāda and show the intimate connection of this sūtra with the Vijñānavāda of the Yogācāra.

In spite of the use of these doctrines, however, the *Laṅkāvatāra*

30. *RGV*, p. 74.5-6.

31. Tib. *rnam par śes pa gaṅ lags pa*, Peking Edition, vol. 24, p. 260.5.1. See Takasaki, *Nyoraizō shisō no keisei*, pp. 350–366.

was never regarded as an authority in the early days of the Yogācāra. Quite unlike the *Saṃdhinirmocana* and the *Mahāyānâbhidharmasūtra*, the name of this sūtra never appeared in the works attributed to Maitreyanātha or Asaṅga, nor even in the works of Vasubandhu, although, as referred to at the beginning of the present study, similar verses of this sūtra are quoted in his *Vyākhyāyukti*. It was only in the works of Sthiramati and Dharmapāla that this sūtra was quoted with explicit reference to its name.[32]

This fact may show that the *Laṅkāvatāra* was in no way the first organiser of these doctrines, nor was it composed by orthodox Vijñānavādin or Yogācāra teachers. It is certain, at least, that the composer or exposers of the *Laṅkāvatāra* were well acquainted with the doctrines of the Vijñānavāda and borrowed its system to express what they intended to make known, but not *vice versa*.

There have already been published many articles that discuss the doctrinal relationship between the *Laṅkāvatāra* and the Vijñānavāda and the Yogācāra, and I shall discuss only the minimum necessary to complement these articles.

1. Appearance of *vijñāna* as *grāhya* and *grāhaka*

As has already been examined in another article by myself,[33] the *Laṅkāvatāra* shares with the *Mahāyānasūtrâlaṃkāra* the use of the term *mana-udgraha-vikalpa* to denote the three kinds of forms of *grāhaka*, the seizer, the subject. Thus, the *Laṅkāvatāra* has:

> *dehaḥ pratiṣṭhā bhogaś ca grāhyavijñaptayas trayaḥ /*
> *mana-udgraha-vijñapti-vikalpo grāhakās trayaḥ //72//*
> (*LAS*, p. 273.14-15)

while the *Sūtrâlaṃkāra* has:

> *trividha-trividhâbhāso grāhyagrāhakalakṣaṇaḥ /*

32. For the reference in Sthiramati's work, see n. 15 above; for that in Dharmapāla's work, see T. vol. 31, p. 10c, etc.

33. "Nyūryōgakyō no yuishiki setsu—*Deha-bhoga-pratiṣṭhābhaṃ vijñānam* no yōrei o megutte," *Bukkyōgaku* 1 (1976), pp. 1–26.

abhūtaparikalpo hi paratantrasya lakṣaṇaṃ //40//
(*MSA*, XI.40)

Vasubandhu comments in his *Bhāṣya* that the first three kinds of appearance (*ābhāsa*) signify appearance as *pada* (basis), *artha* (object), and *deha* (body), while the next three are manifestations as *mana-udgraha-vikalpa*. It is explained further on that here *manas* means that which is always defiled (*kliṣṭaṃ sadā*), *udgraha* means the five aggregates of consciousness (*pañca vijñānakāyāḥ*), and *vikalpa* means consciousness (to function as understanding) (*mano-vijñāna*); of these two kinds, the first three are characterised as *grāhya* (to be seized), and the second group as *grāhaka* (the seizer).

Here the terms denoting the *grāhya*, i.e., the object, in the *Sūtrâlaṃkāra* differ from those in the *Laṅkāvatāra*, but from the contents it is clear that *pada* corresponds to *pratiṣṭhā* in the sense of *bhājanaloka* and *artha* to *bhoga* in the sense of *rūpâdiviṣayāḥ* as sense-objects, while the term *deha*, common to both, is used in the sense of *indriyāṇi*. These terms, *padârthadeha*, are basically accepted in the *Sūtrâlaṃkāra* and often appear in the verses, but the terms *pratiṣṭhā* and *bhoga*, too, are not unknown to it for they appear in v. XIX.49:

pratiṣṭhā-bhoga-bījaṃ hi nimittaṃ bandhanasya hi /
sāśrayāś cittacaittās tu badhyante 'tra sabījakāḥ //

In this verse *āśraya* means *indriyas*, i.e., *deha* in the above, and *bīja* means *ālayavijñāna*.

A set of terms more similar to those in the *Laṅkāvatāra* is found in Vasubandhu's *Bhāṣya* on the *Madhyântavibhāga*. That is, commenting on the latter half of verse III.22, which refers to *saṃskṛtâsaṃskṛtârtha* as the seventh of the ten kinds of skilfulness in the truth (*tattvakauśalya*), he says that here *hetu* in the verse means *ālayavijñāna* in the sense of *bīja* (*bījasaṃgṛhīta*), *nimitta* means the same in the sense of acting consciousness (*pravṛttivijñānasaṃgṛhīta*), i.e., *mana-udgraha-vikalpa*, and that in the sense of *pratiṣṭhā-deha-bhoga* (*pratiṣṭhādehabhogasaṃgṛhīta*).

The *Madhyântavibhāga* has its own system concerning the *grāhya* and the *grāhaka*: *artha* and *sattva* for *grāhya*, and *ātman* and *vijñapti* for *grāhaka*. It may be a more advanced system than that elucidated in the *Sūtrâlaṃkāra*, which has a certain ambiguity. But Vasubandhu seems to prefer the set of terms closer to the *Laṅkāvatāra* here, although the terms *mana-udgraha-vikalpa* are found neither in the verses of the *Sūtrâlaṃkāra* nor in those of the *Madhyântavibhāga*. On the contrary, the set of terms *mana-udgraha-vikalpa* was used only once in the *Laṅkāvatāra*, and is in the "Sagāthakam" and not in the main body, while the other set, *deha-bhoga-pratiṣṭhā*, is used as one of the basic concepts for explaining the doctrine of *cittamātra*. The explanation of this fact would be a central point at issue when we consider the date of the *Laṅkāvatāra* in relation to Vasubandhu.

2. The five *dharmas*

With the *Madhyântavibhāga* the *Laṅkāvatāra* also shares the concepts of the five *dharmas*, otherwise called *pañca vastūni* in the former. That is, the *Madhyântavibhāga* refers to this set of concepts in the chapter on the truth ("Tattva-parivarta") as denoting the involvement or inclusiveness of the truth concerning the fundamental truth, i.e., the *trisvabhāva* (*trividhe mūlatattve saṃgrahatattvaṃ*):

> *nimittasya vikalpasya nāmnaś ca dvayasaṃgrahaḥ /*
> *samyagjñānaṃ-satattvasya ekenaiva ca saṃgrahaḥ* //13//

while in the *Laṅkāvatāra* (chapter VI) is found:

> *nāmanimittasaṃkalpāḥ svabhāvadvayalakṣaṇam /*
> *samyagjñānaṃ tathātvaṃ ca pariniṣpannalakṣaṇam* //6//
> (*LAS*, p. 229.8-9)
>
> (= II.134 and "Sagāthakam" 156, with a variant reading *hi tathatā* instead of *tathātvaṃ ca*)

Here we can observe the fundamental identity between them as regards the involvement of the first three concepts in the first two *svabhāvas*, although they differ from each other in detail. Thus, the *Laṅkāvatāra* explains in the prose section that the *nāman* and the *nimitta*, being subject and object, or conception and its base, respectively, belong to the *parikalpita-svabhāva*, while Vasubandhu comments that only *nāman* belongs to the *parikalpita*. There are many other treatises that adopt a different interpretation: that only *tathatā* is involved in the *pariniṣpanna-svabhōva* and that all other four are involved in the *paratantra-svabhāva*, and this kind of interpretation was regarded as orthodox in the later Yogācāra, as can be seen in the *Vijñaptimātratāsiddhi* of Dharmapāla.[34] The origin of this kind of interpretation was probably in the *Viniścayasaṃgrahaṇī* of the *Yogācārabhūmi*. Compared with this, the *Madhyântavibhāga*'s statement is older, and the *Laṅkāvatāra* might have accepted the idea from it but interpreted it in its own unique way. On this point Vasubandhu is probably quite true to the teaching of Asaṅga and does not rely on the *Laṅkāvatāra*.

3. The four kinds of *śrāvakas*

There is another set of terms which shows the relationship between the *Laṅkāvatāra* and the Yogācāra.

Explaining the four result stages of saints, *srotaāpanna* and so on, the ṣūtra refers to the three kinds of Arhatship of *śrāvakas* (*LAS*, pp. 120.11–121.7). The terms for these three are *ekâyanamārgapratilambhika*, *bodhipraṇidhānâbhyastakuśalamūlasaṃmūḍha*, and *nirmitanairmāṇika* respectively. These terms remind us of the four kinds of *śrāvakas* mentioned in the *Ratnakūṭavyākhyā*, a commentary on the *Kāśyapaparivarta*,[35] which is identical with fascicles 79–80 of the Chinese translation of the *Yogācārabhūmi* (the last part of the *Viniścayasaṃgrahaṇī* on the

34. T. vol. 31, pp. 46c–47b.

35. T. vol. 26, p. 220ab; Peking Edition, vol. 105, p. 174.1.6-7.

bodhisattvabhūmi).[36] The terms for the four in the *Yogācārabhūmi* are to be restored from the Tibetan to *nirmita[nirmāṇa]*, *ābhimānika*, *bodhipariṇamana* and *śamaikāyana*, of which the last is regarded as the lowest kind.

In this case it is not clear which of these borrowed the idea from the other, but judging from other examples, here too the *Laṅkāvatāra* owes its idea to the traditional doctrine of the Yogācāra concerning the varieties of *śrāvaka*s, although it modifies the interpretation in the context of the One Vehicle theory, in opposition to the Yogācāra, which admits the Three Different Vehicles.

* * *

Now we come to the conclusion of our inquiry into the materials used in the *Laṅkāvatāra*. The eight *vijñāna*s theory, which is clearly stated in the *Laṅkāvatāra*, is no doubt a product of the Yogācāra from fairly early days, although it finally reaches a limit in Vasubandhu's *Triṃśikā*. The terms for the eight are *citta* or *ālayavijñāna* for the eighth, *manas* for the seventh, and the six *vijñāna*s common to traditional Abhidharma Buddhism. Of these, the most problematic is *manas*, on which new light has been shed through the efforts of Professor L. Schmithausen.[37] In the light of his analysis, the theory of *manas* in the *Laṅkāvatāra* is rather obscure and seems a bit different from that of the Yogācāra.

Thus *manas* in the *Laṅkāvatāra* is mostly mentioned in a set, *citta-mano-manovijñāna*, with which is sometimes associated a short explanation, for instance, '*manasā vicīyate*' (v. II.106), '*manasā manyate*' (v. II.116), or the like. But we cannot observe any definite function of *manas* as distinct from *ālayavijñāna*. There is no definition of *manas* as *kliṣṭam* (defiled), which is

36. On the four kinds of *śrāvaka*s, see T. vol. 30, p. 744ab; Peking Edition, vol. 111, p. 115.2.3-3.4.

37. "Some Aspects of the Conception of an Ego in Buddhism" (Japanese translation by K. Yokoyama), *Bukkyōgaku* 7 (1979), pp. 1–18. This is a record of his lecture delivered in Tokyo during his visit in 1979.

regarded as the most basic in Yogācāra works.[38] On the other hand, the *Laṅkāvatāra* notes two kinds of *satkāyadṛṣṭi*, one being *sahajā* and the other *parikalpitā*, in relation to saints in the state of *srotaāpanna* (*LAS*, p. 117.17-18). The same is discussed in the *Vijñaptimātratāsiddhi* in terms of two kinds of *ātmagrāha*, where *manas* is considered to offer a seat for the *sahaja-ātmagrāha*.[39] This seems to show that the *Laṅkāvatāra* was not acquainted with the developed Vijñānavāda established by Vasubandhu and that probably the *Laṅkāvatāra* is located a little earlier than Vasubandhu. Also notable in this regard is that there is not observed the use of the concept *pariṇāma* in the same sense as the *vijñāna-pariṇāma* of the *Triṃśikā*.[40]

There is another kind of difficulty for fixing the date and position of the *Laṅkāvatāra* in the history of Buddhist thought. This is the problem of its relation to the *Ratnagotravibhāga*, the most important treatise on the Tathāgatagarbha theory. As is well-known, the *Ratnagotravibhāga*, or *Uttaratantra*, is full of information on those Mahāyāna sūtraṣ that express the doctrine of *tathāgata-garbha* and its background, such as the *Tathāgatagarbha*, the *Śrī-mālā*, the *Mahāparinirvāṇa*, and so on. However, it has no reference to the *Laṅkāvatāra* at all. Also, many influences of the Yogācāra are observed in the *Ratnagotravibhāga* in its use of such terms as *āśrayaparivṛtti*, *tribuddhakāya* beginning with *svabhāvika*, *avikalpajñāna* and *tatpṛṣṭhalabdha-laukikajñāna*, *prakṛti-* and *vaimalya-śuddhi*, and *yathāvadbhāvikatā* and *yāvadbhāvikatā* of *jñāna*, but completely lacking is the use of the most fundamental concepts of the Yogācāra, such as *ālayavijñāna*, *trisvabhāva*

38. On *manas* in the *Laṅkāvatāra*, see J. Takasaki, "The Concept of *Manas* in the *Laṅkāvatāra*" [pp. 118–127 above].

39. T. vol. 31, p. 2a. Cf. L. de La Vallée Poussin, *Vijñaptimātratāsiddhi* (1928), pp. 16–17, esp. note 3.

40. Except for an analogical use showing the relationship of the *pravṛtti-vijñāna*s to the *ālayavijñāna*, compared with waves in the ocean (*LAS*, vv. II.103 and 105).

(*parikalpitâdi*), *vijñaptimātratā* (and *cittamātra*), *grāhya* and *grāhaka*, *kliṣṭa-manas*, etc.

The *Ratnagotravibhāga* was brought to China by Ratnamati in A.D. 509 in the same period as Bodhiruci, who translated the second version of the *Laṅkāvatāra* (the Wei version). Ratnamati and Bodhiruci worked at one time in association in translating the *Daśabhūmika-vyākhyā* of Vasubandhu. Both have left their own translation of the *Saddharmapuṇḍarīka-upadeśa* attributed to Vasubandhu. These circumstances seem to show that both translators were well acquainted with the Vijñānavāda and that both texts of the *Laṅkāvatāra* and the *Ratnagotravibhāga* were treated as belonging to the works of the Yogācāra.

In other words, they received their citizenship in the kingdom of the Yogācāra in the early sixth century at the latest. The *Laṅkāvatāra*, however, was brought to China in the fifth century together with sūtras of the Tathāgatagarbha theory, such as the *Śrīmālā* and the *Aṅgulimālika*. At that time only the *Bodhisattvabhūmi* and a part of the *Saṃdhinirmocana* were among them and almost nothing was known in China of the Vijñānavāda. The *Ratnagotravibhāga* too was not seen by the translators of the fifth century.

Thus the *Laṅkāvatāra* and the *Ratnagotravibhāga* share the Tathāgatagarbha theory, especially that of the *Śrīmālā*, and both are proximate to the Yogācāra, but do not belong to the orthodox Vijñānavāda. Nevertheless they do not show an awareness of each other's existence, or at least we can say that the latter did not use the former as an authority. This would not mean that the *Ratnagotravibhāga* is of an earlier date than the *Laṅkāvatāra*, or *vice versa*, but rather it would show the distance between them, both being on the periphery of the Yogācāra but at opposite poles from each other. Due to their peculiar situation with regard to the Yogācāra, Vasubandhu never referred to either text even though he was acquainted with both of them to some extent. It was only after Vasubandhu, probably by the end of the fifth century, that both texts come to be "enrolled" among the works of the Yogācāra as authorities of a sort, and this fact is shown by their having been translated by the team of Bodhiruci and Ratnamati around 510 along with other works of the Vijñānavāda.

The Structure of the *Anuttarāśrayasūtra* (*Wu-shang-i ching*)*

The *Anuttarāśrayasūtra*[1] is a small but important sūtra which expresses the theory of *tathāgatagarbha*, i.e., the Matrix of the Buddha. At present, only a Chinese version of this sūtra is available, with the title of *Wu-shang-i ching* 無上依經, translated by Paramārtha in the latter half of the 6th cent. A.D. (T. no. 669).

With one glance at this sūtra, one may notice a similarity between its chapter divisions and those of the *Ratnagotravibhāga* (*Uttaratantra*).[2] Leaving aside the first and the last two chapters, which form its introduction and conclusion respectively, the central part of this sūtra consists of four chapters, whose titles are II. "Tathāgatadhātu-parivarta" (如來界品), III. "Tathāgatabodhi-p." (如來菩提品), IV. "Tathāgataguṇa-p." (如來功德品), and V. "Tathāgatakriyā-p." (如來事品). These four titles are identical with those of the first four chapters of the *RGV*, and according to v. I.23 they represent the four aspects of *gotra*.[3] The term *anuttarāśraya* (無上依) seems to signify the Tathāgata who possesses those four aspects.

Furthermore, at the end of each chapter, the sūtra emphasizes the inconceivability (*acintya*) of these four subjects. In the sūtra, they are nothing but an extended explanation of the inconceivability of the Tathāgata given at the start of chap. II as an answer to the question of why the merits of stūpa worship are limitless.

* Originally published in *JIBS* 8-2 (1960), pp. 748–741.

1. This Sanskrit title (abbr. *AĀS*) is restored from the Chinese *Wu-shang-i ching* 無上依經.

2. *The Ratnagotravibhāga Mahāyānottaratantraśāstra*, ed. by E. H. Johnston (Patna, 1950) (abbr. *RGV*). Cf. T. no. 1611.

3. 1) *samalā tathatā* (= *tathāgatagarbha*, *dhātu*, *gotra*), 2) *nirmalā tathatā* (= *bodhi*, *dharmakāya*, *āśrayaparivṛtti*), 3) *buddhaguṇa* (= *buddhadharma*), and 4) *jinakriyā* (= *tathāgatakṛtyakriyā*, *karman*).

However, their description can be traced word by word in the *RGV* in its prose commentary on vv. I.24 & 25, which, in their turn, are commentarial verses on v. 23 (*gotra* is '*viṣayaḥ paramārthadarśinām*'). (*RGV*, p. 21.17-18 = *AĀS*, chap. II, T. 16, p. 470c; *RGV*, p. 22.5 = *AĀS*, chap. III, p. 473c; *RGV*, p. 22.8-9 = *AĀS*, chap. IV, p. 475c; *RGV*, pp. 24.9–25.3 = *AĀS*, chap. V, p. 476bc.)[4]

This fact does not show that the *RGV* imitated the structure of this sūtra, but quite the contrary: it seems to show that this sūtra was composed after the *RGV* as a kind of sūtralization of the latter. This hypothesis will be proved by examining the contents of the sūtra.[5]

This sūtra uses a categorization with respect to the characteristics of *gotra* or *dhātu* similar to that in the *RGV*, but in the chapter on *bodhi*. Its ten divisions are: (1) *svabhāva* (自性), (2) *hetu* (因緣), (3) *paripanthā* (惑障), (4) *phala* (至果), (5) *karman* (作事), (6) *yoga* (相攝), (7) *vṛtti* (行處), (8) *nitya* (常住), (9) *āveṇika* (不共), and (10) *acintya* (不可思惟). This is actually a mixture of the ten meanings of *gotra* and the eight meanings of *bodhi* in the *RGV*. Namely, (2)–(4) are identical with (II) *hetu* and (III) *phala* among the ten meanings of *gotra* in the *RGV*, of which (3) *paripanthā* is included under (II) *hetu* in the case of the *RGV*, while the last six (5)–(10), except for (9) *āveṇika*, are identical with the last five subjects among the eight meanings of *bodhi* in the *RGV*. Although (9) *āveṇika* has no equivalent passage in the *RGV*, the idea is taught here and there. However, in the explanation of (1) *svabhāva*, the idea of which is fundamentally identical with (I) *svabhāva* of *bodhi* in the *RGV*, the sūtra refers to *āśrayaparivṛtti* with its four characteristics, which are not in the *RGV*. On the

4. A comparison of equivalent passages is given at the end of this article.

5. The same hypothesis was made by Prof. Tsukinowa of Ryūkoku University more than two decades ago, but he did not give any detailed comparison of the two works. See "Kugyōichijō hōshōron ni tsuite" [On the *Uttaratantra*], *Nihon Bukkyōgaku Kyōkai Nenpō* 7 (1935).

other hand, the six subjects starting with (V) *yoga* among the ten meanings of *gotra* in the *RGV* are included in the chapter on *tathāgatadhātu* in this sūtra but with a slight difference in arrangement and wording. As for chap. IV, "Tathāgataguṇa-parivarta," the sūtra mentions the 180 *āveṇikadharmas*, including the 80 *anuvyañjanas*, which are not in the *RGV*, but the names for the 32 *mahāpuruṣalakṣaṇas* are identical with those mentioned in the *Ratnagotravibhāga*. It is only the chapter on *tathāgatakriyā* that differs entirely from the *RGV* in its contents.

Besides these similarities with the *RGV*, a stronger factor showing that this sūtra is an imitation of the *RGV* is that this sūtra refers to certain passages which are quotations from other sūtras in the *RGV* as if they were its own words. For instance:

(Chap. II)

1. a passage on the meaning of *gotra* being *ṣaḍāyatanaviśeṣa* taken from the *Ṣaḍāyatanasūtra* (p. 469b; *RGV*, p. 55.16-17);
2. a passage on *anutpādānirodhatā* of the Tathāgata taken from the *Jñānālokālaṅkārasūtra* (p. 469b; *RGV*, p. 9.10-13);
3. a passage on *dharmakāya* endowed with the Buddha's properties, which are *avinirbhāga*, *amuktajña*, *acintya*, etc., taken from the *Śrīmālāsūtra* (p. 469b; *RGV*, p. 12.10-14);
4. a simile of the *vaiḍūrya* stone taken from the *Sāgaramatiparipṛcchā* (p. 469b; *RGV*, p. 49.5-9);
5. a passage on *cittaprakṛti* and *āgantukakleśa* taken from the same sūtra (p. 469bc; *RGV*, pp. 49.9–50.7);
6. a passage on the three states of *dhātu* (*avasthāprabheda*) taken from the *Anūnatvāpūrṇatvanirdeśa* (p. 469c; *RGV*, pp. 40.16–41.5);
7. a passage on the penetration of *tathāgatajñāna* in living beings taken from the "Tathāgatotpattisaṃbhavanirdeśa" of the *Avataṃsaka* (p. 470a; *RGV*, pp. 22.10–24.8);
8. a description of the Buddha, his teaching and disciples, being an authority for the Triple Jewel taken from the

Dhāraṇīśvararājasūtra (p. 470a; *RGV*, p. 3.18);

9. a parable of a householder with respect to the bodhisattva's compassion taken from the *Sāgaramatiparipṛcchā* (p. 470ab; *RGV*, pp. 47.7–48.13);
10. a passage on *dhātu* being the *āśraya* of all *dharma*s, real and unreal, taken from the *Śrīmālāsūtra* (p. 470b; *RGV*, p. 73.2-5);
11. a passage on the inconceivability of *dhātu* taken from the same sūtra (p. 470c; *RGV*, p. 22.1-4);[6]

(Chap. III)

12. a passage on *tathāgatagarbha* covered with millions of defilements taken from the *Śrīmālāsūtra* (p. 470c; *RGV*, p. 79.10);
13. a passage on the *icchantika*s taken from the *Anūnatvāpūrṇatvanirdeśa* (p. 471a; RGV, p. 28.3-4);
14. a passage on those who are proud of their conception of *śūnyatā* taken from the *Kāśyapaparivarta* (p. 471b; *RGV*, p. 28.11-12);
15. a passage on the four *guṇapāramitā*s (*śubha*, *ātma*, *sukha*, *nitya*) taken from the *Śrīmālāsūtra* (pp. 471c–472a; *RGV*, pp. 30.19–31.6);
16. a passage on the epithets of the Tathāgata, viz. *dharmadhātuparama*, *ākāśadhātuparyavasāna*, and *aparāntakoṭiniṣṭha*, taken from the *Daśabhūmikasūtra* (p. 472a; RGV, p. 32.8-9);

(Chap. V)

17. a passage on the inconceivability of *tathāgatakriyā* taken from the *Dhāraṇīśvararājasūtra* (p. 476b; *RGV*, pp. 26.16–27.3).[7]

Another reason for my hypothesis is that the *RGV*, in spite of its abundance of quotations, never uses this sūtra as an authority,

6. See passage (1) quoted at the end of this article.
7. See passage (4) quoted at the end of this article.

while this sūtra is quoted and utilized only in the *Buddhagotra-śāstra* (佛性論) translated by Paramārtha,[8] which, in turn, has a detailed explanation of *tathāgatagarbha* with its ten meanings, similar to those in the *RGV*, and with newly added commentarial passages here and there, among which we find a certain number of parallels in the *Anuttarāśrayasūtra*.

It may now be quite clear that the *Anuttarāśrayasūtra* is a composition based upon the *RGV*, reshaping its contents into the frame of the sūtra style and placing stress on the *bodhi* aspect, which is the ultimate basis (*anuttarāśraya*). As for its introduction and conclusion, the original of chap. I is, as already pointed out by scholars,[9] the *Adbhutasūtra*, versions of which are available in Tibetan and Chinese as well,[10] and whose main subject is the extolling of the merits of stūpa worship as the highest observance of a Buddhist, while chap. VII is a kind of eulogy to the Buddha (*buddhastotra*) and chap. VIII, "Parīndana-parivarta," is an enlarged version of the conclusion of the *Adbhutasūtra* in accordance with the enlargement of the central part. The connection

8. T. no. 1610 (vol. 31, pp. 787–813). Quotations from the *AĀS* in the *Buddhagotraśāstra* are as follows:
1. p. 801c (如無上依經中說…) = *AĀS*, p. 469b = *RGV*, p. 12.6 (part of a quotation from the *Jñānālokālaṅkārasūtra*);
2. p. 806b (故無上依經說…) = *AĀS*, p. 469c = *RGV*, pp. 40.16–41.5 (quotation from the *Anūnatvāpūrṇatvanirdeśa*);
3. p. 806b (如無上依經說…) = *AĀS*, p. 469c = *RGV*, p. 41.13-15 (commentarial passage);
4. p. 812a (如無上依經說…) = *AĀS*, p. 469b = *RGV*, p. 55.16-17 (quotation from the *Ṣaḍāyatanasūtra*).

Paramārtha's translation of the *Mahāyānasaṃgraha-vyākhyā* of Vasubandhu (T. no. 1595) also quotes the *AĀS* (T. vol. 31, pp. 259c–260a = *AĀS*, p. 469bc = RGV, pp. 49.11–50.7, a quotation from the *Sāgaramatiparipṛcchā*). But the quotation is not found either in the Tibetan version or in Hsüan-tsang's translation of the same text. It is probably an interpolation made by Paramārtha himself.

9. E.g., D. Tokiwa, "Introductory Remarks to a Japanese Translation of the *Mujōekyō* 無上依經," *Kokuyaku issaikyō, Kyōshū-bu*, vol. 6 (1932), p. 111ff.

10. T. nos. 688, 689; Tib., Otani Catalogue, no. 985.

of the *tathāgatagarbha* theory with stūpa worship and the eulogy to the Buddha is not at all a merely mechanical and accidental connection, and it shows the existence of an essential interrelation between them. Namely, stūpa worship and the eulogy to the Buddha had originally taken place among a group of Buddhists from which the Mahāyānist community came into existence,[11] and the core of the *tathāgatagarbha* theory lies in its *ekayāna* theory, i.e., the "pure" faith in the Buddha as often referred to in the *RGV*.[12] This being the case, the *Anuttarāśraya-sūtra* may be the most developed expression of the *tathāgatagarbha* theory in its full and pure aspect. (In the case of the *Buddhagotraśāstra*, the *tathāgatagarbha* theory is interwoven with the Vijñānavāda on the one hand, while on the other hand faith in the Buddha in the form of stūpa worship and the eulogy to the Buddha is little referred to owing to the scholastic character of this śāstra.)

Lastly, I shall refer to the date, the author, and the place of composition of the *Anuttarāśrayasūtra*. 1) Coming after the *RGV* and before the *Buddhagotraśāstra*, the date of this sūtra is after Vasubandhu, some time in the late 5th or early 6th century A.D. (Here, Vasubandhu's authorship of the *Buddhagotraśāstra* is rejected because the date of the *RGV* seems to be contemporary to Vasubandhu.)[13] 2) The composer of this sūtra was probably some one in the circle to which Paramārtha, the Chinese translator of this sūtra, had belonged. 3) As Hsüan-tsang 玄奘 translated the *Adbhutasūtra* independently in the 7th century. A.D. and as there

11. Cf. Prof. A. Hirakawa's articles on the characteristics of Mahāyāna Buddhist monasticism (e.g., *Daijō bukkyō no seiritsushiteki kenkyū*, ed. S. Miyamoto [Tokyo, 1954], p. 447ff).

12. Cf. S. Takemura, "Nyoraizō no kugyōsei" [The ultimate nature of the Matrix of the Buddha], *Ryūkoku Daigaku Ronshū* 359 (1958), pp. 39–53.

13. Cf. M. Hattori, "Busshōron no ichi kōsatsu" [A study of the *Buddhagotraśāstra*], *Bukkyō Shigaku* 4 (1955), p. 160ff. I quite agree with Hattori's opinion that the *Buddhagotraśāstra* was written by Paramārtha on the basis of his knowledge of the *RGV*.

is no Sanskrit or Tibetan material which informs us of this sūtra, it might have been unknown to Indians of that time, and hence it seems to have been composed somewhere outside India, e.g., in Sumatra and the like, where Paramārtha stayed on his way to China.

Inconceivability (*acintyatva*) of the Buddha in Four Aspects

AĀS

Chap. II

佛告阿難，佛婆伽婆般涅槃後起刹立塔造像供養，功德福報不可稱量，微塵算數所不能知。云何如此。阿難，如來希有不可思議[1]。所以者何。爲界爲性[2]不可思議。爲菩提爲證得[3]不可思議。爲功德爲法[4]不可思議。爲利益爲作事[5]不可思議。 (T. 16, p. 469b)

(1) 阿難，云何如來爲界不可思議。阿難，是如來界在有垢地，淨不淨法俱在一時，是處不可思惟。依甚深理而得解脫，或阿羅漢，或辟支佛，非其境界。阿難，有二種法不可通達。一者自性淸淨法界不可通達。二者煩惱垢障不可通達。唯阿毘跋致菩薩與大法相應。能聽能受能持。諸菩薩聲聞緣覺信佛語

RGV

tatra *samalā tathatā yugapad ekakālaṃ viśuddhā ca saṃkliṣṭā cêty acintyam etat sthānaṃ gambhira-dharmanayâdhimuktānām api pratyekabuddhānām agocaraviṣayatvāt* / yata āhạ / *dvāv imau*, devi, *dharmau duṣprativedhyau* / *prakṛtipariśuddhacittaṃ duṣprativedhyam* / *tasyaiva cittasyopakliṣṭatā duṣprativedhyā* / *anayor*, devi, *dharmayoḥ śrotā* tvaṃ vā bhaver atha vā *mahādharmasamanvāgatā bodhi-*

1. *adbhūto 'cintyaḥ.*
2. *dhātu*, *gotra*.
3. *bodhi*, *adhigama*.
4. *guṇa*, *dharma*.
5. *artha-kriyā*, *karman*.

故得知此法。阿難，如來爲此界性不可思議。 (p. 470c)

sattvāḥ / *śeṣāṇāṃ, devi, sarvaśrāvakapratyekabuddhānāṃ tathāgataśraddhāgamaniyāv evaitau dharmāv* iti /
(pp. 21.17–22.4)

Chap. III

(2) 阿難，云何如來爲菩提自性不可思議。……復次，眞如本不被染，末無垢污不可思議。阿難，是名菩提不可思議。 (p. 473c)

tatra *nirmalā tathatā pūrvamalâsaṃkliṣṭā paścād viśuddhêty acintyam etat sthānam* / yata āha…… (p. 22.5)

Chap. IV

(3) 阿難，云何如來爲功德不可思議。一切如來恒河沙劫無邊功德，在於惑地及於淨地，相攝相應未曾相離無垢無淨不可思議。 (p. 475c)

tatra *vimalā buddhaguṇāḥ paurvâparyeṇaikāntasaṃkliṣṭāyām api pṛthagjana-bhūmāv avinirbhāgadharmatayā nirviśiṣṭā vidyanta ity acintyam etat sthānam* / yata āha……
(p. 22.8-9)

Chap. V

(4) 阿難，云何如來爲事不可思議。阿難，諸如來事無數無量，世間衆生不能覺知。雖依語言，不能

tatra jinakriyā yugapat sarvatra sarvakālam anābhogenâvikalpato yathâśayeṣu yathāvaineyikeṣu sattveṣv akṣūṇam anuguṇaṃ pravartata ity acintyam etat sthānam / yata āha / saṃkṣepamātrakeṇâvatāraṇârthaṃ sattvānām apramāṇam api tathāgatakarma pramāṇato nirdiṣṭam / api tu, kulaputra, yat tathāgatasya bhūtaṃ *tathāgata karma tad apramāṇam acintyam avijñeyaṃ sarvalokena* /

顯現。不可示人令他悟解。一切佛土處無所閡。一切如來隨順平等。過於意境，無分別相，猶如虛空無有分別。與法界相稱故。

諸善男子[6]，是故佛說如來之事不可思議。行遍一切處。一切處無失，隨行三世處，不滅三寶性。如來住是事中，如來身相不捨虛空性，一切佛土顯現自身。如來言說非音聲性，同其類音而說正法。如來不取心為境界，諸眾生心根性欲樂皆悉通達。阿難，是名如來為事不可思議。 (p. 476bc)

anudāharaṇam akṣaraiḥ /*duḥsaṃpādaṃ parebhyaḥ* / *adhiṣṭhitaṃ sarvabuddhakṣetreṣu*/ *samatânugataṃ sarvâbhogakriyābhyaḥ* / *nirvikalpam ākāśasamatayā, nirnānākaraṇaṃ dharmadhātukriyayā* / iti vistareṇa yāvad viśuddhavaiḍūryamaṇidṛṣṭāntaṃ kṛtvā nirdiśati / *tad anena, kulaputra,*[7] *prayāyeṇaivaṃ veditavyam acintyaṃ tathāgatakarma samatânugataṃ ca sarvato 'navadyaṃ ca* (*trikālânubaddhaṃ ca*)[8] *triratnavaṃśânupacchettṛ ca* / *yathâcintye tathāgatakarmaṇi pratiṣṭhitas tathāgata ākāśasvabhāvatāṃ ca kāyasya na vijahāti sarvabuddhakṣetreṣu ca darśanaṃ dadāti* / *anabhilāpyadharmatāṃ ca vāco na vijahāti yathārutavijñaptyā ca sattvebhyo dharmaṃ deśayati* / *sarvacittârambaṇavigataś ca sarvasattvacittacaritâśayān na prajānātîti* / (pp. 24.9–25.3)

6–7. Note that, instead of the usual Ānanda, the *AĀS* uses here *kulaputra*, which is identical with the *Dhāraṇīśvararājasūtra* quoted in the *RGV*.

8. Words in parentheses are supplied from the Tibetan version of the *RGV*.

Remarks on the Sanskrit Fragments of the *Abhidharmadharmaskandhapādaśāstra**

I

The fragmentary manuscripts to which I wish to refer are at present preserved in the Scindia Institute Museum at Ujjain, India. They are reported to have been brought from the Gilgit area, Kashmir, by an officer of the Indian Army in the early 1950s, but nothing is known to us about the name of the place of discovery and conditions of preservation. Dr. P. V. Bapat procured photostat copies from the Institute for deciphering and editing by staff members of the Department of Buddhist Studies, University of Delhi, and Miss S. Sengupta, lecturer of the said University, was asked to work on them. She brought the typewritten manuscripts transcribed by herself into Roman script when she came to Japan in 1962 for two years' study at the University of Tokyo. I was asked by her to examine them and if possible find equivalent works in Chinese or Tibetan Buddhist texts. In her opinion, these fragments seem to belong to Abhidharma Buddhism, but no title is given in any folio. Furthermore, they are so fragmentary that it is difficult even to determine the exact order of the folios. She stated also that the manuscripts are written in Gupta Brāhmī script which probably dates from the 5th to 6th century A.D., and that they (67 folios in total) were divided into four groups according to paleographical characteristics when she received them.

With this information in mind, I examined the fragments and found that they are to be divided into three groups, rather than the four paleographical groups, according to the subject and line numbers of each folio, and that the group of folios with ten lines,

---

* Originally published in *JIBS* 13-1 (1965), pp. 411–403.

which accounts for more than half of all the folios, is to be identified with parts of the *Abhidharmadharmaskandhapādaśāstra*, one of the fundamental texts of the early Sarvāstivādins, of which only one Chinese version translated by Hsüan-tsang (T. no. 1537, 阿毘達磨法蘊足論) is known to us.

As for the other two groups, one which has 18 folios of six lines and the other 9 folios of nine lines, I have not yet found any correspondences among works available in Chinese or Tibetan translation. Two folios in the first group (folios of 10 lines) for which no parallel passage is found in the *Abhidharmadharmaskandhapāda* seem to be included, according to their contents, in the last group, which has descriptions of *devavimāna*s and other *loka*s.

In the following I will make some comments on the first group of fragments supposedly identifiable with the *Abhidharmadharmaskandhapāda*.

II

First of all, I will present a comparative table of the Sanskrit fragments and the equivalent Chinese version. (Folio numbers of the former are given by me and the pagination of the latter is according to the Taishō editon.)

Skt.	Chinese	Remarks
(A) 1	505c27–506a14	Book 11, chap. 21: *pratītyasamutpāda* (*avidyāpratyayāḥ saṃskārāḥ* /)
2	506a14–506b5	
3	506b5–506c1	
4	506c1–506c24	
5	506c24–507b5	(*saṃskārapratyayaṃ vijñānam* /)
6	507b6–507c2	(*vijñānapratyayaṃ nāmarūpam* /)
7	507c2–507c28	(*nāmarūpapratyayaṃ vijñānam* /)
8	507c28–508b14	(*nāmarūpapratyayaṃ ṣaḍāyatanam* /)

9	508b14–508c13	
10	508c13–509a1	(*nāmarūpapratyayaḥ sparśaḥ* /)
11	509a1–509b7	Book 12
12	509b7–509c3	(*ṣaḍāyatanapratyayaḥ sparśaḥ* /)
13	509c3–509c28	(*sparśapratyayā vedanā* /)
14	509c28–510a21	(*vedanāpratyayā tṛṣṇā* /)
15	510a21–510b23	
16	510b23–510c27	
17	510c27–511b14	Ch. 511a11-26 is omitted in Skt. (*tṛṣṇā-pratyayam upādānam* /)
18	511b14–511c12	
19	511c12–511c29	
20	511c29–512a23	
21	512a24–512b14	([*upādānapratyayo*] *bhavaḥ* /)
22	512b14–512c3	
23	512c3–512c27	(*bhavapratyayā jātiḥ* /)
24	512c27–512c29	Ch. has many omissions
25	512c29–513a14	
26	513a15–513a18	Ch. has many omissions
27	513a18-28, 513b6-11	(*jātipratyayaṃ jarāmaraṇam* /)
28	513b11-14, 513a29–513b6, 513b15–513c6	Skt. has some omissions
29	513c6–513c10;	End of chap. 21; end of work in Ch.
(B)	453c6–454a1	Book 1, beginning of chap. 1: *śikṣāpadāni*
30	454a1–454a25	(*upāsaka*)
31	454a25–454b13	
32	454b13–454c9	
33	454c9-17, 23-26, 455a3-7, 13-18, 454c18-22, 454c27	

	34	454c27–455a2,	
		455a8-12,	
		455c14-16,	
		455a19–455b3,	
		455c17-20	(First of the 5 *śikṣāpadāni* of *upāsaka*)
	35	455c20-27,	
		455b4-18	
	36	455b18–455c14,	
		455c27–456a5	As far as the first few lines of the 2nd *śikṣāpada*
(C)	37	486a12–486b4	Book 7, chap. 12: *apramāṇāni*
	38	486b4–486c6	(*maitrī, karuṇā*)

As is seen in the above table, the fragments cover most parts of chapter 21 (緣起品, *pratītyasamutpāda-varga*) and the beginning of chapter 1 (學處品, *śikṣāpada-varga*) continuously and two folios in the middle separately (part of chap. 12, 無量品, *apramāṇa-varga*). Curious is the fact that the beginning of the work in the Chinese version follows immediately after the very end of the work, and thus neither colophon nor title together with a salutation verse, which are expected from the Chinese version, are found anywhere in the present manuscript. This puzzled us and made it difficult for us to imagine the whole structure of the work in Sanskrit even if available. As for the contents, however, we can trace word-by-word equivalence in most parts between the two versions. In some folios (e.g., folios 17, 24, 26, 28) the contents are abridged by omissions in either of the two versions. But these omitted sentences are mere repetitions of those mentioned in a previous part. A change of order within a subject is also found in folios 27 and 33–36, and it may indicate a difference of recension between the present manuscript and the Sanskrit original used by Hsüan-tsang. But there are found hardly any additions in either version. The only exception is the insertion of the *uddāna* verse in the Sanskrit at the start of each *aṅga* of the *pratītyasamutpāda* up to '*tṛṣṇāpratyayam upādānam*', which is completely lacking in the Chinese translation. On the other hand, the *uddāna* verse kept at the start of chapter 1 in the Chinese translation and representing the table of contents of the whole work is not found in the Sanskrit manuscript, due probably to changes of order between chapters.

When thus examined, we came to the conclusion that, in spite of the lack of a title, the present manuscript is no doubt part of the *Abhidharmadharmaskandhapādaśāstra* and that the two versions probably belong to different recensions. It is difficult, however, to decide which is closer to the original, although the Chinese translation has a better arrangement and seems to show the original form of the work. (The date of the Chinese translation is about the middle of the 7th cent. A.D.) Any further comments seem difficult to make unless we obtain many more fragments of the text.

III

As for the paleographical characteristics, I am not in a position to make any comments as I have not seen the original manuscript kept at Ujjain. A few remarks on grammatical and lexicographical characteristics will be given here.

This manuscript contains special usages observed commonly in Indian Buddhist manuscripts, such as the consonant after 'r' being duplicated (e.g., *karma—karmma*, *vartate—varttate*), *sattva* being written as *satva*, a nasal before a consonant being always replaced by *anusvāra* (e.g., *bhavaṃti* for *bhavanti*), and so on, but otherwise the manuscript is written in Classical Sanskrit. As for *visarga*, it is sometimes dropped before a consonant (e.g., *mithyāsmṛti prabhavati*, fol. 1) and sometimes kept before a vowel (e.g., *dharmāḥ akuśalā-*, fol. 2), but no rules for such irregular forms are to be observed. Generally speaking, the rules of *sandhi* have sometimes been confused due probably to mistakes by the ancient copyist. (A *daṇḍa* is not used between sentences except for the end of a subject, and thus confusion is increased.)

Irregular forms of declension and conjugation are observed in such cases as *nāmasya* (gen. sg. of *nāman)* and *saṃsthihati* (3 sg. ind. pres. of *saṃ√sthā*, Ā). In the latter case, however, the classical form *saṃtiṣṭhate* is also used, and there is no difference in meaning between the two forms. Such irregularity is, however, commonly observed in Buddhist Sanskrit texts and not peculiar to this text. Also there are found some terms unique to Buddhist texts such as *dahra* (for *dahara* 'young', fol. 7), *dhanvam* (for *dhandham* 'slowly', fol. 18), *aihidarśika* (*aihipaśyika*, *ehipaśyika*, wrong form?), etc. (The last is not recorded in Edgerton's *Buddhist Hybrid Sanskrit Dictionary*.) Among the names of *bhikṣus* and others, who appear in quotations as questioners of the Buddha, or names used for the titles of works, we find such names as *svāti bhikṣu kaivartaputra* (Ch. 莎底, Pāli *sātibhikkhu kevettaputta*), *mahānāman licchavī* (Ch. 大名離呫毘, Pāli *mahāli* in corresponding SN passage), *ghoṣila gṛhapati* (Ch. 瞿史羅長者, Pāli *ghosita*), *nādika* (Ch. 那地迦, Pāli *nāgita*), *phalguṇa* (Ch. 頗勒窶那, Pāli *phagguṇa*), *pātāleya* (Ch. 險坑, Pāli *pārileyya*), *paurṇamāṣika* (Ch. 滿月, Pāli *puṇṇamā*), etc. (In the manuscript, *kaivartaputra* is written as *kevalapraśnaṃ*, *kovattapratvi?naṃ*, *kevandapra??naṃ*, *kaivartapurvenaṃ*, etc., but in light of the Pāli, the Sanskrit form must be *kaivartaputra*.) In most cases, the Chinese translation of the name supports the manuscript reading, although linguistic equivalence with Pāli is sometimes uncertain. (*Pātāleya* is rendered in Chinese by a word with the sense of 'dangerous hole', while the derivation of the Sanskrit is rather obscure. Is it derived from *pātāla* 'nether world'?)

IV

The text has many quotations from the Āgamas. Especially in the chapter on *pratītyasamutpāda*, the sources are various and in most cases their titles are mentioned. The following is a list of the Āgamas quoted and their equivalents in the Pāli and Chinese canons. (Pāli references are to the P.T.S. edition.)

(A) Pratītyasamutpāda-varga

1. Source unknown.
   1) fol. 1: *evam uktaṃ bhagavatā / avidyā, bhikṣavo hetuḥ saṃrāgāya*... (Ch. 謂, 世尊說, 苾芻當知...)
2. Title unknown—cf. SN 45.1 (Avijjā); Ch. 雜 28.2-3.
   1) fol. 1: *api khalv evaṃ hy uktaṃ bhagavatā / avidyā bhikṣavaḥ pūrvaṃgamaṃ pūrvanimittaṃ*... (Ch. 復次如世尊說...) (SN, vol. 3, p. 1; Ch. 雜 28.2)
   2) fol. 1: *api khalv evam uktaṃ bhagavatā / ye kecid, bhikṣavo, 'nekavidhāḥ pāpakā akuśalā dharmāḥ saṃbhavanti*... (cf. Ch. 雜 28.3)
3. Kumbhopama-vyākaraṇa—SN 12.51; Ch. 雜 12.10.
   1) fol. 2: *api khalv evam uktaṃ bhagavatā kumbhopame vyākaraṇe / puṇyān eva saṃskārān*... (Ch. 復次瓮喻經中佛作是說...) (SN, vol. 2, p. 82)
   2) fol. 5: *api khalv*... */ tasya puṇyān saṃskārān* (ibid., p. 80f.)
4. Nādikâvavāda-vyākaraṇa—AN 5.30 (Nāgita); cf. Ch. 雜 47.
   1) fol. 6: *api khalv evam uktaṃ bhagavatā nādikâvavāde vyākaraṇe / priyāṇāṃ, nādika, jñātināṃ*... (Ch. 復次教誨那地迦經中佛作是說...) (AN, vol. 3, p. 32)
5. Phalguṇâvavāda-vyākaraṇa—SN 12.12 (Phagguṇa); Ch. 雜 15.10.
   1) fol. 6: *api khalv evam uktaṃ bhagavatā phalguṇâvavāde vyākaraṇe / vijñānaṃ, phalguṇa, āhāram*... (Ch. 復次教誨頗勒窶那經中佛作是說...) (SN, vol. 2, p. 13)
   2) fol. 8; 3) fol. 9; 4) fol. 11; 5) fol. 22 (ibid.)
6. Svāty[avavāda-vyākaraṇa]—MN 38 (Mahātaṇhāsaṅkhāya-sutta); Ch. 中 201 (嗏帝經).

1) fols. 6–7: *api khalv evam uktaṃ svātiṃ bhikṣuṃ kaivartaputram ārabhya / trayāṇāṃ saṃnipātān mātuḥ...* (Ch. 復次敎誨莎底經中佛作是說...) (MN, vol. 1, p. 265)

2) fol. 8; 3) fol. 9; 4) fol. 11 (ibid.)

7. Mahānidānaparyāya-vyākaraṇa (Mahānidānâpavāda-vy., Mahānidānapāda?-vy., Mahānidāna-vy.) (Ch. 大因緣經)—cf. DN 15 (Mahānidānasuttanta); Ch. 長 13 (大緣方便經), etc.

1) fol. 7: *api khalv evam uktaṃ bhagavatā mahānidānaparyāyavyākaraṇe āyuṣmate ānandāya / asti pratyayam, ānanda, nāmarūpaṃ...* (Ch. 復次大因緣經中尊者慶喜問佛...佛告慶喜...) (DN, vol. 2, pp. 62–63)

2) fol. 8: *api khalv evam uktaṃ bhagavatā mahānidānâpavāde /...vijñānaṃ ced, ānanda, nāmarūpapratiṣṭhitaṃ...* (DN, vol. 2, p. 63)

3) fol. 12: *api khalv evam uktaṃ bhagavatā mahānidānapāde yasmin vyākaraṇe āyuṣmate ānandāya / asti pratyayam, ānanda, sparśa iti vistareṇa yāvat...*

4) fol. 14: *api khalv...ānandāya / asti pratyayam, ānanda, vedanā...*

5) fol. 17: *api khalv...mahānidānaparyāye āyuṣmatyānande* (sic.) / *tatrânanda, yā ca bhava-tṛṣṇā...*

6) fol. 22: *api khalv...mahānidāne vyākaraṇe āyuṣmatyānande* (sic.) / *asti pratyayam ānando, 'pādānaṃ...*

7) fol. 23: *api khalv...nidānapādaye? vyakaraṇe āyuṣmatyānande* (sic.) / *asti pratyayam, ānanda, bhavo...*

8) fol. 27: *api khalv...mahānidānapādaye? vyākaraṇe āyuṣmatye* (sic.) *ānande / asti pratyayaṃ, jātir...*

9) fols. 27–28: *api khalv...mahānidānapādaye? vyākaraṇe āyuṣmatyānande / asti pratyayam, ānanda, jarāmaraṇaṃ...*

8. Title unknown—SN 35.129 (Ghosita); Ch. 雜 17.5.

1) fols. 13–14: *api khalv evam uktam ānandena ghosilasya gṛhapater, anye ca gṛhapate, cakṣū dhātur...* (Ch. 復次如契經說尊者慶喜告瞿史羅長者言...) (SN, vol. 4, pp. 113–114)

9. Pancôpādānaskandhika-vyākaraṇa—SN 22.27-28 (Assādo 2, 3); Ch. 雜 1.13-14.

1) fol. 15: *api khalv evam uktaṃ bhagavatā pañcôpādāna-skandhike vyākaraṇe / rūpasyâhaṃ, bhikṣava, āsvādaparyeṣaṇaṃ*... (Ch. 復次取蘊經中佛作是說...) (SN, vol. 3, p. 29)

2) fol. 15: *api khalv... / rūpe ced, bhikṣava, āsvādaś cen na bhaven* (SN, vol. 3, pp. 29–30)

10. Ṣaḍāyatanika-vyākaraṇa—SN 35.15-18; Ch. 雜 9.17-8.

1) fol. 15: *api khalv evam uktaṃ bhagvatā ṣaḍāyatanike vyākaraṇe / cakṣuṣâhaṃ, bhikṣava, āsvādaparyeṣaṇaṃ*... (Ch. 復次六處經中佛作是說...) (SN 35.15, vol. 4, pp. 8–9)

2) fols. 15–16: *api khalv... / cakṣuṣi, bhikṣava, āsvādaś cen na bhaven*... (SN 35.17, vol. 4, pp. 10–12)

3) fol. 16: *api khalv... / rūpasyāhaṃ, bhikṣava, āsvāda-paryeṣaṇam* (SN 35.16, vol. 4, pp. 9–10)

4) fol. 16: *api khalv... / rūpe ced, bhikṣava, āsvādo na bhaven*... (SN 35.18, vol. 4, pp. 12–13)

11. Title unknown—SN 22.60 (Mahāli); Ch. 雜 3.32.

1) fols. 16–17: *api khalv evam uktaṃ bhagavatā mahā-nāmānaṃ licchavīm āgamya / rupaṃ ced, mahānāma, ekā-ntaduḥkhaṃ bhaven*... (Ch. 復次佛爲大名離呫毘說...) (SN, vol. 3, pp. 68–71)

12. Paurṇamāsika-vyākaraṇa—SN 22.82 (Puṇṇamā); Ch. 雜 2.26.

1) fol. 17: *api khalv evam uktaṃ bhagavatā paurṇamāsike vyākaraṇe / yad, bhikṣavo, rūpaṃ pratītyôtpadyate sukham*... (Ch. 復次滿月經中佛作是說...) (SN, vol. 3, pp. 102–103)

13. Pātāleya-vyākaraṇa—SN 22.81 (Pārileyya); Ch. 雜 2.25.

1) fols. 17–18: *api khalv evam uktaṃ bhagavatā pātāleye vyākaraṇe / deśitā, vo bhikṣavo, mayā dharmāḥ skandhā-nāṃ pravicayāya*... (Ch. 復次險坑經中佛作是說...) (SN, vol. 3, pp. 96–97)

2) fols. 18–19: *nahaiva rūpam ātmataḥ samanupaśyaty,*

api tu… (SN, vol. 3, pp. 98–99)

(B) Sikṣāpada-varga

14. Title unknown—AN 5.174.

1) fol. 29: *evaṃ mayā śrutam*… / *yasya kasya cid, bhikṣavaḥ, pañca bhayāni vairāṇy aśāntāni bhavaṃti*… (AN, vol. 3, pp. 204–205)

15. Title unknown—MN 41 (Sāleyyakasutta).

1) fol. 34: *evaṃ hy uktaṃ bhagavatā* / *prāṇâtipāti khalv ihaiko bhavati*… (Ch. 如世尊說, 有殺生者…) (MN, vol. 1, p. 286)

2) fol. 36: *evaṃ hy uktaṃ bhagavatā* / *adattâdāyi khalv ihaiko bhavati*… (Ch. 如世尊說, 有不與取者…) (MN, vol. 1, p. 286)

16. Source unknown.

1) fol. 36: *yathā cāha* /

samantânvāsravī lokaṃ diśa[*ś ca*] *sarvam īritaḥ* /
icched bhavanam ātmānaṃ nâdhigacched aniśritam //
(Ch. 如有頌言, 普隨順世間, 周遍歷方邑, 欲求於勝我, 無所證無依)

It is notable that most of these Āgamas are called *vyākaraṇa*, probably in the same sense as *dharma-paryāya* or *sūtra*, used as a general term for the Āgama. The relationship between this use of the term *vyākaraṇa* and that of the third *aṅga* of the *navâṅga-buddhavacana* (九分教) will be a subject for further investigation.

On the *Myaṅ 'das**

1. The *Myaṅ 'das*, i.e., *Yoṅs su mya ṅan las 'das pa chen po'i mdo* (*Mahāparinirvāṇasūtra*) is an important Mahāyāna scripture famous for its doctrine of the Buddha's nature or the *tathāgatagarbha* and the eternity of the Buddha. There are two translations in the Tibetan Kanjur: one of 13 *bampo*s translated from a Sanskrit original, the other of 56 *bampo*s translated from Chinese materials, namely, Dharmakṣema's translation of the same scripture in 40 fascicles combined with Jñānabhadra's translation in 2 fascicles as a kind of appendix,[1]

In the following I wish to give a survey of the latter, i.e., the *Myang 'das* in 56 *bampo*s.

2. The *Myaṅ 'das* in Tibetan Kanjur Catalogues

The *Myaṅ 'das* is described in Tibetan Kanjur catalogues in the following ways:

1) *lDan dkar ma* (c. 812 / 824 A.D.)
(Lalou[2] no. 249; Yoshimura[3] no. 248)
theg pa chen po'i mdo sde, rgya las bsgyur ba la |
'Phags pa yoṅs su mya ṅan las 'das pa chen po, 12600 śls., 42 bps.

---

* Originally published in Ernst Steinkellner and Helmut Tauscher, eds., *Proceedings of the Csoma de Kőrös Symposium Held at·Velm-Vienna, Austria, 13-19 September 1981* (Wien: Arbeitskreis für tibetische und buddhistische Studien, Universität Wien, 1983), vol. 2, pp. 285–291.

1. T. nos. 374 & 377, respectively.

2. M. Lalou, "Les texts bouddhiques au temps de *Khri-sroṅ-lde-bcan*," *JA* 241 (1953), p. 325.

3. "The Denkar-ma: An Oldest Catalogue of the Tibetan Buddhist Canons," in *Indo daijō bukkyō shisō kenkyū* (Kyoto, 1974), vol. 2, pp. 99–199. (This article was originally published in 1950.)

2) Bu ston, *Chos 'byuṅ chen mo* (IV. dKar chags) (c. 1322 A.D.) (Nishioka no. 368)[4]
(VII) *theg pa chen po'i mdo sde sna tshogs la...*
Mya ṅan las 'das pa chen po'i mdo, rgya las bsgyur ba, 56 bps.

3) *sNar thaṅ bKa' 'gyur* (1730–32 A.D.)
(Takasaki no. 361, cases 78–79)[5]
Myaṅ 'das Ka pa (bps. 1–28, le'us 1–9) & Kha pa (bps. 29–56, le'us 10–15)
Myaṅ 'das chen po...rgya nag gi mkhan po Waṅ phab shun daṅ | dharma'i gźi 'dzin dGe ba'i blo gros | lo tsā ba rGya mtsho'i sde rnams kyis bsgyur ba...

4) *lHa sa bKa' 'gyur*
(Takasaki no. 368, cases 77–78)[6]
Myaṅ 'das Ka pa & Kha pa

5) *sDe dge bKa' 'gyur dKar chags* (1733 A.D.)
(Tohoku no. 119)[7] mDo, Ña & Ta

6) *Peking Edition* (1724 A.D.)
(Otani no. 787)[8] mDo, Ju & Ñu

7) *Co ne bKa' 'gyur*
(Mibu no. 790)[9]

---

4. Soshū Nishioka, "Index to the Catalogue Section of Bu ston's 'History of Buddhism'" (I), *Annual Report of the Institute for the Study of Cultural Exchange, Faculty of Letters, University of Tokyo* 4 (1980), pp. 61–92.

5. J. Takasaki, *A Catalogue of the Lha sa Kanjur Kept in the University of Tokyo* (facsimile edition), 1965 (text numbers of the sNar thaṅ Kanjur are given in the comparative table). Also see Shodo Nagashima, "A Catalogue of the sNar thaṅ Kanjur Kept in Taisho University," *Taishō Daigakū Kenkyū Kiyō* 61 (1975), pp. 760–726.

6. Ibid.

7. *A Complete Catalogue of the Tibetan Buddhist Canons*, ed. by H. Ui & others (Sendai, 1934).

8. *A Comparative Analytical Catalogue of the Kanjur Divison of the Tibetan Tripitaka* (Kyoto: Otani Daigaku Library, 1930–32).

9. Taishun Mibu, "A Comparative List of the bKaḥ-ḥgyur Division in the

3. Date of Translation

There is no record on the date of translation of the *Myaṅ 'das*. Pelliot, in his article on the catalogue of the Kanjur,[10] referring to the transcription of the Chinese name of the translator Wang phab shun (Wang Fa-chouen 王法順 *or* 王法淳), writes that the date may be before 1000 A.D. in light of the transcription *phab*, instead of *fa*, for the term signifying *dharma* or *chos*. Sakurabe, in the *Otani Catalogue*,[11] suggests the identification of the name dGe ba'i blo gros with a co-translator of Atīśa, who belongs to the 11th century. The fact that the *Myaṅ 'das* is mentioned in the *lDan dkar ma* may show an earlier date of translation. The only difficulty in identifying the *Myaṅ 'da*s in the *lDan dkar ma* with that preserved in the present Kanjur is the difference in the number of *bampo*s. But we may surmise that 42 is the number of fascicles in the original Chinese text (40+2) and that initially the Tibetan translation had the same division of fascicles as the Chinese texts.[12]

Co-ne, Peking, sDe-dge and sNar-thaṅ Editions," *Taishō Daigaku Kenkyū Kiyō* 44 (1959), pp. 1–69.

At the Conference information was kindly provided by Dr. G. Bethlenfalvy on the Urga Kanjur. This edition has a similar arrangement to the Derge Edition, and the *Myaṅ 'das* of 56 bps. is located in mDo sde, Ña pa & Ta pa (no. 119). G. Bethlenfalvy, *A Catalogue of the Urga Kanjur*, Śaka-piṭaka Series 246 (New Delhi, 1980).

10. P. Pelliot, "Notes à propos d'un catalogue de Kanjur," *JA* (Juillet-Août 1914), pp. 130–131.

11. *Otani Catalogue* (n. 8 above), p. 287.

12. According to information provided by Dr. H. Eimer of Bonn after the Velm Conference, the *Myaṅ 'das* among the hand-written manuscripts of the Kanjur kept in the British Library in London occupies vols. 98–100 and consists of 42 *bampo*s (vol. 98, bps. 1–14, 315 folios; vol. 99, bps. 15–28, 318 folios; vol. 100, bps. 29–42, 309 folios). Therefore, the identification is almost certain.

As an example of a Tibetan text translated from Chinese sources which has the same fascicle division as the original, we have the *rDo rje tiṅ ṅe 'dzin gyi chos kyi yi ge*. It is, however, curious that the *lDan kar ma* records this sūtra as having 6 bampos (Lalou, no. 254, in the same section as the *Myaṅ 'das*).

4. Characteristics of the Chinese Original

The original of the *Myaṅ 'das* is, as mentioned above, a combination of Dharmakṣema's text and Jñānabhadra's text. According to the biographies of Dharmakṣema,[13] he initially brought the first 10 fascicles with him from India in c. 412–415 A.D., but thinking it incomplete, he went back to India, where he met with his mother's death, and on the way back to China he obtained at Khotan the next portion up to fascicle 20. Afterwards he sent a messenger back to Khotan to get the remaining parts and finally completed the translation in 40 fascicles in 421. Later on, however, a monk from Central Asia informed him of the incompleteness of the text (probably because his translation has no scene of the Preceptor's funeral and distribution of his relics as told in the Hīnayāna *Mahāparinirvāṇa Sūtra*). He therefore asked his sponsor Chü-ch'ü Meng-sun 沮渠蒙遜, the lord of Pei-liang 北涼, for permission to go abroad in search of the remaining text. But soon after starting out, he was killed by subordinates of the lord, who was afraid of his venerated great master's being carried off by the powerful Pei-wei 北魏. Thus in China people began to make efforts to seek this illusory text and continued doing so until finally they were satisfied with Jñānabhadra's translation in two fascicles, which was brought by his disciple to the then capital Ch'ang-an 長安 in c. 676 and was permitted by Empress Wu Tse-t'ien 則天武后 to be propagated in 695. The text was regarded as a continuation of Dharmakṣema's text and was called the "latter part (*hou-fen* 後分)" of the *Mahāparinirvāṇa*.[14]

There are, however, some doubts about the origin of this new text. The text was originally found in Java, where Jñānabhadra lived. Its main part is mostly a description of the facts around the

13. E.g., *Kao-seng chuan* 高僧傳, fasc. 2 (T. no. 2059, vol. 50, pp. 335c–337b). See Fuse Kōgaku 布施浩岳, *Nehan-shū no kenkyū* 涅槃宗の研究 [Studies on the *Mahāparinirvāṇa* sect in China] (Tokyo, 1942; reprint, 1973), vol. 1, pp. 100–138.

14. Fuse, op. cit., pp. 139–146.

Buddha's *mahāparinirvāṇa* as in the Pāli Canon, and a few Mahāyānistic ideas such as the eternity of the Buddha's body are scattered throughout the text. The textual continuation from the final portion of Dharmakṣema's text is technically not perfect. Namely, Dharmakṣema's text ends with Subhadra's attainment of arhatship, while the beginning of the "Latter Part" starts with his obtaining pure dharma eyes after attending the Preceptor's teaching.[15] The Tibetan translation is quite faithful to the Chinese idea of combining both texts and seems not to have noticed this contradiction.[16]

4.2.

Furthermore another mystery exists concerning Dharmakṣema's text. Almost in the same year as the completion of his translation, Fa-hsien 法顯 finished his own translation of the *Mahāparinirvāṇa* in 6 fascicles at Chien-k'ang 建康 (418 A.D.).[17] This text is equivalent to the first 10 fascicles of Dharmakṣema's text. Its authority was lost and replaced by the latter when the latter was brought to Southern China in c. 436, probably with the idea that the latter was more exhaustive and had a deeper consideration of the problem of *icchantika*s. Monks in Chien-k'ang made revisions to Dharmakṣema's translation and arranged the text in 36 fascicles,[18] utilizing the detailed chapter division of Fa-hsien's translation.

Fa-hsien had brought the original text directly from India, the text having been found in the house of a Brahmin at Pāṭaliputra

15. Fuse, op. cit., pp. 148–149.

16. *...śin tu bzaṅ po ni dgra bcom pa'i 'bras bu thob par gyur to || de'i tse śin tu bźan pos bcom ldan 'das las yoṅs su mya ṅan las 'das pa chen po'i chos śin tu zab mo thos nas chos la chos kyi mig rnam par dag par gyur to || ...de bźin gśegs pa las rab tu 'byuṅ bar gsol to* || (Peking Ed., mDo, Nu 319a2-4).

17. T. no. 376. See Fuse, op. cit., pp. 72–81.

18. T. no. 375. See Fuse, op. cit., pp. 156–176.

between 404 and 409. Though short, this text seems to show the original form of the Mahāyāna *Mahāparinirvāṇasūtra* and is complete in itself. The reason for this hypothesis is that the Mahāyāna versions were composed not for the purpose of describing the death of the Buddha, but, borrowing this scene, to express its significance in the light of Mahāyāna doctrines, and this purpose is adequately fulfilled by Fa-hsien's text. At the same time, however, the expression of such ideas has no literal limitation unless it contradicts facts believed by followers. In other words, there is room for fantasy and any continuation is possible, and thus the text is open to further expansion and is not necessarily brought to an end by the death of the Buddha. In this way Dharmakṣema's text also shows a kind of completeness.

Then where was this extension of the text carried out? It was at least not in India proper, because another Tibetan translation of the *Mahāparinirvāṇa* in 13 *bampo*s, which was brought to Tibet directly from India before the beginning of the 9th century, is of equivalent length to Fa-hsien's text and is closer to it in content than to Dharmakṣema's, which has a certain amount of elaboration even in the first 10 fascicles. Another source proving this fact is the fragmentary Sanskrit manuscript of the *Mahāparinirvāṇa* in the collection of Hoernle found in Eastern Turkistan and identified by K. Watanabe (Hoernle, *Manuscript Remains of Buddhist Literature*, pp. 93–97). It is equivalent to a passage towards the end of fasc. 9 and the beginning of fasc. 10 of Dharmakṣema's text,[19] where an important insertion is made by the latter text[20] which plays the role of the link between the former 10 fascicles and the latter 30 fascicles (see below).

---

19. Equivalent to *Myaṅ 'das*, Peking Ed., mDo, Ju 160b4–162a1.

20. Equivalent to the same, Ju 161a6–161b6 (*de nas 'jam dpal gźon nur gyur pas bcom ldan 'das la 'di skad ces gsol to* || ...*tha dad pa yaṅ ma lags par 'tshal to* ||).

5. Characteristics of the Tibetan Translation

The technical terms used in the *Myaṅ 'das* mostly follow the *skad gsar bcad* method. Some important terms different from those used in the text of Indian origin are as follows:

1) *saṅs rgyas kyi raṅ bźin*, for the Buddha's nature, *fo-hsing* 佛性 in the Chinese original, which is usually used for the translation of Skt. *buddhadhātu*. This is suggested by the term *saṅs rgyas kyi khams* used in the equivalent passage in the other version.
2) *log sred can* for *icchantika*, which is usually translated as *'dod chen po*.
3) The term *tathāgatagarbha* is translated as *de bźin gśegs pa'i sñiṅ po*, as usually found in texts of Indian origin, when Dharmakṣema uses the word *ju-lai-tsang* 如來藏 or *ju-lai pi-tsang* 如來祕藏, while it is translated as *de bźin gśegs pa'i gsaṅ ba'i sñiṅ po* when he uses the terms *ju-lai wei-mi-tsang* 如來微密藏 or *ju-lai pi-mi-tsang* 如來祕密藏.
4) *rtag pa gnas pa mi 'gyur mi 'pho ba* for *ch'ang chu wu yu pien i* 常住無有變易, which is sometimes for *nitya*, *rtag pa*, and sometimes for *nitya-dhruva-śāśvata*, *rtag pa brtan pa ther gsug pa*.
5) *bkri ba'i don* for *neyārtha*, which is usually translated as *draṅ don*.
6) The following case is an example of incorrect translation.

   | *thog ma yod la da ltar med* || *thog ma med la da ltar yod* |
   | *dus gsum srid pa'i chos thams cad* || *de ltar bu ni ma yin no* |[21]

   (*pen yu chin wu*   *pen wu chin yu*
   san shih yu fa   *wu yu shih ch'u*
   本有今無　本無今有
   三世有法　無有是處)

21. This verse is what I regard as the link. The same verse appears again in facs. 17, 27 and 28 in Dharmakṣema's text.

This verse appears in the inserted passage in Dharmakṣema's text at the beginning of fasc. 10, corresponding to the Sanskrit fragment referred to above. Here the third *pada* should mean "existence of *dharma* in the three modes of time" and ought to be translated "*dus gsum la ni chos yod pa*." Also in the fourth *pada*, *mi ruṅ ṅo* would be better than *ma yin no*. The Chinese term *wu yu shih ch'u* 無有是處 usually corresponds to Skt. *naitad sthānam*.

6. Initially, I had hoped to make clear the reason why the *Myaṅ 'das* of 56 *bampo*s is separated from the other version and is treated as an independent section in some editions of the Tibetan Kanjur.[22] But due to my laziness I could not find any material that answers this question. Only Bu ston's treatment of the *Myaṅ 'das* gives us some hint. He places the *Myaṅ 'das* of 56 *bampo*s at the end of the group of Mahāyāna sūtras and before the Pāli *Pāritta*s, which had been newly translated by his teacher. In the sNar thaṅ Kanjur these latter were put at the end of the *mDo pa*, that is to say, just before the *Myaṅ 'das pa*.

Also I have not made any attempt to find out how far the

22. According to information provided by Dr. H. Eimer at the Velm Conference, the *dKar chags* of the London manuscript (mentioned above in n. 12) treats the *Myaṅ 'das* as an independent section (in three volumes) and places it after the *rGyud 'bum* and *mDo* and before the *Śer phyin*, etc. In his opinion, another manuscript Kanjur kept in the Tōyō Bunko Library (Kawaguchi Collection), Tokyo, is also to be included in this same group of arrangement because it has the same division of sections and the same number of volumes in the respective sections, and this arrangement of the Kanjur represents an old West Tibetan tradition. The sNar thaṅ and lHa sa Editions, both having the *Myaṅ 'das* as an independent section, seem to belong to this Western group.

On the Tōyō Bunko manuscript Kanjur, see Kōjun Saitō, "Kawaguchi Ekai-shi shōrai Tōyō Bunko shozō shahon Chibetto Daizōkyō chōsa bibō," *Taishō Daigaku Kenkyū Kiyō* 63 (1977), pp. 406–345.

Myaṅ 'das was used or referred to by Tibetan authors.[23] If we examine these points, we will make much clearer the position of the *Myaṅ 'das* in Tibetan Buddhism.

23. Prof. D. Seyfort Ruegg informed me at the Velm Conference of cases regarding Bu ston, who quotes both versions of the *Myaṅ 'das* side by side. Cf. D. Seyfort Ruegg, *Le Traité du tathāgatagarbha de Bu ston rin chen grub* (Paris, 1973).

Textual Problems of the *Mahāyānaśraddhotpāda**

The *Ta-ch'eng ch'i-hsin lun* (*Daijō kishin ron* in Japanese), usually restored to Sanskrit as *Mahāyānaśraddhotpādaśāstra*, is one of the most influential texts in the history of Chinese Buddhism. The work is attributed to Aśvaghoṣa, but in the absence of the Sanskrit original, there has been controversy concerning its authenticity among scholars. There are two versions of its Chinese translation,[1] one translated by Paramārtha, and the other one by Śikṣānanda. Paramārtha's work was first queried by Fa-ching 法經 in his Tripiṭaka Catalogue at the end of the 6th century.[2] Based on this and other evidence observed among Chinese documents, Dr. Mochizuki Shinkō 望月信亨 established his theory that the text is not of Indian origin, but is a compilation by Chinese Buddhists probably belonging to the Ti-lun School 地論宗 (1918).[3] To this

* Originally published in *Annals of the Bhandarkar Oriental Research Institute* 68 (1987), pp. 413–424. A Japanese version of this article appeared in *JIBS* 35-1 (1986) under the title "Kishinron kenkyū no mondaiten—Jisshananda yaku no seikaku o megutte" 起信論研究の問題点——実叉難陀訳の性格をめぐって.

1. (1) T. no. 1666, vol. 32, pp. 575b–583b; (2) T. no. 1667, vol. 32, pp. 584a–591c. The titles of both versions are exactly the same. Hereafter we refer to them by the names of their translators, namely, P for the first and Ś for the second. When referring to the text itself, the title is given in the abbreviated form *Śraddhotpāda*.

2. The so-called *Fa-ching lu* compiled in 594; T. no. 2146, vol. 55, p. 142a.

3. Mochizuki Shinkō, *Daijō kishin ron no kenkyū* (Tokyo, 1922). In this volume, his previous articles discussing the author and the origin of the text (published since 1902) are included as appendices. See also his *Kōjutsu Daijō kishin ron* [Lectures on the *Śraddhotpāda*] (Tokyo: Fuzanbō, 1938), where his final opinion is expressed.

were raised objections by Tokiwa Daijō and others,[4] and since then the controversy has continued for many years among scholars, including Western scholars such as P. Demiéville[5] and W. Liebenthal.[6] Even now the problems have not been finally solved although there are no visible polemics among scholars. Shortage of evidence for both theories made scholars give up on reaching a solution.[7] The present author, personally having doubts about its Indian origin, wishes to make some short observations on the characteristics of both translations and thereby hopes to contribute to some extent towards solving the problems concerning the origin of the text.

Among evidence mentioned by Mochizuki to prove the Chinese origin of the text, that which plays a very important role in establishing his theory concerns the second translation. In reality, the existence of the second translation gave Mochizuki's theory the greatest difficulty. He picked up on the legend that Hsüan-tsang 玄奘 translated the *Śraddhotpāda* into Sanskrit and made it spread among Indian lands when he visited India and that Śikṣānanda brought it again from Central Asia to China, and, together with evidence of the uncertainty of the translation by Śikṣānanda found in the Tripiṭaka catalogues, he rejected this legend, saying that it is merely a camouflage of the fact of its Chinese origin to

---

4. Titles of papers discussing the author, etc., of the *Śraddhotpāda* are listed by H. Kashiwagi in his study on the *Śraddhotpāda* (*Daijō kishin ron no kenkyū* [Tokyo: Shunjūsha, 1981], pp. 498–501).

5. P. Demiéville, "Sur l'authenticité du Ta tch'ing k'i sin louen," *Bulletin de la Maison Franco-Japonaise* II, no. 2 (Tokyo, 1929), pp. 1–28. He argued for the Indian origin of the text though he denied the authorship of Aśvaghoṣa.

6. W. Liebenthal, "New Light on the Mahāyānaśraddhotpādaśāstra," *T'oung Pao*, vol. XLVI, 4-5, pp. 155–216. He supports Mochizuki's opinion.

7. As a recent work on this problem, mention should be made of H. Kashiwagi's work mentioned above (see note 4). He examined all opinions that had so far appeared concerning the authenticity of the text. He himself regards the text as of Indian origin, contrary to Mochizuki.

protect the text and its doctrine from attacks by the Fa-hsiang school 法相宗.[8] The present author has no further evidence to add for or against his theory concerning data about its translation, but from the inner evidence of the text itself he has the confidence to say that the second translation is not necessarily a real translation of a new text brought by Śikṣānanda or anyone else, but is a revised edition of the first translation to respond to the needs of the day, such as to protect its doctrine from the attacks of opponents.

The principal doctrine of the *Śraddhotpāda* is usually held to be the Tathāgatagarbha theory based upon the *Śrīmālāsūtra* and the *Laṅkāvatārasūtra*. To be more specific, the *Śrīmālā*, together with the *Anūnatvāpūrṇatvanirdeśaparivarta* and the *Ratnagotravibhāga*, gives the basis for its doctrine of the mind reality (*hsin chen-ju* 心眞如, *citta-tathatā*), while the *Laṅkāvatāra* gives the basis for its doctrine of mind transformation (*hsin sheng-mieh* 心生滅, **citta-udayavyayatā*).[9] There are many passages which were undoubtedly composed word for word by using these basic texts. By picking up such passages, we can expect to examine the genuineness of the translation, especially when their Sanskrit original is available. As some such passages that involve key words of the doctrine, we have the following.

8. Mochizuki, *Kōjutsu Dáijō kishin ron*, pp. 19–28, esp. p. 24.

9. The *Śraddhotpāda* is a discourse on what is called Mahāyāna and its body, attributes, and function in terms of *sattva-citta*, the mind of living beings, probably in the sense that there is no vehicle without a rider, i.e., the practiser of the path. This *sattva-citta* is discussed from two points: its reality, *citta-tathatā*, and its transformation, *citta-udayavyayatā*. The former is otherwise called *tathāgatagarbha*, *dharmakāya*, and *cittaprakṛti*, while the latter is referred to in terms of *ālayavijñāna*, from which appear *manas* and *manovijñāna*, functioning for transmigration caused by *avidyā*, as well as functioning towards enlightenment by the force of *citta-tathatā* (in the direction of their disappearance).

(I)

P(aramārtha's translation):[10]

Endowed with such unthinkable qualities of the Buddha which are beyond the sands of the Ganges in number, and are inseparable (*pu-li* 不離), uncut (*pu-tuan* 不斷), not different (*pu-i* 不異) (from the reality), and being perfect and of nothing lacking, it is called the Tathāgatagarbha as well as the Dharmakāya of the Tathāgata.

Ś(ikṣānanda's translation):[11]

It is endowed with such unthinkable qualities of the Buddha which are beyond the sands of the Ganges in number, neither equal to nor different from (the realty) (*fei-t'ung fei-i* 非同非異) and have no interruption. In this respect, it is called the Tathāgatagarbha and the Dharmakāya of the Tathāgata.

The main point of difference between both is the use of the terms 'neither equal to nor different from' in Ś against 'inseparable, uncut, not different' in P. As the same terms are used again a few lines later,[12] we come to know that the terms used by the respective translations show their own understanding and are not a result of caprice.

Now, we find the equivalent passage to this in the *Śrīmālāsūtra*, of which the Sanskrit original is collected from quotations in the *Ratnagotravibhāga*:[13]

(duḥkhanirodhanāmnā...) gaṅgānadīvālukāvyativṛttair avinirbhāgair (amuktajñair) acintyair buddhadharmaiḥ samanvāgatas tathāgatadharmakāyo deśitaḥ / ayam eva,

10. T. vol. 32, p. 579a16-17.

11. Ibid., p. 587b20-22.

12. Ś, ibid., p. 587c9-11. Here the terms '*fei-i fei-i*' (*hi-i hi-itsu* in Jp.) are used instead of '*fei-t'ung fei-i*' in the previous case, but the meaning is more or less the same.

13. *The Ratnagotravibhāga Mahāyānottaratantraśāstra*, ed. by E. H. Johnston (Patna, 1950) (abbr. *RGV*), p. 12, ll. 10-14.

bhagavaṃs, tathāgatadharmakāyo 'vinirmuktakleśakośas tathāgatagarbhaḥ sūcyate /

Compared to these Sanskrit sentences, we come to know that P is mostly true to the idea of the original in the use of the terms 'inseparable' (*avinirbhāga*), etc., while 'neither equal nor different' in Ś has no equivalent term in the Sanskrit text of the *Śrīmālāsūtra*. ('Not different' in P is also not found in the original, but it is not so out of place here. But 'not equal to' (*fei-t'ung*) does not fit here at all. The reason will be shown below.)

Actually, however, P seems to be not a literal and direct translation of the original, but rather it seems to have utilized the Chinese translation of the *Śrīmālā* available at the time. Namely, Guṇabhadra's translation of the said sūtra has such terms as 'inseparable' (for *avinirbhāga*), 'unreleased' (for *amuktajña*), and 'not different'.[14]

Also in a similar passage in the *Śrīmālā*, of which the Sanskrit equivalent is again collected from the *Ratnagotravibhāga*,[15] Guṇabhadra gives the terms 'inseparable, uncut, unreleased, and not different' for *sambaddha*, *avinirbhāga*, *amuktajñāna*, and *asaṃskṛta* (*asaṃskṛta* is not translated, and 'uncut' seems to be for *sambaddha*).[16]

To borrow terms or phrases from previous translations is, however, not peculiar to this text, but rather commonly observed among Chinese texts. For example, the very translation of the *Ratnagotravibhāga* by Ratnamati also utilized the translation of

14. *Sheng-man shih-tzu hou i-ch'eng ta fang-pien fang-kuang ching* (abbr. *Sheng-man ching*), T. no. 353, vol. 12, p. 221c7-11.

15. *RGV*, p. 73, ll. 2-5: *tasmād bhagavaṃs tathāgatagarbho niśraya ādhāraḥ pratiṣṭhā sambaddhānām avinirbhāgānām amuktajñānāṃ dharmāṇām* /

16. *Sheng-man ching*, op. cit., p. 222b10-12. One more example of the use of such terms is available in the *Sheng-man ching* and quoted in the *RGV*, namely, *RGV*, p. 76, ll. 8-9: *śūnyas tathāgatagarbho vinirbhāgair muktajñaiḥ sarvakleśakośaiḥ* / *aśūnyo gaṅgānadīvālukāvyativṛttair amuktajñair acintyair buddhadharmaiḥ* / (*Sheng-man ching*, ibid., p. 221c16-18).

the *Śrīmālā* when quoting it.[17] Namely, for the former case it has the terms 'inseparable, unreleased, and not different', while for the latter passage, 'inseparable, inseparable from knowledge (*amuktajñāna*), uncut, unreleased, not different, and unconditioned'.[18] Also for a passage in the *Anūnatvāpūrṇatvanirdeśaparivarta* which shows a similar idea, Bodhiruci's translation has the terms 'inseparable, unreleased, uncut, and not different'.[19]

In contrast, Paramārtha uses new terms in his translations of other texts. For example:

> O Bhagavan, the *tathāgatagarbha* is not empty of the qualities of the Buddha which are equal to the number beyond those of the sands of the Ganges, inseparable (*pu-hsiang-li* 不相離), uncast of *jñāna* (*pu-she-chih* 不捨智), and unthinkable. (Quotation in the *Fo-hsing lun*)[20]

Also,

> As is said in the scripture, this *vijñāna* element is the basis, the support, the foundation for the qualities of the Buddha, which are constantly associated and inseparable, uncut of *jñāna*, unconditioned, equal to the sands of the Ganges in number. (Quotation in the Commentary on the *Mahāyānasaṃgraha*)[21]

This difference of terminology between the *Śraddhotpāda* and other texts among Paramārtha's translations may pose a problem

17. T. no. 1611, vol. 31, p. 824a17-22.
18. Ibid., p. 839a25-28.
19. *Pu-tseng pu-chien ching*, T. no. 668, vol. 16, p. 467a19-21. Quoted in *RGV*, p. 3, ll. 4-5: *yo 'yaṁ Śāriputra tathāgatanirdiṣṭo dharmakāyaḥ so 'yam avinirbhāgadharmā avinirmuktajñānaguṇo yad uta gaṅgānadīvālukāvyatikrāntais tathāgatadharmaiḥ* / See also T. vol. 31, p. 821b2-3.
20. T. no. 1610, vol. 31, pp. 811c29–812a1. This passage is equivalent to *RGV*, p. 76, ll. 8-9, and *Sheng-man ching*, p. 221c16-18. See note 16.
21. T. no. 1595, vol. 31, pp. 156c28–157a2. This passage is equivalent to *RGV*, p. 73, ll. 2-5, and *Sheng-man ching*, p. 221c7-11. See notes 14 & 15.

concerning the genuineness of P, but we should not be in a hurry to give a conclusion since the date of translation of P seems earliest and the assistants for translation were different from those of later translations.[22]

Through the above examination, one thing at least has become clear. Namely, nowhere is used the phrase 'neither equal nor different' as appears in Ś. Doctrinally speaking, it should not be 'neither equal nor different' because the terms 'inseparable', etc., are, as shown in our translation of the quotations, words for showing the relation of the qualities to the qualified as a special case of reality, the reality referred to in terms of *tathatā*, *dharmadhātu*, *dharmakāya* (of the *tathāgata*) (as the result aspect), and *tathāgatagarbha* (as the cause aspect),[23] to which are to be added the following terms unique to the *Śraddhotpāda*: *citta-tathatā*, *sattva-citta* (*chung-sheng hsin* 衆生心), the mind pure by nature, innate enlightenment (*pen-chüeh* 本覺), etc.[24] This reality is, in the doctrine of the *Śraddhotpāda*, said to be always inseparable from qualities unique to the Buddha, of which the most basic is

22. Whether or not Paramārtha translated the *Śraddhotpāda* is the most important issue in polemics concerning the authenticity of the text. According to the *Li-tai san-pao chi*, the *Śraddhotpāda* was translated in the 4th year of T'ai-ch'ing, i.e., 550 A.D., at Fu-ch'un. It was soon after Paramārtha's arrival in China and under such very bad conditions that he was obliged to escape from the capital due to a riot against the Emperor Mu. His main work of translation during this period is the *Shih-ch'i ti lun* (Treatise on the 17 Stages), which is said to be equivalent to the main part of the *Yogācārabhūmi*. But he stopped his work partway through. Even his partial translation in 5 fascicules has now been lost, and we have no way to judge the style of his translations of this period.

23. On these terms used in the *RGV*, see J. Takasaki, *A Study on the Ratnagotravibhāga* (Roma: IsMEO, 1966), pp. 20–31 (Introduction, III. Keypoint of the Discourse).

24. See note 9. The term *pen-chüeh* was used probably for the first time in the *Śraddhotpāda*, and no Sanskrit equivalent is known to us. It is in contrast to *shih-chüeh*, enlightenment *de facto*. But this latter is not different from the former. So it is a kind of postulate for Enlightenment within *sattva*s who are actually not enlightened (*pu-chüeh*).

wisdom. This inseparability is also referred to by the terms 'in association with' (*samanvāgata*), 'not empty of' (*aśūnya*), etc.[25] Furthermore, reality is said to be always accompanied by function, which causes living beings to turn their minds to the highest good, i.e., Nirvāṇa or Highest Enlightenment.[26] This doctrine, being the fundament of the text, is expressed in the initial part of the text in terms of the three meanings of greatness, namely, the greatness of body or substance (*t'i-ta* 體大), the greatness of characteristics or qualities (*hsiang-ta* 相大), and the greatness of function (*yung-ta* 用大).[27] There is no question of whether it be identical or different.

(II) The second point of evidence to show the ungenuine character of Ś is as follows:

P:[28]

> The perfume-like influence of the *tathatā* based upon its own existence and characteristics is as follows: from beginningless time it is endowed with unpolluted qualities and associated with unthinkable functions, and it constructs the nature (or character) of the sense-objects. By these two significances, it always gives influence. Due to this being powerful, it makes living beings loathe Samsaric suffering and turn to desire and wish to get Nirvāṇa (*yao-ch'iu nieh-p'an* 樂求涅槃) through having confidence in the existence of *tathatā* in their own body and resolve to practise the way.

In this passage, 'loathe Samsaric suffering and turn to desire and wish to get Nirvāṇa' (*yao-ch'iu nieh-p'an*) comes from the

25. See notes 15, 16 & 18. See also J. Takasaki, "On the Meaning of the Term *Amuktajña*" (in Japanese), *JIBS* 6-1 (1958).
26. See the next example (II).
27. P, p. 575c20-28; Ś, p. 584b22–c2. A further explanation is given in the text: P, p. 579a12–c18; Ś, pp. 587b16–588a19.
28. P, p. 578b6-8.

Śrīmālā, namely:[29]

> O Bhagavan, if there be no *tathāgatagarbha*, (the living beings) could not get loathing of suffering and the desire and wish for Nirvāṇa.
>
> *tathāgatagarbhaś ced, bhagavan, na syān, na syād duḥkhe 'pi nirvin, na nirvāṇa iccha vā prārthanā vā praṇidhir vā* / (cf. *duḥkhanirvicchamaprāpticchandapraṇidhikarmakaḥ* [*jinagarbho 'yam*]—*Ratnagotravibhāga*, v. I.35cd)[30]

For this passage, Ś reads as follows:[31]

> Let living beings loathe Samsaric suffering and ask for the bliss of Nirvāṇa (*ch'iu nieh-p'an lo* 求涅槃樂).

Here the Chinese word *yao* (*gyō* in Jp.) has been moved after the term for Nirvāṇa with the meaning of 'bliss' (*lo*; *raku*, in Jp.). This concept of the bliss of Nirvāṇa itself is rather common in Buddhist texts (e.g., *vūpasamo sukho*),[32] in contrast to the *duḥkha* of Saṃsāra, but it is not faithful to the usage in the original. Such a change would never occur in the Sanskrit original. And as this same phrase is used thrice in Ś,[33] we cannot ascribe it to a careless mistake.

(III) The third point that shows a clear change in Ś is as follows:

P:[34]

> Next, "Innate Enlightenment under pollution" is by distinction of the two characteristics, both being inseparable

29. *Sheng-man ching*, T. vol. 12, p. 222b14-15; quoted in *RGV*, p. 36, ll. 1-2.
30. *RGV*, p. 30, l. 5 (on 'Karman' of Tathāgatagarbha).
31. Ś, p. 586c12-14.
32. The so-called "verse on transitoriness":
aniccā vata saṅkhārā uppādavayadhammino /
uppajjitvā nirujjhante tesaṃ vūpasamo sukho //
33. Ś, pp. 586c28, 587a13.
34. P, p. 576c5-16.

from Innate Enlightenment. What are the two? The first one is the characteristic of intellectual purification, the second is the characteristic of unthinkable function.

(1) The characteristic of intellectual purification is that, owing to the perfume-like influence of the power of doctrine, (living beings or practisers) practise in accordance with the truth, and completing the means, break the characteristic of the combined *vijñāna* (= *ālayavijñāna*), destroy the characteristic of the continuing mind (= *citta* in *santāna*, *udayavyaya* = *pravṛttivijñāna*), and manifest the *dharmakāya* due to purification of wisdom.

What does it mean? Because all the characteristics of the mind and consciousness are ignorance (*avidyā*), and the characteristic of ignorance is inseparable from the nature of enlightenment (Innate Enlightenment). Nor is it destroyable.

Just as the water in the ocean moves in the form of waves due to the wind, and the characteristic of water and that of wind are inseparable from each other, and still water is not of the nature of movement. When the wind stops, its movement disappears, but its nature of moisture will never be lost. In the same way, the Innate pure mind of living beings moves due to the wind of ignorance, and both the mind and ignorance are of no shape and inseparable from each other. And still the mind is not of the nature of movement. When ignorance disappears, continuity (of the mind through momentary *udayavyaya*) immediately disappears. But the intellectual nature (of the Innate Mind) is never broken.

In this passage, instead of the terms 'inseparable from' and 'inseparable from each other' (*pu hsiang she-li* 不相捨離) in P, Ś uses the phrase 'neither identical nor different' (*fei-i fei-i* 不一不異). Furthermore, Ś gives a somewhat different meaning in the parable portion:[35]

> Just as the water in the ocean and waves are neither identical nor different, waves move due to the wind, but the water is not of the nature of movement. When the wind stops, the movement of the waves may stop, but the nature of water never disappears. The case is similar to living beings. (Their) innate mind is caused by the movement of the wind of ignorance to start the waves of *vijñāna*s. These three (i.e., the Innate pure mind, ignorance, and moving *vijñāna*s) are of no shape and neither identical nor different. And still the pure Innate mind is the root of moving *vijñāna*s, which disappear when ignorance is destroyed, but the intellectual nature will never be destroyed.

Here a simile is given, not between the water of the ocean and the wind, but between water and waves, and they are referred to as being 'neither identical nor different'. In the doctrinal explanation, however, the same kind of relationship is said of the three, i.e., the Innate mind, ignorance, and moving *vijñāna*s. This 'moving *vijñāna*' is a term for the working *vijñāna* (*pravṛtti-vijñāna*) in the Vijñānavāda, which was once used in Ś in place of 'continuing mind' in P mentioned above. The remarkable point is that by adding this 'moving *vijñāna*', Ś laid stress on the relationship between the Innate mind and moving *vijñāna*s instead of that between the Innate mind and ignorance. And this is probably the reason why Ś changed the term from 'inseparable' to 'neither identical nor different', because the same term (neither identical nor different) is used to denote the relationship between *tathāgatagarbha*, which is the same as the Innate mind, and *ālaya-vijñāna*, which is the principal or fundamental mind for transformation.[36] In this case P also uses the same term. This means that

35. Ś, p. 585b1-10 (parable portion: 585b5-10).

36. P, p. 576b7-8. It goes on to say of the Mind transformation that, on the

in P the 'neither identical nor different' relationship is recognised only between two forms of the mind, *citta-tathatā* and *citta-udayavyayatā*, while the relationship between the Innate mind and ignorance is referred to as being 'inseparable'. This inseparability is, however, not innate like that between reality and its qualities (observed in (I)), but is merely temporary since ignorance is nothing but an illusion signifying a lack of wisdom. (This position of ignorance is usually called *āgantuka* in the Tathāgatagarbha theory, and the *Anūnatvāpūrṇatvanirdeśa* explains it as 'coexisting from beginningless time but not [innately] combined' [*anādisāṃnidhya-asambaddha*] in contrast to the Buddha qualities 'coexisting and innately combined [*sambaddha*] with Reality'.[37] P seems quite faithful to this usage commonly observed in texts of the Tathāgatagarbha theory.)

Then what is the cause of this shift in the point of stress in Ś? Imaginable is the need to make clear the theory concerning the *vijñāna* function in the *Śraddhotpāda* for defending it from attacks of the Fa-hsiang school, but a direct influence seems to have come from the new translation of the *Laṅkāvatāra* by Śikṣānanda,[38] the same person as the translator of the *Śraddhotpāda*.

---

basis of the Tathāgatagarbha (which is of neither origination nor destruction), there arises the mind of origination and destruction, and this point, namely, a combination of non-transformation and transformation, is called *ālayavijñāna*, which is neither identical with nor different from (Tathāgatagarbha). This idea comes from the *Laṅkāvatārasūtra* (6. Kṣaṇikaparivarta). See below.

37. *Pu-tseng pu-chien ching*, T. vol. 16, p. 467b25-29. The *RGV*, using this idea, explains the characteristic of Tathāgatagarbha in the following way:

ity etad aparāntakoṭisamadhruvadharmatāsaṃvidyamānatām adhikṛtya daśavidhena arthena tathāgatagarbhavyavasthānam uktam / punar anādisāṃnidhyāsambaddhasvabhāvakleśakośatām anādisāṃnidhyasambaddhasvabhāvaśubhadharmatāṃ cādhikṛtya navabhir udāharaṇair aparyantakleśakośakoṭigūḍhas tathāgatagarbha iti yathāsūtram anugantavyam / (p. 59, ll. 11-14)

38. *Ta-ch'eng ju leng-ch'ieh ching*, T. no. 672 (so-called T'ang version). On the passage referred to, see note 42 below.

The *Laṅkāvatāra* was, as mentioned previously, one of the basic texts for the compilation of the *Śraddhotpāda*, especially for its portion on the transformation of the mind. And the very analogy of the ocean and the wind is adopted from this *Laṅkāvatāra* but with a slight modification. The original for the analogy of water, wind and waves in the *Laṅkāvatāra* runs as follows:[39]

> *udadheḥ pavanāhatā iva, Mahāmate, viṣayapavana-cittodadhitaraṅgā avyucchinnahetukriyālakṣaṇā anyonya-vinirmuktāḥ karmajātilakṣaṇasuvinibaddha-rūpasvabhāvānavadhāriṇo, Mahāmate, pañcavijñānakāyāḥ pravartante* /[40]
>
> Just like (waves of) the ocean agitated by wind, Mahāmati, so (do) waves (of the *vijñāna*) (appear on) the ocean of the mind (due to) the wind-like outer world having the characteristics of being uninterrupted from (?) the work of the cause (i.e., *ālayavijñāna*) and inseparable from each other, and not noticing the nature of the (sense-objects,) colour (and others), which are well connected with the characteristic of function (of the working *vijñāna*) and that of origination (i.e., *ālayavijñāna*). (Thus,) O Mahāmati, the group of the five *vijñāna*s starts to work.

In the *Laṅkāvatāra* what is compared to the wind is the outer world, but in the doctrine of the Vijñāna(mātra)vāda, it is not

39. *Laṅkāvatāra*, ed. by B. Nanjio (Kyoto, 1923) (abbr. *LAS*), p. 44, ll. 10-14. See also *LAS*, p. 220, ll. 9-16 (Kṣaṇikaparivarta):

> *tathāgatagarbho, Mahāmate, kuśalākuśalahetukaḥ sarvajanmagatikartā ... anādikālavividhaprapañcadauṣṭhulyavāsanāvāsita ālayavijñānasaṃśabdito 'vidyāvāsanabhūmijaiḥ saptabhir vijñānaiḥ saha mahodadhitaraṅgavan nityam avyucchinnaśarīraḥ pravartate ...*

And ibid., p. 221, ll. 12-13:

> *aparavṛtte ca tathāgatagarbhaśabdasaṃśabdita ālayavijñāne, nāsti saptānāṃ pravṛttivijñānānāṃ nirodhaḥ* /

40. The Chinese translations, etc., suggest *anyonyâvinirmuktāḥ* for *anyonya-vinirmuktāḥ* followed by a sentence break and °*suvinibaddhā rūpa*° for °*suvinibaddha-rūpa*°.

admitted as real since it is a mere product of the mind due to ignorance. For the Vijñānavāda, what is real is the mind called *ālaya-vijñāna* or *citta* associated with its functional appearance, i.e., the *pravṛttivijñāna*s. Now, there are three versions of this sūtra among Chinese translations. Of these, the first one, the Sung version[41] translated by Guṇabhadra, reads *avyucchinna* separately as denoting the movement of waves, and for Skt. *anyonyavinirmukta* it reads as if it were *anya-ananya-avinirmukta* (or *saṃyukta*) (*i pu-i ho* 異不異合) and connects it with *hetukriyālakṣaṇa*, and inserts a compound between *-suvinibaddha* and *rūpa-*. The second translation, the Wei version[42] translated by Bodhiruci, reads as if it were *anyonya-avinirmukta* (*pu hsiang she-li* 不相捨離) instead of *anyonya-vinirmukta* in the Nanjo Ed., while the third translation, the T'ang version,[43] instead reads 'neither identical nor different' (*fei-i fei-i* 非一非異; *naika-nānya*?) and connects it with *hetukriyālakṣaṇa* in the same way as the Sung version does. (This reading of the T'ang version has a certain similarity with the Tibetan translation from the Sanskrit original, which reads *gcig dang tha dad pa las rnam par grol ba = eka-anya-vinirmukta = ananyānyavinirmukta*?)[44]

Now, a very interesting fact is observed here. Namely, there is a fine equivalence between the Wei version and P on the one hand and the T'ang version and Ś on the other, the former group using the term 'inseparable from each other', while the latter group uses the term 'neither identical nor different' instead.

What conclusion could be drawn out from this fact? There are

41. *Leng-ch'ieh a-pa-t'o-lo pao-ching*, T. no. 670, vol. 16, p. 414a16-19.
42. *Ju leng-ch'ieh ching*, T. no. 671, vol. 16, p. 523a23-25.
43. T. no. 672, vol. 16, p. 594b19-22.
44. Peking Ed., no. 775, Kanjur Nu, 79a2-3; Reprint Ed., vol. 29, p. 33, 5.1-2. Cf. Peking Ed., no. 776 (translated from the Sung version of the *Laṅkāvatāra*), Nu 218a7-218b1; Reprint Ed., vol. 29, p. 89, 4.7-5.1. (The passage in question reads: *rgyu dang bya ba'i mtshan nyid tha dad pa dang tha dad ma yin pa gcig tu 'dres pa*.)

various possibilities, including a change of reading in the Sanskrit original of the *Śraddhotpāda* in accordance with that in the *Laṅkāvatāra*, but most probably it shows the simple fact that Ś borrowed the terms from the T'ang version of the *Laṅkāvatāra* for revision of the text in accordance with the introduction of the Vijñānavāda. Unfortunately, Ś applied this new term (i.e., 'neither identical nor different') so widely beyond its doctrinal limitations that doubt about its genuineness was produced among us.

PART III
TECHNICAL TERMS AND BASIC CONCEPTS OF THE *TATHĀGATAGARBHA* THEORY

The "Tathāgatôtpattisaṃbhava-nirdeśa" of the *Avataṃsaka* and the *Ratnagotravibhāga*: With Special Reference to the Term *Tathāgata-gotra-saṃbhava* (如來性起)*

The point I wish to make here is the discovery of the use of the compound noun *tathāgata-gotra-saṃbhava* in the *Ratnagotra-vibhāga* (*RGV*; *Uttaratantra*), which seems to be the original Sanskrit for 如來性起, one of the important terms in the philosophy of the Hua-yen 華嚴 sect of Chinese Buddhism, but is actually not found in the *Avataṃsaka*, the basic scripture of that sect.

The passage where this term is found is in the prose explanation of v. 27 of chap. I (Skt., p. 26.8-9). The commentator of the *RGV*, i.e., the author of the supplementary verses as well as the prose commentary on the basic verses,[1] refers there to the three meanings of the term *tathāgatagarbha* given in v. 27, of which the third is *tathāgata-gotra-saṃbhava-artha*, while the other two are *tathāgata-dharmakāya-parispharaṇa-artha* and *tathāgata-tathatā-avyatibheda-artha*. V. 27, the basic stanza for which this explanation is given, runs as follows:

buddha-jānântargamāt sattva-rāśes
tan-nairmalyasyâdvayatvāt prakṛtyā /
bauddhe gotre taṭ-phalasyôpacārād
uktāḥ sarve dehino buddha-garbhāḥ //

(The multitudes of living beings are included in the

* First published in *JIBS* 7-1 (1958), pp. 348–343.

1. For the textual structure of the *RGV*, see my article "Kugyōichijō hōshōron no kōzō to genkei" 究竟一乘實性論の構造と原型 [Textual structure of the *Ratnagotravibhāga* (*Uttaratantra*) and the supposed form of its original text], *Shūkyō Kenkyū* [Journal of Religious Studies] 155 (1958).

Buddha's Wisdom,
Their immaculateness is non-dual by nature,
Its result manifests itself in the Germ of the Buddha;
Therefore it is said: all living beings are possessed of the Matrix of the Buddha.)

The three meanings mentioned above correspond one by one to the first three lines in the verse which form the three reasons for the statement "*sarvasattvās tathāgatagarbhāḥ*." At the same time, the commentator regards these three points as the threefold own-nature of the Essence of the Tathāgata (*tathāgata-dhātos trividhaḥ svabhāvaḥ*). In other words, *dharmakāya*, *tathatā* and *gotra* are said to show the three aspects of *tathāgata-dhātu*. This is explained once as 'powerfulness' (*prabhāva*), 'identity' (*ananyathābhāva*) and 'being moist' (*snigdhabhāva*) with similes of a jewel, sky and water respectively (p. 27.1-11). A further detailed explanation is given in the commentary on the nine illustrations on how the Essence is polluted by the covers of defilements based upon the *Tathāgatagarbha-sūtra*, where the nine modes of *dhātu*, corresponding to the nine kinds of defilements, are summarised into the said threefold own-nature in the following way:

1. *dharmadhātu*, 2 & 3. *tan-niṣyanda* —— I. *dharmakāya* (vv. 145–7)
4. *tathatā* (*suvarṇavat*) —— II. *tathatā* (v. 148)
5. *prakṛtistha-gotra*, 6. *samudānīta-gotra*, 7. *svabhāva-*, 8. *saṃbhoga-* & 9. *nirmāṇa-kāya* —— III. *gotra* (vv. 149–152)

Now, special attention is to be paid to the third group. In the prose commentary which follows vv. 149–152 (p. 72.7-14), this *gotra* is explained as *trividha-buddhakāya-utpatti-gotra* since Tathāgatahood is manifested (*prabhāvita*) in the form of the triple Body of the Buddha, for whose acquisition the cause (*hetu*) is the Essence (*dhātu*) of the Tathāgata. Here we know that *gotra*, being synonymous with *dhātu* (and *garbha*, too), is used in the sense of *hetu* from which the triple *buddhakāya* originates. This is exactly what is meant by the third line of v. 27, and is also identical with what is signified by *ratna-gotra* in the title (= *gotraṃ ratna-trayasya*, v. 24; that from which the *ratna-traya* originates, *-sargako yataḥ*, v. 23; *ratna-traya* = *buddha-ratna*, par excellence = *dharmakāya*, the basis of the triple *kāya*, p. 7, etc.). An important authority for this statement is sought in a scriptural passage, which runs as follows:

> *tatra ca sattve tathāgata-dhātur utpanno garbhagataḥ saṃvidyate, na ca te sattvā buddhyante.*
>
> (And now, in every living being, there exists the Essence of the Tathāgata arisen, in the form of an embryo. But these living beings do not know about it.)

Unfortunately we have not yet come to know the name of this scripture, but it seems no doubt to be a sūtra belonging to the same group as the *Tathāgatagarbha-sūtra*. Here the term *dhātu* is used instead of *gotra* in the *RGV*, but the significance is exactly the same as the latter in its content: *sattve utpanno*, but *garbha-gataḥ*. It means that *gotra* or *dhātu* is on the one hand identical with *dharmakāya*, the essence of the Buddha, but is on the other hand *garbha-gata*, i.e., in an unmanifested state in contrast with the *dharmakāya*'s being the manifested state in the form of *tri-vidha-buddhakāya*.

Then what does the term *saṃbhava* mean? From the explanations given above, terms like *sarga*, *utpatti*, *upacāra*, *prabhāvita*, and *utpanna* are to be noticed for their synonymous sense of 'manifestation (origination)' for *saṃbhava* or 'manifested' for *saṃbhūta*. There are, however, two usages of this 'manifestation': 1) *sattva* is a manifestation of *dhātu* or *gotra* being 'essence', i.e., *dharmakāya*, because of his being penetrated by the latter; and 2) *buddhakāya* is the manifestation of *gotra* within *sattva* being the 'cause' for it. The second point is just what is meant by *gotra-*

saṃbhava as the third aspect of *tathāgata-garbha*, and hence this compound is to be resolved into *gotrāt saṃbhavaḥ* (origination from cause) in its literal sense. At the same time, because of the essential identity between both cause and result (this is shown by the second aspect, *tathatā*: *tathāgatagarbha* = *samalā tathatā*, while *dharmakāya* = *nirmalā tathatā*), it means *gotrasya saṃbhavaḥ*, i.e., manifestation of *gotra* itself. Furthermore, *gotra*, being *dharmakāya*, is all-pervading, and hence this manifestation takes place in *gotra* itself, i.e., *gotre saṃbhavaḥ*.

This interpretation seems, however, not to have been accepted by either the Tibetan or the Chinese translations of the *Ratnagotravibhāga*. They translate *saṃbhava* as 'existence' (Tib. *yod pa*, Ch. 有). This is not completely wrong because the text itself refers often to *gotra-astitva* (e.g., vv. I.160, V.8), but the simple sense of *astitva* is, in my opinion, not enough here to show the connotation of *saṃbhava*.[2]

V. 27 is, according to the commentator, said to have been taken from the *Tathāgatagarbha-sūtra* as a whole. The very sūtra which consists merely of nine illustrations of the *tathāgata-garbha* expresses its fundamental idea in the first illustration, a Buddha sitting in the interior of every lotus flower:

> With the Buddha's eyes, I observe that all living beings, though they are among the defilements of hatred, anger and ignorance, have the Buddha's Wisdom, Buddha's Eye, Buddha's Body sitting firmly in the form of meditation. — Thus, in spite of their being covered with defilements, transmigrating from one path (*gati*) to another, they are possessed of the Matrix of the Tathāgata, endowed with

2. There is another passage where the term *gotra-saṃbhava* is used: *na khalu kaścit prakṛti-viśuddha-gotra-saṃbhavād atyantaviśuddhi-dharmā bhavitum arhati* (p. 37.3-4). Here both interpretations seem possible: existence of *gotra* = manifestation of *gotra* (in everybody) (manifestation in the sense of 1)).

> virtues, always pure, and hence are not different from me. — Having thus observed, the Buddha preached the doctrine in order to remove the defilements and manifest the Buddha-nature (within living beings).[3] (abridged translation from Ch., T. 16, p. 457c)

It may be easy to pick up the three points taught in the *Ratnagotravibhāga* from this passage. One may at the same time easily notice, at one glance of this passage, the similarity of the idea with that taught in the "Tathāgatôtpattisaṃbhava-nirdeśa" of the *Avataṃsaka* by means of the simile of an atom which encloses the whole universe.

This simile, being the tenth illustration of the mental activity (*manas-karman*) of the Tathāgata which, in turn, forms the fourth mode (*lakṣaṇa*) of the tenfold manifestation of the Tathāgata (*tathāgata-utpatti-saṃbhava*) (如來性起十相), has an important significance in this sūtra. The mental activity, otherwise called *cittôtpatti* according to the Tibetan version (*thugs skye ba*), is understood to be essentially the activity of *tathāgata-jñāna*, which is brilliant like the sun, all-pervading like space, and is so essential that without it there is no *bodhi*, nor *buddha*. This being so, this *tathāgata-jñāna* is duly termed *tathāgata-gotra* or *-dhātu*, the Essence of the Tathāgata. Because of its all-pervadingness, every *sattva* is understood to be penetrated by this *jñāna* or to be within this *jñāna* (*buddhajñānântargama*). The *Avataṃsaka* refers to this point and says:

> Just as the whole universe is enclosed within an atom and became useless, similarly the *tathāgata-jñāna* is uselessly enclosed within each *sattva*. Due to attachment to misconceptions, *sattva*s remain without knowing what is inside.

3. For the last phrase, 'to manifest the Buddha-nature' (顯現佛性), Tib. instead reads: *de bsgrubs paḥi de bshin gśegs pa rnams ni yaṅ dag pa ñid du gnas so* (having completed this, the Tathāgatas establish themselves perfectly) (Peking Ed., Kj. Mdo Shu, p. 263a1).

> Now I (= the Buddha) will break the covering of bondage and let them know the *tathāgata-jñāna* within them. (abridged translation from the quotation in the *RGV*, pp. 22.10–24.8)[4]

There is, however, no use of the term *tathāgatagarbha* in the *Avataṃsaka*. It was probably the *Tathāgatagarbha-sūtra* that for the first time called this *buddhajñāna* within living beings *tathāgata-garbha*, following the idea of the "Tathāgatôtpattisaṃbhava-nirdeśa." The unknown sūtra of which a passage is quoted above seems also a successor to the same sūtra. And lastly the *RGV* systematised this *tathāgatagarbha* theory as a whole, concentrating its basic point in this idea of the all-pervadingness of *buddhajñāna*. V. 27 is the verse expressing this fundamental idea deriving from the *Avataṃsaka*.

Now we have to find out the relationship between the two terms *tathāgata-utpatti-saṃbhava* and *tathāgata-gotra-saṃbhava*. The former is, needless to say, the fundamental idea in the said sūtra of the same title, of which one aspect is expressed by the all-pervadingness of *tathāgata-jñāna*. In that sūtra, *tathāgata* always means the *dharmakāya*, and its *saṃbhava* (or *utpatti*) signifies the manifestation of all kinds of the Buddha's activity as the natural outflow of the *dharmakāya* caused by the Buddha's great compassion towards *sattva*s. This is, however, a kind of Mahāyānist modification of the idea taught since the early days of Buddhism in which the acquisition of enlightenment by Śākyamuni is meant by the term *tathāgata-utpatti*. In other words, *tathāgata-utpatti* is understood originally to mean the acquisition of wisdom by a unique personality (cf. Pāli AN I.13, "Ekapuggala-vaggo"). From the Mahāyānist standpoint, the possibility of enlightenment

4. The *RGV* quotes the entire illustration as an authority for the identification of *tathāgatagarbha* with *tathāgata* because of its endowment of virtues identical to those of the Buddha. For the original in the *Avataṃsaka*, see T. 9, pp. 623c–624a.

by all *sattva*s is emphasised, and to prove this possibility the *Avataṃsaka* developed the doctrine of the *dharmakāya*'s manifestation in all living beings. Thus the *buddha-jñāna* in each *sattva* is called a form of *tathāgata-saṃbhava*. This second kind of *tathāgata-saṃbhava* is easily replacable by the term *gotra-saṃbhava* or *dhātur utpannaḥ*, although this was not actually done in the *Avataṃsaka*. The role of the *RGV* was to resolve this knot kept unrevealed. It referred to this *buddhajñāna* in each *sattva* directly as *gotra* and characterised it as the cause of the actual manifestation of the Buddha (*buddhakāya-utpatti* = *tathāgata-utpatti* or *-saṃbhava*). In other words, *tathāgata* is the result of *gotra-saṃbhava*, i.e., the acquisition of *bodhi* by any one of the *sattva*s. This may be called the third interpretation of the term *tathāgata-utpatti-saṃbhava* but with the special sense of *gotra-saṃbhava*. It is certain that this interpretation was introduced into China along with the *Avataṃsaka-sūtra* when the Chinese Hua-yen sect established its *hsing-ch'i* 性起 theory.

The Description of Ultimate Reality by Means of Six Categories in Mahāyāna Buddhism*

To describe the characteristics of the *tathāgatagarbha* (the matrix of the Tathāgata, i.e., the Buddha's nature), the *Ratnagotravibhāga* (*RGV*) uses in chap. I the following ten categories: namely, (1) *svabhāva*, (2) *hetu*, (3) *phala*, (4) *karman*, (5) *yoga*, (6) *vṛtti*, (7) *avasthāprabheda*, (8) *sarvatraga*, (9) *avikāra*, and (10) *asaṃbheda*. Similar terms are used in chap. II as categories for describing ultimate reality, i.e., the *phala* aspect of the *tathāgatagarbha*. Of its eight categories in all, the first six categories are the same as those used in chap. I, i.e., (1) *svabhāva* to (6) *vṛtti*, while the remaining two are (7) *nitya* and (8) *acintya*.

As for the ten categories in chap. I, the *RGV* says in the commentary that there is a (tenfold) category by which all kinds of explanations of the meaning of the *tathāgatagarbha* exist (i.e., are made) with no variance anywhere in the scriptures.[1] After a brief explanation of the threefold meaning of the term *tathāgatagarbha* made on the basis of v. I.27,[2] the statement mentioned above probably means that these ten categories are commonly used in the scriptures for describing the *tathāgatagarbha*, while the threefold meaning is unique to the *RGV*.

This statement, however, needs to be corrected to some extent

---

* Originally published in *JIBS* 9-2 (1961), pp. 740–731.

1. *yenârthena sarvatrâviśeṣena pravacane sarvâkāraṃ tad(= tathāgatagarbha)-arthasūcanaṃ bhavati tad api…* (*RGV*, p. 26.10-11).

2. *RGV*, p. 26.5-10. The three meanings are: *dharmakāyaparispharaṇârtha*, *tathatâvyatirekârtha*, and *gotrasaṃbhavârtha*. On this threefold meaning, see my article "The 'Tathāgatôtpattisaṃbhava-nirdeśa' of the *Avataṃsaka* and the *Ratnagotravibhāga*: With Special Reference to the Term *Tathāgatagotra-saṃbhava* (如來性起)" [pp. 201–207 above].

by the following descriptions in the same *RGV*. Namely, after explaining the sixth category, *vṛtti*, the commentary says:

> After this passage, with reference to this very category of *vṛtti*, the other (remaining) four categories are to be known through separate explanations.[3]

And also:

> All those teachings on immaculate Ultimate Reality (*anāsravadhātu*) taught by the Lord in detail through various forms of doctrines are condensed in brief into these six categories, i.e., *svabhāva, hetu, phala, karman, yoga* and *vṛtti*.[4]

What we come to know from these passages is that a set of categories that is commonly used and hence the basic one is not all of the ten categories, but the first six categories beginning with *svabhāva*, and that the object to which this set of six categories is applied is not the *tathāgatagarbha* alone, but Ultimate Reality in any aspect, inclusive of the aspect of *tathāgatagarbha*, and thirdly that the *RGV* added four categories to the regular set in order to explain the mode of manifestation (*vṛtti*) of the *tathāgatagarbha*. This is proven from the use of the same set of categories in chap. II, where the seventh and eighth categories are said to be included in the sixth, *vṛtti*,[5] as showing special characteristics of the *vṛtti* aspect of Ultimate Reality characterised as *bodhi* or *āśraya-parivṛtti*.

Then how is this set of six categories used in the scriptures (*pravacana*) and what is meant by the term *pravacana*?

First, we shall see how it is applied in the basic verses (*śloka*)

---

3. *ataḥ paraṃ etam eva vṛttyartham ārabhya tadanye catvāro 'rthāḥ prabhedanirdeśād eva veditavyāḥ* (*RGV*, p. 40.5-6).

4. *ye kecid anāsravadhātunirdeśe nānādharmaparyāyamukheṣu bhagavatā vistareṇa nirdiṣṭāḥ sarve te ebhir eva samāsataḥ ṣaḍbhiḥ svabhāva-hetu-phala-karma-yoga-vṛttyarthaiḥ saṃgṛhītāḥ....* (*RGV*, p. 40.12-14).

5. *tribhir gāmbhīryaudāryamāhātmyaprabhāvitair buddhakāyair nityam ā bhavagater acintyena prakāreṇa vartanaṃ vṛttiḥ* (*RGV*, p. 79.16-18).

of the *RGV*.

sadā prakṛty-asaṃkliṣṭaḥ śuddharatnâṃbarâmbuvat / ...... (1)
dharmâdhimukty-adhiprajñā-samādhi-karuṇânvayaḥ //
(v. I.30) .... (2)
śubhâtmasukhanityatva-guṇapāramitā-phalaḥ /[6] .... (3)
duḥkhanirvic-chamaprāpticchandapraṇidhi-karmakaḥ //
(I.35).............. (4)
mahôdadhir ivā 'meyaguṇaratnâkṣayâkaraḥ /
pradīpavad anirbhāgaguṇayukta-svabhāvataḥ // (I.42)..... (5)
pṛthagjanārya-saṃbuddha-tathatâvyatirekataḥ / .... (6)
sattveṣu jinagarbho 'yaṃ deśitas tattvadarśibhiḥ // (I.45)

(Being always undefiled by nature, like the pure [character] of a treasure, the sky and water:

Following after faith in the [Mahāyāna] doctrine, the excellent intellect, Meditation and Compassion: ——

Having the climax of qualities with respect to purity, unity, happiness and eternity as its result;

Having aversion of Suffering and desire for and vow to the attainment of Quiescence as its functions; ——

Being, like an ocean, an imperishable receptacle of treasures of innumerable qualities,

As being by nature united with its properties inseparably, as a lantern [is inseparable from its light and so on]; ——

And as its [various manifestations in the forms of] ordinary beings, the sages and the Buddhas are not differentiated from Reality,

[There exists] this Matrix of the Victor (= Tathāgata) among living beings; ——

Thus is taught by those who perceived the Truth.)

These four verses, though they are interrupted by commentarial passages, were no doubt composed in a series, whose subject

6. *-tā phalam /* in the text. The reason for my correction will be given below.

word is *jinagarbha* in the last verse[7] and in which is applied a mode of the set of six categories previously known to the author.

A quite similar application of the same mode of description in a series of verses is found in the *Mahāyānasūtrâlaṃkāra* (*MSA*).

sarvadharmadvayâvara-tathatāviśuddhi-lakṣaṇaḥ /
vastujñāna-tadālamba-vaśitâkṣaya-lakṣaṇaḥ // (v. IX.56) (1)
sarvatas tathatājñāna-bhāvanā-samudāgamaḥ / .... (2)
sarvasatva-dvayâdāna-sarvathâkṣayatā-phalaḥ //[8] (IX.57) (3)
kāyavākcittanirmāṇa-prayogôpāya-karmakaḥ / .... (4)
samādhi-dhāraṇī-dvāradvayâmeya-samanvitaḥ // (IX.58) (5)
svabhāva-dharmasaṃbhoga-nirmāṇair bhinnavṛttikaḥ / ... (6)
dharmadhātuviśuddho 'yaṃ buddhānāṃ samudāhṛtaḥ //
(IX.59)

(Its characteristic is the purification of the two kinds of obscurations with regard to the Reality of all phenomena,
And is the inexhaustible controlling power over knowledge of the nature and object of its cognition; ——
It has originated from the practices of wisdom with regard to Reality in all respects;
It is the result of the inexhaustible formation of the two (i.e., benefit and happiness) by all possible means for the sake of all living beings; ——
Its function is the transformation of body, speech and mind as the means of application;
It is endowed with the gates of meditation and mystical formulae and with the immeasurable accumulation of the two (i.e., bliss and wisdom); ——
It manifests itself variously by the Body of its own essence, by that of Enjoyment of the doctrine, and by that of

7. Being appositional to *jinagarbho 'yaṃ*, the reading *-pāramitā-phalaḥ* as a *bahuvrīhi* compound should be accepted. See note 6.

8. ...*tā phalam* / in the text has been corrected for the same reason as above. See also Tib., which has *ḥbras bu can*.

incarnation: ——

[Thus] is explained this immaculate Ultimate Reality of the Buddhas.

These four verses in a series are said to be the *śloka*s on the topic of *dharmadhātuviśuddhi*, which is, at the same time, like *jinagarbha* in the example in the *RGV*, the subject word of the whole sentence.

Thus in their application of the same mode of description, the *RGV* and *MSA* show a close interrelationship, and as the *RGV* quotes the *MSA* in its commentary, there is no doubt that it was the *RGV* that imitated the *MSA*. This is especially certain regarding chap. II of the *RGV*, which, though there is no example of the application of the same mode in a series of verses as above, has many traces of the influence of the *MSA* in its doctrines (e.g., the triple *kāya* theory, *avikalpajñāna* and *tatpṛṣṭhalabdha*, etc.).[9]

But the *MSA* cannot claim originality in the use of the six categories, because according to Prof. Nishio's information,[10] almost

9. The same can possibly be said about the commentarial passage in chap. I, but, as for the *śloka*s or basic verses in chap. I, the influence of the *MSA* is scarcely observed except for the application of the six categories mentioned above.

10. Kyōyū Nishio, *Butchikyōron no kenkyū* [Studies on the *Buddhabhūmi-sūtra* and the *Buddhabhūmi-vyākhyāna*; Studies, translation and Tibetan texts], 2 vols. (Nagoya, 1940). The following is a comparison of the four verses of the *BBS* and *MSA* in their Tib. versions.

BBS (Nishio's text, p. 23)	*MSA* (Peking Ed., Mdo-'grel, Phi, 12b2-5; repr., vol. 108, p. 7)
/ chos rnams kun gyi de bshin ñid /	*/ chos rnams kun gyi de bshin ñid /*
/ sgrib gñis ldan dag mtshan ñid can /	*/ sgrib gñis dag paḥi mtshan ñid can /*
/ dngos po śes pa de dmigs pa /	*/ dṅos po śes pa de la dmigs /*
/ dbaṅ tshad mi śes mtshan ñid can //	*/ dbaṅ zad mi śes mtshan ñid do //*
/ de bshin ñid śes thams cad nas /	*/ de bṣhin ñid śes thams cad nas /*
/ bsgoms la yaṅ dag ḥgrub pa can /	*/ bsgoms pa las ni yaṅ dag ḥbyuṅ /*
/ sems can kun la gñis bskyed pa /	*/ sems can kun la rnam kun tu /*
/ rnam kun mi bzad ḥbras bu can //	*/ gñis bskyod mi zad ḥbras bu can //*

the same verses as in the *MSA* mentioned above are found in the *Buddhabhūmisūtra* (*BBS*) towards the end of the text as a kind of concluding verses. Also there are other passages in the *MSA* where the doctrines taught in the *BBS* are summarised, and hence originality would seem better ascribed to the *BBS*.

It is, however, still difficult to regard the *BBS* as the only source of the set of six categories. The *Yogācārabhūmi* (*YB*), in which is also found mention of the same set of categories,[11] has not so clear a theory as found in the *BBS* on the *buddhakāya* and has no exposition of the four kinds of wisdom (i.e., *ādarśa-jñāna*, *samatā-jñāna*, *pratyavekṣā-jñāna*, and *kṛtyânuṣṭhāna-jñāna*), both of which are central topics of the *BBS*, and at present we have no objective proof for determining the order of composition of the two treatises. Furthermore, also curious is the manner in which the said categories are mentioned in the *YB*. Namely, they are found in a passage where the science of grammar (*śabda-vidyā* or *vyākaraṇa*) is explained as one of the five sciences (*vidyā-sthāna*), but without any detailed comment. There seems to be no use of such a set of terms in Sanskrit grammars, although most of the terms used for the six categories are technical terms of grammar. In this respect, I suppose that the set of terms was placed, or

---

/ lus daṅ ṅag daṅ sems sprul paḥi /	*/ sku daṅ gsuṅ daṅ thugs sprul paḥi //*
/ sbyor baḥi thabs kyi las can yin /	*/ ḥbyor baḥi thabs kyi las can te /*
/ tiṅ ṅe ḥdsin daṅ gzuṅs sgo daṅ /	*/ tiṅ ṅe ḥdsin daṅ gzuṅs sgo daṅ /*
/ dpag tu med pa gñis daṅ ldan //	*/ dpag tu med pa gñis daṅ ldan //*
/ raṅ bshin chos rdsogs loṅs spyod daṅ /	*/ raṅ bshin chos rdsogs loṅs spyod daṅ /*
/ sprul pas tha dad ḥjug pa can /	*/ sprul de dag gi(s) tha dad ḥjug /*
/ saṅs rgyas rnams kyi chos kyi dbyiṅs /	*/ ḥdi ni saṅs rgyas rnam dag gi /*
/ rnam dag ḥdi ni yaṅ dag brjod /	*/ chos dbyiṅs rnam par dag par bśad //*

11. *YB*, (Tib.) Peking Ed., Mdo-'grel, Dsi, 230a5-6 (repr., vol. 109, p. 304); (Ch.) T. vol. 30, p. 361a. The six terms in Tibetan are as follows: *ṅo bo ñid*, *rgyu*, *ḥbras bu*, *bya ba* (*kriyā*), (*khad par du*) *sbyor ba* (*viśeṣa-yoga*), and *ḥjug-pa*.

rather inserted, in that passage in connection with the word *artha* (meaning) just because there was a traditional usage of these terms as a mode of description among the Vijñānavādins even at the time of the composition of the *YB*. What is meant by the term *pravacana* in the *RGV* is, therefore, not necessarily to be fixed to any special scripture or treatise, but is to be understood as 'the word of predecessors'.

Now we shall proceed to examine the extent of the application of the said categories. Besides their application to *dharmadhātu-viśuddhi*, there is another mode of application in the *MSA*. It is found in a couple of verses at the end of the work, which are a kind of eulogy to the Buddha. They run as follows:

niṣpanna-paramārtho 'si, sarvabhūmi-viniḥsṛtaḥ / .... (1, 2)
sarvasatvâgratāṃ prāptaḥ, sarvasatvavimocakaḥ //
(XX–XXI.60) ... (3, 4)
akṣayair asamair yukto guṇair, lokeṣu dṛśyase / .... (5, 6)
maṇḍaleṣv apy, adṛśyaś ca sarvathā devamānuṣaiḥ // (61) (6)

(Thou art the one who is perfect-transcendental,
Who has come out of [the practices in] all the stages,
Who has attained the highest point among all living beings, and makes them liberated; ——
And who is endowed with virtues, inexhaustible and unequalled;
Thou art perceived in various worlds and in the circles [of the assembly of Bodhisattvas through thy two apparitional Bodies],
However invisible is thy [Body of Essence] by all means to those who belong to the world of gods and human beings.)

According to the commentary, these two verses refer to the characteristics of the Buddha (*buddhalakṣaṇa*), among which we find the triple-body theory under the category of *vṛtti*.

The same verses are quoted in the *Mahāyānasaṃgraha* (*MS*)

by Asaṅga,[12] explaining that they refer to the highest qualities of the Absolute Body (*dharmakāya*), and it is commented-by Vasubandhu that "the highest" means "unique to the Mahāyāna, i.e., not shared with the Hīnayāna."[13] This seems to show that the use of this set of categories is unique to the Mahāyāna.

The third mode of application of the six categories is found in the first two of the dedicating verses placed at the start of the *Abhidharmasamuccaya-vyākhyā*, a commentary on the *Abhidharmasamuccaya* (*AS*) of Asaṅga. They run as follows:[14]

/ *rtogs pa des gnas dri med don* / .... (1)
/ *gaṅ spyod rgya mtshoḥi pha rol gśegs* / .... (2)
/ *chos kun dbaṅ phyug, bsam mi khyab* / .... (3), (4)
/ *ḥdul baḥi thabs kyis ḥdren pa can* // .... (4)
/ *gshal med legs gyur yon tan ni* / .... (5)
/ *raṅ daṅ gshan don gñis la brten* / .... (6)
/ *saṅs rgyas chos daṅ ḥphags pa yi* /
/ *tshogs laḥaṅ de phyir phyag ḥtsal lo* //

(I bow to the Buddha, and to the Doctrine and Holy Community as well, because ——
He is [by nature] the realization and the immaculate truth established by it,
Having reached the other shore of the ocean of practices,
And having [attained] controlling power over phenomena,
He leads [living beings] by skillful means and in an inconceivable manner; ——

12. *MS*, (Ch.) T. vol. 31, pp. 111a (no. 1592), 131a (no. 1593), 150b (no. 1594); (Tib.) Peking Ed., Mdo-'grel, Li, 46b3-6 (repr., vol. 112, p. 234).

13. 於大小乘中不與他共故無有上 (T. vol. 31, p. 258a). However, this is found only in Paramārtha's translation (no. 1595), and Vasubandhu's authorship is somewhat doubtful.

14. *AS Vyākhyā*, Peking Ed., Mdo-'grel, Śi, 143b3-5 (repr., vol. 113, p. 141). Cf. T. vol. 31, p. 694b: 諸會眞淨究竟理　超聖行界昇彼岸　證得一切法自在 善權化導不思議　無量稀有勝功德　自他竝利所依止　敬禮如是大覺尊　無等妙法諸聖衆.

He is endowed with immeasurable and marvellous qualities,
And is the foundation of the benefits of his own and of others.)

Commenting on these verses himself, the commentator[15] says that by the first two verses there are shown the six categories with respect to the excellent qualities of the Buddha, i.e., the categories of *svabhāva*, *hetu*, etc.[16] This explanation is exactly in line with the *MS*.

Through the above examination we have got, I think, a fairly good account of the idea of the six categories and their applications to Ultimate Reality, however it may be called, in treatises of the Vijñānavāda. Before concluding this investigation, I must lastly refer to the *Abhidharmasamuccaya*, in which there is an explanation of this set of categories as one of the seven methods for interpreting a topic of discussion (*sāṃkathya-viniścaya*) under the name of *artha-viniścaya*.[17]

The *Abhidharmasamuccaya* is a kind of classified lexicon of technical terms of the Mahāyāna Abhidharma, i.e., the works of the Yogācāra school or the Vijñānavādins. It is divided into two parts, one a collection of terms concerning phenomena (*lakṣaṇa*), the other of terms concerning interpretation (*viniścaya*), and the "Sāṃkathya-viniścaya" is the last of the four chapters belonging to the latter part. Being thus situated, and in comparison with the other six methods, i.e., commentary (*vyākhyā*), exhibition of difference (*prabhidyasaṃdarśana*), questioning (*saṃpraśna*), summary (*saṃgraha*), dialogue or logic (*vāda*), and implication (*abhisandhi*), this *artha-viniścaya* is clearly a mode of description or interpretation recognized by the authority of the Vijñānavāda.

15. According to Chinese tradition, it is ascribed to Sthiramati, while in Tibet, to Jinaputra (Rgyal baḥi sras).

16. *AS Vyākhyā*, op. cit., p. 144a2-3.

17. *AS*, (Tib.) Peking Ed., Śi, 344a4–345a8 (repr., vol. 113, no. 5555); (Ch.) T. vol. 31, p. 693b; (Sthiramati) ibid., p. 765bc; (Skt.) ed. by P. Pradhan (Santiniketan, 1950), pp. 102–103 (this passage is restored from the Tibetan and Chinese).

The explanation of the six categories in the *AS* is, however, unsatisfactory for us. It gives us merely the terms of three to five kinds of each category,[18] but gives no example of the application of the whole set as examined above.

Rather, it seems difficult to limit its application exclusively to Ultimate Reality, because the subdivisions of the six categories include all the varieties so that by using one of them any kind of subject, *saṃskṛta* or *asaṃskṛta*, of impure or pure character, can be described. This may be natural from a logical point of view as the terms used for the six categories do not contain any evaluation in themselves. Actually, however, there is no example of their application to any subject other than Ultimate Reality, and taking the explanation in the *RGV* referred to at the beginning of this article into consideration, we may safely say that there was a traditional use of the set of six categories among the Vijñānavādins for describing Ultimate Reality, and that the latest example available to us is observed in the *AS Vyākhyā*.

Additionally, I will offer some cursory observations on the modified use of this set of categories in works belonging to the so-called Tathāgatagarbha theory. The *RGV*, though it was written by one of the Vijñānavādins (this may be certain at least from his knowledge of the use of the said categories), established the system of the Tathāgatagarbha theory, and to describe its doctrine, it modified the six categories according to its own needs but without losing their original character. But this modification continued

18. (1) *svabhāva*: 1. *parikalpita*, 2. *paratantra*, 3. *pariniṣpaṇṇa*.
(2) *hetu*: 1. *utpatti-*, 2. *pravṛtti-*, 3. *siddhi-*.
(3) *phala*: 1. *vipāka-*, 2. *niṣyanda-*, 3. *adhipati-*, 4. *puruṣakāra-*, 5. *visaṃyoga-*.
(4) *karman*: 1. *upalabdhi-*, 2. *kāritra-*, 3. *vyāvasāyaka-*, 4. *pariṇati-*, 5. *prāpti-*.
(5) *yoga*: 1. *sāmūhiko y.*, 2. *ānubandhiko y.*, 3. *sāṃbandhiko y.*, 4. *āvasthiko y.*, 5. *vaikāriko y.*
(6) *vṛtti*: 1. *lakṣaṇa-*, 2. *avasthāna-*, 3. *viparyāsa-*, 4. *aviparyāsa-*, 5. *prabheda-*. (Skt. terms are acc. to Pradhan's text.)

until their character as categories of general use disappeared by the mixing or replacing of new terms that show the characteristics of the Absolute unique to the Tathāgatagarbha theory. As such examples we have the ten categories of *tathāgatabodhi* in the *Anuttarāśrayasūtra* (*AĀS*, 無上依經), the ten categories of *tathāgatagarbha* in the *Buddhagotraśāstra* (*BGŚ*, 佛性論), and the twelve categories of *bodhicitta* in the *Dharmadhātvaviśeṣaśāstra* (*ḌAŚ*, 大乘法界無差別論).[19]

19. *AĀS*, T. vol. 16, p. 470c: 1. 自性, 2. 因緣, 3. 惑障, 4. 至果, 5. 作事, 6. 相攝, 7. 行處, 8. 常住, 9. 不共, 10. 不可思惟.

BGŚ, T. vol. 31, p. 796b: 1. 自體相, 2. 因相, 3. 果相, 4. 事能相, 5. 總攝相, 6. 分別相, 7. 階位相, 8. 遍滿相, 9. 無變異相, 10. 無差別相.

DAŚ, T. vol. 32, p. 892a: 1. 果, 2. 因, 3. 自性, 4. 異名, 5. 無差別, 6. 分位, 7. 無染, 8. 常恒, 9. 相應, 10. 不作義利, 11. 作義利, 12. 一性.

(All these works are preserved only in the Chinese Tripiṭaka, and their Sanskrit titles have been restored from the Chinese.)

A Comment on the Term *Ārambaṇa* in the *Ratnagotravibhāga*, I.9*

The term *ārambaṇa* is a technical term unique to Buddhism. Being equivalent to Pāli *ārammaṇa* and classical Sanskrit *ālambana*, it is usually used in the sense of 'basis of cognition' or 'sense-object', e.g., *rūpa* as the *ārambaṇa* of *cakṣurvijñāna*, or *dharma* as that of *manovijñāna*. The usual equivalent of this term in Tibetan and Chinese is *dmigs pa* and 所緣, respectively.[1]

What I am going to examine here is whether or not the same meaning mentioned above can be applied to this term used in the *Ratnagotravibhāga* (*RGV*),[2] I.9. The passage in question is as follows:

> *tasmai dharmadivākarāya vimalajñānâvabhāsatviṣe*
> *sarvârambaṇarāgadoṣatimiravyāghātakartre namaḥ* /
> (I.9cd)

These lines, being the latter half of the second Kārikā (i.e., 'basic stanza on which the commentary is made') of the *RGV*,[3] refer to the "Jewel of the Doctrine" (*dharmaratna*) as the Truth of the Path (*mārgasatya*) by means of a simile of the sun (*dharmadivākara*, the sun of the Doctrine, or the sunlike Doctrine). The

---

* Originally published in *JIBS* 10-2 (1962), pp. 757–750.

1. As for the meanings contained in the terms *ārambaṇa* and *ārammaṇa*, see F. Edgerton, *Buddhist Hybrid Sanskrit Dictionary*, q.v., and R. C. Childers, *A Dictionary of the Pāli Language*, q.v. An etymological analysis of the term *ārambaṇa* in relation to Pāli *ārammaṇa* and Skt. *ālambana* is beyond the scope of this article.
2. Ed. by E. H. Johnston, Patna, 1950.
3. As for the identification of Kārikās among the verses of the *RGV*, see my article "The Texual Structure of the *RGV* and Its Original Form" (in Japanese), *Journal of Religious Studies* 155 (Sendai, 1958).

similarity of the Dharma to the sun is, according to the commentary (vv. I.10–12, and prose section, p. 12), to be explained in three respects, namely, 1) purity (*śuddhi*) by *vimala-jñāna*, 2) manifestation (of everything) (*vyakti*, *abhivyaktikaraṇa*) by *avabhāsatviṣ*, and 3) antidote (of darkness) (*vipakṣa*, *tamaḥ-pratipakṣa*) by *sarvârambaṇarāgadoṣatimiravyāghātakartṛ*).

Of these three, the subject with which we are concerned at present is the last one. The detailed explanation given in the commentary (*RGV*, p. 13) can be summarised thematically in the following manner.

[*vipakṣatā*] (*K.* = terms in I.9)
K. dharmadivākara = *sarvârambaṇarāgadoṣatimiravyāghātakartṛ*
(Tib. *dmigs pa kun la chags pa daṅ sdaṅ daṅ rab rib rnam par ḥjoms mdsad…*)
(Ch. 能破諸曀(or翳)障 覺觀貪瞋癡 一切煩惱等)[4]
(A) *K. timira*[5]
= *tamas* = *sarvâkāratattvadarśanavibandha*[6] (*K. sarvârambaṇarāgadoṣatimira*)
= *abhūtavastunimittârambaṇamanasikāra-pūrvikā* (I) *rāgadveṣamohôtpattiḥ* (which, in its turn, causes *karman* and *janman* to rise successively) (II)
(I) *abhūtavastunimittârambaṇamanasikāra* (= *ayoniśomanasikāra*)

---

4. Tibetan translation of the *RGV*, Tohoku no. 4025, Sde-dge Ed., 79b7; Chinese translation, T. no. 1611, vol. 31, p. 823c. The passages corresponding to those in this summary can be found at Tib. 81a4–81b6 and Ch. p. 824b.

5. *Timira* in the Kārikā stands for a) *ajñāna* or *avidyā* as the counterpart of *jñāna*, and b) *moha* as one of the three kinds of *kleśa*. Ch. translates them as 曀障 or 翳障 and 癡, respectively, although Tib., which is of quite a literal character, translates *timira* as *gti mug* as representing *moha*. Note that the sun is called *timira-cchid*, *-nāśana*, *-nud*, *-ripu*, *-ari*, etc., in the sense of 'darkness-breaker' and the like.

6. *satyadarśana* in the text (p. 12.19) is corrected in the light of Tib. *de kho na mthoṅ ba* and *tattvadarśana* on p. 13.17.

(*K. ārambaṇa*)

ye bālāḥ (Ignorants, they are ignorant of *eka-dhātu*)

1. *anuśayavantaḥ*

   (*anuśayataḥ kleśa-paryutthānaḥ*)

2. *nimitta-grāhiṇaḥ*

   abhūtaṃ (= *atatsvabhāvaṃ*) *vastu śubha-(pratigha-, avidyā-)ākāreṇa nimittaṃ bhavati rāga-(dveṣa-, moha-) utpattitaḥ.*

3. *ārambaṇa-caritāḥ* (*ārambaṇa-kurvantaḥ*)

   rāgadveṣamoha-nimittam ayathābhūtam ārambaṇaṃ kurvanti.

teṣām

ayoniśomanasikāraḥ samudācarati (= *cittaṃ paryādadāti*).

(II) *sarvâkārakleśakarmajanmasaṃkleśasamudayaḥ* (*K. rāgadoṣa-timira*)

(B) *K. timira vyāghātakartṛ*

= *sarvâkāratattvadarśanavibandha-pratipakṣa*

= (*ekadhātu-yathābhūtadarśana*)

sa (= *saṃkleśa*) *ca tathā draṣṭavyo yathā parigaveṣayan na tasya kiṃcin nimittam ārambaṇaṃ vā paśyati.*

= *sarvadharma-samatā-abhisaṃbodha*

by *samatā-jñāna* of:

1. *asato* (= *abhūta, ayathābhūta*) *nimitta-ārambaṇasya adarśanam*
2. *sato yathābhūtasya paramārthasatyasya darśanam* (*sa* [= *parigaveṣayat*] *yadā na nimittaṃ nârambaṇaṃ vā paśyati tadā bhūtaṃ paśyati.*)

= *avikalpajñāna* (*dharmakāyaprāptihetur darśanabhāvanā-mārgaḥ*)

(*dharma* as *mārgasatya* or *virāgahetu*)[7]

---

7. The *Fo-hsing lun* (佛性論, **Buddhagotraśāstra*, *BGS*) (T. no. 1610) has a similar passage to this *RGV* passage in a condensed form under the heading *virāgahetu* (離欲因) in the chapter on *yoga* (總攝) (chap. V of sect. IV) (T.

Thus we are told in these passages of the process of origination of *saṃkleśa* (*duḥkha* in general, or *saṃsāra*) and the method of its removal. What has come out of this summary is that *ārambaṇa* in the Kārikā is interpreted as *abhūtavastunimittârambaṇamanasikāra*, i.e., *ayoniśomanasikāra*, which, being a technical term in the *RGV*, is equivalent to *vikalpa* in the orthodox Vijñānavāda.[8] The Chinese equivalent of this term seems therefore to be 覺觀[9] in the sense of 'wrong discrimination', i.e., *vikalpa*, while the Tibetan version has the usual word *dmigs pa* for it.

How, then, is *ārambaṇa* able to represent the whole process contained in the compound *abhūtavastunimittârambaṇamanasikāra*? In the light of the commentary, this compound is to be resolved as "the *manasikāra* whose *ārambaṇa* is the *nimitta* of the *abhūta-vastu*," or "the *manasikāra* which takes *abhūta-vastu-nimitta* as its *ārambaṇa*." For *ārambaṇa* here, the Tibetan version has *yul* (= *viṣaya*). This may be correct, though its relation to other component words in the compound is not clear.[10] On the other hand, the Chinese version translates the whole compound as 取不實事相 虛妄分別念, and *ārambaṇa* seems to have been replaced by the verb 取 (to take). The same translation is used for '*nimittaṃ bhavati*' '*...nimittaṃ...ārambaṇaṃ kurvatām*' (不實事相), and also for '*na nimittaṃ* (*na*) *ārambaṇaṃ vā paśyati*' (不取相). In these cases the Tibetan version uses *dmigs pa* for *ārambaṇa*.

Thus the Chinese version always implies a subjective or

---

vol. 31, p. 801b). It says: 眞見暗障 (*tattvadarśanavibandha*) consists of 1. 具足想, 2. 煩惱難, 3. 業難, and 4. 果報難. Of these, 1 corresponds to A-I and 2–4 to A-II in the above summary.

8. *vikalpa ucyate karmakleśasamudayahetur ayoniśomanasikāraḥ* (*RGV*, p. 12.3).

9. 覺觀 is usually used for *vitarka-vicāra*. There are observed in the Chinese translation of the *RGV* two other cases where 觀 seems to be used for *ārambaṇa*. Namely, 1) 心所念觀 for *cittārambaṇa* (*RGV*, p. 25.2), and 2) 無觀 (without perception?) for *nirālamba* (supportless) (*RGV*, p. 110.14).

10. *yaṅ dag pa ma yin paḥi dṅos po rgyu mtshan gyi yul yid la byed pa* for the entire compound.

functional sense in *ārambaṇa*, while the Tibetan, an objective sense. From the context in the Sanskrit, however, both interpretations are not incorrect, one being an implied meaning, the other a literal translation. This relates fundamentally to the character of *ārambaṇa*. The term *ārambaṇa* is a term for all the *dharmas* when viewed as objects of *vijñāna*.[11] It is called *ārambaṇa* because *vijñāna* functions depending upon it (*ā√ramb* = *ā√lamb*, to hang down, to depend upon). Chinese 所緣 is its literal translation. At the same time, *ārambaṇa* is not a purely objective thing itself (*vastu*), but is that which is perceived in the mind, i.e., an idea, thought or concept. Tibetan *dmigs pa* has this sense.[12] And thus '*ārambaṇaṃ √kṛ* or *√car*' can be translated as 'to perceive, cognise, imagine, grasp, take in mind, etc.' Chinese 觀 (to perceive) and 取 (to take, grasp) can also be construed in this way.[13] As this function is basic to *manasikāra*, which is in turn the cause of *saṃkleśa*, the Kārikā makes *ārambaṇa* represent the whole process of origination of *manasikāra*. It was not a difference in terminology or word meaning but in contextual interpretation that caused the difference between the Chinese and Tibetan versions.

There is another question about *ārambaṇa*. It concerns, namely, the difference between *nimitta* and *ārambaṇa* or between

11. Cf. Sylvain Lévi, French translation of the *Mahāyānasūtrâlaṃkāra*, IV.1, note on *ālambana* (*Lè Mahāyāyasūtrālaṃkāra de Asaṅga*, Tome II, p. 32); Th. Stcherbatsky, *The Central Conception of Buddhism* (Calcutta: Susil Gupta Ltd., 1956), p. 81.

12. The word *dmigs pa* originally means 'to fancy, imagine, conceive', etc. As a noun it has two opposite meanings: 1) 'function of conceiving' as used for Skt. *upalabdhi* or *upalambha*, and 2) 'that which is conceived' as used for *ārambaṇa* (*ālambana*). The former is probably a derivation of the present tense in active voice, while the latter of the past tense in passive voice (like p.p.p. in Skt.).

13. Cf. note 9. 心所念觀 (that which is perceived by the mind) shows a more accurate use. But *sarvacittârambaṇavigata* (used as an epithet of *tathāgata*) may also mean *avikalpa*. In the same way *nirālamba*, being an adjective qualifying *ākāśa*, can be translated as 'inconceivable', 'invisible'.

nimittaṃ √*grah* and *ārambaṇaṃ* √*kṛ* or √*car* as observed in a sentence such as '*ṇa tasya kiṃcin nimittam ārambaṇaṃ vā paśyati*' (he perceives neither its *nimitta* nor its *ārambaṇa*). Once these two terms are combined with a singular case ending and the adjective *asat* (*asataś ca nimittârambaṇasya*). As for the function *nimittaṃ* √*grah* (*bāla*s are *nimittagrāhin*), the commentary says: *abhūtaṃ...vastu śubhâkāreṇa nimittaṃ bhavati rāgôtpattitaḥ*. It means: (to the ignorants) an unreal thing 'is characterised' by the mental mode (*ākāra*) of being pleasant due to the rise of passion. Thus this function is to be called 'characterisation of a thing by this and that mental mode' and *nimitta* has a similar character to *ārambaṇa*, being a kind of reflection in the mind, though it belongs to a thing as its feature or mark. As a matter of process, this 'characterisation' proceeds to 'cognition' (*ārambaṇam* √*kṛ*), and hence, without the former, there is no function of the latter. This may be the reason why both terms are mentioned sometimes side by side, sometimes in a compound. In this respect it is also possible to understand Chinese 取相 as a translation of *nimittaṃ* √*grah* in which is implied the next function *ārambaṇaṃ* √*kṛ*.[14]

To further clarify these points discussed above, I will consult a passage from the *Prajñāpāramitāsūtra*, which is regarded by the *RGV*'s commentator as the authority for this passage on 'Dharma as the Truth of the Path' (*sa khalv eṣa dharmakāyaprāptihetur avikalpajñānadarśanabhāvanāmārgo vistareṇa yathāsūtraṃ Prajñāpāramitânusāreṇânugantavyaḥ*, p. 13.19-20). The text of the

14. The *BGS* (see note 7) defines 具足想 (complex thought, which corresponds to *abhūtavastunimittârambaṇa* in the *RGV*) as 以隨眠煩惱爲因, 五塵欲爲緣, 不正思惟爲俱起因, 此三具足故名爲具足相 (It makes *anuśaya-kleśa* its cause, desire for *pañcârthāḥ* (?) its condition, and *ayoniśomanasikāra* its *samudācāra-hetu*. As it is accompanied by these three, it is called a complex thought). Here the attachment to objects probably signifies either *nimittaṃ* √*grah* or *ārambaṇaṃ* √*kṛ*. Instead of '*na tasya kiṃcit*, etc.', the *BGS* says 'neither 想 (*manasikāra*) nor 境 (*viṣaya*)', and comments that 境 means *parikalpita* and 想 *paratantra* (i.e., *ālayavijñāna*, *vikalpa*). Here too, either or both *nimitta* and *ārambaṇa* are implied by 境.

RGV has no quotation from the said scripture, nor does it refer to the section or chapter used as the authority. But, from the context, the section concerned is in the chapter on gratification and maturing (*anumodanā-pariṇāmanā-parivarta*), which is chapter VI in the *Aṣṭasāhasrikā* (*ASP*) for example. This chapter teaches the realisation of the 'inconceivability' (*anupalambha*) of everything as the inevitable condition for maturing towards Perfect Enlightenment (*anuttarāyāṃ samyaksaṃbodhau pariṇāmanā*), and is, according to the *Abhisamayâlaṅkāra* (*AA*) and *Āloka* (*AAA*), said to belong to the second Abhisamaya, *mārgajñatā* (Wisdom of the Path). It may well correspond to the *RGV* passage entitled *avikalpa-jñāna-darśana-bhāvanāmārga*.

The following are excerpts of passages where the terms *vastu*, *ākāra*, *nimitta*, *ārambaṇa*, etc., are used.[15]

> 1. *tatra bodhisattvayānikaḥ pudgalo yair vastubhir anumodeta* (or *pariṇāmayet*) *yair ārambaṇair yair ākārais tac cittam utpādayet, api nu tāni vastūni tāni vā ārambaṇāni te vā ākārās tathôpalabhyeran yathā nimittīkaroti.* (*ASP*, p. 332)

Here *ārambaṇa* is mentioned along with *vastu* and *ākāra*, being the concept of an object depending on which *citta* starts to function, and this mental action is called *nimittī√kṛ*. To this question, Bodhisattva Maitreya gives an answer to the questioner Subhūti with a negation, saying that these *vastu*s, *ārambaṇa*s, and *ākāra*s are 'not conceived' (*na upalabhyante*) as they are 'characterised' (*nimittī√kṛ*), that is, they are not existent in reality. Haribhadra in the *AAA*, commenting on this section, says that *ālambanāni* (for *ASP ārambaṇāni*) means '*śīlâdiskandhāḥ sarvadharmāḥ*' (all the *dharma*s grouped into *śīla* and others),[16] *ākārāḥ* means '*tad-*

15. The text used here is the *Abhisamayâlaṅkārâloka*, ed. by U. Wogihara (Tokyo, 1936), in which are combined the *ASP* and *AA*. Cf. Tib. (*ASP*), Lhasa Ed., Case 29 (brGyad stoṅ), 125a7f.; Ch. T. vol. 7, p. 791bf. (4th *pariṣat*), p. 880cf. (5th *pariṣat*) (大般若); vol. 8, p. 547cf. (小品般若), etc.
16. Viz. *śīla*, *samādhi*, and *prajñā* (Ch. 三學).

(= *alambanānāṃ*)*grahaṇaparicchedāḥ*' (kinds of their cognition), and *citta* means '*vikalpa*', the cognizer.

> 2. *yadi so 'saṃvidyamānaṃ vastu asaṃvidyamānam ārambaṇam ārambaṇī-kuryān nimittī-kuryāt, tat katham asya saṃjñāviparyāsaś cittaviparyāso dṛṣṭiviparyāso na bhavet.* (p. 333)

Here it is taught that to make an *ārambaṇa* or *nimitta* of an unreal thing or object is the cause of the three kinds of erroneous conception (*viparyāsa*), viz. that on account of *saṃjñā*, *citta*, and *dṛṣṭi*. The *AAA* comments that *ālambanī√kṛ* means 'to make the individual characteristic its sense-object' (*svalakṣaṇaviṣayīkaraṇa*), while *nimittī√kṛ* means 'to distinguish the general feature' (*sāmānyarūpapariccheda*). And further, defining the three kinds of *viparyāsa*, it says: *saṃjñā* (notion, idea) is 'of the nature of abstracting *nimitta*' (*nimitta-udgrahaṇa-ātmikā*), *citta* (mind) is '*vijñāna* which catches *ālambana*' (*ālambanagrāhaka-vijñāna*), and *dṛṣṭi* (view) is 'of the nature of distinguishing *ākāra*' (*ākāraparicchedarūpā*), otherwise called *prajñā*, which has the nature of judgement (*saṃtīraṇa-ātmikā*).

These definitions are more or less common to Abhidharma treatises[17] and are accepted traditionally. They are acceptable for the *RGV* passages, too. Thus we come to the conclusion that *nimittaṃ √grah*, being identical with *nimittī√kṛ*, is the function of *saṃjñā*, general characterisation,[18] on the basis of which there arises the function of *vijñāna* or *vikalpa* (= *manasikāra*) characterised as *ārambaṇaṃ √kṛ* (discriminative cognition), which again gives rise to the succession of *saṃkleśa*, being bondage (*vibandha*) to

17. E.g., for *saṃjñā*, see Th. Stcherbatsky, op. cit., p. 15; for *prajñā*, ibid., p. 84.

18. Its modes (*ākāra*) are said to be three, viz. *śubha*, *pratigha*, and *avidyā*. *Ākāra* here may be defined as *nimittagrahaṇaprakaraṇa*, being *prakaraṇa* of *saṃjñā*. (In the Vijñānavāda, *ākāra* is always *ālambanagrahaṇaprakaraṇa*.)

true perception (*tattvadarśana*); and that, being the object of *vikalpa*, *ārambaṇa* as used in the *RGV* has no special meaning other than the usual form *ālambana*, or *ārambaṇa* as translated into Chinese as 所緣.

Before bringing this article to a close, it may be my duty to give a translation of the Kārikā passage in question. It is as follows:

> I bow before the sun of the Doctrine
> Which, with rays of light of immaculate Wisdom,
> Destroys all kinds of darkness
> (In the forms of) passion, hatred (and ignorance)
> With respect to the basis of cognition.

(This research was partially supported by a grant-in-aid for scientific research from the Ministry of Education for 1961.)

Dharmatā, *Dharmadhātu*, *Dharmakāya* and *Buddhadhātu*: The Structure of the Ultimate Value in Mahāyāna Buddhism*

I

The fundamental structure of Buddhism may be summarized in the following way: The Buddha, having realized the Dharma by himself, preached the Dharma for the sake of others. The Dharma realized by the Buddha through introspection is said to be the law of causation (*pratītyasamutpāda*), which is explained through the Buddha's voice in the form of the four *āryasatya*s and so on.

In this structure, the ultimate value in Buddhism is fundamentally the Dharma, the truth, and the Buddha is merely a mediator who conveyed the truth to people by means of words understandable to them. As for religious feeling, however, the Buddha is considered to be the ultimate value, an object of worship, since he is the law-giver and a practical ideal in the sense that one should attain Enlightenment (*bodhi*) (i.e., become *buddha*) through the Buddha's instruction, the Dharma. Thus the Buddha is the first of the *triratna*, and the Dharma comes second, which is interpreted as the Buddha's instruction (*buddhaśāsana*), the authority of which lies in the Buddha himself. But, again, the Buddha's authority lies in the belief that the Buddha revealed the truth, and on the basis of this belief the Buddha is called *tathāgata*, thus gone or come, which is interpreted as having become one with the truth or reality (*tathatā*).

Thus the ultimate value in Buddhism is of a combined character, consisting of the subjective or practical ideal represented by

* Originally published in *JIBS* 14-2 (1966), pp. 919–903.

the Buddha and the objective or theoretical truth represented by the Dharma, both being inseparable from each other. The best formula to show this structure is found in a scripture:

> *yaḥ pratītyasamutpādaṃ paśyati sa dharmaṃ paśyati, yo dharmaṃ paśyati sa buddhaṃ paśyati* / (*Śālistamba*)[1]

II

The investigation of this fundamental structure of the ultimate value in Buddhism was a task for the followers after the death of their preceptor. But Abhidharma Buddhism was not adequate to engage in this task since it was mainly aimed at the interpretation of the *dharma*, the Buddha's teaching, which resulted in an objective understanding of the *dharma*, and the subjective purpose was neglected. The Buddha gradually became super-humanised, but the link between the Buddha and the followers was lost and the link between the Buddha and the truth was forgotten. The motive of Mahāyāna Buddhism was to recover these two kinds of links and to make the Buddha the ultimate value, which involves both subjective and objective aspects.

In the course of developing the Mahāyānistic system of thought, however, the first efforts were mainly devoted to establishing a correct conception of the Buddhist truth against the Abhidharmic *sarvadharma-asti* concept. The term *śūnyatā* was the answer, and representing *pratītyasamutpāda*, the truth revealed by the Buddha, this *śūnyatā* is called *dharmāṇāṃ dharmatā* or *tathatā*, *tattvasya lakṣaṇa*, *bhūtakoṭi*, etc.[2] Here, *dharma* in the plural means *sarva-dharmāḥ*, all things or phenomena, as defined in

1. Ed. by Aiyaswami Sastri (Adyar, 1950), p. 1. Cf. Pāli SN: *yo kho Vakkali dhammam passati so mam passati / yo mam passati so dhammam passati* /; MN I.190-1: *yo paṭiccasamuppādaṃ passati so dhammaṃ passati, yo dhammaṃ passati so paṭiccasamuppādaṃ passati* /

2. As for the usages of these terms and their interrelationship, see Prof. H. Nakamura's article in *Kegon shisō* (Kyoto, 1960), pp. 95–127, where the discussion is centred on the Chinese term 諸法實相.

Abhidharma Buddhism, while *dharma* as the truth is meant by the term *dharmatā*. This term meant originally nature or natural condition, and thus it is synonymous with *prakṛti*, *svabhāva*, etc. This meaning is common to Abhidharma Buddhism,[3] but the Mahāyānist, defining the nature of things as *śūnya* or *niḥsvabhāva*, removed the concept of substantiality from this term. A typical formula showing that *dharmatā* signifies the truth, i.e., *pratītya-samutpāda*, is found in the *Śālistamba*:[4]

> *tatra bhagavatā pratītyasamutpāda-lakṣaṇaṃ saṃkṣepe-ṇoktam / idaṃpratyatā-phalam utpādād vā tathāgatānām anutpādād vā sthitaivaiṣāṃ dharmāṇāṃ dharmatā yāvad yaiṣā dharmatā dharmasthititā dharmaniyāmatā pratītya-samutpāda-samatā tathatā aviparīta-tathatā bhūtatā satya-tā aviparītatā aviparyayatā iti //*

As can be readily noticed, this formula has its source in the Āgama of Primitive Buddhism. Namely, in the *Saṃyutta Nikāya* we find the following sentences referring to *pratītyasamutpāda*:[5]

> *jātipaccayā, bhikkhave, jarāmaraṇam uppādā vā tathā-gatānam anuppādā vā tathāgatānaṃ / ṭhitā va sā dhātu dhammaṭṭhitatā dhammaniyāmatā idappaccayatā /*

These sentences are found in a passage where a comparison between *paṭiccasamuppāda* (*pratītyasamutpāda*) and *paṭicca-samuppannā dhammā* (*pratītyasamutpanna-dharmāḥ*) is discussed, the latter being represented by each *aṅga* of the twelvefold chain of causation, *avidyā*, etc. The term *pratītyasamutpanna-dharmāḥ* is, however, nothing but a designation for all phenomena, mental and material, according to the Buddhist conception of truth,

---

3. E.g., *Abhidharmakośa-vyākhyā*: *dharmatā dharmaprakṛtir dharmasva-bhāvo dharmaśailîty arthaḥ* / (Wogihara's Ed., p. 181).
4. Aiyaswami Sastri's Ed., p. 4. Cf. *Prasannapadā* (ed. by de La Vallée Poussin), p. 40, n. 2.
5. SN II, p. 25.

namely, all phenomena make their appearance through causes and conditions.

In comparison with this Pāli passage, the term *dharmatā* in the *Śālistamba* is understood to be a term for *sā dhātu*, both being explained as *dharmasthitatā*, *dharmaniyāmatā*,[6] while *dharmāṇām* may be interpreted as *pratītyasamutpannānāṃ dharmāṇām*.

The term *dhātu*, being a derivative from the root √*dhā*, has the meaning 'that which places or sustains something (*ādhāra*)', and hence it is a similar concept to *dharma*. It can stand for *dharma* in the sense of rule, principle or truth. But the independent use of this term in this sense as observed here (*ṭhitā va sā dhātu*) is rather rare in Primitive Buddhism, and throughout Abhidharma Buddhism the concept of 'element', 'essence' or 'essential nature' is predominantly applied to this term, as observed in terms such as '18 *dhātu*s',[7] etc. In other words, it was understood as something substantial. This is probably the reason why the Śūnyavāda avoided the use of this term and accepted the term *dharmatā* instead, which is of a more abstract character in its verbal construction (*dharma+tā*).[8]

---

6. *Dharma* in these compound words may be interpreted as 'nature' (*svabhāva*). These terms are often used to show the eternity of the truth, e.g., *Saddharmapuṇḍarīka*: *dharma-sthitiṃ dharmaniyāmatāṃ ca nityasthāpitaṃ loki imāṃ akampyām* / (Wogihara's Ed., p. 51). Also noticeable is that the phrase '*utpādād vā tathāgatānām anutpādād vā* (*tathāgatānām*)' is idiomatically used when any statement concerning the truth is expressed. Examples will be seen below.

7. The Pāli commentary interprets this *sā dhātu* as *paccaya-sabhāva*. Various meanings of this term are discussed in the *Visuddhimagga* (HOS Ed., pp. 411–412). On this information, see Prof. K. Kawata's article in *Komazawa Daigaku Kenkyū Kiyō* 21, pp. 25–31. But note that *dhātu* does not mean literally *pratyaya* or *pratītyasamutpāda*.

8. For example, the use of the term *dhātu* in such an important sense is not observed in the *Madhyamakakārikā* (see index appended to *Daijō bukkyō no seiritsushiteki kenkyū*, comp. by S. Miyamoto, Tokyo, 1954).

III

It was in the sūtras and śāstras composed after the establishment of the Śūnyavāda by Nāgārjuna that the term *dhātu* recovered its place among terms which show the ultimate value in its objective aspect. A good example is found in the *Saṃdhinirmocana*:

> *de la de bshin gśegs pa rnams byuṅ yaṅ ruṅ / ma byuṅ yaṅ ruṅ ste / chos gnas par bya baḥi phyir chos ñid gaṅ yin pa de ni chos ñid kyi rigs pa yin no // (= *tatra utpādād vā tathāgatānām anutpādād vā dharmasthāpanāya yā dharmatā dhātu-sthititā sā dharmatāyuktiḥ /)*[9]

This reference is the definition of *dharmatā-yukti*, being a mode of argument in which *dharmatā* is used as *yukti* (or *nyāya, naya*).[10] But attention should be paid to the use of the term *dhātu-sthititā* (or *-sthitatā*), which seems to be synonymous with *ṭhitā va sā dhātu* or *dhammaṭṭhitatā* in the Pāli scripture. A further concrete explanation of this idea is observed in the *Laṅkāvatāra*. Namely, explaining the statement of *avacana* by the Buddha between the night of Mahābodhi and that of Mahāparinirvāṇa, it refers to the two characteristics of the *dharma* as *pratyātma-dharmatā* and *paurāṇasthiti-dharmatā*. In the definition of the latter, it says as follows:[11]

> *dharmadhātu-sthititotpādād vā tathāgatānām anutpādād vā tathāgatānāṃ sthitaivaiṣāṃ dharmāṇaṃ dharmatā dharmasthititā dharmaniyāmatā paurāṇanagarapathavat /*

And again:[12]

> *evam eva, Mahāmate, tan mayā taiś ca tathāgatair*

9. Ed. by E. Lamotte, p. 158 (Sanskrit reconstruction is my own).
10. Cf. *Ratnagotravibhāga*, p. 73 (ed. by Johnston, 1950): (*...dharmāṇāṃ dharmatā...*) *yaiva câsau dharmatā saivâtra yuktir yoga upāyaḥ paryāyaḥ / evam eva tat syāt / anyathā naiva tat syād iti /*
11. Ed. by Nanjio, p. 143.
12. Ibid., p. 144.

adhigataṃ, sthitaivaiṣā dharmatā dharmasthititā dharmaniyāmatā tathatā bhūtatā satyatā /

This *paurāṇasthiti-dharmatā* is no doubt a synonym of *dharmāṇāṃ dharmatā* or the truth concerning phenomena, which is revealed by the Buddha as *pratītyasamutpāda*. Being revealed by introspection, the same *dharmatā* is called *pratyātma-dharmatā*, i.e., '*tathāgatair adhigataṃ svapratyātmagatigocaraṃ*'.[13] This definition of the truth in two aspects is unique to this sūtra and quite important in showing the subjective-objective relationship within the ultimate value. As for the point of this discussion, notable is the introduction of the concept *dharmadhātu*.

The term *dharmadhātu* here may be interpreted as the nature (*dhātu*) of things (*dharma*), or the truth concerning things. Anyway, it is understandable in the same context as the phrase *dharmāṇāṃ dharmatā* (a *ṣaṣṭi-tatpuruṣa* compound). But the usage and definition of this term in Abhidharma Buddhism is 'the element (*dhātu*) called *dharma*' (a *karmadhāraya* compound), which, being one of the eighteen *dhātu*s, signifies the object (*viṣaya*) of *manas*, or the basis of cognition (*ālambana*) by *manovijñāna*. In a narrow sense, it excludes the *dharma*s belonging to the other seventeen *dhātu*s, but as everything knowable is perceived by *manas* directly or indirectly, all things or all phenomena could be called *dharmadhātu* when they are cognised by the mind. Thus *dharmadhātu* signifies the entire phenomenal world or the universe, i.e., *sarvadharmāḥ*. In this sense, *dhātu* may be translated as 'sphere' or 'region', of which similar uses are found in such terms as *lokadhātu, traidhātuka*, etc.

Thus *dharmadhātu* has two characteristics, one being *dharmatā*, i.e., the law of *pratītyasamutpāda*, and the other being *sarvadharmāḥ*, i.e., the entire sphere of *pratītyasamutpanna-dharmāḥ*. Remarkable is the combination of the two aspects of *dharma* in

13. Ibid., p. 143.

one word, such being not the case with the term *dharmatā*. As for the term *dharmatā*, it is used for distinguishing the first aspect from the second as observed in the *Dharmadharmatā-vibhāga*, where the *dharma*s to be abandoned (*prahātavya*), i.e., those belonging to the world of *saṃsāra*, are meant by *dharma*, while the *dharma* to be realized (*sākṣātkaraṇīya*), i.e., the truth or the ideal state of *nirvāṇa*, is meant by *dharmatā*.[14] Naturally it led to the use of this term in the sense of 'logical ground' as observed in the example from the *Saṃdhinirmocana* mentioned above, such use not being found in the case of *dharmadhātu*. What is identified with *dharmatā* in this last sense is *dharmadhātu-sthititā*, but not *dharmadhātu* itself, as appeared in the example from the *Laṅkāvatāra*.

Then what is the significance of the use of the term *dharmadhātu* with these twin characteristics? It may be summed up in three points, namely, 1) the positive evaluation of *sarvadharma*, 2) the emphasis of the subjective value behind this evaluation, and 3) the reintroduction of a kind of substantial concept in its outlook. These points are inseparable from each other and were generally created by the reintroduction of Abhidharmic doctrine, but with modifications on the basis of the Śūnyavāda. As for the first point, we must remember first of all a fundamental idea of Indian thought in general that 'that which holds its nature (or quality, attribute), i.e., *dharma* (*dharmin*)', is also called *dharma*.

---

14. The opening stanza and following sentences of the *Dharmadharmatā-vibhāga* read as follows (in Tibetan): / *gaṅ phyir śes nas ḥgaḥ shig spaṅ bya shiṅ // gshan dag ḥgaḥ shig mṅon sum bya baḥi phyir // des na de dag mtshan ñid las rnam dbye // byed par ḥdod nas bstan bcos ḥdi mdsad do // ḥdi dag tham cad ni gñis kyis bsdus de / chos daṅ chos ñid kyis so // chos kyi ñe bar mtshon pa ni ḥkhor baḥo // chos ñid kyis ñe bar mtshon pa ni theg pa gsum gyi mya ṅan las ḥdas paḥo //* (ed. by J. Nozawa in *Studies in Indology and Buddhology, Presented in Honour of Prof. S. Yamaguchi on the Occasion of his Sixtieth Birthday*, Kyoto, 1955, p. 11). Cf. S. Takeuchi's article in *JIBS* 6-1, p. 205.

(It may be termed a *bahuvrīhi* concept.)[15] The definition of *dharma* in Abhidharma Buddhism is along these lines, and *saṃskṛta-dharma* (standing for *pratītyasamutpanna-dharma*) claims its reality (*astitva*) with the same right as *asaṃskṛta-dharma*, which stands for *pratītyasamutpāda*, and both kinds of *dharma* are included in the term *sarvadharma*. Thus *dharmadhātu*, being *sarva-dharmāḥ*, may represent exclusively the *saṃskṛta-dharma* as *dharmin* on the one hand, and the totality of *saṃskṛta-* and *asaṃskṛta-dharmas* on the other hand. From a practical or subjective standpoint, however, *saṃskṛta-dharma*, which represents *saṃsāra*, is denied its value and distinguished from *asaṃskṛta-dharma*, which represents *nirvāṇa*, while the latter is understood as nothingness in its content. The Mahāyānistic conception is quite the opposite in this regard. It denies the reality of *sarvadharma*, but positively evaluates the latter as expressed in the idea of the oneness of *nirvāṇa* and *saṃsāra*, by the reason that everything is nothing but a manifestation of the ultimate reality. Thus *sarvadharma* is called *dharmadhātu* because it is the manifestation of the latter. Here again we must remember the Abhidharmic definition that *dharmadhātu* is the object of the mind. By the denial of the reality of *sarvadharmāḥ*, only the mental element (*citta*, *manas*, or *vijñāna*) could remain as the reality. This leads to the idealism of the *citta-mātratā* and *vijñaptimātratā*, to which we will refer later on. In the present context, notable is that the ultimate reality should be of a mental character or of a subjective value. In other words, there is anticipated the existence of the ultimate reality of the subjective value which represents *dharmadhātu*, or the *dharmin* of the *dharmadhātu*, the truth.

As for this last point, notable is the definition of *dharmadhātu* given in Mahāyāna texts. The most common is that *dharmadhātu*

---

15. E.g., *saṃskriyate anena iti saṃskāraḥ*; *saṃskriyate etad iti saṃskāraḥ*. Cf. Th. Stcherbatsky, *The Conception of Buddhist Nirvāṇa*, p. 11, fn. 1. The same structure is observed between cause and result, means and purpose.

means the origin or cause (*dhātu* = *hetu*) of the *āryadharma*, the teaching of the Buddha.[16] It seems that here is implied the ultimate value of the Buddha over the *dharma*, since the Buddha as the *dharma*-giver is worthy of being called the source of the *dharma*. The term for the Buddha as the source of the *dharma* is *dharmakāya*. An example to show the *dharmakāya* of this character is observed in a verse of the *Ratnagotravibhāga*:[17]

> *dharmakāyo dvidhā jñeyā dharmadhātuḥ sunirmalaḥ /*
> *tanniṣyandaś ca gāmbhīrya-vaicitryanaya-deśanā //* (I.145)

Commenting on this, the text explains that the first aspect stands for *pratyātma-adhigamadharma* and the second for *deśanā-dharma*, which is the *niṣyanda* of the *dharmadhātu* as well as the cause for attaining it (*tatprāptihetu*). This explanation reminds us of the fundamental structure of Buddhism, to which we referred at the beginning. But the conception involved in the term *dharmakāya* is quite complicated, especially in its relation to *dharmadhātu*. We must further investigate this subject in the next section.

IV

The first use of the term *dharmakāya* seems to go back to Primitive Buddhism, with only one example being found in the *Dīgha Nikāya*,[18] where it is used as a synonym (*adhivacana*) of *tathāgata*.

16. E.g., *Madhyântavibhāga-bhāṣya*: *āryadharmma-hetutvād dharmma-dhātuḥ / āryadharmmāṇān tad-ālambana-prabhavatvāt / hetv-artho hy atra dhātv-arthaḥ /* (ed. by G. Nagao, Tokyo, 1964, p. 23f.); Sthiramati on the *Triṃśikā Vijñaptimātratā*: *āryadharma-hetutvād dhātuḥ / hetvartho hy atra dhātuśabdhaḥ /* (ed. by S. Lévi, p. 44). The latter refers actually to *anāsrava-dhātu*, which is in its turn almost synonymous with *dharmadhātu* as the ultimate value.

17. Ed. by Johnston, p. 70.

18. DN III, p. 84: *Bhagavato 'mhi putto oraso mukhato jāto dhammajo dhammanimitto ti. Taṃ kissa hetu? Tathāgatassa h'etaṃ, Vāseṭṭha, adhivacanaṃ dhammakāyo iti pi brahmakāyo iti pi, dhammabhūto iti pi brahmabhūto iti pīti /*

Its exact meaning is not clear, but judging from the fact that it appears together with such terms as *dhammaja*, *dhamma-nimitta*, *dhamma-dāyāda* and *dhammabhūta*, it seems to mean 'one whose body is the *dharma*, i.e., the teaching in which is combined the sense of truth'. This matches well with what we referred to above and shows its origin in the *dharmin* concept. But the Abhidharmic interpretation of this term was 'the body consisting of the five aggregates (*skandha*), beginning with *śīla*', being the nature of the Buddha, which distinguishes the Buddha from ordinary *sattva*s, who consist of the five *skandha*s, beginning with *rūpa*. On the basis of this analysis, Mahāyāna Buddhism developed this idea into the Buddha as representing the truth itself, in contrast to the *rūpakāya*, which signifies the historical Buddha but is considered to be of secondary value. Thus the *dharmakāya* recovered its original character through the efforts of Mahāyānists.

The systematic investigation of the *dharmakāya* started after Nāgārjuna, along with the introduction of the concept of *dharmadhātu*. The identification of the *dharmakāya* with the *dharmadhātu* gave the former many meanings. Among these, their identification regarding the aspect of truth may be understandable from what we observed above. One point to be noted here is that there is a kind of substantial character retained by the *dharmakāya* due to its identification with *dharmadhātu* as representing the entire sphere of *dharma*s, as observed in such a phrase as '*dharmadhātuvipula ākāśadhātu-paryavasāna aparântakoṭi-niṣṭha*', which is frequently used in the *Avataṃsaka*.[19] This idea is probably a result of the religious sentiments of Buddhists who regarded the Buddha as a universal god. Doctrinally it is interpreted as signifying the unlimited extension[20] of the Buddha's light of *jñāna* in

19. E.g., *Daśabhūmika* (Rahder's Ed., p. 14).
20. With reference to this, the character of the *dharmakāya* is often called *yāvadbhāvikatā*, while that representing truth is called *yathāvadbhāvikatā*. Cf. *Saṃdhinirmocana*, pp. 98–99; *Ratnagotravibhāga*, pp. 14–15.

time and space, of which symbolic features are the Buddha Vairocana, the Buddha Amitābha, and so on.

This last point, that *jñāna* is considered to be the essential character of the *dharmakāya*, is quite significant since it is unique to the *dharmakāya* being the subjective ultimate value and is not associated with the concept of *dharmadhātu* itself. From this standpoint, the *dharmakāya* may be interpreted as 'the Body consisting of virtuous qualities (*dharma*) acquired as the result of enlightenment (*bodhi*)'. The *dharmas* as such are generally called *buddhadharma* as used in the case of the eighteen *āveṇikabuddhadharmāḥ*. *Jñāna* is no doubt one of them and is often referred to as *buddhajñāna*, *tathāgatajñāna* or *tathāgatabodhijñāna*. At the same time it is the necessary means (*upāya*) of *bodhi*, or the cause of the attainment of *bodhi* in the sense of 'that by which is attained'.[21] Thus *jñāna* has again a dual character, means and purpose or cause and result combined in one. These two aspects of *jñāna* are referred to by the terms *prajñā* and *jñāna*, or *avikalpajñāna* and *tatpṛṣṭhalabdha* respectively. This structure corresponds to that of *dharmakāya* and *dharmadhātu* observed above, and applying the latter, *prajñā* (= *prajñāpāramitā*) or *avikalpajñāna* is said to represent the truth, *adhigamadharma*, *paramārthasatya*, *jñāna* as *svārthasaṃpatti*, of *lokottara* character, *yathāvadbhāvikatā*, etc., while *pṛṣṭhalabdha-jñāna* represents the universe or the whole entity, *deśanādharma*, *saṃvṛti* or *vyavahārasatya*, *karuṇā* as *parārthasaṃpatti*, of *laukita* character, *yāvadbhāvikatā*, etc., from various aspects, respectively.[22]

In relation to this, notable here is the idea of the threefold body of the Buddha (*trividhabuddhakāya*). As can be readily understood, the division of the *buddhakāya* into the *dharmakāya*

---

21. *prāpyate anena iti prāptiḥ* (*Ratnagotravibhāga*, p. 79). This is referred to in explaining *jñāna* as representing the *hetu* aspect of the *dharmakāya*. See n. 15 above.

22. See for example the passages from the *Ratnagotravibhāga* referred to in nn. 17, 20 and 21.

and the *rūpakāya* corresponds to the dual characteristics of *jñāna*. Namely, the latter represents the Buddha for *parārthasampatti*, giving *deśanā* for *sattva*s, based on his *karuṇā*, while the *dharmakāya* in this sense stands for the Buddha as *svārthasampatti*, whose essence is *jñāna*. This *rūpakāya* is again divided into two according to its functions, the *saṃbhogakāya* for *bodhisattva*s and the *nirmāṇakāya* for ordinary *sattva*s. There are, however, many problems concerning the *trividhabuddhakāya* in Mahāyāna texts, especially the *saṃbhogakāya*. To discuss these is rather beyond our purpose here. We will refer to just one point in relation to the concept of the *dharmakāya*.

The *Mahāyānasūtrālaṅkāra*, referring to *dharmadhātu-viśuddha*, regards the threefold *buddhakāya* as its manifestation (*vṛtti*), namely:

> *svabhāva-dharmasaṃbhoga-nirmāṇair bhinnavṛttikaḥ /*
> *dharmadhātur viśuddho 'yaṃ buddhānāṃ samudāhṛtaḥ //*
> (IX.59)[23]

The same set of the threefold *buddhakāya* is explained in the *Ratnagotravibhāga* as the manifestation of the *dharmakāya*.[24] And we know that *svabhāva-kāya* (*svābhāvika*) is a designation for the *dharmakāya* as representing the pure *dharmadhātu*. This reminds us of another pair of aspects of the *dharmakāya*, one being the truth itself and the other being the acquisition of realization, just as in the division of *dharmatā* into *paurāṇasthiti*- and *pratyātma*- in the *Laṅkāvatāra* referred to above. Also the *Buddhabhūmisūtra*, probably utilizing the verse from the *Mahāyānasūtrālaṅkāra* and its explanation of the four *buddhajñāna*s, beginning with *ādarśa-jñāna*, regards the pure *dharmadhātu* and four *buddhajñāna*s together as the five *dharma*s (elements) of the *buddhabhūmi*.[25] This seems to remove the *jñāna* aspect from the *dharmadhātu*, and this

23. Ed. by S. Lévi, p. 44.
24. *Ratnagotravibhāga*, p. 85.
25. *Buddhabhūmisūtra* and its *Vyākhyāna*, ed. by K. Nishio (Nagoya, 1940).

problem relates to the definition of the second *buddhakāya* as *dharmasaṃbhoga*. But later Tantric Buddhism regards the five *dharma*s of the *buddhabhūmi* as the fivefold *jñāna* of the Buddha Mahāvairocana.[26]

V

Now we must proceed to the last and most important subject deriving from the concept of the *dharmakāya* as representing *buddhajñāna*. This *jñāna* aspect, as observed above, is to be termed the 'result aspect' in its relation to the *dharmadhātu* aspect. From a religious or practical point of view, however, there is a quite different kind of relationship concerning the *dharmakāya*. Namely, being the *buddha*, it stands in opposition to *sattva*s, who are to be characterized as *abuddha* or *bodhya*.[27] In this relationship, the *dharmakāya* represents *nirvāṇa* as the practical goal of *sattva*s who are actually wandering in *saṃsāra*. This being so, how is it possible to find a link between both, or a character common to both?[28] In one sense this is a question of how to understand the idea of the identification of *nirvāṇa* and *saṃsāra*.

The answer is given by introducing the *dharmadhātu-sarvadharma* relationship as referred to above (III). Namely, the *dharmakāya*, being a universal entity, pervades (*pari√sphar*, or *sarvatraga*) or penetrates into (*pra√viś*) every *sattva*, or nobody exists outside the *dharmakāya*, and hence the nature of the Buddha and the nature of the *sattva* are the same. Therefore, the Buddha's nature exists in every *sattva*, the only difference being that this

26. *Mahāvairocanasūtra*. Cf. Kawata, op. cit., p. 38.
27. E.g., *abudhabodhanârtham* (*Ratnagotravibhāga*, p. 7, l. 10; *abudha* = *abuddha*); *bodhyaṃ bodhis tadaṅgāni bodhanêti* (ibid., p. 25, l. 4).
28. In Buddhist terminology pertaining to the *hetu-phala* relationship, it is called a *vipāka* relationship. Doctrinally, however, the Buddha is regarded as *visaṃyoga-phala*, while the relationship between the two aspects of *dharmakāya*, *dharmadhātu*, etc., is to be termed a *niṣyanda* relationship. The answer to this question is to interpret it as this *niṣyanda* relationship.

nature is hidden and unknown to *sattva*s. The *Avataṃsakasūtra* explains this structure of the *dharmakāya* and its relation to the *sattva* in terms of *tathāgatajñāna* with the analogy of the whole universe concealed within an atom.[29] On this basis, the *Tathāgatagarbhasūtra* calls the *sattva tathāgatagarbha* in the sense that the *sattva* is an embryo of the *tathāgata* or is possessed of the embryo of the *tathāgata* within him. The statement '*sarvasattvās tathāgatagarbhāḥ*' as the truth (*dharmāṇāṃ dharmatā*) follows on from this explanation.[30]

What is involved in this concept was previously sought for in the terms *cittaprakṛti*[31] and *tathāgatagotra.*[32] The former, standing in contrast to the concept of *āgantuka-kleśa*, reminds us of the idea of *cittamātra* in its negation of the reality of *kleśa*, while the latter, whose literal meaning is the family (*kula*) or lineage (*vaṃśa*) of the *tathāgata*, reminds us of the concept of *dhātu* as a classifying principle of groups.[33] In these respects and as the logical conclusion of the explanation given above, this *tathāgatagarbha* is duly to be termed *dhātu* in every respect. Thus the *Mahāparinirvāṇasūtra*, on the basis of the *Tathāgatagarbhasūtra*, modified

29. Quoted in the *Ratnagotravibhāga*, pp. 22–24. Cf. J. Takasaki, "The 'Tathāgatôtpattisaṃbhava-nirdeśa' of the *Avataṃsaka* and the *Ratnagotravibhāga*" [pp. 201–207 above].

30. Quotation in the *Ratnagotravibhāga*, p. 73: *yathoktam / eṣā kulaputra dharmāṇām dharmatā utpādād vā tathāgatānām anutpādād vā sadaivaite sattvās tathāgatagarbhā iti /*. See n. 10 above.

31. This idea goes back to the idea of *citta-prabhāsvaratā* as mentioned in the Pāli AN I, p. 10.

32. It often appears in the *Avataṃsakasūtra* (Tib. *de bshin gśegs paḥi rigs*). On this, see J. Takasaki in *Kegon shisō* (mentioned above), pp. 238–309.

33. Cf. *Abhidharmakośa*, I.20 (*gotra* = *dhātu*); *Bodhisattvabhūmi* (ed. by Wogihara), p. 3 (*gotra* = *bīja*), etc. The term *gotra* is often used to classify *sattva*s according to their faculties in relation to the three *yāna*s, and there is a difference of interpretation regarding this term between the *ekayāna* theory and the *triyāna* theory. The idea *tathāgatagotra* = *tathāgatagarbha* represents the former theory.

the statement into '*asti buddhadhātuḥ sarvasattveṣu*'.[34] The *buddhadhātu* (or *tathāgatadhātu*) is on the one hand, signifying the nature (*dhātu* = *svabhāva*, *dharmatā*) of the *buddha*, perfectly equal to the *dharmakāya*, but on the other hand, being the cause (*dhātu* = *hetu*) of the *buddha*, i.e., the cause from which the *buddha* arises (*buddhakāya-utpattihetu*), it is quite different from the *dharmakāya* in its status. To be more precise, it is the hypothetical Buddha in the sense that the Buddha originates from it. The aim of positing the existence of the *buddhadhātu* in all *sattva*s was nothing other than this practical hypothesis to make a link between *sattva*s and the Buddha in order to encourage them to attain enlightenment. The link between the cause and the result is the nature (*dhātu*) common to both, which is nothing other than the *dharmadhātu*. This structure of a triple relationship within the *dhātu* is called in the *Ratnagotravibhāga* the '*trividhasvabhāva* of the *tathāgatadhātu*', namely, *dharmakāya* representing the result, *tathatā* (for *dharmadhātu*) the link, and *tathāgatagotra* the cause, respectively.[35]

There is another example showing this structure of the *dhātu* in a different way.

---

34. Cf. Tib.: *ḥdi na dge sloṅ la la de bshin gśegs paḥi sñiṅ poḥi mdo sde chen po* (*Tathāgatagarbhasūtra*) *ston par byed do // sems can thams cad la ni saṅs rgyas kyi khams* (*buddhadhātu*) *yod la*... (Peking Ed., Reprint, vol. 31, p. 185-5-6).

35. Pp. 69–73. From the aspect of *tathatā*, the cause and the result are called '*samalā tathatā*' and '*nirmalā tathatā*', respectively (ibid., p. 21). Other terms to be noted in this connection are: *gotra*, *prakṛtistha-* and *samudānīta-* (for the cause and the result, resp.), p. 71 (cf. *Bodhisattvabhūmi*, p. 3); *āśraya-parivṛttilakṣaṇo dharmakāyaḥ* (*dhātu*, the cause, is meant by *āśraya*), p. 79f. For reference, a set of three terms concerning the structure of the object of faith (*śraddhā*) used in works of the Vijñānavāda will be mentioned, since it shows the same triple relationship observed here. Namely, 1. *astitva* (*dharmakāya* as *dharmadhātu*), 2. *guṇavattva* (*dharmakāya* as *tathāgatajñāna*), and 3. *śaktatva* (*dharmakāya* as *āśrayaparivṛtti*, or the result in relation to *buddhadhātu*). On this, see J. Takasaki in *Komazawa Daigaku Kenkyū Kiyō* (Faculty of Buddhism) 22, pp. 86–109.

anādikāliko dhātuḥ sarvadharma-samāśrayaḥ /
tasmin sati gatiḥ sarvā nirvāṇādhigamo 'pi ca //

The significance of this famous verse from the *Mahāyānābhidharmaṣūtra* may be clear from the above considerations. Namely, the first line shows the structure of the ultimate value in its objective aspect, the *dhātu* being the common nature of the *saṃskṛta-* and *asaṃskṛta-dharmas*, but in particular standing for the *asaṃskṛta-dharma*, i.e., the *dharmadhātu*, while the second line shows the same in its subjective aspect, the *dhātu* being the common nature of *sattvas* in *saṃsāra* and in *nirvāṇa*, but in particular standing for the former, i.e., the *buddhadhātu*. But these two lines ultimately signify the same truth, since what is meant by the term *sarvadharma* in contrast to *dharmadhātu*, i.e., *saṃskṛta-dharma* in particular, is nothing but the phenomena of *saṃsāra*.

Now we encounter another problem. The interpretation of *dhātu* as *buddhadhātu* mentioned above is actually given in the *Ratnagotravibhāga* from the standpoint of the so-called Tathāgatagarbha theory.[36] The Vijñānavāda, on the other hand, interprets this *dhātu* as meaning *ālayavijñāna*.[37] This *ālayavijñāna* is, as is well-known, a designation for *citta* given by the Vijñānavāda in order to interpret the idea of *cittamātra* on the basis of the epistemological relationship between the mind and its objects, i.e., between *manovijñānadhātu* and *dharmadhātu* in Abhidharmic terminology. This being so, it may be called *dhātu* by applying one aspect of the *dharmadhātu-sarvadharma* relationship (see III). But notable is that it is actually the principle or the cause (*dhātu*) of the *saṃskṛtadharma*, i.e., the cause for the origination of the *saṃkleśadharma* or *saṃsāra*, and being homogeneous with them, it is by nature of unreal character (*śūnya*, *niḥsvabhāva*). Therefore,

36. P. 72.

37. E.g. Sthiramati on the *Triṃśikā*, p. 37. Paramārtha, in his translation of the *Mahāyānasaṃgrahabhāṣya* by Vasubandhu, gives both interpretations side by side (T. vol. 31, p. 157a).

its relationship to the *dharmakāya* is, quite contrary to the case of the *buddhadhātu* or *tathāgatagarbha*, of a negative character in the sense that the realization of the *dharmakāya* is possible only by its negation.[38] In the case of the Tathāgatagarbha theory, such a negative relationship is observed between *cittaprakṛti* and *āgantuka-kleśa*, the latter being completely outside the *citta*. On the other hand, by involving the cause of the *saṃkleśadharma* within the *citta*, the Vijñānavāda seems to recognize this negative relationship in the inside of the *citta* as its fundamental structure.

In this respect, it should be remembered that the *dharmadhātu-sarvadharma* relationship signifies ultimately the truth of *pratītyasamutpāda*, within which the *pratītyasamutpāda-dharma* and the *pratītyasamutpanna-dharmāḥ* stand in a negative relationship. It is quite significant in this regard that the *ālayavijñāna* is said to stand for *paratantra-svabhāva*, being a term for *pratītyasamutpāda*, as one of the *trisvabhāva*, the other two being *pariniṣpanna-* and *parikalpita-svabhāva*. It is clear that *pariniṣpanna* represents the *asaṃskṛta-dharma* or *nirvāṇa*, while *parikalpita-svabhāva* represents the *saṃskṛta-dharma* or *saṃsāra*, and that, being the link between the two, *paratantra* is to be called *dhātu*, which is, in turn, nothing but *citta* itself. By regarding this *citta* as of two aspects standing in a negative relationship to each other, the verse of the *Mahāyānābhidharmasūtra* can be understood more clearly.[39]

In conclusion, we may say, as the most important point we

38. The term *āśrayaparāvṛtti* (*āśraya* for *ālayavijñāna*) implies this sense. As for the different use of the terms *āśrayaparivṛtti* and *āśrayaparāvṛtti*, see J. Takasaki in *Nihon Bukkyō Gakkai Nenpō* 25, pp. 89–110.

39. In the history of the Vijñānavāda, the *trisvabhāva* theory and the *ālayavijñāna* theory are of different origin. Their combination was probably established by Asaṅga in his *Mahāyānasaṃgraha*. The present interpretation is according to his view. But there were various opinions among the Vijñānavādins before and after him concerning the interpretation of the *trisvabhāva* as well as the character of the *ālayavijñāna*.

should never forget, that the ultimate value of Buddhism is, however it may be termed, after all the truth of *pratītyasamutpāda*, which is to be established by the negation of all *dharma*s, the negation of their reality, and that it was by the introduction of the *dhātu* aspect, be it the *buddhadhātu* or the *ālayavijñāna*, that the structure of ultimate reality as involving such a factor of negation was established.

On *Upādāna/Upādāyaprajñapti*[*]

§1. *Introduction*

The *Mūlamadhyamakakārikā* (*MK*), XXIV.18 runs as follows:

> *yaḥ pratītyasamutpādas tāṃ śūnyatāṃ vyācakṣmahe /*
> *sā prajñaptir upādāya pratipat saiva madhyamā //*

In this verse Nāgārjuna aimed to emphasize the synonymity of four important terms which elucidate the fundamental concepts of Buddhism, namely, 1) *pratītyasamutpāda*, 2) *śūnyatā*, 3) *upādāya-prajñapti*, and 4) *madhyamā pratipad*. Of these four, in contrast to the other three which were already known to Buddhists at that time, *upādāya-prajñapti* (*prajñaptir upādāya* in the *Kārikā*) seems to be a term newly coined by Nāgārjuna.[1] In spite of its importance,

---

* This article was originally written in Japanese and published under the same title ("Upādāna ni tsuite") in the commemoration volume for Professor Yoshirō Tamura on his sixtieth birthday entitled *Bukkyō kyōri no kenkyū* (Tokyo: Shunjūsha, 1982, pp. 39–52), and its English version was submitted and read at the fifth conference of the International Association of Buddhist Studies (Oxford, August 1982). The present article is a revised edition of the latter and was originally published in G. Gnoli and L. Lanciotti, eds., *Orientalia Iosephi Tucci Memoriae Dicata*, vol. 3, Serie Orientale Roma 61-3 (Roma: Istituto Italiano per il Medio ed Estremo Oriente, 1988), pp. 1451–1464.

1. This is the only occurrence of the term in Nāgārjuna's works as far as the available texts are concerned. It is, therefore, quite uncertain whether he regarded this term as a solid technical term or not. But the concept was quite clear for him, and commentators eventually made it into a compound word. Candrakīrti clearly uses this term once as a compound word: *paramagambhīrasya pratītyasamutpādasya śāśvatocchedarahitasya upādāyaprajñaptyabhidhānasya* (*Prasannapadā*, ed. by de La Vallée Poussin, p. 215, l. 1). In the light of this use, the same term in the very passage commenting on v. XXIV.18 may safely be regarded as a compound word although the editor kept *upādāya* and *prajñapti* separated (*saiva śūnyatā upādāya prajñaptir iti vyavasthāpyate* /, ibid., p. 504, l. 8). As for the possibility of making a compound by using a gerund in its first member, there is no rule in the Pāṇinian

however, this term has not been seriously studied by scholars.[2] Especially significant is its identification with *pratītyasamutpāda*, and its similarity with the latter in its verbal construction (gerund + noun) has escaped scholarly observations. I am now going to investigate this concept mainly on the basis of the *Mūlamadhyamakakārikā* and its commentary, the *Prasannapadā*, written by Candrakīrti.[3]

§2. *Upādāyaprajñapti*

First of all, let us see how Candrakīrti explained the term as used in the *Kārikā*. He states:

yā ceyaṃ svabhāvaśūnyatā "sā prajñaptir upādāya" / saiva

Grammar, but the very term *pratītyasamutpāda* is a good example in Buddhist use (cf. Wackernagel, *Altindische Grammatik*, II, i, p. 69: § 28-γ; L. Renou, *Grammaire sanscrite*, p. 87: §77. Premier membre). Also we have a compound term *upādāya-rūpa* denoting materials made out of the four material elements (*mahābhūta*): *aṣṭau dravyāni catvāri mahābhūtāni catvāri côpādāyarūpāṇi rūparasagandhaspraṣṭavyāni* / (*Abhidharmakośabhāṣya*, ed. by Pradhan, 2nd ed., Patna, 1975, p. 53, l. 1); *Mahāvyutpatti*, 1846 (Sakaki edition). Cf. Pāli *upādā-rūpa*, *upādāya-rūpa* (*upādā* = *upādāya*). A further remarkable term is the compound *upādāpaññattānuyoga* appearing in the *Kathāvatthu*, p. 45 (§§171–199), which is replaced by *upādāyapaññatti-* in the *Atthakathā*. See *PrasP.*, p. 285, n. 4. The meaning of these compounds I will refer to later on.

2. Among the few articles referring to *upādāya-prajñapti*, the only detailed investigation is found in S. Yamaguchi's work *Bukkyō ni okeru u to mu to no tairon* [Controversy between being and non-being in Buddhism] (Kyoto, 1941; reprint, Tokyo: Sankibō Busshorin, 1975), pp. 15–37 (referring to *prajñapti* in Nāgārjuna's doctrine and *vijñapti* in the Yogācāra doctrine). J. May's *Candrakīrti Prasannapadā Madhyamakavṛtti* (Paris, 1959) gives notes on *upādāya-prajñapti*, *upādāna* and other related terms, but his investigations are not linked to each other.

3. *Prasannapadā nāma Madhyamakavṛttiḥ. Mūlamadhyamakakārikā (Madhyamikasūtra) de Nāgārjuna avec la Prasannapadā commentaire de Candrakīrti*, éd. par L. de La Vallée Poussin, Bibliotheca Buddhica IV (St. Petersbourg, 1903–13) (abbr. *PrasP.*). Corrections to the text are given, whenever necessary, according to J. W. de Jong, "Textcritical Notes on the *Prasannapadā*," *IIJ* 20 (1978), pp. 25–29, 217–252.

> *śūnyatā upādāya(-)prajñaptir iti vyavasthāpyate / cakrādīny upādāya rathāṅgāni rathaḥ prajñapyate / tasya yā svāṅgāny upādāya prajñaptiḥ sā svabhāvenānutpattiḥ / yā ca svabhāvenānutpattiḥ sā śūnyatā //* (*PrasP.* 504, 8-10)

Here there is no direct interpretation of the term *upādāya-prajñapti*, but the explanation by means of the analogy of *ratha* tells us its basic meaning—viz. a concept or verbal expression (*prajñapti*) (conceived) on the basis of something (as its stuff or material).[4] Any concept has its counterpart among things material or immaterial, existent or nonexistent. What is referred to here is that of which the counterpart is regarded as other than its own substance. In Buddhist philosophy a chariot exists merely as a conceptual thing (*prajñaptitaḥ sat*), while its component parts exist essentially (*svabhāvataḥ sat*) or exist substantially (*dravyataḥ sat*).[5] In the same way Ātman or 'self' is doctrinally deprived of substantiality and is said to be merely conceptual, but the aggregates of the five elements, *rūpa* and others, are regarded as the stuff (*upādāna*) for making up this concept. This understanding is explained by Candrakīrti as follows:

> *skandhān upādāya prajñapyamānaḥ pudgala ātmêty ucyate /* (*PrasP.* 303, 6-7)

The problem is this: to what extent may things be regarded as existent merely as a concept or verbal expression? The scope of

4. The section on *upādāpaññattānuyoga* in the *Kathāvatthu* referred to above deals with the concept of *puggala* made on the basis of (*upādāya*) *rūpa* and others and discusses the characteristics of *puggala*. So the term *upādāyapaññatti* used in its *Atthakathā* should have the same meaning as this *upādāyaprajñapti* against that given in *A Critical Pāli Dictionary*, s.v., p. 494 (the concept "with reference to, accessory to."Also q.v. 'upādā-paññatti').

5. A famous example of this analogy of a chariot is observed in the *Milinda-pañho* where the passage is concluded with the quotation of a gāthā:
yathā hi aṅgasambhārā hoti saddo ratho iti,
evaṃ khandesu santesu hoti satto ti sammutīti. (P.T.S. ed., p. 28)

'*prajñaptitaḥ sat*' seems to differ in Buddhism from sect to sect, from school to school. To this I will refer later.

§3. *Upādāna*

In the previous section, the term *upādāna* was understood as the 'stuff' for making a concept.[6] Thus, the aggregates of the five elements 'taken' as the stuff for the concept of *ātman* are called *pañcôpādānaskandhas* or *pañca upāttaskandhāḥ* in contrast to *pañcaskandhas* as the elements of *dharma* in general.[7] Used in such a manner, *upādāna* is defined in the following way:

> *upādīyata ity upādānaṃ pañcôpādānaskandhāḥ* / (*PrasP.* 212.18)

This sentence is found in the commentarial passages on verse 15 of chap. X, *Agnîndhana-parīkṣā* (*ātmôpādānayoḥ* in *MK*). As is shown in the chapter title, the analogy for *upādānaskandha* is *indhana* (fuel), i.e., fire stuff, which is also called *upādāna*. (This usage is peculiar to Buddhist texts.) For example, we have the following statement:

> *tad yathâgnir upādānapratyaye sati jvalaty, upādānavaikalyān*

6. Bhavaviveka, in his *Prajñāpradīpa*, a commentary on the *Madhyamakakārikā*, when giving a definition of the term *upādāyaprajñapti*, uses *upādāna* to denote stuff in general for making a concept.

> *rten ciṅ 'brel par 'byuṅ ba shes bya ba / stoṅ pa ñid gaṅ yin pa de ni brten nas gdags pa* (*upādāya-prajñapti*) *ste / 'jig rten pa daṅ jig rten las 'das pa'i tha sñad 'dod pas ñe bar len pa dag la brten nas gdags pa yin no* // (**laukikalokottaravyavahārârthinā upādānāny upādāya prajñapyate*). (Derge Ed., Tohoku no. 3853, Tsha 230b4-5)

7. See *PrasP.*, p. 285, n. 3. In Pāli commentaries, the term *upādānakkhandha* is traditionally interpreted as 'the *skandhas* as the basis of *upādāna* (clinging)' (*upādānassa paccayabhūtā*) or 'those as the object of *upādāna*' (*upādānānam ārammaṇabhūtā*; *upādānagocarā*); also it is explained as 'those produced by *upādāna* or producing *upādāna*' (*upādānena janitā upādānajanakā vā khandhā upādānakkhandhā*). See *A Critical Pāli Dictionary*, 'upādāna-kkhandha', q.v. To this meaning of *upādāna* (clinging, attachment) I will refer later (§6).

na jvalati / (*PrasP*. 568.13; quotation from *Śālistamba-sūtra*)[8]

A similar definition is given in another passage:

ihopādīyata ity upādānaṃ karma / (*PrasP*. 576.10)

Here, again, the term *upādāna* in the *Kārikā* (*kathaṃ hi nāmôpādānam upādātā bhaviṣyati* // v. XXVII.6cd) refers to the *pañcôpādānaskandha*s, *upādāna* being *karman* (object of action) in contrast to *upādātṛ* being *kartṛ*.

§4. *Upādāna* and *Upādātṛ*

The *pañcôpādānaskandha*s are said to be the stuff of the concept of Ātman on the one hand, and those which are taken or seized by the *upādātṛ*, one who seizes, on the other. This *upādātṛ* is, in common parlance, no other than what is called Ātman; so the 'conceptuality' of Ātman, i.e., the state of being merely a verbal expression, is to be proved through the conceptuality of *upādātṛ*. Thus, the relationship between the *pañcaskandha*s and *ātman* is repeatedly discussed in the *Madhyamakaśāstra* in terms of the *upādāna-upādātṛ* relationship.

The concept of *upādātṛ* first appears in the *Prasannapadā* in a passage in chapter I, where a debate is held between the Logicians and the Mādhyamika concerning the phrases '*śilāputrakasya śarīraḥ*' (body of a torso) and '*Rāhoḥ śiras*' (Rāhu's head) (*PrasP*. 66.1–68.4). As Buddhists, the Logicians maintain that the verbal expression *upādātṛ* can be assumed even in regard to a torso as that which possesses a body as its stuff (*saśarīrôpādāna*) though there is a body only, or in regard to Rāhu, who possesses a head only. The Mādhyamika indicates the improperness of this example as an analogy for Ātman, because it is only linguistically

8. In the *Śālistambasūtra*, *upādāna* is used as an analogy for *kleśa* and *karman*, by which power the *vijñāna* in the maternal womb grows into *nāmarūpa*. See *PrasP*. 568.13-16. On its significance, see §7 below.

possible, while the Ātman, though not existent apart from *rūpa* and other stuff, still admits of its existence as a worldly convention (*lokasaṃvṛti*) on the basis of the aggregates of elements (*skandhān upādāya*). Here the difference between them is not so clear, but Candrakīrti probably wished to maintain that *ātmaprajñapti* is a kind of *upādāya-prajñapti* and hence is within the scope of *saṃvṛti-satya*, but a torso or Rāhu is not as they both are *saṃvṛtimātra*, mere convention.[9]

The main concern of the author of the *Madhyamakaśāstra* is, however, to prove the relativity or mutual dependence (*parasparâpekṣitā*) of *upādāna* and *upādātṛ*, and hence the non-substantiality (*śūnyatā*) of both. And this problem of relativity is the underlying subject throughout the text.

The discussion on the *upādāna-upādātṛ* relation begins with v. 13 of chap. VIII, *Karmakāraka-parīkṣā*, where the author insists upon the application of the same *parasparâpekṣitā* between *karma*, the work that is done, and *kāraka*, the doer, to *upādāna*.[10] Commenting on the term *upādāna*, Candrakīrti says:

---

9. See S. Yamaguchi, *Chūron-shaku* (Japanese translation of the *Prasannapadā*) (Kyoto: Kōbundō, 1947), vol. I, p. 201, n. 15. Yamaguchi's statement is based upon Candrakīrti's *Madhyamakāvatāra* VI.28 and the commentary thereon.

10. *pratītya kārakaḥ karma, tam pratītya ca kārakaṃ* /
karma pravartate, nânyat paśyāmaḥ siddhikāraṇaṃ // (*MK*, VIII.12)
evaṃ vidyād upādānaṃ vyutsargād iti karmaṇaḥ /
kartuś ca, karmakartṛbhyāṃ śeṣān bhāvān vibhāvayet // (ibid. 13)

Thus chapter VIII in general and verse 12 in particular are the general statement of the *parasparâpekṣitā** between *karma* and *kāraka* (*karmakārakayoḥ parasparâpekṣiki siddhi*), while verse 13 is the statement of the application of this principle to the *upādāna-upādātṛ* relationship (and other similar ones) concerning *bhāvas*. The actual application accompanied with examples concerning *upādāna* and *upādātṛ* starts from the next chapter and continues to chapter X and further, as will be shown below. (*The term **parasparâpekṣitā* is not recorded anywhere in the *Prasannapadā*. The present author introduced it for convenience' sake [*parasparâpekṣā* > °*apekṣin* > °*apekṣi* + *tā*, the state of being in mutual dependence].)

> *upāttir upādānaṃ / anena côpāttikriyām āha / sā ca svasādhanaṃ kartāram upādātāraṃ karma côpādānaṃ saṃnidhāpayati* / (*PrasP*. 189.13-14)
> (*Upādāna* here means 'taking'. And by this the action of taking is referred to. And this action combines *upādātṛ* as *kartṛ*, agent, and *upādāna* as *karman*, object.)

This sense of 'taking' (or 'seizing', 'depending', ' basing on', etc.), i.e., *upādāna* as *kriyā*, is grammatically more basic to the term, and in contrast to it, *upādāna* as *karman* is called *upādeya*, the object to be taken (ibid. 189.15–190.2).

The same idea is discussed in the next chapter (IX, *Pūrvaparīkṣā*) with the example of *darśana*, *śravaṇa* and other sense actions in their relationship to *pudgala*, the seizer or the possessor of these sense actions. Discussion is held with the Pudgalavādins (Sammitīyas), who maintain the pre-existence of *pudgala* without actions. The Mādhyamika objects to this view by saying that in that case the *upādānas* such as *darśana* and so on could be existent without an agent (*PrasP*. 193.11-15),[11] and concludes that, as in the case of *karman* and *kartṛ*, *upādāna* and *upādātṛ*, too, are to be relatively established (*parasparâpekṣā siddhiḥ*) and not by themselves (*na svābhāvikī*) (ibid. 200.3).[12]

To this conclusion, the opponent objects by saying that even those things, like fire and fuel, that have their own existences (*sāsvābhāvya*) can depend on each other (at the beginning of chap. X, *Agnîndhana-parīkṣā*, *PrasP*. 202.3-8). Here again the Mādhyamika maintains that the *parasparâpekṣitā* of the kind between *upādāna* and *upādātṛ* applies to the relationship between fuel (consumed)

11. *yadi manyase darśanādibhyaḥ pūrvam pudgalo nāmâsti, sa darśanādikam upādānam upādatta iti* /

12. *tasmāt karmakārakavad evôpādānôpādātroḥ parasparâpekṣā siddhir, na svābhāvikîti sthitam* //

The same is said in the previous chapter in a similar way, viz.:

tayoś côpādeyôpādātroḥ parasparâpekṣayoḥ karmakārakavad eva siddhir, na svābhāvikī // (*PrasP*. 189.4-15)

and fire (consumer), clay (material) and pot (manufacture), as well as to the *pañcaskandhas* and *ātman*, in view of a fivefold investigation of their relationship. Thus it is stated:

> *indhanaṃ punar agnir na, nâgnir anyatra cêndhanāt* /
> *nâgnir indhanavān, nâgnāv indhanāni, na teṣu saḥ* // (*MK*, X.14)
> *agnîndhanābhyāṃ vyākhyāta ātmôpādānayoḥ kramaḥ* /
> *sarvo niravaśeṣeṇa sārdhaṃ ghaṭapaṭādibhiḥ* // (ibid. X.15)

The term *upādāna* in v. X.15 refers to the *pañcôpādānaskandhas* as mentioned above (§3. *Upādāna*), while *ātman* in the same verse is explained by Candrakīrti as follows:

> *yas tān* (= *pañcôpādānaskandhān*) *upādāya prajñapyate sa upādātā grahītā niṣpādaka ātmety ucyate* / (*PrasP*. 212.18-19)

The fivefold way of investigation is, as shown in v. X.14, 1) *ekatva* of both, 2) *pṛthaktva* of both, 3) *agni* or *ātman*'s possession of *upādāna*, 4) inclusiveness of *upādāna* to *upādātṛ*, *agni* or *ātman*, and 5) vice versa. In the following passage, referring to *ghaṭa* and *paṭa*, 3) is generalized in terms of a *lakṣaṇa-lakṣya* or *guṇa-guṇin* relation, while 4) and 5) are said to be in an *avayavâvayavin* relation, and to them is added the *kārya-kāraṇa* relation (*PrasP*. 213.15-16).

The same way of investigation beginning with *ekatva* and *anyatva* is repeatedly applied to prove the relativity and non-substantiality (*niḥsvabhāvatā*) of *ātman* and *upādānas* in chap. XVI (*pañcadhā mṛgyamāṇo 'sau nâsti kaḥ saṃsariṣyati*, v. 2cd, and *PrasP*. 284.8 with quotation of v. X.14–15), chap. XVIII, *Ātma-parīkṣā* (vv. 1–2: *ekatva* and *anyatva*, *PrasP*. 341.5-7, 342.2: quotation of v. XXVII.6), chap. XXII, *Tathāgata-parīkṣā* (v. 1, *PrasP*. 431.3–436.3; vv. 8–11, *PrasP*. 439.6–444.10: *tattva*, *anyatva*, *tadvat*(*tva*), *ādhāra*(*tva*) and *ādheya*(*tva*), 439.8-11),[13]

13. *skandhā na, nânyaḥ skandhebhyo, nâsmin skandhā, na teṣu saḥ* /

and chap. XXVII, *Dṛṣṭi-parīkṣā* (vv. 4–8, *PrasP*. 574.11–578.8).

In v. XXVII.8, the author expresses his conclusion to this problem thus:

> *evaṃ nânya upādānān na côpādānam eva saḥ /*
> *ātmā nâsty anupādāno nâpi nâsty eṣa niścayaḥ //*[14]
>
> (Thus Ātman is neither different from *upādāna* nor the same as *upādāna*.
> There is no Ātman without *upādāna*. Also we cannot decide its non-existence.)

About this, Candrakīrti gives the following commentary:

> Of what is verbally expressed on the basis of *upādāna*, how can we deny its existence? Indeed a son of a barren woman, which is non-existent, is never assumed (to exist) on the basis of *skandhas* (since it is a contradiction in terms). Then how is it reasonable to say that there is no *upādātṛ* when *upādāna* exists? Therefore, non-existence is also not applicable to it (= *ātman*). And hence to decide that Ātman does not exist is not reasonable. (*PrasP*. 578.4-6)

The same conclusion is expressed more positively thus:

> *evaṃ tāvat sāṃvṛtaṃ bimbākāram upādātāram upādānaṃ câbhyupetyâpi śāśvatādidṛṣṭyasaṃbhavam pratipādya...* (*PrasP*. 591.1-2)
>
> (Even though admitting the conventional shadow-shaped *upādātṛ* and *upādāna*, still we do not fall into eternalism

---

tathāgataḥ skandhavān na, katamo 'tra tathāgataḥ // (*MK*, XXII.1)

and

tattvânyatvena yo nâsti mṛgyamāṇaś ca pañcadhā /
upādānena sa kathaṃ prajñapyate tathāgataḥ // (ibid. 8)

14. The two previous verses run as follows:
na côpādānam evâtmā vyeti tat samudeti ca /
kathaṃ hi nāmôpādānam upādātā bhaviṣyati // (*MK*, XXVII.6)
anyaḥ punar upādānād ātmā naivôpapadyate /
gṛhyate hy anupādāno yady anyo na ca gṛhyate // (ibid. 7)

and other views,...)

That is to say, both *upādātṛ* and *upādāna* are non-existent by themselves, i.e., have no own existence (*svābhāvena śūnya*) (this point is called *śūnyatā*), but they are said to exist from the worldly point of view (*saṃvṛtitaḥ*), i.e., as worldly convention and as verbal expression (*prajñaptitaḥ*) based upon (*upādāya*) certain stuff or a cause (*upādāna*, *nimitta*). This is what is meant by the term *upādāya-prajñapti*. Thus, being neither existent nor non-existent, this *upādāya-prajñapti* is defined as the *madhyamā pratipad*. From this we can know that the main theme of the *Madhyamakaśāstra* is to show the middle way of non-being and no non-being from the two standpoints of the highest and ultimate truth (*paramārthasatya*) and the conventional truth (*saṃvṛtisatya*).

§5. *Anupādāya*

The saying '*ātmā nâsty anupādānaḥ*' in the last verse mentioned above leads to another problem.

In chap. XVI, *Bandhanamokṣa-parīkṣā*, the author rejects the Ātmavāda of the opponents through discussing whether Ātman is *sa-upādāna* or *an-upādāna* when it shifts from this life to another in the course of transmigration. The author says:

> *nirvāsyāmy anupādāno nirvāṇam me bhaviṣyati* /
> *iti yeṣāṃ grahas teṣām upādāna-mahāgrahaḥ* // (v. XVI.9)
> (If someone had the belief "having no *upādāna* I shall enter Nirvāṇa, Nirvāṇa will be with me," then he would have a big false belief concerning *upādāna*.)

The second *upādāna* in the verse is commented upon by Candrakīrti as '*ahaṃkāramamakārâkhyaṃ satkāyadṛṣṭyupādānam*', namely, the attachment to the view of the existence of personality. What is rejected here is the doctrine of the Heretical or certain Hīnayānistic concepts of Nirvāṇa that there exists a substantial Self as the subject of transmigration that will attain Emancipation or Nirvāṇa after getting rid of its *upādāna*. From the discussion at the beginning of the chapter in question, we understand that *upādāna* means 'body' or 'support'. But here another meaning 'clinging' or 'attachment', a well-known meaning in Buddhist doctrine, is introduced. Actually, here *upādāna* seems to carry the two meanings of 'support' and 'attachment'. Buddhist doctrine admits the correlation between *anupādāna* and Nirvāṇa by taking *upādāna* in either of the two meanings. The same view is held by the author of the *Madhyamakaśāstra*. In chap. XXV, *Nirvāṇa-parīkṣā*, we find the following verse:

> *bhāvaś ca yadi nirvāṇam, anupādāya tat katham* /
> *nirvāṇaṃ nânupādāya kaś cid bhāvo hi vidyate* // (v. 6)
> (If Nirvāṇa is something, how could it be without *upādāna*? There is not a single thing, indeed, without *upādāna*.)

Commenting on *upādāya*, Candrakīrti says that it means '*svakāraṇa-sāmagrīm āśritya*' (depending on the totality or the congregate of one's own causes) (*PrasP*. 526.11-12).

In the next two verses,[15] the opinion that Nirvāṇa is non-existent (*abhāva*) is also rejected because, according to Candrakīrti, *abhāva* is a kind of *upādāyaprajñapti* in the *lakṣaṇa-lakṣya* relation with regard to *bhāva* (*PrasP*. 527.13–528.4).[16] Finally in v. 9, the definition of Nirvāṇa is given in the following way:

---

15. *bhāvo yadi na nirvāṇam, abhāvaḥ kiṃ bhaviṣyati* /
nirvāṇaṃ yatra bhāvo na, nâbhāvas tatra vidyate // (*MK* XXV.7)
yady abhāvaś ca nirvāṇam anupādāya tat kathaṃ /
nirvāṇaṃ na hy abhāvo 'sti yo 'nupādāya vidyate // (ibid. 8)

16. *lakṣaṇam āśritya lakṣyam prajñapyate, lakṣyam āśritya ca lakṣaṇaṃ / ataḥ parasparâpekṣikyāṃ lakṣyalakṣaṇapravṛttau kuto lakṣyaṃ bhāvam anapekṣya anityatā bhaviṣyati / tasmād abhāvo 'py upādāya prajñapyate / tatrâbhāvo 'nityatā vā bhāvam upādāya prajñapyate / kharaviṣāmādīnām anityatânupalambhāt* /

Here *abhāva* is replaced by *anityatā* (impermanence) in the sense of 'cessation of something' in contrast to the 'absolute non-existence' of horns on the head of a donkey. See Th. Stcherbatsky, *The Conception of Buddhist Nirvāṇa*, p. 194.

ya ājavaṃjavībhāva upādāya pratītya va /
so 'pratītyânupādāya nirvāṇam upadiśyate //
(When that which is moving to and fro in Saṃsāra depending on something or caused by something becomes not depending or not caused by anything, then this is indicated as Nirvāṇa.)

Here *upādāya* and *pratītya* are mentioned side by side and it is explained respectively in the commentary that this (transmigrating one) is sometimes assumed to exist depending on the aggregate of various causes and conditions (*hetupratyayasāmagrīm āśrityâstîti prajñapyate*) just as long and short, and is sometimes assumed to be originated (*utpadyata iti prajñapyate*) just as a light (is produced from) a lantern and a germ (is grown from its) seed; therefore, it is established that this (migrating one) is always assumed either on some basis (*upādāya prajñapyate*) or as originating by depending on something (*pratītya jāyate*) (*PrasP.* 529.3-6). Thus here the definitions of *upādāyaprajñapti* and *pratītyasamutpāda* can be said to be synonymous with each other as mentioned in v. XXIV.18. They are synonymous with each other in that both show the state of things, not of Nirvāṇa. The commentary defines Nirvāṇa as follows: whenever there is non-function (*apravṛtti*) of this (transmigrating one characterized as the) successive connections of birth and death (*janmamaraṇaparaṃparāprabandha*) by reason of not depending on or not being based upon (or not taking anything) (*apratītya vânupādāya vā*), this non-function is established as Nirvāṇa (ibid. 529.6-7).

There is another connotation of *anupādāya* in relation to Nirvāṇa. Just after the passage, Candrakīrti quotes a passage from the *Tathāgataguhyaka* in order to authenticate his view:

yāṃ ca rātriṃ, Śāntamate, tathāgato 'nuttarāṃ samyaksaṃbodhim abhisaṃbuddho yāṃ ca rātrim anupādāya parinirvāsyati, atrântare tathāgatenaikam apy akṣaraṃ nôdāhṛtaṃ na vyākṛtaṃ nâpi pravyāharati nâpi pravyāhariṣyati / (*PrasP.* 539.3-5)

The cliché '*yam ca rātriṃ*, etc.' is commonly used in Buddhist scriptures. In Pāli we find *anupādisesāya nibbānadhātuyā parinibbāyati*' instead of '*anupādāya parinirvāsyati*',[17] and this *anupādisesa* is replaced in Buddhist Sanskrit texts by *anupadhiśeṣa.*[18] Thus we can know that *anupādāya* means *upādānaṃ śarīram anupādāya* and signifies the Perfect Nirvāṇa of the Buddha, and that *upādāna* in the sense of *upādisesa* or *upadhiśeṣa* has a meaning of body as the remnant of attachment. And this equivalency reminds us of another connotation concerning *upādāna*.

§6. *Upādāna* to *Bhava*

In contrast to *anupādāya*, which leads to Nirvāṇa, *upādāya* is the cause of *bhava*, i.e., Saṃsāra. This is nothing but what is meant by the saying '*upādānapratyayo bhavaḥ*' in the Twelvefold Chain of Causation (*pratītyasamutpāda*). In the *Madhyamakaśāstra*, this problem is dealt with in chap. XXVI, *Dvādaśâṅgaparīkṣā*, where '*upādānapratyayo bhavaḥ*' is explained in the following way:

upādāne sati bhava upādātuḥ pravartate /
syād dhi yady anupādāno mucyate, na bhaved bhavaḥ // (v. 7)

Here by *upādāna* is meant the fourfold attachment or clinging,

17. E.g., *yañ ca rattim anupādisesāya nibbānadhātuyā parinibbāyati* (Itiv. §112). See *PrasP.*, p. 366, n. 1.

18. At the beginning of chap. XXV, Candrakīrti explains two kinds of Nirvāṇa, viz. *sôpadhiśeṣa* and *anupadhiśeṣa*, and gives the definition of *upadhi* as follows:

tatrôpadhīyate 'sminn ātmasneha ity upadhiḥ / upadhiśabdenâtmaprajñaptinimittāḥ pañcôpādānaskandhā ucyante / (*PrasP.* 519.9-10)

and of *anupadhiśeṣa-nirvāṇa*:

yatra tu nirvāṇe skandhamātrakam api nâsti tan nirupadhiśeṣaṃ nirvāṇam / (*PrasP.* 520.1)

beginning with *kāma*, as shown in the previous verse (v. 6), namely, *upādāna* in the sense of *kriyā* with the meaning of *kleśa*, defilement. And in relation to this, *upādātṛ* is explained in the commentary as *grahītṛ*, seizer or one who affectionally clings to *upādāna*, and consequently, *utpādayitṛ*, producer (of *bhava*) (*PrasP.* 556.4).

This *upādātṛ* is what we call *pudgala* or Ātman, which is defined as *avidyānivṛtaḥ* and is said to make *saṃskārā*s that land it in *bhava*, Saṃsāra (v. 1), while *bhava* is said to be '*pañca skandhāḥ*' (v. 8a) as the product of *upādāna* and to have a threefold *karman* which determines future existence or rebirth (*punarbhava*) (*PrasP.* 556.8–557.3).

The same kind of use of *upādāna* is observed in the following case.

mamêty aham iti kṣīṇe bahirdhādhyātmam eva ca /
nirudhyata upādānaṃ tat kṣayād janmanaḥ kṣayaḥ //
(v. XVIII.4)

The commentary says that because of annihilation of this (*ahaṃkāra* and *mamakāra*), i.e., *satkāyadṛṣṭi*, due to no perception of 'I' and 'mine', the fourfold *upādāna* beginning with *kāma* is annihilated, and due to annihilation of the latter, there is the extinction of life (*janman*) characterized as rebirth (*punarbhavalakṣaṇa*) (*PrasP.* 349.12-14).

A similar interpretation is given for *anupādāna* used in chap. XVI. Namely, in verse 3 *vibhava* is said to be *anupādāna*[19] and is explained as that which is separated (*vigata*) from or that which lacks *bhava*, i.e., *pañcôpādānaskandhāḥ* (so *upādāna* = *bhava*?) (*PrasP.* 285.6-7),[20] while in verse 6 *upādāna* is equated with

19. *upādānād upādānaṃ saṃsaran vibhavo bhavet /*
vibhavaś cânupādānaḥ kaḥ sa kiṃ saṃsariṣyati // (*MK* XVI.3)

20. *Anupādāna* is otherwise explained as *prajñaptyupādānakāraṇarahita* (lacking the stuff for concept): *yaś ca vibhavo 'nupādānaḥ sa skandharahitatvāt prajñaptyupādānarahitatvān nirhetukaḥ syāt / yaś cânupādāno nirañjano*

bandhana[21] (*rāgâdikam upādānâkhyaṃ bandhanabhūtam asti...*, *PrasP.* 290.14-15: this is the opinion of an opponent), and *anupādāna* is explained as *bandhanarahita*, that which has no bondage (*PrasP.* 291.2-3).

Also we have another example of *anupādāya* used in the sense of 'without *upādāna*, attachment' in a quotation from the *Ratnakūṭa* (*Kāśyapaparivarta*):

> *atha teṣāṃ pañcānāṃ bhikṣuśatānām anupādāyâśravebhyaś cittāni vimuktāny abhūvan* / (*PrasP.* 48.12)
>
> (At that time these five hundred *bhikṣu*s getting rid of attachment emancipated their mind from evil influences [*āśrava* = *āsrava*].)

§7. *Conclusion*

There are more than a hundred occurrences of terms derived from *upa-ā-dā-*, *upādāya*, *upādāna*, etc., in the *Prasannapadā*, but their varieties in usage and meaning have, I believe, been referred to in previous sections. In summary, a diagram may be given in the following way.

A. 1) *upādāna*(*karman*) = *pañcôpādānaskandha* (= *upadi*, *upadhi*) = *upādeya*, *upātta*.
   2) *upādāna*(*kriyā*) = *upātti* in general, *darśana*, *śravaṇa*, etc.
   3) *upādāna*(*kriyā*) = *caturvidha-upādāna* (*kāma*, *dṛṣṭi*, *śīlavrata* and *ātmavāda*) (which is caused by *tṛṣṇā* and is the *pratyaya* of *bhava*).

B. 1) *upādānam* (A.1) *upādāya prajñapyata ātmā* (*upādātṛ*).
   2) *upādāya* (by action of *upādāna* (A.3)) *bhava upādātuḥ pravartate*.

C. 1) *anupādāya* (without *upādāna* (A.l)) *parinirvāsyati*.

'vyakto nirhetukaḥ sa na kaś cit saḥ / *nâsty èva sa ity arthaḥ* // (*PrasP.* 285.7–286.2).

21. *bandhanaṃ ced upādānaṃ sôpādāno na badhyate* /
badhyate nânupādānaḥ kim avastho 'tha badhyate // (*MK* XVI.6)

2) *anupādāya* (without *upādāna* (A.3)) *cittaṃ vimucyate* (or *nirvānaṃ adhigamyate*).

B.1 is *upādāyaprajñapti*, B.2 is *pratītyasamutpāda*.

Schematically speaking, Ātman is a kind of *upādāyaprajñapti* or *upādāyaprajñapta*, that which is conceived or assumed on the basis of *pañcôpādānaskandha*,[22] while all the *dharma*s classified into *pañca skandhāḥ* are *pratītyasamutpannāḥ*. According to the Sarvāstivāda, Ātman is deprived of its substantiality because of its being presumed on the basis of *upādāna*, while the *upādāna-skandha*s, being *dharma*s, are regarded as substantial (*sasva-bhāva*). The Mādhyamika, on the contrary, opposed this substantial view of *dharma*s and maintained the non-substantiality (*niḥ-svabhāvatā*) of *dharma*s, just as in the case of Ātman, in terms of *śūnyatā*, which in turn is explained as *parasparâpekṣitā* of *upādāna* and *upādātṛ*, of *kārya* and *kāraṇa*, etc. This means that, according to the Mādhyamika, all *dharma*s are, like Ātman, merely *upādāya-prajñapti*, and thus *pratītyasamutpāda* is equated with *upādāya-prajñapti* through the intermediary of *śūnyatā*.[23] Close observation

---

22. Another typical example of this kind of *upādāyaprajñapti* is *kāla* (time). The Mādhyamika says: though it is admissible that time is presumed on the basis of *rūpa* and other phenomena in conditioning (*rūpādīn eva sa saṃ-skārān upādāya prajñaptaḥ kālaḥ* / (*PrasP.* 387.4), still,

> *bhāvaṃ pratītya kālaś cet kālo bhāvād ṛte kutaḥ* /
> *na ca kaś cana bhāvo 'sti kutaḥ kālo bhaviṣyati* // (*MK* XIX.6)

Here *pratītya* is explained as *upādāya* by Candrakīrti. *Kāla* is not counted among *dharma*s by the Sarvāstivādins.

23. J. May calls *upādāyaprajñapti* a 'désignation métaphorique' and says that to the Mādhyamika this metaphor is in two degrees, viz. Ātman is 'désignation métaphorique des ensembles' and *dharma*s are 'désignation métaphorique de la réalité absolue' (May, op. cit., p. 161, n. 494).

The difference of range between *pratītyasamutpāda* and *upādāya-prajñapti* is due also to that between the two gerunds. Namely *upādāya* has a variety of meanings and usages, viz. 'on the basis of, based upon', 'clinging to, attached to', 'depending on' (*pratītya, niśritya, āśritya*), 'with reference to' (*adhikṛtya, ārabhya*), 'beginning with' (*ārabhya*), 'implying' (*saṃdhāya*), 'compared to' (*āpekṣya*), etc., while the meaning of *pratītya* is almost fixed

discloses a wider scope of *upādāyaprajñapti* than that of *pratītya-samutpāda*: viz. in contrast to the limitation of *pratītyasamutpāda* to *saṃskṛtadharma*, *upādāyaprajñapti* is applicable to any concept denoting *saṃskṛta* and *asaṃskṛta* alike, e.g., Nirvāṇa, *śūnyatā*, etc., these being concepts by which the truth which is unutterable is denoted.[24] In other words, it covers the same range as the *saṃvṛtisatya* in Nāgārjuna's terminology.[25] But in this case, *upādāya* should not be understood as 'based upon attachment' because Nirvāṇa is *anupādāya*. Rather it may be interpreted as 'by means of verbal expression' (with *vyavahāra*), because Nirvāṇa, being *paramārthasatya*, is *anupādāya* (beyond *vyavahāra*).

After Nāgārjuna two problems remained. One was how to explain *upādātṛ* as the agent of transmigration under the doctrine

---

in Buddhist doctrine.

24. E.g., *śūnyam iti na vaktavyam aśūnyam iti vā bhavet /*
ubhayaṃ nobhayaṃ ceti, prajñaptyarthaṃ tu kathyate // (*MK* XXII.11)

25. Commenting on the verse mentioned above (see n. 24), Candrakīrti says: *sarvam etan na vaktavyam asmābhiḥ / kiṃ tv anukte yathāvad-avasthitaṃ svabhāvam pratipattā pratipattuṃ na samartha ity / ato vayam api āropato vyavahārasatya eva sthitvā vyavahārârthaṃ vineyajanânurodhena śūnyam ity api brūmaḥ, aśūnyam ity api...* (*PrasP.* 444.3-6).

Also see Bhāvaviveka's definition of *upādāyaprajñapti* (n. 6 above). Avalokitavrata gives a detailed comment on the term *laukika-lokottara-vyavahāra* (*'jig rten pa daṅ 'jig rten las 'das pa'i tha sñad*) with examples such as eyes (grown from foetus), a germ (from seed), a vase (based upon earth and other conditions), cloth (out of thread and other conditions), and *bālapṛthagjana* on the basis of *karman*, *kleśa* and others as *laukika-vyavahāra*; *śrāvaka* and *pratyekabuddha* are assumed on the basis of *padapātha* and *kleśâvaraṇa-prahāṇa*, etc., *bodhisattva* and *tathāgata*, on *bhūmi* and *pāramitā*, and *daśabala* and other virtues as *lokottara-vyavahāra*. (Of these, the examples up to vase and cloth are metaphors for *pratītyasamutpāda*, while after *bālapṛthagjana* are the *pudgala-prajñapti*.) Furthermore, he says that all these are, including those like *tathāgata* and others who realized the truth (*bden pa gzigs pa* = *dṛṣṭasatya*, *satyadarśin*), explained from the empirical standpoint (*saṃvṛtitaḥ*) as '*svabhāvena śūnya*'. From the highest standpoint (*paramārthataḥ*), however, they are said to be '*svabhāvena śūnya*' because they are by no means produced from these conditions (*pratyaya*) (*Prajñāpradīpa-ṭīkā*, Tohoku no. 3859, D. Za, 241a4-b3).

of *anātman*, and the other, related to the first, was how to interpret the relationship between *upādātṛ* and *upādāna* in the doctrine of the twelvefold chain of causation. As for the second problem, a certain kind of solution had been given even in the Canon of Early Buddhism where we observe the *parasparâpekṣitā* between *vijñāna* and *nāmarūpa*, being *upādātṛ* and *upādāna* respectively.[26] Another case found in the Pāli Canon is the *upādāna-upādāniya* relation in the doctrine of the fivefold chain of causation beginning with *taṇhā* (SN, Nidānasaṃyutta, no. 52: *Upādāna*), where the succession of mental activities, *taṇhā* and *upādāna*, is said to be caused by *upādāniya dhamma*s and results in *bhava* and, in sequence, in the origination of sufferings, and where its process is again analogized with the burning of fire by supplying fuel. Here we may observe a triple relationship between *upādāniya* (= *upādāna* as *karman*), *upādāna* (as *kriyā*, attachment), and *upādātṛ* (hidden behind *upādāna-kriyā* as the possessor of it).

It was the Yogācāra who gave the answer to these problems by taking this triple relationship in the chain of causation into consideration. They gave the name *ālayavijñāna* to the *upādātṛ*, the agent of transmigration, which is said to be originated on the basis (*pratītyasamutpanna*) of the two kinds of *upādāna*,[27] one being *rūpîndriya*, i.e., the body with its faculties, equivalent to *nāmarūpa* or *pañcaskandhāḥ*, and the other being *vāsanā* (biotic force), equivalent to *saṃskāra*, which is the result of its own actions (i.e., *upādāna*) in previous times and lives and which is

26. As observed in the doctrine of the ninefold (or tenfold) chain of causation (SN, Nidānasaṃyutta, no. 67: *Nalakalapiyam*), where the relationship between *vijñāna* and *nāmarūpa* is said to be reciprocal and is compared to a bundle of reeds (*naḍakalāpa*, *nalakalapiya*). Also the *Śālistamba* refers to '*naḍakalāpa-yogena*' (quotation in *PrasP.* 561.11).

27. *Mahāyānasaṃgraha*, I. jñeyāśraya, 5. definition of *ādāna-vijñāna* (T. no. 1594, vol. 31, p. 133bc; Nagao Gajin, *Shōdaijōron: wayaku to chūkai* [Japanese translation of the *Mahāyānasaṃgraha* with notes], vol. 1 [Tokyo: Kōdansha, 1982], pp. 85–89). Because of this function (taking two *upādānas*), *ālayavijñāna* is called *ādāna-vijñāna* (*ādāna* = *upādāna*).

characterized as conceptualization and discrimination (*vyavahāra* and *vikalpa*). This function, i.e., taking (*upādā-*) these two *upādānas*, is also called *vijñapti*. As long as *ālayavijñāna* continues to take *upādānas*, *bhava* or *saṃsāra* continues to exist. Also the Yogācāra maintains that any assumption (*upacāra* = *prajñapti*) of Ātman or *dharmas* appears as the changing process (i.e., continuation) of this *ālayavijñāna* (*vijñānapariṇāma*),[28] and thus all phenomena as the world of *prajñapti* are reduced solely to the *ālayavijñāna* in terms of *vijñaptimātratā*. In this new scheme, all *dharmas* and *ātman* are regarded as *upādāyaprajñapti* as explained by the Mādhyamika, while the *ālayavijñāna* recovered the character as representing *pratītyasamutpāda* being the *upādāna* (basis as well as attachment) of *prajñapti*.

28. *Triṃśikā Vijñaptimātratāsiddhi*, v. 1.

On *Upādāna* (II)
Ālayavijñāna and Its Two Kinds of *Upādāna**

1.

At the 5th Conference of the IABS, held at Oxford in 1982, I read a paper entitled "On *Upādāna*," referring mainly to the concept of *upādāna* as used in the *Madhyamakakārikā* of Nāgārjuna, and in its commentary, the *Prasannapadā* composed by Candrakīrti.[1] In that paper, I tentatively suggested that *upādāna* has two meanings, namely, (1) 'that which takes (something)' and (2) 'that which is taken'; that the latter is otherwise termed *upādeya*; and that this *upādāna-upādeya* relationship constitutes the core of the doctrine of *pratītya-samutpāda* as symbolically expressed in the formulae '*upādānapratyayo bhavaḥ*' and '*anupādāya nirvāṇam*'.

I also suggested that Nāgārjuna, by identifying *pratītya-samutpāda* with *upādāya-prajñapti*, expanded the latter to the whole sphere of *dharma*s in contrast to the Abhidharmic understanding in which *upādāya-prajñapti* is applied only to *ātman*. In other words, in the philosophy of Nāgārjuna, or Mahāyāna Buddhism in general, all *dharma*s are, like *ātman*, deprived of their substantiality (*niḥsvabhāva*, *śūnya*). In the present paper, I wish

---

* This paper was first read at the 8th Conference of the International Association of Buddhist Studies held at Berkeley in August 1987. The original text of this paper was published in Japanese under the title "Arayashiki to engi—shūju/upādāna to no kanren" [*Ālayavijñāna* and dependent origination: In relation to the concept of *upādāna*], in *Bukkyō shisō no shomondai* (dedicated to Prof. A. Hirakawa on his 70th birthday; Tokyo: Shunjūsha, 1985), pp. 33–53. This English version was originally published in N. K. Wagle and F. Watanabe, eds., *Studies on Buddhism in Honour of Professor A.K. Warder* (Toronto: Centre for South Asian Studies, University of Toronto, 1993), pp. 149–159.

1. J. Takasaki, "On *Upādāna/Upādāyaprajnapti*" [pp. 246–264 above].

to examine how these concepts relating to *upādāna* developed after Nāgārjuna in the doctrine of the Yogācāras.

2.

Our observations will start with the following passage from the *Triṃśikā-kārikās*:[2]

> *tatrālayākhyaṃ vijñānaṃ vipākaḥ sarvabījakam //2//*
> *asaṃviditakopādisthānavijñaptikaṃ ca tat /*

These *pādas* belong to the passage describing the *ālayavijñāna* as the first of the three *vijñānapariṇāmas*, on the basis of which are produced various kinds of access (through verbal designation) to *ātman* and the *dharmas* (*ātmadharmopacāra*; *upacāra* = *prajñapti*). The first line gives the explanation of the 'body' of *ālayavijñāna*, and the second line its object, or basis (*ālambana*) and the feature or content of cognition (*ākāra*). The point in question is the meaning of the term *upādi* in the compound *asaṃviditakopādi-sthānavijñaptikaṃ* and how to resolve this compound.

In his *Triṃśikā-bhāṣya*[3] Sthiramati begins the explanation of this line with the following introductory comments:

> [Objection] If there be an *ālayavijñāna* which functions apart from the acting consciousness (*pravṛttivijñāna*), it should always have its own basis and feature in its capacity as consciousness.
>
> [Answer] Indeed, it does have its own basis and feature as consciousness, but they are quite indistinct (*aparicchinnāsaṃviditaka*) because the *ālayavijñāna* acts in two ways:
>
> (1) internally, as cognition (*vijñapti*) of stuff (*upādāna*), and

---

2. S. Lévi, *Vijñaptimātratāsiddhi, Deux traités de Vasubandhu ... Viṃśatikā et Triṃśikā* (Paris, 1925), pp. 18.21–19.25 (vv. 2cd, 3ab, and commentary thereon).

3. Ibid., p. 19.2-8.

(2) externally, as cognition of the receptacle world of indistinct feature (*aparichinnākāra-bhājanavijñaptitaḥ*).

Here, 'internal stuff' (*adhyātma-upādāna*) means:

(a) residue of inclination towards things construed by thought (*parikalpitasvabhāvābhiniveśavāsanā*),

(b) faculty stuff and the body as its foundation (*sādhiṣṭhānam indriyarūpam*), and

(b') mental stuff (*nāma ca*) (i.e., *vedanā*, *sañjñā*, *saṃskāra*, *vijñāna*).

In the explanation following the verse, however, Sthiramati interprets the compound in a different manner. Namely, he resolves it into 'that which has *asaṃviditakopādi* and *asaṃviditakasthāna-vijñapti*.'[4] Furthermore, *upādi* (= *upādāna*) in this verse is explained as being of two kinds, as in the introductory comment, but in a little more detail.

The first of these two, i.e., residue, is explained as being (a) the residue of cognition (discrimination or construction in thought) of *ātman*, etc. (*ātmādivikalpavāsanā*), and (b) the residue of *dharma*s, material and so on (*rūpādidharmavikalpavāsanā*). This residue is called *upādāna* because, owing to its existence, *ātman* or form, etc., are taken (*upātta*) by *ālayavijñāna* as the result of construction. This means that residue is the stuff (*upādāna*) to be taken (*upādeya*) by the agent (*upādātṛ*), i.e., *ālayavijñāna*, for its act of *vikalpa*. Here *vikalpa* is synonymous with *vijñapti* or *upacāra* (in *ātmadharmopacāra*, v. 1). The second kind of *upādi*, on the other hand, is explained as being *āśrayopādāna*, i.e., the taking of the basis.[5] Namely, *upādāna* is used here to denote the function of taking, while by *āśraya* is meant *upādāna* as in (b) and (b') of the foregoing passage, i.e., *sādhiṣṭhānam indriyarūpaṃ nāma ca*. And the function of *upādāna* is further explained as

4. Ibid., p. 19.10-16.
5. Ibid., p. 19.16-25.

'*ekayogakṣematvena upagamana*', i.e., to have access or become one through sharing bliss with one another. This is the orthodox definition of the function of *vijñāna* as sustaining the individual body throughout life. In addition, it is said that in the spheres of desire and the material, both mental and material bases are taken, but in the sphere of the non-material, mental stuff only. This does not mean that there remains nothing material in the non-material world, but that the material remains there only in a state of residue.

3.

Sthiramati's interpretation is somewhat obscure, and contains some unique points in comparison with other Yogācāra texts. Firstly, Dharmapāla's *Vijñaptimātratāsiddhi*, available only in Chinese translation, interprets it in the following manner:[6]

> *Vijñapti* in the verse signifies *ākāra*, while *sthāna* means *bhājanaloka* and together with *upādi* (= *upādāna*) represents *ālambana*. There are two kinds of *upādāna*, i.e., *bīja* and **sendriyakāya*. Of these two, *bīja* means **nimitta-nāma-vikalpa-vāsanā*, while *sendriyakāya* means *rūpīndriya* and *indriyādhiṣṭhāna*. These are both taken (*upātta*) by *vijñāna*, made as one with it, and 'share security and danger' with it. [This is the usual expression in Chinese, corresponding to *ekayogakṣematva*.] *Ālayavijñāna*, when it receives its body, transforms itself internally into *bīja* and *sendriyakāya*, and externally into *bhājanaloka*, and making what is transformed its own basis, i.e., supported by them (as by sticks), obtains its feature of cognition (*ākāra*).

Here both *upādi* and *sthāna* are regarded as the objects of *vijñapti*. This agrees with Sthiramati's first interpretation. As for the interpretation of *bīja* or *vāsanā*, as is well-known, Dharmapāla's

6. T. vol. 31, p. 10a.

interpretation is based on the *Saṃdhinirmocana,*[7] while Sthiramati's is based upon the *Viniścayasaṃgrahaṇī* of the *Yogācārabhūmi,*[8] but both are fundamentally identical because both signify the sphere of thought construction impressed upon consciousness. The biggest difference is the addition of '*nāma ca*' by Sthiramati to '*sādhiṣṭhānam indriyarūpaṃ*', which is not observed in any other text. We shall consider this point later.

Another point in question is the ambiguity of the meaning of *upādāna* in relation to *vijñapti.* This we shall now examine by searching for the background to its use in the Abhidharmic tradition.

4.

The concept *upādāna* as equivalent to *chih-shou*[9] in Chinese is used for denoting the function of sustaining the individual throughout life by collecting materials into the body. Its agency is sought in the mind, and the materials sustained in the body are called *upātta* (*yu-chih-shou*). According to the *Abhidharmakośabhāṣya*, *upātta* is defined as follows:[10]

> [What is called 'the material sustained in the body' is] that which is taken up (*udgṛhīta*) by the mind and its associated mental functions as being the foundation [of their activity] (*adhiṣṭhāna*). It is because they (the *upātta* and the mind) are conforming to each other (*anyonyānuvidhāna*) in both accepting [things good for them] and rejecting [things not good for them] (*udgraha-upaghātābhyām*). It is what is called sensual (*sacetana*) in the world.

Among all *dharmas* as classified into the eighteen elements, (1) the seven mental elements (six *vijñānadhātu* and

7. T. vol. 16, p. 692b (Tib.: E. Lamotte, ed., 1935, p. 55).
8. T. vol. 30, p. 580a.
9. Not *ch'ü*, which is used for denoting the ninth *bhavāṅga*.
10. T. vol. 29, p. 8b; *Abhidharmakośabhāṣya*, ed. by P. Pradhan (Patna, 1975 [rev. ed.]), p. 23.7-27, *ad* I.33.

manodhātu), *dharmadhātu* and *śabdadhātu* (sound) are always 'not taken' (*anupātta*);

(2) of the five elements beginning with the eyes, i.e., the five faculties, those existing in the present are *upātta*, and those belonging to the future and the past are *anupātta*; and

(3) of the remaining four elements, i.e., colour, smell, taste and the touchable, those existing at present and connected with the five faculties (namely, materials constituting a living body) are *upātta*, and all others (the outer world, including a corpse, excrement, most parts of the hair, etc., which are capable of being cut off) are *anupātta*.

The same grouping of elements is accepted by the texts of the Yogācāras, such as the *Yogācārabhūmi* (Ch., fasc. 66),[11] *Abhidharmasamuccaya*,[12] and *Mahāyāna-pañcaskandhaprakaraṇa*.[13] Among the definitions given in these texts, the definition of *upātta* as materials which offer the foundation for the origination of sense (*vedanotpattyāśrayarūpa*) in the *Abhidharmasamuccaya* is equivalent to *sacetana* in the *Abhidharmakośabhāṣya*, while *anyonyānuvidhāna* in the latter has the same import as *ekayogakṣematva* mentioned previously.[14] Notable is the fact that throughout these texts the mind and its associated functions (*citta-caitta*), i.e., the four *skandha*s beginning with *vedanā*, or *nāman* of *nāmarūpa*, are always excluded from the group of *upātta*s.

Now, in the doctrine of the *Abhidharmakośa* and other texts of the Sarvāstivāda and other similar schools, this function of *upādāna* or the *upādāna-upātta* relation exists between *citta-caitta* and *sādhiṣṭhānam indriyarūpa*, and the former is denoted (if we

11. T. vol. 30, p. 666a.
12. T. vol. 31, p. 672a; *Abhidharmasamuccayavyākhyā*, ed. by N. Tatia (Patna, 1976), p. 43 (§43).
13. T. vol. 31, p. 850c.
14. Cf. *Yogācārabhūmi*, Ch. fasc. 100 (T. vol. 30, p. 880a), where *ekayogakṣematva* is explained by *anyonyānuvidhānatva* in *udgraha-upaghāta* between *rūpa* and *citta-caitta*s.

apply it in the process of the present life according to the doctrine of dependent origination) by *vijñāna* at the moment of conception, *nāman* (of *nāmarūpa*), and *mana āyatana* (among the *ṣaḍ-āyatana*) in the following stages. To this a query is raised by the Yogācāras in view of the fact that even in a swoon life continues to be sustained, and thus they assumed the existence of a subconsciousness behind the acting mind and named it *ālayavijñāna*.

For example, among the eightfold testimony concerning the *raison d'être* of the *ālayavijñāna* given at the beginning of the *Viniścayasaṃgrahaṇī* of the *Yogācārabhūmi*,[15] the first is called 'the impossibility of sustaining the basis (*āśrayopādānāsaṃbhavatva*) without *ālayavijñāna* (*antareṇālayavijñānam*)'. (The Sanskrit terms are taken from the quotations in the *Abhidharmasamuccayavyākhyā*.)[16] This statement is made on account of five reasons, of which the first is as follows:[17]

> The *ālayavijñāna* is caused by the formative forces of the previous life, while the eye-consciousness and other acting consciousnesses are caused by the conditions of the present life. (*ālayavijñānaṃ pūrvasaṃskārahetukam / cakṣurādipravṛtti-vijñānaṃ punar vartamānapratyayahetukam /*)

This means that the *vijñāna* of the first moment in this life must be *ālayavijñāna* and not the acting consciousness (*pravṛttivijñāna*), and this characterisation of *ālayavijñāna* naturally leads to its being regarded as the substratum of formative forces since the time of death. Thus the eighth statement, 'the impossibility of the transmittance [of life] by consciousness without *ālayavijñāna* (*vijñānacyutyasaṃbhavatva*)', is explained in the following manner:[18]

In the case of the dying *vijñāna* leaves the body from either

15. T. vol. 30, p. 579a.
16. *Abhidharmasamuccayavyākhyā*, p. 11 (§9B).
17. Ibid., p. 12 (§9B, 1(a)).
18. Ibid., p. 13 (§9B, viii); *Yogācārabhūmi*, T. vol. 30, p. 579c.

> above or below, gradually making it cool. This *vijñāna* cannot be *manovijñāna* because it does not function sometimes even during life. Therefore it is observed that the body becomes cool or insentient (*dehāpratisaṃvedana*) when the *ālayavijñāna* that sustains the body (*dehopādānaka*) leaves it, not on account of the leaving of the *manovijñāna*.

A description of *ālayavijñāna* as the substratum of biotic forces in *saṃsāra* is found in the *Manobhūmi* section of the *Mūlabhūmika* of the *Yogācārabhūmi*. Namely, it is said in short that[19]

> after *vijñāna* has left its foundation (i.e., the body), making it cool, a new sort of foundation (*āśraya*) is produced out of the seed (*bīja*) [of *vijñāna*] owing to the impressing force of frivolous discrimination and good or evil acts, and becomes an intermediate existence (*antarābhava*). When the time has come, and it is conceived in the womb, *ālayavijñāna*, consisting of all seeds (*sarvabījaka*) and of the nature of the matured (*vipākasaṃgṛhīta*), attaches to it (i.e., the foundation of *antarābhava*) (?) by sustaining it and congeals into a body (*sammūrcchati*). Thus, inside the womb there grows a *kalala* consisting of *kāya-indriya* only as its foundation for taking.

Because of this function of sustaining the individual throughout life or taking the foundation (*āśrayopādāna*), *ālayavijñāna* received its name of *ādānavijñāna* as observed in the *Saṃdhinirmocana* and other works.[20]

---

19. *Yogācārabhūmi*, ed. by V. Bhattacarya (Calcutta, 1957), pp. 15.7–25.1 (p. 24.3-5: ... *tatra sarvabījakaṃ vipākasaṃgṛhītam āśrayopādānād ālayavijñānaṃ sammūrcchati*); T. vol. 30, pp. 281b–283a.

20. *Saṃdhinirmocana* (T. vol. 16, p. 692b); *Abhidharmasamuccaya* (T. vol. 31, p. 701c); *Abhidharmasamuccayavyākhyā*, p. 11 (§9A: *punaḥ punaḥ pratisaṃdhibandhe ātmabhāvopādānād ādānavijñānam*); *Mahāyānasaṃgraha* (T. vol. 31, p. 133bc; Tib. sDe-dge ed., p. 3b, 3-5; Sanskrit reconstruction by Nagao: *kiṃ kāraṇam ādānavijñānam ity ucyate* / (a) *sarvarūpendri-*

In the passage following this in the *Yogācārabhūmi*, however, *bīja* is explained as being synonymous with *ālaya*, *upādāna*, etc., besides *satkāyadṛṣṭyadhiṣṭhāna*, etc.[21] Hence we learn that *upādāna* has the character of *kleśa* or affection, which causes saṃsāric existence and that this function of 'taking' is involved in *bīja* itself. In other words, (in the state of *antarābhava*) there exists nothing but *ālayavijñāna* in the form of *bīja*s, and on the one hand it produces *upādāna* or the foundation out of itself, but at the same time it sustains the latter (*āśrayopādāna*). But how is it possible for *ālayavijñāna* to work in two ways simultaneously? This relates to another function *of ālayavijñāna*, i.e., the function of cognition.

In addition, mention should be made of a passage in the *Mahāyānasūtrālaṃkāra* referring to the momentariness of *dharma*s (*MSA* XVIII.83 & comm.),[22] where the momentariness of *sarvasaṃskārāḥ* is explained as being established, among other things, through their relationship as cause and effect to the mind which is admitted to be momentary. Namely, for the mind *rūpa* and other *saṃskāra*s are the cause—this is referring to '*saṃskārapratyayaṃ vijñānam*'—but they are also its effect because they are 'taken' (*upātta*) by the mind and governed (*adhipatya*) by the mind. As regards *upāttatva*, the text goes further on to say that all the formative forces, i.e., the mental faculties of the eyes, etc., and their foundations are 'taken' (or sustained) by the mind and together with it congealed into a body as being in association with its benefit (*cittena hi sarve saṃskārāḥ cakṣurādayaḥ sādhiṣṭhānā upāttāḥ saha sammūrcchanāḥ tadanugrahānuvṛttitaḥ* /). For this passage an authority is given in quotation as '*vijñāna-*

---

yopādānatvena (b) *sarvātmabhāvopādānāśrayatvena ca* / *tathā hi* (a) *tena pañcarūpīndriyāṇy upādīyante vināśāya yāvad āyur anuvartate* / (b) *pratisaṃdhibandhe ca tadabhinirvṛttyupādānatvenātmabhāva upādīyate* / *evaṃ tad ādānavijñānam ity ucyate* / [Tokyo: Kōdansha, 1982, pp. 11–12]); and *Vijñaptimātratāsiddhi*, T. vol. 31, p. 14c.

21. *Yogācārabhūmi*, Skt., p. 26.17-18; T. vol. 30, p. 284c.

22. *Mahāyānasūtrālaṃkāra*, ed. by S. Lévi (Paris, 1904), pp. 150.27–151.8.

pratyayaṃ nāmarūpam'. Thus we come to know that this passage is referring to the causal chain of co-origination around *vijñāna*, the third limb, and that here lies the fundamental model of *ālayavijñāna* defined as *vipākasaṃgṛhīta* and *sarvabījaka* as well as *ādāna*. This model may be illustrated by means of the following diagrams:

(*hetu*) *saṃskārāḥ* → *citta* (= *vijñāna*) → (*phala*) *nāmarūpam* (*cakṣurādayaḥ sādhiṣṭhānāḥ*)

Diagram I

[*bīja*] *saṃskārāḥ* (*karmavāsanā*) → [*bīja*] = *ālayavijñāna* [*upādāna*] → *indriyarūpaṃ sādhiṣṭhānam* [*upātta*]

Diagram II

5.

Of the two kinds of *upādāna* what has remained unexplained is the *upādāna* as *vāsanā* of *ātma-dharma-vikalpa*. According to the *Saṃdhinirmocana*, it is termed **nimitta-nāma-vikalpa-vyavahāra-prapañca-vāsanopadāna* (*upādāna* [characterised as] the residue of frivolous multiplicity in verbal expression about characteristics and names and discrimination; acc. to Tib.).[23] It is otherwise called **nāma-vāsanā or *nāma-bīja* in contrast to the **karma-bīja* or *-vāsanā* which causes *saṃsāra*. It is related to cognition as the proper function of *vijñāna*. Namely, it is a kind of impression

23. T. vol. 16, p. 692b; Lamotte ed., p. 55.

stored within *ālayavijñāna* as a result of cognition. This impression is also waiting for a chance to be expressed, as in the case of *karma*, but it is not of any long term as in the latter case, but of every moment. In this cognition of every moment, *ālayavijñāna* keeps the result of cognition and, making this the basis, creates the next cognition. In this respect Sthiramati designated *vāsanā* or *bīja* as '*upādāna* of *vikalpa*'. Hence *upādāna* means the stuff of cognition, being synonymous with *ālambana*.

What was termed the 'result of cognition' above is generally referred to in terms of *ātman* and the *dharma*s. It is a mere product of thought construction and of no reality. This is the fundamental standpoint of the Vijñānavāda. As for *ātman*, however, its non-reality is recognised even in the Abhidharmic doctrine, as observed in the *Abhidharmakośa*.[24] Namely, *ātman* is a verbal construction (*prajñapti*) on the basis of (*upādāya*) the five *skandha*s as stuff (*upādāna*). In the *Madhyamakakārikā*, however, besides *ātman*, all the *dharma*s, i.e., the five *skandha*s too, are regarded as '*upādāya prajñapti*'.[25] The Vijñānavāda school took over this doctrine, but restored the reality of the stuff of *upādāna* in *upādāya prajñapti*. Thus they (hypothetically) established *ālayavijñāna* consisting of *vāsanā* or *bīja*s as the basis (*upādāna*) of the cognition of *ātman* and the *dharma*s, i.e., *upādāna* of the verbal construction (*prajñapti* = *upacāra*) of *ātman* and the *dharma*s, and regarded it alone as real (*sad*), being dependently originated (*pratītyasamutpanna*), with the name of *paratantra-svabhāva*. As *bīja* or *vāsanā* it is stuff (*upādāna* or *upātta*), but functionally it is the taking (*upādāna*) or taker (*upādātṛ*). In this sense 'taking' is synonymous with *vikalpa*, *vijñāna* and *prajñapti* (in the active sense of *prajñāpayati*).

24. T. vol. 29, p. 152c; *Abhidharmakośabhāṣya*, p. 461.20-21: *adhyātmikān upāttān vartamānān skandhān upādāya pudgalaḥ prajñapyate* /.
25. *Madhyamakakārikā* XXIV.18. See Takasaki, op. cit., n. 1.

6.

I have indicated above the two kinds of functions of *upādāna*, namely, (1) sustaining the individual body and (2) cognition or verbal construction. From the standpoint of the monism of *vijñāna*, however, these two are again reduced to the latter function. Namely, sustaining is a kind of function of *vijñāna*, and cognition of the outer world is also a kind of *upādāna* in the latter sense. Embracing these two, the function of *vijñāna* is technically called *vijñapti*, 'making known' or 'information'. Within this 'information' the whole world is divided into subject and object, or *ālambana* and *ākāra*, and while in that state, into impression and expression (*bīja* and **abhinirhāra*), standing in turn for cause and effect, and thus constituting the process of time. This whole is otherwise called *vijñānapariṇāma*, or 'the transformation of consciousness', in which the 'cognition' of *ātman* and *dharma*s and the 'taking' of their residue are repeated alternately.

If we divide the same process into internal and external, information of the outer world is nothing but the cognition of *dharma*s, and its result, i.e., the content of cognition, is impressed in the form of residue. But as far as it is cognised as the outer world, it is never taken (*upātta*) or made to constitute an individual body. On the other hand, internal *dharma*s are taken by *vijñāna* and continue to exist (in a continuity of momentary change: *santati*, *santatipariṇāma*) and at the same time originate the cognition of *ātman*, while the physical elements 'taken' by *ālayavijñāna* put their residue of *karma* in *ālayavijñāna* and make themselves the stuff of *saṃsāra*.

Thus we learn that what are the same in cognition are divided into the internal and external in accordance with the function of 'taking'. It may also be said that in the direction from *bīja* to *abhinirhāra* there is the distinction of being internal or external, but in the direction from *abhinirhāra* to *bīja* both are simultaneously directed towards the internal.

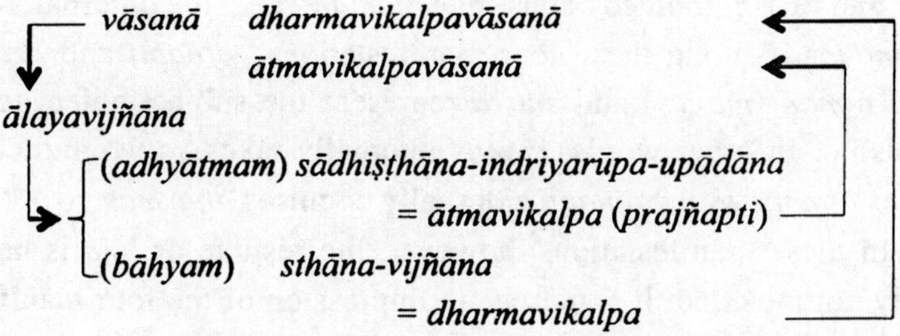

Diagram III: Structure of *ālayavijñāna*

Now, lastly, we should solve the problem of the inclusion by Sthiramati of *nāman* in the internal *upādāna*. The answer may be found in the difference of scope in *upātta* and the cognition of *ātman*. In the traditional doctrine only the physical body and faculties are 'taken' for the sake of maintenance. But we usually include in individuality our consciousness which 'takes' the body. *Nāman*, or mental elements, are not the 'taken', but they are necessary for the cognition of *ātman*. Being internal to individuality they are well said to be at one with *ālayavijñāna* by sharing bliss with it. They are, namely, *manas* and the six *vijñāna*s.

In order to show the position of these acting *vijñāna*s within the whole process of *vijñāna-pariṇāma*, the fourfold manifestation of *vijñāna* described in the *Madhyāntavibhāga* (I.4)[26] is most helpful for our understanding. Namely, (a) manifestation as the object (*artha*) means the six objects (*ṣaḍviṣaya*), which corresponds to the cognition of the outer world; this is *anupātta*; (b) manifestation as sentient beings (*sattva*) means the five (physical) faculties (*pañcendriya*), which corresponds to *sādhiṣṭhāna-indriya-rūpa*; while (c) manifestation as *ātman* (self) means *manas* or *mana-indriya*; and (d) manifestation as making known (*vijñapti*) means the six acting *vijñāna*s (*ṣaḍ vijñānāni*). These last two, i.e.,

---

26. *Madhyāntavibhāga*, ed. by G. M. Nagao (Tokyo, 1964), v. I.3: *arthasattvātmavijñapti-pratibhāsaṃ prajāyate / vijñānaṃ nāsti cāsyārthas tadabhāvāt tad apy asat //*.

(c) and (d) combined, constitute *nāman*, i.e., the internal four *skandhas*. Among these four manifestations, *vijñapti* and *artha*, and *ātman* (*manas*) and *sattva* represent the subject-object relationship. In other words, *manas* internally takes *sattva* and cognises *ātman*, while *vijñapti* externally cognises *dharmas*.

In these manifestations, however, the residue or *bīja* is naturally not included. It is merely an impression of the four manifestations, which in turn is worthy of being called *vijñapti* or expression. The relationship of *ālayavijñāna* to this *vāsanā* or *bīja* is, on the other hand, not suitable to be called *vijñapti* or expression. Rather, it may be better called *upādāna* or 'taking'. It is also notable that this *upādāna*, i.e., the taking of *vāsanā* by *ālayavijñāna*, involves the sense of 'affection' or 'clinging' which causes saṃsāric existence (*bhava*) through the repetition of transformation between *bīja* and the manifestation, impression and expression within *vijñāna*.[27]

---

27. On this subject I consulted the following works:

G. Nagao, "Shoen gyōsōmon no ichimondai" [A problem concerning *ālambana* and *ākāra*], in *Chūgan to yuishiki* (Tokyo: Iwanami Shoten, 1978), pp. 373–388.

S. Suguro, "Arayashiki no gogi" [The meaning of the term *ālayavijñāna*], in *Bukkyō kyōri no kenkyū* (Prof. Tamura Felicitation Volume) (Tokyo: Shunjūsha, 1982), pp. 52–56.

K. Yokoyama, *Yuishiki no tetsugaku* [The philosophy of the Vijñānavāda] (Kyoto: Heirakuji Shoten).

The same subject was discussed by S. Takeuchi in his article "Yuishikigaku ronsho ni okeru shūju no futatsu no imi" [On the two usages of *upādāna* in Vijñaptimātratā treatises], in *Bukkyō to ishūkyō* (Prof. Kumoi Felicitation Volume) (Kyoto: Heirakuji Shoten, 1985), pp. 267–278.

Prof. L. Schmithausen's recent work, *Ālayavijñāna: On the Origin and Early Development of a Central Concept of Yogācāra Philosophy*, 2 pts., Studia Philologica Buddhica, Monograph Series IVa, b (Tokyo: International Institute for Buddhist Studies, 1987), discusses the *upādāna* function of *ālayavijñāna* (pp. 69–73: §§4.3-4), and reference to and criticism of my article in Japanese (in Hirakawa Felicitation Volume, 1985) are given (notes 512, 513, 517, 518, 526 and 529).

This whole process is shown in the diagram below:

ālayavijñāna '*asaṃviditakopādisthānavijñaptikaṃ*'

= vijñāna

[adhyātmam]

upādāna (bīja)

vāsanā = saṃskāra ātmavikalpavāsanā

(bīja) dharmavikalpavāsanā

....

ātmabhava (āśraya) = nāmarūpa

(pañcopādānaskandha) (abhinirhāra)

sādhiṣṭhānam indriyarūpaṃ

—sattva (pañca indriyāni)

↑↓ ....ātmavikalpa

nāma ca —ātman (mana-indriya)

—vijñapti (ṣaḍvijñāna)

↑↓ ....dharmavikalpa

[bahirdhā]

sthāna (bhājanaloka) —artha (ṣaḍvijñāna)

([bāhya] pañcaskandhāḥ)

Diagram IV: *vijñapti-mātra*

On *Gotrabhū**

The following is a summary of my works published in Japanese 25 years ago. I am going to publish it here in the belief that it is still worth publishing even after the publication of two remarkable papers by Seyfort Ruegg and von Hinüber,[1] both of whom did not refer to my papers. My papers in Japanese are as follows:

1. "Gotrabhū to gotrabhūmi" [*Gotrabhū* and *gotrabhūmi*]. In *Felicitation Volume Dedicated to Prof. E. Kanakura on the Occasion of his 70th Birthday* (Kyoto: Heirakuji Shoten, 1966), pp. 313–336.
2. "Gotrabhūmi oboegaki" [A note on *gotrabhūmi*]. *Komazawa Daigaku Bukkyō Gakubu Kenkyū Kiyō* (Memoirs of Faculty of Buddhism, Komazawa University), No. 25 (1967), pp. 1–27.

My papers contain information on materials given in the works of the so-called Northern tradition written in Sanskrit and Chinese translations equivalent to them, which have mostly escaped the attention of both professors.

In my old papers I started the work with the question—as did other scholars who were interested in this term—where this Pāli word of a unique form originated from. As this term *gotrabhū* used in the Canonical texts is explained in the Pāli commentaries with

* Originally published in *Wiener Zeitschrift für die Kunde Südasiens* 36 (Supplementband, 1992), pp. 251–259.

1. D. Seyfort Ruegg, "Pāli *Gotta/Gotra* and the Term *Gotrabhū* in Pāli and Buddhist Sanskrit," in *Buddhist Studies in Honour of I. B. Horner* (Dordrecht, 1974), pp. 199–210; Oscar von Hinüber, "*Gotrabhū*: Die sprachliche Vorgeschichte eines philosophischen Terminus," *ZDMG* 128 (1978), pp. 326–332. The same subject was discussed by Prof. Wijesekara: O. H. de A. Wijesekara, "The Etymology of the Pali *Gotrabhū*," in *Studies in Pali and Buddhism*, ed. by A. K. Narain, 34 (1979), pp. 38ff.

the analogy of the family using another form, *gotta*, equivalent to Skt. *gotra*, such as *ariyagotta* and *putthujanagotta*, it seemed clear to me that this term was borrowed from outside. Limited use of this term to certain portions of Canonical texts which are thought to be of later dates will support my assumption. In this point I side with Seyfort Ruegg, who maintained the term was an example of Sanskritism in Pāli. In the following I will pick up mostly Chinese materials referring to this term. Some of them show equivalence to Pāli passages, others are available only in Chinese texts. In addition, I will refer to similar concepts in Sanskrit materials.

(1) Mention must be made first of all of the *Chieh-t'o tao lun*, the Chinese translation of the *Vimuttimagga* (or *Vimuktimārga*), which is regarded as a kind of source material for Buddhaghoṣa's *Visuddhimagga*[2] and was clearly transmitted from Sri Lanka to China. There are two passages in this text referring to *gotrabhū-ñāna*, of which parallel passages are found in the *Visuddhimagga*. Quite interesting is the Chinese translation of *gotrabhū* as *hsing-ch'u* in this text, which literally means "nature removal" (nature for *gotra* and removal for *bhū*). This reminds us of von Hinüber's theory of **gotrahan*.[3] Indeed this term is explained in the following way:[4] "To remove the *dhamma*s of ordinary people is called 'nature removal': what is not to be removed by *dhamma*s of ordinary people is also called 'nature removal'. [In this latter case] nature means *nibbāna*." Further, it goes on to say: "Those who hear the seed of *nibbāna* are called [of the] 'nature removal', as is said in the Abhidhamma: 'to remove origination is called "nature

2. On the relationship between both texts, see P. V. Bapat, *Vimuttimagga and Visuddhimagga: A Comparative Study* (Poona, 1937). A summary of this work was previously published in *Indian Culture* 1935, pp. 455–459.
3. Wijesekara is of the same opinion.
4. *Vimuttimagga*, T. vol. 32, p. 457a. Cf. Bapat, op. cit., p. 119. Cf. *Visuddhimagga*, pp. 672–673 (no definition of *gotra* as *nibbāna*).

removal," to enter non-origination is called "nature removal"' (*uppādam abhibhuyyantīti gotrabhū, anuppādaṃ pakhandatīti gotrabhū*), and so on." This quotation of the Abhidhamma comes from the *Paṭisambhidāmagga* (I.66). So we come to know that this translator attached importance to the process of removal of the nature of ordinary beings rather than on becoming a member of the saints. The word *-bhū* is here understood in the sense of *abhi-bhuyyati*, 'to be conquered'.

A similar interpretation is given in another passage[5] where again an Abhidharma passage is quoted. Namely: "As is said in the Abhidhamma: 'to remove origination in order to attain the way to enter the stream is called "nature removal," to remove origination in order to attain the result of entering the stream is called "nature removal." Thus in all cases.'" This passage is identified with the *Paṭisambhidāmagga* (I.68), which is quoted in the *Visuddhimagga*:[6] *sotāpattimaggapaṭilabhattāya uppādam abhibhuyyatīti gotrabhū, sotāpattiphalasamāpattattāya uppādam abhibhuyyatīti gotrabhū. evaṃ sabbattha.*

(2) The next example of the use of *gotrabhū* in the Chinese equivalent is observed in the Ekottarāgama,[7] which is regarded as belonging to the Mahāsaṅghika or the Dharmaguptaka, the latter being more likely. The term *gotrabhū* is translated as *hsiang chung-hsing jen*, "one who is (moving) towards the lineage," who is listed just below the one in the 8th stage of the Saint, usually called *srotaāpattimārga*, also called *aṣṭamaka* (the eighth) otherwise. This latter name is often referred to along with *gotrabhū*, an example being observed in the *Kathāvatthu* (243–247), where a debate is held between the Theravāda and the Andhakas or the

5. T. ibid., p. 460c; cf. Bapat, op. cit., p. 125.
6. *Visuddhimagga*, pp. 699–700.
7. T. vol. 2, p. 767bc. This is equivalent to Pāli AN IX-10, Ahuneyya (vol. 4, p. 373).

Sammitīyas. So we come to know that the ranking of *gotrabhū* as a stage just below *aṣṭamaka* was widely adopted among various sects on the continent.

(3) In this connection, notable is the use of the term in the *She-li-fu a-p'i-t'an lun* (*Śāriputrābhidharmaprakaraṇa*), which is held to belong to the Dharmaguptaka. This text has a passage[8] where, like the *Puggalapaññatti*, various kinds of persons are arranged according to their rank, among which we find *hsing jen*, "man of *gotra*." This *hsing jen* is ranked above ordinary beings and those non-ordinary beings who have obtained the five holy faculties, but below Śrāvakas, Pratyekabuddhas, Bodhisattvas and the Samyaksambuddha, and it is explained that if one dwells gradually on the superior *dharma*s of ordinary beings and when (finally) these *dharma*s have disappeared, he ascends to (the state of) fixation in the right way (*samyaktvaniyāma/ -nyāma*), then he is called "a man of *gotra*." It is also explained that if one accomplishes the *gotra dharma* (*hsing fa*), he is called a man of *gotra*. This *hsing jen* is most probably a translation of the term *gotrabhū*.[9]

(4) The next example in a work belonging probably to the same Dharmaguptaka is that in the *P'i-ni mu ching* (*Vinayamātṛkā*), where seven ranks of persons are enumerated by the names of stages (*bhūmi*), *gotrabhūmi* being one of them. It runs as follows:[10] "Because of accomplishment of *chung-hsing ti* (*gotrabhūmi*) it is called ordination (*upasampadā*). The eighth stage (*aṣṭamakabhūmi*) of the four processes and four results (of *ariya*s, ending with Arhatship), the stage of perceiving (*darśanabhūmi*),

8. T. vol. 28, p. 548c.

9. In most cases in Chinese translations, *-bhū* of *gotrabhū* is not translated. So if we apply the same tendency to the case of *hsing fa* above, *gotrabhū-dharma* is another possible way of rendering it. See below.

10. T. vol. 24, p. 801b.

the stage of weakening (of defilements [*tanubhūmi*]), the stage of removal of desire (*vītarāgabhūmi*), the stage of those who have done (what is to be done [*kṛtāvibhūmi*]), and as far as the Pratyekabuddha, all of them are called [of] ordination." And specially commenting on *gotrabhūmi*, it says:[11] "Why is it called *gotrabhūmi*? If one would be sitting in the Buddha's vicinity and having listened to his teaching, would strive with body and mind, and would accomplish moment by moment his practice, then he would, due to this mind, suddenly realize the *dharma* by himself and would attain the state of *srotaāpatti(phala)*. This *srotaāpatti* is the *gotra* (i.e., cause or seed) of [transworldly] virtues." (This commentary sounds contradictory to the main text, where *gotrabhūmi* is clearly located before *aṣṭamaka*, which is to be equivalent to *srotaāpattimārga*.)

What is notable here is the use of the term *gotrabhūmi* instead of *gotrabhū*. Also notable is that the same series of stage names is used in the *Prajñāpāramitāsūtras*.[12] Sanskrit terms for these stages are actually collected from the *Prajñāpāramitāsūtra*. This would suggest that the Mahāyānists who composed the *Prajñāpāramitāsūtra* would have had in their origins certain contact with the Dharmaguptakas, from whom they borrowed the stage system as part of their ten-stage theory covering three vehicles. I will refer to this again at the end of this paper.

As for the interrelation between *gotrabhū* and *gotrabhūmi*, I will here only indicate that due to the equivocality of *-bhū* as a verbal noun in the sense of being, or being born, on the one hand, and as a noun in the sense of earth, being a synonym of *bhūmi*, on the other, it is easily replaced by *bhūmi* when *gotrabhū* is interpreted to denote a certain stage or rank of practitioners. This possibly is supported by examples of the Tibetan translation of *gotrabhū* as *rigs kyi sa* as observed in the *Laṅkāvatāra*, v. X.15.

11. Ibid. Possibly an insertion by the translator.
12. See the table below.

(5) Another example which seems to show the stage relationship between *gotrabhū* and *aṣṭamaka* is observed in the *Samayabhedopacaraṇacakra*, a book on the division of sectarian Buddhism seen from the eyes of the Sarvāstivādins. Namely, referring to the doctrines common to all subsects of the Mahāsaṅghika, there is a passage saying:[13]

> *brgyad pa* (= *aṣṭamaka*) *yung ring(s) du gnas par yang byed do shes bya ba nas, rigs kyi chos* (= *gotra[bhū]dharma*) *kyi bar las kyang, yongs su nyams par 'gyur ro / shes brjod par bya'o / rgyun du zhugs pa* (= *srotaāpanna*) *ni yongs su mi* (?) *nyams pa'i chos can no / dgra bcom pa* (= *arhat*) *ni yongs su mi nyams pa'i chos can no /*

Chinese equivalents in Hsüan-tsang's translation[14] of *brgyad pa* and *rigs kyi chos* are *ti pa ti* and *hsing ti fa* respectively, and suggest the existence of the term *bhūmi* (*ti*) in the original, but two other Chinese translations literally agree with the Tibetan translation.[15] So it might be an insertion by Hsüan-tsang, but I cannot deny the possibility of the form *gotrabhūdharma* in the original.[16]

Sarvāstivādins, the reporters of the *Samayabhedopacaraṇacakra*, however, do not use the term *gotrabhū* or *gotrabhūmi* as a name of the stage just below *srotaāpattimārga*. Instead they use the term *laukikāgradharma*. It is explained that it is called so because in this stage there appears the last moment of the mind of an ordinary being and that this state of mind has the power to reject the nature of ordinary beings (*pṛthagjanagotra*) and to obtain

13. The *gShung lugs kyi bye brag bkod pa'i khor lo*. Peking Ed., no. 5639, Reprint, vol. 127, p. 250.3.4.

14. T. vol. 49, p. 15c.

15. Ibid., p. 18b (*chung-hsing fa*) and p. 20c (*hsing fa*) (both translated by Paramārtha).

16. An example of the use of the form *gotrabhūdharma* is observed in the *Prajñāpāramitā*. See the table below.

the nature of the saints (*āryagotra*).[17] It is also said that in the *laukikāgradharma* the *jñāna* called *duḥkhadharmakṣānti* is ready to appear, and this point is explained as obtaining the *āryagotra*, just like a burnt cloth (the analogy means that even if just a slight part is burnt, it is called so; in the same way a practitioner who has partially burnt his fire of *kleśa* by his *jñāna* is worth being called an *ārya*).[18]

Thus, to denote the state of practitioners situated on the boundary between ordinary beings and saints, Sarvāstivādins use a term expressing their being at the top of worldly beings in contrast to the Theravāda, the Dharmaguptakas, and the Mahāsaṅghikas, who express the same state from the transworldly side.

(6) There may arise then a new question about which term was used earlier, *gotrabhū* or *laukikāgradharma*. My impression is that *laukikāgradharma* is a term newly invented by the Sarvāstivādins who established a detailed stage theory of practitioners ranked below *ārya*s, i.e., the four stages of Nirvedabhāgīya, beginning with *uṣmagata* and ending with *laukikāgradharma*, and this invention appeared after the use of the term *gotrabhū* had already prevailed among various sects.[19]

A positive proof of their earlier use of the term *gotrabhū* is found in a passage of the Chinese translation of the Madhyamāgama,[20] which is regarded as a work of Sarvāstivādins (not the orthodox group, but a certain branch), the passage being equivalent to the Pāli *Dakkhināvibhāṅgasutta* of the Majjhimanikāya (no. 142). It runs as follows: "In the future there will be those

17. The *Mahāvibhāṣāśāstra*, T. vol. 27, p. 6b (*sheng-che chung-hsing* for *āryagotra*).

18. Ibid., p. 12b (*sheng-hsing* is probably for *āryagotra*).

19. The *Mahāvibhāṣā* mentions as an opinion of someone that this is called *chung-hsing ti fa* (*gotrabhūdharma*) and should not be called *laukikāgradharma* (ibid., p. 6a).

20. Madhyamāgama, no. 180, *Ch'ü-t'an-mi ching*, T. vol. 1, p. 722b.

mendicants who, though being members of the family (*ming hsing chung* [lit. *nāmagotrajāti*, but probably for *gotrabhū*]), are lazy and, wearing *kaṣāya* robes, do not strive at all. Even to such lazy members, you should donate offerings because of their laziness. Then, because [of donations] for the sake of the community, to the community, respecting the community, and based on the community, the donor would, I dare to say, receive immeasurable, innumerable, and uncountable bliss and would receive good fortune and happiness." This passage is in a section attached to the description of the seven kinds of Saṅgha worthy to receive donations and refers to the merit of such donations for the Saṅgha.[21] So *ming hṣing chung* or *gotrabhū* here may mean a member of the community, regardless of his being an *ārya* or not. And out of the two kinds of use of the term *gotrabhū*, this seems to be the original.[22]

Now, how shall we understand this fact that *gotrabhū* is used in both powerful sects, Sarvāstivāda and Theravāda? In a way it

21. At a glance, the Madhyamāgama counts this type of donation, i.e., donations to the Saṅgha through *gotrabhūs*, in between the fifth and the seventh, but in its content the passage mostly agrees with the Pāli equivalent, and the Chinese counting seems to be an error by the translator.

22. For this assumption, the following passage in the *Mahāvibhāṣā* would be worth being considered: "And next, to recommend to become a mendicant means to recommend people to enter the saintly *dharma* (*āryadharma*). Therefore the scripture says: There are two kinds of entrance to the saintly *dharma*. One is worldly (*saṃvṛti*), the other is of ultimate sense (*paramārtha*). The former means to abandon the family *dharma* to enter a state of no home, shaving hair and wearing the yellow robes, and to accept the pure moral codes with a pious mind of faith. The entrance in the ultimate sense is to ascend from the *laukikāgradharma* to enter the knowledge called *duḥkhadharmakṣānti*." The parallelism with the two kinds of *gotrabhū* is visible especially in abandonment of the family *dharma* (*kuladharma*, but also possibly *gotradharma*) for the first kind, and of the *laukikāgradharma* (i.e., *pṛthagjanagotradharma*) in the second kind. The Sarvāstivādins retained the first kind of *gotrabhū* in the Madhyamāgama, but replaced the second kind of use by *laukikāgradharma* probably because there was no such use in their authorized scriptures.

is possible to consider that the introduction of the term *gotrabhū* had taken place before the schism of the community. Circumstances for its introduction would be the Buddhist penetration into Hindu society around Aśoka's reign, on the one hand, and the arising of Hindu reaction on the other, both factors having caused Buddhists to feel themselves united not by the name of the Sakiya clan, as they did before, but by the name of Bauddha or analogically a family whose ancestor is the Tathāgata, or having Tathāgata as their *gotra*. As for the development of this concept, however, neither the Sarvāstivāda nor Theravāda could claim their contribution. Most probably it was the Dharmaguptaka who developed the concept for the name of a stage linked with the *aṣṭamaka* and the other four stages ending with *kṛtāvin* and transmitted this system to the Mahāyānist who composed the *Prajñāpāramitā*.

(7) Lastly, I will mention the use of the term *gotrabhū* in the *Prajñāpāramitāsūtras*.[23] For reference I will present here a table of the ten-stage theory in the *Prajñāpāramitāsūtras*.[24] From this table we can get a coherent use of terms denoting a set of persons, qualities, and the stage qualified. In the case of *gotrabhū*, it denotes a person who stands below *aṣṭamaka*, who is endowed with qualities called *gotrabhūdharma*, and whose stage is called *gotrabhūmi*.[25]

23. *Śatasāhasrikā* (ed. by P. Ghosa), p. 1263. But in the equivalent passage, the *Pañcaviṃśatisāhasrikā* uses *gotrabhūmi* (and *aṣṭamakabhūmi*).
24. The table has been copied from my earlier paper no. 2.
25. In this paper I have not discussed the etymology of the term *gotrabhū*. In a question posed after the presentation of my paper, Prof. A. Wayman expressed his opinion that *bhū* in *gotrabhū* meant originally the earth, i.e., a stage (*bhū* = *bhūmi*, f.). I think it unlikely because such a meaning is not applicable to the first kind of use. But to regard *-bhū* in the compound as a verbal noun is also problematic. It is grammatically difficult to solve this compound into 'to be (or become, be born) in the *gotra*'. To become *gotra* is also

A *pudgala*		B *dhạrma*		C *bhūmi*
				1. *śuṣkavipaśyanābh.* (*śuklavipaśyanābh.*, *śuklavidarśanābh.*)
1. *gotrabhū* (*gotrabhūmi*)		1. *gotrabhūdharma*		2. *gotrabhūmi*
2. *aṣṭamaka*		2. *aṣṭamakadh.*		3. *aṣṭamakabh.*
3. *srotaāpanna*	(1)	3. *srotaāpannadh.* (*srotaāpannaphala*)	(1)	4. *darśanabh.*
4. *sakṛdāgāmin* (*sakṛdāgāma*)	(2)	4. *sakṛdāgāmidh.* (*sakṛdāgāmiph.*)	(2)	5. *tanubh.*
5. *anāgāmin* (*anāgāma*)	(3)	5. *anāgāmidh.* (*anāgāmiph.*)	(3)	6. *vītarāgabh.*
6. *arhat*	(4)	6. *arhaddharma* (*arhattva*)	(4)	7. *kṛtāvibh.* 7a. *śrāvakabh.* (1–7)
7. *pratyekabuddha*	(5)	7. *pratyekabuddhadh.* (*pratyekabodhi*) (*pratyekabuddhatva*)	(5)	8. *pratyekabuddhabh.*
8. *bodhisattva*	(6)	8. *bodhisattvadh.* (*bodhisattvatva*) (*mārgākārajñatā*)	(6)	9. *bodhisattvabh.*
9. *buddha* (*tathāgato 'rhan samyaksambud-dha*)	(7)	9. *buddhadharma* (*buddhatva*) (*sarvākārajñatā*)	(7)	10. *buddhabhūmi* (*samyaksambuddha-bh.*)
I 1–8		III ... (1)–(7)		II, III 1–10
III ... (1)–(7)		Vb .. (1)–(5), (7)		Va .... 1–7, Vc 7a–10
IV ... 1–9		IV ... 1–9		VI 2–7**
XI ... 1–9				VII, X ... 1–10
				VIII 1–8
				IX 1–8, B8*, B9*

B8* = *mārgākārajñatā*; B9* = *sarvākārajñatā*; ***ŚsP* B1–2, C4–7; *pṛthag-*

---

meaningless. This is one of the reasons why scholars seek for an original form other than *-bhū* as the latter part of the compound, *-han* being most likely. However, I suppose from the result arrived at in this paper, a wrong Sanskritization, so to say, of *-han* into *-bhū* took place not in the Pāli tradition but in the outside before its introduction to Sri Lanka.

janabh. for C1 in Hsüan-tsang's translation.

I *PvP*, p. 169.8-14; *ŚsP*, chap. vii, p. 1263; *Chih-tu lun*, T. vol. 25, p. 383ab; *Nyi khri*, P. vol. 18, p. 116.1.2-4.
II *PvP*, p. 225.13-19; *ŚsP*, pp. 1472.14–1473.18; *Chih-tu lun*, pp. 411a, 419c; *Nyi khri*, p. 146.4.4-6.
III *PvP*, pp. 230.14–231.10; *ŚsP*, p. 1520; *Chih-tu lun*, p. 421c; *Nyi khri*, p. 153.3.3-8.
IV *PvP*, p. 233.8-14; *ŚsP*, pp. 1555–1557; *Chih-tu lun*, p. 423a; *Nyi khri*, pp. 154.5.7-8, 156.3.3-6.
V *PvP*, p. 235.18-22; *ŚsP*, pp. 1562–1563: *Chih-tu lun*, p. 424c; *Nyi khri*, p. 157.4.3-5.
VI *PvP*, p. 238.21-24; *ŚsP*, pp. 1582–1583; *Chih-tu lun*, p. 426a; *Nyi khri*, p. 163 (Ti 4a6-b8).
VII *Chih-tu lun*, pp. 585a (Sūtra), 585c, 586a; *Nyi khri*, P. vol. 19, p. 34 (Thi 178b7–179b1).
VIII *Chih-tu lun*, p. 652bc (Sūtra); *Nyi khri*, p. 101 (Di 27a1-a6).
IX *Chih-tu lun*, p. 659bc (Sūtra); *Nyi khri*, pp. 110–111 (Di 51b8–52b3).
X *Chih-tu lun*, pp. 664bc (Sūtra), 665b; *Nyi khri*, p. 117 (Di 67b8–68b2).
XI *Chih-tu lun*, pp. 718b (Sūtra), 719c; *Nyi khri*, p. 178.5.6-8.

Abbreviations

PvP *Pañcaviṃśatisāhasrikā Prajñāpāramitā*, ed. by N. Dutt, Calcutta, 1934.
ŚsP *Śatasāhasrikā Prajñāpāramitā*, ed. by P. Ghosa, Part I, Calcutta, 1902–13.
T. Taishō Tripiṭaka.
P. Peking Reprint Edition.

PART IV
TATHĀGATAGARBHA DOCTRINE IN GENERAL

The Buddhist Concept of the Spiritual Family*

As is well-known, Buddhism is a teaching fundamentally for those who have renounced the world.

> *kesamassuṃ ohāretvā kāsāyāni vatthāni acchādetvā agārasmā anagāriyaṃ pabbajatī.* (*Dīgha Nikāya*, I, 60)
> (Shaving off hair and beard, putting on the yellow robes, he wanders forth out of home into the state of no home.)

Monks are required not only to keep celibacy but also to cut off relations with the family they belonged to before renunciation. The word "renunciation" means renunciation of home, renunciation of family, of class, of social state or designation, of wealth—of everything belonging to the worldly life. In the Buddhist Order, family name and caste appellation have no value at all.

Thus, after initiation into the Order, monks lose their family name and clan or caste appellation, and instead obtain, regardless of their origin, the appellation of 'a son of the Sākyas'.

"Just as the great rivers Gaṅgā, Yamunā, Aciravatī, Sarabhū and Mahī, when they flow into the sea, lose their original names and obtain one and the same name of the sea, in a similar manner, those who belonged to various castes of Kṣatriya, Brāhmaṇa, Vaiśya or Śūdra, when they are initiated into the Discipline of the Law (*dhammavinaya*) settled by the Tathāgata, wandering in the homeless state, lose their former name of family and clan, and obtain the appellation of 'a wanderer, a son of the Sākyas'."

> *—evam eva—cattāro 'me vaṇṇā khattiyā brāhmaṇā vessā suddā, te tathāgatappavedite dhammavinaye agārasmā*

* Originally published in *Buddhist Annual* (1967), pp. 85–88.

anagāriyaṃ pabbajitvā jahanti purimāni nāmagottāni, samaṇā Sakyaputtiyā tveva saṃkhaṃ gacchanti. (*Aṅguttara Nikāya*, IV, 202)

But why are they called *Sakyaputtiyā*, sons of the Sākyas, or the Sākyan clan? At first sight, it seems contradictory to the Buddhist idea of 'homeless state' (*anagāriya*). *Sakyaputta* originally signified a member of the Sākyan clan, the Buddha Gotama Śākyamuni himself being an example. And being followers of the Buddha, a *Sakyaputta*, Buddhist monks are called *Sakyaputtiyā*. It was a general custom in those days to call *samaṇa*s by the name of their leader's family or clan. Thus *Sakyaputtiyā* was originally a name given by the people in the same way as the Buddha himself was called *Śākyamuni*, the sage of the Sākyas. But what is the value of the clan name for monks? It is sometimes liable to lead monks of Sākyan origin into an uncalled-for sense of pride in their clan.

An article of the Buddhist Precepts concerning the punishment prescribed for those who speak ill of their companions who advise them against misconduct (the 12th of the *saṅghādisesa*, *Vinaya*, III, 177ff.) refers to the reason for the enactment of the rule. Bhikkhu Channa, who had committed some offence, rejected his companions' advice on the grounds that he belonged to the same noble family as his preceptor, and therefore his companions, being of various clans, had no right to advise him on such a matter. The direct reason for his punishment was his ill-speaking, but the root cause was his pride in the Sākyan clan. Such pride is rather unbecoming of a monk. The appellation *Sakyaputtiyā* is nothing but a symbol of equality of membership in the Buddhist Order.

Buddhist evaluation of a man is basically by his conduct, not by his origin.

"Not by birth is he an outcaste, not by birth is he a Brāhmaṇa;

by conduct is he an outcaste, by conduct is he a Brāhmaṇa."
na jaccā vasalo hoti na jaccā hoti brāhmaṇo,
kammanā vasalo hoti kammanā hoti brāhmaṇo. (*Suttanipāta*, 136)

In the same way monks deserve to be called so because of their conduct. Members in the Order are ranked according to their seniority reckoned from the date of their higher ordination (*upasampadā*). They are evaluated by the progress they have achieved in their religious practices, i.e., by their spirituality. They could be proud of their spirituality.

This pride of Buddhist monks is observed in a canonical passage in the form of a dialogue between the Buddha and a Brāhmaṇa who is proud of his high caste. The point under discussion is that the Brāhmaṇas are proud of their origin, saying that they are the sons of Brahmā, his legal sons, born from his mouth, born out of Brahmā, incarnations of Brahmā, and are heirs of Brahmā, while the *samaṇas*, the *Sakyaputtiyās*, should say that they are the sons of the Bhagavat, his legal sons, born from his mouth; they are born out of the Dhamma, incarnations of the Dhamma, and heirs of the Dhamma: *bhagavato 'mhi putto oraso mukhato jāto dhammajo dhammanimmito dhammadāyādo* (*Dīgha Nikāya*, 27: *Aggañña-suttanta*, DN III, 80ff.; cf. *Itivuttaka*, 100: *tassa me tumhe puttā orasā*, etc.).

Thus the concept of *Sakyaputtiya* is authorized in terms of the Buddha with the interpretation *bhagavato putro*, etc. Also, we meet with a similar term *putrā buddhassa orasā* in another passage (e.g., *Saṃyutta Nikāya*, III, 83), and the same idea is developed into such terms as *buddhaputta* (*buddhaputra*), *dharmarājaputra*, etc., in later scriptures, including Mahāyāna Buddhism, while the corresponding family concept for the Buddhist Order is expressed by such terms as *tathāgata*(or *buddha*)-*kula* (family of the Buddha), -*vaṃśa* (lineage), -*gotra* (lineage or clan), and so on.

There is no space to discuss in detail the development of these concepts here. I will refer only to the concept of *gotra*, which played the most important role in later Buddhism, especially in Mahāyāna.

Gotra is a word for clan, or exogamous unit, used in Brāhmanical society. Each *gotra* bears its *gotra* name based on the name of an ancient Ṛṣi, *Gautama*, *Kāśyapa*, and such others as are believed to be the ancestors of its members. The same usage appears in the Pāli canon with its Pāli equivalent *gotta*. In the case of a Kṣatriya clan, its *gotra* name is said to be based upon that of the *purohita*, the royal Brahmin teacher of its clan. *Gotama*, by which the Buddha Śākyamuni is often addressed, is thus probably his *gotta* name.

In the Pāli canon there is no special use of the term *gotta* with a doctrinal interpretation. Instead, however, we find there the unique term *gotrabhū*, denoting one of the ranks of monks who have entered the path of discipline. This term, being a compound of *gotra* and the root *bhū*, means literally 'to become a member of a clan' or 'to be born into a clan', and this clan (*gotra*) is doctrinally explained by later Pāli commentaries as 'the clan of the nobles' (*ariyagotta*), the latter being 'spiritual nobles', i.e., Buddhist sages, in contrast to the group of ordinary beings, *puthujjana-gotta*. Technically the term *gotrabhū* is used to denote monks who have just entered the group of sages (*ariya-puggala*), being the lowest class, placed below the path of Stream-winning (*sotāpattimagga*).

It is remarkable that the form *gotrabhū* is clearly of Sanskrit origin and not proper to Pāli. It is uncertain when and by whom this term was introduced to the Pāli canon, but at least it can be said without any fear of contradiction that the introduction of this term occurred in the Nikāyas only thrice and is found mostly in the part regarded as later additions.

If it be the case, namely, that the term is of Sanskrit origin, it would be safe to infer that the concept involved in it, too, must have been borrowed from some other sect of Buddhism which used Sanskrit as the language of the scriptures. Unfortunately we have not yet found any material from Sectarian Buddhist texts which proves directly this hypothesis, and we cannot trace the use of this term back to its origin. However, the same term appears in the *Prajñāpāramitā Sūtra* (Sūtra of the Perfection of Wisdom) of Mahāyāna Buddhism in a similar context to that in the Pāli canon mentioned above (*Śatasāhasrikā*, ed. by P. Ghosha, p. 1263). The term is certainly derived from the same origin. But in other parts of the same text and in corresponding passages in other texts, the form *gotrabhū* is replaced by *gotra-bhūmi*, the stage of *gotra*, probably due to a change of interpretation of *bhū* to 'earth' (= *bhūmi*). This latter form became a technical term in later Mahāyāna Buddhism.

Besides the change of form to *gotrabhūmi*, there occurred a change of concept involved in the term *gotra* itself. As was observed before, the *gotra* concept signified the members of the Order as one spiritual family. On the other hand, however, it served to distinguish the members of the two groups of 'nobles and ordinary beings' by their powers acquired after religious practices. This function of distinction is observed in a much developed form in Mahāyānistic doctrine. In accordance with the introduction of the Vehicle (*yāna*) concept, a *gotra* name is given to each group belonging to any one of the three vehicles, viz. the vehicle of the Disciples (*śrāvaka*), of the Self-Enlightened Ones (*pratyekabuddha*), and of the Buddhas-to-be (*bodhisattva*), the last one being the Great Vehicle, i.e., the Mahāyāna. The significant point is that such a division of *gotra* is said to be determined by nature, i.e., by the innate faculty of each member, just as the *gotra* name among Brāhmins is determined by birth. Furthermore, only Mahāyānists are recognized as being possessed of the faculty able to acquire perfect Enlightenment under the name of *tathāgata-gotra*, while the existence of those who cannot attain Nirvāṇa forever under the name of *agotra* (of no *gotra*) is also recognized, both being in a similar relation to Brāhmin caste and outcastes in Brāhmanical society. Also noteworthy is the fact that the term *gotra* is interpreted as something internal, a special kind of faculty transmitted from the outset, just like blood in the case of a clan. This idea is specially strong in a school of Mahāyāna called Yogācāra.

It is clear, however, that such an idea is quite against the fundamental purpose of Mahāyāna Buddhism, which declared itself to be the 'great way' as it saves all human beings regardless of their faculties. There is another and more general current among Mahāyānists which, regarding the *gotra* divisions mentioned above as conventional, admits ultimately the capacity of enlightenment in all living beings under the name of *tathāgata-gotra*, the spiritual lineage of the Buddha. Furthermore, this innate faculty is newly called *tathāgata-garbha*, the womb which bears the Tathāgata, or *buddha-dhātu*, the essence or nature of the Buddha, the existence of which equates all living beings to the Buddha by nature. We should remember that almost all sects of Mahāyāna Buddhism in China and Japan accepted fundamentally this idea of Buddha-nature.

The *Tathāgatagarbha* Theory in the *Mahāparinirvāṇa-sūtra*[*]

I

The *Mahāparinirvāṇa-sūtra* (*MPS*) is a Mahāyāna scripture in which is taught the 'real' meaning of the Buddha's *mahāparinirvāṇa* on the basis of the Mahāyānistic interpretation, borrowing the scene of his Great Death at Kusināra as depicted in a scripture of the same title in the Āgama of Primitive Buddhism (e.g., *Dīghanikāya* no. 15). The Sanskrit original of this sūtra seems to have been lost, and we have at present the following translations in the Chinese and Tibetan Tripiṭakas.

C1: tr. by Dharmakṣema, in 40 vols. Taishō Ed., no. 374.
2: tr. by the same and rearranged by Hui-yen 慧嚴, in 36 vols. Taishō Ed., no. 375.
3: tr. by Fa-hsien 法顯, in 6 vols. Taishō Ed., no. 376.
4: (Additional part) tr. by Jñānabhadra, in 2 vols. Taishō Ed., no. 377.
T1: tr. by Wang phab shun, etc., from a Chinese source, in 2 cases. Peking Ed., no. 787.
2: tr. by Jinamitra, etc., in 13 *bampo*s. Peking Ed., no. 788.

Among these, *T1* is a translation of *C1* and *C4* combined. *T2* is a direct translation of an Indian source, and, though greater in volume, it is equivalent to *C3* in its contents. This *C3* corresponds to only the first one-fourth of *C1* in its contents, but it seems to show the original form of this sūtra. The originality of the remaining part of *C1* as being from India is rather doubtful.

There are 3 fragmentary portions known to us in Sanskrit:

---

[*] Originally published in *JIBS* 19-2 (1971), pp. 1024–1015.

Fr. 1: a passage on *parādhyāśaya* and *pṛcchāvaśa*, being part of chap. VIII of *C3*. A manuscript found at Kōyasan Monastery, Japan, of which an edition is included in the Taishō Tripiṭaka, vol. 12, p. 604 (*T2* (L)[1] 73a4–74a6; *C1*, 385c–386a; *C3*, 868bc).

Fr. 2: a passage on the propagation of this sūtra, being a scripture of the *tathāgatagarbha* theory. A manuscript found in Central Asia by Hoernle and mentioned in his *Manuscript Remains*, p. 93. It has been identified with the *MPS* and re-edited in comparison with *C1* and *C3* by Kaikyoku Watanabe in his collected works, *Kogetsu zenshū*, pp. 574–577 (*T2* (L) 201a7–202b2; *C1*, 422bc; *C3*, 895a).

Fr. 3: a passage on the true notion of *nitya*, *ātman*, *sukha* and *śubha* in relation to the Tathāgata, with a parable of water sport, quoted in the *Ratnagotravibhāga* (*RGV*), pp. 74–75 (Johnston's Ed.) (*T2* (L) 45b3–46a6; *C1*, 377c–378a; *C3*, 862b).

As all of these fragments are found in sections corresponding to *C3* and *T2*, this part is at least certainly of Indian origin. This is confirmed by the fact that the index of the contents of the sūtra spoken in the form of questions by Bodhisattva Kāśyapa (*T2* (L) 52a1–53a3; *C1*, 379c–380a; *C3*, 863c) refers only to this part and not beyond it. For this reason, I will refer in this article exclusively to this same part.

According to the *MPS*, *mahāparinirvāṇa* means the eternity of the *tathāgata*, being *dharmakāya*, and the death of the Preceptor is merely a conventional appearance for the sake of living beings, all of whom he regards 'as his only son'. This doctrine of the eternity of the Tathāgata is interwoven with the theory of the *tathāgatagarbha* as a *sine qua non*, and because of this theory the

1. References to page numbers in *T2* are here basically according to the Lha-sa Edition (*Mdo Ña pa*, no. 122).

MPS declares itself the ultimate scripture (*rgyud phyi maḥi yaṅ phyi ma = uttarottara-tantra*?), being the secret word (*sandhā-vacana*) of the Tathāgata. The purpose of the sūtra is to establish the Buddhist Community by means of this supreme doctrine at the time of a crisis of decline that will occur in the near future: "There remain only about 80 years before the destruction of the *saddharma*" (*C1* 421c).

The sūtra is characterized in the colophon of *T2* in the following way:

> *yoṅs su mya ṅan las ḥdas pa chen poḥi mdo chen po, dam paḥi chos* (*saddharmaḥ*), *gsuṅ rab thams cad kyi sñiṅ por gyur pa* (*sarvapravacanasārabhūtaḥ*), *rgyud phyi ma lta bu* (*uttaratantra iva*) *rtogs par dkaḥ baḥi chos kyi ḥbyuṅ gnas* (*duṣprativedhadharmākaraḥ*), *gcig tu de bshin gśegs paḥi sñiṅ po ston paḥi mdo* (*ekadhā tathāgatagarbhanirdeśa-sūtram*). (L. 222b2-3)

II

Then how is this *tathāgatagarbhanirdeśa* expressed in the *MPS*?

The fundamental statement of the *tathāgatagarbha* theory in this sūtra is found in the following sentence: *sems can thams cad la saṅs rgyas kyi khams yod do* (L. 138a2). It may be restored to Sanskrit in the following way: *asti buddhadhātuḥ sarvasattveṣu*. This statement is spoken of as coming from the *Tathāgatagarbha-sūtra* (*TGS*), but the formula in the latter is *sarvasattvās tathā-gatagarbhāḥ*, as observed in the *RGV* (p. 25). The same connotation is expressed often using the term *tathāgatagarbha* instead of *buddhadhātu* (e.g., L. 119a2-3), and we come to know that the modification took place in the *MPS* by introducing the concept of *dhātu* in order to explain *tathāgatagarbha*. The term *buddha-dhātu* (or *tathāgatadhātu*), which does not appear in the *TGS*, *An-ūnatvāpūrṇatvanirdeśa* (*AAN*) or *Śrīmālāsūtra* (*ŚMS*), the three basic scriptures on the *tathāgatagarbha* theory, seems to be used for the first time in the *MPS*. Thus, the *tathāgatagarbha* theory in the *MPS* will be defined as the theory of *dhātu-astitva*. Let us now go into details.

According to *C1*, the fourth chapter is named 如來性, which is equivalent to *tathāgatadhātu*, though translated as "*de bshin gśegs paḥi sñiṅ poḥi leḥu*" in *T1*. This chapter covers about two-thirds of the first ten volumes, in which is included the passage attributed to the *TGS*. The same part is divided into chapters VII to XVII in *C3*, and the title *Tathāgatadhātu* is given exclusively to chap. XIII. The chapter divisions of *C3* are based on the sūtra index referred to above, and chap. XIII corresponds to the following question:

> *thub pa, byaṅ chub sems rnams kyis //*
> *ji ltar brtag dkaḥ khams mthoṅ ḥgyur //* (L. 52a6)

Here *brtag dkaḥ khams* (*duṣprativedha-dhātu*) signifies the *tathāgatagarbha*, which is said to be accessible only to the Buddha. Actually, the characteristics of *tathāgatagarbha* are also mainly discussed in this chapter. At the same time, the naming and division of *C1* are also reasonable since the references to *tathāgatagarbha* are scattered throughout the part equivalent to chap. 4 of *C1*. We will first of all examine the description of *tathāgatagarbha* in these parts before considering chap. XIII of *C3*.

III

Including the statement *asti buddhadhātuḥ sarvasattveṣu*, the main and typical examples referring to the *tathāgatagarbha* theory are as follows:

1) To cut out the way (*lam chad pa*) means that by practising the notion of *nirātman*, one perceives *nirātman* without cutting the stream. Then, by practising the notion of *ātman*, one perceives *ātman* without cutting the stream, and thus after practising in both ways, one perceives the existence of

the *buddhadhātu*. This is *mokṣa*. What is *mokṣa* is the Tathāgata. (*T2* (L) 106b5-7, (P) 177.3.7; *C1*, 395b; *C3*, 875a, chap. VIII on the four ways of preaching)

2) The Bhagavat, who is regarded as *nitya*, *dhruva*, *śāśvata* and *susukha* (?), teaches "*asti tathāgatagarbhaḥ sarvasattveṣu*." (*T2* (L) 119a2-3, (P) 180.5.1; *C1*, 399a; *C3*, 877c, chap. IX)

3) A *bhikṣu* maintained that (the Bhagavat) taught in the *Tathāgatagarbha mahāsūtra* "*asti buddhadhātuḥ sarvasattveṣu*" and, being possessed of this *dhātu*, *sattva*s, after eliminating defilements, become enlightened, with the exception of *icchantika*s, and thus he, too, is possessed of the *buddhadhātu*. Such a statement by a *bhikṣu* does not commit the fault of 'going beyond human morals' (*miḥi chos las bla mar gyur pa* = *naradharma-atisāra*?) (or is not guilty of the *pārājikā* of false speaking), so long as he keeps himself within the Buddha's precepts and discipline.

This doctrine of *tathāgatagarbha-astitva* is not taught in the teaching of nine divisions (*navāṅga-śāsanā*), i.e., in the Āgama of the Hīnayāna, nor is it taught in the Mahāyāna, which is also based upon the doctrine of *nirātman*. Even so, such a statement does not commit the fault of going beyond human morals since this teaching has not been taught only because it is not within the scope of *śrāvaka*s and *pratyekabuddha*s. Rather, those who think that there exists the *tathāgatagarbha*, being the seed of enlightenment (*saṅs rgyas su ḥgyur baḥi sa bon de bshin gśegs paḥi sñiṅ po*), and that they will attain the state of the Buddha after extirpating defilements, and that not only themselves but all other *kalyāṇamitra*s, too, have the *buddhadhātu* and can attain the *buddhabhūmi*—they are my real disciples and are worthy of being called *bodhisattva*s. (summary) (*T2* (L) 138a2–142a5, (P) 185.5.6–187.1.3; *C1*, 404c–405c; *C3*, 881b–

882a, chap. X on the distinction between the true doctrine and false ones)

4) If someone says that what is meant by the extinction of suffering (*duḥkhanirodha*) is the extinction of everything through the practice of *śūnyatā* and so the *tathāgatagarbha* too ought to be non-existent, this is absolutely unreasonable. On the contrary, through practice in the existence (*astitva*) of the *tathāgatagarbha*, *sattva*s, though possessed of defilements, can get rid of those defilements. To realize this fact (that is, to enter the *tathāgatagarbha*, *tathāgatagarbhapraveśa*) is indeed what is called the *duḥkhanirodhasatya* in the Buddha's teaching. (summary) (*T2* (L) 145b3–146a4, (P) 187.5.5–188.1.3; *C1*, 406c; *C3*, 883a, chap. XI on the four *satya*s)

5) To posit the existence of *ātman* on top of *nirātman* is a misconception (*viparyāsa*). To posit the non-existence of *ātman* on what is *ātman* is also a misconception.. Here, to practise the *nirātman* concept, maintaining that in the Buddha's teaching, as in worldly things (*saṃvṛti*), there is absolutely no *ātman* and hence there should not be even the term *tathāgatagarbha*, this is the third misconception. (*T2* (L) 147a5-7, (P) 188.2.6-8; *C1*, 407c; *C3*, 883b, chap. XII on the four *viparyāsa*s)

Thus we come to know that, in these passages, what was of primary concern to the sūtra-composer was to establish the *astitva* of *tathāgatagarbha* as a synthesis of the doctrines of *ātman* and *nirātman*. Also notable is that, in spite of these frequent references, nothing is explained about what the *tathāgatagarbha* is and how it is the *dhātu*. This task is taken up in the next chapter, the chapter on the *tathāgatadhātu*.

IV

Chapter XIII of *C3* starts with the question of whether or not *ātman* exists. The reply is that what is called *ātman* is nothing but the *tathāgatagarbha* and there exists the *buddhadhātu* in all living beings but they cannot see it because it is hidden by various defilements. This point is called 'the difficulty of understanding the *dhātu*', and it is explained with various analogies, beginning with a treasure under the ground of a poor woman's house. The whole passage can be divided in the following way:

1) The *tathāgatagarbha* is the *ātman* from the highest and supermundane point of view.
   1. The parable of a treasure. (*T2* (L) 147b4–148b5; *C1*, 407b; *C3*, 883b)
   2. The significance of this *ātman* theory after preaching the *nirātman* theory. The example of a mother who applied poison to her breast. (*T2* (L) 149b2-5; *C1*, 407c; *C3*, 883c)
   3. The reason why differences exist among *sattva*s in spite of the existence of *ātman*, the *tathāgatadhātu*. Examples of a jewel on the forehead of a wrestler who does not know it, and of the medicine of one taste grown in the Himālaya which changes its taste according to conditions. Although the *buddhadhātu* is unchangeable and indestructible, variations occur due to the power of *karman*. (*T2* (L) 149b5–154b4; *C1*, 407c–408c; *C3*, 883c–884a)

2) The *dhātu*, being the essence of the Tathāgata, is the ultimate refuge. The Three Jewels are the *śaraṇa* since they are of the nature of my *dhātu*, i.e., the essence of the Tathāgata. Therefore, one should take refuge only in the Tathāgata. Further, he himself should be the refuge since he has the *buddhadhātu* within him. (*T2* (L) 154b4–157a6; *C1*, 409a–410b; *C3*, 884a–885b)

3) The method of understanding the *tathāgatagarbha* (*tathāgatagarbhapraveśa*), *advayatā* of *ātman* and *nirātman*,

vidyā and *avidyā*, etc., being the *madhyamā pratipad*. The teaching of *duḥkha*, *anitya*, *anātman* and *śūnya*, and the *tathāgatagarbha* theory. Parable of *sarpis*, the best of which is produced from the milk of a cow which has eaten a kind of grass grown in the Himālaya called *snum can* (肥膩). (*T2* (L) 157a6–161b6; *C1*, 410b–411c; *C3*, 885b–887a)

4) The *tathāgatagarbha* or *buddhadhātu* is difficult to see even for those *bodhisattva*s who have obtained the tenth stage (*daśabhūmi*). The *tathāgatagarbha* is the sphere accessible only to Tathāgatas. Ten examples beginning with a *taimirika*. (*T2* (L) 161b6–164b5; *C1*, 411c–412b; *C3*, 887ab)

5) The *buddhadhātu* is the real *ātman*. Example of a real sword in the possession of a prince. (conclusion) (*T2* (L) 164b5–166a6; *C1*, 412b–413a; *C3*, 887bc)

Notable points in this chapter are:

1) A positive expression of the *tathāgatagarbha* in terms of *ātman*. This is no doubt related to the definition of the *dharmakāya* as being *nitya*, *ātman*, *sukha* and *śubha*, which is one of the essential doctrines of this sūtra as observed in the parable of water sport quoted in the *RGV*. Because of this *ātma-vāda*, which would seem to run counter to the *anātma-vāda* of Buddhism, the *MPS* refers to itself as the *sandhāvacana*.

2) Emphasis on the worship of the *dhātu* as the only *śaraṇa*. This is, on the one hand, an expression of the *ekayāna* doctrine similar to that of the *ŚMS* and shows its close connections with the *Saddharmapuṇḍarīka*. At the same time, however, it seems to be related to relic (*dhātu*) worship, which is supposed to be one of the origins of the Mahāyāna movement ("I should worship the relics of the Buddha and the *caitya* without neglecting the *dharmakāya*," (L) 155b3-4). We may be allowed to assume that in accordance with

changes in the conception of the Buddha from the *rūpakāya* to the *dharmakāya*, the *dhātu* to be worshipped has also been changed from the relics to the abstract essence of the Buddha, which is nothing but the essence of things (*dharmadhātu*) and is at the same time identical with the essence within *sattvas*, i.e., the *buddhadhātu*.

Another point of which one is reminded in this regard is the teaching of *attadīpa* or *attasaraṇa* in the *Mahāparinibbāna-suttanta*. The existence of *buddhadhātu* seems to show the basis of this teaching.

3) There are various explanations of the nature of the *tathāgatagarbha*, such as:

1. The *tathāgatagarbha* is *bcud kyi khams daṅ ḥdra ba* (L. 152b1) (*bcud* = *rasa*, *amṛta*).
2. *bdud rtsi rtag pa khams kyi dbyiṅs* (eternal and *amṛta*-like essence) (L. 154a2), *bdud rtsi mchog gi khams de ni ṅaḥi khams yin* (L. 154a3) (This highest *amṛta*-like *dhātu* is my essence).
3. The *tathāgatagarbha* is *yaṅ dag paḥi khams* (L. 158b1), with which one should extinguish all the elements (*sarvadhātu* = *saṃskṛtadharmas*) and establish oneself in what is eternal. It is innate nature (*prakṛtidharmatā*) (L. 158b3).
4. *bde baḥi sa bon* (L. 158b3), existing within a body.
5. *chos kyi skuḥi sa bon* (L. 158b5), existing within a body.
6. Although *tathāgatagarbha* is the essence which is unartificial from the beginning (*thogs nas bcos ma ma yin paḥi khams* [*ādy-akṛtrimadhātu*]), various defilements have arisen like temporary guests (*glo bur*, *āgantu*), and those who wish to be enlightened should extinguish these defilements (L. 161a4-6).

V

Another important chapter with respect to the *tathāgatagarbha* theory is chap. XVII, entitled "Questions of the Bodhisattva."

This chapter can be divided into the following three parts on account of the *tathāgatagarbha* theory.

1) On *icchantika*s, who are regarded as having no cause of enlightenment. (*T2* (L) 183b4–195b3; *C1*, 417b–420c; *C3*, 891b–894a)
2) Characteristics of this *MPS*, which preaches the *tathāgatagarbha* theory as the secret word (*sandhāvacana*) of the Tathāgata, and the purpose of its propagation. (*T2* (L) 195b3–202a6; *C1*, 420c–422b; *C3*, 894a–895a)
3) Non-discrimination of the *dhātu* in essence and its differentiation in appearance. (*T2* (L) 202a6–206b4; *C1*, 422c–423c; *C3*, 895a–896a)

Among these, 1) the question of the *icchantika* is another important subject not only of this sūtra but of the *tathāgatagarbha* theory in general. At present, however, as we have no space to discuss this question, I will just recommend an article by Prof. Kōshō Mizutani, in which all passages referring to the *icchantika* in the *MPS* have been extracted from *T2*, in comparison with *C1* and *C3*, and commented on in detail (*Bukkyō Daigaku Kenkyū Kiyō* 40, pp. 63–105).

In section 2), this sūtra is compared to pure *sarpis* in comparison with other teachings, which are like watered milk 'sold by *gopī*s'. The definition of *tathāgatagarbha* as being 'of manly character' is also notable.

3) The third point is more remarkable. Here, at the request of Bodhisattva Kāśyapa, the Buddha explains *tathāgata-pratyekabuddha-śrāvaka-bodhisattva-dhātunirnānākaraṇa(-tva)* (*Fr.* 2) with an analogy of cow milk. Namely, cow milk is of the same quality in spite of differences in the colour of cows. This seems to

show the *prakṛtiviśuddhatā* of the *dhātu*, while another example, of a mine of gold, shows the *vaimalyaviśuddhatā* in the sense that gold comes out of the mine after having been purified. At the same time, the sūtra never forgets to refer to the difference between the Buddha, bodhisattvas and ordinary beings, and this is explained by an analogy of the process of making *sarpis* from milk in five stages. Namely, the difference is considered to be merely a difference of stages or circumstances, and the essential identity throughout the whole process is implicitly maintained.

VI

Following the above examination, we may draw the following conclusions regarding the characteristics of the *tathāgatagarbha* theory in this sūtra.

1) The biggest contribution of the *MPS* to the history of the *tathāgatagarbha* theory was the establishment of the concept of *buddhadhātu* for explaining the nature of *tathāgatagarbha*. This *dhātu* concept as showing the essence or nature common to *sattva*s and the Tathāgata seems to have been introduced by the *AAN*, but the *MPS*, coming after the *AAN*, utilized it to its full scope, in which are involved various other meanings of the term *dhātu* developed in Buddhism, such as relics of the Buddha, the eighteen component elements, the four gross elements, the sphere of the *dharma*, the essence of *dharma*s (e.g., the *tathāgatakāya* is not [consisting] of elements of collected materials [*bsags paḥi khams*], but of the essence of the *dharma* [*chos kyi khams*] [L. 110a1-2], which suggests that *dharmakāya* is *dharmadhātu-kāya*), the root of a word, etc.

2) The most unique expression of this sūtra with respect to the *tathāgatagarbha* is *ātman*, which is regarded as a sort

of taboo in Buddhism.[2] The connotations of this term in the text are completely identical with *dhātu*.

3) In spite of the use of such an abstract concept, the *MPS* is far from presenting a systematization of the theory in comparison with the *AAN* and *ŚMS*. Especially the relationship between *tathāgatagarbha* and *dharmakāya*, the problem of the pure mind and defilements, etc., are not discussed explicitly as in the *ŚMS*. In this respect, I hesitate a little to place the date of the *MPS* after the *ŚMS*.

4) In spite of frequent references to the *icchantika*, the term *agotra* is not used. In general, the *gotra* concept is lacking in the *MPS*. This point is common to the *AAN* and *ŚMS*.

(This research was partially supported by a grant-in-aid for scientific research from the Ministry of Education for 1969.)

---

2. One of the sources of this concept in Buddhism is sought in the *Sammitīya-śāstra* (T. no. 1649) by K. Venkata Ramanam in *Visvabharati Annals* 5 (Santiniketan, 1953), pp. 219–220 (n. 28). He mentions three passages from the *MPS* (T. vol. 12, pp. 525b, 502c–3a, 556a) as evidence, all of which are found in the part we regarded as later additions. (This reference is due to J. Rahder in his review article of my *Study on the Ratnagotravibhāga* [Rome, 1966] in *JIBS* 15-1.)

Tathagātagarbha and the Community of Bodhisattvas*

I

The *Ratnagotravibhāga* (*RGV* in the following),[1] a Mahayana treatise on Tathāgatagarbha thought, has, in its introductory passage, the following verse which explains the inherent connection (*anuśleṣa*) between the seven subjects elucidated in the text.

> *buddhād dharmo dharmataś cāryasaṁghaḥ*
> *saṃghe garbho jñānadhātvāptiniṣṭhaḥ /*
> *tajjñānāptiś cāgrabodhir balādyair*
> *dhamair yuktā sarvasattvārthakṛdbhiḥ //3//*[2]

In this verse, *saṃghe* in the second line is of a doubtful form, since, according to the editor's note, both Chinese and Tibetan translations interpret it as if it were *saṃghād*, though manuscript B clearly reads *saṃghe.* The editor himself accepted the manuscript reading with the understanding that "as the Tathāgatagarbha is in each member of the community and by its working leads to the acquisition of knowledge and the realization of the *dhātu*."[3]

To this is raised an objection by Hakuju Ui, who adopted the reading *saṃghād* in his Japanese translation of the *RGV*, saying that this verse simply shows the order of succession of the seven subjects given in the text as understood by the Chinese translation, which renders the term *anuśleṣa* as 'order' (*krama*), and

* Originally published in V. N. Jha, ed., *Kalyāṇa-Mitta: Professor Hajime Nakamura Felicitation Volume*, Bibliotheca Indo-Buddhica 86 (Delhi: Sri Satguru Publications, 1991), pp. 248–255.

1. The *Ratnagotravibhāga Mahāyānottaratantraśāstra*, ed. by E. H. Johnston (Patna, 1950).
2. *RGV*, p. 7.1-4.
3. *RGV*, p. 7, n. 1.

that the existence of the Tathāgatagarbha is not limited to the members of the community.[4] In my English translation of the *RGV*, on the contrary, I followed the reading of Johnston without giving any positive reason for it.[5]

Reviewing my work, Prof. J. W. de Jong raised a hand for Ui's opinion, and translated the passage in the following way:

> "From the Community comes the Matrix which culminates in the obtaining of the Element of Wisdom—"[6]

Prof. L. Schmithausen, on the contrary, while also reviewing my translation, accepted the editor's reading with the reasons that, the Ms reading being very clear, there is no positive reason for changing the reading, and that the context is understandable by regarding *jñānadhātvāptiniṣṭha* as a predicative to *garbha* in the sense that "in the community *garbha* is led to the acquisition of the Wisdom."[7]

Taking these opinions into consideration, I here wish to re-examine the context of these lines from the contents of the whole text of the *RGV*.

II

First of all, I will fix the meaning of the term *anuśleṣa*, which is used for showing the theme of this verse (*kaḥ punar eṣām anuśleṣaḥ*).

Being a derivative from *anu* + *ślis*, its literal meaning is 'attachment of something to another' or 'connection of a subject with the previous one without interruption'. For this, the Tibetan

4. Hakuju Ui, *Hōshōron kenkyū* (Tokyo: Iwanami Shoten, 1959).

5. Jikido Takasaki, *A Study on the Ratnagotravibhāga (Uttaratantra)*, S.O.R. 33 (Roma: IsMEO, 1966), p. 148.

6. J. W. de Jong, in *Indo-Iranian Journal* XI (1968), pp. 36–54 (p. 41).

7. Lambert Schmithausen, "Philologische Bemerkungen zum Ratnagotravibhāga," *Wiener Zeitschrift für die Kunde Südasiens* 15 (1971), pp. 123–127 (p. 133). (Contents summarized here by Takasaki.)

translation here simply gives *grel pa*, a word for 'relation', which is otherwise used for *saṃbandha* and so on, while the Chinese gives, as mentioned above, a term equivalent to *anukrama* (order). It is true that the text is arranged in the same order as given in this verse to the seven subjects. But what is the use of such a statement about the order as a mere repetition of that already given in verse 1?[8] There should be a special purpose and significance for this verse. It must be to make clear the logical sequence between subjects.

Namely, the text mentions the Buddha as the first subject, which is followed by the Dharma. The reason is that the Dharma is taught by the Buddha; without the appearance of the Buddha, or his Enlightenment, there is no Dharma. In the same way, the Saṃgha comes after the Dharma in the sense that on the basis of the Buddha's teaching there arises the community of disciples who strive after the Buddha's teaching. The sequence of these three subjects is shown by an ablative case-ending to the previous subject. This much may be clear in the light of the history of the founding of the Buddhist community.

Also clear is the relation between the latter three subjects, the sixth and the seventh being connected with the fifth by the instrumental case-ending, the last one being predicative to the sixth. Namely, supreme enlightenment is endowed with the ten powers and other qualities unique to the Buddha which work for the benefit of all sentient beings. By these three subjects (*bodhi*, *guṇa* and *karman*), the Dharmakāya accompanied by Wisdom and Compassion and its activity are shown. Thus these three refer actually to the Buddha, which is taught in the first subject.

The most crucial and unique point of the text is the relation between the *garbha* or embryo of the Buddha and the Dharmakāya of the Buddha. In one sense the whole text of the *RGV* is

8. They are called the seven adamantine subjects (*vajrapadāni sapta*) (*RGV*, p. 1).

devoted to making clear this point. A well-known expression is that the embryo of the Tathāgata is a name for the Dharmakāya when it is covered with the sheath of mental defilements as shown in the *Śrīmālāsūtra*.[9] Here the *garbha* is defined as *jñāna-dhātvāptiniṣṭha*, "the element of Wisdom aiming at its acquisition," according to my translation, or "that which culminates in the obtaining of the Element of Wisdom," as translated by de Jong, while supreme enlightenment, the fifth subject, is explained as the acquisition of this Wisdom. In view of this definition of *bodhi*, the *garbha* is, I think, worthy of being termed the source (*dhātu*) of Wisdom. The *garbha* is potential wisdom, and hence sentient beings, who are possessed of the embryo, are potentially buddhas. With this link between the fourth and the fifth subject, both are otherwise called *samalā tathatā* (Thusness mingled with pollution) and *nirmalā tathatā* (Thusness freed from pollution), respectively.[10] In this is observed the difference between them in spite of their basic equality, and this difference is required to be removed by the movement of the *garbha* from a polluted state to an unpolluted state. For this movement, each sentient being, although he has the embryo of the Buddha within himself, is required to commit to training, the practice of the path (*mārga-bhavanā*). From this context we may suppose that the community must be the place for the training. To give a conclusion to this problem, however, we should see further the characteristic of the community described in the text. The third subject 'Community' is versed as follows:[11]

> *ye samyak pratividhya sarvajagato nairātmyakoṭiṃ śivāṃ*
> *taccittaprakṛtiprabhāsvaratayā kleśāvabhāvekṣaṇāt /*
> *sarvatrānugatām anāvṛtadhyaḥ paśyanti saṃbuddhatāṃ*

9. Quotation in the *RGV*, p. 12.14: *dharmakāyo vinirmuktakleśakośas tathāgata-garbhaḥ sūcyate*.
10. *RGV*, v. I.23.
11. *RGV*, p. 14.1-4; commentary thereon: ibid., pp. 13.21–17.13.

tebhyaḥ sattvaviśuddhyanantaviṣayajñānekṣaṇebhyo namaḥ //13//

(I bow before those who, having perfectly penetrated into the quiescent extremity of non-substantiality of all the world,
Owing to their perception of the unreality of defilements through the brightness of the innate mind of the people,
Perceive, with uncovered intellect, the Buddhahood pervading everywhere;
To those whose eyes of wisdom have their object in the purity and infinitude of sentient beings.)

This basic stanza is explained by the following five verses and the prose commentary thereon. According to these, this stanza refers to the community of Bodhisattvas who have attained the non-retrogressive state (*avaivartikabodhisattva-gaṇa*), but not to the community of disciples (*śrāvaka-saṃgha*). Notable here is the use of the term *gaṇa* instead of *saṃgha* for the community of Bodhisattvas. This probably means the Bodhisattvas' community is free from the regulations of the Saṃgha (or is situated outside the traditional Saṃgha of disciples) in the sense that it is a spontaneous group inclusive of the laity.

Then how are they worth being venerated? It is because of their pure perception in two ways: to perceive the world 'as it is' (*yathāvat*) and to perceive it 'as far as' (*yāvat*). The first perception is explained as the understanding of the non-substantiality of the world usually described in terms of personality and entities (*pudgaladharmākhya*). in a way that they are quiescent from the outset. So much is a common understanding in Mahayana, but the text further states that this understanding is based upon the observation of the unreality of defilements from the outset because of the innate purity of the mind. This doctrine of the innate purity of the mind is a core of the Tathāgatagarbha theory, the innate mind being identified with the embryo of the Tathāgata. The second perception, characterised as being 'as far as', is explained as to perceive the existence of this innate pure mind as the embryo of the Tathāgata in all sentient beings, characterised here as the pervasion of Buddhahood. This perception has its root, via the teaching of the *Tathāgatagarbhasūtra*, in the chapter on the "Appearance of the Tathāgata" in the *Avataṃsakasūtra*, where the perception is explained in terms of the omniscience of the Buddha.[12] Namely, the finding of the pervasion of Buddhahood is due to the omniscience of the Buddha; rather, the omniscience of the Buddha is explained in the scripture as the reason for the omnipresence of Buddhahood. This is the most crucial point in the Tathāgatagarbha theory.

The perception in two ways being like this, Bodhisattvas are required to obtain this perception through the Buddha's teaching, and its first sight is expected to be obtained at the first stage of the Bodhisattva, which is equivalent to the Path of Perception (*darśanamārga*) in the Abhidharmic system. From this we come to know that the community of Bodhisattvas worth being venerated is that consisting of those Bodhisattvas who are abiding in the first stage and beyond, i.e., Bodhisattvas who deserve the title of the noble (*ārya*). They are also qualified as being non-retrogressive.[13]

The description of the community of Bodhisattvas in the text ends here. In the following passage,[14] the text speaks of the altruistic nature of the Bodhisattva as his qualification for being an object of veneration in comparison with the Śrāvaka, who is striving only for himself and hence is not worth being venerated. But there is no further explanation of the altruistic nature of the Bodhisattva. For this we must seek for another passage.

12. Quoted in *RGV*, pp. 22.8–24.8.
13. As for the equivalency of the *avaivartika* state and the stage (*bhūmi*) system, there are various theories. In another passage of the *RGV* it is equated with the eighth stage of the Bodhisattva (p. 53.2-3). But this passage belongs to a later interpolation by a different author.
14. *RGV*, pp. 16.15–17.13.

III

There are many passages in the *RGV* where Bodhisattvas are referred to. Being a kind of sentient being who is possessed of the embryo of the Tathāgata, the text generally locates them in between ordinary beings (*pṛthagjana*) and the Tathāgata. Namely, the text speaks of Bodhisattvas as one of three modes of manifestation of the embryo, characterised as the state of impure and pure (at once) (*aśuddhasuddhāvastha*).[15] Referring to the unchangeability (*avikāritva*) of the embryo or the innate mind in this impure and pure state of the Bodhisattva,[16] the text gives the following stanza:

nirvṛttivyuparamarugjarāvimuktāṃ[17]
asyaiva prakṛtim ananyathāvagamya /
janmādivyasanam ṛte 'pi tannidānaṃ
dhīmanto jagati kṛpodayād bhajante //66//

(Having known its innate nature as it is being free from origination and extinction, as well as from illness and decrepitude,
The wise [= Bodhisattvas] are of no cause of calamity. Still, moved from the rising of compassion towards the world,
They assume the calamity of birth and so forth.)

Here by his perception of the innate mind as being free from birth and so forth, the Bodhisattva is regarded as being in the pure state, namely, he himself is freed from calamity as he has no

15. *RGV*, pp. 40.5–41.5 (v. I.47).

16. *RGV*, pp. 46.5–53.8. The following verse (v. 66) is the basic stanza of this section.

17. Text reading *-vimuktā* is corrected in the light of the Chinese translation and v. I.54: *na pradahaty enaṃ mṛtyuvyādhi jarāgnayaḥ* (*enam* = *prakṛtim*). See Takasaki, op. cit., p. 243, n. 321. Also see Schmithausen, op. cit., p. 149. But the reading *-vimuktā* (adj. for *dhīman*) is also not impossible, since by his perception the Bodhisattva has no cause of calamity, and is consequently freed from birth, etc. The commentary seems to follow this reading. But he is actually not freed from birth, etc., though they are regarded as *anāsrava*.

karmic forces and defilements which cause such a calamity, whereas by his assuming of life in this world due to compassion towards the world, namely, to make other sentient beings freed from calamity, he remains in the impure state. This state is otherwise called unstable Nirvāṇa[18] and is regarded as the ideal of the Bodhisattva.

If we compare the description in this stanza to that of the stanza on the community of Bodhisattvas, we easily come to know that the perception which brings him into a pure state is to be identified with the perception 'as it is' (*yathāvad* = *ananyathā*), while his assuming of birth, etc., moved by compassion, should have an inevitable connection with his perception 'as far as'. For the latter point, the passage in the *Avataṃsaka* referred to above[19] offers a good explanation. Namely, the Buddha, having perceived the existence of the wisdom of the Tathāgata in every sentient being although it is not noticed by sentient beings because of their being captured by wrong conception, starts his preaching of the eightfold noble path in order to remove their bondage made by wrong conceptions. This is nothing but the manifestation of the Buddha's Great Compassion. The Bodhisattva's perception in two ways also corresponds to the two kinds of Buddha's Wisdom, i.e., the Non-discriminative Wisdom that works for his Enlightenment and the Worldly Wisdom obtained based upon the former that works for the benefit of others.[20] Bodhisattvas are following the Buddha's way. To accomplish their compassion, however, they must assume the Samsaric life by their own will (*saṃcintya*), and thus they are obliged to remain in this world forever, since the sentient beings to be released are inexhaustible.

---

18. On unstable Nirvāṇa (*apratiṣṭhita-nirvāṇa*), see *RGV*, p. 35.3-16.
19. See n. 12.
20. On these two kinds of Wisdom, see *RGV*, p. 59.13-14. The terms were originally invented by the Yogācāra.

IV

So far we have talked about the Bodhisattva worth being venerated. The remaining problem connected with the subject of the present paper is how ordinary beings are related to this state of the Bodhisattva. There is a passage in the *RGV* where a suitable answer seems to be given.

Commenting on the stanzas which explain the purpose of the teaching (*deśanaprayojana*) of the Tathāgatagarbha theory,[21] the commentator gives the following verses:

tathā hy aśravaṇād asya bodhau cittaṃ na jāyate /
keṣāṃ cin nīcacittānām ātmāvajñānadoṣataḥ //161//
bodhicittodaye 'py asya śreyān asmīti manyataḥ /
bodhyanutpannacitteṣu hīnasaṁjñā pravartate //162//
tasyaivaṃmatinaḥ samyagjñānaṃ notpadyate tataḥ /
abhūtaṃ parigṛhṇāti bhūtam arthaṃ na vindate //163//
abhūtaṃ sattvadoṣās te kṛtrimāgantukatvataḥ /
bhūtaṃ taddoṣanairātmyaṃ śuddhiprakṛtayo guṇāḥ //164//
gṛhṇan doṣān asadbhūtān bhūtān apavadan guṇān /
maitrīṃ na labhate dhīmān sattvātmasamadarśikām //165//
tacchravāj jāyate tv asya protsāhaḥ śāstṛgauravam /
prajñā jñānaṃ mahāmaitrī pañcadharmodayāt tataḥ //166//
niravajñaḥ samaprekṣī nirdoṣo guṇavān asau /
ātmasattvasamasnehaḥ kṣipram āpnoti buddhatām //167//

(Indeed, if [people] have not heard of this [teaching],
Some of them, being possessed of depressed mind,
May have a fault of self-depreciation, and hence
The will towards Enlightenment does not arise in them.
Even if someone has resolved towards Enlightenment,

21. *RGV*, I.156–157. They are explained by the following 10 verses (*RGV*, pp. 77.9–78.20). Of these, vv. 158–160 are not quoted here.

Then he, being proud of it, saying, "I am superior to [others],"
Will produce the notion of inferiority of those
Whose mind is not aroused towards Enlightenment.
With him who thinks like that,
The true knowledge will never arise, and hence
He clings to unreal things [as if they were real]
And does not cognize the real object.
[Indeed] the defects of living beings are unreal
Because they are non-genuine and accidental,
But the non-substantiality of such defects is real
[Which is represented by] their virtues, of pure nature.
As long as he is grasping the unreal defects and depreciating the virtues which are real,
[A Bodhisattva, though] wise,[22] cannot obtain benevolence
By which one regards living beings as equal to oneself.
On the contrary, if he hears of this teaching,
There arises in him a great exertion, respect [for all living beings] as for the teacher,
Intuition, wisdom and great benevolence.
These five virtues having become originated,
He, being free from [self-]depreciation,
Having equal regard [towards others],
Being devoid of defects and possessed of virtues,
Having love equally for himself and for living beings,
Will attain the state of the Buddha at an early date.)

Here is clearly shown a contrast between those who have not heard of this teaching of the 'existence' of the embryo of the Tathāgata in 'every' sentient being, and those who have heard of it. Firstly, those who were previously taught that everything is

22. *dhīmat* here may mean simply a Bodhisattva who undertakes the path for the first time.

empty (*śūnyaṃ sarvam*)[23] but never heard of this teaching might have a thought of self-depreciation that enlightenment will never occur to them. To teach the 'existence' of the Embryo within themselves will effect them to remove such self-depreciation and encourage them to awaken the mind towards Enlightenment, namely, let them become Bodhisattvas. Secondly, there may be Bodhisattvas who have awakened their mind through other teachings, but often they are proud of their position and look upon others as inferior to themselves. By teaching them that 'everybody' is equally possessed of the Embryo, they will remove this defect and have the thought of the equality of sentient beings and arouse respect towards them.

From this statement of the two kinds of effects of the teaching, we easily observe a correspondence between this and the Bodhisattva's perception in two ways as well as the Bodhisattva's Wisdom and Compassion. Namely, for the acquisition of the perception 'as it is' or acquisition of his own Wisdom, the starting point is the arousing of the will for Enlightenment (*bodhicitta*), while for his acquisition of the perception 'as far as' or completion of compassion, to embrace the thought of equality is required at the beginning. The latter point is further emphasized as the fifth of the five merits effected by the hearing of this teaching in terms of equal love for others as for self, which is given as a remedy for self-affection (*ātmasneha*).

A similar explanation of the merit of this teaching is elucidated towards the end of the *RGV*,[24] where the will for Enlightenment is explained as the receptacle of the five virtues of zeal, striving, memory, contemplation and intuition, etc.,[25] and the training towards the goal is much emphasized.

---

23. *RGV*, I.156.

24. *RGV*, pp. 116.6–117.4 (vv. V.7–15), the commentary passage on the merit of hearing and accepting the teaching.

25. *RGV*, v. V.10: *chandavīryasmṛtidhyānaprajñādiguṇabhājanaṃ bodhicittam.*

V

Now we have nearly arrived at the time to conclude our inquiry. Every sentient being is said to have the Embryo of the Tathāgata within himself by nature. The purpose of this teaching is not only to indicate this fact but also to let this innate potentiality be actualised. For the actualisation of Buddhahood, one should tread the path of training as a Bodhisattva. In this sense the Embryo is moved to its goal, the acquisition of Wisdom which works for the benefit of others, only in the community of Bodhisattvas. Thus the reading '*saṃghe garbho*...' is justified.

And I will revise my translation of these lines in the following way.

> In the Community [of Bodhisattvas]
> The Embryo [of the Tathāgata], being the element of Wisdom, is [expected] to be culminated in its acquisition,
> And the acquisition of this Wisdom is the Supreme Enlightenment,
> Accompanied with ten powers and other [Buddha's] properties
> Which work for the benefit of sentient beings.

Lastly, following the description given in verse 3, I will give here a diagram which shows the whole process of this realisation of the Embryo.

Buddha → Dharma → Saṃgha (Bodhisattva)
|| ||
Buddha-virtues, Buddha-activities
Bodhi ←———————— Tathāgatagarbha
(Transformed Dharma-body) (Dharmakāya concealed)
(Untainted Thusness) (Tainted Thusness)

This cyclic process reminds us of the doctrine of the fourfold purity of the Dharma-realm taught in the *Mahāyānasaṃgraha* of

Asaṅga.[26] A diagram to be inferred from the teaching is as follows:

(Pure Dharma-realm)		(Teaching)		
Innate Purity	→	Purity of the Support	→	[Saṃgha]
‖				‖
Taintless Purity	←	Purity of the Path	←	Innate Purity
(Untainted Thusness)				(Tainted Thusness)

A visible difference between these two diagrams is that this latter is speaking of the whole process in terms of the Dharma-realm in contrast to the former one, which is speaking of it in terms of the Dharma-body.

Another difference is the lack of the item of Path in the former diagram, though it is implicit, as observed above. As a Yogācāra, the author of the *RGV* probably had this theory of the *Mahāyāna-saṃgraha* in mind when he wrote the commentary.

Tathāgatagarbha thought is usually held to be a doctrine which teaches the existence of Buddha-nature in every sentient being. What is more important in this doctrine is, however, the self-realisation of this innate Buddhahood consisting of Wisdom and Compassion through practice of the Path of a Bodhisattva. Mere existence of the Embryo has no significance at all unless it is realised by oneself.

I will close this article by quoting a passage from Dōgen's *Shōbōgenzō bendōwa*:

> There is a dharma transmitted from one Buddha to another. This dharma, though possessed by everybody, cannot be manifested without practice, nor be attained without realisation (by oneself).

26. *Mahāyānasaṃgraha* (Chinese translation by Hsüan-tsang, T. vol. 31). Terms for the four purities in Sanskrit are as follows: *prakṛtiviśuddhi* (Innate Purity), *vaimalyaviśuddhi* (Taintless Purity), *ālambanaviśuddhi* (Purity of the Support), and *mārgaviśuddhi* (Purity of the Path).

Ethische Implikationen der *Tathāgatagarbha*-Lehre*

I. Die Unterrichtung Aṅgulimālas

In den Tagen Buddha Śākyamunis lebte in der Stadt Śrāvastī (Sāvatthī) ein berüchtigter Mörder. Er hatte es sich zur Gewohnheit gemacht, am Straßenrand zu stehen, um Vorbeigehende zu ermorden und nahm sich jeweils einen Finger von jedem Opfer, um einen Fingerkranz herzustellen. So wurde er von den Bewohnern Aṅgulimāla genannt, d. h. jemand, der einen Kranz (*mālā*) aus Fingern (*aṅguli*) trägt.

Als Buddha über seine Schüler von dem Mörder erfuhr, beschloß er, sich ihm entgegenzustellen, um ihn zu bekehren. Aṅgulimāla, der einen *śramaṇa* (pali *samaṇa*)[1] den Weg entlangkommen sah, freute sich; denn damit bot sich ihm die Gelegenheit, seinen Wunsch zu erfüllen, einen Kranz von hundert Fingern herzustellen, war doch aus Furcht, von ihm ermordet zu werden, schon seit vielen Tagen, nachdem er den neunundneunzigsten Finger an sich gebracht hatte, niemand mehr an ihm vorbeigekommen.

So näherte er sich mit dem blanken Schwert in der Hand Buddha. Darauf drehte sich Buddha um[2]. Aṅgulimāla rannte hinterher, vermochte aber Buddha nicht einzuholen. Erschöpft schrie er schließlich: „Bleib doch stehen! *Śramaṇa*, bleib stehen!" Buddha entgegnete: „Ich stehe doch die ganze Zeit hier. Du solltest aufhören zu rennen." Derart von Buddhas wunderbarer Macht

---

* Originally published in *Hōrin* 4 (1997), pp. 96–108.

1. Wanderer (der sein Essen erbettelt), Asket etc. Behelfsmäßig „buddhistischer Mönch".

2. Er ergriff die Flucht.

überwältigt, warf Aṅgulimāla Buddha sein Schwert zu Füßen und verbeugte sich, um sich ihm zu unterwerfen. Buddha sprach: „Du bist willkommen. Ich erlaube Dir, mein Schüler zu werden." Und er begleitete Aṅgulimāla zum *saṃgha*[3].

So wurde Aṅgulimāla ein *bhikṣu* (pali *bhikkhu*) und ein Mitglied des buddhistischen *saṃgha*. Er bereute sein früheres kriminelles Verhalten, beachtete sorgfältig die von Buddha gelehrten Vorschriften und vermittelte sie den buddhistischen Laien.

Als er eines Tages auf dem Weg in die Stadt war, um sich sein Essen zu erbetteln, bemerkte Aṅgulimāla eine schwangere Frau, die unter starken Wehen litt. In der Absicht, sie von der Gefahr, in der sie sich befand, zu befreien, teilte er die Sache Buddha mit und fragte ihn, was zu tun sei. Buddha antwortete: „Du solltest die Frau aufsuchen und ihr sagen, daß Du seit Deiner Geburt niemanden getötet habest. Aufgrund der Macht dieser wahren Worte (*sacca-kiriyā*, *sacca-vacana*) wird sie dann sicher gebären." Überrascht von diesen Worten, befürchtete Aṅgulimāla die Vorschrift, nicht zu lügen, zu verletzen, falls er dies sagen würde. Aber Buddha erklärte ihm: „Das verletzt die Vorschrift überhaupt nicht; denn als Du ein *bhikṣu* wurdest, wurdest Du neu geboren." So befolgte Aṅgulimāla Buddhas Rat, und die Frau brachte ihr Kind sicher zur Welt.

Eines anderen Tages wurde Aṅgulimāla von Steinen verletzt, die jemand, der sein früheres Verhalten kannte, nach ihm geworfen hatte. Aber er ertrug diese Gewalttat geduldig und vervollkommnete die Tugend der Geduld. So erreichte er schließlich Arhatschaft[4].

In Gedanken an seine frühere Zeit verfaßte er in seinen letzten Tagen das folgende Gedicht:

---

3. Der institutionalisierten Gemeinschaft sozusagen professioneller Buddhisten. Behelfsmäßig oft mit „buddhistischem Orden" übersetzt.

4. D. h. er wurde zu einem Arhat, einem „Edlen", einer idealen buddhistischen Persönlichkeit.

„Wer in seiner Jugend die Moral verletzte,
sie aber späterhin in vollkommener Weise annahm,
erleuchtet die Welt wie der Mond,
den eine Wolke freigegeben hat.“[5]

Die wiedergegebene Geschichte ist eine wohlbekannte Legende. Vielleicht wegen ihrer Besonderheit als Erzählung von der Bekehrung eines unmoralischen Menschen wurde sie von den Mitgliedern des *saṃgha* von Generation zu Generation zu Predigten benutzt und schrittweise in Länge und Inhalt weiterentwickelt.

Aṅgulimāla war zunächst ein hochrangiger Schüler eines brahmanischen Lehrers. Während der Abwesenheit seines Lehrers verlangte dessen Frau nach ihm, aber er verweigerte sich ihr. Daraufhin wurde sie so wütend, daß sie ihrem Mann die Lügengeschichte erzählte, Aṅgulimāla habe sie vergewaltigt, und ihn bat, Aṅgulimāla zu befehlen, hundert Menschen zu töten und so einen Kranz aus hundert Fingern herzustellen, so daß er (nach seinem Tod) in die Hölle fahre.

Was das zitierte Gedicht angeht, so findet es sich als Nummer 172 auch im *Dhammapada*. Und Buddhaghosas Kommentar (*DhP Atthakathā*) enthält die Legende von Aṅgulimāla als ein Beispiel. So ist die Autorschaft Aṅgulimālas etwas zweifelhaft.

Wie im Gedicht ausgedrückt, liegt die Relevanz der Legende in der Lehre, daß selbst Verbrecher, die in so ungeheurer Weise die Moral verletzen wie Mörder, ihre Vergehen bereuen und wiedergutmachen können, wenn sie sie bekennen und sich bemühen, den (sc. buddhistischen) Vorschriften zu folgen. Nicht nur können sie ihre Vergehen bereuen und ausgleichen: sie können auch das letzte und höchste Ziel, Nirvana, erreichen. Das mag das Prinzip buddhistischer Moral sein. Das heißt: Ob jemand nach seinem Tod ein Verdienst zu Teil wird (wie in den Himmel geboren zu werden) oder eine Vergeltung widerfährt (wie in die

5. *Theragāthā* 871.

Hölle hinab zu stürzen), hängt allein von seinem Verhalten während seines Lebens in dieser Welt ab. Dabei ist moralisches Verhalten eher geeignet, Verdienste zu erwerben denn unmoralisches Verhalten. Insbesondere für *śramaṇa* ist das Befolgen der von Buddha gelehrten Vorschriften – beginnend mit *ahiṃsā*, der Regel, keinem Lebewesen Gewalt anzutun und es so zu verletzen – die höchste Moral, die sie zum Nirvana führt. Durch Abkehr (sc. von früherem unmoralischem Leben) oder Eintritt in den *saṃgha* werden sie neu geboren und machen frühere Vergehen wieder gut.

Die buddhistische Ethik sei in den folgenden drei Punkten zusammengefaßt:

1. dem Verhalten (und nicht der Geburt) Relevanz zuzuschreiben,
2. der Empfehlung, Gutes zu tun, und dem Verbot, Böses zu tun, und zwar in dem Glauben an die Lehre vom Karma, der Vergeltung der Taten (Handlungen),
3. der schließlichen Befreiung selbst von der weltlichen Ethik, gegründet auf der Idee von der Vergeltung der Taten.

Diese Punkte sind im Mahayana-Buddhismus im Grunde gleich. In ihren Implikationen unterscheidet sich der Mahayana-Buddhismus freilich recht stark von der älteren Form des Buddhismus. Solche Unterschiede lassen sich in der Mahayana-Version der Aṅgulimāla-Legende, im *Mahāyāna-Aṅgulimāla-sūtra*, feststellen. Dieses Sutra, das im Chinesischen und Tibetischen Tripiṭaka erhalten geblieben ist, umfaßt in Guṇabhadras chinesischer Übertragung vier Faszikel und ist über 30mal länger als die kürzeste Fassung der Legende im *Saṃyukta-āgama*.

In der angesprochenen Mahayana-Version wird Aṅgulimālas Mordtat als bloße illusorische Handlung einer illusorischen Person erklärt, als Transformation eines Bodhisattva, um Menschen ans andere Ufer zu führen[6]. Außerdem demonstriert Aṅgulimāla unmittelbar nach seiner Bekehrung, als Bodhisattva, seine über-

6. Das heißt, zu erleuchten bzw. zu erlösen.

natürlichen Kräfte vor himmlischen Gottheiten wie dem Indra Śakra und anderen, und vor älteren Schülern wie Śāriputra und Maudgalyāyana, schilt sie wegen ihrer hinayanistischen Ansicht und lehrt sie die Mahayana-Doktrinen. Die grundlegenden Doktrinen seiner Predigt sind die auf dem *Lotos-Sutra* basierende Lehre vom Einen Fahrzeug und der Einen Zuflucht und die auf dem *Mahāyāna-mahāparinirvāṇa-sūtra* basierende *Tathāgatagarbha*-Lehre oder Lehre von der Buddha-Natur.

Was die grundlegenden Moralvorschriften angeht, so formuliert letzteres Sutra mit den sechs moralischen Verhalten – beginnend mit „dem Töten des Feindes, der den Geist verunreinigt" – paradoxe Lehren. (1) Insofern man Verunreinigungen des Geistes töten soll, da sie einen auf dem Weg zum Nirvana behindern (dasselbe Konzept läßt sich in der Volksetymologie des Ausdrucks *arhat*/*arihat* < *ari-han* – *ari* = Feind, *han* = zu töten – feststellen), lehrt es nämlich, daß man die Vorschrift des Nicht-Tötens nicht notwendigerweise einzuhalten brauche. (2) Buddhas Wort, daß er ins Nirvana eingehen werde, das seiner ewigen Existenz entgegensteht, ist (wie es im *Lotos-Sutra* gelehrt wird) eine konventionelle Doktrin, um die Menschen (sc. zum Nirvana) zu leiten, und deshalb ist es kein Vergehen zu lügen. (3) Man solle den Wein der höchsten Lehre des *tathāgatagarbha* trinken, um die Glückseligkeit der Erleuchtung zu genießen. (4) Man solle stets mit der Glückseligkeit der Meditation als seiner Gattin verbunden sein, so daß man den reinsten *dharma* (er)tragen könne. (5) Man solle für sich die höchste Erleuchtung annehmen, die von niemand anderem gegeben werde. (6) Um die Mahayana-Lehre vom *tathāgatagarbha* zu preisen, solle man Mahayana-Sutren mit einem Musik-Ensemble rezitieren – im Widerspruch zu der Vorschrift, keine Musik zu spielen und nicht zu tanzen.

Solcherart paradoxe Lehren sind ein recht allgemeiner Zug des Mahayana, das auf die Förderung freien Denkens zielte – gerichtet gegen die Tendenz zu starker Formalisierung, die unter den traditionellen, von konservativen buddhistischen Gemeinschaften, den sogenannten Hinayanisten, überlieferten Lehren auftrat. Um solch eine paradoxe Doktrin aufzubauen, ist das Beispiel eines Mörders wie Aṅgulimāla – neben Ajātaśatru, der gescholten wird, weil er seinen Vater Bimbisāra getötet hat, und Devadatta, der gescholten wird, weil er den Buddha töten wollte und die buddhistische Gemeinschaft zerstörte, indem er sich von ihr abspaltete – eines der geeignetsten Gegenstände. Es zeigt ein Motiv, nicht nur die weltliche Moral, sondern auch die Ethik der traditionellen buddhistischen Gemeinschaft zu transzendieren.

II. Die *Tathāgatagarbha*-Lehre als eine Grundlage der buddhistischen Praxis

Die *Tathāgatagarbha*-Lehre ist für eine bestimmte Art des Mahayana-Buddhismus kennzeichnend. Dieser Buddhismus wird durch eine Gruppe von Schriften konstituiert, die allen Sinnenwesen die Möglichkeit zusprechen, Buddha zu werden. Diese Möglichkeit wird *tathāgatagarbha*, Embryo des Tathāgata[7], oder *buddhadhātu*, Ursache oder Grund, ein Buddha zu werden, genannt. Die Lehre wurde zuerst in einem kurzen Sutra mit dem Titel *Tathāgatagarbha-sūtra* formuliert, und zwar mit der Behauptung *sarvasattvās tathāgatagarbhāḥ*. Wörtlich genommen bedeutet dies, daß alle Sinnenwesen innerlich vom *tathāgata* besessen seien oder daß sie den *tathāgata* in sich enthielten (*-garbha* als letzter Teil eines Bahuvrihi-Kompositums hat die Bedeutung „A im Innern habend"; *garbha* im Sinne eines Schoßes, eines Behälters, und nicht eines Embryos oder Inhalts).

Das *Tathāgatagarbha-sūtra* drückt diese Idee einfach mithilfe von neun Beispielen aus, und wir erfahren, daß dabei mit *tathāgata* die Weisheit des Tathāgata oder die tugendhaften Eigenschaften des Tathāgata gemeint sind, die untrennbar mit seiner Buddhaschaft verbunden sind. Weiter, daß dieser *tathāgata* oder

7. D. h. des Buddha.

diese Weisheit des *tathāgata* im Innern eines Sinneswesens von geistigen Verunreinigungen verdeckt ist: Unwissenheit und andere Unreinheiten bedecken den Geist von Sinnenwesen, so daß sie die Existenz des *tathāgata* nicht wahrnehmen. Nur der Buddha erkennt sie und unterrichtet in seiner Anteilnahme die Sinnenwesen von dieser Tatsache, so daß sie den aktuellen (realen) Zustand eines Buddhas erreichen können, indem sie die Unreinheiten beseitigen, die ihren Geist bedecken.

Was als Tathāgata im Innern eines jeden Sinnenwesens gilt, ist deshalb kein wirklicher, sondern ein möglicher Buddha, ein Buddha der Potentialität nach. So wird dieser Buddha später auch als *tathāgatagarbha* im Sinne eines Embryos des *tathāgata* bezeichnet, und zwar in Schriften wie dem *Śrīmālā-sūtra*, dem *Anūnatvāpūrṇatvanirdeśa* und dem *Laṅkāvatāra-sūtra*, während das *Mahāparinirvāṇa-sūtra* des Mahayana vom *buddhadhātu*, dem *hetu*, der Ursache und/oder dem Grund (sc. der Buddhaschaft), oder dem *svabhāva*, der Natur des Buddha spricht. So wird jedem Sinnenwesen Buddha-Natur in Form eines Embryos zugesprochen.

Und diese Natur, welche bewirkt, daß ein Sinnenwesen Buddhaschaft erreicht, wird erneut im Geist gesucht, der als von Natur aus rein gilt, bzw. in der ursprünglichen und angeborenen Reinheit des Geistes. Der Begriff dieser Reinheit des Geistes, die von zufälligen Unreinheiten versehrt ist, findet sich bereits in den frühen *Āgamas*, obwohl sie dort nicht als ursprünglich-angeboren betrachtet wurde. Das zitierte, Aṅgulimāla zugeschriebene Gedicht aus den *Theragāthā* ist als eine Ausdrucksform dieses Begriffs anzusehen.

All diese Begriffe verbindend, formulierte das *Ratnagotravibhāga-mahāyānottaratantra-śāstra*, die Abhandlung, die die *Tathāgatagarbha*-Lehre zum ersten Mal systematisch darstellte, das folgende Gedicht:

> „Die Weisheit Buddhas durchdringt die Menge der Sinnenwesen.

Ihre Unversehrtheit[8] ist von Natur aus kein Zweites (non-dual) (neben dem Buddha).

Ihre Wirkung (d. h. der Zustand der Buddhaschaft) ist im Samen des Buddha angelegt.

Aus diesen Gründen wird (in der Schrift) gelehrt, daß alle Sinnenwesen den Embryo des Buddha besitzen."[9]

Daß jedem Sinnenwesen, ohne Ausnahme, von Natur aus der reine Geist eignet und daß dies die Ursache seiner Erleuchtung ist – diesen Sachverhalt mag man aus ethischer Sicht als die Lehre von der angeborenen (inneren) Gutheit der menschlichen Natur bezeichnen. Was immer der Mensch an Falschem und Schlechtem tut, gehört ihm nicht von Natur aus an, sondern ist nur ein vorübergehendes Akzidenz und deshalb leicht zu beseitigen. Dieser recht optimistische Charakter der *Tathāgatagarbha*-Lehre steht geradewegs im Gegensatz zur *Yogācāra*-Theorie vom *ālaya-vijñāna*, dem Speicherbewußtsein, die den menschlichen Geist (Verstand) in dessen natürlichem Zustand als Ursache der Transmigration betrachtet.

Das *ālayavijñāna* ist nämlich das Bewußtsein (*vijñāna*), in dem die Erfahrungen, die das Bewußtsein in einem früheren Augenblick oder in früheren Augenblicken gemacht hat, gespeichert sind, und (sc. ineins das Bewußtsein) welches das Bewußtsein in diesem Moment oder in zukünftigen Momenten beeinflußt, gerade so, wie ein Speicher voller, im Herbst geernteter Reiskörner, die im kommenden Frühling ausgesäht werden (sollen). So wird es auch als „das, welches aus allen Samen besteht" (*sarvabījakam*) bezeichnet. Die vergangenen Erfahrungen besitzen die Kraft, zukünftige Handlungen und Zustände zu bestimmen – was nichts anderes besagt als das, was im Buddhismus traditionellerweise Karma-Doktrin heißt. So ist das *ālayavijñāna* der Träger des Karma: ein Konzept, angenommen, um zu erklären, wie ein Karma

8. D. h. Reinheit.
9. *RGV*, V. I, 27.

von einem Leben in ein anderes überführt werden kann, wenn kein ewiges Selbst (Ich) existiert. Als ein Bewußtsein ist das *ālayavijñāna* selbst etwas Momentanes, aber es besitzt die Kraft, Gruppen körperlicher und geistiger Elemente in einer individuellen Form der Kontinuität momentaner Aufeinanderfolge aufzubewahren, und wenn das Karma einer Lebensspanne erschöpft ist, bewegt sich das *ālayavijñāna* von dem Individuum, das es gestützt hat, zu einer anderen Gruppe körperlicher Elemente, um ein anderes Leben zu bilden. Derart ist die Kontinuität des Karma in der Transmigration gesichert. In diesem Sinn ist das *ālayavijñāna* eine Kraft oder Funktion, die ein Individuum verursacht, zu transmigrieren, und so muß es ausgelöscht werden, um das Nirvana zu erreichen. Seine Rolle steht deshalb in starkem Kontrast zu der des *tathāgatagarbha*, welcher ein Individuum verursacht, das Nirvana zu erreichen.

Die *Yogācāra*-Schule, eine Gruppe von Meditations-Übenden, die die *Ālayavijñāna*-Theorie auf der Grundlage der im *Daśabhūmika-sūtra* (einer zum *Avataṃsaka*-Buddhismus gehörigen Schrift) erklärten Lehre vom bloßen Bewußtsein schufen, erhielt ihren Namen, weil sie anstrengende Meditation für wichtig hielt, um das Nirvana oder höchste Erleuchtung zu erreichen, und zwar, um den Geist zu kontrollieren oder die Verunreinigungen zu beseitigen, die sich seit anfangsloser Zeit hartnäckig mit dem Geist eines Individuums verbinden. Die *Yogācāra*-Vertreter glaubten grundsätzlich nicht an die Existenz eines ursprünglich-angeborenen Vermögens aller Sinnenwesen, Buddhaschaft zu erreichen. Sie glaubten eher, daß die Sinnenwesen in ihren Vermögen, Buddhaschaft zu erreichen, nicht gleich seien. Für sie ist die Lehre vom Einen Fahrzeug eine konventionelle Doktrin, um bestimmte Menschen zu ermutigen oder zu bekehren, die sich noch nicht für eines der Drei Fahrzeuge entschieden haben. In diesem Sinn sind sie Realisten. Im Gegensatz zu denen, die an die *Tathāgatagarbha*-Lehre glauben und die man als Idealisten oder Optimisten bezeichnen mag, sind sie pessimistisch.

Trotz ihres gegensätzlichen Charakters stimmen *Tathāgatagarbha*-Lehre und *Ālayavijñāna*-Theorie in dem folgenden Punkt überein: Sie befassen sich in erster Linie mit dem Schicksal des Individuums im Prozeß der Transmigration. Mit anderen Worten: Ihr gemeinsames Interesse gilt nicht den Problemen, wie die essentielle Natur der Dinge objektiv zu sehen sei, ob die Dinge substantiell existieren oder bloße substanzlose Erscheinungen seien, sondern wie die grundlegenden Charakteristika existentiell verstandener Individuuen auf der Suche nach ihrem Weg zur Befreiung subjektiv zu sehen seien.

Solch ein praktisches Anliegen ist freilich nicht nur für diese zwei Lehren kennzeichnend, sondern ist genau das, was von Anfang an das erste Anliegen des Buddhismus war, symbolisch zum Ausdruck gebracht in der Lehre von Buddhas Weigerung, metaphysische Fragen zu beantworten.

Schematisch gesprochen, war der von Buddha aus einem rein praktischen oder pragmatischem Interesse heraus (d. h. auf der Suche nach *ariya*, Nirvana als höchster Sicherheit) begründete Buddhismus nämlich in den hauptsächlich theoretisch interessierten *Ābhidharma*-Buddhismus umgewandelt worden. Unterdessen wollte die neue Bewegung des Mahayana-Buddhismus das pragmatische Anliegen des ursprünglichen Buddhismus wieder zur Geltung bringen, und zwar in der Form des Glaubens an den vergöttlichten Buddha wie z. B. an den Amitāyus oder Amitābha des *Sukhāvatīvyūha* oder den ewig in Gṛdhrakūṭa predigenden Śākyamuni des *Lotos-Sutra*. Im Zuge der Entwicklung des Mahayana-Buddhismus kam dann erneut theoretisches Interesse auf. Es zielte darauf, die Mahayana-Lehre der Substanzlosigkeit zu etablieren: die Theorie der Leere der *Prajnāpāramitā* und Nāgārjunas als notwendiges Vorgehen gegen die substantialistische Sicht der *dharmas* durch den Sarvāstivāda. Wir sagen nicht, daß Nāgārjuna sich nicht für das Schicksal von Individuen interessierte. Vielmehr ist für ihn die Erkenntnis der Substanzlosigkeit das pragmatische Anliegen, und nichts sonst; denn vom höchsten Standpunkt aus gesehen gibt es weder *dharmas*, die zu erkennen wären[10], noch Individuen, die erkennen. Nāgārjunas erstes Anliegen war, was wahre (vollendete) Erkenntnis (*prajñāpāramitā*) sei.

Von dieser Doktrin der Substanzlosigkeit oder Leere ausgehend, begann die *Yogācāra*-Schule, nach der praktischen Subjektivität in deren Verhältnis zur wahren Erkenntnis zu suchen. Sie betonte die empirische Existenz des *ālayavijñāna* als Subjekts der Praxis, seiner letztlichen Substanzlosigkeit ungeachtet – des Subjekts der Praxis, das wir gewöhnlich als *ātman* auffassen und das dieser falschen Auffassung zufolge transmigriert, von dem jedoch erwartet wird, vermittels der Praxis der wahren Erkenntnis der Substanzlosigkeit das Nirvana zu erreichen.

Ein weiterer Punkt, den die *Yogācāra*-Schule betonte, war die letztendliche Existenz der Substanzlosigkeit (*śūnyatā*) als, so der Name, Solchheit oder Soheit (*tathatā*). Die (Existenz der) Soheit ist danach eine objektive, erkennbare Wahrheit, aber zugleich auch das Ziel, das es für die Übenden zu erreichen gilt; denn der Buddha, der Tathāgata, ist derjenige, der die Solchheit (*tathatā*) erreicht (*āgata*) hat oder mit ihr eins geworden ist. Mit anderen Worten: die *Yogācāra*-Vertreter ließen die Existenz der Wirklichkeit als eine von der Subjektivität der Übenden ungetrennte Wahrheit zu.

Die gleiche Denkweise kennzeichnet die *Tathāgatagarbha*-Lehre. Diese Lehre steht ebenfalls in der Nachfolge Nāgārjunas. Sie begann die Suche nach der Subjektivität der Übenden beim *tathāgatagarbha*, der in seiner Natur mit dem Tathāgata identisch ist, der seinerseits als ewige und letzte Wirklichkeit gilt. Der *Tathāgatagarbha*-Lehre lieferte der *Yogācāra* mit seiner positiven Behauptung von der letzten Existenz der Substanzlosigkeit die

10. Das heißt, es existieren keine Erkenntnisobjekte.

theoretische Unterstützung. Ein entsprechender *Yogācāra*-Einfluß ist im *Ratnagotravibhāga* klar zu erkennen. Der Verfasser des *Ratnagotravibhāga* dürfte ein *Yogācāra*-Vertreter gewesen sein, der wahrscheinlich zur Zeit Asaṅgas und Vasubandhus, die die *Ālayavijñāna*-Lehre begründeten, lebte.

Ein weiterer Schritt der Annäherung der *Tathāgatagarbha*-Lehre an den *Vijñānavāda* findet sich im *Laṅkāvatāra-sūtra*, in dem die beiden Begriffe *tathāgatagarbha* und *ālayavijñāna* miteinander identifiziert werden, in dem Gedanken, daß beide gleicherweise die Basis für die Transmigration wie auch der zum Nirvana führenden Praxis repräsentieren. Zuvor hatte schon das *Śrīmālā-sūtra* die Idee, daß der *tathāgatagarbha* sowohl Stütze der Transmigration als auch des (Eingangs ins) Nirvana sei, zum Ausdruck gebracht; während eine ähnliche Idee in bezug auf das *ālayavijñāna* in den Versen des *Mahāyāna-abhidharma-sūtra* formuliert ist, die mit den Worten *anādikāliko dhātuḥ* beginnen, „die Basis, die seit anfangsloser Zeit existiert". Das *Mahāyānasaṃgraha* Asaṅgas zitiert diesen Vers als *āgama* oder Schriftautorität für die Existenz des *ālayavijñāna*, während das *Ratnagotravibhāga* die seit anfangsloser Zeit existierende Basis als Hinweis auf den *tathāgatagarbha* ansieht und die Bedeutung des Verses mithilfe von Zitaten aus dem *Śrīmālā-sūtra* erklärt. Aber die Abhandlung enthält keinerlei Bezugnahme auf das *ālayavijñāna*. Die *Yogācāra*-Vertreter wiederum eigneten sich die *Tathāgatagarbha*-Lehre als Doktrin der Natur in deren Vollkommenheit (*pariniṣpanna-svabhāva*) an.

Das letzte Stadium der Identifikation der beiden Begriffe *ālayavijñāna* und *tathāgatagarbha* ist im *Mahāyānaśraddhotpāda*, dem „Erwachen des Mahayana-Glaubens", zum Ausdruck gebracht. In ihm wird der Geist der Sinnenwesen (**sattvacitta*) als das Subjekt der Praxis erörtert. In seiner Essenz repräsentiert dieser Geist den Körper des Mahayana – die Solchheit aller *dharmas* und ausgestattet mit unzähligen inneren Tugenden (des Tathāgata) sowie als Ursache aller Formen kausaler Beziehungen des Guten inner- und überweltlich handelnd. Von diesem Standpunkt aus betrachtet, wird der Geist der Sinnenwesen die Solchheit des Geistes (*cittatathatā*) genannt. In seiner Existenz, d. h. als individueller Geist, wird derselbe Geist als Geist in der Entstehung und Zerstörung bezeichnet (**udayavyayacitta*), der auf der Basis des *tathāgatagarbha*, d. h. der Solchheit des Geistes, erscheint.

Der aktuelle (wirkliche) Zustand des Geistes der Sinnenwesen, der als Verbindung von dem, was ohne Entstehen und Zerstörung ist, mit dem, dem Entstehen und Zerstörung eignen, charakterisiert wird, heißt *ālayavijñāna*.

In China wurde die *Tathāgatagarbha*-Lehre das erste Mal mit dem *Mahāparinirvāṇa-sūtra* eingeführt, und die Bezeichnung *buddhadhātu*, die als *fo xing*, „Buddha-Natur", übersetzt wurde, wurde geläufiger als die Bezeichnung *tathāgatagarbha*, die man als *ru lai zang*, „Speicher des Tathāgata", übersetzte. Aber nach der Verbreitung des *Mahāyānaśraddhotpāda* und insbesondere mit den Bemühungen des *Hua-yan*-Vertreters Fa Zang setzte sich die Lehre selbst Schritt für Schritt in den Köpfen der Chinesen fest. Fa Zang begründete die *Hua-yan-*(*Avataṃsaka-*)Lehre vermittels der Einführung der *Tathāgatagarbha*-Lehre, und der Kern seiner Doktrin wird, symbolisch, im Begriff *xing qi*, „Aufstehen der Natur"[11], gesucht. Gemeint ist das Aufstehen (Buddhas) in der Natur oder Buddha als das Aufstehen der ursprünglich-angeborenen Natur. Diese Lehre wird oft mit der Lehre der *Tian-tai*-Schule verglichen, deren Kern im Begriff *xing ju* gesehen wird, der „inneren Eingeschlossenheit", d. h. dem Besitz der Möglichkeit, Buddha zu werden, als höchstem, und der Möglichkeit, in die Hölle zu fallen, als niedrigstem Potential der eigenen inneren Natur.

---

11. Vielleicht verständlicher: (Selbst-)Aktualisierung der ursprünglich-angeborenen Buddha-Natur.

Diese beiden gegensätzlichen Doktrinen werden manchmal mit Menzius' Doktrin, daß die menschliche Natur ursprünglich-innerlich gut sei, und Xun Zis Doktrin, daß sie böse sei, verglichen. Doch als buddhistische Lehren sollte man sie besser mit den *Tathāgatagarbha-* und *Ālayavijñāna*-Konzepten des *Mahāyānaśraddhotpāda* vergleichen.

III. Die ethischen Implikationen der *Tathāgatagarbha*-Lehre

Kommen wir auf das Problem der ethischen Implikationen der *Tathāgatagarbha*-Lehre zurück. Die ethischen Prinzipien des Buddhismus werden oft im folgenden Gedicht gesehen:

> „Keinerlei böses Verhalten.
> Förderung jeder Art guten Verhaltens.
> Reinigung des eigenen Geistes:
> Das ist die Lehre der Buddhas (in den drei Dimensionen der Zeit[12])".

Von daher gesehen, ist die *Tathāgatagarbha*-Lehre eine Doktrin, die sich insbesondere auf die Reinigung des Geistes als Basis für die Vermeidung bösen und die Förderung guten Verhaltens bezieht und die dabei die Kraft der Reinigung als dem Geist innerlich eigen betrachtet.

Was die Frage angeht, was im buddhistischen Sinn gut ist, so besteht, wie oben angesprochen, ein doppelter Standard. Für *śramaṇas* sind das Nirvana und die zu ihm führenden Übungen das höchste und einzige Gut. Man mag es überweltliches Gut nennen. Für die buddhistischen Laien aber predigte Buddha die Beobachtung moralischen Verhaltens als weltliches Gut.

Dieser Doppel-Standard ist im Grunde auch dem Mahayana-Buddhismus eigen. Doch behauptet er ihn in einer etwas anderen Weise. Zunächst einmal kritisierte er die traditionellen Buddhisten als egoistisch. Sie würden der Abkehr von weltlichen Dingen zu-

12. Das heißt, in Vergangenheit, Gegenwart und Zukunft.

viel Bedeutung zuschreiben und sich nicht um die kümmern, die in der Welt[13] blieben. Dagegen betonten die Mahayanisten ihren eigenen, altruistischen Weg, die Laien vermittels der mahayanistischen Lehre zu retten. Dieser altruistische Weg wird im Namen der Anteilnahme und des Mitleids verkündet, die Buddha gegenüber den Sinnenwesen empfindet, gleich, wie ihre Lage, ob *śramaṇas* oder Laien. Der Nachdruck, der auf die Vervollkommnung der Tugend des Gebens gelegt wird, ist ein Exempel für den altruistischen Weg. So beginnt beispielsweise die Doktrin von den sechs *pāramitās* mit der *dāna-pāramitā*, der Vervollkommnung der Tugend des Gebens; und aus der Reihe der traditionellen Vorschriften werden die folgenden Regeln besonders geschätzt: die vier Arten des unbegrenzten Geistes (*apramāṇāni*), nämlich Freundlichkeit (*maitrī*), Mitleid (*karuṇā*), Fröhlichkeit/Frohsinn (*mudita*) und Gleichmut oder Gleichgestimmtheit jedem gegenüber (*upekṣā*), und die vier Grundeinstellungen als Mittel, alle Menschen in die Erlösung zu führen (*saṃgrahavastu*), nämlich Freigebigkeit (sowohl in bezug auf materielle Güter wie auch heilige Lehren), freundliche Rede (*priyāvavādita*), wohltuende Handlungen (*arthacaryā*) und Gleichheit oder die Betrachtung anderer, als seien sie man selbst (*samāna-arthatā*).

So ist der Nachdruck, der auf altruistische Tugend gelegt wird, der fundamentale und auffälligste Zug mahayanistischer Ethik oder Moral – dem *Śūnyavāda* des *Mādhyamika*, dem *Vijñānavāda* des *Yogācāra* und der *Tathāgatagarbha*-Lehre gemeinsam. Aber er ist ganz besonders für die *Tathāgatagarbha*-Lehre kennzeichnend, gründet sie doch ihre Doktrin des ursprünglich-angeborenen reinen Geistes aller Sinnenwesen als der Möglichkeit, Buddhaschaft zu erreichen, auf der Weisheit Buddhas, die, durch dessen Mitleid bedingt, alles durchdringt, und fordert die Übenden zu altruistischer Praxis auf: als dem Weg der Bodhisattvas, die Buddha in ihren Handlungen nachfolgen. So gesehen, ist es recht

13. Das heißt, in ihrem normalen Leben.

bedeutsam, daß der *Ratnagotravibhāga* den Zweck der Lehre (*deśanā-prayojana*) wie folgt zusammenfaßt:

> „Der Buddha lehrte früher, daß alles leer (an eigener Substanz) sei,
> so wie die Wolken, Illusionen und Dinge im Traum, und so fort.
> Aber warum wird in dieser Abhandlung gelehrt,
> daß die Ursache des Buddha(seins) (*buddhadhātu*) in jedem Sinnenwesen existiert?
> Um die fünf Arten von Fehlern zu beseitigen
> und die fünf Arten von Tugenden zu verwirklichen.
> D. h.:
> (1) Menschen, denen die Entschlossenheit fehlt, weil sie meinen, sie hätten kein Vermögen zur Erleuchtung, lehre man die Existenz des *garbha*, so daß sie den tapferen, auf Erleuchtung gerichteten Geist entwickeln mögen.
> (2) Jene, die stolz auf ihre Entschlossenheit zur Erleuchtung sind und auf die herabsehen, die ihren Geist noch nicht entschlossen auf Erleuchtung gerichtet haben, lehre man, daß jeder gleichermaßen den *garbha* besitzt, so daß sie wegen dieser Gleichheit ihnen gegenüber – wie gegenüber Lehrern – den Geist der Achtung entwickeln mögen.
> (3) Jene, deren Geist dazu neigt, unwirkliche Dinge für wirklich zu halten, lehre man, daß, gesehen durch die Intuition der *prajñā*, die geistigen Unreinheiten leer sind, so daß sie der Fehler der Verunreinigungen ledig werden.
> (4) Jene, die die letzthöchste Wahrheit vernachlässigen, lehre man, daß, gesehen durch Buddhas Weisheit, Buddhas tugendhafte Merkmale in ihnen existieren, so daß sie sich selbst dieser Tatsache vergewissern können, und
> (5) jene, die eine starke Liebe zu sich selbst besitzen, lehre man, auf der Grundläge der Freundlichkcit, anderen gleiche Liebe zukommen zu lassen, so daß sie das letzte Stadium

der Buddhaschaft erreichen mögen."[14]

Hier sind die Stufen der Kultivierung des Geistes der Übenden beobachtet (gezeichnet), die mit der Entschlossenheit des Geistes, Erleuchtung zu erreichen, beginnen; im Glauben an die Existenz der Buddha-Natur im Inneren ihrer selbst und genauso in allen anderen, gradweise fortschreitend in der Kultivierung von Intuition, Weisheit und Mitleid und im schließlichen Erreichen der Buddhaschaft endend. Es ist bemerkenswert, daß der Nachdruck dabei zunächst auf die Erkenntnis der Gleichheit von einem selbst und anderen gelegt wird, was liebende Zuneigung bewirkt (*sattva-ātma-samadarśikā maitrī*), und dann erneut auf die Gleichheit der Liebe zu sich selbst und anderen (*ātmasattvasama-sneha*) als dem Ausdruck der großen Mitmenschlichkeit oder Freundlichkeit. So würde der Kern der *Tathāgatagarbha*-Lehre in der (Auffassung von der) Erkenntnis der Gleichheit (aller Sinnen-wesen) und der Achtung vor allen Sinnenwesen liegen, Faktoren, die in der gleichen Liebe zu sich selbst und anderen resultieren. Dies mag der ethisch wichtigste Punkt der Lehre genannt werden.

Was den Weg angeht, diesen Geist gleicher Liebe zu verwirklichen, so verweist der *Ratnagotravibhāga* auf die Lehre vom instabilen Nirvana (*apratiṣṭhitanirvāṇa*) des Bodhisattva, der aufgrund seiner wahren Intuition (*prajñā*) nicht in der Welt verharrt und aufgrund seines Mitleids (*karuṇā*) mit der Welt nicht im Nirvana bleibt, und gibt Beispiele von Bodhisattva-Aktivitäten, indem er aus verschiedenen Mahayana-Sutren zitiert. Diese Idee ist erneut allen Mahayanisten gemein und keine Besonderheit der *Tathāgatagarbha*-Lehre, aber die Einzigartigkeit der *Tathāgatagarbha*-Lehre liegt in ihrem Nachdruck auf der positiven Empfehlung gleicher Liebe auf der Grundlage der Würde der Sinnenwesen als dem Embryo des Buddha. Einige Mahayana-Texte drücken diese Liebe als Vorstellung des einzigen Sohnes (*eka-*

14. *RGV*, Vv. I, 156f., sowie der dazugehörige Kommentar, ibd.,158–167.

putrakasanjñā) aus, so z. B. das *Mahāparinirvāṇa-sūtra*, nach dem der Buddha die Sinnenwesen wie seinen einzigen Sohn Rāhula betrachtet. Die Idee entstammt den Worten Buddhas im *Lotos-Sutra:* „Alle Sinnenwesen in den dreifachen Welten der Transmigration sind meine Söhne". Der Geist gleicher Liebe ist in Wirklichkeit der Geist Buddhas.

Abschließend gehe ich auf die Sitte, fleischliche Nahrung zu verbieten, ein; ein Beispiel einer ethischen Implikation der *Tathāgatagarbha*-Lehre hinsichtlich der Vorschrift der Gewaltlosigkeit (*ahiṃsā*).

Es ist wohlbekannt, daß das *Laṅkāvatāra-sūtra* mit Kapitel 8 ein selbständiges Kapitel einschließt, das dem Verbot fleischlicher Nahrung (*māṃsabhakṣaṇa*) gewidmet ist. In ihm wird der Bodhisattva, der von Natur aus Mitleid empfindet, gelehrt, kein Fleisch zu essen, um so die Praxis zu üben, die Geisteshaltung aller Sinnenwesen zu kultivieren, als seien sie sein einziger Sohn (*sarvasattva-ekaputrakasanjñā-bhāvanā-artham*). Die Vorschriften des frühen *saṃgha* verboten den *śramaṇas* allgemein die Gewohnheit des Fleischessens, von den folgenden drei Ausnahmen abgesehen: 1. Fleisch, das für sie getötet wurde, ohne daß die *śramaṇas* es gesehen hatten, 2. Fleisch, das für sie getötet wurde, ohne daß sie es gehört hatten, und 3. Fleisch, das zweifellos nicht für sie getötet wurde. *Śramaṇas*, die diese Arten Fleisch aßen, wurden nicht bestraft. Im *Laṅkāvatāra-sūtra* jedoch ist selbst das Essen dieser Arten „reinen" Fleisches verboten. Und in Vers 16 des angesprochenen Kapitels erklärt das Sutra, daß dieses Verbot von Buddha gelehrt sei, und zwar in Sutren wie dem *Hastikakṣya*, dem *Mahāmegha*, dem (*Mahā*)*parinirvāṇa*, dem *Aṅgulimālika* und dem *Laṅkāvatāra*.

Wir können nicht feststellen, ob diese Behauptung uns eine gewisse historische Evidenz liefert, was die Geschichte des Verbots fleischlicher Nahrung im Mahayana-Buddhismus angeht, aber es ist wahr, daß diese Sutren Stellen zur Sache enthalten. Bemerkenswerter ist, daß all diese Sutren derselben Gruppe angehören, die die *Tathāgatagarbha*-Lehre präsentiert. Aus diesen Tatsachen dürfen wir vielleicht schließen, daß es eben die Lehre vom *tathāgatagarbha* war, die – aufgrund der (von ihr behaupteten) essentiellen Würde (aller Sinnenwesen) – das strenge Verbot fleischlicher Nahrung und der Verletzung von Tieren unter den Mahayanisten förderte.

Aus dem Englischen übersetzt und mit zusätzlichen Erläuterungen versehen von Gregor Paul. Vom Verfasser überprüfte und autorisierte Fassung.

Thoughts on *Dhātu-vāda* and Recent Trends in Buddhist Studies*

The first thing that comes to mind in considering the major trends of the past ten years in Buddhist studies is the claim made by Hakamaya Noriaki and Matsumoto Shirō that the idea of *tathāgata-garbha* (which happens to be my area of specialization) is a pseudo-Buddhist way of thinking, or is not Buddhist at all.[1] Frankly, the claim came as something of a shock to me, and even now continues to weigh heavily on my mind. Since I have known Hakamaya and Matsumoto from the days when they attended my lectures as students and have kept up friendly relations with them ever since, I was not altogether unaware of their way of thinking and the path by which they arrived at their conclusions.

The idea that *tathāgata-garbha* thought has much in common with the teachings of the mainstream of Indian thought as represented by the Upaniṣads and Vedānta philosophy is a point I have often made myself, and was hardly any cause for alarm. But it is quite another thing to conclude that such a way of thinking is "not Buddhist" simply because it is similar to the mainstream of Indian thought. Here I part company with them.

As a form of Indian thought, it is only natural that Buddhism should have certain things in common with the mainstream of Indian thought that it would not, for example, have in common with

---

* Originally published in Jamie Hubbard and Paul L. Swanson, eds., *Pruning the Bodhi Tree: The Storm Over Critical Buddhism* (Honolulu: University of Hawai'i Press, 1997), pp. 314–320.

1. I do not know exactly when Hakamaya Noriaki and Matsumoto Shirō began their critique of *tathāgata-garbha* thought and *hongaku shisō*, but the first time I myself ran across it was in Hakamaya's "Thoughts on the Ideological Background of Social Discrimination."

Christianity or Islam. The problem, as I see it, is how one defines "Buddhism." Some definitions may even permit one to speak of "non-Buddhistic" forms of "Buddhism." But such talk is relative to the world of intra-Buddhist theoretical debate and should not be taken as absolute. But when I first heard the claim that "the doctrine of *tathāgata-garbha* is not Buddhist" I was reminded of Nichiren's attack on other Buddhist schools—that *nenbutsu* leads to hell, Zen followers are devils, Shingon is the ruin of the nation, members of the Ritsu school are traitors, and so forth—and dismissed them as having nothing to do with normal academic debate.

Leaving to one side the question of whether or not *tathāgata-garbha* thought is Buddhist (a gesture to which the proponents of the idea will no doubt object), I would like to have a brief look at Matsumoto's proposed neologism *dhātu-vāda* as pointing to the specific structure of the doctrine of *tathāgata-garbha*.

Tathāgata-garbha thought and Buddhist Vijñaptimātravāda thought in many ways stand opposed to each other. For instance, the doctrine of *tathāgata-garbha* teaches the practice and attainment of a single vehicle (*ekayāna*), while the Vijñaptimātravāda teaches three vehicles (*triyāna*). Even so, I find the term *dhātu-vāda* a rather accurate expression of the common structure found in both. In this sense, it is a useful tool for discussing that question.

The idea of *dhātu-vāda* takes as its model terms such as *anādikāliko dhātuḥ* (a beginningless substance or basis), as expounded in the verses of the *Mahāyāna-abhidharma Sutra*,[2] or *eko dhātuḥ* (the one realm), as found in the even older *Anūnatvāpūrṇatvanirdeśaparivarta*.[3] These terms refer to the idea that samsara and nirvana exist together or share a single "place" or "realm." This "place" is the context within which one passes, through practice, from samsara to nirvana. Those who experience this place as

2. A text quoted as the basis for the *Mahāyāna-saṅgraha*, but no longer extant.

3. *Sutra of Neither Increase Nor Decrease*, T. no. 668, 16.466-468.

samsara are ordinary sentient beings; those who experience it as nirvana are Buddhas. For ordinary sentient beings, the *tathāgata-garbha* refers to the hoped-for result of Buddhahood, from the perspective of that potential. The *ālaya-vijñāna* (store consciousness) has as its basis the causes of samsara, and these must be "overturned" or "converted" for one to attain nirvana. In the *tathāgata-garbha* tradition, the manifestation of the bodhi-wisdom of the Dharma Body, which remains unmanifested in ordinary sentient beings, is called "the Dharma Body that bears the mark of the conversion of the ground (of enlightenment)." Certainly one may speak of this way of thinking as a "*dhātvasti-vāda*" rather than a "*śūnya-vāda*." Nonetheless, the "way of being" (*asti*) referred to here is not of a substantialist or essentialist sort, but existential. It is a kind of being that lacks selfhood (*anātman*). This is clearly the case at least in the teachings accompanying the two examples I have given. I refer to this idea of the continuity of samsara and nirvana through practice as *ekadhātu-vāda*.[4]

What, then, is the basis for this *ekadhātu-vāda*, the unity or continuity of samsara and nirvana? This is where the idea of the *dharmadhātu* enters into the picture. The interpretation given in the Yogācāra tradition is that the *dharmadhātu* is equivalent to causality (*pratītyasamutpāda*); in this sense it is the ground of the noble Buddha Dharma, the teachings of the Buddha.[5] If one pursues the question further, one finds that this idea is based on the teaching of *dharmadhātu* in the *Avataṃsaka Sutra*, where the term was used in an attempt to explain the meaning of the Buddha's attainment of enlightenment. Still further back one discovers

4. I have published an expanded discussion of this topic under the title "'Mushi jirai no kai' saikō" 「無始時来の界」再考 [A reexamination of *anādikāliko dhātuḥ*], in *Suguro Shinjō hakushi koki kinen ronbunshū* 勝呂信静博士古稀記念論文集 [Festschrift for Dr. Suguro Shinjō] (Tokyo: Sankibō Busshorin, 1996), pp. 41–59.

5. Skt. *āryadharmahetutvād dharmadhātuḥ*; see *Madhyāntavibhāga-bhāṣya*, ad v. I.16.

in the *Saṃyuttanikāya* of the Pāli canon the term *sā dhātu* in the sense of "the nature of all dharmas" (*dharmatā*).[6] There is yet another, distinct, meaning of *dharmadhātu* given in the Abhidharma tradition, that is, as the "things" or "phenomena" that are the direct and indirect objects of our consciousness (as one of the eighteen categories of "things").

The term *dhātu*, then, has at least two meanings: the sense of "realm" or "place" (or the collection of "things" in that place), and the sense of a "cause" (or the common features that allow the classification of all the "things" into a single group). This double meaning is basic to the notion of *dhātuvāda*. Such double (or multiple) meanings are not uncommon in Buddhist terms. One need look no further than the word *dharma*, which can refer as well to a phenomenon itself as to the nature of a thing that distinguishes it from other things. The original Indian meaning was closer to the second meaning of the "nature" of a phenomenon. Grammatically speaking it is more accurate to use the term *dharmin* to refer to the phenomenon itself.

Or again, consider the term *pratītyasamutpāda*. Originally it referred to the "causal" side of the process of conditioned arising, in contrast to *pratītyasamutpanna*, which refers to the resultant side of the process. Tachikawa Musashi has pointed out recently that in Nāgārjuna's *Mūla-madhyamakakārikā*, the term *pratītyasamutpāda* must be understood as including the meanings of both the causal and the resultant side.[7] Tachikawa goes on to note that Nāgārjuna deliberately avoids distinguishing between these two meanings so as to preserve them both in his use of the term. Nāgārjuna recognized that *pratītyasamutpāda* expresses the nature of all phenomena (*dharmatā*), and that this is the meaning of emptiness (*śūnyatā*). He did not, however, use the term *dharmadhātu*

6. *Saṃyuttanikāya* II, 25 (*Nidāna-saṃyutta*, 20, *paccaya*); see also T. 2.84b.
7. See Tachikawa Musashi 立川武蔵, *Chūron no shisō* 中論の思想 [The philosophy of the *Middle Treatise*] (Kyoto: Hōzōkan, 1994), p. 226.

in its causal sense because he did not wish to acknowledge an independent "dharma-nature" apart from the phenomena themselves. In this sense Nāgārjuna's position could be called *adhātu-vāda*, though he did not deny dharma-nature in the sense of *pratītya-samutpāda* or emptiness, nor did he deny nirvana as the goal of Buddhist practice.

In the Vijñaptimātravāda tradition, the relationship between phenomena (dharmas) and the *dharmadhātu* is spoken of in terms of the unity of samsara and nirvana, that is, as the "realm" (*dhātu*) that is the basis for conditioned and unconditioned dharmas. This "realm" is none other than the unconditioned dharma of nirvana. The *tathāgata-garbha* tradition follows the same structure, except that it speaks in terms of the *dharmakāya* and Buddha; that is, a Buddha is one who has correctly perceived dharmas (or the *dharma-dhātu*), and such a one is called a Dharma Body because he "has the Dharma as his body."

Examples can be found in the Āgama Sutras, where this *bahu-vrīhi* compound is used adjectivally, but it is the *tathāgata-garbha* tradition that first uses "Dharma Body" as an independent technical term. It is interesting to note that this term is also used in the sense of "the accumulation of dharmas" to mean the whole of the Buddha's teachings, or *sarvadharma*, such as in the teaching of the collection of dharmas in five parts, of which the Buddha's qualities consist.[8] The tendency to perceive the Buddha as one with the Dharma he has realized shares the same conceptual structure as the Upaniṣads, which teach that one "becomes" something by coming to know it.

The problem comes down to this. Is *dhātu-vāda*, or the way of thinking that is associated with *dhātu-vāda*, an essential element of Buddhism? If it is essential, how far back in the history of

8. The idea that the enlightened are endowed with, or have as their "body," the five qualities of keeping the precepts, samadhic concentration, wisdom, liberation, and the insight of liberation.

Buddhist thought can it be traced? Can its origin be found in the thinking of the Buddha Śākyamuni himself? The reference to *sā dhātu* in the *Saṃyuttanikāya* mentioned above speaks of the establishment of this *dhātu* (that is, dependent origination as the regular nature of dharmas) as a "law" or truth in such a way that it is established from the outset, "whether or not a Tathāgata appears in the world" to discover and perceive it correctly. But this particular passage seems to stem from a period after *pratītyasamutpāda* had become established as the basis of the Buddha's teaching. The same idiomatic phrase ("whether or not a Tathāgata appears in the world") is used in the *Aṅguttaranikāya* to speak of the "three characteristics of dharmas," beginning with "the transience of all things," as the established law or truth, but this also appears to be a later development.[9] Hence it is difficult to prove that the idea of *dhātu* as *pratītyasamutpāda* is directly connected with the Buddha himself.

There is, however, a passage in the *Sutra of the Castle City* [*Nagara*] of the *Saṃyuttanikāya* that, while not linked to the doctrine of *pratītyasamutpāda*, refers to the Buddha as simply one who has "discovered" the Dharma.[10] In this context the "Eightfold Path" is presented as the same path that all Buddhas from time out of mind have trod. The same may be said of the discovery of the truth of *pratītyasamutpāda*.

The opening "Chapter on the Buddha" of the *Nidāna-saṃyutta* (section XII of the *Saṃyuttanikāya*) claims that the Seven Buddhas of the Past all realized the teaching of *pratītyasamutpāda*, and that "eyes, wisdom, insight, and light were aroused concerning the undiscovered Dharma."[11] While these may not be the direct words of the Buddha, it is certainly true that the Buddha did not present himself as the author of the Path but only as one who

9. *Aṅguttaranikāya*, I, 286; no equivalent in the Chinese canon.
10. *Saṃyuttanikāya* II, 106; T. 2.80c.
11. *Saṃyuttanikāya* II, 1-11; T. 2.101c.

discovered what was already there, one who "saw" the Dharma and thus awoke as a Buddha to become himself a teacher of that same Dharma. The Dharma is what the Buddha saw and what he taught. It is the foundation of Buddhism. In this sense Buddhism is different from the Indian mainstream that takes the idea of atman=brahman as its foundational doctrine, which is where we find the origin of *dhātu-vāda* in Buddhism.[12]

After the Buddha passed away, he was idealized and apotheosized, and this process of religious divination expanded the concept of *dhātu-vāda*. Mahayana Buddhism, in turn, emphasized the Buddha more than the Dharma, in contrast to the Abhidharma tradition, which maintained a central focus on the Dharma.[13] Mahayana Buddhism was also in closer contact with day-to-day life in Hindu society. These factors may have contributed to making Mahayana Buddhism more susceptible to influence by Hindu ways of thought.

Matsumoto bases his discussion on the assumption that Buddhism should not permit influence from other Indian ways of thinking. This may explain why he tries to proscribe any teaching that even slightly resembles non-Buddhist Indian thought or that seems to smack of *dhātu-vāda* tendencies. This leads him to reject samadhic concentration as well as the ideas of liberation and nirvana as non-Buddhist, and explains why he confines Buddhism

12. For a more detailed discussion see my essay "Bukkyō shisō ron" 仏教思想論 [Theories on Buddhist thought], in Iwanami Kōza Tōyō Shisō Series 9 (Tokyo: Iwanami Shoten, 1988).

13. A shift in emphasis from impersonal Dharma to personal Buddha is one of the characteristics of early Mahayana scriptures. That is, the Buddha was required to be an eternal refuge (*saraṇa*) for believers, one who teaches dharmas in order to lead people to the highest enlightenment that is equal to that of the Buddha. Such a concept appears in the *Lotus Sutra*, for example, as the Tathagata of Immeasurable Life (chapter 16). Also, it is symbolically given the names of the Buddha Amitāyus (immeasurablc life) and Amitābha (immeasurable light) in the *Sukhāvatīvyūha*. Theoretical absolutization of the Buddha followed this through identification with the *dharmadhātu*.

to insight into *pratītyasamutpāda*. Still, the Buddha did experience both samadhic concentration and nirvana, and it cannot be denied that he instructed his disciples on these matters. There is also no evidence that he ever taught anything that would refute these teachings.

We might note that one of the reasons Matsumoto insists that *tathāgata-garbha* thought is not Buddhist is that it holds to seemingly substantialist ideas such as a "Great Self" or the four "positive" traits of nirvana as "eternal, blissful, selfhood, and pure." These ideas are undeniably similar to the idea of an atman, and it is hardly surprising that they should come up for question. An even stronger reason for Matsumoto's claim is that the *tathāgata-garbha* tradition served as the source of the development of the thought of original enlightenment (*hongaku shisō*) in Japanese Buddhism. His critique of the doctrine of *tathāgata-garbha* gives him the wedge he wants to drive into contemporary Japanese Buddhism and pry open the minds of its scholars. This aspect of Matsumoto's work runs parallel with the efforts of Hakamaya, and has provided his colleague with support for his own arguments. Of late Matsumoto's critique has been aimed at the source of Japanese Buddhism, namely, Chinese Buddhism and in particular the Ch'an tradition.[14] His arguments are sharp, but at times he lets his expectations overshadow the evidence and forces the facts to fit his theories.

Hakamaya, meantime, has focused the sights of his critique of *hongaku shisō* on Dōgen, claiming that the twelve-fascicle *Shōbōgenzō* written by Dōgen in his later years contains his true position, and that the earlier writings should be rejected in favor of the later ones.[15] Dōgen specialists have not been convinced.[16]

---

14. I am referring here to Matsumoto's *Zen shisō no hihanteki kenkyū* 禅思想の批判的研究 [Critical studies on Zen thought] (Tokyo: Daizō Shuppan, 1993).

15. See Hakamaya Noriaki, *Dōgen to Bukkyō—Jūnikanbon* Shōbōgenzō *no*

Even Matsumoto criticizes Hakamaya for having over-idealized Dōgen and argues that the *dhātu-vāda* way of thinking found in early works of Dōgen such as the "Bendōwa" were not rejected by Dōgen even in his later years. I must say, I agree.

➢ ➢ ➢

There are further undercurrents to Hakamaya's and Matsumoto's criticism of the present state of Buddhist studies. One senses a dissatisfaction with the strong emphasis that has been put on objective textual studies in mainstream Japanese Buddhology. In the same vein, one cannot fail to feel a disillusionment with religious studies in general for having taken the ideal of value-free judgments to the point that almost anything claiming to be a religion deserves equal scholarly attention. Hakamaya and Matsumoto have taken the approach that Buddhology should concern itself with the question "What is Buddhism?" and pursue the truth of Buddhism from a subjective perspective, rejecting what is non-Buddhist or anti-Buddhist. They call this "Critical Buddhism." It is my view that such judgments may serve to advance the cause of particular schools or sects within Buddhism, but that they are not the stuff of Buddhology. But now I understand that this very view has become the target of criticism.

[*Translated by Paul L. Swanson*]

Dōgen 道元と仏教—十二巻本『正法眼蔵』の道元 [Dōgen and Buddhism: Dōgen in the 12-fascicle *Shōbōgenzō*] (Tokyo: Daizō Shuppan, 1992).

16. See Kagamishima Genryū 鏡島元隆 and Suzuki Kakuzen 鈴木格禅, eds., *Jūnikanbon* Shōbōgenzō *no shomondai* 十二巻本『正法眼蔵』の諸問題 [Issues concerning the 12-fascicle *Shōbōgenzō*] (Tokyo: Daizō Shuppan, 1991).

The Tathāgatagarbha Theory Reconsidered: Reflections on Some Recent Issues in Japanese Buddhist Studies*

The Tathāgatagarbha theory is an influential yet controversial part of the Buddhist tradition. This essay examines some of the issues related to this tradition that have been discussed recently by Buddhist scholars: the dhātu-vāda thesis and the critique of "original enlightenment," the relationship between the terms tathāgatagarbha and padmagarbha, the interpretation of dependent origination in the Ratnagotravibhāga, the role of relics worship in the Mahāparinirvāṇa-sūtra, and the Tathāgatagarbha theory in Tibetan Buddhism.

Nearly fifty years have passed since the publication of the *Ratnagotravibhāga*, the earliest and most basic Sanskrit text of the Tathāgatagarbha theory. Since then many studies of this text and the Tathāgatagarbha theory have been published, including my English translation of the *Ratnagotravibhāga* (Takasaki 1966), my work in Japanese on the formation of the Tathāgatagarbha theory in Indian Mahāyāna Buddhism (1974), and D. Seyfort Ruegg's works on the Tathāgatagarbha theory in Tibetan Buddhism (1969, 1989). Recent notable publications on this topic include S. K. Hookham's *Buddha Within* (1991) and Shimoda Masahiro's work on the *Mahāparinirvāṇa-sūtra* (1997), indicating that the Tathāgatagarbha theory is a continuing (and continually

* This essay is an expanded revision of a paper given at the XIIth Conference of the International Association of Buddhist Studies at Lausanne, Switzerland, August 1999. Originally published in *Japanese Journal of Religious Studies* 27-1/2 (2000), pp. 73–83.

controversial) topic of interest among Buddhist scholars.

In the 1980s voices of criticism were raised against the Tathāgatagarbha theory, claiming that it contradicted the Buddha's teaching of *anātma-vāda*. The objection was first raised by Matsumoto Shirō (1989), who characterized the Tathāgatagarbha theory as a *dhātu-vāda*, a theory that admits the existence of something basic (*dhātu*) as the ground of all ephemeral phenomena. Matsumoto maintained that this *dhātu-vāda* is akin to the *ātma-vāda* of the "heretics" and contradicts the Buddhist *śūnya-vāda* or theory of coarising, thus claiming that the Tathāgatagarbha theory is not Buddhist at all. This position was also promoted by Hakamaya Noriaki (1989, 1990), and is gradually being echoed by Buddhist scholars of the younger generation, leading to waves of "critical" studies of Buddhism along this line.[1]

In my opinion, the *dhātu-vāda* hypothesis—as denoting a current of doctrine within folk Buddhism and common to both Tathāgatagarbha theory and *vijñāna-vāda* in contrast to *śūnya-vāda*—is quite useful. It covers all Buddhist thought that takes a monistic view with regard to dharmas, including esoteric Buddhism—the *dharmakāya* of Tathāgatagarbha theory and esoteric Buddhism, *dharmadhātu* of the *vijñāna-vāda*, and even *śūnyatā* of the Mādhyamika. The development of such a monistic view in Buddhism may have been influenced by Hinduism; it is a topic worthy of further investigation. In any case, such topics must be tackled before deciding whether such theories should be considered "within" or "outside" of Buddhism.

Among the criticisms of the Tathāgatagarbha theory there has been a critique of the doctrine of "original enlightenment" (*hongaku* 本覺) in Japanese Buddhism. This critique has sweeping implications; in effect it calls for a reevaluation of Japanese Buddhism in general and in comparison with Buddhism in other

1. A collection of studies related to this issue was published recently as *Pruning the Bodhi Tree* (Hubbard and Swanson 1997).

regions of the world. It cannot be denied that Buddhism in Japan, and in East Asia in general, was and continues to be strongly influenced by Tathāgatagarbha thought. The topic has been debated at length among Japanese scholars in Buddhist studies, not least because of its implications for understanding Buddhism in Japan. As the scholarship has been largely confined to Japanese publications, I would like to address the topic in English, and in the process advance the debate by discussing some of the important recent works on the topic, including those that criticize my work. To my regret, until now I have not yet publicly addressed these criticisms in detail. I find the fundamentalistic opinions of "Critical Buddhism" problematic in many ways, and yet they offer valuable suggestions worthy of acceptance and/or discussion. In this essay I shall highlight these suggestions and examine their significance.

Tathāgatagarbha and Padmagarbha

Among various points raised by Matsumoto Shirō, I will first take up his valuable suggestion concerning the original meaning of the term Tathāgatagarbha in the *Tathāgatagarbha-sūtra* and its relation to the term *padmagarbha*, which he offered in an essay entitled "*Padmagarbha* and *Tathāgatagarbha*: Thoughts on the Formation of Tathāgatagarbha Thought."[2] The subtitle of his essay reflects his intention to prove that this way of thinking is basically an adoption of *ātma-vāda*. In this article his arguments are philologically sound as he investigates the original use of the term *padmagarbha* ("lotus-womb") in relation to the concept or idea of a buddha sitting in a *padma* or *padmagarbha*, or born from a *padma*. He investigates similar examples of a miracle performed by the Buddha at the beginning of the *Tathāgatagarbha-sūtra* and

2. "Nyoraizō to rengezō—nyoraizō shisō no seiritsu ni kansuru ichi kōsatsu" 如来蔵と蓮華蔵—如来蔵思想の成立に関する一考察. This lengthy essay can be found in chapter 4 of Matsumoto 1993, pp. 411–543.

also found in the sūtras belonging to the *Avataṃsaka* group, and concludes that the original use of the term is the one found in the *Tathāgatagarbha-sūtra*, while the examples found in the *Gaṇḍa-vyūha* are derivations. He also points out an example found in the present Sanskrit edition of the *Daśabhūmika* that is a later interpolation, as it is not found in the old Chinese editions of the same text.[3] As for the previous history of the concepts, he thinks that the direct influence came from the *Saddharmapuṇḍarīka*, especially from the chapter on the "rising of bodhisattvas from the earth,"[4] though he admits that there may have been some influence from the Pure Land sūtras.

Matsumoto's hypothesis is directly connected with the question as to the first or earliest use of the term *tathāgatagarbha*. In my early work (Takasaki 1974, p. 520) I suggested that the term, appearing in the *Gaṇḍavyūha* as an epithet for Sudhana, was used without any connection to the doctrinal background of later Tathāgatagarbha theory, and that this use provided a clue for identifying the author of the *Tathāgatagarbha-sūtra*. Matsumoto argues against my theory and suggests that use of the term *tathāgata-garbha* as an epithet for Sudhana without any explanation means that the term was already known in the Buddhist circles of those days. His suggestion is most reasonable and worthy of being considered in further investigations on the history of the formation of the Tathāgatagarbha theory.[5]

3. The present Sanskrit edition and the Chinese translation of the *Avataṃsaka* have a series of names of bodhisattvas who are attending the Buddha's preaching. Among these we find the name of Padmagarbha (see the Rahder ed., p. 2, l. 5). However, this series of names is not found in the oldest Chinese edition translated by Dharmarakṣa (see T. no. 285, vol. 10, p. 458a).

4. Chapter 15 of the Kumārajīva version of the *Lotus Sutra*.

5. I still think that the term *tathāgatagarbha* as an epithet for Sudhana is a synonym of *buddha-putra* or *jina-putra*, denoting a bodhisattva, and not an epithet for an ordinary being as used in general in the *Tathāgatagarbha-sūtra*. In any case, as far as we know from the extant Sanskrit texts, this is

As for the original meaning of the term *tathāgatagarbha* in the *Tathāgatagarbha-sūtra*, Matsumoto and I are in fundamental agreement in that it was used as a kind of epithet for a *sattva* or all *sattvas*, denoting the idea that the Tathāgata dwells inside beings, and not as a technical term fixed in later works (such as the *Śrīmālā-sūtra*) denoting some potential that makes a *sattva* become a buddha, and always used in the masculine singular. One difference is that Matsumoto newly suggests the meaning of "container" or "receptacle" for *garbha* in the sense that all *sattvas* are "containers" for the Tathāgata, while I translated the term as a *bahuvrīhi* compound to mean "one who bears a Tathāgata in the inside." As this Tathāgata is hidden under the sheath of defilements, I interpreted the meaning to have gradually shifted to "one who is possessed of the embryo of a Tathāgata." This interpretation was influenced by the Tibetan translation of *tathāgatagarbha* as *de bshin gśegs paḥi sñiṅ po can*. With this translation, however, I faced a difficulty in translating the first sentence given in the *Ratnagotravibhāga* as one of the threefold meanings of *tathāgatagarbha*. My English translation of the *Ratnagotravibhāga* was complicated, and after receiving critical suggestions from Professor L. Schmithausen, I changed the translation in my Japanese translation of the *Ratnagotravibhāga* into simply "embryo of the Tathāgata." Matsumoto indicated that this translation is wrong in the case of the *Tathāgatagarbha-sūtra*, and suggests the term "receptacle" instead.

This suggestion is acceptable in the light of the Chinese translation *ju-lai-tsang* 如來藏, a "storehouse" of the Tathāgata. At the same time I feel a certain uneasiness about limiting the meaning simply to "storehouse," in comparison to the term *kośa*, which is used only in the sense of "store" or "sheath." The term *garbha* is truly ambiguous, but this point was not fully utilized by the followers of the Tathāgatagarbha theory. In light of this point, further

---

the only example of the term being used as an epithet for a single person.

efforts are needed to find a more suitable translation.[6]

As for the textual reading of the *Tathāgatagarbha-sūtra*, I recently received information that in old manuscripts such as those at the Newark Museum, there is no use of the suffix "*can*" at the end of *de bshin gśegs paḥi sñiṅ po*,[7] and that one doubtful passage in the fifth illustration where the term *tathāgatagarbha* is used (in the light of the Chinese equivalent, the term should actually be *tathāgata-jñāna*), the Newark edition clearly shows the term *de bshin gśegs paḥi ye shes*.[8] This information supports my opinion, though the term *sñiṅ po* has a sense of something like a kernel, as used elsewhere to translate the Sanskrit *hṛdaya* or *sāra*.

Finally, as for the significance of the idea of the penetration of the Tathāgata, or the wisdom of the Tathāgata, into all *sattva*s, I will merely say that this idea is exactly the same as the idea of the all-pervadingness of Brahman into individuals in the form of *ātman*. The simile of *ākāśa* (space, or ether) is commonly used for this idea in both Hinduism and Buddhism. (In this sense, *sattva*s are instead in the inside of the Tathāgata as embryos.) I do not deny the influence on Buddhism of this rather common way of thinking in Hinduism in the days when Tathāgatagarbha thought was developing.

The Doctrine of Dependent Origination in Tathāgatagarbha Theory

The denial or neglect of the doctrine of dependent origination

6. "Embryo" is not unfit, being a term relating to the concept of *putra* ("child"). "Womb" is also acceptable as a literal meaning of *garbha*.

7. These manuscripts are a Kanjur, originally found in Batang and now kept at the Newark Museum in New Jersey, USA.

8. My thanks to Michael Zimmermann, a student of Professor Schmithausen at Hamburg, for pointing out this information. Zimmermann is preparing a critical edition of the *Tathāgatagarbha-sūtra* as a part of his doctoral thesis to be submitted to the University of Hamburg.

(*pratītyasamutpāda*) is another reason for branding Tathāgatagarbha theory as a *dhātu-vāda*, or regarding it as non-Buddhist. This blame is based on the admittance of a single *dhātu*, *dharmadhātu*, or *buddhadhātu*, as a non-causal basis on which the dependent origination of phenomena occurs.

Doctrinally speaking, however, the term *dharmadhātu* is used and interpreted by the Yogācāra as the cause of phenomenal dharmas, in the sense that it is the truth of *pratītyasamutpāda* realized by the Buddha which causes the rise of *āryadharma* or the holy teachings of the Buddha. This principle of *pratītyasamutpāda* penetrates all dependently arising (*pratītyasamutpanna*) phenomenal and ephemeral dharmas. In this sense, *dharmadhātu* is the unchanging nature (*dharmatā*) of all dharmas. This unchangeability is here called *asaṃskṛta* (unconditioned), in contrast to *saṃskṛta* (conditioned), or *pratītyasamutpanna* (dependently originated). This interpretation is the same as that of Nāgārjuna, although he did not use the term *dharmadhātu* in this sense. He identified *dharmatā* with *śūnyatā*, and furthermore added another definition to it as being conditioned verbal expression (*prajñaptir upādāya*) in order to avoid the idea that *śūnyatā* is something that exists outside of all dharmas that are *śūnya*, empty of independent existence of their own (*niḥsvabhāva*).

In the case of the Tathāgatagarbha theory, much more attention was paid to the soteriological problem, and the *dhātu* is often expressed with the term *dharmakāya* as denoting the Buddha or Tathāgata in the sense of "the one whose body is Dharma," or "the one who has become one with the *dharmadhātu* or *dharmatā* through its realization." The same *dharmakāya* is called *tathāgatagarbha* or *buddhadhātu* when hypothetically admitted in all *sattva*s as the potentiality and postulate of their enlightenment. In this soteriological sense, *dharmakāya* or *buddhadhātu* cannot remain simply as *asaṃskṛta*, that is, "it" or "he" (or "she") has powers and activity towards, or that lead to, enlightenment. These virtuous powers are called *anāsravadharma*s: that is, dharmas that are without the "flow" or pollution of defilements, and the *dhātu* itself is also referred to as *anāsravadhātu*. Concerning these *anāsravadharma*s, the *Ratnagotravibhāga* explains their dependent origination, in comparison with the usual twelvefold chain of causation, as also characterized as *sāsrava*, accompanied by defilements. Actually, however, this dependent origination of "flowless" dharmas is presented in order to explain how bodhisattvas, who are free from the flow of defilements, can remain in the world of *saṃsāra* (or *bhava*) for the altruistic purpose based on compassion, and whose practice is the realization of non-abiding *nirvāṇa* (*apratiṣṭhita-nirvāṇa*).

The process of this dependent origination of "flowless" dharmas referred to in the *Ratnagotravibhāga* is based on the doctrines taught in the *Śrīmālā-sūtra*. It begins with the *avidyāvasabhūmi* (dwelling base of ignorance), which causes the *anāsravakarman* (flowless action). The latter results in the birth of the form of bodhisattvas (and other *ārya*s of the two vehicles) as *manomayakāya* (body made of mind) and their deaths as inconceivable transformations (*acintyā pāriṇāmikī cyuti*). The *Ratnagotravibhāga* applies this process of dependent origination to the system of three divisions of that which is defiled (*saṃkleśa*): that in the form of defilement (*kleśa-saṃkleśa*), that in the form of action or force (*karma-saṃkleśa*), and that in the form of birth (*janma-saṃkleśa*). This last form represents the repetition of birth and death in *saṃsāra*, characterized as suffering (*duḥkha*). The term *saṃkleśa* was originally used for denoting those dharmas belonging to the truth of suffering and the truth of the origination (of suffering), in contrast to those dharmas belonging to the truth of extinction (of suffering) and the truth of the way (toward extinction), which are called purification (*vyavadāna*), or "the purified." Therefore the application of the term *saṃkleśa* for *anāsravadharma*s is inconsistent from the standpoint of the Abhidharma system of doctrines. Besides attaching powers to the *asaṃskṛta-dhātu*, the *Ratnagotravibhāga* has dared to violate Abhidharmic rules for the sake of its own doctrine.[9]

Recently I received a paper on this subject entitled "Theories of the immaculate dependent origination in Tathāgatagarbha thought" from the author Kubota Chikara.[10] In this article Kubota analyzes in detail the passage of the *Ratnagotravibhāga* referred to above and indicates a certain kind of doctrinal contradiction caused by combining the four kinds of impediments with the three stages of *saṃkleśa*. According to his argument, the *Ratnagotravibhāga* violated the system of the twelvefold chain of dependent origination by inserting *sāsrava-/anāsrava-karman* before *bhava/manomayakāya*, which is included in the *janma-saṃkleśa*. At the same time, he suggests that the *Ratnagotravibhāga* intended to emphasize a bodhisattva's altruistic action in this world (as I summarized above), but the explanation he provides is not complete, especially in regard to the character of the *manomayakāya*. He emphasizes the double role of the *manomayakāya*: the defiled side shown as impediments for the attainment of the supreme qualities of the Tathāgata, and the pure side shown as the result of a bodhisattva's altruistic intention. He finds the most elevated figure of the latter in the description of the *manomayakāya* in the *Laṅkāvatāra-sūtra* (see Kubota 1998). As for the bodhisattva's altruistic intentions, the *Ratnagotravibhāga* expresses it in a more positive way in the section on the pure and impure state of the bodhisattva in terms of *saṃcintya-bhavôpapatti* ("intentional birth

9. The passage where this process of the *anāsrava* actions is taught is in the section on the supreme virtues (*guṇapāramitā*) of the Tathāgata, and, in comparison to them, the shortcomings of the bodhisattvas' qualities characterized by four kinds of impediments. See Takasaki 1966, pp. 214–221; T. no. 1611, vol. 31, p. 830bc.

10. The author is a graduate of Tohoku University and at present teaching at the Tohoku University of Art and Design in Yamagata. See Kubota 1999.

in the world of migration").[11]

The Significance of Buddha Nature (buddhadhātu) in Relation to the Worship of Relics in the Mahāyāna Mahāparinirvāṇa-sūtra

In addition to *garbha* there are other terms used synonymously as key words to express the meaning of "kernel" in the Tathāgatagarbha theory, such as *dhātu*, *gotra*, and *prakṛti*. Each of these terms has its own range of equivocal meanings associated with each other, and, combining these terms, the Tathāgatagarbha theory established its system of "pregnant" thought centering around the *tathāgatagarbha* or Buddha nature.

The term *buddhadhātu*, usually translated as "Buddha nature," is a term used for the first time in the *Mahāyāna Mahāparinirvāṇa-sūtra* to denote the concept equivalent to *tathāgatagarbha* in the sense of the nature or essence of the Buddha existent inside every *sattva* or sentient being, such as in the formula *asti buddhadhātuḥ sarvasattveṣu* (or *sarvasattvakāyeṣu*: that is, "all beings have Buddha nature"). At the same time, there is the use of this term in the *Mahāyāna Mahāparinirvāṇa-sūtra* used in the sense of the Buddha's relics worshiped in the stūpas.

Recently Shimoda Masahiro has published a mammoth work entitled "A study of the *Mahāparinirvāṇa-sūtra*, with a focus on the methodology of the study of Mahāyāna sūtras" (1997), investigating how and why the term *buddhadhātu*, which originally referred to the relics (*śarīradhātu*), came to be used in the *Mahāparinirvāṇa-sūtra* in place of the concept of *tathāgatagarbha*. He concludes that the author (or authors) of the *Mahāparinirvāṇa-*

---

11. See Takasaki 1966, pp. 248–246; T. 31, p. 833bc. The *Ratnagotravibhāga* uses the term *bhava* always as synonymous with *saṃsāra*, but not in the sense of the power or *karman* that causes future existence, as in the Sarvāstivāda.

sūtra were originally leaders and advocates of stūpa worship. Wishing to reform their religious group into a more morally rigorous community, and armed with doctrine suitable to their purpose, they introduced or accepted the teaching of the *Tathāgatagarbha-sūtra* and reshaped the significance of *dhātu* worship from that of the physical relics of the Buddha to that of the inner Buddha as a principle of salvation.

Shimoda attempts to prove this process through an examination of the textual formation of the *Mahāparinirvāṇa-sūtra*. He shows that the early or basic sections are equivalent to the first Chinese translation in 6 volumes (T. no. 376), translated by Fa-hsien in 418. He divides the text into two diachronic stages, the first stage including chapters 1–4, 6, and 7 of the sūtra, and the second stage including chapters 5 and 8–18, the latter being divided again into chapters 8 and 9–18. Of these, the first expresses faith in the body of the Buddha as the eternal *dharmakāya*, instead of the physical body, while the second part expresses mainly the Tathāgatagarbha theory in which it is taught that the Buddha within the body of each *sattva* is the eternal *ātman*. The first portion of the second part shows a transitional stage in teaching and in the formation of a new order. Shimoda characterizes this transition as a shift from the worship of the outer stūpa to that of the inner stūpa.

The aim of Shimoda's work is not to clarify the history of Tathāgatagarbha theory per se, but to investigate the formation of Mahāyāna sūtras with a new methodology and using the *Mahāparinirvāṇa-sūtra* as an example. This is not the place to give a full survey of his whole work, but I wish to add one point by introducing his interpretation of the significance of stūpa worship as the expression of a prayer for the eternity of the Buddha throughout the history of Buddhism, after the Buddha's *mahāparinirvāṇa*, by both mendicants and lay believers. Shimoda thus denies the hypothesis that Mahāyāna Buddhism was a new movement caused by the existence of groups of lay believers. As for the process of the formation of Mahāyāna scriptures (which is itself nothing but the formation of Mahāyāna Buddhism), he seems to suggest the need for investigating the connection or relation of the composer with one of the traditional Buddhist sects. He also suggests the importance of making clear the continuity and discontinuity of Mahāyāna Buddhism with the Buddhism of the traditional sects.

In light of Shimoda's work, it can be said that Tathāgatagarbha theory is an expression of this rather emotional prayer of all Buddhists necessary for Buddhism as a religion, in addition to the hermeneutics of doctrine based on the confidence in the eternity of the Dharma. Shimoda's work also suggests further questions: if the Tathāgatagarbha theory was imposed on the *Mahāparinirvāṇa-sūtra* from the outside, how should we consider the formation of the Tathāgatagarbha theory itself? Can we connect the concept of the rise of the Buddha from the lotus in the *Tathāgatagarbha-sūtra* to the concept of the stūpa of Prabhūtaratna rising up out of the earth in the *Lotus Sutra*? Again, these are issues in need of further consideration.

Is the Tathāgatagarbha Theory a Teaching of Ultimate Meaning or Conventional Meaning?

As a final point I would like to refer to the significance of the work of S. Hookham in *Buddha Within* (1991), specifically the question of whether the Tathāgatagarbha theory is a teaching of ultimate meaning (*nītārtha*) or conventional meaning (*neyārtha*), as stated in the debate in Tibet between the school claiming the doctrine of the emptiness of others (*gshan stoṅ pa*) and that claiming the doctrine of self-emptiness (*raṅ stoṅ pa*). The main efforts of Hookham were dedicated to finding out the source materials on the Tathāgatagarbha theory, which was accepted positively in the

Buddhist tradition of Tibet. Hookham sought for materials in the works of the Jo nang pa and others, materials that are characterized as belonging to the Shen tong pa tradition in contrast to the Rang tong pa (to which belongs the Ge lugs pa school). Consequently Hookham revealed that the pioneering work of Seyfort Ruegg on the Tibetan tradition of interpreting the Tathāgatagarbha theory was based solely on materials belonging to the Rang tong pa, which interprets Tathāgatagarbha theory as of convenient character, leading to the ultimate truth of self-emptiness. In contrast, the Shen tong pa claims the ultimate character of the Tathāgatagarbha theory, regarding the *śūnyavāda* as incomplete and provisional, and hence of conventional meaning. This work by Hookham seems to recover the ultimate position of Tathāgatagarbha theory as declared in the *Ratnagotravibhāga* as *uttaratantra* (ultimate), the term interpreted by the Shen tong pa as signifying the theory and contents of the *Ratnagotravibhāga* and *Tathāgatagarbha-sūtra* as the third (and final) promotion of the wheel of the Dharma.

Upon further consideration, however, it seems to me that the debate between the Rang tong pa and the Shen tong pa concerns the point of whether to put ultimate value in the Dharma or in the person of the Buddha, whether on self-realization of the Dharma or on salvation by the Buddha, and not on the question of which is ultimate or not, much less on the question of which is right or not. Both sides complement each other and are necessary for Buddhism as a religion. Again I would emphasize that the follower of the Tathāgatagarbha theory would be content with the evaluation of this teaching as "conventional," because any teaching of the Buddha is, after all, a convention or means for the sake of deliverance or religious awakening.[12]

12. In a personal correspondence, Professor Yamaguchi Zuihō informed me that Bu ston was a Rang tong pa who was eager to discuss this point.

Summary

I have briefly discussed a few points with regard to the Tathāgatagarbha theory that have recently become issues of debate among Buddhist scholars. These points indicate that there is still much to be discussed and clarified concerning the Tathāgatagarbha theory, and that the issue is one of continuing controversy and interest among Buddhist scholars both in Japan and abroad.

REFERENCES

Hakamaya Noriaki 袴谷憲昭

1989 *Hongaku shisō hihan* 本覚思想批判. Tokyo: Daizō Shuppan.

1990 *Hihan bukkyō* 批判仏教. Tokyo: Daizō Shuppan.

Hookham, S. K.

1991 *Buddha Within: Tathagatagarbha Doctrine According to the Shentong Interpretation of the Ratnagotravibhaga*. Suny Series in Buddhist Studies. Albany: State University of New York Press.

Hubbard, Jamie, and Paul L. Swanson

1997 *Pruning the Bodhi Tree: The Storm Over Critical Buddhism*. Honolulu: University of Hawai'i Press.

Kubota Chikara 久保田力

1998 "Manasu no torikkusutā-sei (II): Ishōshin no keifu to *Ryōgakyō*" マナスのトリックスター性 (II)—意生身の系譜と『楞伽経』. *Tōhoku Geijutsu Kōka Daigaku Kiyō* 5: 14–69.

1999 "Nyoraizō shisō no muro-engi setsu: *Hōshōron* no shishō, sanzōzen setsu o megutte (jō)" 如来蔵思想の無漏縁起説—『宝性論』の四障・三雑染説をめぐって（上）. *Tōhoku Geijutsu Kōka Daigaku Kiyō* 6: 4–26.

Matsumoto Shirō 松本史朗

1989 *Engi to kū—Nyoraizō shisō hihan* 縁起と空—如来蔵思想批判. Tokyo: Daizō Shuppan.

1993 *Zen shisō no hihanteki kenkyū* 禅思想の批判的研究. Tokyo: Daizō Shuppan.

Seyfort Ruegg, David

1969 *La théorie du Tathāgatagarbha et du Gotra: Études sur la sotériologie et la gnoséologie du bouddhisme*. Paris: École Française d'Extrême-Orient.

1989 *Buddha-nature, Mind, and the Problem of Gradualism in a Comparative Perspective: On the Transmission and Reception of Buddhism in India and Tibet*. London: School of Oriental and African Studies, University of London.

Shimoda Masahiro 下田正弘

1997 *Nehangyō no kenkyū—Daijō kyōten no kenkyū hōhō shiron* 涅槃経の研究—大乗経典の研究方法試論. Tokyo: Shunjūsha.

Takasaki Jikidō 高崎直道

1966 *A Study on the Ratnagotravibhāga (Uttaratantra), Being a Treatise on the Tathāgatagarbha Theory of Mahāyāna Buddhism*. Roma: Istituto Italiano per il Medio ed Estremo Oriente.

1974 *Nyoraizō shisō no keisei* 如来蔵思想の形成. Tokyo: Shunjūsha.

1998 "Nyoraizō shisō: Indo kara Chūgoku e" 如来蔵思想—インドから中国へ. *Indotetsugaku Bukkyōgaku* 13: 163–179.

PART V
JAPANESE AND EAST ASIAN BUDDHISM

A History of East Asian Buddhist Thought: The Formation of a Sphere of Chinese-Canon–Based Buddhism*

I. THE THREE SPHERES OF BUDDHISM

In Japan it is often said that Buddhism has been transmitted through three lands, meaning that it has its origins in India, the birthplace of Śākyamuni, passed through China, and then reached Japan, and this calls to mind the great distance travelled by Buddhism in the course of its eastward dissemination. The fact that Buddhism passed through China in the course of its transmission to Japan has been an important factor in determining the character of Japanese Buddhism, for it has meant that Japan has relied on Chinese translations of the Buddhist scriptures, and the same conditions have also applied to Buddhism in Korea as well as in Vietnam. What I shall refer to here as 'East Asian Buddhism' is none other than that form of Buddhism based on Chinese translations of the Buddhist scriptures.

If we consider Buddhism today, we find that, typologically speaking, there are, in addition to East Asian Buddhism based on Chinese translations of the Buddhist scriptures, the sphere of the Southern tradition of Buddhism centred on Sri Lanka and found throughout Southeast Asia and the sphere of Tibetan Buddhism that spread from Tibet to Mongolia. Of these two latter spheres, that of the Southern tradition is based on the Early Canon written in the sacred language known as Pāli, while that of Tibetan Buddhism has its foundations in the scriptures that were translated into the Tibetan language. This division into three types is, in

* Originally published in *Acta Asiatica* 66 (1994), pp. 1–32.

other words, based on differences in the languages used in their respective scriptures. As regards their doctrines, the Southern tradition follows the Theravāda school, while the other two spheres adhere to Mahāyāna Buddhism. These three types have their origins in the historical circumstances surrounding the propagation of Buddhism, but they were also strongly influenced by the cultural circumstances of the lands into which Buddhism was received. This was especially so in the case of East Asian Buddhism, which evolved through its contacts with a highly developed alien cultural sphere in the form of Chinese culture. In considering the distinctive features of East Asian Buddhism, let us first survey for comparative purposes the circumstances under which the other two spheres of Buddhism evolved.

Buddhism was a product of Indian culture. With the unification of India under the Mauryan dynasty this ancient civilization, rivalling that of China, extended its influence in neighbouring regions to the north and south and gradually created an Indian cultural sphere sometimes referred to as 'Greater India'. In scope it went beyond Gandhāra and Afghanistan in the north and extended as far as the various regions of Central Asia, while to the south, starting from Sri Lanka, it spread throughout Southeast Asia as far as Indonesia and Indochina. In these regions settlement by Indians continued until the seventh and eighth centuries and led to the establishment of Indianized kingdoms. The peoples in the surrounding areas basked in the benefits of Indian culture and thereby gradually became civilized. The advance of Islam put an end to this state of affairs, but even today its influence remains in Southeast Asia in, for example, the traditional culture of the performing arts associated with the Rāmāyaṇa legend.

Buddhism spread throughout this Indian cultural sphere together with Hinduism, but it is to be surmised that there were some differences in the manner in which these two religions disseminated. This was because Buddhism, with adherents among traders, would have spread quickly from one town to another and because the monastic community actively undertook to propagate its teachings. The existence of monks who had quite literally distanced themselves to a certain degree from Indian society doubtless facilitated the propagation of Buddhism among peoples of differing manners and customs. By way of contrast, the spread of Hinduism required the advance and settlement of Hindus in the form of Indian society itself.

In other respects, however, Buddhism as found in this Indian cultural sphere was nothing other than Indian culture itself, and its scriptures were written in Indian vernaculars and later in Sanskrit. In regard to interchange on a personal level too, many Indian monks resided in Central Asia, some of them also visiting China, and Kumārajīva (Chiu-mo-lo-shih 鳩摩羅什) of Kucha (Kuei-tzu 龜茲) for example, who later went to China where he became a renowned translator, underwent training as a monk during his youth in Kashmir. (Translator-monks in China with the surname Chu 竺 were either Indian monks or the disciples of Indian monks.) Under the rule of the Kushan (Kuei-shuang 貴霜) dynasty, founded by the Greater Yüeh-chih 大月氏 and with its capital at Gandhāra, Gandhāran was made the official language, and it is thought that Gandhāran was also regarded as the sacred language of the Buddhist scriptures. A similar situation prevailed in Southeast Asia too, where it was easy to travel by sea in the region extending from Bengal and Suvarṇabhūmi (Myanmar) as far as Sumatra and Fu-nan 扶南 (Cambodia), and Indian monks were always travelling back and forth. Paramārtha (Chen-ti 眞諦), who was invited to China by Emperor Wu 武帝 of the Liang 梁 dynasty, was at the time a monk of renown in Fu-nan, but he had been born in Ujjain in western India. Fu-nan and Sumatra served as bases for Chinese monks on pilgrimages to India. In addition, although the present-day Theravāda school of the Southern tradition has copied the Buddhist scriptures in the respective scripts of Sri Lanka, Myanmar, Thailand and Cambodia, the language used is the one and same Pāli. What is more, this Pāli is not even the Sinhalese language indigenous to Sri Lanka, the home of Theravāda Buddhism, but derives from the west Indian language of the monastic community—the language of Magadha with elements of west Indian vernaculars—that was used when Buddhism was introduced to Sri Lanka around the third century B.C. and became established as the language of the scriptures (viz. Pāli). When considered in this light, the Buddhism of the Indian cultural sphere, including present-day Theravāda Buddhism, may be said to represent an extension of Indian Buddhism. In this sense the Buddhism of the Southern tradition is no different from the Buddhism of Nepal, where monastic communities have continued to exist down to the present day and Mahāyāna scriptures written in Sanskrit continue to be preserved.

Even following the advances of Islam, Theravāda Buddhism survived in Southeast Asia, and it was in fact subsequent to these advances that it built up its present strength. Prior to this it had been late Indian Buddhism in the form of Mahāyāna Buddhism and Tantrism (or Esoteric Buddhism) that had enjoyed the greatest influence in Southeast Asia. Tantrism in particular has close connections with Hinduism and may almost be described as an amalgam of Buddhism and Hinduism (as may be seen for example in the ruins of Borobudur), and for this reason it is thought to have shared the fate of Indian society when the latter disappeared from this region. By way of contrast, the Theravāda school preserved the traditions of early Indian Buddhism, with a strong monastic organization, and this perhaps provided the energy behind the subsequent revival of Buddhism. It is at any rate evident from the fact that Buddhism vanished from India proper when it lost the last stronghold of its monastic community in Bengal in the thirteenth century that within the Indian cultural sphere the continuing existence of the monastic community was a *sine qua non* for the survival of Buddhism. Once Buddhism, which lacked any lay organization, was deprived of its leadership, its eventual engulfment by Hindu society was probably inevitable.

Next, moving on to the sphere of Tibetan Buddhism, we find that although Tibet lies next to India, she had no contacts with India because of the rugged mountains separating the two regions until the establishment of a unified state within Tibetan society in the seventh century. But from this time onwards Tibet began to import Buddhism along with other cultural institutions from both Nepal and China. Modelling themselves on Indic scripts, the Tibetans also created a Tibetan alphabet and began translating Buddhist scriptures into Tibetan. Buddhist scriptures were introduced from both India and China, but they were invariably translated. This was a phenomenon peculiar to Tibet, not to be found in either the lands of Southeast Asia or the countries of East Asia apart from China, and as a result, although wedged in between two ancient civilizations, Tibet was able to develop a sphere of Buddhist culture independent of these two neighbouring cultural spheres. It is especially remarkable that, in spite of frequently finding herself under the political control or influence of China, Tibet managed to maintain her cultural independence of China. Tibet's relations with India, on the other hand, revolved around Buddhism, and especially after Indian monks triumphed in their debate with representatives of Chinese Buddhism there was a steady stream of Indian monks entering Tibet, and Buddhist scriptures and treatises were translated in rapid succession. Following the disappearance of Buddhism from India proper, Tibet gained importance as a centre for preserving the traditions of late Indian Buddhism. Tibetan Buddhism, based on the Tibetan translations of Buddhist texts, was later adopted by the Mongols of the Yüan 元 dynasty and spread throughout Inner Asia, resulting in the translation of Buddhist scriptures into Mongolian, while under the Ch'ing 清 dynasty they were also translated into Manchu, the native tongue of the founders of this dynasty. But the foundations of doctrine and monastic organization lay in Tibetan Buddhism, and in this sense this entire sphere of Buddhism may be referred to simply as Tibetan Buddhism.

When the sphere of Chinese-canon–based East Asian Buddhism is compared with the above two types of Buddhism, the source of its distinguishing features is found to lie in the fact that in this case Buddhism left the cultural sphere of its origins and was transplanted into an already established alien culture where, as a result of conflict, reconciliation and interaction with local culture, as well as control by and compromise with powerful political forces, it underwent major changes when compared with the Buddhism of its original home in India. In addition, when it spread from China to neighbouring countries it underwent still further changes. But it is perhaps worth noting that once Buddhist texts had been translated into Chinese they were revered as sacred scriptures throughout all of East Asia and were not translated into the languages of other East Asian countries. This was, however, nothing but a reflection of the enormous influence exerted by Chinese culture, and it means in effect that all the countries of East Asia fell within the cultural sphere of Chinese writing. It is also probably necessary to add as a further distinctive feature of East Asian Buddhism the fact that under the ancient Chinese tribute-investiture system the propagation of Buddhism carried highly political overtones.

II. THE ACCEPTANCE OF BUDDHISM IN CHINA

According to a widely circulated tradition, Buddhism was first introduced to China in Yung-p'ing 永平 10 (A.D. 67) during the reign of Emperor Ming 明帝 of the Later Han 後漢 when Chia-yeh Mo-t'eng 迦葉摩騰 (Kāśyapa Mātaṅga?) and Chu Fa-lan 竺法蘭 (Dharmaratna?) came to Lo-yang 洛陽 from the land of the Greater Yüeh-chih and translated the *Ssu-shih-erh-chang ching* 四十二章經

(Sūtra in Forty-two Sections). Today this tradition is regarded as a fictitious product of later times, first appearing in Hui-chiao's 慧皎 *Kao-seng chuan* 高僧傳 (Biographies of Eminent Monks). But according to another account found in the *Hou-Han shu* 後漢書 (History of the Later Han), in Yung-p'ing 7 the same Emperor Ming saw a "golden man" in a dream and sent envoys to the western regions in order to seek out *fu-t'u* 浮圖, or Buddhism. This too cannot be regarded as a factual account, but Emperor Ming did have a half brother, Prince Ying of Ch'u 楚王英, who does in fact appear to have embraced Buddhism. Going back further in time, the first reference to Buddhism in Chinese historical sources concerns a national university student (*po-shih ti-tzu* 博士弟子) by the name of Ching Lu 景盧 who in Yüan-shou 元壽 1 (2 B.C.) during the reign of Emperor Ai 哀帝 of the Former Han 前漢 received oral instruction in the Buddhist scriptures from I-ts'un 伊存, an envoy from the Greater Yüeh-chih. This too is probably based on fact, but this alone cannot be said to have constituted the transmission of Buddhism to China. By way of contrast, the account concerning Prince Ying of Ch'u indicates that by the second half of the first century A.D. Buddhism was beginning to be accepted in some form or another. By mentioning the name of Emperor Ming, later Chinese historians probably sought to gain official recognition for the introduction of Buddhism.

As is evident from the above traditions, Buddhism first entered China by way of Central Asia. On the Chinese side the conditions for its transmission were created by China's subjugation of the western regions, which had been initiated by Emperor Wu of the Former Han, while in Central Asia the determining factor was the existence of the Greater Yüeh-chih. Buddhist images and scriptures would have been circulating among the Central Asians under the latter's rule, and the spearhead of this movement would have reached Chinese territory. Thus occurred the initial introduction of Buddhism into China.

But what sort of interest did the Chinese evince in Buddhism? In the first place, they would appear to have been attracted by Buddhist images, which they called "golden men" (*chin-jen* 金人), and they seem to have installed these images for the same reasons that they worshipped the Yellow Emperor (Huang-ti 黃帝) and Lao-tzu 老子, namely, out of a desire for longevity and immortality. The aforementioned account of Prince Ying of Ch'u notes that he worshipped the Yellow Emperor and Lao-tzu alongside the Buddha, while a gloss on the biography of Śākyamuni as related by I-ts'un speculates that after having gone through the pass to the west and traversed the western regions, Lao-tzu may in fact have gone to India, where he instructed the barbarians and became the Buddha. This legend of Lao-tzu's conversion of the barbarians was gradually elaborated on, leading to debates between Buddhists and Taoists over the relative merits of Śākyamuni and Lao-tzu, and as a result Śākyamuni's dates were gradually pushed back and works such as the *Lao-tzu hua-hu ching* 老子化胡經 (Sūtra of Lao-tzu's Conversion of the Barbarians) were composed. It is at any rate to be surmised that the Chinese took a keen interest in Buddhism because they sensed in the doctrines of Buddhism some affinities with the teachings of Lao-tzu. From the development of so-called *ko-i* 格義 ("matching the meaning") Buddhism, whereby Buddhism was interpreted through the medium of the thought of Lao-tzu and Chuang-tzu 莊子 (Lao-Chuang thought), to the establishment of Ch'an 禪 this was to exert considerable influence far into the future, while on the Taoist side a monastic organization was to be established under the influence of Buddhism and scriptures were compiled, developing into popular Taoism and the Taoist Canon (*Tao-tsang* 道藏).

The inevitability of Buddhism's links with Lao-Chuang thought may also be seen in the translation of Buddhist scriptures into Chinese. The fact that the Chinese set about attempting to understand an alien culture expressed in a foreign language by first translating it into their own language was probably a reflection of Chinese pride in their own culture. At the time, this was without a doubt an epoch-making event for Buddhism. Central Asian Buddhism appears to have been largely dependent upon scriptures written in Indic languages, and although there are some Buddhist texts in Khotanese, it would not have been particularly difficult to translate from an Indic language into Khotanese since the latter belongs to the same Indo-Aryan family of languages. By way of contrast, the Chinese language not only bespoke an alien culture, but also belongs to a totally different family of languages. In order to surmount the resultant difficulties the translators had no choice but to adopt the method of first borrowing terms from Lao-Chuang thought and then adding explanations as required.

The history of the translation of Buddhist scriptures into Chinese begins with An Shih-kao 安世高 in the mid-second century. An Shih-kao was a native of Parthia (An-hsi 安息) who came to China during the reign of Emperor Huan 桓帝 (r. 147–167) of the Later Han, and for more than thirty years he spread the Buddhist teachings by expounding and translating the Dharma. He exerted considerable influence and endeared himself to the Chinese, being known as a 'Bodhisattva'. According to the *Ch'u san-tsang chi chi* 出三藏記集 (Collection of Notes concerning the Translation of the *Tripiṭaka*), the oldest extant record of Chinese translations of Buddhist texts, An Shih-kao translated thirty-five texts in forty-one fascicles. Of these more than a dozen are known to have been preserved down to the present day, and it is thus possible to acquaint ourselves with his achievement. The majority of the texts that he translated were either manuals for the practice of meditation or outlines of Buddhist doctrine, and it is to be surmised that they were put to practical use in the propagation of Buddhism. Representative of his translations are the *An-pan shou-i ching* 安般守意經 (Sūtra of *Ānāpāna* Meditation) and *Yin-ch'ih-ju ching* 陰持入經 (Sūtra of the Aggregates, Realms, and Sense-

Fields). '*An-pan*' in the title of the former is a transliteration of *ānāpāna*, a compound of *āna* (inhalation) and *apāna* (exhalation), and refers to the observation of incoming and outgoing breath, an elementary exercise for regulating the breath during meditation, while '*shou-i*' means to control and stabilize the mind through the regulation of the breath and signifies 'meditation' or 'concentration'. This text begins with an explanation of *ānāpāna* and then describes each of the thirty-seven factors of enlightenment (*bodhi-pakṣa* / *bodhy-aṅga*). Meditation based on the regulation of the breath is also found in Lao-Chuang teachings, and in this text it is in fact explained as resembling the Lao-Chuang practice and was probably adopted as such. The practice of employing as deemed appropriate both transliteration and translation in rendering Buddhist terms, as evidenced in the title of this text, was to become an established tradition in the translation of Buddhist texts into Chinese. The use of the term *an-pan*, a corrupt form corresponding to Sanskrit *ānāpāna*, is probably evidence of the fact that Buddhist texts written in an Indic language were circulating in Parthia. The *Yin-ch'ih-ju ching*, on the other hand, presents an outline of all the constituent elements of existence as subsumed under the five aggregates (*skandha*), eighteen realms (*dhātu*), and twelve sense-fields (*āyatana*), and it is an Abhidharmic text. An Shih-kao received the assistance of disciples such as Yen Fo-t'iao 嚴佛調, and he was thus able to pass his work down to posterity. In addition to the translation of Buddhist texts, such personal contacts were also an important factor in the dissemination of Buddhism.

The next figure of importance in the history of the translation of Buddhist texts into Chinese was Chih Lou-chia-ch'en 支婁迦讖 (Lokakṣema). He was a native of Yüeh-chih 月氏 (Scythia) of the Greater Yüeh-chih or Kushan dynasty and came to China in the final years of Emperor Huan's reign. During the reign of Emperor Ling 靈帝 (r. 178–189) he translated for the first time a number of

Mahāyāna scriptures, including the *Tao-hsing pan-jo ching* 道行般若經 (corresponding to the *Aṣṭasāhasrikā Prajñāpāramitā*), *Pan-chou san-mei ching* 般舟三昧經 (corresponding to the *Pratyutpanna-buddhasammukhāvasthitasamādhi-sūtra*), and *Shou-leng-yen ching* 首楞嚴經 (no longer extant but corresponding to the *Śūraṃgama-samādhi-sūtra*). As a result of these translations Chinese Buddhism was introduced to a variety of Buddhism differing from that transmitted by An Shih-kao. Today it is considered that these Mahāyāna texts were introduced to China not long after having made their appearance in India and that it was a period during which many similar works were being composed. As a result Chinese Buddhism was subsequently visited by a veritable flood of scriptures, both old and new, and was faced with the task of translating and cataloguing them and of classifying and interpreting their teachings.

Lokakṣema's work was carried over by his disciple Chih Liang 支亮 and, through him, Chih Ch'ien 支謙. Avoiding the upheavals of the final years of the Later Han, Chih Ch'ien betook himself to Wu 吳 where, receiving the patronage of Sun Ch'üan 孫權, he devoted himself to the translation of Buddhist texts, translating in addition to the *Ta-ming-tu ching* 大明度經 (another version of the *Aṣṭasāhasrikā Prajnāpāramitā*) Mahāyāna scriptures such as the *A-mi-t'o ching* 阿彌陀經 (a version of the *Larger Sukhāvatīvyūha*) and *Wei-mo-chieh ching* 維摩詰經 (corresponding to the *Vimala-kīrtinirdeśa-sūtra*). Chih Ch'ien is also an important figure in that he propagated Buddhism in Chiang-nan 江南, but similar recognition for services in the dissemination of Buddhism must also be accorded K'ang Seng-hui 康僧會, who founded the monastery Chien-ch'u-ssu 建初寺 in Chien-k'ang 建康, the capital of Wu, and devoted his energies to expounding the Buddhist scriptures. He is said to have been born into a family hailing from Samarkand (K'ang-chü-kuo 康居國) and travelled with his father from India to Chiao-chih 交趾 (in Chiao-chou 交州), where he was orphaned at the age of ten and joined the Buddhist order. Buddhism had probably reached Chiao-chih via the sea route from the south, and there would have been many Indian monks there too. The southern districts as far as Chiao-chih lay within the domain or under the influence of Wu, and Buddhism entered Wu through its trade with this region. K'ang Seng-hui is considered to have been the first person to introduce Buddhism to Wu from the south.

The final years of the Later Han and the Three Kingdoms (San-kuo 三國) period were a time of great upheaval in the history of ancient China, and in the realm of philosophy the teachings of Lao-tzu and Chuang-tzu were supplanting Confucianism, providing the ideology for social reform movements such as the Wu-tou-mi-tao 五斗米道 (Five Pecks of Grain Movement) and absorbing many elements from folk religions, eventually developing into Taoism. Buddhism would appear to have taken advantage of these circumstances, and during the subsequent Western Chin 西晉 and Eastern Chin 東晉 dynasties it won social acceptance. There were also developments in the interpretation of Buddhist doctrine, although it was still understood in the light of Lao-Chuang thought. In particular, with the successive translations of Prajñāpāramitā texts by Lokakṣema and Chih Ch'ien affinities were discovered between the doctrine of 'emptiness' (*śūnyatā*) in Mahāyāna Buddhism and the teachings of 'nothingness' (*wu* 無) or the 'way' (*tao* 道) in Lao-Chuang thought, and as a result the method of interpreting Buddhist scriptures along such lines (*ko-i*) flourished. In the field of translation Chu Fa-hu 竺法護 (Dharmarakṣa), who was born in Tun-huang 敦煌 but had the ethnicon 'Chu' (denoting India) prefixed to his Chinese name because he joined the Buddhist order under an Indian monk, was active during the years 266–307 and was known as the 'Bodhisattva of Tun-huang'; he is regarded as the preeminent translator-monk prior to Kumārajīva.

At the start of the fourth century, following Dharmarakṣa's

death, the Chin dynasty was forced to abandon its capital at Ch'ang-an 長安 on account of the incursions of foreign tribes (316) and moved to the southeast, establishing the Eastern Chin dynasty. In central China the so-called sixteen states of the five "barbarian" or non-Chinese tribes coexisted or succeeded one another, and we enter the period of division between the north and the south. During this period Buddhism faced a turning point in the process of its Sinicization. In the first place, it was accorded reverence by successive foreign dynasties and Buddhist monks were appointed to positions of trust, and in the second place, consequent to the policies of these foreign dynasties, Han Chinese were granted official permission to join the Buddhist order and the foundations for monastic organization were laid. The figures to render the greatest services in this respect were Fo-t'u-teng 佛圖澄 and his successor Shih Tao-an 釋道安.

Fo-t'u-teng was born into the Po 帛 clan and is thought to have been a native of Kucha. Since he claimed to be one hundred years old when he arrived at Lo-yang in 310, he was obviously already of an advanced age, and he was renowned as a thaumaturge and miracle-worker. Upon hearing of his abilities, Shih Lo 石勒 of the Later Chao 後趙 summoned him, appointed him advisor in military and political affairs, and is said to have utilized his magical powers. But for his part Fo-t'u-teng also made use of the trust placed in him by Shih Lo and his son Shih Hu 石虎, promoting the construction of Buddhist monasteries and the dissemination of Buddhist rites, and he also prevailed upon Shih Hu to grant Han Chinese official permission to join the Buddhist order. This latter measure was to be of considerable importance in allowing Buddhism to take root in China. Fo-t'u-teng was also held in high regard as a strict disciplinarian, and he attracted many disciples, including Shih Tao-an, Seng-lang 僧朗 (who lived in seclusion on T'ai-shan 泰山), and Chu Fa-ya 竺法雅, the leading exponent of the *ko-i* method of exegesis.

Shih Tao-an (312–385) was the first great Buddhist of Han Chinese origin. Winning the respect of Fu Chien 符堅 of the Former Ch'in 前秦, he not only contributed to the establishment of the Buddhist order in northern China, but is also said to have sent many disciples to the south in order to expand the order there too. His disciples included Hui-yüan 慧遠 of Lu-shan 廬山, who laid the foundations for the development of a practice-oriented Buddhism in the subsequent period.

On account of his contributions to scriptural hermenutics and to the compilation of records relating to the translation of Buddhist texts into Chinese, Tao-an is today considered to have made one of the greatest contributions in the history of Buddhism. But nor can he be overlooked in regard to the establishment of the code of discipline governing the Buddhist order in China, for the rules that he formulated for discoursing on the scriptures, for meals and other aspects of monastic life, and for rituals such as the semimonthly meeting days (*upavasatha* [*pu-sa* 布薩]) and confession were to provide the models for the regulations established in later times. It was also Tao-an who advocated that Buddhists adopt the surname of Shih 釋, corresponding to 'Śākya'. As a result of Tao-an's activities Buddhism may be said to have truly taken root in China.

III. THE EVOLUTION OF CHINESE BUDDHISM AND ITS DISSEMINATION THROUGHOUT EAST ASIA

The second epoch in the history of Chinese Buddhism corresponds to the period of approximately two hundred years between the arrival of Kumārajīva (*ca.* 340–409) in Ch'ang-an in 401 and the unification of the Northern and Southern dynasties by the Sui 隋 dynasty. The distinguishing features of this period may be given as follows: (1) Kumārajīva's translations of various Buddhist texts led to rapid advances in the Chinese understanding of Buddhism, as a result of which correct interpretations according with

Buddhism proper gradually supplanted the *ko-i* Buddhism of the foregoing period, thereby laying the foundations for the formulation of the doctrines of the subsequent period; (2) state control of Buddhism increased, especially under the different Northern dynasties, thus preparing the way for the establishment of a state Buddhism under the Sui and T'ang 唐 dynasties; (3) as a result of this state policy of protecting (or sometimes suppressing) Buddhism, Buddhism infiltrated into Chinese society, thereby leading to the evolution of popular cults; and (4) again as a result of state policies Buddhism was exported under the tribute system to the countries of East Asia. Generally speaking, this period (including the Sui and the early T'ang) may be described as the period during which Buddhism was the most ostensibly active in the entire history of China. Insofar that Buddhism took root in the Han Chinese society of the Southern dynasties and was accepted by the intellectual élite, it was in particular the period during which Buddhism exerted its greatest influence on the thought and culture of China.

As was noted earlier, Kumārajīva was born in Kucha, joined the Buddhist order and studied Buddhism in Kashmir (Chi-pin 罽賓), and further studied the Mahāyāna in Kashgar (Su-lo 疏勒). He returned to Kucha and was enjoying a growing reputation when Kucha was invaded by Lü Kuang 呂光, a general under Fu Chien of the Former Ch'in. Kucha fell in 382, and Kumārajīva was taken prisoner and moved to Liang-chou 涼州 (Ku-tsang 姑臧), where he appears to have mastered the Chinese language. He was subsequently invited to Ch'ang-an by Yao Hsing 姚興, who had overthrown the Former Ch'in, and during a period of less than ten years he produced a steady stream of translations, many of them outstanding translations that were to earn a place in history. He did have the assistance of a translation centre, but his prodigious output would have been inconceivable without his mastery of Chinese while in Liang-chou. In addition to texts such as the

Saddharmapuṇḍarīka-sūtra and *Vimalakīrtinirdeśa-sūtra*, which have been read on a daily basis down to the present age, his translations also included the *Pañcaviṃśatisāhasrikā Prajñāpāramitā*, *Aṣṭasāhasrikā Prajñāpāramitā*, and *Ta chih-tu lun* 大智度論 (Treatise on the Great Perfection of Wisdom), the latter being a commentary on the *Pañcaviṃśatisāhasrikā Prajñāpāramitā*, and he is recognized in particular for having translated for the first time works such as the *Madhyamaka-kārikā* by Nāgārjuna and the *Śataka-śāstra* by Āryadeva, thus providing the Chinese with access to the orthodox Indian interpretation of the Mahāyāna doctrine of emptiness. As a result the earlier understanding of *prajñā* based on *ko-i* thinking was rectified and the foundations for the development of the San-lun 三論 (Three Treatise), T'ien-t'ai 天台, and other schools of thought were laid.

The period of translation continued further, and the task of translating the scriptures was pursued with ever greater zeal. A variety of texts reflecting the various doctrines that had developed after the *Prajñāpāramitā-sūtra*s were translated in rapid succession: these included translations of the *Avataṃsaka-sūtra* by Buddhabhadra (Fo-t'o-pa-t'o-lo 佛陀跋陀羅), who followed Kumārajīva to the Eastern Chin, the Mahāyāna *Mahāparinirvāṇa-sūtra* by Dharmakṣema (T'an-wu-ch'en 曇無讖), who had been invited to Northern Liang 北涼 on account of his occult powers, and the *Laṅkāvatāra-sūtra* and *Śrīmālādevīsiṃhanāda-sūtra* by Guṇabhadra (Ch'iu-na-pa-t'o-lo 求那跋陀羅) under the Sung 宋 dynasty. As a result Buddhist circles in China were busied with the task of absorbing these new teachings. The Mahāyāna *Mahāparinirvāṇa-sūtra* in particular, with its doctrine of the eternal nature of the Tathāgata, was avidly studied in southern China on account of the novelty of its ideas when compared with the *Prajñāpāramitā-sūtra*s, and this led to the establishment of a Nieh-p'an 涅槃 (Nirvāṇa) school. This represented a turnabout in doctrine from nonexistence to existence. The number of Chinese making pilgrimages to India also increased. One of these pilgrims was Fa-hsien 法顯, who set out in search of a manuscript of the *Vinaya-piṭaka*, but he also brought back another version of the Mahāyāna *Mahāparinirvāṇa-sūtra* and wrote the *Fo-kuo chi* 佛國記 (Record of Buddhist Kingdoms), an account of his travels.

In the early sixth century Bodhiruci (P'u-t'i-liu-chih 菩提流支) and Ratnamati (Lo-ṇa-mo-t'i 勒那摩提) arrived in the capital of Wei 魏 (508) and transmitted for the first time the views of Vasubandhu by translating works such as the *Daśabhūmikasūtra-śāstra* and various Yogācāra texts, and this resulted in the establishment of the Ti-lun 地論 (Stage Treatise) school devoted to the study of these works. Further Yogācāṛa texts were subsequently introduced by Paramārtha, who came to China by the invitation of Emperor Wu of Liang in 549 and translated Asaṅga's *Mahāyānasaṃgraha*, which led to the establishment of the She-lun 攝論 (Compendium Treatise) school. Paramārtha's views were influenced by the concepts of *tathāgatagarbha* and Buddha-nature propounded in the Mahāyāna *Mahāparinirvāṇa-sūtra*, *Śrīmālādevīsiṃhanāda-sūtra*, and the *Ratnagotravibhāga* translated by Ratnamati. Following the translation (ascribed to Paramārtha) of the *Mahāyānaśraddhotpāda-śāstra* (*Ta-ch'ęng ch'i-hsin lun* 大乘起信論 [Treatise of the Awakening of Faith in the Mahāyāna]), the *tathāgatagarbha* theory swept Chinese Buddhist circles, but Paramārtha's interpretations of Yogācāra doctrine were a little too original, arousing doubts in the minds of many, and this later induced Hsüan-tsang 玄奘 to undertake his journey to India.

In this manner the study of Buddhist doctrine (called *i-hsüeh* 義學) made marked advances, but it was not without its problems. For instance, karma, transmigration, and rebirth, all important concepts in Buddhist doctrine, were explained in terms of the indestructibility of the Chinese notion of *shen* 神 or 'soul' and Buddha-nature as expounded in the Mahāyāna *Mahāparinirvāṇa-sūtra* was also understood along these lines. (Emperor Wu of

Liang, for example, defined Buddha-nature as '*chen-shen*' 眞神 or 'true soul'.) The debate over the destructibility or indestructibility of the soul had its origins in the Confucian criticism of transmigration and rebirth, with its advocacy of the destruction of the soul after death, and in order to counter the Confucian arguments Buddhist apologists appear to have obstinately insisted upon the indestructibility of the soul. This tendency was to reappear later in other forms too, such as a theory equating Buddha-nature with 'spiritual intelligence' (*ling-chih* 靈知).

Chinese Buddhism was faced with one other major problem, namely, that presented by the flood of scriptures ranging from the Early Canon to the Mahāyāna and all allegedly expounded by the Buddha. Finding it difficult to determine which texts represented the true Buddhist teachings, Chinese Buddhist circles set about classifying with typically Chinese rationality the entire corpus of teachings believed to have been expounded by Śākyamuni during the course of his life. This was the so-called 'critical interpretation of the aspects of the doctrine' (*p'an-chiao* 判教 or *p'an chiao-hsiang* 判教相, In Japan it is usually referred to as *kyōsō hanjaku* 教相判釋 or in abbreviation *kyōhan* 教判), and by this means Chinese Buddhists sought to establish a basis for evaluating the tenets of the different schools of Buddhist thought. The prevalent tendency during this period was to regard the *Saddharmapuṇḍarīka-sūtra* or the Mahāyāna *Mahāparinirvāṇa-sūtra* as the supreme scripture and to set greatest value on the one-vehicle bodhisattva path. This too was to become a line of thought basic to Chinese Buddhism.

The second of the aforementioned features characterizing the Buddhism of this period was the development of a state Buddhism, the beginnings of which may be traced back to the policies of the Northern Wei 北魏 dynasty. Emperor T'ai-tsu Tao-wu 太祖道武帝, who ascended the throne after having overthrown the Northern Liang dynasty, took over the Buddhism of Northern

Liang and made efforts to support it, founding numerous monasteries, but at the same time he also appointed monastic authorities (*seng-kuan* 僧官) and established an organization for supervising monks and nuns. His Buddhist faith was, however, born at best out of a desire to ensure peace and prosperity for himself and other members of the ruling classes and for his dynasty, and he hoped to gain the requisite merits through the erection of monasteries and Buddhist images. The images found in the famous caves at Yün-kang 雲崗 and Lung-men 龍門 were one such example, and they are moreover said to have been modelled on the features of the emperor himself. But just as the patronage of Buddhism was at the mercy of the emperor's whims, so too was there an immediate danger of persecution if his displeasure should be incurred. For their part, Buddhist monks ingratiated themselves with the authorities, likened the emperor to the Buddha, and suggested that he be worshipped as a Tathāgata. In India Buddhism had been 'supramundane' (*lokottara*), standing above and free of the norms of state and society, and even though the Buddhist order might receive the patronage of the rulers, it was a matter of principle that the ruler's authority did not extend within the order. In addition, India had rarely been under the rule of powerful dynasties, and as a result state control of Buddhism such as that in China did not evolve. In China too there had been no such tradition in the earlier Han Chinese dynasties, and it had been possible for monks such as Hui-yüan to argue that "a monk did not pay homage to a king." But the state control of Buddhism under the Northern Wei dynasty was later taken over by the Sui and T'ang, and the views of people such as Hui-yüan were to have little influence. This state control was also inherited by the Buddhism of other countries in East Asia, whither Buddhism began to spread during this period.

The dissemination of Buddhism to the countries of East Asia presupposes the establishment of political contacts between

China and these countries, and these took the form of what may be described in a word as the tribute-investiture system. Within the framework of this system neighbouring countries paid tribute to China primarily for the purpose of enjoying the benefits of her culture through trade, while in return their rulers were granted certain titles and ranks by the Chinese emperor and these countries became tributary states of China or entered into a dependent relationship with her. It was, in other words, an alliance of non-equals. For the countries concerned, participation in this system was an effective means of gaining an advantage over neighbours and intimidating internal forces, but its greatest influence came through the importation of Chinese culture with its writing system. Buddhism too was bestowed as a favour by the Chinese in the form of gifts of images and copies of the scriptures, and the receiving party doubtless welcomed these as symbols of culture.

The first official record of the transmission of Buddhism to neighbouring countries concerns Koguryŏ 高句麗. According to the *Samguk sagi* 三國史記 (History of the Three Kingdoms), in 372 Fu Chien of the Former Ch'in dispatched envoys with Buddhist images and scriptures as well as a monk by the name of Shun-tao 順道. Then in 384 the foreign monk Mo-lo-nan-t'i 摩羅難提 is said to have been dispatched to Paekche 百濟 from the Eastern Chin in return for tributes sent by Paekche. Koguryŏ and Paekche were in a state of continual conflict, and they sent tribute to the Northern and Southern dynasties respectively. The transmission of Buddhism to both of these countries clearly took the form of an imperial gift, and it is considered to have admitted of no refusal.

The events surrounding the transmission of Buddhism to Śilla 新羅 and Japan (known at the time as Wo-kuo / Wakoku 倭國), on the other hand, differed somewhat from the situation in Koguryŏ and Paekche. In the case of Silla, it is recorded that during the reign of Pŏphŭng 法興 a monk by the name of Mukhoja 墨胡子

introduced it from Koguryŏ, and if this was in fact so, it would have been a natural form of transmission just as when Buddhism entered China from Central Asia. But on the other hand, in 521 King Pŏphŭng of Silla followed Paekche's example in dispatching a tributary mission to Liang, and there is a record that would suggest that a monk was sent in return by Liang, in which case Buddhism would have been introduced to Silla in the same manner as it was introduced to Paekche. King Pŏphŭng emulated Emperor Wu of Liang in embracing the Buddhist faith, and he is also said to have adopted the Buddhist name of Pŏpkong 法空. As for the transmission of Buddhism to Japan, a Buddhist image and copies of the Buddhist scriptures were sent to the Japanese court by Sŏngmyŏng 聖明, king of Paekche, in either 538 or 552. These did not, however, represent a royal gift, but appear to have been a token of gratitude for Japan's alliance with Paekche, and evidence of this may be seen in the debate that took place in the Japanese court over whether or not to recognize Buddhism (see Tamura Enchō).

In the case of Japan, Buddhism would in fact have been transmitted earlier than the official date, for it is thought to have had adherents among the immigrants from the Korean peninsula. In the context of the contemporary establishment, however, the fact of official transmission would have borne considerable weight.

In this manner, the transmission of Chinese Buddhism accompanied the dissemination of Chinese culture, and Confucianism and popular forms of Taoism would also have been introduced at about the same time. By accepting these as a single set, the countries concerned were incorporated within the Chinese cultural sphere, and the Chinese translations of Buddhist texts have been preserved as sacred scriptures down to the present day without being retranslated into the indigenous languages of these countries.

It may also be noted that Chinese translations of Buddhist texts found their way westwards too. Many texts no longer extant in China proper have been discovered at Tun-huang, formerly a gateway for the importation of Buddhism to China, and during the T'ang period it became a centre of cultural exchange with the newly emerging state of T'u-fan 吐蕃, or Tibet. As a result many Chinese translations entered Tibet via Tun-huang, but unlike in the case of the countries to the east of China the Tibetans retranslated them into Tibetan. As was noted in Section I, however, the Tibetans attached greatest value to the Buddhism introduced directly from India and eventually rejected the Buddhism of Chinese provenance. But texts that had been translated into Tibetan were preserved in the Tibetan Canon, and there were in fact some treatises, such as the *Fa-hua hsüan-tsan* 法華玄贊 (Profound Eulogy of the *Lotus* [*Sūtra*]), by the T'ang scholar-monk Chi 基 of Tz'u-en-ssu 慈恩寺, and the *Chieh shen-mi ching shu* 解深密經疏 (Commentary on the *Saṃdhinirmocana-sūtra*), by Wŏnch'ŭk 圓測, that continued to be valued and utilized in later times.

Developments in the Buddhism of Korea and Japan will be dealt with in Section V below. While on the subject of the transmission of Buddhism to different parts of Asia, however, I wish to touch on two further countries, although the period in question is somewhat later in time.

The first is Parhae (Po-hai) 渤海. This country was founded by survivors of Koguryŏ after it had been overthrown by the T'ang, and during the reign of Munwang 文王, who acceded to the throne in 737, it entered into the T'ang's tribute system. Buddhism here does not appear to have gone beyond the stage of building monasteries and erecting Buddhist images, but Parhae also had contacts with Japan, and Japanese envoys to T'ang China called at her ports on their voyages to and from China.

The second country I wish to mention is Vietnam. During the Sung period, when it was known as Nan-yüeh 南越, it entered into the Sung's tribute system, and the history of its Buddhism is said to have begun in 931 with the bestowment on Wu Chen-liu 呉眞

流, controller of monks (*seng-t'ung* 僧統), of the title K'uang-chen Ta-shih 匡眞大師 (Great Master K'uang-chen). Northern Vietnam corresponded to former Chiao-chih and Chiao-chou, and, as was noted earlier, Buddhism had existed here already around the second century. But this would have represented a forefront of the Indian cultural sphere (just as Tun-huang represented the forefront of the Indian cultural sphere in Central Asia), and it cannot be said to have formed part of the sphere of Chinese-canon–based Buddhism. From the T'ang period onwards it instead became a gateway to India, serving as a point of departure for many Chinese pilgrims to India. The prevailing form of Buddhism in Vietnam is that of the Ch'an traditions.

IV. THE CONSUMMATION OF CHINESE BUDDHISM: THE SUI, T'ANG, AND SUBSEQUENT PERIODS

As if in reaction to the persecution of Buddhism under Emperor Wu of the Northern Chou 北周 (574–578), Emperor Wen 文帝 of the Sui dynasty, which was heir to the Northern Chou and eventually unified the Northern and Southern dynasties, made Buddhism the spiritual mainstay of the unified state, and he not only had constructed the monastery Ta-hsing-ch'an-ssu 大興禪寺, but also restored many other monasteries and lent his protection to the Buddhist clergy.

The persecution of Buddhism under the Northern Chou dynasty had acted as a warning to Buddhist circles of the need for reform, and the doctrines of T'ien-t'ai Chih-i 天台智顗 (538–597) are said to have been born out of Chih-i's reflections on this experience. Another figure to formulate a doctrinal system during this period was Chi-tsang 吉藏 (549–623) of the San-lun school, but his doctrines were in essence not very different from those of the existing schools. By way of contrast, the doctrines of Chih-i may be described as representing an original system of thought which he formulated by selecting on the basis of his own experiences certain teachings from among the various types of Buddhism that had been thitherto introduced to China.

In the lineage of the T'ien-t'ai school Chih-i is looked upon as the third patriarch, following on from Hui-wen 慧文 and Hui-ssu 慧思, but if one goes back still further in time, his teachings may be said to have been born out of the traditions of the practice-oriented Buddhism that followed on from Tao-an and Hui-yüan. The essence of his teachings was the practice of *chih-kuan* 止觀 or 'calm and insight', expounded in his *Mo-ho chih-kuan* 摩訶止觀 (Great Calm and Insight), and he asserted that in regard to spiritual cultivation he was following the orthodox traditions of Buddhism. In the realm of doctrine, he attributed ultimate authority to the *Saddharmapuṇḍarīka-sūtra* and the Mahāyāna *Mahāparinirvāṇa-sūtra* on the basis of his system of doctrinal classification into 'five periods and eight teachings'; to the teachings of these two scriptures he added the doctrines of the *Madhyamaka-kārikā* and, on the basis of the doctrine of the threefold truth of emptiness, conventionality, and the middle (*k'ung-chia-chung* 空假中), propounded the 'true aspect of phenomena' (*chu-fa shih-hsiang* 諸法實相), while on the basis of the doctrine that "one thought is equivalent to the three thousand (modes of existence)" (*i-nien san-ch'ien* 一念三千) he advanced the idea of 'intrinsic inclusiveness' (*hsing-chü* 性具). His school was called the T'ien-t'ai school because he made Mt. T'ien-t'ai his base, and this tradition of a form of Buddhism based in the mountains was later brought to Japan by Saichō 最澄. The theories of the T'ien-t'ai school represented the highly specialist doctrines of the higher élite among Buddhists, but equally important were the new Buddhist movements that had spread among the general populace as a result of the persecution of Buddhism under the Northern Chou, the forerunner of which was the lay Buddhism advocated by P'ing-yen-ssu 平延寺. The persecution of Buddhism was interpreted as heralding the advent of the 'last [days of the] Dharma' (*mo-fa* 末法), and as countermeasures Hsin-hsing 信行 (540–594) propounded the San-chieh-chiao 三階教 or 'Teaching of Three Stages', while Tao-ch'o 道綽 (562–645) advocated the Pure Land (Ching-t'u 浄土) teachings. On the basis of the ideas of *tathāgatagarbha* and Buddha-nature, the San-chieh sect taught that all living beings were in essence future Buddhas and were as such equally worthy of respect, and it encouraged 'inexhaustible almsgiving' as a form of social practice, but its activities subsequently met with suppression by the authorities and the movement died out. The Pure Land teachings, on the other hand, had their origins in T'an-luan 曇鸞 of the Northern Wei and, following on from Tao-ch'o, Shan-tao 善導 (613–681) brought them to their final codification. He advocated the recitation of the name of Amitābha and placing absolute trust in this Buddha. The Pure Land faith later transcended sectarian bounds to spread far and wide among both the Buddhist clergy and the laity.

It may be appropriate to touch briefly here on the thought surrounding the notion of the last days of the Dharma. This was based on the belief that following Śākyamuni's death his teachings would be gradually abandoned in three stages, referred to as the period of the true Dharma, the period of the imitative Dharma, and the period of the last days of the Dharma respectively, and it was held that because the final stage of the last days of the Dharma was approaching or had in fact already arrived, it was necessary to advocate the practice of teachings befitting these times. A precursor of this idea of dividing the duration of the Buddhist teachings into three periods in China may be seen in Hui-ssu (515–577), whose vows recorded in a document entitled the *Li shih-yüan wen* 立誓願文 (558) contain the following passage: "The true Dharma is for five hundred years, the imitative Dharma for one thousand years, and the last Dharma for ten thousand years." According to his calculations, he had been born in the eighty-second year of the period of the last Dharma. Chi-tsang put forward a different theory, according to which each of the three periods lasted for one thousand years, but it was Hui-ssu's view that prevailed at the time. The names of these three periods appear in the *Mahāyānābhisamaya-sūtra* (*Ta-ch'eng t'ung-hsing ching* 大乘同性經 [Sūtra of the Sameness of the Great Vehicle]), while the *Mahāsaṃnipāta-sūtra* (*Ta chi ching* 大集經 [Great Collection of Sūtras]) makes mention of five periods of five hundred years each, and the theory of three periods would appear to be based on these references. The situation in regard to Indian Buddhism as a whole, however, is not necessarily clear. In China there was of course the notion of a 'degenerate age' (*chiao-chi* 澆季), while in India the concept of *kaliyuga* was also an old one. In Buddhism the first such theory to appear was that according to which the true Dharma would face the danger of extinction five hundred years after Śākyamuni's death, references to which are found in a number of early Mahāyāna sutras, and the *Saddharmapuṇḍarīka-sūtra*, for example, is rooted in such a sense of crisis. The notion of 'an evil world with five defilements', mentioned in the *Sukhāvatīvyūha* and other texts, is based on a similar awareness. The five hundred years following the first five hundred years were known as the 'subsequent five hundred years', when only a semblance of the Dharma would be practised, but there was no mention of the still later advent of the last days of the Dharma. The first reference to this is found in the *Candragarbha* section of the *Mahāsaṃnipāta-sūtra*, and it has been suggested by Yamada Ryūjō (1959) that the direct cause behind its sudden appearance in this text lies in the persecution of Buddhism by Mihiragula (enthroned in 515) of the Ephthalites, a branch of the Hūna or Huns who overthrew the Gupta dynasty. It is to be surmised that Narendrayaśas (Na-lien-t'i-yeh-she 那連提耶舍), who arrived in China in 556 and translated the *Candragarbha* and other sections of the *Mahāsaṃnipāta-sūtra*, and Jñānayaśas (She-na-yeh-she 闍那耶舍), who arrived in China in 564 and translated the *Mahāyānābhisamaya-sūtra*, both brought with them in addition to scriptural texts accounts of the persecution of Buddhism in Kashmir. The persecution under the Northern Chou would then have reinforced the sense of crisis and convinced people of the advent of the last days of the Dharma.

In order to establish the date of the advent of the last days of the Dharma, it was however necessary to determine the date of Śākyamuni's death. In his *Li-tai san-pao chi* 歷代三寶紀 (Chronological History of the Three Treasures) Fei Chang-fang 費長房 of the Sui states that Śākyamuni lived between the reigns of King Chuang 莊王 and King K'uang 匡王 of the Chou 周 (687–609 B.C.), but in addition he also mentions six other views. One of these was that advanced by Fa-shang 法上 (495–580), which makes Śākyamuni a contemporary of King Chao 昭王 and King Mu 穆王, also of the Chou dynasty, and this became the generally accepted view from the T'ang onwards. This type of chronological discussion was peculiar to China, and because the relative merits of Lao-tzu and Śākyamuni had been debated on the basis of their respective dates, the date of Śākyamuni's death was taken back as far as the ninth century B.C. (Kusuyama Haruki 1985). When this was coupled with Hui-ssu's aforementioned view assigning five hundred years to the period of the true Dharma and one thousand years to the period of the imitative Dharma, it meant that the Sui and early T'ang coincided with the advent of the last days of the Dharma. It is equally possible that this new theory concerning Śākyamuni's dates was conversely born as a result of the influence of this notion of the last days of the Dharma. It may also be noted that although the exact textual authority for the view in Japan identifying the advent of the last days of the Dharma with Eishō 永承 7 (1052) during the reign of the emperor Go-Reizei 後冷泉 is not clear, it is based on a combination of the above date for Śākyamuni's death with the theory attributing one thousand years to each of the three periods of the Dharma.

The policy of the T'ang dynasty towards Buddhism was basically no different from that of the Sui dynasty. On the basis of the contention that the imperial family's surname (Li 李) was the same as that of Lao-tzu, Kao-tsu 高祖, the first emperor of the T'ang dynasty, gave precedence to Taoism, but from the next emperor T'ai-tsung 太宗 onwards the court reverted to its deference to Buddhism. Worthy of special mention during the early T'ang are the translation activities of Hsüan-tsang (602–664). He travelled to India in search of the authentic Yogācāra teachings and, returning in 645, brought back with him a large number of new scriptures and treatises, which he then proceeded to translate with the full support of the state. He prided himself in producing faithful renditions of the original texts that remedied the inadequacies of earlier translations and corrected their errors, and his 'new translations' (*hsin-i* 新譯) are distinguished from the earlier 'old translations' (*chiu-i* 舊譯). They did not, however, supplant the translations already in general circulation.

Another of Hsüan-tsang's achievements was his introduction of the entire corpus of Yogācāra thought, and this bore fruit in the establishment of the Fa-hsiang 法相 school by his disciple Chi. The theories of this school were the most subtly intricate of the various schools of thought produced by Chinese Buddhism, and in addition to Yogācāra thought they also incorporated Abhidharma doctrine. The Fa-hsiang school flourished for about forty years, but was then superceded by the newly emerging Hua-yen 華嚴 school. One reason for its decline was the fact that, being a direct import from India, it did not suit the Chinese temperament, and its theory of 'five distinct natures' (*wu-hsing ko-pieh* 五姓各別), according to which there were some sentient beings who would never attain enlightenment, also placed it in conflict with the idea of universal enlightenment through the one vehicle that had already won over the Chinese.

The traditions of the Hua-yen school may be traced back to the tradition of expounding Buddhabhadra's translation of the

Avataṃsaka-sūtra in sixty fascicles during the period of the Northern and Southern dynasties, but it became an independent school by combining the meditative practices of Tu-shun 杜順 (557–640), which were encapsulated in his *Fa-chieh kuan-men* 法界觀門 (Gate for Meditating on the Dharma-Realm), with the doctrines of Chih-yen 智儼 (602–668), and the codification of its doctrines was completed by Fa-tsang 法藏 (643–712). Referring also to the new translation of the *Avataṃsaka-sūtra* in eighty fascicles by Śikṣānanda (Shih-ch'a-nan-t'o 實叉難陀) and incorporating the Yogācāra thought of the Fa-hsiang school, Fa-tsang established the doctrine of 'dependent co-arising of the mind alone' (*wei-hsin yüan-ch'i* 唯心緣起). According to this theory, all phenomena constitute an inexhaustibly interpenetrating Dharma-realm, and this is referred to as the 'arising of intrinsic nature' (*hsing-ch'i* 性起). This world view identifying the whole with its constituent parts was welcomed by the establishment as serving the purposes of the T'ang state, finding special credence with Empress Wu 武后, and as a result the Hua-yen school flourished. The term 'Dharma-realm' (*dharmadhātu*; *fa-chieh* 法界) originally signified the basis of Śākyamuni's teachings and referred to his experience of enlightenment. The *Avataṃsaka-sūtra* describes Śākyamuni's enlightenment, and this scripture was given the highest ranking in the Hua-yen doctrinal classification as representing the 'consummate teachings' (*yüan-chiao* 圓教). The 'arising of intrinsic nature' means that all sentient beings are suffused with the light of the Buddha's wisdom, which constitutes the latent cause of their potential enlightenment. But when the T'ang emperor was tacitly likened to the Buddha, there was a danger of this doctrine degenerating into a form of establishment Buddhism that simply affirmed the *status quo*. Be that as it may, the Hua-yen school subsequently became the leading current of Chinese Buddhism and served as the mainstay of the ideology of state Buddhism. Its traditions were quickly taken over by the Buddhism of Silla on the

Korean peninsula and by the Buddhism of the Nara 奈良 period in Japan.

A further development of importance in connection with monastic organization during the T'ang was the establishment of the Discipline school of the Southern Mountain (Nan-shan Lü-tsung 南山律宗) by Tao-hsüan 道宣 (596–667). Tao-hsüan is renowned for works such as the *Hsü kao-seng chuan* 續高僧傳 (Further Biographies of Eminent Monks) and *Ta-T'ang nei-tien lu* 大唐内典錄 (Catalogue of Buddhist Scriptures of the Greater T'ang), but he also laid down the rules for the ordination of monks on the basis of the *Caturvargika-vinaya* (*Ssu-fen lü* 四分律 [Four-Part Vinaya]) and elaborated on the theoretical significance of ordination, thus laying the foundations for his Discipline school. As a result the method of ordination based on the *Caturvargika-vinaya* won general acceptance. I-ching 義淨 travelled to India in search of the complete corpus of the Vinaya and brought back the text of the *Mūlasarvāstivāda-vinaya*, which he then translated, but it was not actually used instead of the *Caturvargika-vinaya.* Chien-chen 鑑眞 (687–763), the founder of the Discipline school in Japan, also belonged to this school founded by Tao-hsüan, and he was invited to Japan expressly for the purpose of establishing the institution of ordination there.

The last wave of Buddhism to enter China from India was that of Esoteric Buddhism, which began with the arrival of Śubhākarasiṃha (Shan-wu-wei 善無畏; 637–735) during the reign of Hsüan-tsung 玄宗. Elements of the doctrines of Esoteric Buddhism existed already in Mahāyāna scriptures, and they were systematized with the compilation of the *Mahāvairocanābhisambodhi-sūtra* and then the *Sarvatathāgatatattvasaṃgraha* in the second half of the seventh century. This new wave of Buddhism (which Hsüan-tsang and I-ching had not encountered during their travels in India) had thus reached China already by the early eighth century. Śubhākarasiṃha translated the *Mahāvairocanābhisambodhi-sūtra* with the assistance of his disciple I-hsing 一行 and others, and then Vajrabodhi (Chin-kang-chih 金剛智; 669–741) arrived in China in 720 and translated part of the *Sarvatathāgatatattvasaṃgraha*. His disciple Amoghavajra (Pu-k'ung 不空; 705–774) won the trust of Hsüan-tsung and translated many scriptural and ritual texts relating to Esoteric Buddhism, thereby establishing Esoteric Buddhism in China. His disciples included Hui-kuo 惠果 (?–805), who initiated Kūkai 空海 from Japan into the teachings and rites of Esoteric Buddhism, and Kūkai then transmitted them to Japan for the first time. But Esoteric Buddhism did not particularly flourish in China, and it did not survive for long as an independent school before disappearing.

The last of the schools of Buddhism to flourish during the T'ang was the Ch'an school. The lineage of the Ch'an school goes back to Bodhidharma (P'u-t'i-ta-mo 菩提達磨), who came to China during the Northern Wei, and it is then said to have been transmitted together with the teachings of the *Laṅkāvatāra-sūtra* to Hui-k'o 慧可 and Seng-ts'an 僧粲. 'Ch'an' corresponds to Sanskrit '*dhyāna*', signifying 'meditation', and represents the basis of Buddhist practice. (Śākyamuni is said to have passed through four meditative stages, or 'four meditations', on the occasion of his enlightenment, and the six perfections include the 'perfection of meditation' [*dhyāna-pāramitā*].) In China there were many practitioners of Buddhism who were renowned for their practice of meditation, including Chih-i with his method of *chih-kuan*, and they belonged to a variety of lineages. The lineage that looked upon Bodhidharma as its founder is considered to have been established by a group consisting of Hui-neng 慧能 (638–713), a contemporary of Fa-tsang, and his disciples. Hui-neng is counted as the sixth legitimate patriarch in this lineage stemming from Bodhidharma, and the record of his sayings is known as the *Liu-tsu t'an-ching* 六祖壇經 (Platform Sūtra of the Sixth Patriarch). At about the same time as Hui-neng there also existed various other lineages, including the Northern school of Shen-hsiu 神秀, who enjoyed the patronage of Empress Wu; the Ho-tse 荷澤 school of Ho-tse Shen-hui 荷澤神會, who was Shen-hsiu's rival; the Niu-t'ou 牛頭 school founded by Niu-t'ou Fa-jung 牛頭法融; and the Ching-chung 淨衆 school, believed to be that to which Mo-ho-yen 摩訶衍, who introduced Ch'an to Tibet, belonged. It is, however, thought to have been ultimately due to the efforts of Ma-tsu Tao-i 馬祖道一 and Shih-t'ou Hsi-ch'ien 石頭希遷, both disciples of Hui-neng at one remove, that the Ch'an schools as they are known today were established and that a lineage recognizing the line of transmission from Bodhidharma as the legitimate tradition, superceding all others, was created (see Yanagida Seizan 1972). The Ch'an schools advocate a 'separate transmission outside the teaching' (*chiao-wai pieh-chuan* 教外別傳), according to which it is their avowed aim to transmit the Buddha-mind underlying the teachings of the scriptures, and through the practice of meditation the practitioner seeks to make manifest his own intrinsic nature and thereby achieve sudden enlightenment by immediately entering the same state as that of a Buddha. In the place of scriptures, special importance is attached to records of the experiences of individual practitioners and their dialogues (*yü-lu* 語錄 ['recorded sayings']), and these were subsequently used as *kung-an* 公案, or 'cases', to assist people in their practice of meditation. In their mode of expression these *kung-an* reflect daily life in contemporary Chinese society and also make free use of Lao-Chuang thought, and in this respect the Ch'an schools created the most non-Indian form of Buddhism, one that was peculiar to China. A further point worth noting in the de-Indianization of Buddhism was the formulation of rules for Ch'an monasteries by Ma-tsu's disciple Pai-chang Huai-hai 百丈懷海 (720–814). These were known as 'pure rules' (*ch'ing-kuei* 清規), and the basic emphasis is on a self-sufficient mode of life. (By way of contrast, the monastic regulations of Indian Buddhism permit of no productive activities whatsoever.)

This was also a form of resourcefulness to enable the monastic community to survive repeated persecutions without, namely, the patronage of the rulers, and the effectiveness of these measures may be seen in the fact that whereas most other schools of Buddhism were virtually decimated by the Hui-ch'ang 會昌 persecution of Buddhism in 845 towards the end of the T'ang, the Ch'an schools alone survived to subsequently flourish to an even greater degree than before. Ch'an Buddhism was thus a religion free of the restrictions of state Buddhism, but partly because of the rigorousness of its practice it tended to win supporters from among the intellectual élite rather than from the general populace.

China experienced further social upheavals at the end of the T'ang period, and following the unification of China under the Sung dynasty Confucianism regained its earlier strength after a long lapse. With the increasing external pressure from Liao 遼, Chin 金, and Mongolia in the north, there was an upsurge of nationalism, and the Ch'an schools also found themselves incorporated within the resultant establishment. As a means of survival under these circumstances, there were some who advocated the integration of the three teachings of Confucianism, Buddhism and Taoism, and Buddhism had by now lost all its earlier strength and vitality. It is, however, worth noting that the printing of the Buddhist canon began during the Sung dynasty and was continued as a state undertaking during the Liao, Chin, Yüan, Ming 明, and Ch'ing dynasties. It may also be pointed out that the doctrines of the Hua-yen school and the thought of the Ch'an schools exerted influence on Confucianism through the intellectual élite and stimulated the speculations of Neo-Confucianism and the school of Wang Yang-ming 王陽明. There is also said to be evidence of the philosophical influence of Buddhism in the reformist and modern schools of K'ang Yu-wei 康有爲 and others. As a religion of the general populace, Buddhism has survived in a form combined with Taoism and various other folk beliefs, and it is now concerned primarily with ancestor worship and fulfilling the material desires of its adherents.

V. THE DEVELOPMENT OF BUDDHISM IN KOREA AND JAPAN

In the aftermath of the Chinese expeditions against Koguryŏ during the Sui and early T'ang periods the Korean peninsula experienced major upheavals, which eventually resulted in the fall of Koguryŏ and Paekche and in the unification of the peninsula by Silla, and it was only after some military engagements with the T'ang that stability returned to the region in 680. Prior to its unification of the Korean peninsula, Silla had been making active overtures to the T'ang, and under the tribute-investiture system it sent many monks to study in China, importing both the doctrines and organization of T'ang Buddhism and establishing its own form of Silla Buddhism. The central figures in these movements were Ŭisang 義湘, who had studied Hua-yen philosophy under Chih-yen, and Wŏnhyo 元曉, who studied the Hua-yen doctrines under Ŭisang, and as a result of their activities the Hua-yen school was established on the Korean peninsula. It is especially noteworthy that through his commentaries (known as the 'commentaries from across the sea in the east' [*Hai-tung shu* 海東疏]) Wŏnhyo became well-known even in China. There were also monks such as Wŏnch'ŭk who remained in China to pursue their activities, and the speed with which Silla absorbed Chinese culture far surpassed that of Japan. The Buddhism of Silla was also strongly tinged by elements of state Buddhism, and the monks themselves actively strove to serve the state, one example of which may be seen in the 'five secular precepts' advanced by Wŏn'gwang 圓光. Wŏnhyo, who remained a layman, propagated the Buddhist teachings among the masses and exerted considerable influence with his teaching of *ho-cheng* 和諍, or the ultimate reconciliation of all doctrinal differences. The philosophical influence of Buddhism among the élite groups of nobles known as *hwalang* 花郎 was also considerable, and the Maitreya cult enjoyed great popularity. From the time of Wŏnhyo onwards there was a growing interest in the study of the Pure Land scriptures, which led to original developments in this sphere, and these developments are in turn thought to have exerted a great influence on the Pure Land teachings of Japan during the Heian 平安 period.

In 935 Silla was supplanted by Koryŏ 高麗, the successive rulers of which revered Buddhism, and under their patronage the Ch'an school and the newly introduced T'ien-t'ai school flourished. The foundations of the latter were laid by Ŭich'ŏn 義天, who introduced it from China, and it took root to the extent of superceding the Hua-yen school. The Ch'an Buddhism of Koryŏ originally derived from the Fa-yen 法眼 school, but later Chinul 智訥 appeared and developed his own form of Ch'an, which was to become the basis of the present-day Chogye 曹溪 school. An event of importance for Buddhism during this period was the printing of the Koryŏ edition of the Chinese Buddhist canon, based on an edition received from Liao. The wood blocks of this edition were, however, burnt during the Mongolian invasion and were recarved in the years 1236–51 with prayers for the repulsion of the Mongolian forces. This corresponds to the present Koryŏ edition, which was used as the base text in compiling the Taishō Tripiṭaka.

The subsequent Yi 李 dynasty aimed at a state governed by Confucian principles, and because it did not grant any special favours to Buddhism, the development of Buddhism more or less halted with the fall of Koryŏ. It is to be noted, however, that when the Japanese leader Toyotomi Hideyoshi 豐臣秀吉 invaded Korea in the late sixteenth century the monks, under the leadership of Hyujŏng 休靜 (Sŏsan Taesa 西山大師 [Great Master Sŏsan]), organized an army of volunteers and participated in the resistance movement against the Japanese invasion, thus demonstrating that the traditions of Buddhism serving the needs of the state continued to live on. Following the persecution of Buddhism by the king Yŏnsan'gun 燕山君 in 1475, Buddhism became entirely a matter of personal faith and lost all social influence.

The development of Buddhism in Japan after its original transmission was initially due to the policies and personal faith of Shōtoku Taishi 聖德太子 (Crown Prince Shōtoku). In his role as representative of the state, it was probably his intention to establish a state system not only modelled on Chinese institutions such as her bureaucracy but also rooted in a form of international culture as represented by Buddhism. To this end he himself embraced Buddhism of his own accord, erected temples, invited eminent monks from the Korean peninsula, sent Japanese monks to Sui China for the purpose of studying Buddhism, and generally endeavoured to edify his fellow countrymen to the extent of even giving lectures himself on Buddhist scriptures in the presence of the empress Suiko 推古. In this respect he is thought to have emulated Emperor Wu of the Liang dynasty. His lectures have been preserved in the form of the "Commentaries on the Three Sūtras" (*sangyō gisho* 三經義疏), which commentate the *Saddharmapuṇḍarīka-sūtra*, *Śrīmālādevīsiṃhanāda-sūtra* and *Vimalakīrtinirdeśa-sūtra*. Even though he may have received instruction from foreign monks and may have referred to earlier Chinese commentaries on which to base his interpretation, there is no denying the fact that these commentaries express the views of Prince Shōtoku. After his death he came to be revered as the manifestation of a bodhisattva or as a reincarnation of Hui-ssu, and this gave birth to a cult centred on him.

Contacts between Japan and Silla ceased with the defeat of the Japanese and Paekche forces in the battle of Hakusukinoe 白村江 in 663, but there was a sudden revival of contacts from the reign of the emperor Tenmu 天武 onwards, and new Chinese schools of Buddhist thought were introduced to Japan in rapid succession via Silla. The schools of Buddhism that were introduced prior to the Nara period either by monks who went to study on the continent or by foreign monks who came to Japan were as follows. (1) Sanron 三論 sect (corresponding to the Chinese San-lun school), which was introduced at the time of Prince Shōtoku by Hyegwan 慧觀 (Jp. Ekan) from Koguryŏ; (2) Jōjitsu 成實 sect (corresponding to the Chinese Ch'eng-shih school), which was introduced by Tojang 道藏 (Jp. Dōzō), who arrived in Japan from Paekche in 721; (3) Hossō 法相 sect (corresponding to the Chinese Fa-hsiang school), which was brought back to Japan in 653 by Dōshō 道昭, who had studied under Hsüan-tsang; and (4) Kuṣha 俱舍 sect (corresponding to the Chinese Chü-she school), affiliated to the Hossō sect and devoted to the study of the *Abhidharmakośa-bhāṣya*. The Hossō sect was subsequently transmitted a further four times in the years up until the end of the Nara period. (5) During the Nara period itself Shinjō 審祥, having returned from Silla, was invited by Rōben 良辯 to lecture for the first time on the *Avataṃsaka-sūtra* at Tōdaiji 東大寺 temple, and on the basis of his teachings Rōben founded the Kegon 華嚴 sect (corresponding to the Chinese Hua-yen school). (6) Lastly, after five abortive attempts, Chien-chen finally succeeded in crossing over to Japan and transmitting the Discipline school. The above six sects are known as the "six sects of the southern capital (*viz.* Nara)" (*nanto rokushū* 南都六宗), and their doctrines generally reflect the state of Chinese Buddhism between the period of the Northern and Southern dynasties and the early T'ang. Chien-chen's journey to Japan stemmed from an invitation by Japanese monks, and as a result the admission of monks to the monastic order in accordance with the prescribed ordination ceremony became possible for the first time in Japan.

The Buddhism of the Nara period was a wholesale importation of the state Buddhism of the T'ang. The legal codifications (*ritsuryō* 律令) of the period included a section governing the conduct of the Buddhist clergy, based on a registry system (*sōgō* 僧綱), and although the number of monks and nuns permitted to be annually ordained was restricted, they were ensured of a place to pursue their studies and their livelihood was guaranteed by the state. The system of provincial temples (*kokubunji* 國分寺), with their headquarters at Tōdaiji, was modelled on Ta-hsing-shan-ssu of the Sui and Ta-yün-ssu 大雲寺 and K'ai-yüan-ssu 開元寺 of the T'ang. In addition, the Great Buddha enshrined at Tōdaiji represents Vairocana, the expositor of the *Avataṃsaka-sūtra*, and not only does it (needless to say) symbolize the world view of the *Avataṃsaka-sūtra*, but it also hints at a unified state structure culminating in the emperor. But Japanese Buddhism, with its partial origins in the private faith of immigrants, was nevertheless not completely divorced from the masses. There were monks such as Gyōki 行基 who proselytized among the general populace by performing public works, but the government did not welcome such moves and suppressed them. Yet when it came to erecting the Great Buddha at Tōdaiji, the authorities availed themselves of Gyōki's influence by placing him in charge of the collection of donations for this undertaking.

In order to put an end to the collusion of politics and Buddhism in the capital Nara and to remedy the resultant abuses, the emperor Kanmu 桓武 moved the capital first to Nagaoka 長岡 and then to Kyōto 京都, and it was Saichō who in response to the emperor's demands founded a new school of Buddhism based in the mountains to serve as a stronghold for protecting the state and training true servants of the nation. In addition to visiting China and transmitting the T'ien-t'ai (Jp. Tendai) school to Japan, Saichō also succeeded in obtaining permission to ordain a number of monks annually at his headquarters on Mt. Hiei 比叡山, and in place of the ordination ceremony performed by the Nara sects he established rules of ordination based on the 'perfect and sudden precepts' (*endonkai* 圓頓戒), in turn based on the bodhisattva precepts of the Mahāyāna. This was an institution recognized in China only in the case of lay people, and its adaptation to the ordination of monks is peculiar to Japan. With the aim of transforming Mt. Hiei into a centre for the comprehensive study of Buddhism, he also encouraged the study of Ch'an (Jp. Zen), the Pure Land teachings, and Esoteric Buddhism in addition to Tendai doctrine. In the case of Esoteric Buddhism, he initially sought to master it by receiving an initiation from Kūkai, who had visited China at the same time as Saichō himself, but he later sent his own disciple Ennin 圓仁 to study it in China and retransmit it in proper form to Japan. This branch of Esoteric Buddhism is called 'Taimitsu' 台密, meaning the Esoteric Buddhism of the Tendai sect.

Kūkai had been initiated into Esoteric Buddhism by Hui-kuo, and after his return to Japan he founded the Shingon 眞言 sect, establishing a monastery on Mt. Kōya 高野山. At the same time he also set up a base at Tōji 東寺 temple in Kyōto, and by approaching the imperial court and winning the trust of the emperor Saga 嵯峨, he gradually established his influence. In contrast to the Taimitsu of the Tendai sect, the Shingon sect is referred to as 'Tōmitsu' 東密, or the Esoteric Buddhism of Tōji. Unlike Saichō, Kūkai maintained cordial relations with the Nara sects and observed the precepts prescribed by the traditional form of ordination, and this tradition came to be preserved as the Shingon Discipline sect (Shingon Risshū 眞言律宗). In addition, as in the case of Gyōki, he also endeavoured to perform works for the public good, and his influence lives on today in the form of a cult centred on him, to be seen for example in the Shikoku 四國 pilgrimage. During the Heian peiod the Tendai and Shingon sects created a structure for answering the requirements of the court and the nobility, and they became a form of quasi-state Buddhism. The court and nobility required a form of Buddhism that would answer their prayers for attracting good fortune and averting ill fortune, and the Tendai and Shingon sects sought to provide this primarily by means of the rites of Esoteric Buddhism. But at the same time the Pure Land teachings gradually spread among the clergy and the nobility, and they developed as a private faith of those aspiring to rebirth in the Pure Land. In the subsequent Kamakura 鎌倉 period this gave birth to Pure Land sects such as the Jōdo 浄土 sect and Jōdo Shin sect (Jōdo Shinshū 浄土眞宗), and as a result Buddhism finally took root in Japan as a religion of personal salvation. It also evolved into a purely Japanese form of Buddhism with doctrinal developments that were original to Japan.

Underlying factors in the growing popularity of the Pure Land teachings were the collapse of the *ritsuryō* system and the political instability of the provinces. These combined with the fear of the advent of the last days of the Dharma and gave rise to hopes for rebirth in the Pure Land. Members of the newly emerging warrior class, uneasy about their precarious way of life, also sought solace in the Pure Land faith. But once they founded the Kamakura *bakufu* 幕府 after the conclusion of the war between the Taira 平 and Minamoto 源 families and established their rule over the country, they sought a new culture and guiding principle in the Zen sects that happened to be entering Japan from the Sung and gave them their patronage and encouragement. This parallelled the situation in China, where Ch'an Buddhism had been adopted by the intellectual élite. In this manner the social precedence of the new Zen sects was established during the Kamakura and Muromachi 室町 periods. It is true that the succinct teachings and methods of practice of the Zen sects were suited to the spiritual discipline of the warriors, but the Zen sects were regarded above all as bearers of a new culture. Examples of Zen monks who became advisors to members of the warrior class, ranging in rank from the *shōgun* 將軍 down to local proprietary lords (*ryōshu* 領主), are too numerous to mention here. This state of affairs continued until the early years of the Edo 江戸 *bakufu* and the activities of Sūden 崇傳. Confucian studies were also preserved by Zen monks under the name of Gozan 五山 literature. It was only after one of these monks, Fujiwara Seika 藤原惺窩, renounced the monkhood that Confucian studies became an independent field of study, leading to the consolidation of Confucianism as the ruling ideology of the shogunate. Insofar that this occurred not as a natural consequence of academic theory but through the demands of politics, one may see here an extension of the system of state Buddhism. On the pretext of suppressing Christianity, the Edo *bakufu* instituted the *danka* 檀家, or 'parishioner', system and created a new method for controlling Buddhism. Although there had been large-scale uprisings by, for example, adherents of the Pure Land faith during the Sengoku 戰國 period (known as 'Ikkō *ikki*' 一向一揆, which were uprisings by protest leagues composed of those with exclusive faith in Amida 阿彌陀 or Amitāyus), Japanese Buddhism does not appear to have been able to transcend the constraints imposed by the ruling authorities.

The typically Japanese sects of Buddhism originating in the Kamakura period were founded by monks such as Hōnen 法然, Shinran 親鸞, Dōgen 道元, and Nichiren 日蓮, who had all studied on Mt. Hiei but failed to find satisfaction in the form of Buddhism prevailing there. Their common target of criticism was the doctrine of 'innate enlightenment' (*hongaku* 本覺). This doctrine was based on the *Shih Mo-ho-yen lun* 釋摩訶衍論, a commentary on the *Mahāyānaśraddhotpāda-śāstra* that had been brought to Japan by Kūkai, and developed within the Esoteric branch of the Tendai sect (Taimitsu), and it represents an amalgamation of *tathāgatagarbha* thought and the doctrine of 'enlightenment with this very body' (*sokushin jōbutsu* 即身成佛) propounded by Kūkai. It may be considered to have suited the ethos of Mt. Hiei, closely linked as it was to secular power, and brought about the indolence and decadence of the monks living there. Through the cultivation of unsullied faith and unsullied practice, the new currents of Buddhism sought to restore Buddhism to its pristine form. Representative examples of their views may be seen in Shinran's identification of Buddha-nature with 'the mind of great faith' and

Dōgen's advocacy of 'practice grounded in realization' and the 'identity of practice and realization'.

A further issue in regard to Japanese Buddhism is the question of the amalgamation of Buddhism with Shintō 神道 and existing religious customs in the course of its domestication. There is no denying the fact that this, together with ancestor worship and concepts of the soul found also in China and Korea, has caused Japanese Buddhism to develop in a manner differing considerably from Indian Buddhism. Even though traditional interpretations of Buddhism may be preserved within the doctrines of the various sects, it is no easy matter to undermine this syncretic tradition in situations where Buddhism comes in direct contact with society, such as in funeral rites. The Shin sect, in particular, would be expected to have preserved a Buddhist faith in its purest form and rejected all elements of folk beliefs, and yet in its organization it is the most purely Japanese sect, being characterized by laicism and hereditary succession.

Ever since its introduction into Japan, Buddhism had long enjoyed a dominant position in Japanese society as a symbol of foreign culture, but there had also existed an undercurrent of anti-Buddhist thought in the traditions of Shintō, and with the emergence of National Learning (*kokugaku* 國學) in the wake of the revival of Confucian studies from the mid-Edo period onwards this gradually surfaced, eventually leading to the persecution of Buddhism in the early years of the Meiji 明治 era. Although the persecution soon ended, Buddhism was completely deprived of its former position of dominance following the subsequent ascendancy of modern Western culture. But with advances in Buddhist scholarship and educative efforts through the written word the merits of Buddhism are being reevaluated by intellectuals, and there has been a revival in aspirations towards the heights of its thought. An important issue for Japanese Buddhism in the future will be the question of how to reconcile these aspirations with the

Buddhism of traditional rites and rituals.

REFERENCE WORKS

There are not many studies dealing with the Buddhism of China, Korea, and Japan from the perspective of East Asian Buddhism. Even in the field of historical studies the method of examining the state of affairs in East Asia from the sixth to eighth centuries in an integrated fashion does not have a very long history. I recall having been struck about twenty years ago by the originality of the term 'tribute-investiture system' (*sakuhō taisei* 冊封体制) proposed by Nishijima Sadao 西嶋定生 (Nishijima Sadao, "Roku-hasseiki no Higashi Ajia" 六—八世紀の東アジア [East Asia during the sixth to eighth centuries], in *Iwanami kōza: Nihon rekishi 2, Kodai 2* 岩波講座　日本歴史 2　古代 2 [Iwanami lecture series: The history of Japan 2—The ancient period 2], Iwanami Shoten 岩波書店, 1962). Further development of this perspective led to the establishment of an "East Asian world" within the field of historical studies (Nishijima Sadao, "Sōsetsu" 総説 [General remarks], in *Iwanami kōza: Sekai rekishi 4* [*Kodai 4, Higashi Ajia sekai no keisei I*] 岩波講座　世界歴史 4 [古代 4, 東アジア世界の形成 I] [Iwanami lecture series: World history 4 (The ancient period 4: The evolution of the East Asian world)], Iwanami Shoten, 1970). As the mainstays of this East Asian world, Nishijima gives (1) culture based on Chinese writing, (2) Confucianism, (3) the *ritsuryō* (Ch. *lü-ling*) system, and (4) Buddhism (ibid.). A survey of the history of Buddhism along these lines may be found in:

Kamata Shigeo 鎌田茂雄, "Chūgoku Bukkyō no tenkai to Higashi Ajia Bukkyō ken no seiritsu" 中国仏教の展開と東アジア仏教圏の成立 [The development of Chinese Buddhism and the establishment of the sphere of East Asian Buddhism], in *Iwanami kōza: Sekai rekishi 6* (*Kodai* 6), Iwanami Shoten, 1971.

A researcher who has been long engaged in the study of the

history of the transmission of Buddhism to Japan from the same perspective is Tamura Enchō 田村円澄, and the results of his research have been brought together in:

Tamura Enchō, *Nihon Bukkyō shi 1: Asuka jidai* 日本仏教史 1 飛鳥時代 [The history of Japanese Buddhism 1: The Asuka period], Hōzōkan 法蔵館, 1982.

———, *Nihon Bukkyō shi 4: Kudara, Shiragi* 日本仏教史 4 百済・新羅 [The history of Japanese Buddhism 4: Paekche and Silla], Hōzōkan, 1983.

There are various histories of Chinese Buddhism, including:

Tsukamoto Zenryū 塚本善隆, *Chūgoku tsūshi* 中国通史 [A general history of China], vol. 1, Shunjūsha 春秋社, 1979.

More recently there have appeared:

Kamata Shigeo, *Chūgoku Bukkyō shi* 中国仏教史 [The history of Chinese Buddhism], vol. 1 (Shodenki no Bukkyō 初伝期の仏教 [Buddhism during the initial period of transmission]), Tōkyō Daigaku Shuppankai 東京大学出版会, 1982.

———, *Chūgoku Bukkyō shi*, vol. 2 (Juyōki no Bukkyō 受容期の仏教 [Buddhism during the period of acceptance]), Tōkyō Daigaku Shuppankai, 1983.

———, *Chūgoku Bukkyō shi*, vol. 3 (Nanbokuchō no Bukkyō 南北朝の仏教 [Buddhism during the Northern and Southern dynasties], I), Tōkyō Daigaku Shuppankai, 1984.

———, *Chūgoku Bukkyō shi*, vol. 4 (Nanbokuchō no Bukkyō, II), Tōkyō Daigaku Shuppankai, 1990.

As an introductory work, the following book may be recommended:

Kamata Shigeo, *Chūgoku Bukkyō shi*, Iwanami Shoten, 1978.

In regard to Korean Buddhism, the first general history to have appeared is:

Kamata Shigeo, *Chōsen Bukkyō shi* 朝鮮仏教史 [The history of Korean Buddhism], Tōkyō Daigaku Shuppankai, 1987.

On the subject of Chinese or East Asian Buddhism considered from the standpoint of the history of Buddhism as a whole, reference may be made to:

Takasaki Jikidō 高崎直道, "Sōsetsu: Daijō Bukkyō no 'shūhen'" 総説　大乗仏教の〈周辺〉 [General remarks: The "periphery" of Mahāyāna Buddhism], in *Kōza Daijō Bukkyō 10—Daijō Bukkyō to sono shūhen* 講座大乗仏教 10—大乗仏教とその周辺 [Lecture series on Mahāyāna Buddhism 10: Mahā-yāna Buddhism and its periphery], Shunjūsha, 1985.

Okabe Kazuo 岡部和雄, "Chūgoku shakai to Daijō Bukkyō" 中国社会と大乗仏教 [Chinese society and Mahāyāna Buddhism], ibid.

Fukui Fumimasa 福井文雅, "Chūgoku shisō to Daijō Bukkyō" 中国思想と大乗仏教 [Chinese thought and Mahāyāna Buddhism], ibid.

The first study to raise the question of interaction between Chinese thought and Buddhism, and still required reading on this subject, was :

Tsuda Sōkichi 津田左右吉, *Shina Bukkyō no kenkyū* シナ仏教の研究 [Studies in Chinese Buddhism], Iwanami Shoten, 1957.

Recently Fukunaga Mitsuji 福永光司 has been undertaking various studies focusing especially on Taoist thought, in regard to which reference may be made to:

Iwanami kōza: Tōyō shisō 岩波講座　東洋思想 [Iwanami lecture series: Oriental thought], vols. 13, 14 (*Chūgoku shūkyō shisō* 中国宗教思想 [Chinese religious thought], 1, 2), Iwanami Shoten, 1990.

Under the direction of Fukunaga many younger researchers are pursuing the study of the translation of the Buddhist scriptures into Chinese and other aspects characteristic of Buddhist thought in China; see for example:

Yoshikawa Tadao 吉川忠夫, "Uchi to soto" 内と外 [The inner and the outer], in *Iwanami kōza: Tōyō shisō*, vol. 13.

A point worth noting is the fact that in China the Buddhist scriptures are referred to as the 'inner scriptures' (*nei-tien* 内典)

and that generally speaking anything associated with Buddhism is regarded as 'inner' while Confucianism is called the 'outer teachings' (*wai-chiao* 外教). This usage of 'inner' and 'outer', which would appear to run counter to our normal conception of Buddhism as having been introduced to China from without and Confucianism as being indigenous to China, seems to be based on a contrast between that which is concerned with the individual's internal and spiritual well-being and that which is associated with the external social order. But even so it is worth taking note of the fact that Buddhism, of external provenance, should have won the trust of the Chinese as a religion concerning itself with the soul of the individual.

This trust placed in Buddhism is also reflected in the fact that enlightenment was referred to as the 'way' (*tao* 道) and Buddhism as the 'teaching of the way' (*tao-chiao* 道教) and that its teachings were regarded as 'holy' (*sheng* 聖; as in *pa-sheng-tao* 八聖道 ['eightfold holy path'] and *sheng-chiao* 聖教 ['holy teachings']) and 'true' (*chen* 眞; as in *chen-ju* 眞如 ['true suchness': *tathatā*] and *chih-chen* 至眞 ['one who has attained the truth': *arhat*]). Although one must be ever mindful of the fact that terms such as these are also used in Taoism and that they therefore facilitated the exertion of Taoist influence on Buddhist thought and the application of Taoist interpretations in Buddhism, the fact that the Chinese people placed great hopes in Buddhism should also not be overlooked.

As for the formation of the Ch'an/Zen tradition, which has continued down to the present day, see:

Yanagida Seizan 柳田聖山, *Shoki Zenshū shisho no kenkyū* 初期禅宗史書の研究 [Studies in historical records of the early Ch'an sect], Hōzōkan, 1972.

In regard to research on the history of Chinese Buddhism by Western scholars, I shall restrict myself to mentioning only the following works:

P. Demiéville, *Choix d'études bouddhiques*, Leiden, 1973.

E. Zürcher, *The Buddhist Conquest of China*, Leiden, 1959 (rev. ed. 1972).

Kenneth Ch'en, *Buddhism in China: A Historical Survey*, Princeton, 1964.

On the subject of the notion of the last days of the Dharma and debates surrounding the date of Śākyamuni's death, reference may be made to:

Yabuki Keiki 矢吹慶輝, *Sangaikyō no kenkyū* 三階教の研究 [Studies in the Teaching of the Three Stages], Iwanami Shoten, 1927 (repr. 1973).

Kusuyama Haruki 楠山春樹, "Chūgoku Bukkyō ni okeru Shaka shōmetsu no nendai" 中国仏教における釈迦生滅の年代 [The dates of Śākyamuni's birth and death in Chinese Buddhism], in *Hirakawa Akira hakushi koki kinen ronshū: Bukkyō no shomondai* 平川彰博士古稀記念論集　仏教の諸問題 [Collected papers in honour of the 70th birthday of Dr. Hirakawa Akira: Various issues in Buddhism], Shunjūsha, 1985.

Yamada Ryūjō 山田龍城, *Daijō Bukkyō seiritsuron josetsu* 大乗仏教成立論序説 [An introduction to the study of the establishment of Mahāyāna Buddhism], Heirakuji Shoten 平楽寺書店, 1959 (esp. part 2, chapter 8: "Kōki kyōten no haikei" 後期経典の背景 [The background to the later scriptures]).

The cultural significance of the acceptance of Buddhism in Japan has been dealt with in various studies by Nakamura Hajime 中村元, but here I wish to mention only the "Introduction" of the following work:

Nakamura Hajime (ed.), *Nihon no meicho 2: Shōtoku Taishi* 日本の名著 2　聖徳太子 [Japanese classics 2: Shōtoku Taishi], Chūō Kōronsha 中央公論社, 1983.

On specific subjects concerning the Buddhism of China, Japan and other parts of East Asia, reference may be made to:

Iwanami kōẓa: Tōyō shisō, vol. 12 (*Higashi Ajia no Bukkyō* 東アジアの仏教 [East Asian Buddhism]), Iwanami Shoten, 1988.

In addition, I wish to mention my recent article on Shōtoku Taishi which appeared as "an explanatory note on authors and their works" in

Takasaki Jikidō (ed.), *Daijō butten (Chūgoku Nihon hen) 16: Shōtoku Taishi, Ganjin* 大乗仏典（中国日本篇） 16—聖徳太子・鑑真 [Mahāyāna Buddhist Texts (China and Japan) 16: Shōtoku Taishi and Chien-chen], Chūō Kōronsha, 1990.

"Japanization" of Buddhism*

1. Japanese Initiation to Buddhism

Buddhism was introduced to Japan in the middle of the 6th century A.D. via Korea. It was a form of Buddhism that was based upon the scriptures translated into Chinese, which spread throughout East Asia together with Chinese culture. Compared with the original Buddhism in India, it may be termed 'sinicized Buddhism' in the sense that it had gone through a great deal of transformation under the influence of the Chinese cultural tradition. The Japanese accepted this form of Buddhism as a part of Chinese culture and as a symbol of civilization and the internationalization of the country.

According to the official record in the *Nihongi* or *Nihon shoki*, the oldest chronicle of Japan compiled in 720 A.D., Seimei Ō, the king of Kudara (Paekche), presented Kinmei Tennō with a statue of the Buddha together with rolls of scriptures in 552 A.D. (Another record transmitted in Hōryūji Temple gives the date as 538 A.D.) In actuality, however, Buddhism was brought earlier, by people of Korean origin who settled in Japan. But the significance of the official transmission of Buddhism and its final acceptance by the Yamato court lies in the fact that it shows the strong desire of the state to become part of the international order of East Asia at that time. Paekche itself received Buddhism from the emperor of the last Chin dynasty towards the end of the 4th century. Japan in the 4th to 5th century was far behind compared with the Korean states in its level of civilization. However, Japan was strong in military power, with which it had a certain influence in the

* Originally published in Ishizuka Harumichi, ed., *Japanization: From Ancient to Modern Times* (Tokyo: Kyûko Shoin, 1999), pp. 15–25.

Korean peninsula. Efforts to civilize the country were actively made, especially in the early 7th century by a government led by the regent Prince Shōtoku, who sent a delegate directly to the emperor of the Sui dynasty and tried to introduce the Chinese bureaucracy and institutions to Japan together with Confucianism and Buddhism as their ideological background. The ideas of Prince Shōtoku finally ripened a century later in the policies of Tenmu Tennō and his consort and successor Jitō Tennō. The birth of '*Nihon koku*' (change of the state name from *Wa* 倭 to *Nihon* 日本 = *Nippon*, *Jih-pen* = Japan) was officially announced to China in 701.

Buddhism was thus accepted in Japan first by the court and high officials, who were the intellectuals of those days, and its spread to the common people was not accomplished easily or without problems. Even for the intellectuals, except for a few like Prince Shōtoku, Buddhist doctrine was far beyond their understanding. As is shown in a story about a conflict between clans concerning the acceptance of Buddhism, Buddhism was regarded as a kind of *kami* cult of foreign (western) lands. The question was whether or not to worship the Buddha (a foreign deity) besides the *kami* (the indigenous deities of Japan). The main issue being whether its worship would bring merit or demerit to the country, there was strong expectation of magical power from such a new cult. (The case was more or less similar in China at the beginning of the spread of Buddhism. The decisive difference is that in Japan from the beginning Buddhism was introduced from above through the initiative of the state.) Thus by donations of the court and high officials who longed for the prosperity of the country and their families, or for individual merits, Buddha statues were built and enshrined in the magnificent *kapala*-roofed new-style temples, which attracted a lot of people. The importation of scriptures and commentarial texts and invitations to priests and monks from Korea and China followed thereafter. As for the initiation and training of monks and nuns, the government issued severe regulations by law. By the end of the 8th century (during the Nara period), Buddhism had really established itself in Japan, though still under the control of the government, with its order and system of discipline for monks and nuns. They also developed the study of the doctrines of the various Buddhist schools then flourishing in China. (They are called the six schools of Nanto, the Southern Capital, i.e., Nara.) As the best monument to the prosperity of Buddhism in those days, we have the statue of the Daibutsu (Great Buddha) at the Tōdaiji temple. In all these processes mostly the model of China was followed with quite little transformation. In other words, Buddhism remained a mere importation.

2. Buddhist Acculturation to the Japanese Religion

To enter more deeply into the heart of the Japanese people, however, Buddhism needed to have some connection with the *kami* cult and other forms of the primitive customs of the Japanese people. In the process of this spread of Buddhism, Buddhism proved its pliability in assimilating itself with the Japanese *kami* cult, resulting in a unique strain of syncretism. Buddhism received a great deal of transformation in accordance with the needs of the Japanese people, social, spiritual, as well as intellectual. This phenomenon is here called the 'Japanization' of Buddhism. There are many other phenomena that show the characteristics of Buddhism that are peculiar to Japan, such as maintaining a stress on simple faith and practice rather than on logical implications. Furthermore, there is a strong inclination to laicism, which gives minor attention to moral discipline, etc. All these phenomena seem to be the result of contact with the Japanese religion. In this sense, the author wishes to focus his account on the phenomenon of syncretism.

The syncretism of Buddhism with the *kami* cult is usually called *shinbutsu shūgō* 神佛習合, 'overlapping' or 'piling up' of the *kami* (i.e., Shinto) and the Buddha (i.e., Buddhism), in other words, Shinto-Buddhist amalgamation or *shinbutsu konkō* 神佛混淆, a mixture of Shinto with Buddhism. These terms have as their antonym *shinbutsu bunri* 神佛分離, separation of Shinto from Buddhism, or removing of the Buddhist elements from Shinto shrines. This separation was conducted politically in 1872 by the government of the Meiji restoration in the so-called *shinbutsu hanzen* order (*hanzen* = distinction). Before then, i.e., towards the end of the Edo period, *shinbutsu shūgō* was commonly observed all over Japan. Even today this custom remains in the daily life of the Japanese people. In this sense, syncretism of Buddhism with the Shinto or *kami* cult is the most conspicuous characteristic of the Japanese religion.

As a religious phenomenon, syncretism is not peculiar to Japan. When cultures with differing traditions encounter each other, there occur mutual influences between them that result in a certain kind of assimilation. In the case of one of them being much more developed than the other, the latter is often assimilated to the former and loses its own traditions. A typical example is that of the Germanic and other European peoples that were confronted with Christianity. They were obliged to convert to Christianity and have lost their former faith and cults. Only a few elements remained that were adopted by Christianity. The case is quite different with Buddhism. Wherever it spread, it never destroyed the native cult but tried to accept the native cult by giving a reasonable meaning to it. In its homeland, Buddhism developed surrounded by the Vedic or Hindu cult of deities, and received recognition by Indian society as a supra-worldly order of mendicants that did not interfere with the worldly order established by Hinduism. Lay Buddhists remain at the same time Hindus in their daily life. Doctrinally Buddhism accepted Hindu deities (e.g., Indra and Brahmā at the top) as beings that believe in the Buddha's teaching and that protect Buddhism. Mahayana Buddhism, which adopted laicism within its doctrine, enlarged its scope further into the Hindu pantheon and created new figures of deities. Also in this new form of Buddhism many Buddhas and Bodhisattvas were created and became objects of worship. Behind them the existence of the absolute Dharma body, or the Buddha as the truth, is supposed, the Buddhas being apparitional bodies or incarnations of it. Finally, Esoteric Buddhism created a pantheon of Buddhas, Bodhisattvas, and deities and demons of its own. In all cases, however, Buddhas and Bodhisattvas held priority over Hindu deities. As a result of this active assimilation with Hinduism, however, Buddhism lost its purity as a religion independent from Hinduism, and when the order of mendicants was destroyed by the invasion of the Muslims, Buddhism was absorbed into the Hindu world.

With this tolerant character towards different beliefs, Buddhism spread beyond the borders of India or the Hindu world and could penetrate into different countries and peoples of various regions, without destroying their native cults and deities. In all cases, however, Buddhism retained its own field aloof from the secular world by the efforts of the members of the order, and by doing so it could maintain its identity in foreign lands. The syncretism of Buddhism with the Japanese *kami* cult is usually thought to have come about through identification of Japanese deities with Buddhas, Bodhisattvas and Indian deities as their incarnations. This theory is called *honji suijaku setsu*. The terms used in this phrase are originally Chinese, used by Taoism. *Honji* 本地 means 'an original basis or state', and *suijaku* 垂迹 means 'to make the appearance of its trace', i.e., apparitional forms. The first use of these terms in a Buddhist text is found in Seng-chao's commentary on the *Vimalakīrtinirdeśa* translated by Kumārajīva. So it may be said that this is a Chinese way of interpreting the Indian theory of incarnation. A typical example of this kind of identification is the following: Amaterasu Ōmikami, the sun goddess and the highest deity in the Japanese pantheon as the ancestor of the lineage of the Japanese emperors, is said to be the incarnation of Mahāvairocana, or Dainichi (the great illuminator or the sun), who is the highest Dharma body and the Preceptor of the Esoteric scriptures as well. Scattered examples of identification appear in the 9th century at the earliest, but the systematic application of this theory belongs rather to the later period of the 11th to the 14th century.

Syncretism started from the side of Shinto. As has been said before, the policy of the Japanese government under Tenmu and his successors was to establish a regal state united under the power of the emperor. For this purpose, the government tried to control local political powers together with the local *kami* cult conducted by the respective local powers. In order to achieve this, the government reorganized local deities in hierarchical order, putting the ancestor god of the emperor at the top. In this process, those local deities that were not ranked high gradually lost their magical power and influence in the area, but were often rescued by their contact with Buddhism. It is to be noted that many local deities that were originally representing natural phenomena in animistic beliefs, such as spirits dwelling on the mountains and in the sea, or the supra-human powers of rain, storm and thunder, were gradually personified at that time. They were regarded as ancestors of local political powers and their subordinates in the same way that had happened in the central government in the case of the emperor and his subjects. New myths and related narratives were composed for them: these newly personified local deities wished to become disciples of the Buddha so that they could receive stronger power and good fortune for themselves. As a famous example we have the record of Tado Jingū (a *kami* shrine in Tado, Ise county, in present-day Mie Prefecture) in the 8th century. The deity worshipped there was simply called *Tado no ōkami* (*ōkami* = great god). He expressed through the words of a shaman his plight of growing weak due to his sinful deeds committed in previous lives and his wish to become a Bodhisattva with the help of Buddhist monks. With permission of the government people built a temple for him to practise Buddhist training for enlightenment. This kind of temple was called a *jingūji*, literally 'a (Buddhist) temple of a *kami* shrine'. The name itself represents the syncretism that was involved. The establishment of *jingūji* gradually increased in number and even Ise Jingū, where Amaterasu Ōmikami is enshrined, had its own *jingūji* towards the end of the 8th century. The next stage, in the following period, was the affiliation of these local *jingūji* to Buddhist headquarters such as Hiei-zan of the Tendai sect or Tōji of the Shingon sect. Buddhism in the central capital area thus started to exert its influences in local Japan through connection with local deities and local powers by means of the *jingūji*. Another example of a Bodhisattva deity is Hachiman or Bahan Shin 神 at Usa in Kyushu. His original form is uncertain, but in the middle of the 8th century he suddenly appeared in the central area of Japan and claimed to be the incarnation of Ōjin Tennō, who was believed to be the direct ancestor of the imperial family. Declaring himself to be the protector of Buddhism, he demanded from the government the title of a Bodhisattva. He was then worshipped and enshrined at Tamukeyama, in the compound of Tōdaiji. This Bodhisattva diety, called Hachiman Daibosatsu, gradually increased its power all over Japan and was popularized as a god of warriors, having the Minamoto family as their chief, because they were proud of their lineage as descendants from Ōjin Tennō via Seiwa Tennō.

3. The *Goryō* Cult and the Japanese Concept of Soul

The next stage begins with the shift of the capital from Nara to Kyoto (at first briefly at Nagaoka and then to Heiankyō) by Kanmu Tennō towards the end of the 8th century, when two Buddhist schools were newly founded by Saichō and Kūkai, namely, the Tendai sect and the Shingon sect. In this second stage of syncretism,

Buddhist influence over Shinto reached its peak, along with the development of these new sects, especially through the efforts of Kūkai and his followers. In other words, Buddhism found its way into Japanese society by its mystical powers that were especially connected with the Esoteric doctrine of the Shingon sect. The Tendai sect also adopted the Esoteric doctrine as an important part of its cult. Armed with this Esotericism, Buddhism enjoyed prosperity all over the country and received the confidence of those of high society down to the common people in local areas. But this intimate connection with the local *kami* cult and other traditional customs inevitably also caused changes to Buddhism concerning its doctrines.

A conspicuous phenomenon, which started at the beginning of this second stage of syncretism, that can be observed is the *goryō* worship. *Goryō* here means the soul of a deceased person who unjustly received the death sentence, or died after receiving some other heavy sentence from the government, and who was as a result believed to repay the emperor and the government officers who were responsible for the matter in a dreadful way. Among early examples, the *goryō* of Prince Sawara, a younger brother of Kanmu Tennō, posthumously received the title of Tennō (Sudō) from Kanmu for fear of his revenge for the misfortune he had unjustly received. A much more famous and influential *goryō* is that of Sugawara Michizane, a minister at the time of the reign of Uda Tennō, who on the basis of false charges was sent to Kyushu as a criminal. After his death he was believed to cause various disasters in the capital, e.g., the burning of the palace, the death of high officers, the illness of the emperor, and so on. He was regarded by the people to have become a *tenjin*, a celestial god who originally represented thunder, but was declared to be a subordinate of Taishakuten, i.e., *Śakro devānām Indra*. To stop his anger, or for the requiem of his soul, the government enshrined him at Kitano and restored to him the rank and post of his living days. At the same time, ex-Emperor Uda, who had become a monk after resigning from the throne, sent his disciple Nichizō to Yoshino Ōmine. This was the centre of the Shugendō mountain religion and a product of syncretism, which concentrated on the training of mystic powers by means of Esoteric Buddhism. The aim of Nichizō's meeting was that the *goryō* could be pacified by his mystic power.

It is notable that, although only the power of Esoteric Buddhism could finally pacify his soul, the *goryō* itself remained among the pantheon of the *kami*. Generally speaking, Buddhism never rejected the *kami* cult, but wished rather to give meaning to the cult in the background. Also notable is that in the syncretism of this period the power of the *Onmyōdō*, an astrological school based upon the philosophy of Yin and Yang in China, functioned as a part of the officially recognized *kami* ceremonies. Also a certain influence of Taoism can be observed, along with Confucian customs.

In relation to this new form of worship of dreaded souls, a certain change occurred in the concept of 'soul' within Buddhist folklore. As is well-known, according to its doctrine Buddhism teaches the non-existence of the self, which is believed by the orthodoxy, especially in the philosophy of the Upanishads, to be eternally existent in the form of a soul beyond lives. At the same time Buddhism never denied the existence of future lives and the transmigration of the soul. For the Buddhist the biggest problem to be doctrinally solved was how transmigration is possible without the existence of an eternal soul. The final solution was given by the Yogācāras, who hypothetically admitted the subconsciousness, which functions (though itself existent only momentarily) to make the appearance of the continuity of an individual by the force of *karma* which is preserved in that subconsciousness (consciousness as a container, *ālayavijñāna*). This subconsciousness loses its function, and hence its existence too, when the individual obtains Nirvana.

But this doctrine of no-self was too difficult for ordinary lay believers. Especially in China, Buddhism was obliged to maintain the non-destruction of the soul beyond this life in the presence of Confucianism, which claims the existence of a soul without the body. The Mahayana doctrine of the eternity of the Buddha and, as its counterpart in living beings, the existence of Buddha nature, which causes any sentient being without exception to obtain Buddhahood, gave a strong support for this admission of the soul, and this concept gradually substantialized in China. Buddhism in Japan had from the beginning this sinicized tendency and had thus no objection to worship of the souls of the dead. In the genuine Japanese cult the soul in terms of *tama* or *tamashihi* was believed to be active even after death, having a strong power over living people. This power is specially strong immediately after death and, growing gradually weaker, is finally lost when the soul loses its individual character and enters the realm of the ancestors. Among the dead, those considered to be the founder of a clan or heroes of the country were buried and served in a cemetery and often worshipped as *kami*, but ordinary deceased persons were left unburied. The revengeful souls mentioned above were considered to belong to the first category. These powerful souls were thought to be living in the cemetery or nearby to protect their descendants against evil. Buddhism started to take part in funerals first for those ordinary deceased persons who were not worshipped as *kami*. Towards the end of the medieval age (the 15th century), Buddhism monopolized the funeral ceremonies of the common people and memorial services were given up to the 33rd year after one's death. In this way Buddhism in Japan entered into the daily life of the Japanese, mainly by these funeral ceremonies and memorial services. The concept of transmigration of the soul has been lost in actuality among Japanese, except for the belief in rebirth in the Pure Land.

4. The *Mono Imi* and the Concept of Pure and Impure

Another concept, commonly held among the Japanese, which caused Buddhism to transform, and more specifically to develop the Pure Land faith with special enthusiasm, was the concept of purity and impurity. That is, the importance of keeping pure in daily life and avoiding impurity. Among impure things the decaying, defiled, dead body was the worst, as is shown in the myth of Izanami in the *Kojiki*. In order to avoid defilement by the impurity of death, people were required to perform *misogi*, a ceremony of purification as Izanaki, the husband of Izanami, performed after he returned from *yomi*, the underworld. For this purification, the power of the *kami* was invoked, but not that of Buddhism, because the latter had a special connection with funeral ceremonies. In the middle of the Heian period, i.e., from the 11th century onwards, a rapid spreading of the *mono imi* custom can be observed, as can be seen in the *Tale of Genji*, and in this connection Buddhism was gradually regarded as something impure and became an object of avoidance. (*Mono imi* literally means avoidance of the power of an ill spirit, a custom of avoiding impure things and matters before and during a Shinto ceremony.) This contradiction of making peace with souls on the one hand and being impure due to this connection with death on the other perhaps caused Buddhism to propagate the Amida cult of Pure Land Buddhism. The earnest wish for purity by all people, from high society down to the common people, brought forth their faith in Amitābha, through whom one could obtain rebirth in the Pure Land. The Pure Land of Amitābha is far better than the dark *yomi* land of the underworld. Detailed descriptions in the *Ōjō yōshū* by Genshin (985) on the brightness of the Pure Land are in stark contrast to the terrible and painful *jigoku* (*naraka*), which was thought to be located underground, and were welcomed emotionally by the people.

Of course the concept of purity and impurity is not strange to Buddhism. Buddhism emphasizes the value of purity in various points. The concept of Buddha nature is based upon the doctrine of the innate purity of the mind. The mind of sentient beings is pure by nature, and it is polluted temporarily and incidentally by defilements which are unreal and mere shadowy products of the mind. This doctrine of Buddha nature, otherwise called the *tathāgatagarbha* doctrine, was enthusiastically accepted in China and developed into the concept of original enlightenment (*hongaku*), the term originally used in the *Daijō kishin ron* (*Mahāyānaśraddhotpāda*). This concept was fruitfully used especially by Kūkai and the followers of Esoteric Buddhism both in Shingon and Tendai (for Kūkai, to establish the doctrine of enlightenment with this body in this life, and for the Tendai sect, as an interpretation of the One Vehicle doctrine), and a kind of secret tradition was established of this teaching, called *hongaku hōmon*. This doctrine gave strong support to the doctrine of rebirth in the Pure Land. Also it offered the basis for the establishment of the *honji suijaku setsu* in the next stage of Japanese Buddhism.

The merit of the *hongaku hōmon* lies in its concept of the equality of all sentient beings, human beings par excellence, with regard to attaining Buddhahood. Its demerit, on the other hand, was that it was said to make monks lazy in the practice of training and cause degeneration in Buddhist orders, which became the cause of new reform movements in the Kamakura period.

The concept of purity and impurity also prevailed in Hinduism. The rigid distinction between pure and impure, and disgust of the latter, in Hinduism caused in India the severe social discrimination of the caste system. The same tendency was partially brought to Japan with Buddhism, where it mixed with the already existing Japanese concept of *kegare* (impurity) and produced a Japanese-style discrimination, i.e., social discrimination on the basis of occupation. The Buddhist concept of equality could not dispel this discrimination. Equality is expected only beyond this life, in the Pure Land.

5. The Establishment of the *Honji Suijaku Setsu* and Thereafter

A memoir of an aristocrat in the 12th century records details of a cult in Kumano. Kumano was regarded by the ancient Japanese as a kind of world of the dead, due to its location far south of the capital and behind the Yoshino and Ōmine mountains, facing the great ocean beyond which the island Hōrai, the land of longevity as described in ancient Chinese legends, was believed to exist. Buddhist efforts in those days (in the 11th and 12th centuries) were aimed at making Kumano a holy land of Buddhism on the basis of the doctrine of the *honji suijaku setsu*. According to the said memoir, the three main shrines in Kumano were regarded as the abode of Buddhas who are the *honji*, i.e., the original basis (or substratum) of the respective *kami* manifested and enshrined there. Namely, the *kami* enshrined in the main shrine (*hongū*) is a manifestation of the Buddha Amitābha, and being the abode of Amitābha, the shrine is the entrance to Sukhāvatī, the Pure Land in the west. The *kami* in Nachi is a female manifestation of the Bodhisattva Avalokiteśvara with a thousand hands who leads people to the Pure Land of Potala in the south. And the *kami* in Hayatama is a manifestation of the Buddha Bhaiṣajyaguru (teacher of medicine) whose Pure Land, the Pure Vaiḍūrya (Jōruri), is located in the north. So Kumano was regarded as the best basis to approach any of the pure lands according to one's preference. The prosperity of Kumano can be seen in the *Ryōjin hishō*, a collection of popular songs of that time, compiled by Go-Shirakawa Tennō. In this book we also find many songs which express the doctrine of the *hongaku hōmon*.

The active movement of Buddhism towards Shinto in the form of the amalgamation of *kami* with Buddhas reached its zenith in the 12th and following centuries, resulting in the reorganization of Shinto deities in accordance with the Buddhist pantheon through identification of a respective *kami* with a certain Buddha or Bodhisattva, and in rewriting the myths of the *kami* in accordance with Buddhist doctrine. Also new Shinto doctrines were established based upon interpretations of the Shinto faith by means of Buddhist doctrine: for instance, the Sannō Ichijitsu Shinto derived from the Tendai sect, and the Ryōbu (Shūgō) Shinto derived from the Shingon sect.

From the 14th century onwards, during the civil war period of the Northern and Southern dynasties, the situation of Buddhism and Shinto began to turn into mutual equality in accordance with the rise of a nationalistic view of the Japanese tradition, as seen for example in the idea of *shingoku* (country of *kami*) in Kitabatake Chikafusa's *Jinnō shōtōki*, which caused the rise of Ise Shinto and Yoshida Shinto. They demanded pure Shintoistic doctrines and wished to give preference to Shinto *kami* over Buddhas. Also through a policy of the Tokugawa shogunate, which looked to Confucianism for moral support, the Japanese people became inclined to secularism and rationalism, and Buddhism lost its spiritual leadership in society. Finally, a new and modern nationalism rose in the 19th century, establishing a new government under the emperor, and this government of the Meiji restoration planned the separation of Shinto and Buddhism and wished once and for all to annihilate Buddhist power from the country. This last effort failed, but the policy of the government to centralize Shinto continued as far as the end of the Second World War. In spite of such changes in policy, however, syncretism of Buddhism and Shinto can be seen even today in the daily life of the Japanese people. Most Japanese are Buddhist in the sense that they have a grave in a Buddhist temple and receive religious services from a Buddhist priest (especially the funeral service), but at the same time they are Shintoists, as they belong to the local shrine of the village where they live and join in the annual festival of the shrine or perform their marriage ceremony in front of a *kami* through the services of a Shinto priest. Thus the Japanese people use Buddhism and Shinto, each in accordance with their purposes. This may be termed 'Japanese conventionalism'.

References

Kitagawa, Joseph M.

1987 *On Understanding Japanese Religion*. Princeton: Princeton University Press.

Murayama, Shūichi

1959 *Shinbutsu shūgō shichō*. Kyoto: Heirakuji Shoten.

1974 *Honji suijaku*. Tokyo: Yoshikawa Kōbunkan (rev. ed. 1995).

Sueki, Fumihiko

1992 *Nihon Bukkyō shi*. Tokyo: Shinchōsha.

1993 *Nihon Bukkyō shisō shi ronkō*. Tokyo: Daizō Shuppan.

Tsuji, Zennosuke

1944 *Nihon Bukkyō shi: jōsei hen*. Tokyo: Iwanami Shoten.

Yoshie, Akio

1996 *Shinbutsu shūgō*. Iwanami shinsho. Tokyo: Iwanami Shoten.

The Ekayāna (One Vehicle) Doctrine as the Basis of Japanese Buddhism*

The One Vehicle Doctrine in India

The *ekayāna* or "one vehicle" doctrine is one of the principal doctrines of Mahāyāna Buddhism. It was stated for the first time in the *Saddharmapuṇḍarīka-sūtra* (*Lotus Sūtra*), and teaches that the purpose of the Buddha's appearance in this world is to lead all sentient beings to the highest enlightenment, identical with that attained by the Buddha himself. There is, it is said, only one way to attain Buddhahood: the "Buddha vehicle" (*buddhayāna*).

In the *Lotus Sūtra*, at the beginning of the second chapter, the very core of the text, the one vehicle doctrine is stated as follows:

> Śāriputra, the Buddha appeared in the world with one task (*ekakṛtya*), one duty (*ekakaraṇīya*), one great task, one great duty. What, then, is the single great task of the Tathāgata, the single great duty of the Tathāgata, for the sake of which he appeared in this world? It is that the Tathāgata appeared in this world in order to inspire sentient beings with the vision of the Tathāgata's intuition (*jñāna*); in order to show the vision of the Tathāgata's intuition to sentient beings; in order to cause sentient beings to enter into the vision of the Tathāgata's intuition; in order to enlighten sentient beings with the vision of the Tathāgata's intuition; in order to cause sentient beings to enter upon the path which leads to the vision of the Tathāgata's intuition. This, Śāriputra, is the single great task, the single great duty of the Tathāgata.

---

* Originally published in Minoru Kiyota et al., eds., *Japanese Buddhism: Its Tradition, New Religions, and Interaction with Christianity* (Tokyo and Los Angeles: Buddhist Books International, 1987), pp. 24–33.

This is his sole motive for appearing in this world (*ekaprayojanaṃ loke prādurbhavāya*).

Thus, Śāriputra, the Tathāgata alone is able to pursue this one great task, this one great duty. Why? Because, Śāriputra, I myself am the only one who inspires (sentient beings) with the vision of the Tathāgata's intuition; I myself am the only one who shows the vision of the Tathāgata's intuition (to sentient beings); I myself am the only one who causes (sentient beings) to enter into the vision of the Tathāgata's intuition; I myself am the only one who enlightens (sentient beings) with the Tathāgata's intuition; I myself am the only one who causes (sentient beings) to enter upon the path which leads to the vision of the Tathāgata's intuition.

I will therefore, Śāriputra, preach dharma for the sake of sentient beings, dharma which refers to the one vehicle, namely, this very Buddha vehicle (*ekam evāhaṃ śāriputra yānam ārabhya sattvānāṃ dharmaṃ deśayāmi yad idaṃ buddhayānam*). Śāriputra, there is no second or third vehicle other than this (*na kiṃ cic chāriputra dvitīyaṃ vā tṛtīyaṃ vā yānaṃ saṃvidyate*). Śāriputra, this truth is all-pervasive, in the ten directions of the world (*sarvatraiśā śāriputra dharmatā daśadigloke*).[1]

Further, the verse section of the same chapter says:

There is not a single sentient being who cannot become a Buddha after hearing the dharma; indeed, the vow of the Tathāgatas is: "After practicing (myself) I shall practice for the sake of the enlightenment of others." [*SPS*, 100]

They will elucidate in the future thousands of millions of varieties of the dharma; exhibiting this one vehicle they will preach dharma concerning Tathāgatahood (*tathāgatatve*).

---

1. *Saddharmapuṇḍarīka-sūtra* (hereafter cited as *SPS*) (ed. Vaidya), p. 27.7-22.

[*SPS*, 101]

> Certainly, this dharma-method is always firmly established; the nature of phenomena is always brilliant. Knowing this, Buddhas, supreme among human beings, will explain this one vehicle. [*SPS*, 102]
>
> The establishment of the dharma, the determinacy of the dharma, its permanent establishment and firmness in the world—Buddhas on the throne of enlightenment will explain this to the world with skillful means. [*SPS*, 103]

The doctrine of one vehicle is said to be taught for the first time in this text, as against the doctrine of the three vehicles taught previously as skillful means (*upāya-kauśalya*). But in fact the sūtra declares that the Buddha has never taught this ultimate truth previously in the forty years of his teaching career following upon his enlightenment, and that he has now resolved to teach the one vehicle doctrine for the benefit of those who wish to attain the highest enlightenment.

The same doctrine is taught in the third chapter of the *Lotus Sūtra*, using the illustration of the burning house in the following way: a rich householder, realizing that his children are playing in a room of a burning house without knowing that they are in danger, tells them, in order to get them to leave the house, that waiting for them outside are three beautiful carts, one drawn by a sheep, another by a deer, and a third by an ox. In actuality, when the children leave the burning house, they find only a great cart drawn by a white bull. In the same way, it is said, when the Tathāgata finds many thousands of sentient beings wishing to escape from the sufferings of the world, he teaches them the way to the highest nirvāṇa, and the way that he teaches them is single (*ekayāna*, *buddhayāna*) even though it may appear to specific individuals that it is different. Some may see it as a deer-cart, others as an ox-cart, and so forth, when in reality there is only the cart drawn by a white bull.

The doctrinal point is that three different ways (*yāna*) are taught as expedient methods (*upāya*) in accordance with the different inclinations of sentient beings, while in reality there is only one course (*yāna*) to the highest enlightenment, a course open to all sentient beings in virtue of the fact that they are all sons of the Buddha (*buddhaputra*). Some beings, of course, may mistake the expedient teaching for the ultimate. This point is explained in the fourth chapter of the *Lotus Sūtra* with the story of a rich man's son who left his native country and wandered without knowing his good birth and lineage. He discovered it through the mercy of his father only when working as a servant in his father's house.

In the seventh chapter of the *Lotus Sūtra* there is a somewhat different illustration of the one vehicle doctrine. There it is said that, just as the leader of a caravan might create a magical illusion of a castle in order to encourage his followers to endure through a difficult part of the road, so the Buddha, knowing the depression to which individuals can become subject during their passage to nirvāṇa, might make two resting places on the way, designating one as appropriate to disciples (*śrāvaka*) and another as appropriate to Pratyekabuddhas, while in reality there is only one resting place—the nirvāṇa of the Buddha.

Thus the *Lotus Sūtra* claims its priority concerning the one vehicle doctrine. However, a similar statement is found also in the *Aṣṭasāhasrikā-prajñāpāramitā-sūtra*. Towards the end of the chapter on Suchness (*tathatā*) from that text it is said:

> According to the method of dharma-teaching elucidated by Subhūti, no teaching is retrievable from the highest enlightenment. Also, he said that three kinds of persons belonging to the Bodhisattvayāna are referred to by the Tathāgata, but there is no distinction of these three. It is really as Subhūti has said, that there is only one vehicle, namely, the Buddhayāna or Bodhisattvayāna (*ekam eva yānaṃ bhavati*

yad uta buddhayānaṃ bodhisattvayānam).[2]

The "three kinds of persons" mentioned here are those belonging to the vehicles of disciples, of Pratyekabuddhas, and of Bodhisattvas. All of them are called Bodhisattvas. In this case too, as in the *Lotus*, the vehicle of Bodhisattvas has a double role. On the one hand it is one among three, and on the other it is one alone, equivalent to the vehicle of the Buddhas (*buddhayāna*). In the *Prajñāpāramitā-sūtra*, however, references to one vehicle are comparatively rare, and the three vehicles are referred to mostly by the names of the three kinds of stages (*bhūmi*), or sometimes as particular teachings (*dharma*), with the stage of Bodhisattvas and the teachings of Mahāyāna being judged superior to those of the other two vehicles, which are collectively called the "lesser" or "inferior" vehicle (*hīnayāna*).

The three vehicles as different courses which lead to different results were originally taught among abhidharmic schools in terms of *śrāvakayāna*, *pratyekabuddhayāna* and *buddhayāna* respectively. For these schools the *buddhayāna* is limited to those who have become Buddhas in any of the three times (not in the ten directions). The *Prajñāpāramitā* literature stood against this exclusive view of the Buddhayāna and made it open to all Bodhisattvas, i.e., to anyone who aspires to highest enlightenment. The question remains as to whether this course is exclusive to Mahāyānists or inclusive of those in the vehicle of disciples and Pratyekabuddhas. The sūtra states inclusiveness of all in terms of equality of *tathatā*, or suchness, to all, but in practice emphasis was laid on the superiority of the Mahāyāna and of Bodhisattvas over those of the other two vehicles. The *Lotus Sūtra* was somewhat critical of this tendency of the *Prajñāpāramitā*, and emphasized inclusiveness in the name of the Buddha's mercy, a mercy shown by his prophesying (*vyākaraṇa*) to Śāriputra and others that they

2. *Aṣṭasāhasrikā-prajñāpāramitā-sūtra* (ed. Mitra), p. 319.14-15.

would become enlightened in a future life. Indian Mahāyāna Buddhism after the *Lotus* developed speculations on the one vehicle vis-à-vis the three vehicles in terms of the similarity of persons in their essence and differences in their practical abilities. Roughly speaking, there were two tendencies, one being the Tathāgatagarbha theory, which emphasized the ultimate equality of sentient beings, and the other the Yogācāra doctrine, which laid stress upon the practice of yoga and consequently maintained the existence of differences in the faculties of sentient beings.

The Tathāgatagarbha theory was elucidated for the first time in the *Tathāgatagarbha-sūtra*. The theory teaches the existence of the nature of the Buddha in every sentient being, using the term *tathāgatagarbha*—"embryo of the Tathāgata." The *Tathāgatagarbha-sūtra* owes its doctrines largely to the *Avataṃsaka-sūtra*, especially the chapter of that text which deals with the appearance of the Tathāgata. The *Avataṃsaka* teaches, using the image of an atom containing the whole universe, the all-pervasiveness of the wisdom of the Buddhas among sentient beings. The doctrine is another expression of the equality of *tathatā* as taught in the *Prajñāpāramitā*. *Tathatā*, or Suchness, is otherwise called *dharmāṇāṃ dharmatā* ("the real nature of all phenomena"), or *dharmadhātu* ("the basis of phenomena"), and the Tathāgata is explained as one who has reached (*āgata*), and thus become one with, *tathatā*. Then the Tathāgata, thus identified with *tathatā*, is called the *dharmakāya*, or the "body of Dharma," which is in turn essentially associated with the wisdom of enlightenment. Thus, because of the equality or non-distinction of *tathatā* in every phenomenon, speaking impersonally, and because of the all-pervasiveness of the wisdom of the Tathāgata, speaking personally, sentient beings are given the epithet "those who have the embryo of the Tathāgata" (*tathāgatagarbha*). This means that they have the ability to become a Buddha. The same point is expressed with terms such as "sons of the Buddha" (*buddhaputra* or *jinaputra*) or "those who belong to the Tathāgata's lineage" (*tathāgatakula* or *tathāgatagotra*). This last meaning is otherwise explained as the "mine" (*gotra*) from which come forth Tathāgatas who are like precious gems.

The *Tathāgatagarbha-sūtra* does not use the term "one vehicle," but the *Śrīmālā-sūtra*, which developed the *tathāgatagarbha* theory, explains it in terms of the one vehicle. In this text Śrīmālādevī, after making a vow to embrace the true doctrine (*saddharma*—the same term used in the title of the *Lotus Sūtra*), being helped by the Buddha, explains that the Mahāyāna is the only true doctrine which leads to ultimate nirvāṇa, and that the nirvāṇas of the Arhats and Pratyekabuddhas are only partial, taught by the Buddhas for reasons of expediency. She goes on to say that this Mahāyāna is synonymous with *buddhayāna*, which ends with the attainment of the *dharmakāya*, and thus that it is the "ultimate point of the one vehicle." She concludes that the practice of two vehicles (*śrāvaka* and *pratyekabuddha*) is simply a means used to accord with the inclinations of sentient beings, a means which leads always to the Mahāyāna. In the ultimate sense there is only the one vehicle which involves each of the three vehicles. For Śrīmālā, then, the *tathāgatagarbha* theory is simply the ultimate teaching of the Mahāyāna, a teaching which conforms to the ultimate purpose of the one vehicle.

In the *Mahāparinirvāṇa-sūtra*, another of those texts which expresses the *tathāgatagarbha* theory and uses one vehicle ideas, we find the famous expression that all sentient beings possess the nature of a Buddha (*buddhadhātu*), a term which is synonymous with *tathāgatagarbha* as used in the *Śrīmālā*. The *Mahāparinirvāṇa* compares its own teaching—aimed at making sentient beings perceive their own Buddha-nature, with the teaching of the *Lotus Sūtra* in which prophecies are made of the Buddhahood belonging to 8,000 *śrāvaka*s.[3] The text also teaches that just as cow's milk is always white, no matter what color the cow that gave it, so also Buddha-nature is possessed by all sentient beings. The only differences have to do with differences in degree of maturation, just like the differences between milk, sour milk, cream, cheese and butter:[4] At the same time, this sūtra emphasizes that no attainment of Buddhahood by *icchantika*s, those who have only worldly desires, is possible because of their lack of faith in this teaching. This raises the question of differences in ability among sentient beings in spite of their identity of essence.

It is the Yogācāras, otherwise called the Vijñānavādins, who lay stress on the importance of practice for the attainment of enlightenment rather than upon the innate possibility of becoming a Buddha possessed by all sentient beings. Also, the Yogācāras admit differences of many different kinds among practitioners, making use of the term *gotra*—"(religious) lineage"—to describe these differences. Five *gotra*s are enumerated, including those who have no *gotra*, that is, no ability to become enlightened. It may well be said that the followers of the Yogācāra were more realistic than those of the Tathāgatagarbha concerning the possibility of attaining highest enlightenment. From this perspective the Yogācāras dared to say that the *ekayāna* doctrine was an expedient and not an ultimate teaching.

Referring to the purpose of the one vehicle, the *Mahāyānasūtrālaṃkāra* has this to say:

> [The Buddha has intentionally taught] the one vehicle (*ekayānatā*) with [the following seven] reasons:
>
> 1. Equality (*tulyatva*) of truth (*dharma*).
> 2. Equality (*tulyatva*) of egolessness or non-substantiality (*nairātmya*).
> 3. Equality (*tulyatva*) of emancipation (*vimukti*) (in all

3. *Mahāparinirvāṇa-sūtra*, T. vol. 12, p. 420a.
4. Ibid., pp. 422, 423b.

groups).

4. Difference (*bheda*) of religious lineage (*gotra*) (i.e., that it is especially for those not yet fixed in any one of the three lineages).
5. Attainment of (the same) mental disposition (*āśaya*) by both (Buddhas and those fixed in the *śrāvakayāna* —i.e., that Buddhas have the intention of becoming one with sentient beings, and Śrāvakas, after preparing themselves for enlightenment, have feelings of equality with Buddhas).
6. [Entering into nirvāṇa in the same way as Śrāvakas] by virtue of the apparitional (*nirmāṇa*) body of the Buddha.
7. [Buddhahood] as ultimate goal.[5]

But, as the *Mahāyānasūtrālaṃkāra*[6] and Vasubandhu's commentary thereto make clear, this does not mean the non-existence of the three different vehicles. Vasubandhu explains the meaning of the term *yāna* in each of items (1) through (4) in the above extract in the following way: (1) *yāna* means *yātavya* ("that which is to be gone to"), which is *dharmadhātu*. (2) *yāna* means *yātṛ* ("the goer"), which is that which has no ego (*nairātmya*). (3) *yāna* means *yāti* ("the action of going"), which is emancipation (*vimukti*). (4) *yāna* means *yānti* ("the vehicle by which one goes"), which is *gotra*. He goes on to say:

> Buddhahood (*buddhatva*) is thus the one vehicle (*ekayāna*). It is in accordance with this, by various intentions and in various sūtras, that one-vehicle-ness should be understood. But it is not the case that the three vehicles do not exist. With what purpose, then, have the Buddhas taught one vehicle?
>
> To invite some and to retain others

5. *Mahāyānasūtrālaṃkāra* (hereafter cited as *MSA*) (ed. Lévi), p. 68.15-16.
6. *MSA*, p. 11.53.

> The Buddhas have taught one-vehicle-ness
> To those whose lineage is not yet fixed. (v. 54)

> "To invite some" refers to those who are of the Śrāvakagotra, but who are not yet fixed therein (*aniyata*). "To retain others" refers to those who are of the Bodhisattvagotra but who are not yet fixed therein.

After this the text explains (in vv. 55–59) various stages of the path belonging to those who are in the Śrāvakayāna but who are not yet fixed therein. He refers to those for whom the Śrāvaka, the Pratyekabuddha and the Buddha are stages within the long process of transmigration, and ends by quoting the following sentence from the *Śrīmālā-sūtra* (although the sentence is not found in the present text of that sūtra):

> First they are Śrāvakas, then Pratyekabuddhas, and finally they become Buddhas.[7]

The Yogācāras thus admit the existence of three vehicles, but they finally regard the one vehicle doctrine as an expedient used to invite as many beings as possible into the Mahāyāna. Sthiramati, the author of a sub-commentary on the *Mahāyānasūtrālaṃkāra*, clearly makes this point, saying that there is a group of sūtras which teaches one vehicle and another that teaches three, and those that teach one-vehicle-ness do so in order to lead people into the Mahāyāna by means of intentional language. This latter group are therefore to be called those sūtras whose meaning is not yet finally established (*neyārtha*), whereas only those teaching the three vehicles as real are the sūtras whose meaning is finally established (*nītārtha*).

In later times the Mādhyamikas opposed the Yogācāras and recovered the ultimate position of the one vehicle doctrine—as in the Tathāgatagarbha theory—but they were at one with the Yogācāras in putting stress on practice rather than on innate original

7. *MSA*, 70.8.

enlightenment. For example, Candrakīrti in the *Madhyamakāvatāra* regarded the Tathāgarbha theory as *neyārtha* because it teaches the "existence" of Buddha-nature in order to deliver people from the fear caused by the doctrine of the non-existence of the Self (*ātman*).

The One Vehicle Doctrine in China

The *Lotus Sūtra* was first translated into Chinese by Dharmarakṣa at the end of the third century A.D., but it was about a century later that the text was enthusiastically accepted by Chinese intellectuals through the medium of a new and more fluent translation by Kumārajīva (406 A.D.).

Studies on the *Lotus Sūtra* were begun almost immediately by followers of Kumārajīva, men such as Dōshō (Tao-sheng 道生, 353–434 A.D.), Ekan (Hui-kuan 慧觀, died between 426 and 453 at the age of 71), Sōei (Seng-jui 僧叡, died at the age of 64) and others. A point disputed by such commentators was whether the Mahāyāna (Buddhayāna) as the one vehicle should be identified with the Bodhisattvayāna considered as one of the three vehicles. Much of the discussion centered around the story of the burning house already mentioned, and those commentators who considered the bullock-cart to be different from the three carts pulled by sheep, deer and ox were called "four-carters," while those who thought of the one vehicle (Buddhayāna) as identical with the Bodhisattvayāna were called "three-carters." Among the followers of Kumārajīva, Dōshō and Sōei are three-carters and Ekan is a four-carter. Similarly, among later commentators Kichizō (Chitsang 吉藏, 544–623) of the San-lun 三論 school and Kiki (K'ueichi 窺基, 632–682) of the Fa-hsiang 法相 school belong to the three-carters.

However, a more influential interpretation in Chinese Buddhism was that of the four-carters led by Chigi (Chih-i 智顗, 538–597) of the T'ien-t'ai school 天台 and Hōzō (Fa-tsang 法藏, 643–

712) of the Hua-yen 華嚴 school. The four-carters may perhaps be regarded as typical of Chinese interpretation on this issue. On the other hand, Dōshō, Kichizō and Kiki, the three-carters, were more intimate with the Sanskrit texts than the followers of T'ien-t'ai, and their interpretation is thus more or less representative of the Indian position. We can see in their interpretations doctrines of Indian texts introduced into China after Kumārajīva, texts such as the *Śrīmālā-sūtra*, the *Laṅkāvatāra-sūtra*, and Vasubandhu's *Upadeśa* on the *Saddharmapuṇḍarīka*, as well as other texts belonging to the Vijñānavāda. In what follows I shall consider each line of interpretation according to its historical position.

Prior to examining them, mention should be made of Hōun of Kōtakuji (Fa-yün 法雲 of Kuang-chai-ssu 光宅寺, 467–529), famous as one of the three great dharma-teachers in the Liang 梁 dynasty. His commentary on the *Lotus Sūtra* is important not only for its influence upon Chigi and Kichizō in the next period, but also for its use by Prince Shōtoku 聖德 (574–622) of Japan. According to Hōun, the *Lotus Sūtra* teaches that the Buddha preached the dharma in three ways in accordance with the followers of the three vehicles, though the truth behind these teachings is one and is identical with the one vehicle. Also, he says that the three carts represent the Arhat, the Pratyekabuddha and the Bodhisattva, and that each of them is an expedient leading to the ultimate fruit of Buddhahood illustrated by the great bullock-cart.

Almost a century after Hōun a typical one vehicle doctrine was established by Chigi, who found the *Lotus Sūtra* the most basic teaching of the Buddha. He clearly stated that the one vehicle of the true doctrine (*saddharma*) is the Buddhayāna, the only true doctrine, and that the doctrines of the three vehicles are merely provisional expedients. He thus stressed the difference between the one and the three, and listed ten meanings concerning the relationship between the one and the three:

1. Breaking attachment to the doctrine of three vehicles

in order to make clear the one wisdom of the Buddha.

2. Abandoning the convenient teaching of the three vehicles in order to manifest the ultimate teaching of the one vehicle.

3. Opening the three ways to the people of the three vehicles in order to let them enter the Buddhayāna.

4. Combining the three ways of convenient practice in order to make clear the practice of the one vehicle.

5. Abiding in the one vehicle to manifest (the essence of the Buddha) as it really is.

6. Abiding in three vehicles to manifest the one (as a means for leading people).

7. Abiding in neither three vehicles nor one in order to manifest the truth as one.

8. Covering over the three vehicles in order to remove attachment and in order to manifest one vehicle without removing their teaching.

9. Abiding in three vehicles in order to use one vehicle (the standpoint of the Śrāvakas).

10. Abiding in one vehicle in order to use the three vehicles (the standpoint of the previous vow of the Buddha?).

Also, Chigi teaches the doctrine of "four ones": teaching, practice, person and reason. He says: (1) In the chapter on skillful means the Buddha elucidates the teaching of "opening three vehicles to manifest one" by referring to "teaching" and saying that there is only one vehicle, not two or three. (2) Through the illustration of the burning house the Buddha preaches the same doctrine by referring to "practice" and saying that by rejecting means (*upāya*) he preaches the highest enlightenment directly. (3) Through the illustration of the poor son the Buddha preaches the same doctrine by referring to "person" and saying that he educates Bodhisattvas only. (4) Through the illustration of an illusory castle in the seventh chapter the Buddha preaches the same doctrine by referring to "reason" and saying that truth, firmly established, always appears in the world.

Chigi's other contribution to Chinese Buddhism was the establishment of the doctrine of the five periods of the Buddha's teaching. He regards the *Lotus Sūtra* together with the *Mahāparinirvāṇa-sūtra* as the fifth and ultimate period of teaching, classifying all the preceding ones as provisional and expedient.

At about the same time Kichizō put forth his doctrine of the middle way as non-perception of any way, whether three or one, and interpreted Chigi's "joining three into one" and "joining two (lesser vehicles) into one (the Mahāyāna)" as being finally the same, just as a man holding a single fruit in his hand says that he has three. His interpretation of "without second or third" is the same as Dōshō's, while his view that the three vehicles are conventional and that the one vehicle is true is similar to Hōun's. At the same time, though, the following explanation shows a standpoint close to that of the four-carters:

> Bodhisattvas live among people in order to educate them; thus they are like oxen. Disciples, following the Teacher, also live in the world; thus they are like sheep. Pratyekabuddhas never educate the world, neither do they follow the Teacher; thus, being wild animals, they are like deer. Finally, the great bullock-cart represents the great wisdom of equality. As a cart signified ten thousand qualities of the fruit of being a Buddha, the Buddha is illustrated as a person on the cart.[8]

About a century later, Kiki of the Fa-hsiang school, following Genjō (Hsüan-tsang 玄奘) and Vasubandhu's *Upadeśa*, firmly stands on the side of the three-carters, saying that the essential body of the Mahāyāna is not excluded from the three (the Bodhisattvayāna being the Mahāyāna), that the illustration of the poor

8. *Hokke gisho* (*Fa-hua i-shu* 法華義疏), T. vol. 34, pp. 525c, 528b.

son secretly deprives the two (Śrāvakayāna and Pratyekabuddhayāna), and that the illustration of an illusory castle represents the two as a resting place on the way to final nirvāṇa. In contrast to Kichizō, however, Kiki finally assents to the five-*gotra* theory, including the idea that there is a group of beings incapable of attaining enlightenment, and declares the ultimacy of the three vehicles. He says that there are two kinds of truth and expedient relation. In the doctrine of the five different groups, three vehicles —those of Śrāvakas, who are fixed in their *yāna*, and those of Pratyekabuddhas and Buddhas—are true and real, while the preaching of the one vehicle is an expedient for inviting the group of people not fixed in any one of the three vehicles into the Mahāyāna. Secondly, as far as the group of those not fixed in any vehicle is concerned, they have the capacity to attain the fruits of the three vehicles, and at first they obtain the nirvāṇa-with-residue after practicing any one of the three vehicles. Then, converting to the Mahāyāna and practicing the vehicle of Bodhisattvas, they finally attain the fruit of Buddhahood. Therefore, for them the Bodhisattvayāna is the one vehicle and is true and real, while the other two vehicles are merely expedients. According to Kiki, the *Lotus Sūtra* thus represents an expedient teaching.

Finally, let us look at the doctrine of Fa-tsang, who established the Hua-yen doctrine against the Fa-hsiang school of Kiki. Unique to Fa-tsang is his division of the one vehicle doctrine into two. The first belongs to the *Avataṃsaka-sūtra*, which sees itself as the ultimate one vehicle as distinct from the teaching of three vehicles. The second belongs to the *Lotus Sūtra*, which preaches, according to Fa-tsang, the one vehicle as identified with the three vehicles, as represented by the three carts outside the burning house. The former is called the one vehicle as separate teaching and the latter is called the one vehicle as common teaching. The former is the root and the latter the end of the Buddha's teaching.

Fa-tsang also teaches the doctrine of five kinds of one vehicle.

The first and highest two are those belonging to the *Avataṃsaka* and the *Lotus* as already mentioned. The third is the *ekayāna* as "beyond imagination," taught in the *Laṅkāvatāra*. The fourth is the one vehicle of the equality of Buddha-nature as taught in the Tathāgatagarbha texts. And the fifth is the one vehicle doctrine considered as intentional or provisional teaching, as taught in the *Mahāyānasaṃgraha* (which Fa-tsang takes to belong to the "elementary teaching of the Mahāyāna").

Fa-tsang also teaches a threefold division of the one vehicle doctrine. First, the one vehicle retaining the three vehicles as final. This is the teaching of the *Mahāyānasaṃgraha*, which, without removing attachment to the three vehicles, and without joining the fruits of practice in the two vehicles to the fruits of the Mahāyāna, teaches the one vehicle merely as signifying the equality of the truth of emptiness. Second, the one vehicle removing the three vehicles. This is the teaching of the *Lotus*, which, joining the fruits of practice in the two vehicles to those of the Mahāyāna, removes attachment to the distinctions between the three vehicles and preaches the doctrine of one vehicle. Third, the one vehicle directly manifested. This is the teaching of the *Avataṃsaka*, which, ignoring the maintenance of the (other) two vehicles because of their being empty but at the same time manifesting its universe like the dharma-body, elucidates the meaning of the enlightenment of the entire dharma-sphere solely for the sake of the great Bodhisattvas.

Fa-tsang's standpoint, then, was at first against the three-vehicle doctrine of the Fa-hsiang school, and was intended to emphasize the ultimacy of the *Avataṃsaka* against the T'ien-t'ai school, which supported the ultimacy of the *Lotus Sūtra*. Such scholastic conflicts continued, but there developed no new unique doctrine which surpassed those mentioned.

The Japanese Initiation to the One Vehicle Doctrine

Japan was introduced to Buddhism in the middle of the sixth century A.D. via Paekche 百濟 on the Korean peninsula, where the Buddhism of Southern China had flourished. This Buddhism was characteristically of the one vehicle variety, closely connected with *Prajñāpāramitā* doctrine and with the *Mahāparinirvāṇa-sūtra*. Prince Shōtoku, who bears the title of preceptor of Japan, has also the honor of being the principal Buddhist scholar of his country. He wrote commentaries on the *Lotus Sūtra*, the *Vimalakīrtinirdeśa-sūtra*, and the *Śrīmālā-sūtra*. Among these texts, the *Śrīmālā* stands for the one vehicle of the Tathāgatagarbha, while the *Vimalakīrti* belongs to the exclusive Mahāyāna, which rejects the two lesser vehicles. The selection of these sūtras by Prince Shōtoku was no doubt due to his ideal of introducing the Japanese to the all-embracing Mahāyāna, but at the same time we must observe the influence of the Buddhism of the Southern Dynasties.

A typical instance can be seen in the *Hokke gisho* 法華義疏, a commentary on the *Lotus Sūtra*. In writing this commentary, Prince Shōtoku used Hōun's interpretation of the chapter on skillful means. Also, quoting Hōun's text, Prince Shōtoku clearly says that the term *shohō* (in the expression *shohō jissō* 諸法實相, *dharmāṇāṃ dharmatā*) means the three kinds of teaching about the three vehicles, and the term *jissō* means the one truth of the one vehicle.

At the same time there is perceptible in Prince Shōtoku's works some influence from T'ien-t'ai doctrines, such as that of the "four ones" already discussed together with that of the five periods. For example, Shōtoku says that the *Lotus* teaches that to illuminate the object of the four ones is called true wisdom, and to illuminate the three objects of the three faculties is called expedient wisdom. Here "the object of the four ones" means that one person with one faculty experiences one teaching and teaches one truth. In response to this the Tathāgata gives one teaching to one faculty and educates one person by manifesting one truth. "The three objects of the three faculties" means that three persons with three kinds of faculties experience three objects, and the Tathāgata, in response to three faculties, educates three persons by means of three teachings.

The introduction of these T'ien-t'ai doctrines was probably a result of Prince Shōtoku's communication with the great Sui 隋 in 607 A.D., ten years after the death of Chigi. Japanese Buddhism did not, however, exhibit a direct development of the T'ien-t'ai version of the one vehicle doctrine until the beginning of the ninth century A.D., when Saichō 最澄 brought T'ien-t'ai doctrines from T'ang 唐 China. Before this, Japanese Buddhism had received direct influence from the new currents of Buddhism belonging to the T'ang dynasty in China. Soon after the revolution of 645, the same year that Genjō returned from India, the Japanese government sent monks to China, and Dōshō 道昭 was among those who brought the doctrines of the Fa-hsiang school to Japan for the first time in about 653. These doctrines were finally established as the Japanese Hossō 法相 school in the middle of the eighth century. This was the most influential school during the Nara 奈良 period, until the beginning of the ninth century, and thus the doctrine of the ultimacy of the three vehicles was much in vogue during that period.

During the reign of Sokuten Bukō (Empress Wu Tse-t'ien 則天武后, 685–705), another new school flourished, the Hua-yen, which was introduced to Japan around 736 A.D. and immediately came to occupy an influential position under the policies of a government looking for an ideology which could be used to unify the country. Thus the one vehicle theory of the Hua-yen school, which goes with the Tathāgatagarbha theory, began to influence the minds of Japanese Buddhists, and this was particularly visible in the case of Kūkai 空海, who studied the *Shih mo-ho-yen lun* (*Shaku makaen ron* 釋摩訶衍論), a Chinese commentary on the *Ta-ch'eng ch'i-hsin lun* 大乘起信論 (*Mahāyānaśraddhotpāda-śāstra*), and made its doctrine of intrinsic enlightenment (*hongaku* 本覺) the basis of his esoteric Buddhism.

Lastly comes the T'ien-t'ai school, established by Saichō, who supported the one vehicle doctrine of Japanese Tendai 天台 based upon the *Lotus Sūtra*, a doctrine which was dominant in Japan for many centuries. Before its establishment, however, he was forced to have disputes with the upholders of the doctrine of three vehicles, among whom Tokuichi 德一 was the major representative, and also with Kūkai, who supported the ultimacy of esoteric Buddhism against the exoteric Tendai. It was after Saichō's death that Kūkai's doctrines of intrinsic enlightenment began to appear in Tendai. This doctrine of intrinsic enlightenment (*hongaku hōmon* 本覺法門), a characteristic feature of Japanese Buddhism in the medieval period, represents the amalgamation of the one vehicle doctrine and esoteric Buddhism.

Kōbō Daishi (Kūkai) and *Tathāgatagarbha* Thought*

Introduction

In the Buddhism of Kūkai 空海 (posthumously given the honorific title Kōbō Daishi 弘法大師), the text of the *Shih Mo-ho-yen lun* 釋摩訶衍論 (Commentary on the Mahāyāna Treatise) was apparently an important influence. Kūkai was already well-versed in the text before his trip to T'ang China. It is possible that he was instructed in the text by the monk Gonzō 勤操, who is said to have gotten it directly from Kaimyō 戒明 (of Daianji 大安寺 temple), the monk responsible for introducing the book into Japan.

The *Shih Mo-ho-yen lun* is a commentary on the *Ta-ch'eng ch'i-hsin lun* 大乘起信論 (Treatise on Awakening Faith in the Mahāyāna) supposedly deriving from India, but from the record regarding the circumstances of its "translation" and other unfavorable evidence, it was already labeled a forgery by Ōmi no Mifune 淡海三船 in his letter to Kaimyō soon after the text's arrival in Japan, and the same allegation was repeatedly laid upon it thereafter by Saichō 最澄 and others affiliated with the Tendai 天台 school.[1] In spite of this, Kūkai not only relied on the commentary in such major works of his as the *Jū jūshin ron*, *Hizō hōyaku*, and *Ben kenmitsu nikyō ron* (described below) as the authoritative work of Nāgārjuna 龍樹 (also called Nāgārjuna Bodhisattva 龍樹菩薩), but even went so far as to number the text among the basic

* Originally published in *Acta Asiatica* 47 (1985), pp. 109–129.

1. Mochizuki Shinkō 望月信亨, *Bukkyō kyōten seiritsushi ron* 佛教經典成立史論 [Historical study in the history of Buddhist texts] (Kyoto: Hōzōkan, 1946), pp. 651–670, latter part, chapter 12, section 3: "Ryūju ni kataku seraretaru *Shaku Makaen ron*" 龍樹に假託せられたる釋摩訶衍論 [The *Shih Mo-ho-yen lun* attributed to Nāgārjuna].

sutras and treatises for study of the doctrines of his sect of (esoteric) Buddhism, being a required text for study and promulgation by the faithful. One cannot but wonder what Kūkai's intention was in making such important use of the book as a true work of Nāgārjuna, even though there is no doubt that Kūkai was aware of the label of forgery on the book. Understanding this point may also help clear up some of the questions regarding Kūkai's uncertain biography before his trip to China.

For the present paper, the author was assigned the topic of the relationship between Kūkai and *tathāgatagarbha*[2] thought. Since the *Shih Mo-ho-yen lun* is a commentary on the *Ta-ch'eng ch'i-hsin lun*, which in turn clearly belongs to the lineage of texts

2. *Tathāgatagarbha* 如來藏: Buddhism (*Buddhadharma*) is often pointed out as being not only the teaching of the Buddha ("enlightened one"), but also the path leading to the stage of buddhahood. However, historically it does not appear that this was the universally accepted view in India, where in the non-Mahāyāna sects the highest attainable condition of perfection was considered that of the *arhat*. Against this, the Mahāyāna view was that the true intention of Buddhism was more than just the personal enlightenment of the *arhat*, but the salvation (bringing to enlightenment) of all sentient beings while aiming at no less than the complete, perfect enlightenment of the Buddha—the *bodhisattva* ideal. Even within the Mahāyāna, some held that the path of the bodhisattva was not accessible to all (ruling out, e.g., the "selfish" pursuants of the personal enlightenment of the *arhat*; focus on the individual abilities of the devotees), and yet others believed that limitless compassion and wisdom must surely lead all to the highest stage (focus on the absolute perfection of the Buddha). This latter view, that *all* beings possessed the potential to attain buddhahood, found an expression in the concept of *tathāgatagarbha*. *Tathāgata* 如來 is a synonym of the Buddha ("one who has gone to [or gone to and returned from, i.e., to guide others] the transcendental state"), and *garbha* 藏 is a word with such meanings as womb/matrix as well as that contained therein, i.e., fetus, embryo, etc. In the sense of possession of the potentiality of buddhahood, it is taken as meaning "containing the *tathāgata*" (*garbha* as the final element in compounds can mean "containing [the earlier element]"), or in the sense of one's ultimately attaining buddhahood, it means "*tathagata*-fetus," or future *tathāgata*. Another term often used synonymously is *buddha-dhātu* / *buddha-gotra* 佛性, often translated "buddha-nature."

dealing with *tathāgatagarbha* and represents the final stage of development of the concept that passed through earlier stages represented by the *Śrīmālādevī-siṃhanāda* and *Laṅkāvatāra* sutras, it seemed appropriate to seek the connection between Kūkai and *tathāgatagarbha* thought in terms of Kūkai's usage of the *Shih Mo-ho-yen lun* in his own works.

I

Kūkai's fundamental position was *Shingon Mikkyō* 眞言密教, or Esoteric (Tantric) Mantrayāna Buddhism. *Mikkyō*, lit. the "secret teaching," is of course a designation made in distinction to *kengyō* 顯教, the exoteric, or "openly manifest" teachings, and represents the latest development among the Buddhist schools, proclaiming itself to be the highest and most profound of teachings and dismissing all other schools of Buddhism under the name of *kengyō*. Kūkai's system of classification of the Buddhist teachings and schools (*kyōhan* 教判), stemming from the above *Mikkyō* position, is basically presented in the *Ben kenmitsu nikyō ron* 辯顯密二教論 (Distinguishing the Exoteric and Esoteric Teachings), and in more concrete fashion in the *Himitsu mandara jū jūshin ron* 祕密曼荼羅十住心論 (Secret Maṇḍala of the Ten Stages of the Development of Mind, hereafter referred to as *Jū jūshin ron*) and *Hizō hōyaku* 祕藏寶鑰 (Precious Key to the Secret Treasury), where the relative ranking of the various schools of exoteric (*kengyō*) Buddhism is expressed along with Kūkai's theory of the ten classes, or stages of development, of human mind (*jūshin* 住心). On the other hand, Kūkai's statement of the profound essence of the teachings is of course his *Sokushin jōbutsu gi* 即身成佛義 (The Attainment of Buddhahood in This Very Existence).

Within the context of Kūkai's thinking on the classification of the Buddhist teachings, the text *Shih Mo-ho-yen lun* figures heavily in the role of providing the criterion for the distinction between exoteric and esoteric teachings. For instance, taking the text *Ben kenmitsu nikyō ron*, the following passage is found at the end of the section of questions and answers on the distinction between exoteric and esoteric teachings occurring early on in the text.

> As it says in the *Commentary on the Mahāyāna Treatise* by the bodhisattva Nāgārjuna:
>
> All sentient beings possess, from the beginningless past, intrinsic enlightenment (*pen-chüeh*, *hongaku* 本覺; original enlightenment, enlightenment by nature), never losing it for a moment. Why, then, is there a distinction of past, future, and present in the attainment of buddhahood? Furthermore, there are those who diligently practice and those who backslide; those who are brilliant and those who are quite dull; what of these uncountable distinctions?
>
> Given the uniform possession [among sentient beings] of the state of intrinsic enlightenment, all beings should as one give rise to the resolution to attain the highest enlightenment (*fa* [*p'u-t'i-*]*hsin*, *hosshin* [*hotsu bodaishin*] 發[菩提]心), cultivate, and arrive at the unsurpassed object (*tao*, *dō* 道 = *p'u-t'i*). Is this because of differences in the excellence and inferiority in the possessed buddha nature of intrinsic enlightenment? [Or] is this because of the heaviness or lightness of the [covering of the] passions bred of ignorance (*wu-ming fan-nao*, *mumyō bonnō* 無明煩惱)?
>
> Whosoever would put forth the view like the former [mentioned above] would be mistaken; it is not due to any such [distinction of excellence-inferiority (*ch'iang-lieh*, *gōretsu* 強劣)]. And why? Because the intrinsically enlightened buddha nature fully possesses the [Buddha's] virtues (*kung-te*, *kudoku* 功德) surpassing the number of grains of sand in the Ganges River, and shows no increase or decrease.
>
> Should one put forth the view like the latter [mentioned above], he would likewise be mistaken; it is not due to any such [distinction of heaviness-lightness (*hou-po*, *kōhaku* 厚

薄)]. And why? Because the notion of cutting off [all ignorant passions/delusions] at one and the same stage of spiritual development (*i-ti tuan i*, *itchi dan no gi* 一地斷義) is not viable. All of the above-mentioned innumerable, multifarious distinctions owe their continuing [apparent] existence (*chu-ch'ih*, *jūji* 住持) to ignorance; within the domain of the highest principle (intrinsic enlightenment), they are of no concern.

Supposing that to be so, (1) then if all those practicing the discipline were to cut off all evils, practice all good, surpass the ten stages [of the bodhisattva's path] to reach the highest level, perfectly realize the three bodies [of the Buddha], and become endowed with the four virtuous attributes (*te*, *toku* 德): would such practitioners (supply "an understanding of the practitioners"; similarly for each question and answer) be of the stage of wisdom or the stage of ignorance?

Such [an understanding of the] practitioners would be of the stage of ignorance and not of the stage of wisdom.

If so, (2) then the pure intrinsic enlightenment does not depend upon practice and is not something gained by the power of others; by nature the virtuous attributes are complete, and intrinsic wisdom is present; [it] is both beyond the four modes of description (*catuṣ-koṭi*, *ssu-chü*, *shiku* 四句) and the five biased views (*wu-pien*, *gohen* 五邊). The expression "conforming with reality" is incapable of conforming with [true] reality (*tzu-jan chih yen pu neng tzu-jan*, *jinen no gon jinen-taru atawazu* 自然之言，不能自然); the [expressible] "mind of purity" is incapable of [true] purity (*ch'ing-ching chih hsin pu neng ch'ing-ching*, *shōjō no shin shōjō-taru atawazu* 清淨之心，不能清淨). [It] is utterly surpassing, utterly surpassing (transcendent of thought or expression) (*chüeh li chüeh li*, *zetsuri zetsuri* 絶離，絶離).

Is such a state (*pen-ch'u*, *honjo* 本處) one of wisdom or of ignorance?

Such a state belongs to merely a limited realm of ignorance (*wu-ming pien-yü*, *mumyō no hen'iki* 無明邊域) and does not represent the stage of wisdom (*ming fen-wei*, *myō no bun'i* 明分位).

If so, (3) then the mind of the absolute [one] dharma realm (*i fa-chieh hsin*, *ippōkai no shin* 一法界心) is not related to the hundred negations (corresponding to *k'ung*, *kū* 空, insubstantiality), withdraws before the thousand affirmations (corresponding to *chia*, *ke* 假, impermanent, conditional), and is not to be found in between (corresponding to *chung*, *chū* 中, the synthesis of the preceding two); not [even] being in the middle, turns from [the realm of] heaven; turning from heaven, [even] the most eloquent of speech loses its drive and ceases, and the manifold speculations lose their means and come to a halt.

Is this absolute [one] mind to be considered wisdom or ignorance?

Such an absolute [one] mind belongs to merely a limited realm of ignorance and does not represent the stage of wisdom.

(4) Regarding the Mahāyāna dharma of the one [absolute] mind with its three inherent aspects (= the three "greatnesses" of suchness spoken of in *The Treatise on Awakening Faith in the Mahāyāna*, i.e., greatness of substance, greatness of attributes, and greatness of function) (*san-tzu i-hsin Mo-ho-yen fa*, *sanji isshin Makaen no hō* 三自一心摩訶衍法), the word "one" does not indicate [the ordinary meaning of] "one," but the term "one" is borrowed as a means to aid spiritual progress; the word "mind" does not indicate [the ordinary meaning of] "mind," but the term "mind" is borrowed as a means to aid spiritual progress.

> [Likewise,] while in fact not being named "I" (*wo*, *ga* 我), still the convention is established to call me "I"; even though it does not [truly] refer to myself, still "myself" (*tzu*, *ji* 自) is arbitrarily connected with me. Even though "I" and other such names be established [in everyday usage], they are not the true "I" [or other entities]; even though referable to by "myself" and other such names, still they are not truly "myself" [etc.]. It is profound, profound—beyond profound; remote, remote—beyond remote.
>
> Does such a station of mastery (*abhibhv-āyatana*, *sheng-ch'u*, *shōjo* 勝處) constitute wisdom or ignorance?
>
> Such a station of mastery belongs to merely a limited realm of ignorance and does not represent the stage of wisdom.
>
> (5) The non-dual Mahāyāna dharma alone is the non-dual Mahāyāna dharma. Does this non-dual Mahāyāna dharma constitute wisdom or ignorance?[3]

The preceding quotation from the *Shih Mo-ho-yen lun*, referred to as the "five-part dialog," corresponds to a portion of the section commenting on the "meaning of the six perfumings of suchness" in the *Ta-ch'eng ch'i-hsin lun* and is found in the fifth fascicle of the commentary.[4] In the *Hizō hōyaku*, the passages marked with (1) through (4) above are found separately quoted as literary authorities in the sections from that on the sixth stage, *Taen-Daijō-shin* 他緣大乘心 ("the Mahāyāna mind with sympathetic concern for others"), through that on the ninth stage, *Goku-mujishō-shin* 極無自性心 ("the profoundest [exoteric] mind that realizes its lack of immutable nature [own-being]").[5] Therefore,

---

3. T. vol. 77, p. 375bc.

4. T. vol. 32, p. 637bc.

5. Sixth stage: 龍猛菩薩說。一切行者斷一切惡… (T. vol. 77, p. 370b); seventh stage: 那伽羅樹那菩薩說。清淨本覺從無始來… (ibid., pp. 370c–371a); eighth stage: 龍猛菩薩說。一法界心非百非… (ibid., p. 371c); ninth stage: 龍猛菩薩

one would expect that, although he does not clearly state it, Kūkai interpreted the fifth numbered section on "the non-dual Mahāyāna dharma" to correspond with the tenth and final stage, *Himitsu-shōgon-shin* 祕密莊嚴心 ("the glorious mind of the esoteric teachings"). And in fact, after quoting two more sections from the *Shih Mo-ho-yen lun* (beginning "Why is the non-dual Mahāyāna dharma without cause or condition?" and "The profound and immense meaning of the Buddhas comprehensively includes all the teachings heretofore ever expounded"), he sums up, writing:

> Speaking in explanation, what is meant by the non-dual Mahāyāna and the Buddhas of the completely perfect ocean of virtues (*yüan-yüan hai-te chu-fo*, *ennen kaitoku no shobutsu* 圓圓海德諸佛) is none other than the absolute dharmakāya (*tzu-hsing fa-shen*, *jishō hosshin* 自性法身). This is named the treasury of all secrets (*mi-mi-tsang*, *himitsuzō* 祕密藏) and is also called the Vajra-Head Great King of the Teachings (*Chin-kang-ting ta-chiao-wang*, *Kongōchō daikyō-ō* 金剛頂大教王; meaning the *Vajraśekhara Sūtra*). Because the bodhisattva of the fifty-first of the fifty-two stages (*teng-chüeh*, *tōgaku* 等覺) and of the tenth of the ten stages (*shih-ti*, *jūji* 十地) cannot yet know this, it receives the name of secret. Detailed explanation can be found in the *Vajraśekhara Sūtra* (also called *Tattvasaṃgraha-tantra*: *Chin-kang-ting ching*, *Kongōchōkyō* 金剛頂經).[6]

Of the two latter quotes just mentioned, the first comes from fascicle one of the *Shih Mo-ho-yen lun*, where the commentary is discussing the "Section Setting Forth the Teaching" (*Li-i fen*, *Ryūgibun* 立義分) of the *Ta-ch'eng ch'i-hsin lun* in which, as the substance and attributes of the principle (*dharma*) and significance (*artha*) of the Mahāyāna, the three "greatnesses" are listed. There,

---

說。三自一心法… (ibid., p. 373a).

6. T. vol. 77, p. 376a.

the point that the non-dual Mahāyāna dharma is unrelated both to the capacity of the listener to understand the teachings (*chi-ken, kikon* 機根) and to causes and conditions is discussed in contrast with the eight kinds of fundamental dharmas (*pa-chung pen-fa, hasshu no honpō* 八種本法) that arise in accord with the capacity of the listener and with causes and conditions. Not fearing to become a bit tedious, I will quote the section here.

> Again, to quote:
>
> Why is the non-dual Mahāyāna dharma without cause or condition? This dharma is extraordinarily subtle and profound, isolated and exalted. This is because it is unrelated to the spiritual capacity of the listener (*kikon*). Why is it unrelated to spiritual capacity? Because spiritual capacity does not exist. Why must this dharma be established? Because it is not a matter of establishment [in line with the spiritual capacity of the listener]. Is this Mahāyāna dharma what is attained by the Buddhas? It is what causes all Buddhas to attain [realization]. Do the Buddhas attain? No, for which reason bodhisattvas, followers of the two [lesser] vehicles (= *śrāvaka*s and *pratyekabuddha*s), and the common multitudes are also the same; the "perfectly complete ocean of intrinsic virtues" (*hsing-te yüan-man-hai, shōtoku enman-kai* 性德圓滿海) refers to this fact. What is the reason for this? Because [the non-dual Mahāyāna dharma] is unrelated to spiritual capacity, because [it is] unrelated to [any of] the teachings.
>
> The eight kinds of fundamental dharmas arise in accord with causes and conditions. This is because they respond to spiritual capacity, and because they follow the teachings. Why is it that they respond to spiritual capacity? Because of the existence of spiritual capacities. Are these eight fundamental dharmas what are attained by the Buddhas? They are what the Buddhas attain. Attained within the Buddhas,

> because they are not [attained]. The bodhisattvas, followers of the two [lesser] vehicles, and the common multitudes are also thus; the "ocean of the seeds of cause by practice" (*hsiu-hsing chung-yin-hai*, *shugyō shuinkai* 修行種因海) refers to this fact. What is the reason for this? Because of the existence of spiritual capacities; because of the existence of the teachings.[7]

The "eight fundamental dharmas" mentioned here are explained earlier in the same commentary, in the passage beginning "Next, this underlying Mahāyāna (*ken-pen Mo-ho-yen* 根本摩訶衍) includes eight distinctions," as "Mahāyāna of the one substance and one mind (*i-t'i i-hsin Mo-ho-yen* 一體一心摩訶衍) ...," and are apparently composed of two dharmas each corresponding to the "dharma realm of the one mind" (*i-hsin fa-chieh* 一心法界) and the three "greatnesses," which represent the teachings of the Mahāyāna set forth in accordance with the spiritual capacities of sentient beings; against this, the comprehensive underlying substance itself is referred to as the "non-dual Mahāyāna." In the commentation of the "Section Setting Forth the Teaching," these eight are further developed into sixteen attainments, or realizations (*so-ju*, *shonyū* 所入, "what is entered"), and sixteen causes of attainment/realization (*neng-ju*, *nōnyū* 能入, "what can [cause to] enter"), to which is added the non-dual Mahāyāna for a total of thirty-three classes.[8] By this system, the non-dual Mahāyāna becomes reduplicatively classified, but leaving that aside for the time being, these thirty-three dharmas are mentioned in the next quoted passage, as follows.

> Again, to quote:
>
> The profound and immense meaning of the Buddhas (*chu-fo*, *shobutsu* 諸佛) comprehensively includes all the

7. T. vol. 77, pp. 375c–376a; T. vol. 32, p. 601c.
8. T. vol. 32, p. 600a.

teachings heretofore ever expounded. This is because it encompasses the thirty-three dharmas. What does this mean? By "the Buddhas" is signified none other than the non-dual Mahāyāna dharma. This is because the non-dual dharma resembles the Buddhas in terms of their virtues. The *Ta-pen Hua-yen ch'i-ching* 大本華嚴契經 (the larger version [not extant] of the *Avataṃsaka Sūtra*) presents the following statement.

> "The Buddhas of the absolutely complete ocean of virtue (*yüan-yüan hai-te*, *ennen kaitoku* 圓圓海德) are superlative. Not all Buddhas (*i-ch'ieh fo*, *issaibutsu* 一切佛) can realize the absolutely complete ocean of virtue, because of inferiority."

If so, then why is it that the *Fen-liu Hua-yen ch'i-ching* 分流華嚴契經 (the derivative, or current recension [extant] of the *Avataṃsaka Sūtra*) presents the following statement?

> "The three 'worlds' (*san-chung shih-chien*, *sanshu seken* 三種世間: the physical 'world' [器世間], the 'world' of sentient beings [衆生世間], and the 'world' of the Buddha's correct realization of wisdom [智正覺世間]) are the body and mind of [Vai]rocana Buddha (Lu-she-na-fo, Rushana-butsu 盧舍那佛)."

The three "worlds" subsume all dharmas without exception. That Buddha's body and mind likewise encompass all dharmas without exception. Yet even though [Vai]rocana Buddha encompasses all the three "worlds," still it is a case of both encompassing and non-encompassing; for this reason, [in the apparently contradictory statements of the two texts] there is no mistake.[9]

This passage is from near the end of the tenth fascicle of the *Shih Mo-ho-yen lun*, and is commentary on the first line of the concluding verse in the *Ta-ch'eng ch'i-hsin lun*, "The profound and

9. T. vol. 77, p. 376a.

immense meaning of the Buddhas."[10] Since this immense great meaning is said to encompass the thirty-three dharmas, it refers to the Mahāyāna overall, and within this, since it is said that the Buddhas are none other than the non-dual Mahāyāna dharma, then this must indicate dharmakāya in the absolute state (*tzu-hsing fa-shen*, *jishō hosshin* 自性法身) wherein dharma and buddha exist non-dualistically, signifying none other than Vairocana Buddha. This identity of buddha and dharma is the esoteric aspect of this teaching, so that to Kūkai, this non-dual Mahāyāna dharma represented the esoteric teaching, while in comparison with it, the eight fundamental dharmas represented the exoteric teachings, which were taught in response to the varying capacities of the sentient beings belonging to the phenomenal realm. For this reason, speaking in terms of the quoted passages, it was thought that passage (5), which speaks of the non-dual Mahāyāna dharma, corresponds with the tenth stage of development (*jūshin*) while (1)–(4) correspond with the Mahāyāna (*Makaen*) as exoteric teachings. In the quotation (as in the *Shih Mo-ho-yen lun* itself), the reply as to whether the non-dual Mahāyāna dharma is to be considered wisdom or ignorance is not supplied, but it is certainly not a limited realm of ignorance, but rather wisdom itself, the very body of intrinsic enlightenment.

In this way, Kūkai discovered the esoteric import of the non-dual Mahāyāna dharma, which in turn seems to be a key term of central importance in the *Shih Mo-ho-yen lun*. This may be seen from the fact that, as seen in the passages quoted by Kūkai, the concept appears as a unifying theme throughout this commentary on the *Ta-ch'eng ch'i-hsin lun*, in the explanation (fascicle one) on the word "Mahāyāna" in the "Section Setting Forth the Meaning" in the *Ta-ch'eng ch'i-hsin lun*, used to indicate the intrinsically enlightened buddha nature (fascicle five) in the discussion of "perfuming influences" (熏習) within the discussion of the phe-

10. T. vol. 32, p. 668a.

nomenal aspect of mind (心生滅門) in the "Section of the Interpretation," and at the end of the work where the term "the profound and immense meaning of the Buddhas" is understood as referring to it. One can only admire Kūkai's clarity of vision to have discerned the central concept of this treatise and to have established his thesis upon it. The passage that concerns the non-dual Mahāyāna dharma and the eight fundamental dharmas and the commentary on the "profound and immense meaning of the Buddhas," in other words, the passages that form the beginning and end of the *Shih Mo-ho-yen lun*, are quoted by Kūkai in the esoteric commentary on the ninth stage of development in the *Jū jūshin ron*. According to it, the esoteric content of the "profoundest mind (exoteric) that realizes the lack of own being" is explained as the *samādhi* realized by Samantabhadra Bodhisattva (普賢菩薩所證三摩地門) and is also the absolute teaching of the aspiration to enlightenment of Mahāvairocana Tathāgata (大毘盧舍那如來菩提心一門), while as examples of the teachings of the (exoteric) Buddhas and Bodhisattvas, the "complete enlightenment" of the *Sūtra of Complete Enlightenment* (*Yüan-chüeh ching* 圓覺經) and the "Mahāyāna" of the *Ta-ch'eng ch'i-hsin lun* are given, next the *Shih Mo-ho-yen lun* is given, and then a passage is quoted regarding the essential purity of intrinsic enlightenment (性淨本覺) from the discussion of the phenomenal aspect of mind.[11] There then follows a quotation of the section on attainment of enlightenment by the moon-disk meditation (*yüeh-lun-kuan ch'eng-chüeh* 月輪觀成覺) in the *Sūtra of the Dhāraṇī of the Lord Protector of the Borders of the State* (*Shou-hu kuo-chieh-chu t'o-lo-ni ching* 守護國界主陀羅尼經), then again quoting from the *Shih Mo-ho-yen lun*, rounding out the chapter on the "profoundest mind (exoteric) that realizes the lack of own being" with the above-mentioned initial and final two passages.[12] While the *Jū jūshin ron* and *Hizō hō-*

11. T. vol. 77, pp. 357c–358a.
12. T. vol. 77, pp. 358c–359a.

yaku both deal with the same ten categories of the stages of development of mind, the pattern of usage of quotations from the *Shih Mo-ho-yen lun* differs as shown above. However, it is possible to understand that the concept of the non-dual Mahāyāna dharma is employed simply to explain the ninth stage of development from the fact that it is described as not only the *samādhi* realized by Samantabhadra Bodhisattva, but also as none other than the absolute teaching of the aspiration to enlightenment of Mahāvairocana Tathāgata.

II

Thus far we have examined Kūkai's use of the *Shih Mo-ho-yen lun* and considered the reasons for his prominent use of it, but this does not necessarily seem to lead to any conclusions about how Kūkai viewed *tathāgatagarbha* theory. In this regard, the *tathāgatagarbha* theory under consideration here is that such as defined by Fa-tsang 法藏 in the Hua-yen (Kegon 華嚴) doctrine's scheme, that is, a theory directly based on the doctrine of the *Ta-ch'eng ch'i-hsin lun* and indirectly incorporating the doctrines and theories set forth in such sutras as the *Śrīmālādevī-siṃhanāda* and *Laṅkāvatāra* and the treatises *Ratnagotravibhāga* and *Fo-hsing lun* 佛性論 (Treatise on Buddha Nature), and indicating the doctrine referred to under the name of the doctrine of origination dependent on the *tathāgatagarbha* (如來藏緣起宗), also called the doctrine of the true state of reality (實相宗). As for this, in the Hua-yen school's classification of the teachings, it is classified as the final teaching of the Mahāyāna (大乘終教), and yet above this are still to be found the "sudden" (頓) and "perfect" (圓) teachings, so while it represents an important part of the perfect teaching that is the *Avataṃsaka Sūtra* (*Hua-yen ching* 華嚴經), it is not all of it. However, judging from the *Jū jūshin ron*, Kūkai does not seem to deal with *tathāgatagarbha* theory as a cohesive, autonomous entity such as that subsumed under the classification of the doctrine of origination dependent on the *tathāgatagarbha*. From the extent of our investigations, it appears that Kūkai's references to *tathāgatagarbha* theory—which in this case may be taken to be equal in extent to the doctrines comprising the *Ratnagotravibhāga*, which represents the bounds of the theory as it is unmistakably known to have existed in India—are limited to the following:

(1) In the chapter on the sixth stage of development ("the Mahāyāna mind with sympathetic concern for others"), regarding the fifth division of the objective consciousness-only (所觀唯識), the consciousness arrived at by discarding appearances and realizing the essence (遣相證性識), it is mentioned that the *Śrīmālādevī-siṃhanāda Sūtra* refers to this as the "inherently immaculate mind" (自性清淨心);[13]

(2) In the chapter on the seventh stage, *Kakushin fushō jūshin* (覺心不生住心) ("realizing the mind as unborn"), regarding "unconditioned *saṃsāra*..." (無爲生死), this is mentioned as being made clear in the *Śrīmālādevī-siṃhanāda Sūtra* and the *Ratnagotravibhāga* and *Fo-hsing lun* treatises;[14]

(3) Quoting Fa-yün 法雲, of Kuang-chai-ssu 光宅寺 temple, it is stated, "the Buddha-fruit has the four categories of eternity, bliss, personality, and purity (常樂我淨)";[15]

(4) At the end of the eighth chapter, *Ichidō mui jūshin* (一道無爲住心) ("the unconditioned mind of the absolute path"), the *Sūtra Describing the Ritual of the Lotus Sūtra* (法華儀軌經) is quoted in the esoteric interpretation thus: "All sentient beings within their own bodies have the buddha nature, and fully possess the matrix of the tathāgata (*tathāgatagarbha*); there is not one being that is not a vessel for the unsurpassed dharma of enlightenment";[16]

---

13. T. vol. 77, p. 345b.
14. T. vol. 77, p. 347a.
15. T. vol. 77, p. 348a.
16. T. vol. 77, p. 353a.

(5) As part of the discussion of the ninth stage ("the profoundest [exoteric] mind that realizes the lack of own-being"), where the phrase "the dharma realm of suchness (*tathatā*) does not rigidly preserve a self-identity (*svabhāvatā*) but exists following the temporal conditions (*pratyaya*)" (眞如法界不守自性隨緣) is quoted from Fa-tsang's *Treatise on the Five Teachings* (五教章) as illustrating the profound meaning of the *Avataṃsaka Sūtra*, Kūkai quotes in this connection from the *Laṅkāvatāra Sūtra*: "The [supramundane] *tathāgatagarbha* undergoes painful and pleasurable experiences and in line with these causes (*hetu*) arises and dissipates [in the phenomenal realm]," as well as from the *Ta-ch'eng ch'i-hsin lun*: "The inherently immaculate mind, when stirred by the winds of ignorance, moves and becomes defiled."[17]

In addition to these references, in the esoteric interpretation (深祕釋), the previously mentioned reference from the section commenting on the significance of the word "Mahāyāna" in the *Ta-ch'eng ch'i-hsin lun*, the three "greatnesses" referred to are none other than *tathāgatagarbha* theory, and the phrase "intrinsic enlightenment" (本覺) as well is a term from the *Ta-ch'eng ch'i-hsin lun* that signifies the suchness inherent within sentient beings, in other words, *tathāgatagarbha* or *buddhadhātu* (*fo-hsing*, *busshō* 佛性).

From only these scattered quotations, it is not possible to fully ascertain Kūkai's comprehension of *tathāgatagarbha* theory, but one is forced to conclude that he did not have an awareness of it as an autonomous line of doctrine. Nonetheless, underlying the thought of Kūkai, a concept of intrinsic enlightenment that derives from the *Shih Mo-ho-yen lun* and *Ta-ch'eng ch'i-hsin lun* and was inherited from the doctrine of the Hua-yen school undoubtedly plays a major role. It also seems possible to prove this to be the precursor of the intrinsic (original) enlightenment doc-

17. T. vol. 77, p. 353c and p. 354a, respectively.

trine (本覺法門) that later came to exert such great influence on the history of Japanese thought, first appearing in Kūkai and then being transplanted into the esoteric doctrine of the Japanese Tendai sect (*Taimitsu* 台密).[18]

However, along with this there is an even more essential aspect in the relationship of the esoteric Buddhism of Kūkai with *tathāgatagarbha* theory. This is found in the known history of the development of esoteric doctrine in Indian Buddhism, that is, in the line of development from the *Avataṃsaka Sūtra* to the *Mahāvairocana Sūtra* (*Vairocanābhisaṃbodhi-sūtra* 大日經) to the *Vajraśekhara Sūtra*, which is recognizable even from the identity of the central Buddha in all three sutras, namely, Vairocana Tathāgata. In this process of development, *tathāgatagarbha* theory may be viewed as forming a bridge between the *Avataṃsaka Sūtra* and esoteric Buddhism, perhaps in the sense of acting to solidify the doctrines that served as a preparatory stage leading to the appearance of esoteric Buddhism. (In China, *tathāgatagarbha* thought was a kind of catalyst in the formation of the Chinese Hua-yen school. The introduction of esoteric Buddhism into China just during the period when the Hua-yen school was strongly flourishing may be thought to be responsible for the extremely strong coloration by *tathāgatagarbha* theory of esoteric interpretations. Of course Kūkai was heir to this particular line of development, regarding which further discussion will appear later.) As evidence for this, we shall next consider the content of the important authoritative text on which Kūkai based his argument in the *Sokushin jōbutsu gi*, the treatise *P'u-t'i-hsin lun* 菩提心論 (Treatise on the Aspiration to Enlightenment [*bodhicitta*]), more formally known as *Chin-kang-ting yü-ch'ieh chung fa a-nou-to-lo san-miao-san-*

18. See also Tamura Yoshirō 田村芳朗, "Mikkyō to hongaku shisō" 密教と本覺思想 [Esoteric Buddhism and the doctrine of original enlightenment], in *Daijō Bukkyō kara Mikkyō e* 大乘佛教から密教へ [From the Mahāyāna to esoteric Buddhism: Papers collected in honor of Dr. Katsumata Shunkyō's 勝又俊教 seventieth birthday] (Tokyo: Shunjūsha, 1981), pp. 887–897.

p'u-t'i-hsin lun 金剛頂瑜伽中發阿耨多羅三藐三菩提心論 (Treatise on Giving Rise to the Aspiration to the Unsurpassed Enlightenment [*anuttarasamyaksaṃbodhi*] Within the Vajraśekhara Yoga).

III

The *P'u-t'i-hsin lun* is traditionally asserted to be a translation by Amoghavajra (Pu-k'ung 不空) of a work by Nāgārjuna. As was the case with the *Shih Mo-ho-yen lun*, Kūkai evidences no doubts about the supposed authorship by Nāgārjuna, quoting from it in his *Sokushin jōbutsu gi* and *Hizō hōyaku* as "the bodhisattva Nāgārjuna's *Treatise on the Aspiration to Enlightenment*" (龍猛[菩薩]菩提心論). However, there are many dubious points concerning the text's lineage, and it is at least certain that the author was not Nāgārjuna.[19] (This point will be touched upon later.) Be that as it may, content-wise, the text treats the functional aspects (行相) of the aspiration to enlightenment (*bodhicitta*) based on the doctrines of the *Vajraśekhara Sūtra*.

The treatise begins, "The great *ācārya* (teacher) speaks [as follows]" (大阿闍梨云), stating that those of excellent capacity ("roots," or faculties) and excellent wisdom (上根上智) should not desire after the teachings of the heretical paths or two [lesser, i.e., non-Mahāyāna] vehicles, but rather should embark on the Buddha-vehicle and pledge in their hearts to aspire to the unsurpassed enlightenment, and likewise, desiring through *yoga* (瑜伽) to perfect the body of the bodhisattvas (i.e., the esoteric practice) is also to be known as aspiration to [the unsurpassed] enlightenment; the discourse then continues to explain that as functional aspects of the aspiration to enlightenment there are three divisions (門), namely, the highest truth (勝義), the vow of practice (行願), and

19. Mochizuki, op. cit., pp. 671–694, latter part, chapter 12, section 4: "Ryūju-zō to tsutaerareru Kongōchō bodaishin ron" 龍樹造と傳えられる金剛頂菩提心論 [The *Chin-kang-ting p'u-t'i-hsin lun* traditionally ascribed to Nāgārjuna].

samādhi (三摩地) (spiritual concentration attained through meditation).[20] However, "only within the Mantrayāna teachings is there attainment of buddhahood in this very existence, and for this reason *samādhi* is spoken of," so that there is a total of three divisions, but regarding all other (Mahāyāna) "teachings, it is missing and not mentioned." In other words, this *samādhi* is to be found only in the esoteric teachings and is none other than the "*Vajraśekhara-yoga*" referred to in the title.

Next, the functional aspects of the aspiration to enlightenment will be briefly explained in the order of vow of practice, highest truth, and *samādhi*.

The first, vow of practice is defined as the practitioner's constantly giving rise to the thought, "I will benefit (利益) the entire world of beings without exception (無餘有情界) and cause them to have peace of mind (安樂)," while viewing all sentient beings (含識) of the ten quarters (north, northeast, east, etc., and above and below) as being no different from one's own person. In this case, benefit means to cause all beings to become secure in the stage of the highest enlightenment; as proof (in contrast to the view that some beings are unqualified to attain the highest enlightenment), it is stated that the Mantrayāna practitioner knows that "all sentient beings possess the *tathāgatagarbha*," while as doctrinal evidence, the *Avataṃsaka Sūtra* is quoted:

> There does not exist even one sentient being who lacks the Tathāgata's wisdom. It is only a matter of not realizing this due to delusion, misguided views, and false attachments. If delusion is abandoned, then the wisdoms of all-knowledge (一切智), cognition of the self-existent (自然智), and nonobstruction (無礙智) will immediately become manifest.

This is none other than the famous passage of the "Chapter on Origination from the Tathāgata-nature" (如來性起品) that includes

20. T. vol. 32, p. 572bc.

the metaphor of "the thousand worlds contained in a mote" (微塵含千) and is the origin of the *tathāgatagarbha* theory that started in the *Tathāgatagarbha Sūtra*.[21] Next, regarding "causing [them] to have peace of mind," it is explained that the Mantrayāna practitioner does not think lightly of any being because he knows that all beings will ultimately attain buddhahood; because of great compassion, he seeks to provide even unto offering up his body and life in response to the needs of sentient beings; and when sentient beings have entered into a friendly relationship with the practitioner, he uses suitable expedient means to guide them towards enlightenment. This discussion is reminiscent of the passage found in the *Saddharmapuṇḍarīka-upadeśa* (法華經論) explaining the deeds of the bodhisattva Sadāparibhūta (常不輕菩薩) from the *tathāgatagarbha* viewpoint,[22] but is probably better characterized as a generally representative Mahāyāna teaching. In any case, the important point of this passage[23] is the *Avataṃsaka Sūtra* interpretation based on *tathāgatagarbha* theory.

Next, the highest truth is defined as seeing that all dharmas are without immutable substance. Various levels are distinguished among the methods and objects of this meditation, starting with the common folk who hanker after notoriety and material wealth and who are carried away by the three poisons (greed, hatred, and ignorance) and the five desires (corresponding to the five sensory data, or to desire for property, sexual love, food and drink, fame, and sleep) and extending to the followers of the heretical teachings who seek long life and rebirth in the heavens, to the followers of the two (lesser) Buddhist vehicles who are attached to the fourfold Noble Truth and the twelvefold chain of causation, and

21. *Hua-yen-ching* 華嚴經, "Hsing-ch'i p'in" 性起品 (60-fascicle *Hua-yen ching*), T. vol. 9, p. 623c; "Ju-lai ch'u-hsien p'in" 如來出現品 (80-fascicle *Hua-yen ching*), T. vol. 10, p. 272c. The quoted passage is the same as the text of the latter.

22. T. vol. 26, p. 9a.

23. T. vol. 32, pp. 572c–573a.

then to the followers of the Mahāyāna, who have discarded such attachments to these dharmas, given rise to the Mahāyāna mind of seeking to benefit sentient beings, practice the bodhisattva's path, which consists of thousands of deeds corresponding to the six perfections (*pāramitā*) requiring three *asaṃkhyeya* (= 3×10^{52}) *kalpas* of time to complete, and aim to attain the buddha-fruit. In contrast, the Mantrayāna devotee sees the lack of immutable nature of dharmas, with great compassion for all sentient beings transcends the realms of the heretical paths and two (lesser) vehicles, and furthermore by practice of the "highest dharma of *yoga*" surpasses the ten stages of the bodhisattvas; quoting from the *Mahāvairocana Sūtra*, the realization "all dharmas are without distinguishable characteristic, which is called the characteristic of empty space" (諸法無相，謂虚空相), is referred to as the "highest true aspiration to enlightenment" (勝義菩提心), and after explaining this in terms of the "buddha-mind" (佛心) of the *Avataṃsaka Sūtra*, *Kuan Wu-liang-shou ching* 觀無量壽經 (Sūtra of the Meditation on the Amitābha [Amitāyus] Buddha), and *Nirvāṇa Sūtra*, completes the explanation with the famous passage from the *Mahāvairocana Sūtra*: "the aspiration to enlightenment is the cause, great compassion is the root, and expedient means are the completion" (菩提爲因，大悲爲根，方便爲究竟).[24] The division into the various levels or stages of practice mentioned here seems to have been based upon the picture presented in the "Chapter on the Stages of Development of Mind" (住心品) of the *Mahāvairocana Sūtra*, Kūkai's model for his theory of the ten stages, and thus he includes this passage in his *Hizō hōyaku*, dividing the quotation in order among the first stage (common folk [異生]), the third stage (heretics [外道]), the fourth stage (name of text mentioned only, not quoted), the fifth stage (two [lesser] vehicles), and the sixth stage (Mahāyāna); furthermore, in the chapter on the seventh stage, the passage from "[The devotee] will learn that all dharmas

---

24. T. vol. 32, p. 573a-c.

are void, and having realized that dharmas are originally unborn, [he will know that] the essence of mind itself is suchness and will not discriminate body or mind" to "When the illusion ceases, the fountainhead of mind will [return to its] void and tranquil state" is quoted to describe the spiritual state at that stage, while in the chapter on the ninth stage, the passage quoted as a doctrinal authority in the discussion of this stage starts earlier in the text, from the beginning of the definition of "lack of immutable nature" (無自性), where it reads: "The dharmas of the unenlightened realms arise from delusion." (This passage continues to beyond the end of the passage quoted in the chapter on the seventh stage, down to "Whosoever possesses this mind is capable of turning the wheel of Dharma [preaching] for the benefit of himself and others," but is abbreviated and skips most of the earlier quotation except for the end, i.e., "When illusion ceases, the fountainhead mind is void and tranquil.")[25] In short, it may be seen that the discussion of this second functional aspect (行相) is based on the *Mahāvairocana Sūtra* and touches upon the various levels or stages of the premised meditations (reaching to the ninth of Kūkai's ten stages of development of mind).

The discussion of the third functional aspect, *samādhi*, consists of an abbreviated description and commentary concerning the five-phased meditation leading to attainment of the body (of Mahāvairocana) (五相成身觀) as taught in the *Vajraśekhara Sūtra* and represents the ultimate teaching of the *P'u-t'i-hsin lun*, the teaching of the attainment of buddhahood in this very existence, which is the *yoga* unique to the esoteric school. The section con-

25. First stage: 龍猛菩提心論云。謂凡夫執著名聞… (T. vol. 77, p. 364a); third stage: 龍猛菩薩菩提心論云。諸外道等戀其身命… (ibid., p. 365c); fourth stage: 菩提心論證文, 與下文心雜擧… (ibid., p. 368c); fifth stage: 龍猛菩薩菩提心論云。又二乘之人聲聞執四諦法… (ibid., p. 369b); sixth stage: 龍猛菩薩菩提心論云。又有衆生發大乘心… (ibid., p. 370a); seventh stage: 菩提心論云。當知一切法空… (ibid., p. 370c); ninth stage: 龍猛菩提心論云。夫迷途之法… (ibid., p. 372c).

cludes with what is known as the "*Gāthā* Extolling the Aspiration to Enlightenment" (讚菩提心偈):[26]

> If a man, seeking after the wisdom of the Buddha,
> Should complete the aspiration to enlightenment,
> He will, even in the very body produced by his parents,
> Swiftly realize the stage of the Greatly Enlightened One.
> 若人求佛慧，通達菩提心，父母所生身，速證大覺位

This verse and the passage found near the beginning of the *P'u-t'i-hsin lun* that starts, "Only within the Mantrayāna teaching is there attainment of buddhahood in this very existence..." (mentioned above) were highly valued by Kūkai and used by him as doctrinal evidence in his *Sokushin jōbutsu gi*.[27] It should also be noted that the entire text of the above passage explaining *samādhi*, the third functional aspect, was quoted in the *Hizō hōyaku* and serves to weld together chapter ten on "the glorious mind of the esoteric teachings."[28]

IV

The foregoing constitutes a brief look at the content of the *P'u-t'i-hsin lun* and its connection with Kūkai. As touched upon earlier, both this text and the *Shih Mo-ho-yen lun* are forgeries originating in China, but whereas the *Shih Mo-ho-yen lun* seems to have been an intentional misrepresentation from the first, the *P'u-t'i-hsin lun* shows signs of having gained its false attribution after the fact. This is suggested by the existence of a recension (Korean edition) as evidenced by the *Taishō Tripiṭaka* text that has, instead of "The great *ācārya* speaks" (大阿闍梨云), "The *ācārya* Ta-kuang-chih speaks" (大廣智阿闍梨云 [Ta-kuang-chih being one of translator Amoghavajra's titles]), allowing the possibility that the

26. T. vol. 32, pp. 573c–574c.
27. T. vol. 77, p. 381c.
28. T. vol. 77, pp. 373b–374b: 又龍猛菩提心論云。第三言三摩地者....

text constitutes a lecture by Amoghavajra that was noted down by his disciple or disciples. However, even in light of such a possibility, it is hard to explain the presence of such obviously Chinese Buddhist elements as the quotation from the *Mahāvairocana Sūtra* commentary *Ta-jih-ching shu* 大日經疏 under the section on *samādhi* and the appearance of the (T'ien-t'ai) theory of the four levels of the Buddha's enlightenment (四佛智見) corresponding to the *Lotus Sūtra* doctrine of *k'ai-shih-wu-ju* 開示悟入) (opening [making accessible], revealing, causing to realize, and causing to enter the Buddha's enlightenment) being applied to the interpretation of the five esoteric meanings of the Sanskrit letter "*a*" (阿字); if this really is the work of Amoghavajra, one cannot avoid entertaining doubts about just how authentically he appreciated the true intent of the *Vajraśekhara Sūtra*, which he took such pains to bring back to China from his journey to Ceylon.

During the past few years, Dr. Tsuda Shin'ichi has published a number of papers expressing his position that esoteric Buddhism and Mahāyāna Buddhism are mutually exclusive (in his words, esoteric Buddhism stands in a "critical" relationship with respect to the Mahāyāna), and that this esoteric Buddhism is first definitely established with the appearance of the *Vajraśekhara Sūtra*, whereas the *Mahāvairocana Sūtra* represents nothing more than the limit of development of the Mahāyāna position towards esotericism while still remaining within the province of Mahāyāna.[29] This view is put forth based upon the development of esoteric Buddhism in India after the *Vajraśekhara Sūtra*, and seems to have sufficient logical grounds. When one examines the esoteric Buddhism of China and Japan from this point of view, the doctrine that was transmitted along the lineage from Amoghavajra to Hui-kuo 惠果 to Kūkai appears doctrinally as a rather lukewarm compromise. In particular, Kūkai's initiation by Hui-kuo into both

29. Most recently in "Kūkai no kaishakugaku" 空海の解釋學, translated as "The Hermeneutics of Kūkai" in *Acta Asiatica* 47 (1985), pp. 82–108.

garbha and *vajra maṇḍala*s (respectively embodying the *Mahāvairocana* and *Vajraśekhara* doctrines), a fact of which he was extremely proud, seems a most uncritical, even self-contradictory, act in light of the antipathetic relation in which the two exist, as of two soaring steep slopes that share between them but the narrowest of ridges, with the *Mahāvairocana Sūtra* on the one side, representing a religion of gradual practice (*caryā* 行) devoted to the salvation of all beings, versus the *Vajraśekhara Sūtra* on the other side, representing a religion of *yoga* emphasizing direct union with the *dharma*-body of Vairocana. However, the *P'u-t'i-hsin lun* exhibits a similar position, appropriating the attainment of buddhahood in the present lifetime as its ideal of *yoga*, but simultaneously integrating the meditative practices of the *Avataṃsaka Sūtra* and *Mahāvairocana Sūtra* under the headings of vow of practice and highest truth. In no way can it be accused of trying to set the esoteric and exoteric doctrines against one another, nor does it negate the practice-oriented position of "attainment of buddhahood after three *kalpa*s (三劫成佛)." If, as suspected from the evidence of the documents themselves, this treatise is based on the oral teaching of Amoghavajra, then he also will have to be regarded as a man of compromise. Should this be the case, then in spite of the fact that Amoghavajra was of foreign nationality, it is perhaps best when appraising his thought to bear in mind the fact that he had lived in China ever since his youth. In other words, the very soil on which the Buddhism of China was cultivated may be sought against a background of compromise and adaptation.

To come to the point, the characteristic "soil" underlying the Sinicized form of Buddhism is the basic position of the "sudden" (*tun* 頓) doctrine. An example of this may be seen in the debate held in eighth-century Tibet concerning the Buddhist doctrines imported from China versus those from India (the debate of bSam-yas, 793 A.D.), where the Chinese representative, Hva śaṅ

Mahāyāna (Ta-ch'eng ho-shang 大乘和尚), defended the doctrine of sudden enlightenment (*tun-wu* 頓悟) as his fundamental position, while the Indian representative, Kamalaśīla, presented his position of gradual practice (*chien-hsiu* 漸修). With the victory of the latter, the orthodoxy of Indian Mahāyāna Buddhism became officially recognized in Tibet. The idea of gradual practice is more specifically the *caryā* religion of attainment of buddhahood after three *asaṃkhyeya kalpa*s based on the vow to lead all sentient beings to enlightenment. On the other hand, the foundation of the views of Hva śaṅ Mahāyāna was the Chinese Ch'an (Zen) 禪 sect, but with the *śamatha-vipaśyanā* (*chih-kuan* 止觀; quiescent concentration and insight meditation) practice of the T'ien-t'ai school as an indirect influence. The Hua-yen school established its own position of the "perfectly complete" teaching (*yüan-chiao* 圓教) in contrast to the T'ien-t'ai and the Ch'an "sudden" doctrine and classified it above the latter. In the Hua-yen position can be discovered the attitude of attempting total integration of not only both the "primitive" and "developed" doctrines of the Mahāyāna (始教, 終教), but even the three vehicles altogether, and yet after all it is fundamentally a position that belongs to the "sudden" camp. In the first place, it must be remembered that the *Avataṃsaka Sūtra* itself, while setting forth the ten stages of a bodhisattva's development (十地) and teaching that it requires three *asaṃkhyeya kalpa*s to attain buddhahood, simultaneously declares that "immediately upon the first arousal of the aspiration to enlightenment, perfect enlightenment is attained" (初發心時便成正覺). Since the esoteric developments of *bodhicitta* and attainment of buddhahood in a single lifetime can be said to have evolved from an extrapolation of the doctrinal line represented by the latter *Avataṃsaka* stand, it is obvious that the "sudden enlightenment" position is not exclusively Chinese in origin, but again, it is also difficult to imagine that the Chinese, unlike the Indians, gave much serious consideration to the concept of requiring such an astronomical length of time as three *asaṃkhyeya kalpa*s for attainment of enlightenment and buddhahood. At the very least, it seems quite likely that to the Chinese mind the true intention of the *Avataṃsaka Sūtra* is to be found in the latter of the above two *Avataṃsaka* positions. Dr. Tsuda, in his outline division of the schools of Buddhism into the "religion of *caryā*" versus the "religion of *yoga*" mentioned above, recognizes the membership of Ch'an and T'ien-t'ai, and the Chinese Pure Land (Ching-t'u, Jōdo 淨土) school as well, in the lineage of religions of *yoga*, but by expanding the interpretation of this argument, it is possible to claim that even without need of the importation of esoteric Buddhist influence, the Buddhism of China, being the Buddhism of sudden enlightenment, already exhibited a predilection towards religions of *yoga*. This predisposition may be seen in the Chinese development of *tathāgatagarbha* theory in the form of the emphasis on intrinsic enlightenment (本覺) and the production of the text *Shih Mo-ho-yen lun*.

This inclination found in Chinese Buddhism towards the "sudden" teachings may be thought to have contributed to the ease of acceptance of the esoteric school's doctrines, but in fact this characteristic is only actually found in the form of doctrines of texts such as the *P'u-t'i-hsin lun*, where the scheme "exoteric Buddhism = three *asaṃkhyeya*s to attain buddhahood" versus "esoteric Buddhism = buddhahood in this lifetime" has become somewhat blurred, for example, the doctrine regarding *samādhi* in that text, which is explained as the "*adhiṣṭhāna* of the three mysteries" (*san-mi chia-ch'ih* 三密加持: the doctrine that the three mysteries of Buddha's body, speech, and mind are accessible to men through Buddha's Grace [= sustaining power: *adhiṣṭhāna* 加持] only by performance of the three rituals described next), under which is subsumed the acts of making the prescribed hand-gestures (*mudrā* 印契), uttering the proper formula (*mantra* 眞言), and becoming absorbed in a purifying state of meditation (*yoga*

瑜伽). Looking at it another way, this situation was responsible for the relatively blunted perception by the Japanese and Chinese Buddhist community of the revolutionary nature of the doctrines of the *Vajraśekhara Sūtra* compared to India, thus resulting in a lack of appreciation of the true intent of the scripture.

As is well-known, the popularity of esoteric Buddhism waned in China not long after the time of Hui-kuo and Kūkai. In contrast, the theoretical grounding and systematization of the doctrines by Kūkai in Japan led to esoteric Buddhism's firm and independent establishment, continuation, and position of vitality. In the process of working out this theoretical grounding, the type of *tathāgatagarbha* thought represented by such texts as the *Shih Mo-ho-yen lun* played an important role.[30] The resulting esoteric Buddhist doctrine was admittedly not the kind of doctrine that Dr. Tsuda points out as representing a standpoint "critically" opposed to that of the Mahāyāna, but by the same token, one cannot dismiss it as not esotericism. This is because the Mahāyāna Buddhism of China already possessed a sufficiently strong "*yogic* religious" tendency. In turn, Japanese Buddhism in general became more and more colored by "sudden enlightenment" doctrinal tendencies due to the influence of Kūkai's esoteric Buddhism, showing strong leanings towards the "attainment of buddhahood in this lifetime" position. This tendency is represented by the so-called doctrine of intrinsic enlightenment (本覺法門). This doctrine entered the Tendai school by way of the esoteric branch of the school (*Tai-*

30. Yoshida Hiroaki 吉田宏晢, in his "Mikkyō no tetsugakuteki rikai" 密教の哲學的理解 [A philosophical understanding of esoteric Buddhism], *Gendai shisō* 現代思想 11-9 (1983), pp. 100–123, has pointed out that the conception of the two verses, eight lines, appearing in the *Sokushin jōbutsu gi* (as a summary of the esoteric doctrine) is based entirely on the *Ta-ch'eng ch'i-hsin lun* and *Shih Mo-ho-yen lun* (ibid., p. 111). See also the same author's "Kōbō daishi kyōgaku to *Shaku Makaen ron*" 弘法大師教學と『釋摩訶衍論』 [Kōbō Daishi's doctrine and the *Shih Mo-ho-yen lun*], pts. 1 & 2, *Chizan gakuhō* 智山學報 23 & 24 (1974).

mitsu), eventually swelling into the undercurrent that developed into the various forms of Kamakura-period Japanese Buddhism, including Jōdo and Zen. From the viewpoint of the present author's particular speciality, this stream of thought introduced by Kūkai represents a distinctly Chinese-Japanese development of the *tathāgatagarbha* theory, and will be a topic for further treatment hereafter.

*Saṃsāra eva nirvāṇam**

1.

The *Shushōgi* 修證義 (The Significance of Practice and Realization), the basic holy text of the Sōtō 曹洞 sect in Japan,[1] begins with the following sentences:

> To realize what is life and to realize what is death is the biggest motive for Buddhists. When there is a buddha in Samsaric life, then the latter will be no more. Keeping in mind that Samsaric life is nothing but Nirvāṇa (**saṃsāra eva nirvāṇam*), one should feel neither disgust with Samsaric life nor wish for Nirvāṇa. (When one is able to fulfill this condition,) then one will for the first time be free from Samsaric life.

These sentences are originally found in the *Shōbōgenzō* 正法眼藏 of Dōgen 道元,[2] the founder of the Sōtō sect in Japan. Thus we realize that Dōgen's teaching is fundamentally established on the basis of the idea of the unity of Saṃsāra and Nirvāṇa.

Not only Dōgen or the Sōtō sect but almost all Japanese Buddhist sects also believe in this doctrine of the unity of Saṃsāra and Nirvāṇa, regarding it as the quintessence of Mahāyāna

---

* Originally published in Jonathan A. Silk, ed., *Wisdom, Compassion, and the Search for Understanding: The Buddhist Studies Legacy of Gadjin M. Nagao* (Honolulu: University of Hawai'i Press, 2000), pp. 333–346.

1. The *Shushōgi* 修證義 was originally compiled by Ōuchi Seiran 大内青巒 and recognized with some revision as one of its holy texts by the Sōtō sect in 1890.

2. The first sentence is taken from the section on *shoaku makusa* 諸悪莫作, and the other three from the section on *shōji* 生死. See Mizuno Kōgen 水野弘元, *Shushōgi kōwa* 修証義講話 (Tokyo: Sōtōshū Shūmuchō 曹洞宗宗務廳, 1968): 45.

Buddhism.[3]

What is the significance of this doctrine and where is its origin in Mahāyāna scriptures? The following article is a note on these points.

2.

In our Japanese Buddhist tradition, the Chinese translations of the Tripiṭaka have been used as the sacred canon throughout the ages. In the context of the idea of the unity of Saṃsāra and Nirvāṇa, the origin of the phrase *sheng-ssu chi nieh-p'an* 生死即涅槃 should be sought for first of all in the Chinese Tripiṭaka. In spite of its popularity, however, the first appearance of this phrase has not yet been clarified. Even modern Buddhist scholars have not been able to clarify the source. For example, the *Mochizuki Bukkyō daijiten*, referring to the phrase under the item *shōji soku nehan*, mentions a passage in Paramārtha's translation of the *Mahāyāna-saṃgraha* as its source, and offers an explanation with the help of Vasubandhu's Bhāṣya on the same text.[4] (I will refer to this passage in detail below.) But there is no direct reference to any sūtra sources. Other sources referred to by Mochizuki are Chinese works such as the *Wang-sheng lun chu* 往生論註 of T'an-luan 曇鸞, the *T'ien-t'ai ssu-chiao i* 天台四教儀 and the *Mo-ho chih-kuan* 摩訶止觀 of Chih-i 智顗, and among Japanese sources, Shinran's 親鸞 works. Oda's *Bukkyō jiten*[5] mentions, besides an apparently erroneous reference to a verse of the *Mahāsaṃnipāta-sūtra*, the

3. This idea was often misunderstood under the influence of the doctrine of original enlightenment (*hongaku hōmon* 本覺法門) to mean that there is no use practicing to attain enlightenment. Dōgen corrected this misunderstanding with this statement.

4. Mochizuki Shinkō 望月信亨, *Bukkyō daijiten* 佛教大辭典 (Tokyo: Sekai Seiten Kankō Kyōkai 世界聖典刊行協会): 3.2621a.

5. Oda Tokunō 織田得能, *Bukkyō jiten* 佛教辭典 (New Corrected Edition, Tokyo: Daizō Shuppan 大蔵出版, 1974): 780a. See now the Addendum to this paper.

Mo-ho chih-kuan as the first source, while the *Bukkyōgo daijiten*[6] of H. Nakamura mentions Japanese sources only (the *Ippen goroku* 一遍語錄 and the *Shōshinge* 正信偈), referring in addition to Sanskrit phrases of similar import such as *saṃsāraśānty-ekarasa* from the *Mahāyānasūtrālaṃkāra*.[7]

Generally speaking, in the Buddhist tradition when we meet a phrase consisting of a pair of concepts contrary to each other, we are easily reminded of the doctrine of the entrance into non-duality of the *Vimalakīrtinirdeśa*. And in fact, we find in the *Wang-sheng lun chu* just referred to the following passage:

> The one way (一道) means the unobstructed way. Here "unobstructed" means to know that Saṃsāra is nothing but Nirvāṇa. In this way the doctrine of the entrance into non-duality as such has the characteristics of nonobstruction.[8]

In the *Vimalakīrtinirdeśa*, however, we cannot find exactly the same phrase, although there is a passage expressing a similar meaning. In the chapter called "The doctrine of the entrance into non-duality," we find the following as the words of Bodhisattva Sumati (善意):

> Here "the two" means Saṃsāra and Nirvāṇa. If one sees the nature of Saṃsāra, then to him there is no Saṃsāra. There is neither bondage nor release, nothing is born and nothing perishes. To understand in this way is called entrance into the doctrine of non-duality.[9]

In this way we realize that the non-duality of Saṃsāra and Nirvāṇa is established through an understanding of the nature of Saṃsāra as of no reality, and that this understanding is nothing

---

6. Nakamura Hajime 中村元, *Bukkyōgo daijiten* 佛教語大辞典 (Tokyo: Tokyo Shoseki 東京書籍): 1.707d (s.v. *shōji soku nehan*) and 708a (s.v. *shōji nehan*).

7. *Mahāyāna-sūtrālaṃkāra*, ed. Sylvain Lévi (Paris: Librairie Honoré Champion, 1907): 9 (v. II.3). See below, n. 30.

8. T. vol. 40, p. 843c.

9. 維摩詰所説經, trans. by Kumārajīva, T. vol. 14, p. 551a.

but the attainment of Nirvāṇa. This passage should be regarded as one of the Mahāyāna scriptural sources of the concept in question here, although it does not state the idea literally.

3.

Prior to entering into an investigation of the original text of the passage of the *Mahāyānasaṃgraha* referred to above and its meaning, let us look at the development of the idea in question in those Mahāyāna works which we may suppose to have been composed before the time of Asaṅga and Vasubandhu.

The *Ta chih-tu lun* 大智度論 in one hundred volumes, translated by Kumārajīva, is the greatest source book in the Chinese Tripiṭaka of not only Mahāyāṇistic but also Abhidharmic concepts and doctrines as well. In spite of its encyclopedic character, however, there are rather few references to the idea of the unity of Saṃsāra and Nirvāṇa. Only the following three examples have been found so far.

> 1. (Bodhisattvas) are fearless, having accumulated the powers of immeasurable wisdom and compassion. As is said in the stanzas:
>
> If one could destroy evils, even the smallest ones,
> For him, being of great virtue, there would be no wish unfulfilled.
> This person of great wisdom would have no sufferings in the world;
> Therefore, for one like him, Saṃsāra and Nirvāṇa are but one (生死涅槃一). (T. vol. 25, p. 101a)
>
> 2. And again Bodhisattvas, having known the characteristics of things, do not regard defilements as evils, nor regard virtuous qualities as excellent. And so they do not feel disgust for defilements, nor feel affection for virtuous qualities. Due to this power of wisdom, they are able to practise

patience (*kṣānti*). As is said in the stanzas:

The Bodhisattva has cut off the evils as far as those of atomic size without residue,
His virtues and merits are measureless, actions created by him are never undone.
Due to his power of wisdom the Bodhisattva cannot suffer from defilements;
Therefore, he knows the characteristics of things: Saṃsāra and Nirvāṇa are one and non-dual (生死涅槃一無二). (ibid., p. 169bc)

The stanzas quoted in the above two examples are probably from some canonical works, but I have so far been unable to identify them.

3. And next, in the teachings for Disciples and Self-enlightened ones, it is not taught that the world (Saṃsāra) is Nirvāṇa. Why? Because (their) wisdom cannot penetrate deep into dharmas. (On the contrary,) in the teachings for Bodhisattvas, it is taught that the world (Saṃsāra) is Nirvāṇa, because their wisdom penetrates deep into dharmas. As the Buddha told Subhūti:

> Matter is nothing but emptiness. Emptiness is nothing but matter. (In the same way) sensation, conception, volitions, and cognition are nothing but emptiness. Emptiness is nothing but sensation, conception, volitions, and cognition. (In the same way as far as) emptiness is nothing but Nirvāṇa, Nirvāṇa is nothing but emptiness.

Also it is said in the *Madhyamakaśāstra*:

Nirvāṇa is not different from the world (Saṃsāra), the world is not different from Nirvāṇa,
Because the extreme of Nirvāṇa and the extreme of the world (Saṃsāra) are the same and of no difference. (ibid.,

pp. 197c–198a)

Of the two quotations above, the first one seems to be from the *Prajñāpāramitā*. In Kumārajīva's translation of the *Larger Prajñāpāramitā*, a similar passage is found in the chapter on Māyā (T. vol. 8, p. 240b). A parallel passage in the *Pañcaviṃśati Prajñāpāramitā* reads as follows:[10]

> *punar aparaṃ, Subhūte, bodhisattvo mahāsattvaḥ prajñāpāramitāyāṃ carann evaṃ pratyavekṣate: na rūpaśūnyatayā rūpaṃ śūnyaṃ, rūpam eva śūnyatā, śūnyataiva rūpam* | *na vedanaśūnyatayā ... na vijñānaśūnyatayā ...* (*yāvat*) *buddhadharmā eva śūnyatā śūnyataiva buddhadharmāḥ* |

Here *dharma*s are mentioned in a series as far as the eighteen qualities exclusive to Buddhas. But there is no reference to Nirvāṇa, although insofar as it is a concept Nirvāṇa is a *dharma*, and hence it too is logically to be identified with emptiness.

The original Sanskrit verses of the second quotation of the *Madhyamakaśāstra* are as follows:

> *na saṃsārasya nirvāṇāt kiṃcid asti viśeṣaṇam* |
> *na nirvāṇasya saṃsārāt kiṃcid asti viśeṣaṇam* ||
> *nirvāṇasya ca yā koṭiḥ koṭiḥ saṃsārasya ca* |
> *na tayor antaraṃ kiṃcit susūkṣmam api vidyate* ||
> (XXV.19–20)[11]

From these verses, we understand that the Chinese term *shih-chien* 世間 in Kumārajīva's translation is equivalent to Sanskrit *saṃsāra*. On this basis we are able to suppose that the phrase *shih-chien chi shih nieh-p'an* 世間即是涅槃 is identical in meaning

10. N. Dutt, ed., *Pañcaviṃśatisāhasrikā Prajñāpāramitā* (London: Luzac & Co., 1934): 155.15-22.

11. *Prasannapadā*, ed. L. de La Vallée Poussin (St. Petersburg: Imperial Academy, 1903–13): 535; 中論, trans. by Kumārajīva, T. vol. 30, p. 36a: 涅槃與世間　無有少分別　世間與涅槃　亦無少分別　涅槃之實際　及與世間際　如是二際者　無毫釐差別.

to *sheng-ssu chi nieh-p'an* 生死卽涅槃.

As for the subject of the third example, namely, that the very idea of the unity of Saṃsāra and Nirvāṇa is the teaching exclusively for Bodhisattvas, i.e., Mahāyāna, the *Ta chih-tu lun* refers to it later again in terms of the superiority of Bodhisattvas' wisdom over that of Disciples and Self-enlightened Ones. Here I will freely translate the passage:

> 4. Through two reasons Bodhisattvas are superior to Disciples and Self-enlightened Ones. Firstly they understand through emptiness that all *dharma*s are empty, and still never perceive this emptiness. (They regard) emptiness as equal to, one with, and not different from non-emptiness. Secondly they, with this wisdom (i.e., of emptiness), wish to release all sentient beings (from Saṃsāra) and cause them to attain Nirvāṇa. The wisdom of Disciples and Self-enlightened Ones only perceives the emptiness of all *dharma*s, but cannot perceive that Saṃsāra and Nirvāṇa are but one. For example, there may be two kinds of persons coming out of a prison. One, after making a hole in the wall, himself alone would come out and be released. Another, having himself been released, would destroy the prison, break the chains, and release many others from that prison (兼濟衆人). (T. vol. 25, p. 320a)

Here is emphasized the altruistic attitudes of Bodhisattvas in relation to their perception of the unity of Saṃsāra and Nirvāṇa.

On the basis of the *Ta chih-tu lun*, we know that the idea of the unity of Saṃsāra and Nirvāṇa belongs exclusively to the Mahāyāna, which aims at the salvation of all sentient beings, whose agency is the Bodhisattvas, and that this idea is motivated by the Bodhisattva's desire to work for the salvation of others.

The *Ta chih-tu lun* is traditionally attributed to Nāgārjuna, but modern scholarship has expressed doubts about this attribution and is inclined to view Kumārajīva's participation in the composition of this treatise as crucial. In the present case, however, we cannot deny the identity of the treatise's position with Nāgārjuna's view, as is shown in the stanzas of the *Madhyamaka-śāstra* quoted above.

Besides the two verses in the chapter on the Investigation of Nirvāṇa (chap. XXV) mentioned above, there is another verse that expresses the same idea in the chapter on the Investigation of Bondage and Release (chap. XVI). Namely:

> *na nirvāṇasamāropo na saṃsārāpakarṣaṇam |*
> *yatra kas tatra saṃsāro nirvāṇaṃ kiṃ vikalpyate ||*
> (XVI.10)[12]
>
> Where there is neither superimposition of Nirvāṇa nor diminution of Saṃsāra,
> What Saṃsāra, and what Nirvāṇa, could be constructed in thought there?

*Piṅgala's commentary in Kumārajīva's translation of the *Madhyamakaśāstra* explains this in the following way:

> In the ultimate meaning, which represents the reality of *dharma*s, no elucidation of Nirvāṇa as being apart from Saṃsāra is possible. As is said in the scripture: Nirvāṇa is nothing but Saṃsāra, Saṃsāra is nothing but Nirvāṇa (涅槃即生死 生死即涅槃). The reality of *dharma*s being thus, how can one definitely say that this is Saṃsāra, this is Nirvāṇa? (T. vol. 30, p. 21b)

Unfortunately again, the sūtra passage that expresses the very phrase in question has not yet been identified.

4.

Let us now return to the passage of the *Mahāyānasaṃgraha* mentioned at the beginning of section 2 of this article, *Mahāyāna-*

12. 中論: 不離於生死 而別有涅槃 實相義如是 云何有分別 (T. vol. 30, p. 21b).

saṃgraha IX.3.

1. In Paramārtha's translation the passage runs as follows:

In Saṃsāra and Nirvāṇa, when there arises the knowledge of equality,
Then Saṃsāra is (identified with) Nirvāṇa, since of the two no (distinction of) this or that is observed.
Therefore, of Saṃsāra there should be neither abandonment nor non-abandonment.
Of Nirvāṇa, too, (there should be) neither attainment nor non-attainment.[13]

These two stanzas are probably a quotation of some unknown scripture. They are quoted as a source authority for the doctrine of unstable Nirvāṇa (*apratiṣṭhitanirvāṇa*), whose terminology was newly established by the Yogācāras. The same idea was, however, already transmitted in the *Prajñāpāramitā* as an ideal state of the Bodhisattva in terms of *susthito 'sthāna-yogena* (well standing in a manner of no standing).[14] In the *Mahāyānasaṃgraha*

13. T. vol. 31, p. 129b: 於生死涅槃　若智起平等　生死即涅槃　二無此彼故　是故於生死　非捨非非捨　於涅槃亦爾　無得無不得. Cf. Hsüan-tsang's translation: 於生死涅槃　若起平等智　爾時由此證　生死即涅槃　由是於生死　非捨非不捨　亦即於涅槃　非得非不得.

14. The first use of this phrase is perhaps in the *Aṣṭasāhasrikā* (*ASP*), p. 8.3 in Mitra's edition: *bodhisatvo mahāsatvaḥ prajñāpāramitāyāṃ veditavyaḥ sthito 'vinivartanīyāyāṃ bodhisatvabhūmau susthito 'sthānayogena.*

This sentence is located at the end of a passage in which a bodhisattva's perception of all *dharma*s by means of *prajñāpāramitā* is elucidated and understood by Subhūti to be that no *dharma* exists, so even a bodhisattva is non-existent and is appellation only (*nāmadheyamātra*), and what is appellation only is neither abiding nor not abiding (*na sthitaṃ nāsthitaṃ na viṣṭhitaṃ nāviṣṭhitaṃ*) because it is not existent, and that if a bodhisattva has no fear but has faith with a deep mind when this *prajñāpāramitā* is taught, then he is to be known as abiding in the irreversible stage of a bodhisattva standing firm in perfect wisdom in the manner of non-standing (*ASP*, 7.9–8.3). Cf. Kumārajīva's translation, T. vol. 8, p. 537c: 住無所住 for the phrase.

The same passage is considerably enlarged in the *Pañcaviṃśatisāhasrikā* (*PVP*), pp. 123.14–128.1 in N. Dutt's edition, by enumerating various kinds

unstable Nirvāṇa is defined as the result of a Bodhisattva's abandonment of defilements, which is otherwise characterized as the transformation of the basis (*āśraya-parivṛtti*).[15] Commenting on these verses, Vasubandhu says the following:

> (Both Saṃsāra and Nirvāṇa are products of thought-construction. They are but one and the same suchness. If one attains non-discriminative wisdom, then equality is established between them.)
>
> The impure part of the Dependent nature (*paratantra-svabhāva*) is called Saṃsāra, while the pure part is called Nirvāṇa. (To understand) the non-reality of Saṃsāra and non-substantiality of ego and *dharma*s is nothing but Nirvāṇa. If, attaining non-discriminative wisdom, one perceives the non-existence of Saṃsāra, then he perceives the non-existence of Nirvāṇa. Therefore, there is no distinction

---

of *dharmas*, among which is found the pair *saṃsārika* and *nairvāṇika* (126.11-12). Cf. Kumārajīva's translation (*Larger PP*), T. vol. 8, pp. 234a–235a: 住不住法故 for the phrase. There is no direct reference to Saṃsāra and Nirvāṇa there.

Besides this passage, the *PVP* adds a passage in which this idea of "standing in the *prajñāpāramitā* in the manner of non-standing" is taught, and locates it, probably with the idea of emphasizing the importance of this concept, towards the start of the main part of the sūtra, i.e., immediately after the introductory part: *iha, Śāriputra, bodhisattvena mahāsattvena prajñāpāramitāyāṃ sthitvā 'sthānayogena dānapāramitā paripūrayitavyā aparityāgayogena deyadāyakapratigrāhakānupalabdhitām upādāya* | (18.7-10). Cf. *Larger PP*, T. vol. 8, p. 218c: 以不住法住般若波羅蜜中.

The *dānapāramitā* is followed by other *pāramitā*s, and next by the thirty-seven *dharma*s as the means for the attainment of *bodhi*, etc., up to the eighteen qualities exclusive to the Buddha and compassion. It is with reference to just these passages that the *Ta chih-tu lun* explains these *dharma*s in detail (139a–257c), among which are the references to the unity of Saṃsāra and Nirvāṇa discussed above.

15. The stanzas referred to here are located at the end of the chapter on the result of annihilation, or attainment of Quiescence as the result of a bodhisattva's practices, being the ninth subject of the text. In this chapter, the main topic is *āśrayaparivṛtti*.

> between the two. Then what is the merit of this wisdom?... Though he perceives non-substantiality (of Saṃsāra), he never retires from Saṃsāra. This is the meaning of non-abandonment. Though staying in Saṃsāra, he always perceives non-substantiality. This means non-non-abandonment .... As he obtains no Saṃsāra, then he obtains no Nirvāṇa. This means non-attainment. The point that he perceives supreme quietude in Saṃsāra, this is the meaning of non-non-attainment.[16]

As for the phrase *sheng-ssu chi nieh-p'an* 生死卽涅槃 in the former stanza, Hsüan-tsang's translation uses the same expression, while the equivalent Tibetan translation is *ḥkhor ñid mya ṅan ḥdas par ḥgyur*.[17]

There are some other passages in the *Mahāyānasaṃgraha* where the same idea is expressed in similar phrases.

2. In the chapter on the objects of knowledge (*jñeya*), the second subject out of ten, which elucidates the *trisvabhāva* doctrine, Asaṅga discusses the meaning of the idea of the non-distinction of Saṃsāra and Nirvāṇa with reference to the character of the Dependent nature. A summary of the passage (II.28) runs as follows:

> Q: In the *Brahmaparipṛcchā* the Bhagavat taught that the Tathāgata does not see Saṃsāra, or Nirvāṇa. What was his hidden intention in this teaching?

---

16. T. vol. 31, p. 249ab, according to Paramārtha's translation.

17. Tibetan translation, sDe-dge (D), Ri (*Sems tsam* 12), 37a2-3. The two stanzas are as follows:

ḥkhor ba daṅ ni mya ṅan ḥdas || mthuṅs par śes pa nam kye ba ||
de tshe de phyir de la ni || ḥkhor ñid mya ṅan ḥdas par ḥgyur ||
de yi phyir na ḥkhor ba ni || gtoṅ ba ma yin mi gtoṅ min ||
de phyir mya ṅan ḥdas pa yaṅ || thob pa ma yin mi thob min ||

It is difficult for me to restore the Sanskrit of these verses. A hypothetical sentence for the fourth *pada* of the first verse, which is equivalent to the third *pada* of Paramārtha's translation, would be *saṃsāro nirvṛtir bhavet ||* (*nirvṛti* for *nirvāṇa*, *causa metrica*).

A: The Dependent nature is in one respect the Constructed nature, and is in another respect the Perfect nature. Therefore, there is no difference between Saṃsāra and Nirvāṇa (*ḥkhor ḅa daṅ mya ṅan las ḥdas pa ñid bye brag med pa*). This is the hidden meaning. Thus the Dependent nature is in Saṃsāra due to its part of the Constructed nature, the same is in Nirvāṇa when its part of the Perfect nature is realized.[18]

The Dependent nature is represented by the *ālayavijñāna* and the latter is otherwise characterized as the beginningless basis (*anādikāliko dhātuḥ*), the basis for both paths of Saṃsāra and attainment of Nirvāṇa.[19]

The quoted scripture, otherwise called the *Brahmaviśeṣacintiparipṛcchā*, is also found among Kumārajīva's translations, and we should add this sūtra to the list of sources of the idea in question.[20]

In the same chapter, there is another passage (II.30) in which the Buddha's teaching concerning pairs of concepts contrary to each other, such as *nitya* and *anitya*, is discussed in relation to the *trisvabhāva* doctrine (ibid. 121a). Among the list of such pairs, we find *sheng-ssu nieh-p'an wu-erh* 生死涅槃無二, which we suppose to be equivalent to Sanskrit *saṃsāra-nirvāṇādvaya*. The term is reconstructed (by Nagao) from Tibetan *ḥkhor ba daṅ mya ṅan las ḥdas pa daṅ gñis su med*, which means "Saṃsāra, Nirvāṇa, and the Non-dual," representing the Constructed, the Perfect, and the Dependent nature, respectively.[21] This may be called the

18. D, ibid., 19b4-5; Paramārtha, T. vol. 31, pp. 120c–121a. For the phrase given in Tibetan, Paramārtha has: 生死爲涅槃依無差別義.

19. The term appears in a quotation from the *Abhidharma-Mahāyānasūtra* at the beginning of chap. 1, on *jñeyāśraya*, as its synonym.

20. The passage is in T. no. 586 思益梵天所問經, vol. 15, p. 36c. The sūtra explains the reason for the Buddha's statement by saying that Nirvāṇa is only an appellation and is not perceived (但有名字而有不可得).

21. The Sanskrit reconstruction of the phrase is correct from a doctrinal

Yogācāra interpretation of the doctrine of entering non-duality.

4. In the last chapter of the *Mahāyānasaṃgraha*, on the Buddha's wisdom, we find the following stanza (X.28A [12]):

thabs chen rnams daṅ ldan pa la || ñon moṅs byaṅ chub yan lag ḥgyur ||
ḥkhor ba'aṅ shi baḥi bdag ñid de || de phyir de bshin gśegs bsam yas ||[22]

For one who has accomplished the great means (for salvation),
Defilements become components of enlightenment,
And Saṃsāra becomes Quiescence itself;
Therefore, the Tathāgata is inconceivable.

This verse is quoted in the *Madhyāntavibhāga-ṭīkā* of Sthiramati, and as most of the verse except for the first four syllables was missing in the Sanskrit manuscript, it was restored into Sanskrit by Yamaguchi, the editor, in the following way:

kleśo bodhya*ṅga āpanno mahopāyaprayoginaḥ* |
saṃsāro 'py upaśāntyātmā tato 'cintyas tathāgataḥ ||[23]

Both Chinese translations by Paramārtha and Hsüan-tsang locate the first *pada* of the Tibetan translation (equivalent to *mahopāyaprayoginaḥ*) in the third *pada* without showing any sign of case relations, thus making it very difficult for us to understand the verse. (Paramārtha's 得成大方便 is better than Hsüan-tsang's 具大方便故. 故 is to be located at the head of the fourth *pada*, as

viewpoint, but D here (20b1) has the reading *ḥkhor ba daṅ mya ṅan las ḥdas pa dag kyaṅ gñis su med pa* instead of Nagao's reading. See Gadjin Nagao, *Shōdaijōron: wayaku to chūkai* 摂大乗論・和訳と注解, Indo koten sōsho インド古典叢書 (Tokyo: Kōdansha 講談社, 1982, 1987): 1.382 (§II.30).

22. D, ibid. 40b1-2; Paramārtha, ibid., p. 131b: 諸惑成覺分 生死爲涅槃 得成大方便 故佛難思議; Hsüan-tsang, ibid., p. 150c: 煩惱成覺分 生死爲涅槃 具大方便故 諸佛不思議.

23. *Sthiramati Madhyāntavibhāgaṭīkā*, ed. Susumu Yamaguchi (Nagoya: Librarie Hajinkaku, 1934): 98. Cf. Nagao, *Shōdaijōron*, 2.401-3.

Paramārtha has it.)[24]

The same stanza is quoted in the *Fo-hsing lun* 佛性論, attributed to Vasubandhu and translated by Paramārtha. The passage in which it is quoted is as follows:

> Because of this real way of the reasoning of the essence of *dharma*s (如實法界道理門), what is Nirvāṇa is nothing but Saṃsāra (卽是涅槃卽是生死), and it is impossible to distinguish them. And thus one is able to enter the doctrine of non-duality. And again, both are neither one nor two, as they abide in instability (住無住處故). In other words, one does not stay in Saṃsāra due to his destruction of defilements, nor does he abide in Nirvāṇa due to his previous vow. By means of wisdom he is able to destroy defilements, and by means of compassion he is able to complete his previous vow. So it is taught in a verse of the Sūtra of the Inconceivable (不可思量經—**Acintyatā-sūtra*):
>
> Defilements become components of enlightenment,—
> (and so on).[25]

The scripture whose name is mentioned above has not yet been identified.

According to modern scholarship, the *Fo-hsing lun* is to be regarded as a different version of the *Ratnagotravibhāga*, the basic text for the so-called Tathāgatagarbha doctrine, or rather as a text composed under the influence of the latter.[26] And in fact we find in the *Ratnagotravibhāga* an equivalent of part of this passage:

---

24. Nagao's correction of the third *pada* to *-prayuktataḥ* is not necessary. Tibetan ~ *daṅ ldan pa* may mean "one who is possessed of ~," and *la* may be used here for the genitive case.

25. T. vol 31, p. 799c. The translation of the verse by Paramārtha is as follows: 諸惑成覺分 生死成涅槃 修習大方便 諸佛叵思議 (叵 = 不可).

26. See J. Takasaki, *A Study on the Ratnagotravibhāga (Uttaratantra)* (Rome: Istituto Italiano per il Medio ed Estremo Oriente, 1966): 47–49 (§2. *Buddhagotraśāstra*). I received the suggestion first from Prof. G. Nagao in 1955. I suppose the translator Paramārtha himself was the real author of the text.

> *tad anena dharmadhātunayamukhena paramārthataḥ saṃsāra eva nirvāṇam ity uktam* |
> That by this introduction to the theory of the essence of *dharmas*, it is taught that from the ultimate standpoint Saṃsāra is nothing but Nirvāṇa.[27]

In the *RGV* this passage belongs to the section on the eternity of the embryo of the Tathāgata from the result aspect as representing the Dharma body and is elucidated as commenting on the latter half of verse I.38: *nityaḥ saṃsāranirvāṇasamatāprativedhataḥ*. The sentence mentioned above is immediately followed by an explanation of unstable Nirvāṇa[28] similar to that in the *Fo-hsing lun*. As for the verse quoted in the *Fo-hsing lun*, however, the *RGV* lacks it, and instead has the following verse:

> *chittvā snehaṃ prajñayātmany aśeṣaṃ*
> *sattvasnehān naiti śāntiṃ kṛpāvān* |
> *niḥśrityaivaṃ dhīkṛpe bodhyupāyau*
> *nopaity āryaḥ saṃvṛtiṃ nirvṛtiṃ vā* || 39
> The saint, being full of mercy, does not approach

27. *Ratnagotravibhāga Mahāyānottaratantraśāstra*, ed. E. H. Johnston (Patna: Bihar Research Society, 1950): 35.3 (hereafter *RGV*).

28. The whole passage is in *RGV* 34.18–35.16. The direct reference to unstable Nirvāṇa following the sentence mentioned above runs as follows:

> (That is) because he has realized unstable Nirvāṇa in which both (Saṃsāra and Nirvāṇa) are not discriminated (*ubhayathāvikalpanāpratiṣṭhitanirvāṇa-sākṣātkaraṇataḥ*). — Now, in the world, the Bodhisattva is not entirely involved among all living beings because he has completely rejected all tendencies of desire by means of Wisdom. (At the same time) he is not remote from them owing to his great compassion. This is the means for the acquisition of Supreme Enlightenment, of which instability is the essential nature (*apratiṣṭhitasvabhāva...samyaksambodhi*). Owing to wisdom, indeed, the bodhisattva ... having deep intention towards Nirvāṇa for his own sake, does not stay in Samsaric life as the lineage of no Nirvāṇa (*aparinirvāṇagotra*) does. Owing to Great compassion, however, he never abandons those suffering people, and having activity in the Samsaric world for the sake of others, he does not abide in Nirvāṇa as do those who seek only for Quiescence (*śamaikāyanagotra*).

> Quiescence because of his affection towards sentient beings.
> Thus standing on intellect and mercy, both being the means for enlightenment,
> The saint approaches neither the covered nor the uncovered.[29]

Here the term "the covered" (*saṃvṛti*) means Saṃsāra, while "the uncovered" (*nirvṛti*) means Nirvāṇa. This verse, though counted by the editor as an original verse in its own right, seems to be a quotation from an unknown text. The Chinese translation of the *RGV*, the *Pao-hsing lun* 寳性論, omits this verse, and instead has another which is again not yet identified.[30] It runs as follows:

> A man of indiscriminate (wisdom) discriminates neither the world (Saṃsāra) nor Nirvāṇa; (he perceives) the equality of Nirvāṇa and existence (in Saṃsāra).
> 無分別之人　不分別世間　不分別涅槃　涅槃有平等

In the *RGV* passage quoted above, we met a quite important phrase which looks like it might be the original of our Chinese phrase *sheng-ssu chi nieh-p'an* 生死卽涅槃, namely *saṃsāra eva nirvāṇam*. This is what we have been seeking from the beginning of this paper. Perhaps the reason why this important phrase escaped our notice so far is that neither of the two Chinese translations, the *Fo-hsing lun* and *Pao-hsing lun*, translate the phrase idiomatically. Their translations are, respectively, 卽是涅槃　卽是生死 and 卽世間法　名爲涅槃.

The *RGV* might not be the first text to have used this phrase. The words *ity uktam* seem to show the existence of its idiomatic use at the time of the composition of the *RGV*. However, we should be satisfied now by the discovery of this Sanskrit phrase, *saṃsāra eva nirvāṇam*, and might end our present investigation here.[31]

29. *RGV*, 35.13-16.
30. 究竟一乘寳性論, trans. by Ratnamati, T. no. 1611, vol. 31, p. 831a.
31. I had no chance in the main body of this paper to discuss the term *saṃ-*

Addendum

After sending my manuscript to the editor, I located the source of the erroneously attributed verse, referred to above, cited in Oda's *Bukkyō jiten*, as coming from the *Mahāsaṃnipāta-sūtra*, fascicle 90. The passage is rather from fascicle 90 of the *Mahāratnakūṭa-sūtra* translated by Bodhiruci. This is the *Upāli-parṣat*, the twenty-fourth sūtra of the collection, and there the following verse containing the phrase *sheng-ssu chi nieh-p'an* is found.[32] It reads:

了知諸法如實相　常行生死即涅槃　於諸法中實無染　調伏衆生言離欲

Those who realize the real feature of phenomena
Always practise (the idea that) Saṃsāra is Nirvāṇa.
Though (living) in the phenomenal world, they, without pollution,
Guide living beings (to Nirvāṇa)—they are called desireless.

There is another version of this *Upāli-paripṛcchā* in the Chinese Tripiṭaka, called the *Vinayaviniścaya-sūtra* (決定毘尼經; T.

---

sāraśānty-ekarasa, quoted from the *Mahāyānasūtrālaṃkāra* above (see n. 7). The said term is found in II.3 (Levi's ed., p. 9), which runs as follows:

sarvān satvāṃs tārayituṃ yaḥ pratipanno
yāne jñāne sarvagate kauśalyayuktaḥ |
yo nirvāṇe saṃsṛtiśāntyekaraso 'sau
jñeyo dhīmān eṣa hi sarvatraga evaṃ ||

One who is ready to save all living beings,
Is endowed with skill in the vehicle and all-pervading knowledge,
And has one taste of Saṃsāra and Quiescence in Nirvāṇa,
This Bodhisattva is indeed to be known thus as all-pervading.

The third *pada* is quoted according to Prof. Nagao's correction on the basis of the ms. reading and the Tibetan translation. The Sanskrit original of Vasubandhu's commentary to this verse is missing, while the equivalents to it in Tibetan and Chinese run respectively as follows: *mya ṅan las ḥdas pa kun tu ḥgro baḥi don ni ḥkhor ba daṅ shi ba ro gcig paḥi phyir te | de dag gis ñes pa daṅ yon tan la rnam par mi rtog paḥi phyir | de la ḥkhor ba daṅ mya ṅan las ḥdas pa la bye brtag med do ||* (D, Phi [*Sems tsam* 1], 133b5-7); 四者。寂滅一切遍。生死涅槃體是一味。過惡功德不分別故 (T. vol. 31, p. 593a).

32. T. vol. 11, p. 519a.

no. 325), and there the equivalent verse runs as follows:[33]

觀世寂靜名勇猛　知法實相亦復然　受五欲利常修行　不生染着度衆生

Those who perceive the world as Quiescence are called the brave,
And who know the real feature of phenomena as well.
They, though perceiving five objects of desire, practise constantly,
And having produced no attachment, guide sentient beings (to Nirvāṇa).

This version is said to be a translation by a certain Bodhisattva of Tun-huang (敦煌菩薩), date unknown, and is nearer the Tibetan version of the *Vinayaviniścaya*, whose equivalent verse (Lhasa Kanjur, *dKon brtsegs*, Ca, 244a7-b1) runs as follows:

| *gaṅ dag raṅ bshin med chos ḥdi śes pa* |
| *dpaḥ bo de dag ḥjig rten mya ṅan ḥdas* |
| *ḥdod paḥi yon tan spyod kyaṅ chags med ciṅ* |
| *chags pa rnams spaṅs sems can ḥdul bar byed* |

Again, thanks to information I received from the editor, Dr. Jonathan Silk, I came to know that the same verse is quoted twice in the *Prasannapadā* (in chapters XIV and XIII, La Vallée Poussin's ed., 257.1-4 and 474.7-10, respectively). Both quotations differ from each other in minor points, and Prof. J. W. de Jong offers, in his "Textcritical Notes on the *Prasannapadā*" (*Indo-Iranian Journal* 20 [1978]: 25–57), variant readings from a manuscript kept in the IsMEO in Rome ("R"). In light of a comparison of these variant readings and with the help of the Tibetan translation, we can arrive at the following as the presumed original form of the verse:

ye parinirvṛta loki ta śūrā yehi 'sabhavata ñāt'imi dharmā |

33. T. vol. 12, p. 42a.

kāmaguṇai hi caranti asaṅgā saṅgu vivarjiya satva vinenti ||
(metre *dodhaka*)

We might render this into Sanskrit as follows:

ye parinirvṛtā loke te śūrāḥ yebhiś [*cā*]*svabhāvato jñātā ime dharmāḥ* |
kāmaguṇair hi caranty asaṅgāḥ saṅgaṃ vivarjiya sattvaṃ vinayanti ||

Those who have completely entered *nirvāṇa* (abiding) in the world, and by whom these phenomena have been known as of no own nature—they are the brave. Though following after sensual objects, they have indeed no attachment, and having got rid of attachment, they convert sentient beings.

Turning back to the Chinese translation of this verse, the phrase *sheng-ssu chi nieh-p'an* has been known to be a free rendition of the idea of entering *nirvāṇa* while abiding and acting in the world. This idea is nothing but the later developed concept of *apratiṣṭhitanirvāṇa*. With this concept in mind, the translator Bodhiruci must have used the phrase renowned in China at that time.

As for the *Upāli-paripṛcchā*, a critical Tibetan edition with a French translation was published by Pierre Python (Paris, 1973), who actually identified the verse quoted in the *Prasannapadā* for the first time. On the verse in question, see also Jacques May, *Candrakīrti: Prasannapadā Madhyamakavṛtti* (Paris, 1959): 205 and 417.*

* A Japanese version of the present paper, with slight differences, has appeared in *Tōhōgaku ronshū: Eastern Studies Fiftieth Anniversary Volume* (Tokyo: Tōhō Gakkai, 1997): 753–770.

"Non-Sentient Beings Preaching the Dharma" 無情說法: Buddhist Views on the Environment*

I

My discussion of the significance of 'non-sentient beings preaching the Dharma' is part of a larger endeavour to find out ways in which Buddhism could help to solve the environmental problems of our age. 'Non-sentient beings preaching the Dharma' refers to the fact that natural phenomena such as a stream's murmur and a mountain landscape 溪聲山色 can manifest the Truth preached by the Buddha and become a factor leading to spiritual awakening. This points to the importance of our humbly learning from Nature. The teaching of 'non-sentient beings preaching the Dharma' is expounded in many chapters of Dōgen's 道元 (1200–53) *Shōbō genzō* 正法眼藏, first and foremost in the chapter which actually bears this title, as well as in "The Stream's Murmur and Mountain Landscape" 溪聲山色 chapter, "The Demeanour of the Practising Buddha" 行佛威儀 chapter, etc. My paper, however, will focus on Nan-yang Hui-chung 南陽慧忠 (?–775), with whom the doctrine of 'non-sentient beings preaching the Dharma' originated, and try to trace it back further to the concept of 'environment' in Indian Buddhism.

II

First of all, what is the traditional Buddhist term equivalent to our modern 'environment'? The most appropriate notion appears to be the concept of 'physical world'.

---

* This article is a slightly edited version of a paper presented at Waseda University in January 1999; the original version was translated by Florin Deleanu.

As opposed to the 'sentient world' (*sattvaloka* 有情世間), the concept of physical world or, literally, 'receptacle world' (*bhājanaloka* 器世間) refers to the place where living beings dwell. Sentient beings include beings wandering in the six or five destinations of the rebirth cycle as well as practitioners of the Three Vehicles, i.e., the *śrāvaka*, *pratyekabuddha*, and *bodhisattva.* The receptacle world includes the land where sentient beings dwell as well as the vegetation growing there.[1] Because they lack sensorial functions (*acetana* 無覺),[2] they are called 'non-sentient beings' (*asattva* 非情). The idea that plants are non-sentient runs counter to our modern common sense. Many systems of Indian philosophy, other than Buddhism, actually include vegetation in the *cetana* category. Buddhism itself in its early phase regarded plants as being sentient. It has been suggested that the reason for their inclusion in the non-sentient class might have been the contradiction felt to exist between a plant diet and the non-killing precept.[3]

This distinction between these two 'worlds' appears clearly defined in the *Abhidharmakośa* and was taken over by the Mahāyāna tradition, becoming thus a matter of common sense for Buddhist followers in East Asia. The dichotomy is not found in the Theravāda tradition, but the word *loka* itself was used with the meaning of the place where sentient beings dwell.[4] For us, this is the Earth or, in traditional terms, Jambudvīpa. Different from 'this world' (*ihaloka*), there is a 'world after death' (*paraloka*)

1. *Abhidharmakośabhāṣya* (*AKBh*): 諸穀麥豆金鐵菴羅半娜婆等、亦有自類互相似故 ("Wu-ch'ing t'ung-fen" 無情同分, T. vol. 29,. p. 24a); *śāli-yava-mudga-māṣâmra-panasa-loha-kāñcanādi*.

2. In the *AKBh*., p. 73.20, the corpse which has lost its life, heat, and consciousness is described as *yathā kaṣṭham acetanaḥ* 如木無思覺 (T. vol. 29, p. 27a).

3. L.Schmithausen, *Buddhism and Nature*, Studia Philologica Buddhica, Occasional Papers VII (Tokyo: International Institute for Buddhist Studies, 1991), p. 5, §II.9; p. 6, §II.10.1.

4. For the meaning and illustrations of the usage of *loka*, see PTS *Dictionary*, s.v. *loka*.

which is conceived of as a form of retribution for one's deeds. Heaven and Hell are assumed to be spatial locations occupying the zenith and nadir of existence. This basic frame of the model is the product of Indian thought, but Buddhism further developed it by dividing the realm of gods into various subdivisions following the levels of meditative practice as well as by conceiving of Mount Sumeru as the summit of the Earth. This was further enlarged to include the 'triple-thousand great thousand world' (*trisāhasramahāsāhasralokadhātu* 三千大千世界), i.e., the cube of 1000, which was considered to be the sphere covered by the wisdom of the Buddha. Incidentally, I may remark that the term *sekai* 世界 (*lokadhātu*), which is the modem Japanese word for 'world', represents each individual component (*dhātu*) of this multi-world cosmic system.

The difference between the physical world and the living world, or between non-sentient and sentient beings, is that while sentient beings are born in various realms in accordance with the maturation (*vipāka* 異熟) of their karma, the entities of the insentient world have no karma by themselves. Theravāda regards the physical world merely as a place populated by sentient beings, while the Sarvāstivādins maintain that "the diversity of the world is produced by karma" (*karmajaṃ lokavaicitryaṃ* 世別由業生)[5] and regard it as a dominant result (*adhipatiphala* 增上果) brought about by the common karma (*sādhāraṇakarman* 共業) of sentient beings. The reason for its inclusion in the law of cause and effect is the fact that the physical world, being something composed of the five aggregates 五蘊所成, strictly speaking of the form-aggregate 色蘊所成, belongs to conditioned phenomena (*saṃskṛtadharma* 有爲法). On the other hand, the Sarvāstivādins limited the twelvefold chain of dependent origination (*dvādaśapratītya-samutpāda* 十二支緣起) to sentient beings and developed here the theory of cause and effect spanning the three ages of past, present, and

5. T. vol. 29, p. 67b.

future. As phenomena consisting of five aggregates, both the sentient and non-sentient worlds have a real existence.

The Mahāyāna scriptures postulate the simultaneous existence of various Buddhas in all the quarters of the universe, each having his own land. Following the principle that only one Buddha can exist in one world, it was reasoned that each Buddha must have his own Pure Land. The most typical example is the Sukhāvatī land of Amitābha Tathāgata. This Pure Land appeared as the fruition of Bodhisattva Dharmākara's vow fulfilment, and Sukhāvatī cannot exist without Amitābha Buddha. It is thus different from our world (Sahā, literally 'world of endurance', defined as an impure land, in contradistinction to Sukhāvatī), which had already been in existence before Śākyamuni. The precise definition of the Pure Land concept became a new problem. On the other hand, the Mahāyāna sūtras expound the doctrine of emptiness and criticise the Sarvāstivādin pan-realist theory. Like the self, all phenomena are without own-nature and empty (*asvabhāva-śūnya* 無自性空) and are merely postulated as existent at the linguistic level for the sake of achieving worldly efficiency.[6] Even the Tathāgata is no exception to this principle. But Nāgārjuna and the Mādhyamika school founded by him did not further elaborate on the mechanism which makes possible the postulation of the Tathāgata, sentient beings, and the physical world. It was the Yogācāra school and its ideation-only (*vijñaptimātratā*) doctrine which developed a theoretical model to explain this mechanism.

The ideation-only theory reduces the world of all dependently originating phenomena to a mutually dependent relationship between consciousness (*vijñāna*) and name-and-form (*nāmarūpa*). By introducing here the mutual succession of actualisation

6. The definition of the postulated physical world is almost identical with the Sarvāstivādin conception. E.g., *Prasannapadā* ad XX.16: *idam jagat = ayaṃ bhājanaloka = vāyumaṇḍalādi...akaniṣṭha-bhavana-paryanta* (p. 448): "the physical world, from the air circle at the bottom to Akaniṣṭha Heaven at the top."

(*abhisaṃskāra* 現行) and potentiality, or 'seeds' (*bīja* 種子) in traditional terms, it attempts to explain the rebirth cycle of sentient beings. It is the store-consciousness (*ālayavijñāna*) which activates this mechanism in the following way: all phenomena are stored as seeds in the *ālayavijñāna* and actualised to manifest themselves as phenomena. In the *Madhyāntavibhāga* the manifestation (*pratibhāsa* 顯現) of consciousness is analysed as consisting of four elements: sentience (the five faculties), self, discrimination (the six consciousnesses), and objects (the six sense-objects). This is nothing but stating in different terms the 'metaphor of the self and phenomena' (*ātmadharmopacāra*) of the *Triṃśikāvijñaptimātratāsiddhi*. The self is nothing more than self-consciousness, and its content is provided by the six faculties and six consciousnesses. Phenomena are the sense-objects, which correspond to the physical world. The physical world is basically nothing but the ideated existence of the objects of consciousness outside the self. It might be assumed that other individuals ('other-continuity', *parasaṃtati* 他相續) are included among the sense-objects, but since according to the classification of the *Madhyāntavibhāga* other individuals are listed separately as sentient beings possessing faculties (*sādhiṣṭhānam indriyarūpaṃ* 有根身), sense-objects are interpreted as referring only to the physical world. Sense-objects are also called 'loci' (*sthāna* 處). The term 'ideation-only' (*vijñaptimātratā*) actually comes from the fact that all these loci come into existence as the ideation of consciousness (*vijñapti*).[7]

Being based upon the concept of ignorance (*avidyā*), this model also serves to explain the mechanism of delusion. By spiritual awakening (*bodhi*), nescience becomes science and consciousness is converted into wisdom, and thus the Buddhas, their Lands, and sentient beings come into being. This transformation of the

7. Cf. Takasaki Jikidō, "Ārayashiki to engi shūju upādāna to no kanren" アーラヤ識と縁起執受 upādāna との関連, in *Hirakawa Akira hakushi koki kinen ronshū* 平川彰博士古稀記念論集 (Tokyo: Shunjūsha, 1985), pp. 33–55.

support (*āśrayaparivṛtti*) or transformation of consciousness and obtaining of wisdom 轉識得智 is conceived of as a function of the four types of wisdom (*catvāri jñānāni* 四智). When *ālayavijñāna* becomes great perfect mirror wisdom (*ādarśajñāna* 大圓鏡智) the physical world of the Buddha Land is experienced through the enjoyment body 受用身 or recompense body 報身 (*saṃbhogakāya*), which appears as a result of this wisdom. It follows that this is not different from the Buddha's body that embodies the wisdom of sameness (*samatājñāna* 平等性智), the wisdom of wondrous observation (*pratyavekṣaṇajñāna* 妙觀察智), and the wisdom of accomplishing metamorphoses (*kṛtyānuṣṭhānajñāna* 成所作智) obtained as a result of the transformation of self-consciousness, i.e., defiled consciousness (*kliṣṭamanas* 染汚意) or discriminating consciousness. The ideation-only doctrine succeeds thus in giving a theoretical explanation of the characteristics of the Buddha Lands. (According to this theory, the impure Sahā world could become a Pure Land through the awakening of sentient beings.) Vasubandhu, the great systematiser of the Vijñaptimātratā philosophy, also compiled a *Treatise on the Pure Land* (**Sukhāvatīvyūhasūtropadeśa* 淨土論), which, though not directly expounding the ideation-only theory, nevertheless lends itself to a reading in a *vijñaptimātratā* key.[8]

(In order to teach the ideation-only doctrine, the *Saṃdhinirmocana-sūtra* employs as a simile the fact that all visualisations experienced during meditation are nothing but products of the mind. The image of the Pure Land and its Buddha is obtained through a visualisation meditative practice known as *pratyutpannasamādhi* 般舟三昧. We could speculate that from a historical viewpoint the visualisation techniques of the Pure Land made possible the formation of the ideation-only doctrine.)

8. Yamaguchi Susumu 山口益, *Seshin no Jōdoron* 世親の浄土論 (Kyoto: Hōzōkan, 1962), p. 105ff. (the seventeen types of splendours 十七莊嚴 as the manifestations of mirror wisdom 鏡智).

III

T'an-luan 曇鸞 (476–542), who wrote a commentary on the *Sukhāvatīvyūhasūtropadeśa*,writes the following concerning the pure physical world:

> "This purity is to be known as consisting of two types.... What are these two types? The first one is the purity of the receptacle world. The second one is the purity of the realm of sentient beings. The purity of the receptacle world is the accomplishment of the seventeen splendours of the virtues of the Buddha Land as previously explained. This is called the purity of the receptacle world. The purity of the realm of sentient beings is the accomplishment of the eight splendours of the Buddha's virtues as well as the accomplishment of the four splendours of the Bodhisattva's virtues as previously explained. This is called the purity of the realm of sentient beings. This dharma verse is thus to be known as referring to these two types of purity." 〈Quotation from the *Sukhāvatīvyūhasūtropadeśa*; original text: T. vol. 26, p. 232bc〉

Sentient beings represent the essence 體 of individual fruition 別報 and the Land is the function 用 of common fruition 共報. Therefore, it should be known that "the essence and the function are not identical." *But all phenomena are produced by the mind and there are no [exterior] sense-objects* 諸法心成、無餘境界. Sentient beings and the receptacle 器 [world] can be neither different nor identical. Non-identity refers to their distinct meanings, and non-difference refers to the fact that they are equally pure. The receptacle [world] is the function. Because it is said that this Pure Land is received by these pure sentient beings, it is called 'receptacle'. It is like in the case of using an impure vessel 器 for pure food. The vessel being impure, the food will also become impure. [Or like in the case of] using a pure vessel

> for impure food. The food being impure, the vessel will also become impure. In order to be able to call them 'pure' both of them have to be clean. Therefore, the term 'purity' necessarily includes two types.... (T. vol. 40, p. 841c)

The usual reading for 諸法心成、無餘境界 should be "all phenomena are produced by the mind and there are no [exterior] sense-objects,"[9] which appears to express the theory of ideation-only with no external sense-objects (*ābhāsa* 唯識無境). T'an-luan used the *vijñaptimātratā* doctrine to explain the non-identity and non-difference of sentient beings and the receptacle world as a relationship between essence and function.

T'an-luan's commentary mentions at the beginning of this paragraph that "sentient beings represent the essence of individual fruition and the Land is the function of common fruition." In addition to the essence-function relationship, T'an-luan also introduces the concepts of individual fruition and common fruition. In the case of the Buddha of Sukhāvatī, for example, this fruition means the recompense body 報身 of Amitābha Buddha, which is the fruit of his vow. The bodhisattvas of Sukhāvatī are also reborn in that Pure Land due to the merit accumulated by recollecting the Buddha. Since the sentient beings' rebirth in the Pure Land is the result of each being's karma, this fruition is considered individual. Unlike this, for the Buddha and bodhisattvas, the Pure Land can be said to be a common result. This corresponds to the doctrine which considers that the store-consciousness is different for each individual (*cittasaṃtāna* 心相續), but the similarity of the physical world is the result of common karma. (Strictly speaking, we do not know whether we all perceive exactly the same world.) T'an-luan obviously interprets this paragraph in the light of the

9. Shinran 親鸞 read this as "all phenomena make the mind accomplish the state [of Nirvāṇa] without support." Cf. Hayashima Kyōshō 早島鏡正 and Ōtani Kōshin 大谷光真, *Jōdo ronchū* 浄土論註, Butten kōza 仏典講座 23 (Tokyo: Daizō Shuppansha, 1987), p. 371.

vijñaptimātratā theory.

The translator of the *Sukhāvatīvyūhasūtropadeśa* was Bodhiruci 菩提流支 (?–527), who came to China during the Northern Wei dynasty in the sixth century. He also translated Vasubandhu's *Triśatikāyāḥ prajñāpāramitāyāḥ kārikā saptatiḥ* 金剛般若波羅蜜經論 and its sub-commentary, the *Chin-kang-hsien lun* 金剛仙論 ("Vajrasena 金剛仙 on the *Triśatikāyāḥ prajñāpāramitāyāḥ kārikā saptatiḥ*"). We find in the latter the following paragraph explaining the identity and difference of the three Buddhas, i.e., the Dharma-body, recompense-body, and transformation-body:

> [Such questions] are being asked: "The body of the recompense-Buddha 報佛, with wondrous forms and infinite characteristics and splendours, is not the Dharma-body. Is it considered conditioned (**saṃskṛta* 有爲) or unconditioned(**asaṃskṛta* 無爲)? Is it considered contaminated (**sāsrava* 有漏) or uncontaminated (**anāsrava* 無爲)? Is it considered permanent (**nitya* 常) or impermanent (**anitya* 無常)? Does the Pure Land *dependent upon the fruition* 依報 of the recompense-Buddha consist of conditioned phenomena (**saṃskṛtadharma* 有爲法) or unconditioned phenomena (**asaṃskṛtadharma* 無爲法)? Is it considered to be included in the three realms or not?" Such are the questions being asked. In what follows the sutra explains each [of these questions] and the [answer] will be known. (T. vol. 25, p. 811a)

Let us note here the use of the phrase '[fruition] dependent upon recompense' or 'support-fruition' 依報.

Next we find in connection with the 'inexplicability of the cause' 因不可說 the following passage:

> The essence 體 of the recompense-Buddha is unconditioned and cannot be explained. It is unlike the conditioned which can be explained. The reason is that by his practice the Bud-

> dha eradicates the afflictions 斷惑 and original nature 本有之性 reveals its function 用. This is called the recompense-Buddha. As there exists a principal fruition 正果 of the recompense-Buddha, there must be a true Pure Land [acting as] support-fruition 依報. Because of its unhindered function, it is unconditioned. It is not conditioned. Because it is not orderly 條然 [produced as a result of the common cause and effect law], it is eternal 常. (T. vol. 25, pp. 826c–827a)

The recompense-Buddha is called 'principal fruition' 正果 and the Pure Land is qualified as 'support-fruition' 依報. Three paragraphs later we read:

> The so-called Pure Land is the land of the supreme principle (**paramārthasatya* 第一義) of true wisdom [acting as] support-fruition 依報 for all Buddhas. This land has the essence 體 of Thusness true-nature (**tathatādharmatā* 眞如法性). It is hence the realm of the lotus womb (**padmagarbhalokadhātu* 蓮華藏世界). As regards the essence 體, the Pure Land and the true recompense-Buddhas are similar, but as far as their function 用 is concerned, they are different. This is because this land has been carved out from the supramundane uncontaminated superior cause 勝因 of the practice of the two splendours, i.e., the wisdom and the myriad merits accumulated by the Tathāgata ever since the generation of the aspiration for awakening (**bodhicittotpāda* 發心). (T. vol. 25, p. 827b)

The text explains the relationship between the Buddha and the Pure Land in the following terms: "As regards the essence, they are similar; as far as their function is concerned, they are different." This agrees with T'an-luan's theory. T'an-luan was actually contemporaneous with Bodhiruci, and it appears that he directly studied under the latter.[10]

I would like to note here the occurrence of the terms 'principal fruition' 正果 and 'support-fruition' 依報 in the *Chin-kang-hsien lun*. These terms, as well as the expression 'two types of fruition, i.e., support and principal' 依正二報, are a matter of common knowledge in East Asian Buddhism, but so far we have used them without carefully examining their origin. As far as I know, this is the only instance where these terms appear in a translation of an Indian Buddhist text. (They also occur in the *P'u-sa ying-lo pen-yeh ching* 菩薩瓔珞本業經, but as this is considered to be an apocryphal scripture compiled in China, it cannot be taken as an authentic source.)[11] We do not know whether the *Chin-kang-hsien lun* is in its entirety a translation from an Indian original or whether it also includes Bodhiruci's own lectures glossing the text for the Chinese audience. We can, nevertheless, say that as far as the term 'support-fruition' is concerned, this is its earliest occurrence and all the sources which have been cited so far belong to later periods. At all events, I think we can safely assume that the concept of 'support-fruition' was formed in connection with the interpretation of the Pure Land concept.

I have no time now to examine when the terms 'principal fruition' and 'support-fruition' or, in T'an-luan's usage, 'individu-

10. T'an-luan's biography records the fact that he studied the *Amitāyurdhyāna-sūtra* 觀經 under Bodhiruci. There are scholars who doubt the veracity of this detail, but Bodhiruci translated the *Sukhāvatīvyūhasūtropadeśa* in 531 and the *Chin-kang-hsien lun* in 535. T'an-luan died in 542.

11. As its content is, nevertheless, instructive, I quote here the passage in question: "Sons of the Buddha, 'land' is the name for the place where the righteous and the holy 賢聖 dwell. This is why all sentient beings as well as the righteous and holy people each dwell in the land [corresponding to the] fruition [of their deeds]. Ordinary people 凡夫 live in [the realm of] the five aggregates 五陰, which is the land of principal fruition 正報. The mountains, forests, earth, all these are called the land of support-fruition 依報." (T. vol. 24, pp. 1015c–6a) (The meaning of 'principal fruition' is, however, slightly different here.)

al fruition' and 'common fruition', turned into the fixed phrase 'two types of fruition, i.e., support and principal'. Being closely related to the main topic of this paper, I shall only touch upon these terms as they are used by the San-lun 三論 patriarch Chi-tsang 吉藏 (549–623).

In the *Fa-hua hsüan-lun* 法華玄論 Chi-tsang sums up the characteristics of sūtra-preaching using the concept of the 'three circles' (*trimaṇḍala* 三輪) of the Buddha, i.e., knowing the listener's abilities (*ādeśanāprātihārya* 他心示導), using supernatural powers (*ṛddhiprātihārya* 神通示導), and preaching the Dharma (*anuśāsanīprātihārya* 說法示導):

> Generally speaking, the teaching gate is of two types. One is the principal fruition 正果, which is called the Tathāgata's body. The other is the support-fruition 依報, which is the Land, etc. When he reveals the two types of fruition, i.e., support and principal 依正二果, of all the Buddhas, this is called the circle of supernatural powers 神通輪. When he preaches the two types of fruition, i.e., support and principal, of all the Buddhas, this is called the Dharma-preaching circle 說法輪. (T. vol. 34, p. 365b)[12]

The phrase 依正二果 is identical to 依正二報. At the same time, the passage can be seen as an adaptation of the Amidist Pure Land theory to Śākyamuni's Vulture Peak Pure Land 靈山淨土.

Chi-tsang further elaborated on the non-duality of the two types of fruition, i.e., support and principal, and uses them as the foundation of the doctrine of grass and trees attaining Buddhahood 草木成佛. Among the ten gates discussing Buddha-nature 佛性 in the *Ta-ch'eng hsüan-lun* 大乘玄論, *chüan* 3, the seventh gate entitled "Existence [of Buddha-nature] within and without" 內外

12. Cf. Hirai Shun'ei 平井俊栄, *Hokke genron no chūshakuteki kenkyū* 法華玄論の註釈的研究 (Tokyo: Shunjūsha, 1987), p. 212; id., *Zoku Hokke genron no chūshakuteki kenkyū* 続法華玄論の註釈的研究 (Tokyo: Shunjūsha, 1996), pp. 317, 331.

有無 holds that if one discusses the existence of Buddha-nature from within the Principle 理, i.e., from the viewpoint of Buddhist believers, then the acceptance of the fact that sentient beings have Buddha-nature logically leads to the admittance of the idea that grass and trees equally have Buddha-nature. The reason given for this is:

> The *Viṃśatikāvijñaptimātratāsiddhi* 唯識論 says, "[There is] ideation-only and no [exterior] sense-objects. The mountains, rivers, grass, and trees are all mental representations 心想. There are no phenomena outside the mind." This explains that within the Principle all phenomena are non-dual, whether support or principal [fruition] 一切諸法依正不二. If because of the non-duality of the support and principal [fruition] all sentient beings have Buddha-nature, then grass and trees [also] have Buddha-nature. Based on this doctrine, [it follows that] not only sentient beings have Buddha-nature but also grass and trees have Buddha-nature. If one realises the equality (*samatā* 平等) of all phenomena, one does not see the [differences between] the two aspects of support and principal [fruition]. [Seen from] the Principle there actually is neither attaining nor non-attaining [of Buddhahood]. Since there is no non-attaining, then it can be said in a provisional way 假 that there is attainment of Buddhahood. Based on this doctrine, [it follows that] if sentient beings attain Buddhahood, then all the grass and trees can equally attain Buddhahood. (T. vol. 45, p. 40c)[13]

13. On Chi-tsang's theory of grass and trees attaining Buddhhood, cf. Tokiwa Daijō 常盤大定, *Busshō no kenkyū* 佛性の研究 (Tokyo: Heigo Shuppan, 1930), p. 217; Kamata Shigeo 鎌田茂雄, "Sanron-shū, Gozu-shū, Dōkyō wo musubu shisōteki keifu—sōmoku jōbutsu wo tegakari to shite" 三論宗・牛頭宗・道教を結ぶ思想的系譜—草木成佛を手がかりとして, *Komazawa Daigaku Bukkyō Gakubu Kenkyū Kiyō* 駒澤大學佛教學部研究紀要 26 (1968), pp. 79–89.

This is, however, how things appear from the perspective of the general gate 通門 of the Principle 理. From the viewpoint of the particular gate 別門, the same problem is discussed as follows:

> By elucidating the fact that sentient beings have mental perplexity 心迷, it is possible to account for the meaning of awakening. Since grass and trees do not have mind, they have no perplexity. How could it be possible to account for the meaning of awakening [in this case]? (Ibid.)

Since grass and trees have no Buddha-nature, they cannot attain Buddhahood. Chi-tsang makes this remark having perhaps in mind the *Mahāparinirvāṇasūtra* passage which declares that "Buddha nature is not like fences, walls, tiles, and stones." Grass and trees attaining Budhahood is based upon the theory of the non-duality of the principal and support-fruition, which, in its turn, is grounded on the principle of Thusness true-nature 眞如法性 and the doctrine of ideation-only without exterior sense-objects 唯識無境. This does not mean, however, that grass and trees are therefore regarded as sentient beings.

The doctrine of grass and trees attaining Buddhahood is a vast subject in itself. It is undeniable that its background should be sought in Taoist philosophy. Here I shall content myself only with pointing out the fact that this doctrine is connected to Vasubandhu's *vijñaptimātratā* philosophy and Pure Land theory and is based on the concept of two types of fruition, support and principal.

IV

Finally, we can return to our main topic. Let us discuss in broad terms the doctrine of non-sentient beings preaching the Dharma using Nan-yang Hui-chung's *Recorded Sayings*. The source I shall employ here is the *Kuang-chai-ssu Hui-chung yü-lu* 光宅寺慧忠語錄 text edited by Ui Hakuju.[14] Passages (7) and (19) deal with

14. Ui Hakuju 宇井伯寿, *Daini Zenshūshi kenkyū* 第二禅宗史研究 (Tokyo:

a kōan-like story 話 of non-sentient beings preaching the Dharma.

In passage (7), a certain Chang Fen of Nan-yang begs Hui-chung to teach him the meaning of non-sentient beings preaching the Dharma. Hui-chung curtly answers him that if he wishes to ask such a question, he should ask directly non-sentient beings. Chang Fen then asks, "When concisely explained by means of expedient methods (*upāya* 方便) for sentient beings, what is the foundation of non-sentient beings?" Hui-chung replies:

> Even if you could now use all actions, there is not the slightest difference between the rise and cessation of ordinary people and Saints. This is beyond [the understanding of] consciousness. It does not belong to sentient beings. It energetically displays Awakening and is without any attachment. This is why the six faculties correspond to form and discernment is not consciousness.
>
> 但如今於一切動用之中施爲、但凡聖兩流都無少分起滅。便是出識。不屬有情、熾然見覺、只是無其繫執。所以、六根對色。分別非識。

The meaning is not clear, but let us note here that 所以六根對色分別非識 is found in the *Hsin-ming* 心銘 of Fa-jung 法融, the founder of the Oxhead 牛頭 Chan school, with the only difference being that the latter replaces 色 with 境.[15]

In passage (19) we have a series of dialogues with a monk from the South. Not all of them are, however, directly connected with the doctrine of non-sentient beings preaching the Dharma. The dialogue starts with Hui-chung asking about the tenets of the Southern School. Upon hearing Ma-tsu's 馬祖 (709–788) doctrine that the mind itself is the Buddha 即心是佛, he makes the follow-

---

Iwanami Shoten, 1941), pp. 306–325.

15. Ibid., p. 128, l. 14. On the relationship between Hui-chung and Fa-jung, see Kamata, op. cit. On non-sentient beings preaching the Dharma, cf. Ishii Shūdō 石井修道, "Mujō seppō no seiritsu katei" 無情説法の成立過程, *JIBS* 16-1 (1967), pp. 140–141.

ing comments. In the final analysis, there are two theories concerning Buddha-nature: one is his own teaching of the identity of body and mind 身心一如, which holds that Buddha-nature is completely non-arising and non-perishing 全不生滅; the other, which he criticises, is the doctrine of half arising and perishing and half non-arising and non-perishing 半生滅半不生滅, which claims that "the body is non-sentient but the mind nature is sentient." It is then Hui-chung's turn to put a series of questions to the monk. The latter concludes that the body and mind are not separate from true nature and the characteristic of the world is its lack of characteristics 無相. The end of the story shows Hui-chung approving of the monk's conclusion and the latter frankly accepts that Hui-chung is right.

(It appears, however, that the original story in the *Record Sayings* ended with Hui-chung's explanation of his doctrine of the identity of body and mind, at which the questioner exclaimed that had he not met Master Hui-chung, he would have spent his whole life in vain. Ui claims that the rest of the story follows the *Ching-te ch'uan-teng lu* 景德傳燈錄.)

After the passage containing the criticism of the theory of the mind itself being the Buddha, found at the beginning of this section (in the chapter "Discussing the Mind and Discussing Innate Nature" 說心說性 of the *Shōbō genzō*, Dōgen also comments on this problem), we have a short paragraph with a question concerning 'Buddha's wisdom vision' (*tathāgatajñānadarśana* 佛知見) in the *Saddharmapuṇḍarīka-sūtra*. Then the discussion of the concept of non-sentient beings starts with the question "What is the Buddha-mind" 阿那箇是佛心. (I shall divide the passage into subsections, which are formally marked in the original Chinese text with phrases like "the monk asked" 僧問, "the monk asked again" 僧又問, or "[he] asked again" 又問. As this is the third paragraph of passage (19), I shall start my notation with (C).) In what follows I shall give a free translation slightly paraphrasing the original.

(C) "What is the Buddha-mind?"

"Any and every non-sentient thing like fences, walls, tiles, pebbles, etc., is Buddha-mind."

"Then you contradict the scriptures. In the *Mahāparinirvāṇa-sūtra* it is said, 'It is called Buddha-nature because it is different from non-sentient beings like fences, walls, etc.' Or do you think that Buddha-mind and Buddha-nature are different things?"

"For the deluded, they are different; for the enlightened, they are not different."

"If so, then you differ again from the sutras. It is said in the scriptures, 'The mind and Buddha-nature are different. The mind is impermanent and Buddha-nature is eternal.'"

"You are attached to the literal meaning of the words 語 and do not try to rely on the meaning 義 [behind them]. It is like [the relationship between] water and ice. When deluded, living beings fasten up their [Buddha-]nature and this becomes the mind; when enlightened, the mind melts away and turns into [Buddha-]nature. If non-sentient beings had no Buddha-nature at all, the scriptures would not maintain doctrines like 'the three realms are mind-only' 三界唯心 and 'all phenomena are ideation-only' 萬法唯識. This is why it is said in the *Avataṃsaka-sūtra*, 'All phenomena of the three realms are created by the mind alone.' Let me ask you. Are non-sentient entities within these three realms or are they without? Are they mind or not? If they were not mind, the sūtras would not speak of the three realms being mind-only. If they were mind, you should not say that non-sentient beings have no Buddha-nature."

Hui-chung tries to explain here the principle of non-sentient beings having Buddha-nature by making an appeal first of all to the theories of mind-only and ideation-only. The next paragraph deals with non-sentient beings preaching the Dharma.

(D1) "If non-sentient beings have mind, can we then understand their Dharma-preaching?"

"They always energetically preach the Dharma without stopping a single moment."

"But I can't hear them."

"The fact that you can't hear them does not mean that others can't hear either."

"Who on earth can actually hear them?"

"The Saints."

"So do [ordinary] living beings lack the capability 分 to hear them?"

"I preach for living beings, not for Saints."

"Can you, Master, hear them?"

"I can't hear them either."

"Why?"

"Fortunately 賴 I can't hear non-sentient beings preaching the Dharma. If I could hear them, I would be identical with a Saint, and you could not meet or hear me preaching the Dharma."

"So does it actually mean that no living being can hear non-sentient beings preaching the Dharma?"

"If they could hear them, they wouldn't be [ordinary] living beings any more."

Dōgen quotes this passage at the beginning of the "Non-Sentient Beings Preaching the Dharma" chapter in the *Shōbō genzō*.

Next the scriptural authority is questioned.

(D2) "Is there any scriptural authority for non-sentient beings preaching the Dharma?"

"[True] words don't necessarily rely upon scriptural authority. Nor are they necessarily preached by Superior Men 君子. Isn't it said, however, in the *[Smaller] Sukhāvatīvyūha-sūtra*, 'The lakes, birds, and trees, all these recollect the Buddha, the Dharma, and the Saṃgha'? Birds are indeed living beings. But are trees and lakes sentient beings? The *Avataṃsaka-sūtra* also says, 'The land (*kṣetra* 刹) preaches, living beings preach, everything in the three realms preaches.' Living beings are undoubtedly sentient. But how can the land be sentient?"

Then the dialogue turns to the problem of the Buddha-nature of non-sentient beings. As this passage uses 'sentient beings' 有情 instead of 'living beings' 衆生, its source appears somehow different.[16] Let us quote here only the part relevant to our problem.

(D3) "Let's suppose that both sentient and non-sentient beings have Buddha-nature. While killing and eating a sentient being results in sin and grudges and receives its karmic retribution, I have never heard that doing harm to a non-sentient being or eating things like the five cereals, vegetables, fruits or chestnuts is a sin or causes grudges."[17]

"Sentient beings represent the principal fruition 正報. Having been deluded and perverse 虛妄顚倒 and having falsely conceived of the concepts of 'I' 我 and 'mine' 我所 from beginningless time, sentient beings have borne grudges and received their karmic retribution for it. But non-sentient beings represent the support-fruition 依報. They have had neither false views 顚倒 nor a grudging mind. Therefore, it is not said that they are subject to karmic retribution."

After this dialogue, the monk asks about non-sentient beings attaining Buddhahood: which of the Buddhas of the present aeon (*bhadrakalpa* 賢劫) was originally a non-sentient being having attained Buddhahood? Hui-chung answers that just as everything in the land belongs to the Crown Prince when he inherits the throne, everything in the world belongs to the body of Vairocana Buddha and non-sentient beings do not receive predictions of future Buddhahood (*vyākaraṇa* 授記) separate from the Buddha-body (*bud-*

---

16. 'Sentient beings' 有情 is a term belonging to the 'new translations' period starting with Hsüan-tsang and replaced the earlier 'living beings' 衆生. 'Non-sentient beings', 無情 or 非情, as an equivalent of *asattva* belongs to the same period. I have not checked the earliest occurrences of 無情, but it is also possible that it translates the Sanskrit *acetana*.

17. This is precisely what Prof. Schmithausen describes as the limit of non-killing awareness (cf. n. 3 above).

dhakāya 佛身). The monk remarks that if the whole land were Buddha-body, our excrements would defile it. Is it not a sin? Hui-chung replies that since all living beings are Buddha-body, then who could be held responsible for such a thing? This dialogue shows that the concepts of principal fruition and support-fruition no longer refer to the Pure Land but are considered to represent all sentient and non-sentient beings within Vairocana's Dharma-body.

(E) Upon hearing that all sentient beings are Buddha-body, the monk asks, "It would then appear that all living beings could become liberated 解脱 at the same time by the practice of only one Buddha. Why does this not happen?" Using the doctrine of the six characteristics 六相, especially 'the difference existing within sameness' 同中有異, Hui-chung answers, "Living beings and the Buddha have the same nature, but this does not invalidate the principle that each sentient being achieves what he/she practises 自修自得. It is like not becoming satiated merely by looking at someone else eating."

The next question refers to the doctrine of regarding all entities as manifestations of Thusness 眞如 and Wisdom 般若.

(F) "Amongst the words of the virtuous of yore 古德 we find,

> The verdant bamboo is True Thusness 眞如 root and branch;
> There's no luxuriant chrysanthemum that is not Pure Wisdom 般若.[18]

"If you don't accept it, then this must be a heretical doctrine. There are, however, people who believe it. How should we judge it when they say that this is unfathomable?"

"This is, methinks, the stage of great bodhisattvas like Mañjuśrī and Samantabhadra and cannot be comprehended by common living beings. It agrees with the Mahāyāna scriptures of the Perfect Teaching (*nītārtha* 了義). We find thus in the *Avataṃsaka-sūtra*, 'The Buddha-body permeates the Dharma-realm (*dharma-*

18. The source of this quotation needs to be ascertained.

dhātu 法界) and reveals itself before all living beings. In accordance with the conditions 緣 and fruition 感 [enjoyed by each living being], there is nothing that it does not pervade. And it eternally sits on the Throne of Awakening (*bodhi* 菩提).' If you accept the fact that the verdant bamboo is not outside the Dharma-realm, why shouldn't it be Buddha-body? In the *Mahāprajñāpāramitāsūtra* it is said, 'Since form (*rūpa* 色) is infinite, Wisdom (*prajñā* 般若) is also infinite.' As no flowers are outside the scope of form, why shouldn't they be Wisdom? There is no reason, however, to forsake those who don't pay attention to this profound teaching."

Next the text deals with the problem of liberation (*mokṣa* 解脫).

(G) "There is a spiritual friend (*kalyāṇamitra* 善知識) who advises disciples in the following way: 'The only thing you have to do is to realise fully your original mind 本心. If you discern impermanence, i.e., the moment of death 了無常來時, then you will throw away this wretched body 陋殼子一邊 and the [wrong] perception 覺性 acting as your soul will immediately be abandoned. This is called liberation.' What do you think about it?"

"This is no different from the doctrines of the Two Vehicles 二乘 and of the heretics 外道. All the followers of the Two Vehicles abhor the cycle of life and death of the conditioned realm (*saṃskṛta* 有爲法) and aspire to reach Nirvāṇa without any remaining substratum (*anupadhiśeṣanirvāṇa* 無餘涅槃). Lao-tzu 老子 also said, 'The reason that I have a great affliction is that I have a body' 吾所以有大患者爲吾有身. The saints of the Two Vehicles dwell in meditation all throughout a long aeon and when this *kalpa* comes to an end they convert to Mahāyāna. The heretics dwell in the sphere of neither-perception-nor-non-perception (*naivasaṃjñānāsaṃjñāyatana* 非想非非想天) for eighty thousand aeons, but even after such a long period they cannot avoid the cycle of rebirth (*saṃsāra* 輪廻生死)."

The following section (H) contains the above-mentioned doctrine of the identity of body and mind.[19]

V

This brings my rambling presentation to an end. It appears that as yet Hui-chung's *Recorded Sayings* has not been sufficiently examined. To start with, the question arises as to how much of the text represents Hui-chung's own contribution. Furthermore, the present text seems to be a mixture of early and later layers as well as of different lines of thought. There is no doubt, however, that not later than the ninth century the names of Kuei-shan Ling-yu 潙山靈祐 (771–853) and Hui-chung were being propagated as the main characters of kōan-like stories concerning non-sentient beings preaching the Dharma.

It is undeniable that the theory of grass and trees attaining Buddhahood, which started with Chi-tsang, functioned as the premise for the formation of this story. Besides, we have already seen that it also inherited the tradition of the mind-only conception of Sukhāvatī characteristic of the Chinese Pure Land school, which is based on the *Sukhāvatīvyūhasūtropadeśa*. I surmise there is yet

19. In his *Zen shisō no hihanteki kenkyū* 禅思想の批判的研究 (Tokyo: Daizō Shuppansha, 1994,) Prof. Matsumoto Shirō 松本史朗 distinguishes two traditions of Zen thought according to the interpretation of Buddha-nature. He calls the first one the 'theory of immanent Buddha-nature' 仏性内在論 and includes here the lineage starting with the doctrine of 'the mind itself being the Buddha' 即心是仏, believed to belong to the Southern school of Chan, and continuing with the 'True[ly Enlightened] Man of no rank' 無位真人 of the Lin-chi/Rinzai school. The second one is named the 'theory of manifest Buddha-nature' 仏性顕在論 and denotes the line which stretches from Hui-chung's 'non-sentient beings preaching the Dharma' to Tung-shan 洞山 and Dōgen. Prof. Matsumoto considers that the theory of immanent Buddha-nature originated in the doctrine of 'grass and trees attaining Buddhahood' advocated by Chi-tsang and other Buddhist thinkers, and that the theory of immanent Buddha-nature evolved into the manifest theory because of the influence of Taoist 老荘 thought (p. 101; p. 198, n. 56, etc.). This seems to me a very appropriate interpretation. I am afraid, however, that the uncompromising criticism of the Buddha-nature theory as non-Buddhist is somewhat misleading in the understanding of Zen thought.

another source which made possible the formation of the doctrine of non-sentient beings preaching the Dharma: the theory of 'the Tathāgata not preaching a single word during forty-nine years' 四十九年如來一字不說 expounded in the *Laṅkāvatāra-sūtra*, with which Hui-chung was apparently familiar. This can be inferred from the dialogue concerning *wu* 無 with the monk Ling-chüeh 靈覺 from Ch'ang-chou 常州, found in section (20) of the *Recorded Sayings*. The monk asks, "Mahākāśyapa was at the Buddha's side. Did he hear [the Teaching] or not?" Hui-chung answers, "He heard it without hearing it" or "The Tathāgata preaches by non-preaching." When asked what 'preaching by non-preaching' is, Hui-chung replies, "Though words pervade the world 天下, there is no verbal fault."[20] This corresponds to T'ou-tzu Ta-t'ung's 投子大同 (819–914) words: "Non-sentient beings have no harsh words" 無情莫惡口, quoted at the end of the "Non-Sentient Beings Preaching the Dharma" chapter in the *Shōbō genzō*.

'Non-sentient beings preaching the Dharma' became the subject of a dialogue between Yün-yen 雲巖 (780–841) and Tung-shan 洞山 (807–869), led to the latter's enlightenment based on 'hearing sounds with the eye' 眼處聞聲, and eventually continued with Dōgen's thought. In this tradition the prime interest is not so much whether non-sentient beings preach the Dharma or not, but rather what one hears from non-sentient beings and what listening to the Dharma should actually be like. This viewpoint is connected to the Buddhist tradition of 'thus have I heard' (*evaṃ mayā śrutam* 如是我聞). What does one hear? The answer is the Buddha's words (*buddhavacana* 佛說). What do the Buddha's words speak about? They preach the Truth (*dharma* 法). How did the Buddha obtain this Truth? Dōgen thinks that the Buddha heard the Truth and attained Buddhahood. If so, is not the Truth itself the agency of preaching the Dharma? The beginning of the "Non-sentient Beings Preaching the Dharma" chapter declares that

20. Ui, op. cit., p. 325.

"preaching the Dharma 說法 represents the words of the Truth [itself] 法說." In "The Demeanour of the Practising Buddha" chapter Dōgen states that he learnt this concept of 'the words of the Truth [itself]' from the Path 道 of Hsüeh-feng 雪峰 (822–908) and Hsüan-sha 玄沙 (835–908) as well as from the outstanding teachings of Yüan-wu 圜悟 (1063–1135).[21]

'Non-sentient beings preaching the Dharma' exists as a word of the Truth [itself]. It is not a problem of sentience or non-sentience. Nor is it a question of being conditioned or non-conditioned. "It is caused neither conditionally nor non-conditionally. Nor is it a *dharma* following dependent origination." All Buddhas have heard these words of the Truth [itself] and have established the correct lineage of transmission 正傳. And they have set it up by shaping the words of the Truth [itself] into Dharma-preaching. The transmission of the *Shōbō genzō* based on 'holding a flower and faintly smiling' 拈華微笑 is equally an instance of 'non-sentient beings preaching the Dharma'. Dōgen discovered non-sentient beings preaching the Dharma in the stream's murmur and mountain landscape, and he urges that one should experience it as a meditative technique by listening to the Buddha's acts 佛事 which are revealed by fences, walls, tiles, pebbles, etc. (*Bendōwa* 辨道話).

What should we modern people hear from the environment? We must seriously think it through.[22]

---

21. This view is based on Dr. Tamaki Kōshirō's interpretation. Cf. Tamaki Kōshirō 玉城康四郎, *Gendaigoyaku Shōbō genzō* 現代語訳正法眼蔵, vol. 2 (Tokyo: Daizō Shuppan, 1994), p. 274 ("Gyōbutsu igi, kaisetsu" 行佛威儀・解説), and vol. 4, pp. 195–199 ("Mujō seppō, kaisetsu" 無情説法・解説).

22. My lack of competence prevents me from touching on the modern implications of 'non-sentient beings preaching the Dharma', but the following recent studies will provide important leads for the interested reader: Graham Parkes, "Voices of Mountains, Trees and Rivers: Kūkai, Dōgen, and Deeper Ecology," in Mary Evelyn Tucker and Duncan Ryūken Williams, eds., *Buddhism and Ecology: The Interconnection of Dharma and Deeds* (Cambridge,

MA: Harvard University Press, 1997), pp. 111–128; Ruben L. F. Habito, "Mountain and River and the Great Earth: Zen and Ecology," ibid., pp. 167–175.

Additional Note. The following studies published by Dr. SakamotoYukio 坂本幸男 around 1960 touch on the theory of grass and trees attaining Buddhahood and on the non-duality of the principal and support-fruition as well as their relation to *vijñaptimātratā*: "Hijō ni okeru busshō no umu ni tsuite" 非情に於ける仏性の有無について, *JIBS* 7-2 (1959); "Sōmoku jōbutsu no Nihonteki tenkai" 草木成仏の日本的展開, in *Nakano kyōju koki kinen ronbunshū* 中野教授古稀記念論文集 (Kōyachō: Nakano Kyōju Koki Kinenkai, 1960); "Sōmoku jōbutsu ni tsuite" 草木成仏について, *Ōzaki Gakuhō* 大崎学報 109 (1959). All these studies are included in *Daijō bukkyō no kenkyū* 大乗仏教の研究, vol. 2 of *Sakamoto Yukio ronbunshū* 坂本幸男論文集 (Tokyo: Daitō Shuppansha, 1980).

At about the same time Dr. Miyamoto Shōson 宮本正尊 published the following study on the doctrine of grass and trees attaining Buddhahood, which also takes into consideration Dōgen's 'non-sentient beings preaching the Dharma': "'Sōmoku kokudo shikkai jōbutsu' no busshōronteki igi to sono sakusha" 「草木国土悉皆成仏」の仏性論的意義とその作者, *JIBS* 9-2 (1961); reprinted in *Miyamoto Shōson hakushi Bukkyōgaku ronshū: Bukkyōgaku no konpon mondai* 宮本正尊博士仏教学論集・仏教学の根本問題 (Tokyo: Shunjūsha, 1985).

I have tried in the present paper to investigate some problems left unexamined in these contributions.

Some Problems in the Tibetan Translations from Chinese Materials*

It is a great honour for me to be invited to such an important meeting of distinguished scholars in the field of Tibetology. Being a humble scholar of Indology specialising in the field of Indian Mahāyāna Buddhism, Tibetan studies proper are outside the scope of my research. The present paper is, therefore, a mere by-product of my textual study of the *Laṅkāvatāra*, a famous Mahāyāna scripture, of which the Sanskrit text is available together with three translations in Chinese and two in Tibetan. My special concern at present is the Chinese version of four fascicles translated by Guṇabhadra in 443 A.D., otherwise called the Sung version. This version, the *Leng-ch'ieh a-pa-t'o-lo pao-ching* 楞伽阿跋陀羅寶經, was translated into Tibetan by Chos grub, a famous *lo tsā ba* of Tun-huang. I wish to deal with this Tibetan version of the *Laṅkāvatāra*, titled *ḥPhags pa Laṅ kar gśegs pa rin po cheḥi mdo las Saṅs rgyas thams cad kyi gsuṅ gi sñiṅ po shes bya ba*.

As is well-known, there are a certain number of texts in the Tibetan Tripiṭaka which have been translated from Chinese. Some of them are retranslations from Chinese translations of Indian canonical works, such as the *Laṅkāvatāra* mentioned above, the *Suvarṇaprabhāsottamarājasūtra* (from I-ching's translation), the *Mahāparinirvāṇasūtra* of 40 fascicles, and several scriptures belonging to the *Mahāratnakūṭa* Collections. Some others are of so-called spurious sūtras such as the *Chin-kang san-mei ching* 金剛三昧經, the *Shou-leng-yen ching* 首楞嚴經 in 10 fascicles, etc.

* Originally published in Louis Ligeti, ed., *Proceedings of the Csoma de Kőrös Memorial Symposium Held at Mátrafüred, Hungary, 24-30 September 1976* (Budapest: Akadémiai Kiadó, 1978), pp. 459–467.

There are also translations of commentaries such as the *Nyāya-praveśa* of Śaṅkarasvāmin and the *Ta-ch'eng po-fa ming-men lun* 大乘百法明門論 attributed to Vasubandhu (both translated into Chinese by Hsüan-tsang and retranslated into Tibetan by Chos kyi rin chen). In addition, we cannot overlook two important works by Chinese scholar-monks, namely, the *Miao-fa lien-hua ching hsüan-tsan* 妙法蓮華經玄贊, a commentary on the *Saddharmapuṇḍarīka* (Kumārajīva's translation) by K'uei-chi 窺基, and the *Chieh shen-mi ching shu* 解深密經疏, a commentary on the *Saṃdhinirmocana* (Hsüan-tsang's translation) composed by Yüan-ts'e 圓測. The latter was translated into Tibetan by Chos grub, while the translator of the former is unknown. Both authors, K'uei-chi and Yüan-ts'e, were disciples of Hsüan-tsang.

Among the translators of these texts into Tibetan, whose names are as a rule not recorded, the most brilliant figure was Chos grub, living in Tun-huang in the 9th century A.D. (flourished c. 830–860; cf. Ueyama Daishun 上山大峻, "Daibankoku sanzō hōshi shamon Hōjō no kenkyū" 大蕃國三藏法師沙門法成の研究, *Tōhō Gakuhō* 38, p. 133). His name is recorded seven times in the *dKar chags* of the Tibetan Tripiṭaka as a *lo tsā ba* or *shu chen gyi lo tsā ba* (e.g., Peking nos. 174, 369, 370, 374, 776, 1023 and 5517). Seven sūtras belonging to the *dKon brtsegs* (*Ratnakūṭa*) (Peking nos. 760-7, 11, 13, 14, 18, 20 and 40) are also regarded as his translations. Several other works which have not been preserved must also have been translated by him into Tibetan. For his activities, the status of Tun-huang in those days cannot be overlooked. The close connection of Tun-huang with Tibet as part of her territory (Tibetan occupation of Tun-huang, 781–848) on the one hand, and the prospering of Chinese Buddhism in this area since the beginning of its history on the other, led to the importation of Chinese works into Tibet on a large scale. If Chos grub is identified as Fa-ch'eng 法成 of Ta-fan-kuo 大蕃國, he might have contributed to the translation of some canonical works into Chinese, too. One of the characteristics of Buddhism in Tun-huang in the 8th and 9th centuries was the popularity of Zen Buddhism, a tradition in which we find an important role for the *Laṅkāvatāra* in four fascicles, as is symbolized by the legend of Bodhidharma.

According to the colophon of the Tibetan translation of the Sung version of the *Laṅkāvatāra*, Chos grub was helped by the commentary of Wen-hui (Yüan-hui 圓暉) on the said sūtra, part of which is found among the Tun-huang materials in Tibetan (Stein no. 219, Pelliot no. 609—a small part). This commentary, though lost in Chinese, might have been popular among Zen Buddhists in Tun-huang at that time.

There is another version of the Tibetan translation of the *Laṅkāvatāra* among the Tun-huang materials (Pelliot no. 608). It is reported to be the old version of the translation of the same sūtra from the Sanskrit original now kept in the Tibetan Tripiṭaka, the latter being a revised edition. Chos grub might have consulted this Tun-huang version, too, in his translation of the Sung version into Tibetan. Of this matter, however, I can say nothing definite at present as I have not examined it yet.

In the introductory section of the *sGra sbyor bam po gñis pa* (Tohoku no. 4347, Peking no. 5833, *sGra sbyor*), otherwise called the *Madhyama-vyutpatti*, we find a passage where the *Laṅkāvatāra*, together with the *Dharma Ratnamegha*, is mentioned as a good example of translation (cf. Nils Simonsson, *Indo-tibetische Studien*, I, Uppsala, 1957, pl. 258.). This *Laṅkāvatāra* would be either the Tun-huang version or its revised version, i.e., the present Kanjur text from a Sanskrit source, but not that from the Chinese Sung version. It should be noted, however, that Chos grub was acquainted with the revised Tibetan terminology, the results being collected in the *Mahāvyutpatti*. His translation of the *Laṅkāvatāra* uses the newly accepted terms as much as possible, probably in the light of the then revised *Laṅ kar gśegs pa* from Sanskrit, although its context follows closely the Chinese

Sung version. I wish to show some typical examples of the unique characteristics in his translation.**

Ex. 1

T(2) *dṅos poḥi raṅ bshin don dam paḥi sñiṅ po de daṅ ldan pas de bshin gśegs pa rnaṁs ḥjig rten pa daṅ / ḥjig rten las ḥdas pa daṅ / ḥjig rten las ḥdas pa mchog gi chos ḥphags paḥi śes rab kyi spyan yoṅs su rdsogs nas, raṅ daṅ spyiḥi mtshan ñid rnam par dgod pa la ḥjug ciṅ...* (88: 4.2-4). [Being endowed with that essence of the ultimate meaning, the own-nature of beings, Tathāgatas, having completed the worldly, supra-worldly and most supra-worldly *dharma*s, with the eyes of holy wisdom, enter the establishment of (their) particular and general characteristics.]

C(S) 以性自性第一義心. 成就如來世間出世間出世間上上法聖慧眼，入自共相建立. (483b)

Skt. *...tathāgatānāṃ...bhāvasvabhāvaparamārthahṛdayaṃ yena samanvāgatās tathāgatā laukikalokottaratamān dharmān āryeṇa prajñācakṣuṣā svasāmānyalakṣaṇapatitān vyavasthāpayanti* (40.2-4).

T(1) *dṅos poḥi raṅ bshin daṅ / don dam paḥi sñiṅ po de daṅ ldan pas, de bshin gśegs pa rnams ḥjig rten pa daṅ / ḥjig rten las ḥdas paḥi mchog gi chos raṅ daṅ spyiḥi mtshan ñid du gtogs paḥi* (*pa*?) *rnams ḥphags paḥi śes rab kyi spyan gyis rnam par ḥgod de* (33.1.1-2). [Being endowed with that own-nature of beings and the essence of the ultimate meaning, Tathāgatas establish, with the eyes of the holy wisdom, the worldly and most supra-worldly *dharma*s so as to be of particular and

** *Abbreviations*:

T(1) = Tibetan translation of the *Laṅkāvatāra* from Skt. (Peking Ed., no. 775) (Reprinted Ed., vol. 29).

T(2) = Same from the Chinese Sung version (no. 776).

Skt. = *Laṅkāvatārasūtra*, ed. by B. Nanjio (Kyoto, 1924).

C(S) = Chinese Sung version of the *Laṅkāvatāra* (T. no. 669, vol. 16).

general characteristics.]

In this example, *T(2)*'s reading is, in its context, mostly faithful to the basic *C(S)* and more or less the same as the traditional way of reading this passage in Japan. But as is shown above, *T(2)* differs from *T(1)* in two points, which in its turn is quite faithful to the *Skt*. Namely, *yoṅs su rdsogs nas* in *T(2)*, being equivalent to *ch'eng-chiu* 成就 of *C(S)*, takes *chos* (*rnams*) or *ḥphags paḥi śes rab kyi spyan* as its object, while in *T(1)* this *chos rnams* is taken as the object of the verb *rnam par ḥgod pa*, which is equivalent to the last term, both in *Skt.* and in *C(S)* as well (*vyavasthāpayanti* and *chien-li* 建立 respectively). The other point is *ḥjug ciṅ* in *T(2)*, being the equivalent of *ju* 入 in *C(S)*. It takes *rnam par dgod pa* as an accusative denoting location, while its equivalent in *T(1)*, *gtogs pa*, for *Skt. patita*, takes *raṅ daṅ spyiḥi mtshan nyid* as an accusative denoting location, this being of course true to Sanskrit syntax. Such a difference between the two Tibetan translations is, no doubt, due to the *C(S)* translation and is not the fault of *T(2)* at all. In this case, however, we cannot claim simply that *C(S)* mistook the meaning of the *Skt*. The true cause of this difference is that *T(2)*, like the traditional Chinese commentators (and Japanese readers, too), interpreted the Chinese sentence according to usual Chinese syntax, although the basic Sung version of this passage has a peculiar word order, namely, that of the original *Skt*. Thus, quite contrary to Chinese syntax, the object term comes before the verb, and the instrumental case ending is neglected. At the same time, the Chinese syntax is retained in the case of the compound word *svasāmānyalakṣaṇa-patita* (= *ju tzu-kung-hsiang* 入自共相). On the other hand, there are parts in *T(2)* where Chos grub translated some phrases following *T(1)*, e.g., ... *don dam paḥi sñiṅ po de daṅ ldan pas* and thus *C(S)*'s *ch'eng-chiu* is repeated in this translation, namely, once by *daṅ ldan pas* and secondly by *yoṅs su rdsogs nas*. The Tibetan terms for the Chinese words are, as far as this passage is concerned, exactly the same as in *T(1)*, following probably the latter or accepting standard terms as given in the *Mahāvyutpatti*.

Ex. 2

T(2) Blo gros chen po, mu stegs can de dag rkyen gsum phrad pa las skye shes bya ba yaṅ bya ba daṅ / thabs ni rgyu daṅ ḥbras buḥi raṅ gi mtshan ñid du yod la ḥdas pa daṅ / ma ḥongs pa daṅ / da ltar byuṅ ba ni sa bon yod pa daṅ / sa bon med paḥi mtshan ñid do shes zer te / de ni sṅon gcig nas gcig tu rigs paḥi dṅos po brgyud de ḥongs pa rtogs paḥi rjes su ḥjug ciṅ raṅ gi lta baḥi ñes paḥi bag chags kyis bsgos pas de skad du ston te… (89.1.5-7). [O Mahāmati, these heretics maintain that what is called the birth (of something) after the meeting together of three conditions is that, while action and means are existing as the characteristics of cause and effect, past, future and present are the characteristics of the existence of the seed and the non-existence of the seed. This is what is transmitted by the ground of reasoning in succession from the beginning, (and they) teach thus because, acting after theoretical knowledge, they are polluted by the residue of faults of their own perception.]

C(S) 大慧. 彼諸外道. 說有三緣合生者. 所作方便. 因果自相. 過去未來現在有種無種相. 從本已來. 成事相承. 覺相地轉. 自見過習氣. 作如是說. (483c)

Skt. teṣām api, Mahāmate, trisaṃgatipratyayakriyāyogenopadeśo vidyate hetuphalasvalakṣaṇatayātītānāgatapratyutpannāsatsallakṣaṇāstitāṃ yuktyāgamais tarkabhūmau vartamānā svadṛṣṭidoṣavāsanatayā nirdekṣyanti (41.10-13).

T(1) Blo gros chen po, de·dag la yaṅ gsum phrad paḥi rkyen gyi byed pa daṅ ldan pas rgyu daṅ ḥbras bu daṅ / raṅ gi mtshan ñid du ston pa yod de / ḥdas pa daṅ / ma ḥongs pa daṅ / da ltar byuṅ baḥi yod pa daṅ med paḥi mtshan ñid yod par rigs pa daṅ / gshuṅ gis brtags paḥi sa la gnas siṅ raṅ gi lta ba ñes paḥi bag chags kyis ston te (33.2.3-5). [Furthermore, O Mahāmati, of them are found the teaching of cause and effect and the own-characteristics (of things) by association of action conditioned by the meeting of three (factors). (And they) maintain the existence of the characteristics of being and non-being of past, future and present, by living in the field of theoretical knowledge on the basis of reasoning and traditional teaching, due to the residue of faults of their own perception.]

In this example, we must begin with an examination of some Chinese terms unique to this Sung version of the *Laṅkāvatāra*.

(1) *fang-pien* 方便, meaning *yoga* (in *kriyāyoga*), is often found in this text, and it is correct in cases where *yoga* actually means a practical means. In this case, however, *yogena* means "in association with" or "in connection (of something) with (something)," as is shown in *T(1)*: *daṅ ldan pas*. *T(2)* translated this *yoga* by *thabs* on the basis of the Chinese rendering.

(2) *yu-chung wu-chung hsiang* 有種無種相 is the equivalent of *asat-sal-lakṣaṇa* and would simply mean a characteristic of non-being and being. This peculiar translation is also observed many times. For example, *abhūtvā sat*, *nāsty-asti*, etc., which are in *T(2)* invariably translated as *sa bon med pa daṅ sa bon yod pa*. *Skt. abhūtva sat* means in fact a kind of philosophical opinion concerning the existence of things, namely, existence without cause.

(3) *ch'eng-shih* 成事 and *hsiang-ch'eng* 相承 are here used for *Skt. yukti* and *āgama*, respectively, the meaning being as shown in *T(1) rigs pa daṅ gshuṅ*. The latter Chinese word is understandable in this sense, although *āgama* is usually transliterated as *a-han* 阿含. On the other hand, the former term is quite difficult to understand in the sense of *yukti*. Still, *T(2)* has the term *rigs pa* for *ch'eng* 成. How Chos grub could get this idea is not clear, but as the term *ch'eng* was previously used for translating *yukti* in this sūtra (in the passage of 108 questions and answers), Chos grub must have drawn this peculiar sense of "reasoning" out of

ch'eng. But this time *C(S)* attached another *shih* 事 to it to make a technical term in two syllables, and Chos grub might have been confused and added a term indicating its meaning of "matter" (*dṅos po* corresponding to *Skt. vastu*).

(4) As for the phrase *ts'ung pen i-lai* 從本已來, for which no Sanskrit equivalent is found in this passage, we may be allowed to surmise the existence of such a term as *anādi-* in the original Sanskrit used for *C(S)* in the place of, e.g., *astitām* in the present Sanskrit text. More probably, however, this phrase might be an insertion made in accordance with the interpretation of the term *āgama* as traditional transmittance, and *T(2)* went further along the same line of interpretation.

Another difference between *T(1)* and *T(2)* is again caused by *C(S)*'s rather arbitrary placing of terms in the first sentence without taking care of case-endings. Thus *shuo yu* 說有 is a rendering of *upadeśo vidyate*, and, being a translation of *Skt.*, *C(S)* might be expected to read it in the sense that "those heretics are of the opinion that...," and the terms up to *yin-kuo tzu-hsiang* 因果自相 in the first sentence should be taken as the contents of their opinion. This way of interpretation is reflected in *T(1)*. Anyway, this sentence in *C(S)* is most difficult to read as long as we regard it as standard Chinese. Therefore, we cannot blame *T(2)* for reading the terms up to *yu-chung wu-chung hsiang* as the object of the verb *shuo* 說 (*ston pa*).

Ex. 3

T(2) *deḥi phyir blun po de dag theg pa gsum du smra ba yin te / sems tsam du snaṅ ba rnams snaṅ ba med par mi smraḥo* (93.1.2-3). [Therefore those ignorant folk, being adherents of the Three Vehicle doctrine, never maintain that (worldly) phenomena are, being mind-only, of no appearance (in reality).]

C(S) 是故凡愚. 說有三乘. 說心量趣無所有. (486c)

Skt. *atas te, Mahāmate, mohapuruṣā yānatrayavādino bhavanti, na cittamātragatinirābhāsavādinaḥ* (62.2-3).

T(1) Blo gros chen po, deḥi phyir skyes bu blun po de dag theg pa gsum du smra ba yin te, sems tsam du rtog pa snaṅ ba med par mi smraḥo (36.5.6). [Therefore, O Mahāmati, those ignorant people are adherents of the Three Vehicle doctrine and never maintain that (all phenomena), being realized as mind-only, are of no appearance.]

In this example, anybody would notice at a glance that both Tibetan translations are quite similar, the only difference of great importance being *snaṅ ba rnams* in *T(2)* vs. *rtog pa* in *T(1)*. *T(2)* is clearer than *T(1)* and nearer to the original sense of the *Skt.*, while *C(S)* has, on the contrary, no negative particle in the second part and shows a quite opposite interpretation. There should be a negative particle *pu* 不 before the second *shuo*, so that we can get the same meaning as the *Skt.* Otherwise, we may read the *C(S)* passage as follows: "There is not at all the way of teaching of mind-only" for *shuo hsin-liang ch'ü wu so-yu* 說心量趣無所有. Chos grub might have noticed it and inserted a negative particle *mi* as *T(1)* did. As for the equivalent of *Skt. gati*, Chos grub did not accept *T(1)*'s *rtog pa*, probably considering it different from Ch. *ch'ü* 趣, which, in turn, means paths of transmigration (*ḥgro ba*), and he translated it as *snaṅ ba rnams* in the sense of the world of transmigration as being merely phenomenal, in contrast to reality, which is of no appearance (*snaṅ ba med pa*). In the Sanskrit text, from the context, *gati* here may mean "understanding" or "realization" as rendered in *T(1)* (*rtog pa*), but *T(2)*'s translation has not deviated from what the Sanskrit text wanted to express. Here we observe Chos grub's deliberative attitude toward translation.

The Chinese terms *hsin-liang* 心量 (lit. "mind-measure") for *cittamātra* and *wu so-yu* 無所有 (lit. "of no possession") for *nirābhāsa* are unique to *C(S)*. They are translated usually as *wei-hsin* 唯心 for the former, and *wu ying-hsiang* 無影像 (lit. "without image") or *wu-hsiang* 無相 for the latter. As they are key words for understanding the doctrine of the *Laṅkāvatāra* and are so often used in the text, there would have been no room for misunderstanding these terms.

Some other terms peculiar to *C(S)* and translated into Tibetan correctly in the light of the Sanskrit text are:

1. *C(S) wu-hsien* 無間 for *Skt. abhisamaya*, translated as *mṅon par rtog pa* in *T(2)* (*wu-hsien* is usually rendered as *anantara* "of no interval").
2. *C(S) wang-hsiang* 妄想 for *Skt. vikalpa* or *parikalpa*, translated as *rnam par rtog pa* or *yoṅs su rtog pa*.
3. *C(S) she-shou* 攝受 for *Skt. grahaṇa*, *grāhaka*, translated as *ḥdsin pa*.

Ex. 4

T(2) Blo gros chen po, ḥdod chen po ḥdi dag ni ḥdod chen po ma yin te / ḥjig rten na su shig thar pa la ḥjug par ḥgyur / (93.5.2-3). [O Mahāmati, these Icchantikas are not Icchantikas at all. Whoever in the world will enter into liberation?]

C(S) 大慧. 彼一闡提. 非一闡提. 世間解脫. 誰轉. (487b)

Skt. tatra icchantikānāṃ punar Mahāmate, anicchantikatā mokṣaṃ kena pravartate? (65.17-66.1).

T(1) de la ḥdod chen pa rnams kyi thar par mi ḥdod pa ji ltar ḥbyuṅ she na?... (33.4.4). [Here, how does the non-desiring of liberation of Icchantikas come about?]

In this example, *T(2)* is exactly true to *C(S)*. *C(S)*'s interpretation, though being no doubt a misunderstood rendering of the Sanskrit sentence, if the Sanskrit is correct, sounds reasonable since it makes us recollect the passage of the 108 phrases (*aṣṭottaraśata-pada*), which consist of pairs of words in contradiction. Unfortunately the translator of *C(S)* failed to express the ironical idea of the Sanskrit text involved in the term *anicchantikatā* by transliterating it in the same way as *icchantika*.

Ex. 5

T(2) *gshan gyi dbaṅ gi raṅ bshin gyi dṅos poḥi mtshan ñid ni ḥdu byed kyi dṅos poḥi mtshan maḥi mtshan ñid lta bur snaṅ ste / mṅon par shen paḥi kun brtags paḥi raṅ bshin ni rnam pa gñis yod par rnam par ḥjug ste /* (94.1.6-7). [Characteristics of things of the nature of depending on others (*paratantra-svabhāva*) appearing as the characteristics of the mark of phenomenal things. And the nature of the imagined (*parikalpita-svabhāva*) (which is characterized) as attachment is established...to be of two kinds.]

C(S) 緣起自性. 事相相行顯現. 事相相計著有二種. 妄想自性...所建立. (487c)

Skt. *paratantrasvabhāvo vastunimittalakṣaṇākāraḥ khyāyate / tatra, Mahāmate, vastunimittalakṣaṇābhiniveśaḥ punar dviprakāraḥ / parikalpitasvabhāvaṃ vyavasthāpayanti* [*tathāgatā*...] (67.5-7).

T(1) *gshan gyi dbaṅ gi raṅ bshin ni dṅos poḥi mtshan maḥi mtshan ñid lta bur snaṅ ba ste / Blo gros chen po, de la dṅos poḥi mtshan maḥi mtshan ñid la mṅon par shen pa ni...kun brtags paḥi raṅ bshin daṅ / rnam pa gñis su ḥjog go* (37.5.5-7). [The nature of depending on others is appearing as the characteristics of the mark of things. Here, O Mahāmati, the attachment to the characteristics of the mark of things is established to be the nature of the imagined and of two kinds...]

Here again *C(S)* has a mere row of words or phrases in the same order as the *Skt.*, and *T(2)* has tried to interpret the sentence according to Chinese syntax, but for the words and phrases it uses terms borrowed from *T(1)*, with the exception of *ḥdu byed* (*saṃskāra*) for *hsing* 行, which in turn is for *Skt. ākāra*, which is translated here as *...lta bur* by *T(1)*. Examining it in detail, however, we find some modification of the Chinese sentence by *T(2)*. Namely, if we retranslate *T(2)* into Chinese, it will be as follows:

C(S) 緣起自性(之)事相相(者). 顯現(如)行事相相. 計著妄想自性有二種.

This is probably due partly to the mechanical acceptance of the phrase *dṅos poḥi mtshan maḥi mtshan ñid lta bur snaṅ ba* of *T(1)* and partly to the ambiguous Chinese term *hsing*, which is here not a perfect rendering of the *Skt. -ākāra*. (As for the second part, we must seek some other reason in connection with the sentence following it.)

The above-mentioned are only a few examples, and it might be dangerous to draw any conclusion from such a few examples. But at least we may say that Chos grub's translation of the Chinese Sung version of the *Laṅkāvatāra* poses various problems not only in connection with the *Laṅkāvatāra* itself but also concerning Buddhism in Tun-huang as well as the history of the compilation of the Tibetan Tripiṭaka. For this, however, we shall be required to study Wen-hui's commentary on the *Laṅkāvatāra* together with the manuscript of the Tibetan translation of the *Laṅkāvatāra* from Sanskrit that was found in Tun-huang.

PART VI
BUDDHIST STUDIES IN JAPAN

One Hundred Years of Buddhist Studies in Japan*

Introduction: Buddhism and Traditional Buddhist Studies in Japan

Japan is a Buddhist country since nearly 75% of the whole population is statistically counted as Buddhist in the sense that they have their family graves in a Buddhist temple and ask the priest of that temple to perform funeral ceremonies. They are recognized as patrons and believers of that temple.

At the same time, however, the Association of Shinto Shrines claims statistically more than 90% of Japanese belong to Shintoism. This claim is also actually true in the sense that most Japanese customarily worship at Shinto shrines. This may sound curious to people who follow a form of monotheism. But historically speaking we Japanese have customarily had two religions since the introduction of Buddhism. Buddhism was tolerant of local faiths and customs, and because of this tolerance, it was able to win the hearts of the Japanese people.

This phenomenon is generally called "Shinto-Buddhist syncretism." The Tokugawa government politically adopted this

* From 16th to 21st of August 2004 there was held in Moskva, Russia, the 37th International Congress of Asian and North African Studies (ICANAS). At the opening ceremony of the conference, I delivered the opening address with the title given here in my capacity as president of the International Union for Oriental and Asian Studies (IUOAS), which has responsibility for the continuity of ICANAS. This is the text of the address, with notes newly attached. This paper was originally written in Japanese and published in *Tōhōgaku* 100 (Sept. 2000) with the title "Tōhōgaku no hyakunen." "One Hundred Years of Buddhist Studies in Japan" is an English version of this paper, originally published in *Indian International Journal of Buddhist Studies* 8 (2007), pp. 153–173.

practice for governing the people, but gave precedence to Buddhism by granting protection to Buddhist temples. (All people were asked to become a "patron" or "donor" of a Buddhist temple.)

The situation changed suddenly after the Meiji Restoration in 1868. The new government, aiming at the establishment of a modern nation-state under the authority of the emperor backed by Shinto powers, tried to remove social forces protected by the previous government, such as Buddhism. Thus in 1870 the government ordered the removal of Buddhist social power by a "Decree for the Separation of Shinto and Buddhism" (神佛分離令), and all Japanese were nationally claimed to be Shintoists.

But this policy was actually not very effective, and Buddhism soon recovered its former influence among the Japanese people. The government could not but permit their faith as a private matter. At the same time, the government policy of attaching importance to the national Shinto faith gradually grew in conjunction with the rise of nationalism, and eventually this policy had to be abandoned as a result of Japan's defeat in World War II. It resulted once again, however, in the coexistence of both religions in the daily lives of ordinary Japanese, and this continues to this day.

The situation regarding Buddhist studies in Japan is closely related to these political changes in the premodern Tokugawa period and in the modern period since the Meiji Restoration.

Namely, all Buddhist sects that had prospered under the protection of the Tokugawa government started sectarian studies of Buddhist doctrine traditional to each sect. Source materials for their studies were basically the Chinese scriptures or Buddhist scriptures translated into Chinese and commentaries on them written by Chinese and Japanese monks. This kind of study had almost reached its limits by the end of the Tokugawa period and forms our basic knowledge of Buddhism in general even today. (One of its legacies is knowledge of the *Abhidharmakośa*.)

The crisis encountered at the time of the Meiji Restoration, on the other hand, caused Buddhist orders to feel the need for revolutionary changes in all possible ways. Having received information that the study of Buddhist scriptures in Sanskrit and other Indian materials was growing in Europe, certain Buddhist orders (e.g., the Shin sect) decided to send young students to Europe with the aim of introducing these modern ways of interpreting Buddhist scriptures and in expectation of modernizing their orders by this means.

This new current of Buddhist studies started in Europe forms part of Indology, that is, the study of Indian materials written in Sanskrit and other Indian languages, and is mainly philological in its methodology. As for Buddhist studies, it covers research on:

(1) Buddhist scriptures written in the Pāli language and transmitted in Sri Lanka and other regions of Southeast Asia.

(2) Buddhist Sanskrit scriptures preserved or found in Nepal and other areas in Central Asia. With these materials, scholars first collected and read the manuscripts and edited the texts for publication. They then tried to translate them into modern languages for further interpretation of the doctrines. In this way they approached the doctrines of the founder of Buddhism, Śākyamuni, and of the Mahāyāna and other later developed doctrines distinguished from the original doctrines of Buddhism.

Also they tried to clarify the history of Buddhism, including the founder's biography, by using, besides textual materials, inscriptions, records of travellers, etc. For these philological studies Chinese materials and Tibetan materials are quite helpful for understanding the original forms of the texts, especially when Sanskrit materials are lacking.

This second current of Buddhist studies may be characterized as objective (or scientific) in comparison with the traditional methods of study followed in each Buddhist sect or order, which were surely biased towards Buddhism.

I. Buddhist Studies before 1950

I-1. General Survey

The initiation of the Japanese to the world of modern Buddhist studies was begun by two young monks, Nanjō Bun'yū (a.k.a Nanjio Bun'yiu) (1849–1927) and Kasahara Kenju (1852–83), when they were sent to Oxford to study under Max Müller (1823–1907) by order of the chief priest of Higashi Honganji in 1876.

Prior to their return to Japan, however, Tokyo University started a lecture class on the Buddhist text *Daijō kishin ron* 大乘起信論 (Awakening of Faith in the Mahāyāna), a text in the Chinese Tripiṭaka, which sets forth the so-called Tathāgatagarbha theory (to which I shall refer later) and was commonly used among East Asian Buddhists.[1] The lecturer was Hara Tanzan (1819–92), who belonged to the Sōtō Zen sect. This class signified in a sense the recovery of an old tradition by admission of the government, and it was soon elevated to a regular class called "Indian Philosophy." In other words, Buddhism was officially admitted by the government to be a form of philosophy, but not a religion, a philosophy founded in India.

Quite interesting to us is that this designation "Indian Philosophy," first used to denote Buddhism, gradually extended its scope and unexpectedly gave rise to research on various branches of Indian thought in general, the object of study covered by Indology. Later on, when chairs of Indology were established in imperial universities in Tokyo, Kyoto, and so on, they were named "chair in Indian Philosophy," inclusive of Buddhist studies.

As for the systematic introduction and establishment of Indological methodology, Takakusu Junjirō (1866–1945), who studied

1. As for the process of the foundation of a regular class of "Indian Philosophy," see *Tōkyō Daigaku hyakunen shi* [Hundred Years of Tokyo University], Section on Faculty of Letters, 1985.

under Max Müller after Nanjō, would assume the name of pioneer when Tokyo Imperial University welcomed him and offered him a chair in Sanskrit studies in 1900. In the case of Indian Philosophy, the first chair was established in 1916.

Thus the term "Buddhist Studies," or Buddhology so to speak, was avoided in imperial universities, but in private universities founded by Buddhist sects the term "Buddhology" was used without any hesitation. There are many "Faculties of Buddhism" and "Departments of Buddhism" in Buddhist universities where both methodologies are accepted.

What was sought for by Japanese scholars who had grown up in a traditional Buddhist milieu was—quite unlike Europeans approaching Buddhism from the outside—not only textual and philological studies, but also, on the basis of such studies, an approach to the real teachings of the Buddha Śākyamuni's doctrines transmitted to them from India via China, that is, the Buddhist tradition transmitted through three nations 三國傳來 (India, China and Japan). In this way, investigations into the materials of Chinese and Japanese Buddhism were added to research on Indological materials. Interest in Tibetan materials and in Tibetan Buddhism occurred some time later.

In this way, we Japanese scholars have worked and contributed mainly in the following fields:

(1) Studies on early Buddhism[2] based on the Pāli canon in comparison with the corresponding Chinese translations.

(2) Studies on Mahāyāna scriptures, especially those which have special doctrinal relations with various sects, e.g., the

2. The Japanese equivalent of the term 'Early Buddhism' is *shoki Bukkyō*, while previously this field was called 'Primitive Buddhism', which was translated as *genshi Bukkyō*. We sometimes see the latter term in use even today. Ui Hakuju once proposed the term *konpon Bukkyō* (Original Buddhism) for the first hundred years after the Buddha's Mahāparinirvāṇa. But it is now out of use.

Saddharmapuṇḍarīka for the Tendai and Nichiren sects, and the Pure Land scriptures for the Jōdo and Jōdo Shin sects.

(3) Studies on Mahāyāna treatises written by great Indian masters such as Nāgārjuna, Asaṅga, Vasubandhu, and others. A doctrinal approach to the Mādhyamika and Yogācāra schools is the main object of this research. In this genre, studies of the *Abhidharmakośa*, referred to above, would be included.

(4) Studies on the Chinese Tripiṭaka and on Chinese and Korean Buddhism, philological, doctrinal and also historical.

(5) In the same way studies on Japanese Buddhism, philological, doctrinal and historical, both for the benefit of each sect and as an objective science. A further aim is to modernize sectarian doctrines by such studies.

I-2. Some Important Contributions by Japanese Scholars

Here I shall mention the main important contributions by Japanese scholars before World War II. Mention must be made first of all of:

(1) The publication of a critical edition of the Chinese Tripiṭaka in 100 volumes (1922–34), usually called the "Taishō Tripiṭaka." It was planned by Takakusu and edited by him together with Watanabe Kaigyoku (1872–1933). This edition is now utilized by Buddhist scholars all over the world, and its digitization is almost completed.

Other important works are:

(2) A catalogue of the Chinese Tripiṭaka kept in the palace of the Ming dynasty, edited by Nanjō in 1883.

(3) A catalogue of the Kanjur section of the Peking edition of the Tibetan Tripiṭaka, edited by Yamaguchi Susumu (1895–1976) and others (1932).

(4) A catalogue of the Derge edition of the Tibetan Tripiṭaka kept at Tōhoku University, edited by Kanakura Enshō (1896–

1987) and Tada Tōkan (1890–1967) (1934).

(5) *Bukkyō daijiten* [A Buddhist Encyclopaedia], in 5 volumes and 2 separate volumes, compiled by Mochizuki Shinkō (1869–1948) (1931–36). (This dictionary is usually called "Mochizuki jiten.")

As for editions of Sanskrit texts, mention may be made of:

(6) The *Saddharmapuṇḍarīka-sūtra*, edited by J. H. Kern (1833–1917) and B. Nanjō (1912).

(7) The *Laṅkāvatāra-sūtra*, edited by B. Nanjō (1923).

(8) *Bodhisattvabhūmi: A Statement of Whole Course of the Bodhisattva (Being Fifteenth Section of Yogācārabhūmi)*, edited by Wogihara Unrai (1869–1937) (1930).

and some other texts.

(9) Wogihara also started to compile a Sanskrit-Japanese dictionary, but only the first six parts were published during the war (1940–43), and its completion was postponed until 1964, when Tsuji Naoshirō (1899–1979), the most distinguished Sanskrit scholar in Japan, took over the task and completed parts 7–18 (1964–74).

(10) Another large project worth mentioning here is the publication of the *Nanden Daizōkyō*, in 65 volumes, a Japanese translation of the Pāli Tripiṭaka edited by Takakusu in 1936–41. This series was especially meant for Japanese readers, priests, scholars, and students, and there can be no doubt that it contributed tremendously to the study of early Buddhism in Japan.

(11) There were similar projects in the field of the Chinese Tripiṭaka, namely, the *Kokuyaku Daizōkyō* and the *Kokuyaku Issaikyō* in 150 volumes.

As for Tibetan studies, there were no notable studies published by Japanese scholars during this period, but it should be noted that the Tibetan Tripiṭaka and other materials were brought to Japan by pioneers such as Kawaguchi Ekai (1866–1945) and Tada Tōkan. Kawaguchi also brought back Sanskrit manuscripts to Japan from Tibet, which were kept at Tokyo Imperial University.

(12) A unique project planned by Takakusu and the French scholar Sylvain Lévi (1868–1935) was the *Hōbōgirin* 法寶義林 (or "Groves of Meaning in the Dharma Treasure"), an "encyclopaedic dictionary" written in French by various authors. It was planned when Lévi came to Japan at the invitation of Takakusu. Its publication began in 1926 as *Hōbōgirin: Dictionnaire encyclopédique du Bouddhisme d'après les sources chinoises et japonaises* with P. Demiéville (1894–1979) as its first editor-in-chief. Unfortunately, however, the project was interrupted by the war and remained incomplete after only three fascicles had been published, together with a catalogue of the Taishō Tripiṭaka as a separate volume. Work was resumed in 1955, but still only eight fascicles have been published.

I-3. Main Buddhist Studies outside Japan

World War II, which began in 1939, had a severe impact on the world of scholarship. Not only defeated nations such as Japan, but also scholars belonging to the victorious Allied powers suffered from a lack of freedom to engage in research work. In this sense, the year 1945 was significant for them as the end of the old days and the beginning of a new era and an age of hope.

Before describing the succeeding new Japanese era, I wish to give an overview of the main works and projects in the area of Buddhist studies around the world conducted or planned before the end of the war.[3]

---

3. On the following, see J. W. de Jong, *Bukkyō kenkyū no rekishi* (in Japanese), tr. by Hirakawa Akira (Tokyo: Shunjūsha, 1975). This book is

(1) First of all, in the field of Pāli studies, we should mention the compilation of a Pāli Dictionary by R. C. Childers (1838–76) in 1875. Next comes the founding of the Pāli Text Society by T. W. Rhys Davids (1842–1922) in 1881, with its continuing activities in editing Pāli texts and its compilation of a dictionary called *The Pāli Text Society's Pāli-English Dictionary* (usually called *P.T.S. Pāli Dictionary*) in 1925. Also important was the project for the compilation of a *Critical Pāli Dictionary*. This was initiated in the 1920s through the efforts of Dines Andersen (1861–1940) and Helmer Smith (1882–1956) on the basis of materials collected in card form by V. Trenckner (1824–91). Work was interrupted during the war and resumed after the war in cooperation with Pāli scholars all over the world. By 1999, however, publication had progressed only up to the middle of 'Ka' in Part 6 of Volume 3. Nobody knows how many years it will take before completion.

(2) As for Sanskrit materials or Mahāyāna texts, the case is quite different from that of Pāli texts. Due to the lack of a central authority, as may be found in, e.g., the Catholic church, research was obliged to start with the unearthing and collecting of textual materials that remained in monasteries. As a pioneer in this field, we should mention the name of B. H. Hodgson (1800–94), who collected Sanskrit manuscripts from Nepal for the first time in the period between 1821 and 1841. The discovery of manuscripts as a result of the exploration of Central Asia followed some time later. The last work in this area done before the end of the war was, we could say, the discovery of Sanskrit manuscripts in a Tibetan monastery and their filming by Rāhula Sāṅkṛtyāyana (1937).

---

originally based on a course of lectures at the University of Tokyo in 1973.

Manuscripts, thus collected and critically edited, were published in journals or periodicals first and then finalized in book form. There are several series devoted to Buddhist texts, such as the Bibliotheca Indica of the Asiatic Society of Bengal and the Bibliotheca Buddhica, which started in St. Petersburg. But many materials still remain unpublished. Also expected is the fresh discovery of materials still to be unearthed.

(3) The language used in Mahāyāna texts is—except for *śāstra*s of later times, which are written in almost pure Sanskrit—often called Buddhist Sanskrit in the sense that it is a "mixed" form of Sanskrit that includes vernacular elements.

With regard to this Sanskrit unique to Buddhist texts, F. Edgerton (1885–1963) started his research on its grammar and vocabulary in the 1930s. The results were finally published in 1953, after nearly 20 years of study, under the title *Buddhist Hybrid Sanskrit Grammar, Dictionary and Reader* in 3 volumes. This work has become an indispensable reference tool for Buddhist textual studies and has greatly helped scholars to pursue their research.

II. Buddhist Studies since 1950

II-1. General Survey of World Scholarship

Having entered the 1950s, with Japan's recovery in economic and industrial activity after complete destruction by the war, the world of scholarship and researchers also regained their strength and initiated their activities with new projects under new organization.[4] International academic exchange increased, and information was transmitted more quickly. These phenomena caused the rapid development of study and research in every field. The world

4. As for trends in Buddhist scholarship in Europe, America, and India during and after World War II, see Nakamura Hajime, *Ima no sekai to Tōyō shisō* [The present world and Oriental thought] (Tokyo: Sankibō, 1955).

of Oriental and Buddhist studies was no exception. Especially Japanese scholars enjoyed the freedom of going abroad for study more than ever before. One point to be mentioned was the new tendency to select places of study in countries in Asia where Buddhism was still alive or where it had originated. This tendency was the same among European and American scholars. As a result, we often met and exchanged information in these countries. The study of Chinese and Japanese Buddhism among Western scholars also developed, ending the monopoly of Japanese scholars in this field of study.

Another point that needs to be mentioned in this connection is that the increase of research in countries where Buddhism remains alive has intensified scholars' interest in cultural matters related to Buddhism in these countries, which in turn has caused them to study Buddhism from various approaches, e.g., sociological, historical, religious, and cultural anthropological, besides their basic philological and philosophical approaches. In cooperation with specialists in these fields of study, Buddhist studies has widened its scope and developed further. The need to hold conferences and publish the resulting proceedings consequently resulted in the formation of associations of scholars.

As for academic organizations in Japan, the Science Council of Japan was founded in 1949. This organization is a kind of union of all fields of study. With this acting as a momentum, we scholars in Indology and Buddhism founded the Japanese Association of Indian and Buddhist Studies under the leadership of Miyamoto Shōson (1893–1983) in 1952.

Buddhist scholars also belong to the Japanese Association for Religious Studies, and when this association invited the International Congress of History of Religion to Japan in 1958, many Buddhist scholars participated. It was the first time for Japanese Buddhist scholars to attend an international conference of this kind.

In the same year CIPSH/ICPHS (Conseil International de la Philosophie et des Sciences Humaines / International Council for Philosophy and Humanistic Studies) held the 3rd Congress between Eastern and Western Philosophers in Hawaii and younger scholars, in addition to D. T. Suzuki (1870–1961) and other senior scholars, participated.

Meanwhile, the ICO (International Congress of Orientalists), now called ICANAS (International Congress for Asian and North African Studies), has a long and proud history of over one hundred years as the largest organization covering all fields of study concerning the Orient and Asia. The number of Buddhist scholars participating in this ICANAS has been gradually increasing. When its 31st Congress was held in Tokyo and Kyoto in 1983, our above-mentioned association acted as one of the representative associations in charge of the Congress, to which participants numbered over 1,800. The international activities of our younger scholars are still increasing, with some obtaining degrees abroad.

With the growth of ICANAS in both scale and participants, scholars interested in establishing international associations in every field of study have also grown. In response to this, in the field of Buddhist studies, the International Association of Buddhist Studies (IABS) was established in 1978. It holds a conference every two years (with the first conference having been presided over by Nagao Gadjin) and publishes the annual *Journal of the IABS*.

Prior to the IABS, the International Association of Sanskrit Studies (IASS) was established in 1972 and held its first conference in New Delhi. Since then conferences have been held regularly at intervals of three years.

Throughout the years, various associations concerned with Indology and Buddhist studies have been established, e.g., the International Dharmakīrti Conference (president: E. Steinkellner), which had its first meeting in Kyoto in 1991. It is an academic association for the study of Buddhist *ryāya* or Indian logic.

In addition to the founding of these international associations, the publication of the international journal called the *Indo-Iranian Journal* has been important too (Leiden, since 1959).

As for international projects, besides the publication of the *Critical Pāli Dictionary* mentioned earlier, we also have a project for collecting Buddhist Sanskrit manuscripts in Nepal under the supervision of the Nepalese and German governments, which started in 1975.[5]

Mention should also be made of the fact that Tibetan and Sanskrit materials kept in Tibetan monasteries have been made public with the permission of the Chinese government. According to recent information, the originals of the Sanskrit manuscripts photographed by Rāhula Sāṅkṛtyāyana have been brought to Peking, and Chinese scholars, in collaboration with Tibetan scholars, have started working on these materials. As a result of this new development, there have recently been published critical editions of the *Vimalakīrtinirdeśa* and *Jñānālokālaṃkāra*, edited by study groups of Buddhist Sanskrit Literature at Taishō University (2003). Generally speaking, monopolizing documents has become impossible thanks to the tremendous developments in information media.[6]

II-2. Special Reference to Tibetan Studies

In this connection, I wish especially to refer to studies based on Tibetan materials as a field that has developed particularly since the 1950s.

---

5. As for studies on Buddhist Sanskrit materials, see Yamada Ryūjō, *Bongo butten no shobunken* [Buddhist texts in Sanskrit] (Kyoto: Heirakuji Shoten, 1959); Tsukamoto Keishō, Matsunaga Yūkei, and Isoda Hirofumi, *Bongo butten no kenkyū* [A descriptive bibliography of the Sanskrit Buddhist literature] (Kyoto: Heirakuji Shoten, 1989–93).
6. On Buddhist studies in the world up to the 1970s, see H. Nakamura, *Indian Buddhism: A Survey with Bibliographical Notes* (Hirakata: KUFS [Kansai University of Foreign Studies] Publication, 1980).

Initially, a sudden change occurred in Tibet because of the newly established Chinese Communist Government. Escaping from Lhasa, the capital occupied by Chinese forces, the fourteenth Dalai Lama together with his attendants brought many scriptures to India in 1959. With the help of UNESCO, Tibetan refugee monks were welcomed by scholars in many countries around the world. Being informants on Tibetan matters, they first assisted in the learning of the Tibetan language. In Japan, the Tōyō Bunko (Oriental Library) accepted three informants, and this contributed to the rapid development of Tibetan studies in Japan. Centres in the United States and Switzerland, where many such informants were accepted, and in Dharamsala in India, where the Dalai Lama himself lived, have become favourite places for scholars of Tibetan studies.

Prior to this, the Japanese Association of Tibetan Studies had been established, and a major project for the publication of a printed edition of the Peking edition of the Tibetan Tripiṭaka kept at Otani University, in 150 volumes, started under the supervision of Yamaguchi Susumu and was completed in 1959. This was followed by the publication of the complete works of Tsong-kha-pa and Sa-skya in 18 volumes. The making public of these important materials against monopolistic possession by the few has been of great significance and influence. Using these texts, studies of the doctrines of the Mādhyamika and Yogācāra, as well as research on Indian logic, have made rapid advances. This could be said to be a great achievement in Buddhist studies in the postwar period. Internationally, we should recall that the Tibetan Association for the Memory of Alexander Csoma de Kőrös (1798–1842), a pioneer in Tibetan studies, held an international conference of Tibetan and Mongolian studies in 1976, and this was followed by the establishment of the International Association of Tibetan Studies in 1983. Now research on Tibetan Buddhism has developed to cover dictionaries, grammar, history, doxography (compendia and commentaries), thangka, esoteric ritual, and so on. In addition, investigations into the present situation of Tibetan monks in Nepal and Bhutan are progressing.

In summary, as characteristics of trends in Buddhist studies in the latter half of the twentieth century we may point to (1) the internationalization of research and scholars, (2) the making public of source materials, and (3) the development of instruments of information and documentation.

Regarding this last point, we may add here the decision of the Japanese Association of Indian and Buddhist Studies and the Foundation of Buddhist Studies to produce CD-ROMs of the entire Taishō Tripiṭaka. This plan is supported by Buddhist societies at home and abroad. It was initiated in 2000. There can be no doubt that research trends in the new century will be greatly influenced by developments in the computer sciences.

Next, I wish to select some important and interesting topics in recent years that raise issues at the start of the new century.

III. Some Important Issues in Dispute

III-1. Date of the Buddha's Mahāparinirvāṇa

Ui Hakuju (1882–1962) put forward some bold hypotheses in his attempt to construct a history of Indian philosophy. Among them, first comes the date of the Buddha Śākyamuni's *mahāparinirvāṇa* (i.e., his [physical] death). He opposed the generally accepted theory of the fifth century B.C.[7] Instead, he proposed the year 386 B.C. as the date of Śākyamuni's death.[8] The grounds for his hypothesis lie in his dating of King Aśoka's coronation to about one hundred years after the Buddha's *mahāparinirvāṇa* on the basis

7. For example, Takakusu had proposed 485–486 B.C. on the basis of the *Shushō tenki* 衆聖點記, a chronicle of Buddhist saints transmitted in China. Cf. *Bukkyōgaku no shomondai* [Problems around Buddhist studies], ed. by Association for the Celebration of 2500 Years after Buddha's Birth (1935).

8. Ui Hakuju, "Butsumetsu nendai ron," in *Indo tetsugaku kenkyū* [Studies on Indian philosophy], vol. 2 (Tokyo, 1925), pp. 3–112.

of the "Northern tradition," that is, the tradition transmitted in China, whereas in the Southern tradition it is placed about two hundred years after the death of the Buddha. (The Indian government celebrated 2,500 years of Buddhism in 1955 on the basis of the tradition adopted among present-day Theravāda Buddhist orders, which claim the Buddha died in 544 B.C.)[9]

Ui's disciple Nakamura Hajime (1912–99) proposed the year 383 B.C. on the basis of an adjustment of the date of Aśoka's coronation based on Greek materials concerning Alexander the Great and others. Since then Japanese scholars have generally accepted this hypothesis.

In recent years, a new hypothesis has been advanced by scholars of early Buddhism such as R. Gombrich and H. Bechert. They propose a date midway between the Southern tradition and the Northern tradition. Namely, Gombrich regards the date of Aśoka's coronation to have been 136 years after the Buddha's *mahāparinirvāṇa* as a result of his detailed reexamination of the *Dīpavaṃsa*.

Bechert adopts Herbert Härtel's opinion, advanced after his excavations and archaeological investigations of ancient Indian cities in the Middle Gangetic Plain, that the date of the ruins related to the Buddha's activities cannot go back beyond 500 B.C. But, at the same time, he attaches importance to the legend of succession of the Dharma over five generations between the Buddha's *mahāparinirvāṇa* and Aśoka's reign.

Another point Bechert makes is that at the second council for the collection of the Buddha's Dharma, which is said to have been held during Aśoka's reign, there were a number of elders who had studied directly under the Buddha during his lifetime. With this as evidence, he posits the date of Aśoka's coronation at some time between eighty-five and one hundred years after the

9. P. V. Bapat (ed.), *2500 Years of Buddhism* (New Delhi, 1956). According to Radhakrishnan's article, the date is based upon descriptions in the Kusīnārā (var. Kuśīnagara) inscription.

Buddha's *mahāparinirvāṇa*. Bechert's view was first expressed at a symposium on the date of the Buddha's *mahāparinirvāṇa* held in Göttingen in 1988. Later he modified his opinion somewhat and suggested that the date of Aśoka's coronation fell some time between eighty and one hundred and thirty years after the Buddha's *mahāparinirvāṇa* (1991).

The above scholars refer to their hypotheses as the new short chronicle theory. But it still cannot be said that the Buddha's dates have thus been finalized by their hypotheses. Prof. J. W. de Jong (1921–2000) was of the opinion that the dates of the Buddha cannot be determined beyond the rough hypothesis that he lived some time between 500 and 300 B.C.[10]

Another famous hypothesis Ui advanced was that of Maitreya as a historical figure. That is, Maitreyanātha, legendarily regarded as the founder of the Yogācāra school and the author of the five fundamental texts of this school (*Mahāyānasūtrālaṃkāra*, etc.), was identified at the same time with the future Buddha Maitreya, who is believed to be now residing in Tuṣita Heaven and to be destined to appear in this world after 5,670,000,000 years.

Ui regarded this story as a reflection of the historical fact that a man by the name of Maitreyanātha was actually the teacher of Asaṅga, who established the Yogācāra on the basis of his teachings. He therefore put forward the opinion that Maitreyanātha himself could have been the founder of this school and that he would have lived between about 270 and 350 A.D.[11]

This hypothesis was once supported by G. Tucci (1894–1984), but at present mainstream scholars regard Asaṅga as the actual founder of the Yogācāra. Still, we cannot totally reject Ui's hypothesis. Generally speaking, hypotheses about ancient history, once advanced, are difficult to totally adopt or reject.

---

10. On the above, see also Takasaki, "Saikin jūnen no Bukkyōgaku" [Buddhist studies in the last ten years], *Bukkyōgaku* 36 (1994).
11. Ui Hakuju, *Indo tetsugaku kenkyū*, vol. 1 (1924), pp. 355–414.

III-2. Origins of Mahāyāna Buddhism

As one of the hypotheses advanced by Japanese scholars, we should mention Hirakawa Akira's (1914–2002) hypothesis concerning the origins of Mahāyāna Buddhism. According to Hirakawa, it originated first among lay believers who gathered around the Buddha's *stūpa*s and worshipped his relics.

Hirakawa started his academic career with studies on the Vinaya, or the discipline and rules of the Buddhist order, under the guidance of Miyamoto. While studying the Vinaya texts, he also considered the social background of Buddhism and noticed the importance of lay believers who were originally Hindus. This led him to his hypothesis about Mahāyāna Buddhism. He thought that the upholders of Mahāyāna scriptures, i.e., the original authors of the scriptures and their followers, were the successors to lay believers who had taken charge of the Buddha's funeral.[12] This hypothesis was advanced against the commonly held view at that time that the origins of Mahāyāna Buddhism are to be sought in sectarian Buddhism, the Mahāsāṅghika being a strong possibility as its views are akin to those of the Mahāyāna.

Hirakawa's hypothesis was accepted by Japanese scholars because it explained in rational terms the Mahāyāna criticism of sectarian Buddhism in general and it presupposed the existence of lay bodhisattvas (e.g., Vimalakīrti).

Did there, however, actually exist any Mahāyāna order as such in India? There is in fact no Vinaya in the Mahāyāna, which has only disciplinal principles (*śīla*) of its own. The name "Mahāyāna" appears only in inscriptions dating from the sixth century A.D. and later. Donations to the Buddha's *stūpa*s are sanctioned in the Vinaya side by side with donations to sectarian orders. While worship of the Buddha's relics was permitted in sectarian Buddhism, Mahāyāna sūtras such as the *Prajñāpāramitā* and

12. Hirakawa Akira, *Shoki daijō bukkyō no kenkyū* [Studies on early Mahāyāna Buddhism] (Tokyo: Shunjūsha, 1968).

Saddharmapuṇḍarīka advocate the worship of Mahāyāna scriptures (as the Buddha's remains) instead of the Buddha's relics. With these points as evidence, Hirakawa's hypothesis gradually came to be criticized by various scholars (e.g., G. Schopen in 1979,[13] etc.).

In his recent work on the Mahāyāna *Mahāparinirvāṇa-sūtra*, Shimoda Masahiro (1957–) has reexamined this theory seeking the origins of the Mahāyāna movement in the Mahāsāṅghika and emphasizes its continuity with sectarian Buddhism.[14] He picked out the term *dhātu* as a key word concerning this issue. Namely, the term *dhātu* means "relics" when used to denote relic worship in the sense of the physical essence of the Buddha's body (*śarīra-dhātu*), but this same term reappears in the Mahāyāna *Mahāparinirvāṇa-sūtra* as *buddha-dhātu*, with a different meaning denoting the spiritual essence of the Buddha (which is originally present in all sentient beings, this being the key point of the *sūtra*) (一切衆生悉有佛性).

Shimoda goes on to say that between this new *buddha-dhātu* and the old physical *buddha-dhātu* worship of scriptures in the sense of the "physical relics of the [Buddha's] Body of the Dharma (*dharma-kāya*)" is situated, and that this latter indicates the origins of the Mahāyāna. He also says that *dharmabhāṇaka*s, or Buddhist teachers who composed Mahāyāna scriptures, were originally monks belonging to a certain sect, which they left to start their own new movement. They lived as ascetics in the forest (*āraṇyaka*), and it was only later that they established their own orders.

Shimoda explains this process in conjunction with the origins of the Mahāyāna *Mahāparinirvāṇa-sūtra*, but it remains to be

13. G. Schopen, "Mahāyāna Indian Inscriptions," *Indo-Iranian Journal* 21 (1979), etc.

14. Shimoda Masahiro, *Nehan-gyō no kenkyū: Daijō butten no kenkyū hōhō shiron* [A study on the *Mahāparinirvāṇasūtra*, with a focus on the methodology of the study of *Mahāyānasūtra*s] (Tokyo: Shunjūsha, 1997).

seen whether it can be applied universally to the origins of the Mahāyāna or not. (The Mahāyāna *Mahāparinirvāṇa-sūtra* dates from the fourth century A.D.) In spite of his attractive hypothesis, however, it is still questionable whether it can negate Hirakawa's thesis completely so long as there exists some sort of relationship, even if not positive, between relic worship and *sūtra* worship.

I myself once raised the question of whether or how a single monk could simultaneously have triple qualifications when I studied the biography of Atīśa, an important figure in the transmission of Buddhism to Tibet in the eleventh century A.D. His biography records that he first became an *ācārya*, or a practitioner of esoteric Buddhism, and after a number of years of activity in this capacity, he became a *bhikṣu* or monk in the Mahāsāṅghika order. Still later he studied in the Mādhyamika school and became qualified as a Mahāyāna master (*ācārya*) (perhaps without losing his qualification as a *bhikṣu*). From this fact, I surmised that the Mahāyāna existed only as schools and that being a Mahāyānist did not preclude the possibility of being a *bhikṣu* of one of the sects of sectarian Buddhism. I also suggested that the authors of Mahāyāna scriptures were not necessarily limited to the Mahāsāṅghika, as can be clearly observed in the connections between the Yogācāra and the Sarvāstivādins and Sautrāntikas.[15]

III-3. Critical Buddhism

In 1986, on the occasion of the annual conference of the Japanese Association of Buddhist Studies, Matsumoto Shirō (1950–), now professor at Komazawa University, read a paper with the shocking title "Tathāgatagarbha Thought Is Not Buddhism." This criticism of the Tathāgatagarbha theory triggered by him[16] exerted

15. Takasaki Jikidō, "Daijō Bukkyō no keisei" [The formation of Mahāyāna Buddhism], in *Iwanami kōza: Tōyō shisō* [Iwanami lectures on Oriental thought], vol. 8 (Tokyo: Iwanami Shoten, 1998), pp. 145–195.

16. As representative works by him and his group, I will mention the

great influence both at home and abroad. A book in English related to this debate was published with the title *Pruning the Bodhi Tree*, edited by P. Swanson of Nanzan University in Nagoya and J. Hubbard of Smith College.[17]

The Tathāgatagarbha theory is a current of Mahāyāna thought that appeared after Nāgārjuna together with the Vijñāna theory of the Yogācāra. It did not form any school like the Mādhyamika or Yogācāra in India. But it had an important influence on the rise of esoteric Buddhism in later times. As one peculiar characteristic, it bears a close similarity with Hindu thought as observed in its acceptance of the existence of an unchangeable reality (*dharmatā* or *dharma-dhātu*) behind changeable (*anitya*) phenomena (*dharmas*), including our body and spirit. Matsumoto hypothetically called this theory "*dhātu-vāda*," or the theory that recognizes a *dhātu* or essential reality.

As this Tathāgatagarbha theory has been commonly accepted among Buddhists in East Asia under the influence of the *Awakening of Faith in the Mahāyāna* and other works, including the Mahāyāna *Mahāparinirvāṇa-sūtra* mentioned above, Matsumoto's criticism encompassed almost all aspects of East Asian Buddhism.

What became the focus of his criticism was the doctrine of original enlightenment of the Tendai sect in Japan. Criticism of this doctrine has, however, existed since the Kamakura period, when many reformers, our Dōgen being one of them, descended Mt. Hiei, the main centre of the Tendai sect, to establish new schools. Perhaps based on this fact, and in an attempt to defend Dōgen as the founder of the Sōtō sect to which he belongs, Prof. Hakamaya Noriaki (1943–), who takes the same standpoint as Matsumoto,

---

following: Matsumoto Shirō, *Engi to kū: nyoraizō shisō hihan* [Dependent origination and emptiness: A critique of the Tathāgatagarbha doctrine] (Tokyo: Daizō Shuppan, 1989); Hakamaya Noriaki, *Hongaku shisō hihan* [A critique of the idea of original enlightenment] (Tokyo: Daizō Shuppan, 1989).

17. Jamie Hubbard & Paul Swanson (eds.), *Pruning the Bodhi Tree: The Storm over Critical Buddhism* (Honolulu: University of Hawai'i Press, 1997).

put forward his new view that Dōgen rejected his belief in the Tathāgatagarbhạ doctrine as expressed in the opening chapters of the *Shōbōgenzō*, written in his early years, and returned to the doctrine of impermanence in the twelve volumes later added to the *Shōbōgenzō*.[18] His hypothesis has not been accepted by most scholars. Matsumoto himself is of the opinion that Dōgen too was after all subject to the theory of original enlightenment.

I agree partially with Matsumoto's hypothesis of the *dhātu-vāda* insofar that it applies to the standpoint of the Yogācāra, which interprets *dharma-dhātu* as denoting the doctrine of dependent origination, but I do not agree with his opinion that Tathāgatagarbha doctrine is not Buddhism.

In this regard, one might ask what non–*dhātu-vāda* Buddhism might be. According to Matsumoto, only the theory of dependent origination is the real teaching of the Buddha, and even the theory of emptiness is accepted as Buddhism so long as it gives expression to the theory of dependent origination. What, then, is the theory of dependent origination? Prof. Matsumoto only says that it is the twelvefold chain of causation, and he does not go into any further detail.

The grounds for Matsumoto's views may be found in the doctrines of Tibetan Buddhism, especially in those of the dGe-lugs-pa school, established by Tsong-kha-pa, which propounds the Mādhyamika theory of emptiness as its basic standpoint.

As is well-known, early Tibetan Buddhists rejected the "Chinese Buddhism" introduced by a Chan monk named Mahāyāna, and instead they adopted the Indian current of Buddhism. From this fact we tend to evaluate Tibetan Buddhism as being superior to Chinese Buddhism and the *śūnya-vāda* of the Mādhyamika as being superior to the *vijñāna-vāda* of the Yogācāra. Matsumoto's

18. Hakamaya Noriaki, *Dōgen to Bukkyō: jūnikan-bon Shōbōgenzō no Dōgen* [Dōgen and Buddhism: Dōgen as seen in his *Shōbōgenzō* in 12 volumes] (Tokyo: Daizō Shuppan, 1990).

hypothesis was thus readily accepted in such circumstances. Such is the present situation regarding this debate centring around Tathāgatagarbha doctrine.

Hakamaya and Matsumoto called their standpoint "critical Buddhism."[19] They say the wisdom (*prajñā*) of the Buddha refers precisely to this critical judgement. At the same time, their intention is to criticize the objectivism of modern Buddhist studies. According to them, Buddhist scholars should have their own subjective standpoint or their own judgement on any aspect of Buddhism, such as doctrine, practices, or the system of orders. It is true that modern Buddhist studies have had a tendency to maintain objectivity to an excessive degree in order to preserve their standpoint transcending sectarian methods of study, and there have been other scholars too critical of this tendency (e.g., Tamaki Kōshirō [1915–99]).

At the same time, this stance of overstrict judgement about doctrinal matters will inevitably lead to the establishment of new sects, as was observed during the Kamakura period. If one adheres too strictly to the purity of one's thought, it is apt to lose its universality. Recognizing one's opponent's standpoint is also necessary.

Critical Buddhism should mean the unceasing self-examination of one's own standpoint and attitude. Thus, to be critical is the basic stance of scholars. By being critical of traditional theories and the opinions of authorities we can expect progress in scholarship. But the grounds for such criticism must be based on the objective investigation of research materials.[20]

---

19. Hakamaya Noriaki, *Hihan Bukkyō* [Critical Buddhism] (Tokyo: Daizō Shuppan, 1990).

20. As to the background of "critical Buddhism," its problematic points, desirable direction of development, etc., J. Hubbard discussed these in his article in *Nanzan Shūkyō Bunka Kenkyūjohō* 9 (1999). On the problems in Chinese Buddhism concerning critical Buddhism, see Yoshizu Yoshihide, "Chūgoku Bukkyō kenkyū no ichi dōkō: hihanteki kenkyū ni tsuite" [A ten-

IV. Conclusion

In concluding this discussion, I would like to refer to another kind of criticism from within Buddhism. This is, namely, the voices of scholars giving much attention and importance to matters concerning living Buddhism (e.g., Maeda Egaku).[21]

Buddhist studies needs to widen its scope to cover social and cultural phenomena in general. Towards this end, the cooperation of Buddhist scholars with scholars in neighbouring disciplines, as mentioned before, is absolutely essential.

Lastly, I shall mention one further point. There has been an impressive growth in the number and quality of Buddhist scholars in Buddhist countries in East and Southeast Asia. There can be no doubt that new Buddhist studies will emerge from among them in the near future.

---

dency in studies on Chinese Buddhism: On "critical" research], *Bukkyōgaku* 36 (1994).

21. Maeda Egaku, "Bukkyō to wa nani ka, Bukkyōgaku wa ika ni aru beki ka" [What is Buddhism? What should Buddhist studies be like?], *Bukkyōgaku* 36 (1994).

PART VII
BOOK REVIEWS

Oriental Philosophies. By John M. Koller. Charles Scribner's & Sons, New York, 1970. xiv + 303 pages.*

This book is unique in various respects. Firstly, the author is not a specialist in any of the Oriental philosophies, and he attempts to introduce Westerners to Oriental systems of thought as an antidote to a narrow and parochial understanding of what is called 'philosophy'. According to the author, the term 'philosophy' originally meant the answers given to the basic questions of life; in the Oriental tradition, a much more proper sense of this term is found than in the West, where philosophy is thought of in terms of the classical philosophers of the Western world, or more precisely, in terms of an ivory-tower study, set apart from the needs of daily life.

In the opinion of those of us who have grown up in the Eastern tradition, however, philosophy in the Orient has more or less this same character in as much as it has gradually grown more remote from daily life. But one may certainly agree with the author that any Oriental philosophy has always been inseparably linked with some religious, political or social system and so could not survive independently from the needs of society. But it remains true that some philosophers have been so caught up in their profession that they became too scholastic in their approach to think a great deal about the needs of ordinary people.

All apart from this discussion about what philosophy means for us in the East, we should be grateful to the author for his sympathetic study of Oriental traditions, clearly written and systematically arranged according to the character of each school and thus enabling the reader to obtain easily a clear idea of each tradition.

The book consists of three parts—the Hindu systems, Buddhist philosophies, and Chinese philosophies. Each part begins with a description of the basic characteristics of each tradition,

* Originally published in *Monumenta Nipponica* 26-3/4 (1971), pp. 474–476.

followed by a survey of the historical background, a discussion of specific problems and, finally, an account of contemporary features and problems. In the section dealing with the Hindu systems, the chapter divisions correspond to the different philosophical schools in chronological order; more or less the same plan is followed in the case of Chinese philosophies. As regards Buddhist philosophies, however, the main part is divided into two chapters concerning the nature of self and reality (or ultimate reality), and in each chapter the author compares the teaching of the various schools within the Buddhist fold. The apparent inconsistency in arrangement reflects the skill of the author, who recognizes that Buddhism possesses a unified and universal system of thought in contrast to the other two traditions, deeply imbedded as they are in their native cultures.

As regards contemporary features of these different systems, the author has selected Radhakrishnan and Aurobindo in the Indian tradition, Zen in the Buddhist, and Mao Tse-tung in the Chinese. The reader may be astonished by the inclusion of the last name, for Mao is the leader of a Communist party, the fundamental philosophy of which is Marxism, a product of the Western world. But the author does well to point out that Mao's unique philosophy, although sprung from Marxism, has been nurtured in the field of Chinese tradition. His conclusion on this point may be summed up as follows: Mao continues in the line of Chinese tradition in as much as his practical philosophy is based on two contradictory powers, and these may be termed *yin* and *yang* in the traditional way established by the Neo-Confucians in the Sung period.

As the present reviewer has no deep knowledge of Chinese philosophies, it may be better for him to keep silent and not attempt an evaluation of the author's interpretation of Chinese tradition; instead he will confine himself to some comments about the author's account of Indian and Buddhist philosophies.

When describing the *varṇa* system, the traditional Indian system of social classes, the author maintains, on p. 38, that it is not a system of classification according to birth, in contrast to the caste system expressed by the term *jāti* (birth). Historical evidence makes it quite certain that some foreign tribes who entered India and established dynasties claimed to belong to the *kṣatriya-varṇa*, next to the Brahmin in the *varṇa* system; there were priest classes of Southern India who were Dravidians and not Aryans by origin, yet they were allowed to become Brahmins when they accepted the Aryan pantheon and rituals. But there is no evidence of any individual being able to change his *varṇa* by his conduct, unless, indeed, he was deprived of it on account of misconduct. It is therefore necessary to recognize that the *varṇa* system is entirely a social regulation based on hereditary classification, however ideal the system may be in the eyes of Hindus (see also pp. 49 & 50).

At the same time we cannot overlook the structure of a double-value philosophy of the Hindus. Among the four purposes (*artha*) of life, the fourth, *mokṣa* or the religious aim of freedom, differs from the previous three as regards its supramundane character. Solely in regard to this aim are all men equal, regardless of their *varṇa*. Equality in the sight of god is also based on this premise, and this is emphasized in terms of the *bhakti* way. The Hindu social system is unique in its allowing people to undertake this purpose in their fourth and last stage of life after they have fulfilled their duty in society. The same double-value structure is also basic to Buddhism, a system which also had its origin in the field of India. But Buddhism differs from Hinduism in its emphasis on this supramundane value. It emphasizes the merits of renunciation for the purpose of obtaining *mokṣa*. The renunciation of society, that is, the renunciation of social and hereditary class and of duties towards society, is recommended at the earliest possible opportunity and not merely in the last stage of life, and this is where Buddhism departs from the Hindu tradition.

The author's lack of recognition of the double structure of the value system has to a certain extent obscured his description of the ultimate value in Buddhist thought. Of course, he is aware of this point in his reference to the two truths, mundane and supramundane, or conditioned and unconditioned reality, the latter being unknowable and inexplicable, as emphasized by the Mādhyamika (pp. 171, 179, etc.). He also speaks of a direct insight into this unconditioned reality through religious practices. But he stresses that all the philosophical views of the various Buddhist schools are in themselves contradictory. When speaking of schools other than the Mādhyamika, he regards them as if they definitively and ultimately postulate the existence of reality in exterior matter or forces or in consciousness. But it must be remembered that all Buddhist schools, including the Theravādin, are based on a supramundane value and deny any worldly value. In the case of the Vaibhāṣika and Sautrāntika, unconditioned reality was regarded as a different entity from our worldly or conditioned being. Mahāyāna Buddhism (both the Yogācāra and the Mādhyamika) never sought for the world of unconditioned reality outside the mundane world (*Saṃsāra* is *Nirvāṇa*); but at the same time it did not regard the mundane world, as such, as possessing ultimate value. As the author notes, the Mādhyamika taught the unreality of the mundane world in as much as it is merely a world of concepts and is not reality itself—a reality which cannot be explained in conceptual terms. The same opinion was held by the Yogācāra, but this school, founded after Nāgārjuna, wished to speak quite explicitly on the one hand about the nature of ultimate reality and, on the other, about how our mundane world, or the world of *Saṃsāra*, exists *as a fact*. The theory of *ālayavijñāna*, or seed-consciousness as reality, is nothing but an explanation of the structure of the world of *Saṃsāra*. It is therefore characterized as 'unreal thought construction' (*abhūta-parikalpa*). Knowledge that the world of *Saṃsāra* is merely of 'unreal thought construction' (and is therefore *śūnya*) causes the seed-consciousness to change into Wisdom; the *ālayavijñāna* no longer exists and enlightenment is achieved. But as there is no other world of the unconditioned outside the mundane world, this transformation takes place in consciousness itself as its self-negation. This point is called the revolution of the basis (*āśraya-parāvṛtti*).

The author seems to take a standpoint in favor of the Mādhyamika. It is quite natural and right to regard the Mādhyamika teaching as the ultimate in Buddhism, since it is the most faithful transmission of the original doctrine of the Buddha, who taught that ultimate reality cannot be explained in words and is beyond conceptual thought: one should therefore remain silent. Furthermore, Zen Buddhism faithfully continues this teaching and presents it to the modern world. But this does not mean that other standpoints may be neglected, and we should keep in mind the purpose of the teaching of each school. One of the purposes of the Yogācāra's teaching concerning the reality of 'unreal thought construction' on the basis of *śūnyatā* is to show that the mundane world, which must be abandoned, is at the same time to be saved, for it is the world in which the Bodhisattvas strive for this end, it is the world in which the Buddha's compassion operates in the form of the Wisdom-on-behalf-of-the-mundane-world (*laukika-jñāna*) acquired afterward (*pṛṣṭhalabdha*) on the basis of *Prajñā*.

There are some minor points which need correction. On p. 122 the author says that in Mahāyāna the goal is to become a *bodhisattva*. But however much the Bodhisattva may be the 'ideal' for the Mahayanist, it is not his goal. The goal is to become enlightened, that is, to become a *buddha*. In the Glossary, on p. 288, the term Bodhisattva is defined as 'an enlightened and compassionate being', but doctrinally a Bodhisattva is not 'enlightened' owing to his compassion for living beings. Then on pp. 122–124 the author mentions three Mahāyāna schools, the first of which is the 'suchness' absolutism of Aśvaghoṣa, and he notes that the Mādhyamika and the Yogācāra probably developed out of this philosophy. But recent studies by Indologists and Buddhist scholars have made clear that the *Ta-ch'eng ch'i-hsin lun* (*Mahāyānaśraddhotpāda*), the text that is meant here by 'the "suchness" philosophy of Ashvaghosa', was composed in the period after Vasubandhu, the systematizer of the Yogācāra school. Finally, on p. 141, the author uses the term *Buddhi* when talking about a person who has attained *nirvāṇa* by achieving *Buddhi*; he also defines *Buddhi* as 'enlightenment' in the Glossary on p. 288. Both are probably slips for *Bodhi*.

David Seyfort Ruegg, *La théorie du tathāgatagarbha et du gotra. Études sur la sotériologie et la gnoséologie du bouddhisme*. Publications de l'École française d'Extrême-Orient, Vol. LXX. Paris, 1969. 531 pp.*

The *tathāgatagarbha* theory is one of the current subjects in the field of Buddhist studies. Except in Japan, where traditionally this theory has kept its importance from a religious point of view, it had hardly been studied by scholars, mostly due to a lack of Sanskrit materials. The introduction of Tibetan materials to the study of Buddhism opened the eyes of scholars to this unique field. E. Obermiller was the first to offer useful materials through his English translation of the Tibetan version of the *Ratnagotravibhāga* (*Uttaratantra*), an important source which describes this theory systematically.[1] He also made a valuable contribution by his study of the *Abhisamayālaṅkāra*, in which the orthodox *gotra* theory is expressed.[2] Thus in the 1930s he laid the foundations for the study with which we are presently concerned. The publication of the Sanskrit text of the *Ratnagotravibhāga* by E. H. Johnston and T. Chowdhury in 1950[3] was another milestone. Since its appearance studies on this theory have not only rapidly increased in number but have also developed tremendously in quality.[4] Professor

---

* Originally published in *Indo-Iranian Journal* 15-4 (1973), pp. 292–299.

1. E. Obermiller, "The Sublime Science of the Great Vehicle to Salvation, Being a Manual of Buddhist Monism," *Acta Orientalia* IX (1931).

2. E. Obermiller, "The Doctrine of Prajñāpāramitā as Exposed in the Abhisamayālaṅkāra of Maitreya," *Acta Orientalia* XI (1933), pp. 1–133, Additional Indices, ibid., pp. 334–354; E. Obermiller, *Analysis of the Abhisamayālaṅkāra*, Calcutta Oriental Series 24 (Calcutta), Fascs. 1 (1933), 2 (1936), 3 (1943).

3. *The Ratnagotravibhāga Mahāyānottaratantraśāstra*, edited by E. H. Johnston, seen through the press and furnished with indexes by T. Chowdhury (Patna, 1950).

4. H. Ui, *Hōshōron kenkyū* (Tokyo, 1959) (studies on the *Ratnagotravibhāga*, including a Japanese translation); Z. Nakamura, *Bonkan taishō Kugyō ichijō hōshōron kenkyū* (Tokyo, 1961) (comparative text of the *RGV* in

Seyfort Ruegg's work is the first comprehensive and systematic study of the *tathāgatagarbha* theory (TG theory). He bases his research on this theory, and on *gotra* and other related concepts, on materials mainly transmitted in Tibet up to modern times, including a number of works by Tibetan scholars. He defines the characteristics of the TG theory as 'sotériologie' and 'gnoséologie' in the sense that this theory fundamentally aims at the establishment of the possibility of emancipation of all *sattva*s (sentient beings) through the intuition of the truth by themselves owing to their being or having *tathāgatagarbha* (embryo of the Tathāgata). This *tathāgatagarbha* is said to be essentially identical to the absolute and at the same time to be the cause for the attainment of the absolute, the term 'l'Absolu' (used in his work to denote 'la Réalité absolue') 'fonctionnant comme une expression de valeur virtuellement métalinguistique' (Avant-Propos, p. 1); and it is characterized by two aspects, one being the fruit (*phala*) and the other the cause (*hetu*, 'cause motivante') or the support (*ādhāra*), the support of spiritual exercise which, being a road (*mārga*), links the cause and the fruit. But this Absolute of Buddhism is quite different from, for example, the *advaita* relationship of *brahman* and *ātman* of Vedānta philosophy, which admits a unique substance as the material cause of the universe. The term 'monisme' is more suitable to denote the Vedantic Absolute than the Buddhist Absolute, which is characterized by non-dualism (*advaya*). The TG theory thus represents an expression of the Buddhist

---

Sanskrit and Chinese); J. Takasaki, *A Study on the Ratnagotravibhāga* (*Uttaratantra)*, S.O.R. XXXIII (Roma, 1966); Z. Nakamura: *Zōwa taiyaku Kugyō ichijō hōshōron kenkyū* (Tokyo, 1967) (critical edition of the Tibetan translation of the *RGV* and a Japanese translation, together with indexes of the *RGV*; Skt.-Tib.-Ch. and Tib.-Skt.); Ichijō Ogawa, *Indo Daijō Bukkyō ni okeru nyoraizō busshō no kenkyū* (Kyoto, 1969) (based on Darma Rin chen's commentary on the *RGV*). Furthermore, we should mention the first discussion of this theory as belonging to the school of Sāramati by Prof. E. Frauwallner in his *Die Philosophie des Buddhismus* (Berlin, 1956), pp. 255–264.

theory of the Absolute; and the present work, too, concerns itself basically with the clarification of the characteristics of the Buddhist concept of the Absolute.

There are generally two methods to describe any system of thought: historically or systematically on the basis of the fundamental texts. In the case of the TG theory, there are many scriptures, beginning with the *Tathāgatagarbhasūtra*, quoted as sources in the *Ratnagotravibhāga* (*RGV*), but there is still not enough material to arrange them in historical order and discuss their background. For this reason the author preferred the systematic way and commenced the analysis of the *RGV* with the help of commentaries and explanations written by later Tibetan scholars. In the same way he selected the *Abhisamayālaṅkāra* (*AA*) and its commentaries as the basic texts for the study of the *gotra* concept. His selection of the *RGV* and the *AA* as the basic texts of the TG and *gotra* theory is basically in accordance with Tibetan tradition—both are among the five treatises of Maitreya and have the same character of being Mādhyamic in contrast to the other three, which belong to the Yogācāra. This tradition is problematic in the light of modern studies, but it is certainly the most acceptable one for the explanation of the said theories. As far as the *RGV* is concerned, the concept of *gotra* is completely identical with *tathāgatagarbha*, but in Buddhist thought in general, both are not always the same and the *gotra* concept has its own history and background. As is well-known, it relates to the problem of *ekayāna* and *triyāna*, or universality and non-universality of the possibility of the highest enlightenment for sentient beings. The TG theory is connected with the *gotra* theory in its *ekayāna* standpoint. The concept of *gotra* represents the *hetu* or *ādhāra* aspect of the TG (*tathāgatagotra-svabhāva*, one of the three *svabhāva*s, the other two being *dharmakāya-* and *tathatā-svabhāva* representing the *phala* aspect, so to say).[5] Thus the concepts of *tathāgatagarbha* and *gotra* constitute the two main cores of the whole system of the TG theory, like two centers of an ellipse. In using the *RGV* and the *AA* together with Tibetan materials, Prof. S. Ruegg is truly a successor to Obermiller: his work is no doubt the greatest harvest reaped from the seeds sown by Obermiller 40 years ago. He has published many other articles concerning the TG theory[6] as well as a biography of Bu ston rin po che, a great historian of Tibetan Buddhism.[7] His scholarship in the field of Tibetology is well-known. The present volume will greatly advance Buddhist studies.

The present volume consists of an INTRODUCTION, PREMIÈRE PARTIE: La théorie mahāyāniste du *gotra*, DEUXIÈME PARTIE: L'éveil universel et le véhicule unique, TROISIÈME PARTIE: La théorie du *tathāgatagarbha*, QUATRIÈME PARTIE: La luminosité naturelle de la pensée, APPENDICES, and CONCLUSION.

The INTRODUCTION (pp. 31–70) starts with epigraphical evidence for the existence in the Gupta period of the idea according to which ordinary *sattva*s attain enlightenment and studies the scriptures which contain the TG theory. Subsequently the author examines the Indian tradition of the *RGV* and makes it clear that this

---

5. The author discusses this in chapter 4 of Part III.

6. D. Seyfort Ruegg, "The Jo naṅ pas: A School of Buddhist Ontologists according to the Grub mtha' šel gyi me loṅ," *JAOS* 83 (1963), pp. 73–91; "On the dGe Lugs pa Theory of the Tathāgatagarbha," in *Pratidānam: Indian, Iranian & Indo-European Studies Presented to F. B. J. Kuiper on His Sixtieth Birthday* (The Hague: Mouton, 1968), pp. 500–509; "Ārya and Bhadanta Vimuktisena on the Gotra Theory of the Prajñāpāramitā," in *Beiträge zur Geschichte Indiens: Festschrift für Erich Frauwallner* (Leiden/Köln, 1968), pp. 303–317; "Le Dharmadhātustava de Nāgārjuna," in *Études Tibétaines, dédiées à la mémoire de Marcelle Lalou* (Paris, 1971), pp. 448–471 ; "On the Knowability and Expressibility of Absolute Reality in Buddhism," *Indogaku Bukkyōgaku Kenkyū* 20-1 (1971), pp. (1)–(7).

7. *The Life of Bu ston Rin po che, with the Tibetan Text of the Bu ston rnam thar*, S.O.R. XXXIV (Roma, 1966).

tradition is obscure prior to the time of Maitrīpa, who lived two generations before Sajjana (11th century A.D.), the translator of the *RGV* into Tibetan, and that among Indian texts in which the *RGV* is quoted the earliest ones are the *Bodhicaryāvatārapañjikā* of Prajñākaramati and the *Sākārasiddhi* of Jñānaśrīmitra. Both the *RGV* and the *AA* have one point in common. Their influence began to be felt only many centuries after their coming into existence. In those days the Yogācāra-Mādhyamika, a school whose tenet is a kind of amalgamation of the Yogācāra and the Svātantrika-mādhyamika doctrines, was current and exercised a great influence. This seems to have been the cause for a variety of opinions in Tibet concerning the theoretical standpoint of the *RGV* and the TG theory in general.

In Tibet one finds three systems of interpretation: 1) Yogācāra-Vijñānavāda by Bu ston rin po che, 2) Prāsaṅgika-Mādhyamika by Red mda' ba and Tsoṅ kha pa, and 3) the Grand Mādhyamika by the Jo naṅ pas (pp. 58ff.). Of these, 2) is the youngest but orthodox interpretation. The author seems to agree with this system of interpretation. As for the author of the *RGV*, Prof. Ruegg follows again the Tibetan tradition, according to which the authorship of the verses is attributed to Maitreya and that of the prose commentary (Vyākhyā, *RGVV*) to Asaṅga. Furthermore, he suggests that the name Sāramati, which appears as the author of the *RGV* in the Chinese tradition, might be an epithet of Maitreya Bodhisattva (p. 46). However, this seems quite unlikely.

In the PREMIÈRE PARTIE, the author has followed the example of Tsoṅ kha pa's *gSer phreṅ*, a commentary on the *AA*. He treats the *gotra* theory of the Vijñānavāda in chapter 1, that of the Mādhyamika in chapter 2, and that of the *AA* and its commentaries in India and Tibet in chapter 3. In chapter 1, materials are quoted from such texts as the *Laṅkāvatāra*, the *Mahāyānasūtrālaṅkāra*, the *Bodhisattvabhūmi* and *Śrāvakabhūmi* of the *Yogācārabhūmi*, the *Mahāyānasaṃgraha*, and the *Madhyāntavibhāga*; it ends with

Tsoṅ kha pa's critique of the *gotra* theory of the Vijñānavāda. In chapter 2 texts dealing with the *gotra* theories are quoted from the *Daśadharmaka*, the *Kāśyapaparivarta*, the *Vimalakīrtinirdeśa*, the *Buddhāvataṃsaka*, and the *Madhyamakāvatāra*, following Tsoṅ kha pa's work. To call these materials Mādhyamika (as Tsoṅ kha pa does) is, except for the last one (the *Madhyamakāvatāra*), historically problematic, although their interpretation of *gotra* as being the same as *dharmadhātu* and as being characterised as *asaṃskṛta* may be termed 'Mādhyamic'. It is remarkable that there is very little discussion of the concept of *gotra* in the basic texts of the Mādhyamika, including the *Madhyamakakārikā* and its commentaries (see p. 109).

Chapter 3, dealing with the orthodox theory of *gotra* according to Indian and Tibetan tradition, mentions first of all interpretations of *AA* I.38–39 according to Ārya and Bhadanta Vimuktisena and Haribhadra, and then studies Tibetan traditions through the résumés of the said passage by 'Jam dbyaṅs bśad pa (1648–1722) and Kloṅ rdol bla ma (1719–1805), a detailed explanation given in the *Yid kyi mun sel* of Ña dbon kun dga' dpal (14th cent.) and the *rNam bśad sñiṅ po'i rgyan* of rGyal tshab rje (= Dar ma rin chen, 1362–1432).

The DEUXIÈME PARTIE deals in detail with the *ekayāna* theory. This theory is represented in the statement of *AA* I.39: due to non-differentiation of the *dharmadhātu*, a distinction between various *gotra* is improper. They exist merely due to differences in what is contained in them (*ādheya-dharma*). In chapter 1, general problems concerning the relationship between *dharmadhātu* and *gotra* are discussed. Chapter 2 studies the *ekayāna* theory of the *AA* and that of the dGe lugs pa and also contains a translation of a long passage from the *rNam bśad sñiṅ po'i rgyan*. In chapter 3 a survey of the development of the concepts of *dharmadhātu* and *ekayāna* in the Mahāyāna schools is made on the basis of the *Grub mtha' rin chen phreṅ ba* of dKon mchog 'jigs med dbaṅ po

(1728–1791), while chapter 4 discusses the *ekayāna* theory as it appears in the *RGV*. Special attention is paid to the problem of 'the end of *saṃsāra*', which is related to the interpretation of the term *anavarāgra* as an epithet of *saṃsāra* (p. 205).

The TROISIÈME PARTIE deals with the TG theory. Fundamental importance is given to the *RGV*. Chapter 1 gives a survey of the contents of each chapter of the *RGV*, chapter 2 examines examples of the use of the terms *dhātu* and *garbha* in the *RGV* proper, i.e., the verse section of the present text of the *RGV* (the author uses the abbreviation *RGV* exclusively for this part), and chapter 3 examines examples in the commentary part, i.e., the prose section of the *RGV* (called Vyākhyā, *RGVV*) in comparison with the verse section of the *RGV*. Chapter 4 discusses the essential characteristics of *tathāgatagarbha* in terms of *dharmakāya*, *tathatā*, and *tathāgatagotra* (namely *trividha svabhāva*). This leads us naturally to the problems concerning the relationship between *tathāgatagarbha* and the Absolute in terms of *dharmakāya*, *dharmadhātu*, *tathatā*, *paramārtha*, *śūnyatā*, etc., and to the explanation of theories concerning the Absolute in the following chapters. Chapter 5, namely, deals with the inexplicability and unthinkability of the Absolute; chapter 6 with the inseparable virtues or qualities of the *dharmakāya* as the means of knowing the latter (the Absolute is expressed or represented, *prabhāvita*, by qualities); chapter 7 deals with *tathāgatagarbha* and *śūnyatā*, and chapter 8 with comparative studies of conceptions concerning the Absolute in various texts.

This last chapter, the longest one in this part, seems to be the most important and crucial part of the book. The starting point of the discussion is formed by the verses of the *RGV* I.154–155 and 156, where the fundamental conception of *śūnyatā* in the *RGV* is fully expressed. The first section deals with the *itaretara-śūnyatā* (vacuité relative) of the *Laṅkāvatāra* and 'gshan stoṅ' (*para-śūnyatā*) (vide de l'autre) of the Jo naṅ pas as relating to the interpretation of the famous phrase *yad yatra nāsti tat tena śūnyam; yat punar atrāvaśiṣṭaṃ bhavati tat sad ihāsti*, mentioned in the *RGV* and other texts, and brings out the correctness of the interpretation of the *RGV*, given in chapter 7. Subsequently the author studies the inseparability of qualities with the Absolute mentioned in chapter 6. The problem is examined in three subdivisions: a. *prabhāvitatva*, b. *sarvākāravaropeta-śūnyatā*, and c. *avinirbhāga*, *sambaddha*, and *amuktajña* as unique epithets of the qualities of the Absolute. Thirdly comes the problem of the positive determination of the Absolute, which is unique to the TG theory in comparison with the *Prajñāpāramitā* and the *Madhyamakakārikā*, etc. The positive expression of the Absolute leads to similarities between the TG theory and Vedānta, and thus the author devotes the concluding part of chapter 8 to the indication of the Absolute in Advaita-Vedānta.

Finally, chapter 9 is concerned with the theory of *tathāgatagarbha* and *gotra* of Guṅ thaṅ 'Jam pa'i dbyaṅs (1762–1823).

The author points out that both Buddhism and the Vedānta have in common that they focus attention on the idea of a residue (*śeṣa*), which they explain in opposite ways, the former stressing *śūnyatā*, but the latter *pūrṇaṃ* (plénitude) (p. 336). This point may be worthy of further detailed investigation in the light of the history of Indian thought.

The QUATRIÈME PARTIE treats the problem of the innate purity of the mind (*cittaprakṛti-prabhāsvaratā*, or *-viśuddhatva*). Chapter 1 deals with the background of the concept of *cittaprakṛti* from Primitive Buddhism up to the early Mahāyāna scriptures. Chapter 2 explains the same concept in the *RGV* in connection with the concept of *āśrayaparivṛtti* ('la transmutation de la Base psychique'). Chapter 3 deals with the same in the *Madhyamakakārikā* and early works of the Vijñānavāda, while chapter 4 discusses the *cittaprakṛti* and *ālayavijñāna* theory in the works of Dignāga and Dharmakīrti. In chapter 5 the author studies the theory of *amala-vijñāna* as the ninth *vijñāna* in the *Laṅkāvatāra* and the works of the She-tsung (= *Mahāyānasaṃgraha*) school in China, which follows Paramārtha's translation of the *Mahāyānasaṃgraha*. Chapter 6 discusses the opinion of Guṅ thaṅ 'Jam pa'i dbyaṅs on the purity of the mind.

The APPENDICES consist of three sections: 1. the *gotra* theory in the Pāli canon and Abhidharma works; 2. the notions of *bīja*, *āśraya*, *vāsanā* and *dhātu*, all of which are more or less associated with the fundamental concepts of the TG theory and the Vijñānavāda, and 3. the concept of *sarvajñabīja* in the *Yogasūtra*. In the last section, the author notes the existence of a common background to the TG theory and the Yogaśāstra in the Brahmanic atmosphere of the Gupta period.

In the CONCLUSION the author examines the term *tathāgatagarbha* from grammatical and doctrinal points of view on the basis of the results arrived at in the main part of this work. According to him, this term is very frequently used as a *ṣaṣṭhīsamāsa*, and *garbha* means 'embryo', the embryo of the Buddha. This term is also sometimes used as a *bahuvrīhi* compound; and the Tibetan translation indicates this by adding *can* as an affix, but *can* can be used to distinguish the *tathāgatagarbha* from its possessors, i.e., the *sattva*s, and means that *sattva* is not to be identified with *tathāgatagarbha*. He rejects definitely the interpretation of *garbha* as 'womb', though a number of scholars translate *tathāgatagarbha* as 'womb' or 'matrix of the Tathāgata', and he suggests that such a translation originated under the influence of the Chinese translation *tsang* (store) for *garbha*.

The author also notes two different usages of the term *gotra*, one in the sense of 'lineage', the other in the sense of 'mine', and indicates that the former meaning relates to the principle of classification and distinction (as in the *pañca gotrāṇi* of the *Laṅkāvatāra*), while the latter suggests the process of purification from cause to result (as in the case of *ratnagotra*).

The above is a brief survey of this great work of more than five hundred pages. I cannot help but admire the quantity of materials used, the exactness of the translations, the valuable indications concerning text readings (e.g., p. 74: *śamaikāyana* for *śamaika-yāna* in *RGV*, p. 35, l. 11), and the detailed references for important technical terms to Buddhist scriptures and other Indian sources. The author has made a praiseworthy contribution. However, as a result of my research in the same field of study, I have a different opinion on some points, which I indicate below, leaving the final decision to readers.

(1) The meaning of the term *tathāgatagarbha*. Though I once used 'matrix' or 'womb' for *garbha* in my work, I agree with Prof. Ruegg that *tathāgatagarbha* means the 'embryo' of the Tathāgata, and not 'womb' of the Tathāgata, insofar as it is identified with or regarded as a synonym for *dhātu*. As far as the statement in the *Tathāgatagarbhasūtra* "*sarvasattvās tathāgatagarbhāḥ*" is concerned, the term is used as a *bahuvrīhi* compound (p. 512) in the sense of '(one who) embodies the Tathāgata within himself', and *dharmatā* of the Tathāgata, or *tathatā*, or *tathāgata-jñāna* means 'what is inside', i.e., the contents, while *sattva*s are consequently compared to *garbha*, the container. Except for two cases, there is no use of this term in a singular form denoting the essence of the Tathāgata in the said sūtra. Firstly, *de bshin gśegs pa'i sñiṅ po ma gos de*,[8] which appears in the first verse of the first example, indicates the Buddha sitting in a lotus flower used as an illustration, and the first Chinese translation renders it as *ju lai shen* (= *tathāgatakāya*),[9] which seems to reflect the original meaning. Secondly, in the fifth example, where both Chinese translations use terms equivalent to *jñāna* or *jñānadarśana* for *sñiṅ po*

8. Peking Ed., no. 924, (repr. ed.) vol. 36, p. 241-3-6.
9. T. no. 666, vol. 16, p. 457c.

in the Tibetan translation.[10]

There is no doubt that in the *Tathāgatagarbhasūtra* the term *tathāgatagarbha* was not yet established as a technical term. It appears in scriptures of a later date such as the *Śrīmālāsūtra*, the *Anūnatvāpūrṇatvaṇirdeśa*, the *Mahāparinirvāṇasūtra*, and so on, where, however, the use of this term as a *bahuvrīhi* compound is completely absent.[11] In addition I would like to mention the use of this term in the *Gaṇḍavyūha* as an epithet of Sudhana, the itinerant mendicant who is the hero of this work (ed. by D. T. Suzuki and H. Izumi, p. 221: *fo tsang*, Ch.; *de bshin gśegs pa'i sñiṅ po can*, Tib.).[12] This is the only case, as far as I know, where *tathāgatagarbha* masc. sg. is used as an adjective (for a Bodhisattva). This use is probably older than that in the *Tathāgatagarbhasūtra*.

As for the Chinese translation *tsang* for *garbha*, Prof. Ruegg tentatively suggests that the Chinese translation *ju lai tsang* derives from the identification of *tathāgatagarbha* with *ālayavijñāna* in the *Laṅkāvatāra*, where *ālaya* (in *ālayavijñāna*) is sometimes translated by *tsang* (p. 503). However, this is contradicted by the fact that, prior to the translation of the *Laṅkāvatāra* in 433 A.D., the said term was already used in the translation of the *Mahāparinirvāṇa* and other texts, when the concept of *ālayavijñāna* was unknown and Chinese translators were not acquainted with the *vijñāna* theory of the Yogācāra. If one looks for a concept explaining the translation *tsang* for *garbha* in *tathāgatagarbha*, *ākara* of *dharmākara* (*fa tsang*) and *nidhi* or *nidhāna* (*pao tsang*)

---

10. Peking Ed., ibid., p. 242-3-1; T. vol. 16, p. 458b (no. 666): *ju lai chih chien*; p. 462c (no. 667): *chih hui*. There are many cases where *ju lai tsang* is used in both translations. However, in parallel Tibetan passages we do not find the term *de bshin gśegs pa'i sñiṅ po* except when used as a *bahuvrīhi*.

11. On this point, I read a paper at the 28th International Congress of Orientalists held in Canberra, 1971, under the title "Gotra, Garbha and Dhātu—Fundamental Concepts of the Tathāgatagarbha Theory of Mahāyāna Buddhism." The full text has not yet been published.

12. Peking Ed. (repr.), vol. 26, p. 203-3-1; T. vol. 9, p. 719c (no. 278); vol. 10, p. 368b (no. 279).

may be more closely associated with it than *ālaya*. However, Chinese *tsang* quite well expresses the meaning of *garbha* in a *bahuvrīhi* compound. Also we cannot neglect the ambiguity in the meaning of *garbha*, and we must consider the consequences of the double meaning of 'container' and 'content' in one word for the establishment of this monistic philosophy of Mahāyāna Buddhism. A similar consequence results from the use of *gotra* and *dhātu* as synonyms of *garbha*. *Gotra* means a lineage, each individual of all generations within a family being 'included in the same *gotra*'; at the same time, each member is regarded as 'of the same *gotra*', i.e., possessing the same faculty or character which ensures continuity of the lineage.

(2) The term *amuktajña* (pp. 357ff.), one of the epithets of the *buddhadharma*s in the *Śrīmālāsūtra*. In my book[13] I suggested a new interpretation 'unreleased from Wisdom' (= **ye śes daṅ ma bral ba*). This was criticized by Prof. Ruegg (p. 360) and by Prof. Schmithausen.[14] The problem will be discussed by me on another occasion, but here I will indicate just one mistake concerning this term, namely, in a quotation of the *Anūnatvāpūrṇatvanirdeśa*. Prof. Ruegg writes *avinirmukta*jñānaguṇaḥ for *avinirmuktagunaḥ* as a description of a lantern (*pradīpaḥ*) (p. 361, l. 11). It may be merely a slip of the pen, but it is quite important to consider why the term *jñāna* is added in the case of *dharmakāya* as part of its epithet, and this point seems to be more or less related to the formation of the terms *amuktajñāna* and *amuktajña*. As to the application of the term *muktajña* (*muktajñāna*) to the *buddhadharma*s in the second Chinese translation of the *Śrīmālāsūtra* (at the beginning of the 8th century A.D.) as well as in the Tibetan translation of the same text (9th century A.D.), this is clearly a change

13. *A Study on the Ratnagotravibhāga*, pp. 144–145, etc. Cf. Takasaki, *JIBS* 6-1 (1958), pp. 186–190.

14. Lambert Schmithausen, "Philologische Bemerkungen zum Ratnagotravibhāga," *WZKS* XV (1971), pp. 131–132.

caused by misunderstanding, for example, *muktajñāna* for (*vi-)muktijñāna* (knowledge of liberation), which probably took place in the course of the transmission of the original text from the seventh century onwards. The first Chinese translation of the *Śrīmālāsūtra* (5th century A.D.) uses a term equivalent to *amukta-* in the parallel passage, which supports the term *amuktajña* (*amukta-jñāna*) as the original reading. There seems to be no necessity for further consideration on this point.

(3) To determine the school to which the *RGV* and the TG theory in general belong as the Prāsaṅgika-Mādhyamika may be correct doctrinally insofar as it means the *ekayāna-vāda* or the *śūnya-vāda*, but historically it is quite problematic. Namely, the name Mādhyamika as a school of Mahāyāna Buddhism does not seem to have been used at the time of Asaṅga and Vasubandhu, though I do not know exactly when this name first appeared. Furthermore, as the author writes (p. 35), Bhavya and Candrakīrti regarded the TG theory as *neyārtha* by reason of its similarity with the *ātma-vāda* of the Heretics. A more important point to be taken into consideration is that the tradition of the *RGV* was revived when the Mādhyamika and the Yogācāra formed one school. The *RGV* never teaches the *ālayavijñāna* and rejects the *triyāna* theory, but the fact of its being written by someone who belonged to or had an intimate relation with the Yogācāra must not be overlooked.

(4) To my regret the author follows the Tibetan tradition and does not distinguish two kinds of verses in the *RGV*, one being the basic text and the other containing a commentary. This distinction is not necessarily to be taken as indicating different authors for the two parts, but for the understanding of the doctrinal system of the *RGV* this distinction has an important significance. To make no distinction between the two kinds of verses, in other words, to regard the whole of the verse section as the basic text composed by Maitreya and separate the prose section from it as the commentary (*RGVV*) leaves a certain ambiguity in this volume

with regard to the systematical understanding of the *RGV*.[15]

(5) Finally, some minor points: *Lai yeh yüan ch'i*, a technical term of Chinese Buddhism denoting the theory of dependent origination of the Vijñānavāda, is rendered by Skt. *ālayapratītya-samutpāda* (pp. 56, 427), but *ālayavijñānap°* would be preferable; *śubha* of *śubhapāramitā*, one of the four *pāramitās*, being the qualities unique to the *dharmakāya*, is translated as 'bon' (p. 242, 364 sq.), but, being synonymous with *śuci* (pure), and translated by Tib. *gtsaṅ ba* and Chinese *ching*, it would be better to use 'pur' for it. (The author uses 'pur' once on p. 121, l. 3.) *Udbhāvanā-saṃvṛtti*, being one of three forms of the *saṃvṛti-satya* (conventional truth) in contrast to the *paramārtha-satya*, as mentioned in the *Madhyāntavibhāga* III.10, is doctrinally to be corrected to *saṃvṛti* (pp. 1, 197), though the text (the *Ṭīkā*, ed. by Yamaguchi, p. 124) uses *saṃvṛtti*. Both Nagao's edition of the *Madhyāntavibhāga* and Pandeya's revised edition of the *Madhyāntavibhāga-ṭīkā* adopt the form *saṃvṛti*.[16]

Some minor misprints remain uncorrected in the ERRATA ET ADDENDA: p. 59, n. 5 suite, l. 1: présence (for présnce); p. 97, n. 2, l. 9: *āryadharmahetutvād* (for *°hetuvād*); p. 128, ll. 7-8: *trisarvajñatā-viṣaya* (for *°sarvañatā°*); p. 319, l. 14: *avinirbhāgatva* (for *anivirbhāgatva*); p. 372, ll. 17, 20: *pāramitā°* (for *paramitā°*); p. 374, l. 6: *paramātmapāramitā* (for *paramātmaparamitā*); p. 417, l. 6: *dharmāṇāṃ* (for *dharmaṇāṃ*); p. 424, l. 11: *prakṛtiprabhāsvaratā* (for *prakrtipṛabhāsvaratā*); p. 512, note (suite), l. 2: s'il est (omit the second 'est').

Even this voluminous work does not fully explain the *tathāgatagarbha* theory. Especially to be mentioned are two basic characteristics of this theory which have not yet been sufficiently

15. Cf. Schmithausen, op. cit., pp. 123–130 (1. Zur Struktur des RGV).

16. G. M. Nagao, ed., *Madhyāntavibhāgabhāṣya* (Tokyo, 1964), p. 41, ll. 11-12; R. C. Pandeya, ed., *Madhyāntavibhāgaśāstra* (Delhi, 1971), p. 94, ll. 5-6.

made clear: the importance of the Compassion (*mahākaruṇā*) of the Tathāgata and that of faith in the existence of *tathāgatagarbha*. The background to this theory is another point which needs clarification. Prof. Ruegg makes many references to scriptures, but there still seem to remain many problems concerning the arrangement of the scriptures in historical order. According to what I heard from him, Prof. Ruegg is publishing a second volume on the TG theory which will present us with an anthology of Mahāyāna scriptures of the TG theory on the basis of Bu ston rin po che's treatise. I sincerely hope that he will spread new light in the world of Buddhist studies by this forthcoming publication.

The Lion's Roar of Queen Śrīmālā: A Buddhist Scripture on the Tathāgatagarbha Theory. Translated with Introduction and Notes by Alex Wayman and Hideko Wayman. Columbia University Press, New York & London, 1974. xvi + 142 pp.*

The *Śrīmālā Sūtra* is one of the best-known scriptures of Mahayana Buddhism. It is noted for its unusual format, in which the Buddhist doctrine is elucidated by a pious lady devotee named Śrīmālā. To the Japanese, her name has been familiar since the time of Prince Shōtoku through his commentary on the sutra, the *Shōmangyō-gisho*. The focus of the Queen's elucidation is, as the subtitle of the present work indicates, the Tathāgatagarbha theory. According to this theory, which is based on the One Way (*ekayāna*) theory of the *Saddharmapuṇḍarīka*, every sentient being without exception has the possibility of becoming a Buddha. This important work was veritably unknown to Western Buddhist studies until recent times when Dr. E. H. Johnston published the *Ratnagotravibhāga* (*Uttaratantra*) in which he quoted several passages from it as the main sources of the *tathāgatagarbha* doctrine. In his foreword to the text Dr. Johnston expressed his hope for an early translation of this scripture into a Western language. In this fine work by Dr. and Mrs. Wayman, this hope has now been realized.

The Lion's Roar of Queen Śrīmālā consists of an introduction (55 pages), translation with footnotes (pp. 57–113), appendices consisting of a comparative table of section titles and diagrams made by past Chinese and Japanese writers and a list of works cited in Chi-tsang's commentary, Glossary, Bibliography, and Index.

In the introduction the translators set forth their view concerning the history of the text, its structure, and its standpoint and doctrine. The most original of their assertions is that the *Śrīmālā* is "a composition of the Mahāsāṅghika sect" (preface). They attempt to prove this by citing wording or meanings in the *Śrīmālā* that are similar to the Mahāsāṅghika doctrine, though this is done

* Originally published in *Eastern Buddhist*, n.s., 9-1 (1976), pp. 135–138.

from rather sparse and limited sources. Bold hypotheses are sometimes useful in promoting Buddhist studies, but the present reviewer cannot help confessing that in this case the hypothesis would seem to be inadequate on the basis of available evidence. For example, the statement that the text is a product of South India in the Sātavāhana Dynasty is merely a guess. There is no proof that the *Mahāvastu*, a work of the Lokottaravādin school, one of the northern sub-sects of the Mahāsāṅghika, was known and used in southern Mahāsāṅghika sub-sects as well. It is unclear whether the translators maintain that the *Śrīmālā* alone belongs to the Mahāsāṅghika or that the Tathāgatagarbha theory in general comes from the Mahāsāṅghika. Any statement that a Mahāyāna scripture could be a production of Hinayanic Sectarian Buddhism is not understandable either. Does it mean that this scripture was composed by someone who belonged to or came out of the Mahāsāṅghika? Or does it mean that the *Śrīmālā* belonged to the Mahāsāṅghika canon? In any case, to say at this stage of research, even as a hypothesis, that the present text has been modified in accordance with Mahāyāna doctrine from an original Mahāsāṅghika work would be impossible. The relationship between Mahāyāna Buddhism and Sectarian Buddhism is an important problem for future research, and the reviewer hopes that the authors will consider this problem in a wider scope before attempting to decide the position of the *Śrīmālā*.

Their translation is the result of long years' study of the available sources: the Sanskrit fragments cited in the *Ratnagotravibhāga* and other works, the Tibetan translation, the two Chinese translations, the commentaries in Chinese and Japanese, and the related works of modern scholars. Their method of translation, as expressed in a note, was "to reconstruct and render the original meaning of the scripture, as they came to understand it from the consensus of the versions." This is a reasonable course, and, in most cases, they are successful in making clear the original meaning. In only one point do I have an objection to their evaluation of the Sanskrit fragments quoted in the *Ratnagotravibhāga*. They adopt the reading *muktajña* and *amuktajña* on the authority of the Tibetan and the later Chinese translation, which is a reversal of *amuktajña* and *muktajña* respectively, although the latter reading is supported by the earlier Chinese translation and all versions of the *Ratnagotravibhāga*. (Translation, pp. 98, 99. Cf. Introduction, pp. 48–52. The same holds true for the reading *muktajñāna* and *amuktajñāna* in Translation, p. 105.) The reason for their decision is that they regarded the latter reading as a modification by the author of the *Ratnagotravibhāga*. It is difficult to understand why the translators prefer the versions of the later period (the later Chinese translation was made in the 8th century, and the Tibetan translation in the 9th century) to the versions of the earlier period (the earliest Chinese translation dates from 436; the Chinese translation of the *Ratnagotravibhāga* from 509–10, of which the Sanskrit original might have appeared in the early 5th century).

Another point worth noting is the chapter division, which was suggested by Chinese and Japanese commentaries. They adopt, with a slight modification, the 15 subdivisions given in the Koryŏ Tripiṭaka (the base text of the Taishō Tripiṭaka text), which in turn are based on the 16 names Śākyamuni gives in the epilogue as conveying the merits of the *Śrīmālā*. These subdivisions are then arranged into four main chapters, with a Prologue and Epilogue. The method by which the chapters and subdivisions are divided and the titles given to them are their own.

Chap. I. Eliminating All Doubts (sub. 1–2)
II. Deciding the Cause (sub. 3–4)
III. Clarifying the Final Meaning (sub. 5–13)
IV. Entering the One Vehicle Path (sub. 14–15)

These titles are arrived at by breaking down the Chinese translation of the last, 16th title of the Sūtra: 斷一切疑決定了義入一乘道. The equivalent passage in the Tibetan translation reads : "the elucidation which eliminates all doubts, (and which shows) the final meaning (*nītārtha*), the unique basis to be entered (*ekaprati-saraṇa*)." Although the combination of these four titles does not correspond exactly to the 16th title in the Sūtra, the present division well catches what the *Śrīmālā* wants to convey.

The translation is fluent, literal, and true to the original. The translators are to be praised for their contribution of introducing this important scripture to English readers. Some minor mistakes and misunderstandings of the Sanskrit fragments and other versions as well as of general Buddhist usage are listed below:

p. 60, l. 5: "a court official." Tib. *nan kor ma*. It must mean "a court lady." Her name in the Sanskrit original might be *Candirā*.

p. 82, l. 1: The term *vibhaya-vāda* is mistranslated "analyzes and explains" (p. 81, last line). It should be treated as elsewhere as a technical term, associated with *ekāṃśavāda* (see n. 65), and inserted following "not final meaning."

p. 88, l. 10: "From time immemorial, the nescience entrenchment has been unconscious." The same sentence appeared before (p. 84), where it was translated "the nescience entrenchment which has existed from beginningless time is unconscious," which is perhaps preferable.

p. 92, l. 1: "subjects (*dharmin*) undeceived." This could better be rendered to mean "of an unignorant nature."

p. 93, ll. 6-7: "The second one of these refuges is." It should be "These two refuges are," as it refers to Dharma and Sangha in contrast to Buddha. And hence the sentences which follow the above should be changed: the Dharma which teaches the path of One Vehicle *ends with the realization* of the Dharmakāya, and beyond this [realization] there *remains nothing to be done by the Dharma* which teaches the Path of One Vehicle. (The *Ratnagotra-vibhāga* does not mistake the meaning of the *Śrīmālā* as the translators consider in note 73.)

p. 98, l. 10: "knowing as liberated" for *muktajña* may be all right from the term's literal similarity to *kṛtajña* (knowing what is done), but who or what is "knowing as liberated"? The present reviewer believes that this particular *muktajña* should be taken as *amuktajña* in accordance with the Sanskrit version of the *Ratnagotra* (as discussed above), and should be translated: "never being isolated from (supreme) knowledge," or simply "unreleased from Wisdom" (see *Indo-Iranian Journal*, vol. XV, 4, 1973, p. 298).

p. 99, note 84 (on Voidness), *l. 2*: The Sanskrit sentence means "Whatever is lacking in some place, one observes that *that place is void of that thing.*"

p. 112, l. 11 from below: The 11th title should be translated "Teaching of the one refuge which is permanent, steadfast, calm, and eternal." Cf. *Ratnagotravibhāga*, p. 20, ll. 9-10: *eṣā ca nityadhruvaśivasāśvataikaśaraṇanirdeśo vistareṇāryaśrīmālāsūtrānusāreṇānugantavyaḥ/* (Tib. *rtag pa g'yun drun shi ba brtan paḥi skyabs gcig pu* for *nityadhruvaśivasāśvataikaśaraṇa*).

Indian Buddhism: A Survey with Bibliographical Notes. By Nakamura Hajime. Intercultural Research Institute Monograph No. 9. KUFS Publication, Osaka, 1980. vi + 423 pp. ¥21,000.*

Modern Buddhist studies have a history of almost two centuries in Europe and nearly one hundred years in Japan. These works are countless, and new ones are still appearing day by day. Scholars are required to examine this vast accumulation of papers from the past before they start off on any subject which is new to them. If there were a guide which dealt with the research background on the subject, it would be quite convenient and most welcome for all scholars. Especially for Western or other scholars who are acquainted with only European languages but not Japanese, information in English concerning works written in Japanese would be no doubt of great benefit.[1]

Professor Nakamura, famous for his great scholarship covering the whole area of Indian culture, has taken much trouble to give the world of scholars a survey of research works on Indian Buddhism done by Japanese and foreign scholars, with bibliographical data. His first intention was to introduce recent studies being carried on by Japanese, but, he says in his preface to the present volume, in order to evaluate them he had to pay due attention to the works of Western and Asian (especially Indian) scholars; hence, they have also been included. This change of scheme has made this work more useful and comprehensive. He started this book two decades ago and partially published some of the results first in mimeograph form and next in various periodicals, and every time revisions on the basis of new studies were made. Now it is finally published in a beautiful volume.

The present work consists of the main survey of Indian

* Originally published in *Young East*, n.s., 7-3 (1981), pp. 36–39.

1. For example, Prof. J. W. de Jong once expressed his wish for the publication of bibliographical works on Buddhist studies by Japanese scholars in his book *A History of Buddhist Studies* (Japanese translation, Shunjūsha, Tokyo, 1975, pp. 95–99).

Buddhism in historical order following the development of Buddhist thought, and then detailed notes which give bibliographical information. The style being similar to Moriz Winternitz's *Geschichte der indischen Litteratur*, this work may well deserve to be called the successor to that book in the field of Indian Buddhism.

The text is divided into six chapters and twenty-six subdivisions. Chapter I, entitled "General Survey of Buddhism," deals with general books on Buddhism, including introductions to or outlines of Buddhism, histories of Indian Buddhism, dictionaries and other reference books, and books on some general topics of Buddhism, such as causality, meditation, discipline, etc. Out of 11 pages for chapter I, the main body consists of only 11 lines and the rest is spent on the bibliography. This demonstrates a characteristic of this book.

Chapter II deals with Early Buddhism in about 80 pages under eight subdivisions, including the background of the rise of Buddhism, the life of the founder, the scriptures, and the early history of Buddhism in terms of Original Buddhism and Early Buddhism. Here, Original Buddhism means that which can be known only from older portions of the Pāli scriptures, such as Gāthās of the *Suttanipāta*, etc., of which the criteria are given by the author himself previously in his own work. The characteristics of Original Buddhism, according to the author, are summarized under eight points: (1) technical terms of Buddhism were seldom used, (2) nor was any dogma found, and (3) its teachings have a nuance akin to the Ājīvikas and Jains as depicted in the Aśokan Edicts; (4) Buddhist recluses lived in solitude and (5) their life was quite close to that of hermits, as is mentioned in the Epics; (6) nuns did not exist in the earliest stage; (7) *paṭimokkha*, or the code of discipline, was very simple and basically akin to the Upaniṣadic and Jain precepts; and (8) Gotama the Buddha was looked upon as an excellent personage but was not deified. Besides him, many other Buddhas were recognized. This portion, such being rather rare, has no references to any works other than the author's own.

Chapter III deals mainly with the Abhidharma literature under the title "Conservative Buddhism and Transition to Mahāyāna," covering the period of the Mauryan Dynasty and afterwards. By this title, "Transition to Mahāyāna," is meant the development of the legend of the Buddha and the Avadāna literature together with the works of Aśvaghoṣa, all of which paved the way for the rise of Mahāyāna Buddhism.

Chapter IV deals with Mahāyāna Buddhism and the periods beginning with the Kushan Empire down to the post-Gupta ages. This chapter occupies more than 150 pages, and this shows that Japanese scholars have a great interest in Mahāyāna Buddhism and so made great efforts for its research. This tendency is especially observed in the study of the *Saddharmapuṇḍarīka* (pp. 183–191) and Pure Land Buddhism (pp. 201–209). Including these two, Mahāyāna scriptures are discussed under fourteen minor subdivisions. The latter part of the chapter dealing with the philosophical schools of Mahāyāna consists of: A. Early Mādhyamika (Nāgārjuna and Āryadeva); B. Early Vijñānavādins (Maitreya, Asaṅga, and Vasubandhu); and C. philosophers in later days in both schools. For the explanation of the philosophy of Voidness (*śūnyatā*), the author applies the methods of symbolic logic (pp. 249–250). While the studies of Buddhist logic are treated independently in chapter V (Logicians), this was probably the common ground for debates between the two Mahāyāna schools, between Mahāyāna and Hīnayāna, and between Buddhist and Hindu philosophers as well. Studies of this field are specially well developed in recent times. Chapter VI deals with "Esoteric Buddhism," the final stages in the development of Indian Buddhism. In spite of the importance and influence of this form of Buddhism on later Buddhism outside of India, studies carried on so far are rather few and there remains the impression that further work by younger generations is urgently required.

The book ends with Addenda et Corrigenda (pp. 344–379), Abbreviations and Periodicals, and Index.

Thus surveying Professor Nakamura's survey of Indian Buddhism, the present reviewer cannot but express his admiration for this beneficial volume adorned with the author's thorough and wide knowledge and for his constant efforts supported by his spirit of benevolence.

Even such a great work, however, cannot escape from some kinds of shortcomings. Taking up, for example, passages on the Early Vijñānavādins—this field is the most complicated one among systems of Buddhist thought and, in spite of the efforts of many scholars for over fifty years, no final decision has been given by them as yet concerning the history of the Yogācāra, the historical order of the fundamental texts, and the interpretation of the fundamental doctrines as well—the author has arranged sections and paragraphs according to the order of the texts ascribed to the three great teachers. It may be the most clever way of description for avoiding double references and other confusion, but to understand the fundamental system of philosophy elucidated in these treatises, the author could have given a separate subsection specially for it. There are some minor mistakes—p. 259, l.1: "A partial manuscript of this exists in the Sanskrit original," but the full text of the *Madhyāntavibhāga-bhāṣya* in Sanskrit has been edited and published, as is mentioned in n. 42; p. 261, l.7 or n. 55: a Sanskrit fragment of the *Dharmadharmatāvibhaṅga* is attached to Lévi's edition of the *Mahāyānasūtrālaṃkāra* identified by H. Kawai and reported by H. Ui to S. Yamaguchi—see S. Yamaguchi, *Bukkyōgaku bunshū* [Collected papers on Buddhist studies], vol. I, Shunjūsha, Tokyo, 1972 (pp. 203–211); p. 256, n. 16 and n. 19 are to be replaced by each other.

Index

Personal Names

TEXTS